NBER Macroeconomics Annual 2022

T0295620

NBER Macroeconomics Annual 2022

Edited by
Martin Eichenbaum, Erik Hurst, and Valerie Ramey

The University of Chicago Press
Chicago and London

NBER Macroeconomics Annual 2022, Number 37

Published annually by The University of Chicago Press.
www.journals.uchicago.edu/MA/

Subscriptions: For individual and institutional subscription rates, visit www.journals .uchicago.edu, email subscriptions@press.uchicago.edu, or call (877) 705-1878 (US) or (773) 753-3347 (international). Free or deeply discounted institutional access is available in most developing nations through the Chicago Emerging Nations Initiative (www.journals .uchicago.edu/inst/ceni).

Please direct subscription inquiries to Subscription Fulfillment, 1427 E. 60th Street, Chicago, IL 60637-2902. Telephone: (773) 753-3347 or toll free in the United States and Canada (877) 705-1878. Fax: (773) 753-0811 or toll-free (877) 705-1879. E-mail: subscriptions @press.uchicago.edu.

Standing orders: To place a standing order for this book series, please address your request to The University of Chicago Press, Chicago Distribution Center, Attn. Standing Orders/Customer Service, 11030 S. Langley Avenue, Chicago, IL 60628. Telephone toll free in the U.S. and Canada: 1-800-621-2736; or 1-773-702-7000. Fax toll free in the U.S. and Canada: 1-800-621-8476; or 1-773-702-7212.

Single-copy orders: In the U.S., Canada, and the rest of the world, order from your local bookseller or direct from The University of Chicago Press, Chicago Distribution Center, 11030 S. Langley Avenue, Chicago, IL 60628. Telephone toll free in the U.S. and Canada: 1-800-621-2736; or 1-773-702-7000. Fax toll free in the U.S. and Canada: 1-800-621-8476; or 1-773-702-7212. In the U.K. and Europe, order from your local bookseller or direct from The University of Chicago Press, c/o John Wiley Ltd. Distribution Center, 1 Oldlands Way, Bognor Regis, West Sussex PO22 9SA, UK. Telephone 01243 779777 or Fax 01243 820250. E-mail: cs-books@wiley.co.uk.

The University of Chicago Press offers bulk discounts on individual titles to Corporate, Premium and Gift accounts. For information, please write to Sales Department—Special Sales, The University of Chicago Press, 1427 E. 60th Street, Chicago, IL 60637 USA or telephone 1-773-702-7723.

This book was printed and bound in the United States of America.

ISSN: 0889-3365
E-ISSN: 1537-2642
ISBN: 978-0-226-82821-3 (pb.:alk.paper)
eISBN: 978-0-226-82824-4 (e-book)

Relation of the Directors to the Work and Publications of the NBER

1. The object of the NBER is to ascertain and present to the economics profession, and to the public more generally, important economic facts and their interpretation in a scientific manner without policy recommendations. The Board of Directors is charged with the responsibility of ensuring that the work of the NBER is carried on in strict conformity with this object.

2. The President shall establish an internal review process to ensure that book manuscripts proposed for publication DO NOT contain policy recommendations. This shall apply both to the proceedings of conferences and to manuscripts by a single author or by one or more coauthors but shall not apply to authors of comments at NBER conferences who are not NBER affiliates.

3. No book manuscript reporting research shall be published by the NBER until the President has sent to each member of the Board a notice that a manuscript is recommended for publication and that in the President's opinion it is suitable for publication in accordance with the above principles of the NBER. Such notification will include a table of contents and an abstract or summary of the manuscript's content, a list of contributors if applicable, and a response form for use by Directors who desire a copy of the manuscript for review. Each manuscript shall contain a summary drawing attention to the nature and treatment of the problem studied and the main conclusions reached.

4. No volume shall be published until forty-five days have elapsed from the above notification of intention to publish it. During this period a copy shall be sent to any Director requesting it, and if any Director objects to publication on the grounds that the manuscript contains policy recommendations, the objection will be presented to the author(s) or editor(s). In case of dispute, all members of the Board shall be notified, and the President shall appoint an ad hoc committee of the Board to decide the matter; thirty days additional shall be granted for this purpose.

5. The President shall present annually to the Board a report describing the internal manuscript review process, any objections made by Directors before publication or by anyone after publication, any disputes about such matters, and how they were handled.

6. Publications of the NBER issued for informational purposes concerning the work of the Bureau, or issued to inform the public of the activities at the Bureau, including but not limited to the NBER Digest and Reporter, shall be consistent with the object stated in paragraph 1. They shall contain a specific disclaimer noting that they have not passed through the review procedures required in this resolution. The Executive Committee of the Board is charged with the review of all such publications from time to time.

7. NBER working papers and manuscripts distributed on the Bureau's web site are not deemed to be publications for the purpose of this resolution, but they shall be consistent with the object stated in paragraph 1. Working papers shall contain a specific disclaimer noting that they have not passed through the review procedures required in this resolution. The NBER's web site shall contain a similar disclaimer. The President shall establish an internal review process to ensure that the working papers and the web site do not contain policy recommendations, and shall report annually to the Board on this process and any concerns raised in connection with it.

8. Unless otherwise determined by the Board or exempted by the terms of paragraphs 6 and 7, a copy of this resolution shall be printed in each NBER publication as described in paragraph 2 above.

Contents

Editorial

Martin Eichenbaum, *Northwestern University and NBER,* United States of America

Erik Hurst, *University of Chicago and NBER,* United States of America

Valerie Ramey, *University of California San Diego, NBER, and CEPR,* United States of America

The NBER's Thirty-Seventh Annual Conference on Macroeconomics brought together leading scholars to present, discuss, and debate five research papers on central issues in contemporary macroeconomics. In addition, it included a panel discussion on the future of work. Katharine Abraham moderated the panel, which included Steven Davis, Edward Glaeser, and Joel Mokyr.

This conference volume contains edited versions of the five papers presented at the conference, each followed by two written discussions by leading scholars and a summary of the debates that followed each paper.

The decline in the labor share of income over the past decades has attracted considerable attention. Numerous explanations have been suggested, such as superstar firms, rising price markups, and monopsony power of firms in labor markets. In their paper, "Human Capitalists," Andrea Eisfeldt, Antonio Falato, and Mindy Xiaolan offer a new explanation: the rise of a new class of worker that receives part of its labor income as equity-based compensation. The authors begin by meticulously documenting this phenomenon and the quantitative importance of its rise over time in the United States. For example, in manufacturing they find equity-based labor compensation grew from less than 1% of value added before 1980 to 7% of value added in the 2010s. The authors explain the rise by identifying the accounting and tax incentives favoring this type of compensation.

NBER Macroeconomics Annual, volume 37, 2023.

The implications of the human capitalist story are far-reaching. The most immediate implication is the mismeasurement of labor share. They show that one-third of the decline in the measured labor share can be explained by the rise of equity-based compensation, which is not included in labor income in the national accounts. The second implication concerns the returns to skilled labor and the implied capital-skill complementarity. The authors revisit the classic Krusell, Ohanian, Rios-Rull, and Violante (2000) hypothesis of capital-skill complementarity and argue that the estimated complementarity is even greater than previously estimated once adjustments for equity-based compensation are incorporated.

The discussants praise the work and draw out additional implications. Gianluca Violante adds estimates of capital gains and losses on the equity-based compensation and finds that the augmented measure reduces the labor-share decline even more. He also reexamines the link between the current analysis of capital-skill complementarity and his original work from 2000. Eric Zwick's discussion offers detailed links between the rise of human capitalists and the tax reforms of the 1980s, develops an alternative measurement method that supports the authors' conclusions, and highlights other leading puzzles that can be explained by the rise in human capitalists.

The effect of monetary policy on the economy remains a central topic in academic and policy circles. One of the most popular recent methods for identifying monetary policy shocks to estimate causal effects is "high-frequency identification," which uses movements in financial market data around the time of Federal Open Market Committee (FOMC) meetings. However, the estimated monetary surprises display a puzzling correlation with previously available information. The paper by Michael Bauer and Eric Swanson, "A Reassessment of Monetary Surprises and High-Frequency Identification," builds on their earlier work by providing a new explanation for this correlation, a prescription for how to overcome it, and richer data for estimating key parameters more precisely.

A previous explanation for the puzzling correlation was that the Federal Reserve had superior information to private forecasters, so any deviations from the monetary policy rule confounded true shocks with the revelation of private Fed information. Bauer and Swanson present evidence against this "information effect" explanation. The authors argue instead that the puzzles can be explained by the private sector being uncertain about the parameters of the monetary policy rule and learning about the rule. As Bauer and Swanson document, the monetary rule parameters are time varying, with the Fed increasing the strength of its responses to both the output gap and inflation over time. They show that one can purge these confounding effects from estimated monetary policy shocks by orthogonalizing the shocks with respect to lagged macroeconomic and financial market variables. These new methods, together with rich new data that incorporate information from the Fed chair's speeches between FOMC meetings, yield estimates of effects of monetary policy on macroeconomic variables that are much larger than those estimated previously.

The two discussants of the Bauer and Swanson paper were Simon Gilchrist and Mark Watson. Gilchrist discusses several ways the modeling framework could be extended, and he conducts a more detailed comparison of the magnitude of various effects on asset markets and macroeconomic variables. Mark Watson demonstrates econometrically why Bauer and Swanson's orthogonalization fix leads to weaker identification and therefore why their new data on Fed chair speeches are an important component of their overall method.

How long can initial differences in wealth between two groups persist? An individual's wealth can affect their ability to invest in human capital, their decision to choose occupations, and their decision to allocate their savings across different assets. As a result, any initial wealth differences between two groups can persist for long periods of time through wealth's influence on future labor market and portfolio choice decisions. In their paper, "Reparations and Persistent Racial Wealth Gaps," Job Boerma and Loukas Karabarbounis provide a framework to quantitatively explore the gap in wealth between White and Black Americans over the past 150 years. Using the framework, Boerma and Karabarbounis examine the effectiveness of reparations as a tool to close the racial wealth gap.

Boerma and Karabarbounis's model has three key features. First, during certain periods of history, Black households were restricted from investing in certain types of assets. Second, Black households—both in the past and in current generations—face discrimination and other barriers such that their labor income is lower than White households. Finally, the model has an overlapping generation structure where parents can pass on expectations about asset returns of the various assets to their children. It is this latter assumption that Boerma and Karabarbounis highlight as being quantitatively important in explaining current racial wealth gaps. In particular, because Black households historically have been excluded from investing in certain assets, they have not learned sufficiently that certain asset classes—like entrepreneurship—can generate larger returns. As a result, even as differences in labor market outcomes narrow,

Eichenbaum, Hurst, and Ramey

the racial wealth gap persists because Black households are investing, on average, in lower-return asset classes. Boerma and Karabarbounis then highlight that, although reparations will transfer large amounts of wealth to Black households, they will not generate a permanent convergence in the racial wealth gap unless the transfer also causes a narrowing in racial differences in return beliefs. Instead, Boerma and Karabarbounis argue that large subsidies to asset returns—which subsidize saving broadly and accelerate the learning process—are a more effective tool to permanently close the racial wealth gap.

Both discussants—Ellora Derenoncourt and Jonathan Parker—praise the paper for trying to tackle the important question of what explains the persistent racial wealth gaps in a rigorous way. However, both discussants comment on the importance of belief differences about asset returns as the primary explanation. Derenoncourt raises the issue of whether differences in asset returns between racial groups arose instead from more systematic racial barriers. For example, Derenoncourt notes that businesses started by Black households were more likely to fail, suggesting that there is not only a barrier to entry into a high-return asset such as entrepreneurship but also barriers preventing success conditional on entry. Jonathan Parker provides complementary comments suggesting that forces such as liquidity constraints could explain both low entry into business formation by Black households and increased failures conditional on entry. Distinguishing between beliefs and liquidity constraints, he argues, is important for discussing policy responses. For example, if liquidity constraints are responsible for the low entry of Black households into business ownership, policies such as reparations may have a more long-lasting effect with respect to narrowing the racial wealth gap.

A classic question in macroeconomics is why unemployment is so volatile and countercyclical. In many models, rigid or inertial real wages play a central role in answering this question. For example, inertia in real wages is a standard feature of empirically plausible New Keynesian models. Sluggish real wages play a similar role, albeit for different reasons, in classic search and matching models of the type pioneered by Diamond-Mortensen and Pissarides (DMP).

In his paper, "Stubborn Beliefs in Search Equilibrium," Guido Menzio tackles the issue of why real wages are rigid. He does so by modifying one key aspect of an otherwise standard DMP model. The key change is that some workers do not have rational expectations. Instead, some workers believe that aggregate productivity is constant and equal to the unconditional mean of the productivity distribution. Given his assumption about the bargaining game by which wages are determined, the presence of workers with stubborn beliefs changes the response of wages to technology shocks. Under certain assumptions, wages are too high compared with what a recession would call for; that is, they are downward sticky/rigid. In addition, after a positive technology shock, wages do not rise as much as they would under rational expectations.

Menzio shows that the model with "stubborn beliefs" generates much more volatility in job posting and unemployment than the rational expectations version of his DMP model. The larger the fraction of workers with stubborn beliefs, the more volatile unemployment is. In this sense, the implied model accounts for a key failure of classic DMP models, namely their inability to account for the observed volatility of unemployment. The paper argues that countercyclical employment subsidies can correct the cyclical inefficiencies associated with stubborn beliefs.

The discussants, Ilse Lindenlaub and Richard Rogerson, praise Menzio for the clarity and elegance of his analysis and the way that he conveys strong intuition for his results. The key issue for both discussants is the absence of strong empirical evidence in favor of the specific departure from rational expectations that Menzio entertains. Lindenlaub and Rogerson review the empirical evidence cited by Menzio and argue, in different ways, that the evidence admits other ways of departing from rational expectations that could generate qualitatively different results. Both authors also emphasize that alternative versions of the model, which allows for on-the-job search and different wage-setting mechanisms, could weaken the role of workers' beliefs about their outside options in determining labor outcomes.

In their paper, "Excess Savings and Twin Deficits: The Transmission of Fiscal Stimulus in Open Economies," Rishabh Aggarwal, Adrien Auclert, Matthew Rognlie, and Ludwig Straub investigate the evolution of private savings, current account deficits, and fiscal deficits around the world in the period after 2020. They document three key facts. First, there was a large increase in private savings in many countries, especially in the United States. Second, there was an increase in the current account deficit and the trade deficit in the United States, with a corresponding surplus in the rest of the world. Third, there was a large increase in the fiscal deficit worldwide, especially in the United States.

Aggarwal et al. argue that the third fact is the sole cause of the first two facts. They use a multicountry heterogeneous-agent model in which deficit-financed fiscal transfers simultaneously lead to a large and persistent increase in private savings and current account deficits.

Their basic story is as follows. Countries around the world used fiscal deficits to finance transfers to households. Households partly spent these transfers according to their marginal propensities to consume and initially saved the rest. Current account deficits emerged because part of the spending was on imported goods. But in relatively closed countries such as the United States, the share of imported goods is small. So the initial impact of this spending on the current account deficit was also small.

A quantitative version of the model rationalizes both the timing and the magnitude of the excess saving and the current account patterns observed since 2020 as effects of the worldwide fiscal policy response to the pandemic rather than the effect of the pandemic per se.

The first discussant, Oleg Itskhoki, is skeptical about the importance of heterogeneity in people's marginal propensity to consume for explaining the key macro facts. He argues that the baseline neoclassical model with Ricardian equivalence does a surprisingly good job of accounting for the main international macroeconomic features of adjustment to the pandemic shocks. Itskhoki agrees that household heterogeneity and non-Ricardian features central to heterogeneous-agent New Keynesian models are essential to make sense of microlevel consumption and savings dynamics. But he is not convinced that these features have first-order implications for aggregate savings and current account dynamics at the country levels during the COVID-19 pandemic.

The second panelist, Linda Tesar, reviews the international evidence on private savings, government savings, and the current account. She argues that COVID-19 period did not lead to a dramatic change in the time series behavior of the current account. Like the first discussant, she thinks that the standard neoclassic model captured the first-order effects of the COVID-19 shock on the current account.

Tesar notes that the COVID-19 shock affected countries at different points in time, and governments responded with different types of economic policies, generating asymmetries in income, consumption, and the demand for home and foreign goods. These asymmetries could be as important as asymmetries stemming from differences in the nature of the fiscal response in different countries.

The authors and the editors would like to take this opportunity to thank Jim Poterba and the National Bureau of Economic Research for their continued support for the *NBER Macroeconomics Annual* and the associated conference. We would also like to thank the NBER conference staff, particularly Rob Shannon, for his continued excellent organization and support. We thank the rapporteurs, Fergal Hanks and Ali Uppal, who provided invaluable help in preparing the summaries of the discussions. And last but far from least, we are grateful to Helena Fitz-Patrick for her invaluable assistance in editing and publishing the volume.

Reference

Krussell, Per, Lee Ohanian, Jose-Victor Rios-Rull, and Gianluca Violante. 2000. "Capital-Skill Complementarity and Inequality: A Macroeconomic Analysis." *Econometrica* 68:1029–54.

Abstracts

1 Human Capitalists

Andrea L. Eisfeldt, Antonio Falato, and Mindy Z. Xiaolan

The widespread and growing use of equity-based compensation has transformed high-skilled labor from a pure labor input to a class of "human capitalists." High-skilled labor earns substantial income in the form of equity claims to firms' future dividends and capital gains. Equity-based compensation has increased substantially since the 1980s, representing thirty-six percent of total compensation to high-skilled labor in US manufacturing in recent years. Ignoring equity income causes incorrect measurement of the returns to high-skilled labor, with substantial effects on macroeconomic trends. In manufacturing, the inclusion of equity-based compensation almost eliminates the decline in the high-skilled labor share and reduces the total decline in the labor share by about one-third. Only by including equity pay does our structural estimation support complementarity between high-skilled labor and physical capital greater than that found by Cobb and Douglas decades ago. We also provide additional regression evidence of such complementarity.

2 A Reassessment of Monetary Policy Surprises and High-Frequency Identification

Michael D. Bauer and Eric T. Swanson

High-frequency changes in interest rates around Federal Open Market Committee (FOMC) announcements are an important tool for identifying

NBER Macroeconomics Annual, volume 37, 2023.

the effects of monetary policy on asset prices and the macroeconomy. However, some recent studies have questioned both the exogeneity and the relevance of these monetary policy surprises as instruments, especially for estimating the macroeconomic effects of monetary policy shocks. For example, monetary policy surprises are correlated with macroeconomic and financial data that are publicly available prior to the FOMC announcement. We address these concerns in two ways: first, we expand the set of monetary policy announcements to include speeches by the Federal Reserve chair, which doubles the number and importance of announcements. Second, we explain the predictability of the monetary policy surprises in terms of the "Fed response to news" channel of Bauer and Swanson's recent work and account for it by orthogonalizing the surprises with respect to macroeconomic and financial data that predate the announcement. Our subsequent reassessment of the effects of monetary policy yields two key results: First, estimates of the high-frequency effects on asset prices are largely unchanged. Second, estimates of the effects on the macroeconomy are substantially larger and more significant than the typical findings of previous studies using high-frequency data.

3   Reparations and Persistent Racial Wealth Gaps
Job Boerma and Loukas Karabarbounis

We analyze the magnitude and persistence of the racial wealth gap using a long-run model of heterogeneous dynasties with an occupational choice and bequests. Our innovation is to introduce endogenous beliefs about risky returns, reflecting differences in dynasties' investment experiences over time. Feeding the exclusion of Black dynasties from labor and capital markets into the model as the only driving force, we find that the model quantitatively reproduces current and historical racial gaps in wealth, income, entrepreneurship, mobility, and beliefs about risky returns. We explore how the future trajectory of the racial wealth gap might change in response to various policies. Wealth transfers to all Black dynasties that eliminate the average wealth gap today do not lead to long-run wealth convergence. The logic is that centuries-long exclusions lead Black dynasties to hold pessimistic beliefs about risky returns and to forgo investment opportunities after the wealth transfer. Investment subsidies toward Black entrepreneurs are more effective than wealth transfers in permanently eliminating the racial wealth gap.

4   Stubborn Beliefs in Search Equilibrium
Guido Menzio

I study a search equilibrium model of the labor market in which workers have stubborn beliefs about their labor market prospects; that is, expectations about their future job-finding probability and future wages that do not adjust to cyclical fluctuations in fundamentals. Stubborn beliefs dampen the response of bargained wages to shocks and, in turn, amplify the response of labor market tightness, job-finding probability, unemployment, and vacancies. The amplification caused by stubborn beliefs is inefficient and can be corrected by countercyclical employment subsidies. When only a small fraction of workers have stubborn beliefs, the response of wages and labor market outcomes to negative shocks is the same as when all workers are stubborn. In contrast, the response of wages and labor market outcomes to positive shocks is approximately the same as when all workers have rational expectations. Hence, when only a small fraction of workers have stubborn beliefs, wages and labor market outcomes respond asymmetrically to positive and negative shocks.

5   Excess Savings and Twin Deficits: The Transmission of Fiscal Stimulus in Open Economies
Rishabh Aggarwal, Adrien Auclert, Matthew Rognlie, and Ludwig Straub

We study the effects of debt-financed fiscal transfers in a general equilibrium, heterogeneous-agent model of the world economy. In the long run, increases in government debt anywhere raise the world interest rate and increase private wealth everywhere. In the short run, a country with a larger-than-average fiscal deficit experiences both a large increase in private savings ("excess savings") and a small but persistent current account deficit (a slow-motion "twin deficit"). These patterns are consistent with the evolution of the world's balance of payments since the beginning of the COVID-19 pandemic.

1

Human Capitalists

Andrea L. Eisfeldt, *UCLA Anderson School of Management and NBER,* United States of America

Antonio Falato, *Federal Reserve Board,* United States of America

Mindy Z. Xiaolan, *University of Texas at Austin,* United States of America

I. Introduction

Human capitalists are corporate employees who receive significant equity-based compensation such as equity grants and stock options. These employees are partial owners of US firms, and in return for their human capital input, human capitalists accrue a share of firm profits through firm dividends and capital gains in addition to earning wages. We document the stylized facts describing the evolution of human capitalists' income over time and across industries within the US manufacturing sector.[1] Human capitalists have become an increasingly important class of corporate income earners. Due to measurement challenges, prior work has underestimated the importance of equity pay below the C-suite. Correctly measuring the total income of human capitalists substantially alters conclusions about changes in factor shares and technological complementarity.

Equity-based compensation represents 36% of compensation to human capitalists from 2010 to 2019 and constitutes a 7% share of value added in the manufacturing sector in 2019. Correctly accounting for the total income earned by high-skilled workers has a substantial effect on measured changes in labor shares over the modern era. The addition of equity pay to cash wages reduces the decline implied by the wage-only income share of value added in manufacturing since the 1980s by 32%. Without including equity pay, high-skilled labor's share decreased from 17% in the 1980s to 11% in the most recent decade. The inclusion of

NBER Macroeconomics Annual, volume 37, 2023.

equity-based compensation almost eliminates this decline. The high-skilled share of total labor income increases from one-third at the beginning of the 1960s to two-thirds in the 2010s when equity-based compensation is included.

Firms use equity pay for several reasons. Because it is deferred, it is an effective retention tool. Equity pay may also be used due to favorable tax treatment at the personal level, to incentivize effort, or to boost current earnings (and borrow from employees). Our estimation indicates that, on average, 98% of equity pay has been used to replace wages as compensation for marginal product rather than to increase pay overall. Equity-based compensation is widely used beyond the much-studied executive level. In recent years 78% of equity-based compensation went to employees outside the C-suite.

Our study contributes important new facts to the study of changing factor shares and the implications for the distributions of income and wealth. Elsby, Hobijn, and Şahin (2013) and Karabarbounis and Neiman (2014) show that the labor share measured using national accounting data has declined in the US corporate sector since the early 1980s. Wage growth has been anemic relative to the growth of corporate profits. These facts seem to indicate a secular shift of income away from the providers of labor to the owners of physical capital. However, tackling the capital structure question of who owns firms' profits is necessary to provide a concrete link between changing factor shares and changing income and wealth shares. Human capitalists are laborers and also an important class of firm owners.

Our findings documenting rising equity pay in public manufacturing firms are distinct but complementary to recent work by Smith et al. (2018), which emphasizes the mismeasurement of labor income as capital income compensation in the private sector. The authors argue that, in the private sector, firm owners' equity claims are labor compensation as opposed to passive capital income. Smith et al. (2021) document the effect of the growing share of pass-through enterprises on the decline in the labor share. The authors' focus is on the entrepreneurial labor income of small business owners, whereas ours is on the equity income of high-skilled employees at large corporations. The link between investment in intangible assets and missing labor income in the form of sweat equity is emphasized in McGrattan and Prescott (2010), who document a puzzling increase in hours and capital gains in the 1990s when wages measured in national accounts were low.[2] Further evidence on labor-share mismeasurement is documented in the recent paper Koh,

Santaeulàlia-Llopis, and Zheng (2020), which points out the mechanical negative effect on the labor share of the Bureau of Economic Analysis's (BEA) revision to the capital accounts to include intellectual property products in capital income.[3]

We find that the total labor share has declined since the 1960s even including equity pay in our sample of manufacturing firms. Our sample also displays a relatively flat share of physical capital in value added, consistent with Barkai (2017) and Rognlie (2015). In light of these trends, Karabarbounis and Neiman (2019) coined the term "factorless income" and documented measurement methods to reduce the share of income that is unaccounted for by observable factors. Farhi and Gourio (2018) and Greenwald, Lettau, and Ludvigson (2019) study the quantitative role of markups, intangible assets, or risk premia in driving a growing profit or factorless-income share using the discipline of a larger set of macroeconomic and financial market moments. By appropriately allocating profits earned in exchange for labor inputs to the labor share of human capitalists, equity compensation is an important way to reduce factorless income. In our sample, human capitalists' ownership share of public companies is 10% in the 2010s. Thus, their share of profits reduces factorless income by this amount. Human capitalists in the manufacturing sector earned more than $136 billion annually in equity-based compensation from publicly traded firms on average over the most recent decade. Importantly, not only have firm profits grown, but the ownership share of human capitalists grew as well.

We start by carefully documenting the stylized facts describing the secular evolution of human capitalists' income share. The key measurement challenge is to compute the annual flow of equity-based compensation granted to human capitalists each year. There are two main reasons that the majority of equity pay is missing from standard data sources for annual labor compensation such as the BEA and the Bureau of Labor Statistics (BLS). First, a substantial fraction of equity pay is qualified by the Internal Revenue Service (IRS) to be taxed at the long-term capital gains tax rate. Second, equity pay is substantially deferred, on average, by 5 or more years. Thus, newly granted equity pay does not appear in standard data sources based on current income tax or unemployment data, even if it will be taxed as income once it is vested and exercised. Because equity pay has grown at a very high rate since the 1980s, vested and exercised pay is a small fraction of new grants (NG). To see that the majority of equity pay is not included in national accounting compensation data, note that the IRS reports that the value of income from the exercise of nonstatutory stock options (the only equity pay that flows through the IRS form W2 that underlies the BEA and BLS data) averaged only $55 billion per year over the period 2008–17.[4] This total covers the entire economy, whereas we estimate equity pay to be $100 billion on average within the manufacturing sector alone during this same time period. We provide further details on the treatment of equity compensation in standard data sources in Subsection II.C, and we describe how to estimate the small fraction of equity-based pay that is included in W2 forms and in BEA compensation data. The census payroll series to which we add equity-based compensation to compute total human capitalist income for our main analysis is wages only.

To surpass the challenges in measuring equity pay, we use firm-level data on the value of shares reserved for compensation. By law, firms must reserve shares against compensation grants to disclose the expected resulting dilution to shareholders. Data on shares reserved for employees' unexercised stock options or restricted equity grants are available annually for the universe of publicly traded US corporations via their US Securities and Exchange Commission SEC filings. We obtain data on shares reserved for equity-based compensation from 1960 to 2019 by combining data sets based on SEC filings when available and hand collecting the SEC data otherwise. Using the assembled data on the stock of reserved shares (RSs), along with its law of motion, we construct a measure of the annual flow of new equity-based compensation grants each year. We then aggregate to the industry level and add high-skilled wages from a merged NBER-CES–public-firm sample to obtain a measure of total compensation to high-skilled labor. Our merged NBER-CES–public-firm data set covers a very broad set of manufacturing firms and contains a reliable measure of value added.[5]

A rising share of human capitalist income, along with the observed decline in investment goods prices, is consistent with technological complementarity between human and physical capital. We explore this potential complementarity in two ways. First, we provide robust panel-data evidence for complementarity between high-skilled labor and physical capital at both the industry and the firm level. Second, we conduct a structural estimation that highlights the importance of equity-based compensation when evaluating evidence of complementarity between human capital and physical capital.

Our panel regressions first document a negative relationship within firms and within industries over time between investment goods prices and high-skilled human capital owners' earnings and wealth. Human capitalists' income has increased more in industries and firms that have experienced larger declines in investment goods prices.[6] Thus, the evidence suggests that human capitalists have benefited disproportionately from declining investment goods prices. Next, we use the correctly measured total return to human capitalists to show that, consistent with complementarity, within industries and over time there is a positive relation between the human capital share and the physical capital share. By contrast, and consistent with the cross-country evidence in Karabarbounis and Neiman (2014), we find a negative relation between the low-skilled labor share and capital shares. Our evidence supports substitutability between low-skilled labor and capital.

We develop and study a parsimonious model and then estimate its key parameters (a) to provide structure for the facts that describe the rise of human capitalists and (b) to understand the implications of these facts for shares of value added and income. Our model builds on the model developed in Krusell et al. (2000), who were the first to model and document the complementarity between high-skilled labor and physical capital. Notably, their sample ends in 1992. During the internet boom in the mid-1990s, the decline in high-skilled wage income and the rise in the equity pay of human capitalists accelerated. Indeed, our estimation indicates that the post-1992 steep decline in the high-skilled wage share implies greater substitutability between high-skilled labor and capital than Cobb and Douglas (1928) when equity pay is not included. However, using the total compensation of high-skilled labor, including equity pay, the elasticity of substitution we estimate in our model is nearly identical to that in Krusell et al. (2000) (0.66 vs. 0.67).[7] Thus, including equity pay is crucial for finding complementarity greater than that of Cobb and Douglas (1928) in recent years in which wage income has been replaced by equity pay at the high end of the income distribution.

In addition to constructing a more comprehensive measure of high-skilled labor compensation, we modify the theoretical framework in Krusell et al. (2000) in two key ways to accommodate human capitalists. First, we treat high-skilled human capital as a stock that can be accumulated through investment rather than as a flow labor input. Second, in our framework, this stock of human capital earns an equilibrium return that can depend not only on its current marginal product but also on its outside option (e.g., Eisfeldt and Papanikolaou 2013; Hartman-Glaser, Lustig, and Xiaolan 2019). Importantly, we show that only a small fraction of equity-based pay must be assigned to human capitalists' marginal product to generate a degree of complementarity between physical and human capital that is larger than the complementarity implied by Cobb–Douglas. However, our estimates indicate that in fact 98% of equity pay is used as a substitute for wages to compensate marginal product, as opposed to being used as additional pay or rents from the participation constraint.

Our estimate of the elasticity of substitution between capital and unskilled labor is 1.28 and is not sensitive to the fraction of equity-based pay assigned to marginal product. This finding on the substitutability between capital and unskilled labor is broadly consistent with the estimates in the existing literature (e.g., Krusell et al. 2000; Karabarbounis and Neiman 2014). Our model at estimated parameters and with correctly measured income shares is able to replicate the full set of stylized facts we document when the economy receives the observed sequence of declining investment goods prices.

Our paper contributes to the following related areas of the literature. First, there is an ongoing discussion on the secular evolution of factor shares (e.g., Elsby et al. 2013; Karabarbounis and Neiman 2014; Lawrence 2015; Koh, Santaeulàlia-Llopis, and Zheng 2016; Hartman-Glaser et al. 2019; Autor et al. 2020; Kehrig and Vincent 2021). This literature has established the decline of the aggregate labor share measured using standard sources of realized income (mainly wages). Although our data also support a declining overall labor share, we emphasize the importance of using a more complete measure of total compensation in the modern era. Our new compensation series also contributes important new facts that help make progress on the evolution of total income share dynamics for workers of different skill levels. Our time-series evidence is consistent with the prediction of Hartman-Glaser et al. (2019). When allowing skilled labor to share firm profits, their model predicts an increase in performance-pay relative to wages over time as idiosyncratic volatility increases.

Our focus on investment-specific technological change builds on the earlier macroeconomics and asset pricing literature (e.g., Greenwood, Hercowitz, and Krusell 1997; Krusell et al. 2000; Papanikolaou 2011; Kogan and Papanikolaou 2014). Despite this growing literature, there is still a limited amount of direct cross-sectional evidence on the relation between investment goods prices and factor shares (Acemoglu 2002). We examine the implications of investment-specific technological change on factor shares and use new micro data to characterize the shape of an aggregate production function that employs human capitalists. Our study also contributes to our understanding of who gains and who loses from investment-specific technological change.[8] Including equity-based compensation greatly increases the observed disparity between the compensation of high- and low-skilled labor, deepening concerns regarding the unequal sharing of the gains to technological progress highlighted by Autor (2014, 2019).

Our analysis has related implications for the broader debate on the income distribution between capital and labor, and the concern regarding rising inequality (e.g., Piketty 2014; Caicedo, Lucas, and Rossi-Hansberg 2016; Gabaix et al. 2016; Stokey 2016), which on the finance side has generally focused on the very top of the income distribution (e.g., Gabaix and Landier 2008; Frydman and Saks 2010; Kaplan and Rauh 2010; Frydman and Papanikolaou 2015). Given the data limitations, very little was previously known about the total compensation to the intermediate levels of the income distribution represented by high-skilled laborers. An important exception is Lemieux, MacLeod, and Parent (2009), which documents increasing performance-based pay in the Panel Study of Income Dynamics and the effects on income inequality but does not focus on equity-based pay and the implications for factor shares. Our analysis highlights the importance of equity compensation paid to employees below the very top executive or founder level. Whereas total compensation at the C-suite level appears to have peaked around the year 2000,[9] equity-based compensation to a broader set of high-skilled labor continues to rise.

Finally, a growing literature in macroeconomics and finance highlights the importance of a "missing factor," and in particular, intangible capital embedded in and partially owned by human inputs or organization capital (e.g., Eisfeldt and Papanikolaou 2014; Koh et al. 2016; Barkai 2017; Benzell and Brynjolfsson 2019; Karabarbounis and Neiman 2019). We bring new microdata to the measurement of human inputs. Moreover, we examine the importance of the rents generated by organizational capital from a national income accounting perspective, which, aside from the notable exceptions above, has received limited attention thus far.

II. Human Capitalist Income: Measurement and Stylized Facts

In this section, we first provide a detailed description of our method for measuring the total income to human capitalists, including wages and new equity grants using NBER-CES and Compustat data. Using corrected total human capitalist income, we then document the implications of the revised labor income series for macro trends in factor shares.

Our main findings highlight the large magnitude of human capitalists' equity-based compensation, which has grown markedly over the past 4 decades. Next, we show how to construct total human capitalist income starting from BEA data on compensation. First, we describe the reasons why standard sources largely exclude equity-based pay. In manufacturing, we estimate that only 35% of current equity grants are included in the BEA income measure. Then, we provide a way to estimate the amount of equity pay that is included in BEA data. We document the dampening effect of equity pay on the labor share decline measured with that data.

Following our construction of the main stylized facts documenting the growth in equity pay, we provide panel-data evidence in support of technological complementarity between physical capital and human capital from high-skilled labor. Specifically, we show a robust negative relation between investment goods prices and human capitalists' income shares, which holds in the time series in the cross section of industries as well as within firms over time. We also provide evidence on the relation between investment goods prices and human capitalist wealth.

A. Measuring Total Human Capitalist Income

Data Sources

We describe our main data sources. Additional details appear in the appendix. The income of human capitalists consists of two parts. The first is traditional compensation to high-skilled human capitalists in the form of wages. The second part, which is novel to our analysis, is compensation from restricted equity or stock option grants.

Wages, value added, and investment goods prices are obtained at the four-digit Standard Industrial Classification system (SIC) code level from the NBER-CES Manufacturing Industry Database, which is based largely on the Annual Survey of Manufacturing data sets (Becker, Gray, and Marvakov 2013).[10] The NBER-CES is particularly useful for our purposes, as it provides a "clean" measure of wages; these data are payroll only, and they explicitly exclude fringe benefits and equity compensation, as we document in the appendix.[11]

To surpass the challenges faced by standard data sources using employer or employee tax data, we construct our baseline measure of equity-based compensation using widely available firm-level data on shares reserved for employee compensation from public-firm SEC filings. We utilize firms' reporting of shares reserved for employee compensation to construct our firm-level annual time series of new equity grants. These data are reported by Compustat for the period 1960–95. Compustat data are constructed from 10-K statements filed with the SEC and cover the universe of publicly traded US firms. For the subsequent subsample, for the period 1996–2005, we utilize data from RiskMetrics. RiskMetrics (formerly the Investor Responsibility Research Center [IRRC]) covers firms from the S&P 500, S&P midcap, and S&P smallcap indexes and is also sourced from 10-K statements filed with the SEC. The IRRC data set is aimed at providing compensation and governance information, and thus contains additional useful details on grants and vesting. For the 2006–19 period, we hand-collected the RSs data for the industries covered in the NBER-CES data set from firms' 10-K filings or proxy statements available from SEC Edgar.

The merged public-firm–NBER-CES data set covers all firms in the manufacturing and health sectors as well as roughly half of the firms in the consumer goods and high-tech sectors. The combined data set for the 1960–2019 period is composed of 133 four-digit-SIC code industries and 5,271 firms. The covered sectors represent more than 40% of the aggregate value of sales in the public-firm universe. We show in appendix I that factor share dynamics using wage data only in the full NBER-CES universe are nearly identical to those in our merged sample. When constructing our measure of NG relative to value added, we use industry-level sales from each data source to scale the public-firm data to match the public and private establishment data covered by the NBER-CES data set.

Human Capitalist Income: Wages

We designate the NBER-CES category of nonproduction workers as high-skilled laborers, following the standard treatment of this category in labor economics. The validity of utilizing the category of nonproduction workers to represent high-skilled labor has been previously established in the labor literature by, for example, Berman, Bound, and Griliches (1994), Acemoglu et al. (2014), and Pierce and Schott (2016). The time series of high-skilled wages as a share of value added is plotted in figure 1. Note the pronounced decline in the high-skilled income share using wages only, from 17% in 1960 to 11% in 2019. However, compensation using wages

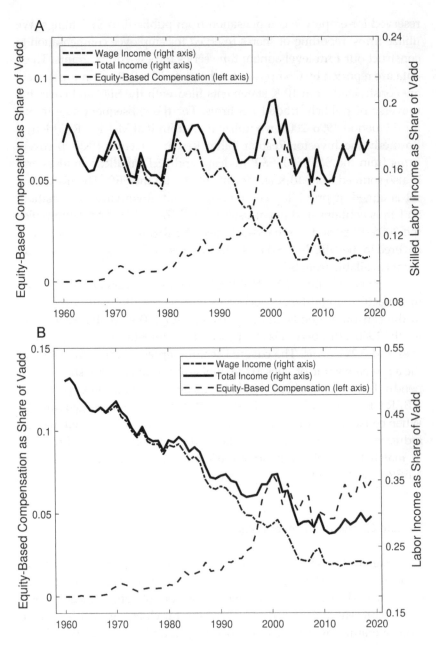

Fig. 1. Human capital share of income and total labor share. Panel *A* reports human capitalists' total income share and its composition. The dotted line is the human capitalists' flow wage income, calculated as the total labor income share minus the production labor income share (from the NBER-CES Manufacturing Industry Database) minus an estimate of the total value of exercised employee stock options. The dashed line is the ratio of equity-based compensation (NG) to value added. The total human capitalists' income share is the sum of

only is incomplete. Equity pay is crucial for fully measuring the differential effects of technological progress on high- and low-skilled labor highlighted by Autor (2014, 2019).

Human Capitalist Income: Equity Pay

Our main measurement challenge is to gather comprehensive information on the equity-based component of current income, which comes from equity grants in the form of restricted stock or unvested stock options. We overcome this challenge using firm-level data on shares reserved for employee compensation to generate annual firm-level observations on the contemporaneous flow of equity-based pay. Securities law requires firms to disclose shares reserved for compensation and thereby disclose the expected dilution to existing shareholders. To be in compliance with the SEC, firms must reserve shares in an amount that reflects the mispricing, and the resulting dilution to existing shareholders, from issuing shares to employees at below-market prices. RSs are authorized by the board of directors and appear as a treasury stock liability on firms' balance sheets. Compustat defines the RS variable as the item that "represents shares reserved for stock options outstanding as of year-end plus options that are available for future grants."[12]

RSs are a stock variable, whereas we are interested in the annual flow of new equity grants. Intuitively, we can convert the stock of RSs into an annual flow by dividing the stock by the average time that a RS remains on the balance sheet before it is granted as compensation. Denote this average granting period as gp. We provide a formal derivation of our flow measure of equity-based compensation, new grants, or NG = RS/gp, in the section "Variable Definitions and Construction" in appendix using a law of motion for RSs that accounts for authorization, exercise, and expiration. We then use the RiskMetrics data from the period 1996–2005 to estimate the weighted-average granting period as the ratio of compensation grants to RSs. During this period, the weighted-average granting period, gp, is 5.69 years.[13] To be conservative, we then use a weighted-average granting period of 6 years to estimate the annual flow of equity-based compensation grants from the end-of-year stock of RSs.

Our equity-based compensation data are obtained from publicly traded firms' accounting statements, whereas value-added data are obtained from the aggregate NBER-CES industry-level database, which includes survey data from manufacturing establishments of both public and private firms. After dropping public firms in industries not covered by the NBER-CES Manufacturing Database, we are left with two remaining potential mismatches when aggregating the firm-level value of NG to the industry level. First, the NBER-CES database includes private firms, causing a downward bias to our NG/value added ratio. Second, publicly traded firms have foreign establishments, and they may grant equity compensation to employees in foreign establishments, whereas the NBER-CES data covers domestic manufacturing establishments only. Therefore, to adjust the new grant series based on public firms to the NBER-CES industry measures of value added, we scale each industry aggregate NG by the corresponding sales ratio between the public-firm industry aggregate and the NBER-CES industry value.[14]

Note that, because our estimates are derived from firm-level data and not worker-level data, we cannot identify the precise recipients of equity-based compensation. We allocate all of equity pay to high-skilled labor. IRS data show that 97% of equity pay goes to earners in the top 10% of the income distribution for the available sample from the period 2008–17, and this fraction is nearly constant over that period.[15] Other auxiliary data sources, such as levels.fyi, suggest that equity-based compensation is used heavily for engineers and for a broad set of managers. We use an expense-based measure below to provide additional evidence that total compensation to white-collar workers has increased from 1980 to 2019. Finally, using ExecuComp, we show that most equity-based compensation (78% in recent years) goes to workers below the C-suite.

Figure 2 reports the aggregate NG as a share of aggregate value added in our sample (the solid line). Income from equity-based compensation grows from less than 1% of value added before 1980 to as much as 7% in the 2010s. We also measure the share of total equity that human capitalists own. We define the ownership share of human capitalists as the ratio of the value of shares reserved for employee equity-based compensation (i.e., RS) to the stock market capitalization of the firm.[16] This share, also plotted in figure 2 (the dotted line), captures the fraction of firm value which is employee-owned. Human capitalists have owned 10% of total public

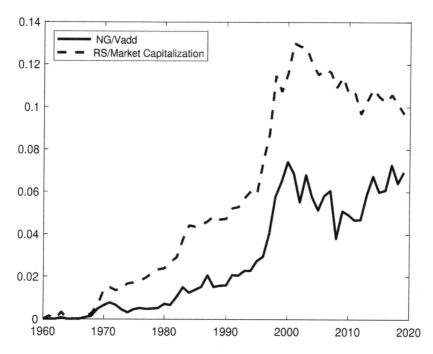

Fig. 2. Equity-based compensation: time series. This plot reports the time series of human capitalists' equity-based compensation in the manufacturing sector, both the annual flow and the stock. The annual flow of total reserved shares (RSs) for employees' equity-based compensation, new grants (NG), is calculated as the aggregate value of outstanding RSs normalized by the average granting period of 6 years. The solid line is the time series of the NG to value-added ratio. The dashed line is the time series of the ownership share, measured by the ratio of the value of RSs for employee equity-based compensation to stock market capitalization.

firms' market capitalization on average over the last decade compared with 3% in the 1980s. The rise of the ownership share indicates that the increase in human capitalists' income is not just driven by rising corporate valuations. Human capitalists have benefited disproportionately from increasing corporate profits because their ownership share also increased.

Human Capitalist Income, Total: Wages plus Equity

Human capitalists earn both wages and equity compensation. Whereas human capitalists' wage share of value added has been trending down, equity pay has replaced wage compensation in recent decades. To construct human capitalists' total income, we add equity pay to wages to form their total compensation. We plot the time series of the total income share along with the wage share and equity-based compensation share in figure 1. The figure shows that the increase in equity-based compensation essentially offsets the decline in high-skilled wage income. The human capitalists' total labor share declined by 1% from the 1980s to 2010s compared with the 6% decline in human capitalists' wage-only share from the 1980s to 2010s. Including the equity-based pay cuts the decline in the wage-only human capitalists' income share by 87%. The fact that the total high-skilled labor share is essentially flat is consistent with our estimate of the fraction of equity pay that is used to compensate marginal product, which is 98%, indicating that, in large part, equity has simply replaced wages, leaving the high-skilled labor share fairly constant.

Human Capitalist Income, Total: Wages plus Equity,
Expense-Based Robustness

As a robustness check, we compare our main approach to measuring total human capitalist compensation as the sum of equity-based compensation using RS data and high-skilled wage data from CES, to an expensed-based measure of the total compensation to human capitalists. Specifically, we compare our measure of total income to a measure based on accumulating the widely available accounting variable *selling, general, and administrative expenses* (SG&A). As detailed in Eisfeldt and Papanikolaou (2013) and the associated appendix I, this variable typically includes the salaries, wages, equity compensation, and bonuses of firms' white-collar workers and managers. However, since SG&A includes other expenses unrelated to employee compensation, we follow the approximation approach from the prior literature (e.g., Eisfeldt and Papanikolaou 2014) and scale the total SG&A expense by 0.3. Our second measure of human capitalist income shares is then constructed in each year by aggregating the firm-level observations of 30% of SG&A to the industry level and then computing the ratio of industry-level $0.3 \times$ SG&A to industry-level value added ($0.3 \times$ SG&A/VADD). This share was 8% at the beginning of the sample period, and it increases to 12% at the end of 2019. As expected, given that wages have trended downward while equity compensation increased substantially, the SG&A based measure increases from 1980 to 2019, but not as dramatically as the measure of equity compensation only.

B.   *Time-Series Evidence: Main Facts*

Table 1 reports the summary statistics of the key variables for our analysis. Panel A reports averages over a longer sample from 1960 to 2019

Table 1
Descriptive Statistics

Panel A: Summary Statistics			
	Mean	St. Dev	Median
	(1)	(2)	(3)
Levels (pct.pt.):			
NG/VADD	2.4	14.1	.2
Skilled wages/VADD	16.5	7.5	15.2
(Skilled wages + NG)/VADD	18.5	8.7	16.9
NG/(Total wages + NG)	10.0	13.8	4.6
SG&A/VADD	11.3	5.2	10.5
Investment/VADD	6.5	4.1	5.4
Total wages/VADD	39.5	12.5	40.5
Unskilled wages/VADD	23	10.1	23.1
Investment good prices	96.6	21.1	98.1
Annual changes (pct.pt.):			
NG/VADD	.22	5.27	0
Skilled wages/VADD	−.09	2.13	−.10
(Skilled wages + NG)/VADD	−.02	3.45	−.06
NG/(Total wages + NG)	.44	6.35	0
SGA/VADD	.09	1.93	.05
Investment/VADD	−.01	2.24	0
Total wages/VADD	−.45	3.71	−.43
Unskilled wages/VADD	−.36	2.21	−.30
Investment good prices	−.76	2.12	−.62
Additional measures (1996–2005, pct. pt.):			
(Employee stock options, Black-Scholes value)/VADD	8.0	25.5	.8
(Employee wealth, Black-Scholes value)/Stock Mkt value	9.3	21.3	4.1
(Nonexecutive employee options, Black-Scholes value)/(Employee stock options, Black-Scholes value)	78.1	18.4	82.7
(Value of exercised options)/Stock Mkt value	1.0	4.8	.4
Number of industries = 133			
Number of observations = 6,303			

Panel B: Time Series Stylized Facts				
	1980–1989	1990–1999	2000–2009	2010–2019
Levels (pct.pt.):				
Human capital wage share (skilled wages/VADD) (%)	17	14	12	11
Total human capital share ([NG + skilled wages]/VADD) (%)	18	17	18	17
Total wage labor share (total wages/VADD) (%)	38	31	25	22
Total labor share ([NG + total wages]/VADD) (%)	39	34	31	28
Equity share of value added (NG/VADD) (%)	1	3	6	6
Ownership share (NG/MktCap) (%)	4	7	12	10
Equity-based pay of total human capital income (NG/[NG+ skilled wages]) (%)	7	18	33	36
Skilled wage share of total wage share (skilled wages/total wages) (%)	44	46	46	47

Table 1
Continued

Panel B: Time Series Stylized Facts				
	1980–1989	1990–1999	2000–2009	2010–2019
Human capital share of total labor share				
(NG + skilled wages/[total wages + NG]) (%)	46	51	56	58
# Skilled workers/total emp (%)	30	30	30	NA
Equity-based pay (billions $)	4.1	29.1	79.5	116.1

Note: Panel A reports descriptive statistics (means, medians, and standard deviations) for our 4-SIC industry-level manufacturing sample between 1960 and 2011. The manufacturing sector corresponds to industries covered in the NBER-CES data set and for which information on their SG&A expenditures or reserved shares is available in Compustat and RiskMetrics. The data set includes 133 unique industries at the 4-SIC level. The first section reports statistics for the total human capital share, unskilled labor share, total labor share, and the structure of skilled labor pay, measured by the ratio of equity-based pay to total pay. The second section reports changes in these variables. The third section reports statistics for equity-based pay based on Black-Sholes valuation from the RiskMetrics sample available 1996–2005. Panel B reports the average of major shares of value added and shares of income for the last 4 decades, during which investment goods prices and the wage share of value added declined steeply. The time period is 1980–2019. See Subsection II.A and the appendix for detailed variable definitions.

and provides the summary statistics that can be used to interpret our cross-section regression coefficients, and panel B reports averages for each decade since 1980 to illustrate the main time-series facts. Both panels show that including equity-based compensation is key to understanding the high-skilled labor share. The wage-only high-skilled labor share averages only 16.5% over the full sample and only 11% over the most recent decade. The equity-pay share of value added is only 2.4% on average in the full sample back to 1960, but it increases to an average of 6% in the most recent decade. Thus, although the wage share of high-skilled labor declined, these workers have transformed into human capitalists—their equity pay has steadily increased over this same period. Including equity pay, the total high-skilled labor share does not change very much; it averages 19% over the full sample and 17% in the most recent decade. Panel A also shows that investment goods prices declined substantially over the full sample, on average 0.76% annually. The correlation between human capitalists' income and investment goods prices is −0.91 from this period, which motivates our study of technical change as a driver of human capitalist income. As investment goods prices declined, the relatively flat share of human capitalists, relative to the declining share of low-skilled labor, is consistent with technological complementarity between high-skilled labor and capital, and substitutability between low-skilled labor and capital. We formalize this intuition in our structural model and estimation.

Figure 2 shows the time series of human capitalists' flow of equity-based compensation as a share of value added. Panel A of figure 1 shows this series along with the time series of human capitalists' wage, and total (wages + equity), compensation as a share of value added. Strikingly, the sevenfold increase in equity-based compensation relative to value added (i.e., a roughly 7 percentage point increase from the 1960s to the end of the sample) almost completely reverses the downward trend in high-skilled labor's wage income share. In fact, panel B of figure 1 shows that the increase in equity-based compensation is strong enough to greatly dampen the decline in the overall labor wage share of value added. Including equity-based compensation cuts the measured decline in the total labor share in our sample by 32%. Note that the wage-based labor share in the NBER-CES sample is lower than that for the overall economy for two reasons. It is manufacturing only (no services), and it does not include any fringe benefits or equity. Despite the lower level, the downward trend is consistent with the prior literature using other labor compensation data. In line with these facts, the human capitalists' ownership share (fig. 2) (i.e., shares reserved for employee equity-based compensation relative to total equity shares outstanding) also displays a pronounced upward trend, increasing from about 1% before the 1980s to about 10% in 2010s. The increase in the ownership share was not driven only by top executives' equity-based compensation, which was relatively stable at around 2.2% on average in the 1990s and 2000s based on ExecuComp data.

Finally, we note that, in the cross section, the increase in equity-based compensation is even more pronounced for small firms (see appendix I).[17] Although our sample focuses primarily on publicly traded firms, the fact that human capitalists in smaller firms receive more equity-based compensation as a share of total sales than those of larger firms indicates that our time series for the share of NG relative to value added could be an underestimate for the whole US economy, including private firms. This increase in equity-based compensation among smaller firms also enhances the divergence between the average and the aggregate total labor share, which is consistent with the evidence in Hartman-Glaser et al. (2019).

C.   *Understanding the Underestimation of Equity Pay
     in Standard Data Sources*

Two key features of equity-based compensation lead to equity income being substantially underestimated in standard data sources such as the BEA and the BLS. These two features are tax treatment and deferral. First, a sizable fraction (one-third to one-half) of equity-based compensation is classified as incentive-based and is thus taxed as capital gains income rather than ordinary income. Second, even pay that is taxed as ordinary income is only taxed after it vests and is exercised, rather than at the time it is granted. Although this would not result in mismeasurement if equity pay were constant, the very high observed growth in equity pay in recent decades means that exercised or vested equity pay severely underestimates current grants. That the majority of equity pay is missing from national accounting data is apparent by observing the publicly available IRS data that reports that the value of equity pay in W2 earnings was only $55 billion over the period 2008–17.[18] This is much smaller than our estimate of equity pay in the manufacturing sector only for the overlapping time period ($100 billion). We discuss the tax treatment and deferred nature of equity pay in turn and then provide a stylized example to illustrate how these two features drive the underestimation of equity pay in standard data sources.

In most of the rest of the literature on the labor share, two main sources of payroll information are used: BEA's National Income and Product Accounts (BEA NIPA) (e.g., Karabarbounis and Neiman 2014) and the BLS Quarterly Census of Employment and Wages (QCEW) (e.g., Elsby et al. 2013). These measures include only payments to employees under plans that are taxed at the personal income tax rate and are either (*a*) reported as payroll by the employer on IRS form 941 or (*b*) reported as wage income by the employee on his or her W-2 form.[19] For this reporting to occur, the equity compensation must be both (i) issued under a plan that treats equity grants as ordinary income for tax purposes and (ii) vested and exercised following deferral.

For measures of the labor share based on BEA NIPA, the BEA technical methodology emphasizes that its labor compensation series only includes vested and exercised nonqualified options. Specifically, the BEA states that "wages and salaries in cash . . . includes employee gains from exercising nonqualified stock options (NSOs). . . . NSOs are regarded as additional, taxable, income at the time they are exercised; in contrast, incentive stock options do not require the reporting of additional income and are taxed as long-term capital gains when sold. The detailed data required for treating NSOs as compensation of employees when the options are granted (as the System of National Accounts [SNA] recommends) are not currently available. Instead, NSOs are valued when they are exercised, and the difference between the market price at the time of the exercise and the price paid by the employee at the time of the exercise is recorded as wages and salaries."[20] For a discussion of the SNA recommendations and the BEA's research on NSOs, see Moylan (2000).

For measures of the labor share based on employer payroll records from the BLS (QCEW), as detailed at the BLS website (https://www .bls.gov/opub/hom/cew/data.htm), the QCEW comes from the administrative tax records of state unemployment insurance (UI) programs. It is similar to NIPA and only includes taxable wages. As such, it includes only the exercise value of NSOs. In addition, as discussed in further detail in the BEA technical note and in the related paper by Moylan (2000), internal BLS surveys indicate that UI records are likely to underestimate even the exercised value of NSOs. That reference states, at the top of page 3, "In addition, although it appears that large technology firms are reporting as wages the exercise of employee stock options, it is not clear that all firms are doing so. Because the annual tax base for UI wages and salaries is capped at $7,000 per employee, states may have little incentive to follow up with firms to ensure correct reporting of special compensation items."

Finally, two other measures of wages from the BLS have also been used in the macroeconomic literature on the labor share; namely, the employment cost index and nonfarm compensation per hour. The former excludes stock options altogether. The latter includes only exercised NSOs, as detailed in table 1 of the FRB technical note in Lebow et al. (1999). Additional details are provided in the appendix, and the links to the relevant technical documentation also provide clear explanations for the treatment of equity compensation for each source. We provide a method for adjusting compensation in standard data sources to fully account for the flow of equity-based compensation, and we describe the impact of including equity pay on the labor share based on BEA data in the next subsection.

Equity Pay and Taxes

Employers can adopt an equity compensation program by approving one of a variety of employee compensation plans, such as a stock option plan, a restricted stock unit plan, an employee stock purchase plan, or an employee stock ownership plan, as well as by placing employee stock grants in retirement and 401(k) plans. For tax purposes, earnings from equity-based compensation may be treated either as income or as capital gains, depending on whether such compensation is derived from nonqualified or qualified plans, respectively. Equity pay that is derived from a plan that is qualified under the IRS code as incentive-based is tax advantaged at the worker level, since the employee can, with proper execution, avoid being taxed at the ordinary income rate and instead pay only long-term capital gains taxes.[21] Preferable personal tax treatment may be one reason that equity pay has grown in importance.

Qualified equity grants are never included in standard sources for labor compensation such as the BEA or BLS. We estimate the fraction of equity grants that are qualified for tax purposes, and thus entirely excluded from standard sources, to be between one-half and one-third. Crimmel and Schildkraut (1999) document that about half of plans surveyed by the BLS offer incentive-based compensation that is qualified for tax purposes and excluded from standard sources. In ExecuComp data, which covers firms' most highly compensated employees, the fraction of equity compensation that is incentive-based and qualified is one-third. Because there is a limit (currently $100,000) on the maximum value of incentive-based options allowed under IRS rules, and it is more likely that executive (vs. nonexecutive) compensation exceeds this limit, we argue that one-third is a lower bound on qualified equity pay for nonexecutive employees.

Vesting and Exercise

Employees receiving equity-based compensation are granted promises of future equity shares, which can only be exercised or vested after a certain period of time has elapsed. In addition to complicating the matching of pay to the year in which labor was provided (and value-added generated), the combination of deferral and the fast growth of equity pay means that even the portion of equity pay that is taxed at normal income rates and should appear on W2 tax returns is a small fraction of current new equity grants. Indeed, in ExecuComp data, vested and exercised options are an order of magnitude smaller than the overall value of granted and unexpired stock options (at about 1% of stock market capitalization relative to 9%, respectively; see table 1).

A Simple Example

The following stylized example illustrates the joint effects of qualified equity pay and the timing of NG versus exercise dates on the underestimation of equity pay in standard sources. Assume that total NG relative to value added grows at an effective annual rate of 12% per year, which is the constant continuously compounded growth rate that connects the beginning and end points of our data on total NG. Assume also that, conservatively, of the total, two-thirds of grants are nonqualified and 100% of grants are exercised immediately after a 5-year vesting period. Because the value of NG grows each year at 12% and grants can only be exercised after the vesting period of 5 years, the value of vested and exercised nonqualified grants (i.e., the portion that might be counted in standard sources) is equal to only 37% of total current grants. With a constant growth rate, this fraction is also constant. It is important to note that, as it is 63% of a growing series, the part of equity compensation that is missing from standard labor share measures grows very substantially in levels in this example, as can be seen in figure 3.

D.   *Adjusting the BEA Manufacturing Labor Share*

In our main analysis, we use NBER-CES payroll data, which only includes wages, to construct human capitalists' total income series. However, in most of the existing literature on the labor share, the standard data sources, from BEA (Karabarbounis and Neiman 2014) or BLS (Elsby et al. 2013), are employed to construct labor share measures. As detailed in Subsection II.C, compensation data from either of these two data sources only includes the fraction of equity-based compensation that is both exercised or unrestricted and nonqualified for tax purposes.

To evaluate the impact of including the equity-based compensation (NG) on the labor share measures based on standard data sources (BEA), we must first estimate a series for wage-only compensation by subtracting income from exercised, nonqualified stock options. Otherwise, some equity pay would be double counted. In ExecutiveComp data, nonqualified equity-based grants are two-thirds of total grants. Although it is likely that nonexecutives are eligible for a higher fraction of qualified grants because they are more likely to have equity compensation below the $100,000 cap on qualified grants, we adopt the conservative assumption that two-thirds of grants to all employees are nonqualified. We assume that 100% of the nonqualified equity grants are

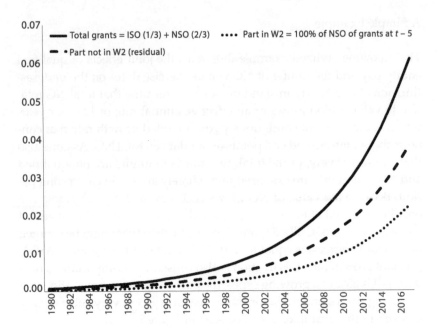

Fig. 3. Equity-based compensation as a fraction of value added. Stylized example of missing equity pay: we construct a stylized example to illustrate the effects of tax treatment and deferral on missing equity pay. We plot total grants (solid line), grants included in standard data sources (dotted line), and grants missing from standard data sources (dashed line). This example uses the observed share of new grants relative to value added in 1975 and assumes that this share grows at a constant rate of 12%, which results in grants as a share of value added that approximately match the empirical share in recent decades of about 6%. From 1980 to 2019, the implied total grants are the top, solid line. The bottom, dotted line denotes grants that could appear in standard labor data, that is, nonqualified, exercised grants. We assume that two-thirds of grants are nonqualified, and that 100% of nonqualified grants are exercised 5 years after they are granted. The calibrated assumptions result in 63% of current grants being excluded from standard data sources, whereas a minority of 37% are included. A color version of this figure is available online.

exercised as soon as they are vested, and we apply the average vesting period of 5 years.

To construct the wage-only labor income in year t, we subtract the estimated amount of current equity grants that are included in the contemporaneous BEA income measure. Assuming all grants are exercised immediately after vesting for 5 years, 100% of two-thirds of equity grants (i.e., all grants that are nonqualified) from year $t - 5$ appear in year t BEA income.[22] Our estimates indicate that, due to deferral and the fact that one-third of grants are qualified, only 35% of current equity grants are accounted for in the BEA data at any given date t. The total labor share is then the sum of estimated wage-only labor income plus the con-temporaneous estimate of NG relative to value added.

Figure 4 reports the aggregate BEA labor share after adjusting for equity-based compensation (NG) for the manufacturing industry (for which we hand-collected the equity pay data for the years after 2006). The manufacturing wage-only labor share declined by 17% since 1980s, and including the equity-based compensation reduces the decline in the labor share based on the BEA manufacturing-sector data by 20%. Although our adjustment focuses on the manufacturing industry broadly defined, the inclusion of equity-based pay should still have large impact on the aggregate labor share given the evidence in Alvarez-Cuadrado, Long, and Poschke (2018) and Aum and Shin (2020) that the downward trend in the aggregate labor share since the 1980 is mainly driven by the decline of labor share in the manufacturing industry.

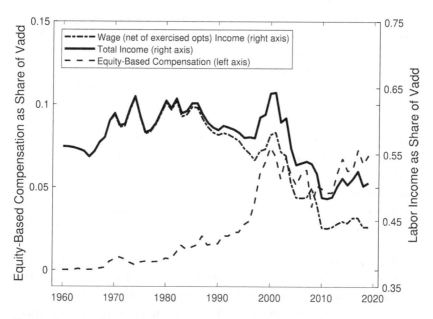

Fig. 4. Aggregate labor share in manufacturing: adjusting BEA labor share. The figure reports the aggregate labor share in manufacturing before and after the adjustment for NG. The dotted line is the aggregate wage income minus the estimate of the total value of exercised employee stock options. The dashed line is the ratio of NG to value added. The total labor income share is the sum of the wage income share and the equity-based income share. Data are from Compustat Fundamental Annual (1960–1996), RiskMetrics (IRRC) (1996–2005), and NBER-CES Manufacturing Industry Database (1960–2011). The total manufacturing labor income and value-added data are from KLEMS industry data set. The nonfinancial corporate sector labor income and value-added data are from NIPA table 1.14. The sample period is from 1960 to 2019. A color version of this figure is available online.

E. Panel-Data Evidence

We next show that cross-industry and cross-firm evidence is consistent with (*a*) a substitution mechanism between human capital and labor and (*b*) complementarity between human capital and physical capital. Complementarity indicates that human capitalists' share of value added declines as costs of physical capital goods become cheaper. We first test whether trends in total human capitalists' share of value added are related to trends in investment goods prices at the industry level. The Kao (1999) cointegration test cannot reject the null hypothesis that there is no cointegration between the human capitalists' share of value added and industry-level investment goods prices.[23] The evidence of cointegration between the human capital share and investment goods prices is consistent with industry-specific investment goods prices being the source of the trend in human capitalists' share of value added. Our regression results also support the idea that the share of equity-based compensation relative to value added, and total human capitalists' share of value added, is strongly and statistically significantly negatively related to the industry-specific path of investment goods prices.

Table 2 reports industry-level multivariate regressions of the human capitalists' share in a given year on both the physical capital share and the unskilled labor share at the four-digit SIC code level of industry aggregation. We follow Karabarbounis and Neiman (2014) and use investment relative to value added to measure the capital share. The physical capital share equals the investment to value added ratio if investment I equals the rental payment to capital rK.[24] Both the grant-based and the expense-based shares are significantly positively (negatively) correlated with physical capital share (unskilled labor share) within industry and over time.

Table 3 reports (4-SIC) industry-level regressions of income shares on investment goods prices. These regressions include year and industry fixed effects and thus examine the change in industry-level share variables across industries and years that were more versus less exposed to the decline in capital goods prices, because the capital mix across capital types that experienced different price changes varies over time and across industries. If there is more complementarity between human capital and physical capital than that between human capital and labor, one should expect to see the total human capital share of value added negatively correlated with the investment goods prices, that is, the coefficient of investment goods prices should be negative. The first three columns

Table 2
The Relation among Factor Shares: Industry-Level Analysis

	Equity Comp Share = NG/VADD		Total H Share = (Skilled Wages + NG)/VADD		SG&A/VADD	
	(1)	(2)	(3)	(4)	(5)	(6)
Physical capital	.004	.056*	.113***	.094***	.010	.031
share	(.11)	(1.72)	(5.46)	(4.49)	(.27)	(.82)
Unskilled labor		−.475***		.171***		−.187***
share		(−4.82)		(2.46)		(−2.21)
Year FE	Y	Y	Y	Y	Y	Y
Industry FE	Y	Y	Y	Y	Y	Y
N	6,207	6,207	6,207	6,207	6,222	6,222
R^2	.345	.378	.074	.094	.141	.153

Note: This table reports industry-level regressions of the human capital share in a given year on the physical capital share at the 4-SIC level of industry aggregation. The specification that is estimated is as follows:

$$Y_{i,t} = \alpha + \beta X_{i,t-1} + \mu_i + \mu_t + \epsilon_{i,t}.$$

All specifications include time (year, μ_t) and industry (μ_i) effects. We report results for three dependent variables: new grants (NG), which are estimated based on the value of reserved shares, and two measures of the human capital share. The main measure is defined as the sum of skilled wages and new grants relative to value added. The second is the expense-based SG&A share. As for the independent variables, the physical capital share is the ratio of investment to value added. The unskilled labor share refers to production workers' wages relative to value added. To ease interpretation, all variables are expressed in standard-deviation units. The interpretation of each reported coefficient is the change in standard deviations of the dependent variable associated with a one-standard-deviation change in the explanatory variable. For example, in the third column, a one-standard-deviation change in the physical capital share is associated with about 11% standard-deviation change in the human capital share. The time period is 1960–2011. See Subsection II.A and the appendix for detailed variable definitions. Standard errors are clustered by industry, with
* denoting significance at the 10% level.
** denoting significance at the 5% level.
*** denoting significance at the 1% level.

show that the share of value added represented by equity-based compensation, total human capitalist income, and the expense-based proxy for total human capitalist income is robustly negative and strongly statistically significant for all measures of human capitalists' income shares. The estimates are also economically significant, as they imply that a one-standard-deviation decline in investment goods prices is associated with up to about 9.4% of a standard-deviation increase in the log human capitalists' income share (col. 2). Columns 4–6 examine the relation of wage shares and investment goods prices. Columns 4 and 5 show that there is a weak negative relation between the total wage share and investment

Table 3
The Human Capital Share of Income and Investment Goods Prices: Industry-Level Analysis

	Human Capital Income			Wage-Only Income			Equity Pay and Ownership Shares	
	NG/ VADD	(Skilled Wages + NG)/VADD	SG&A/ VADD	Total Wages/ VADD	Unskilled Labor Share	Skilled Wages/VADD	(NG)/(NG + Skilled Wages)	Reserved Shares/ Market Cap
	(1)	(2)	(3)	(4)	(5)	(6)	(7)	(8)
Investment goods prices	-.187*** (-3.27)	-.094*** (-2.34)	-.130*** (-2.17)	-.009 (-.23)	.187*** (6.29)	-.119*** (-2.55)	-.028 (-.41)	-.082*** (-1.86)
Time FE	Y	Y	Y	Y	Y	Y	Y	Y
Industry FE	Y	Y	Y	Y	Y	Y	Y	Y
Industry controls	Y	Y	Y	Y	Y	Y	Y	Y
N	6,207	6,207	6,222	6,222	6,222	6,222	4,851	5,855
R²	.367	.090	.163	.646	.724	.304	.502	.347

Note: This table reports (4-SIC) industry-level regressions of the human capital share (cols. 1–3) in a given year on investment goods prices. The specification that is estimated is as follows:

$$Y_{i,t} = \alpha + \beta X_{i,t-1} + \mu_i + \mu_t + \epsilon_{i,t}.$$

All specifications include time (year, μ_t) and industry (μ_i) effects. We report results for three main dependent variables: new grants (NG), which are estimated based on the value of reserved shares, and two measures of the human capital share. The main measure is defined as the sum of skilled wages and new grants relative to value added (col. 2). The second is the expense-based SG&A share (col. 3). The independent variable is investment good prices. We also report results for two additional sets of independent variables, wage-only income (cols. 4–6) and the structure of skilled workers compensation (cols. 7–9). The unskilled labor share refers to production workers' wages relative to value added, and the skilled share refers to nonproduction workers. The structure of skilled workers compensation is measured by the share of equity-based compensation to total skilled workers compensation (col. 7). To ease interpretation, all variables are expressed in standard-deviation units. The interpretation of each reported coefficient is the change in standard deviations of the dependent variable associated with a one-standard-deviation change in the explanatory variable. For example, in the second column, a one-standard-deviation change in investment goods prices is associated with about 18% of a standard-deviation change in the human capital share. The time period is 1960–2011. See Subsection II.A and the appendix for detailed variable definitions. Standard errors are clustered by industry, with

* denoting significance at the 10% level.
** denoting significance at the 5% level.
*** denoting significance at the 1% level.

goods prices, and a stronger positive relationship for the unskilled labor wage share across industries, suggesting substitution between unskilled labor and capital. Although not significant, the negative relation between the total wage share and investment goods prices aligns with the cross-country evidence in Karabarbounis and Neiman (2014). Column 6 shows that the decline in the wage share of high-skilled labor is negatively related to the investment goods prices in the cross section of industries, indicating that the skilled wage share declined less in industries that faced larger declines in capital goods price, consistent with complementarity between high-skilled labor and capital. Note that the coefficient on investment goods prices is much smaller in absolute value in column 6 versus column 1, meaning that equity pay had an increasing share of total pay in industries and years in which capital goods prices declined by more. Column 7 confirms this by showing that declining investment goods prices are correlated with a change in the structure of human capitalists' pay, with equity-based compensation increasing in importance, although the correlation is not statistically significant. Column 8 reports the significant negative relation between the ownership share (which corrects for generally rising share prices) and investment goods prices. A one-standard-deviation decline in investment goods prices is associated with up to about 8.2% of a standard-deviation increase in the human capitalists' ownership share. Overall, the regression analysis confirms the negative time-series relation between investment goods prices and human capitalists' income and ownership shares.

Table 4 confirms the relation between investment goods prices and human capitalists' income and ownership shares at the firm level for specifications with industry fixed effects (panel A) and firm fixed effects (panel B). Columns 1 and 2 show that human capitalists' ownership shares increased more in firm-years with larger investment goods price declines. The relation between investment goods prices and the ownership share is also economically significant. We observe that a one-standard-deviation decline in investment goods prices is associated with an increase of about 10% of a standard deviation in the human capitalists' ownership share at the firm level, based on the estimate in column 2. Using sales to proxy for value added in the firm-level data for which value added is not available, columns 3 and 4 show that equity compensation to sales also increased more in firm-years with larger investment goods price declines. The coefficient estimate in column 4 implies that a one-standard-deviation decline in investment goods prices is associated with an increase of about 2.6% of a standard deviation in the

Table 4
The Human Capital Share, Stock Market Value, and Investment Goods Prices: Firm-Level Analysis

	Value of Reserved Share/Stock Market Value		Equity Comp Share NG/Sales		SG&A/Sales	
	(1)	(2)	(3)	(4)	(5)	(6)
Panel A: Industry and Time Fixed Effects Estimates for the Human Capital Share						
Investment goods prices	−.091***	−.102***	−.032**	−.026	−.042**	−.052*
	(−4.75)	(−4.74)	(−2.52)	(−1.52)	(−2.02)	(−1.95)
Industry FE	Y	Y	Y	Y	Y	Y
Firm FE	N	N	N	N	N	N
Year FE	Y	Y	Y	Y	Y	Y
Firm controls	Y	Y	Y	Y	Y	Y
Industry controls	N	Y	N	Y	N	Y
N	73,027	50,629	73,027	50,629	69,308	47,654
R^2	.321	.331	.707	.714	.624	.668
Panel B: Firm and Time Fixed Effects Estimates for the Human Capital Share						
Investment goods prices	−.071***	−.076***	−.009	−.012	−.022*	−.042**
	(−3.78)	(−3.68)	(−1.09)	(−1.13)	(−1.79)	(−2.90)
Industry FE	N	N	N	N	N	N
Firm FE	Y	Y	Y	Y	Y	Y
Year FE	Y	Y	Y	Y	Y	Y
Firm controls	Y	Y	Y	Y	Y	Y
Industry controls	N	Y	N	Y	N	Y
N	72,476	50,208	72,476	50,208	68,765	47,237
R^2	.625	.633	.830	.834	.899	.907

Note: This table reports firm-level regressions of the human capital share in a given year on investment goods prices. Columns 1 and 2 report results for the ownership share (value of reserved shares to market capitalization ratio). Columns 3 and 4 report results for the NG to sales ratio. Columns 5 and 6 report results for the expense-based measure SG&A to sales ratio. In panel A, we report results for a specification with industry fixed effects, which is as follows: $Y_{j,i,t} = \alpha + \beta X_{j,i,t-1} + \mu_i + \mu_t + \epsilon_{j,i,t}$. All specifications include time (year, μ_t) and industry (μ_i) effects. In panel B, we report results for a specification with firm fixed effects, which is as follows: $Y_{j,i,t} = \alpha + \beta X_{j,i,t-1} + \mu_j + \mu_t + \epsilon_{j,i,t}$. All specifications include time (year, μ_t) and firm (μ_j) effects. The independent variable is investment good prices. To ease interpretation, all variables are expressed in standard-deviation units. The interpretation of each reported coefficient is the change in standard deviations of the dependent variable associated with a one-standard-deviation change in the explanatory variable. For example, in column 1 of panel A, a one-standard-deviation change in investment goods prices is associated with about 9.1% of a standard-deviation change in the ownership share variable. The time period is 1960–2011. See Subsection II.A and the appendix for detailed variable definitions. Standard errors are clustered by industry in panel A and by firm in panel B, with
* denoting significance at the 10% level.
** denoting significance at the 5% level.
*** denoting significance at the 1% level.

human capitalists' income share of sales at the firm level. Columns 5 and 6 show that the expense-based measure of human capitalist income is also negatively related to investment goods prices at the firm level.

Next, we examine the growth of the human capitalists' share relative to the physical capital share as investment goods prices decline. This is an important motivation for complementarity between physical and human capital. Table 5 reports industry-level regressions of the growth of human capitalists' share in a given industry-year relative to the growth

Table 5
The Relative Growth of the Physical Capital and the Human Capital Share and Investment Goods Prices

	ln(NG/VADD) − ln(Investment/VADD)		ln([Skilled Wages + NG]/VADD) − ln(Investment/VADD)		ln(SG&A/VADD) − ln(Investment/VADD)	
	1960–1980	1980–2011	1960–1980	1980–2011	1960–1980	1980–2011
	(1)	(2)	(3)	(4)	(5)	(6)
Investment goods	.381***	−.171**	.169***	−.131**	−.012	−.201**
prices	(4.76)	(−2.36)	(3.53)	(−2.32)	(−.15)	(−2.54)
Year FE	Y	Y	Y	Y	Y	Y
Industry FE	Y	Y	Y	Y	Y	Y
Industry controls	Y	Y	Y	Y	Y	Y
N	2,327	3,880	2,327	3,880	2,306	3,875
R^2	.116	.242	.203	.206	.204	.168

Note: This table reports results of additional industry-level regressions of the human capital share in a given year on investment goods prices. The specification that is estimated is as follows: $Y_{i,t} = \alpha + \beta X_{i,t-1} + \mu_i + \mu_t + \epsilon_{i,t}$. All specifications include time (year, μ_t) and industry (μ_i) effects. New grants (NG) are estimated based on the value of reserved shares. We report results for two measures of the human capital share. The main measure is defined as the sum of skilled wages and new grants relative to value added. The second measure is the expense-based SG&A share. For each measure, we report results relative to the physical capital share. The independent variable is investment good prices. To ease interpretation, all variables are expressed in standard-deviation units. The interpretation of each reported coefficient is the change in standard deviations of the dependent variable associated with a one-standard-deviation change in the explanatory variable. For example, in column 1, a one-standard-deviation change in investment goods prices is associated with about 6.4% of a standard-deviation change in the NG share relative to the physical capital share. The time period is 1960–2011. See Subsection II.A and the appendix for detailed variable definitions. Standard errors are clustered by industry, with
* denoting significance at the 10% level.
** denoting significance at the 5% level.
*** denoting significance at the 1% level.

in the physical capital share on investment goods prices. The coefficient estimates for all measures of relative share changes are negative and statistically significant. A one-standard-deviation decline in investment goods prices is associated with 13% of a standard-deviation faster growth (on average) of the human capitalists' share relative to the physical capital share (col. 4) for the sample from 1980 to 2011. These changes in relative shares drive the identification in our structural analysis below.

We also confirm that our main results are robust to sharpening our measurement by using the more granular information on employee stock option grants that is available for the 1996–2005 period. Our baseline measure has the advantage of being available for a wide cross section of firms over a long time series. For the 1996–2005 period, we have reported data on the value of newly granted options and restricted stock, and we use this information to corroborate the relation between equity-based compensation from granted stock options and investment goods prices. In panel A of table 6, we confirm that the negative relation with investment goods prices also holds for an alternative measure of human capitalists' equity-based compensation: the Black-Scholes value of their earnings from stock option grants relative to the value added (sales) at the industry level (firm level) (cols. 1–2 and 3–4, respectively). Another concern is that our measures include the compensation of the very top executives, and as such, our results may be driven solely by this relatively small subset of human capitalists. Panel B of table 6 shows that the negative relation with investment goods prices holds even after we net out the value of stock option grants for the top five executives. This means that the relation between declining investment goods prices and equity-based compensation is stronger for employees outside the C-suite.[25] Thus, our results for human capitalists' income shares reflect the impact of broad-based employee stock-based compensation, and not executive pay.

Additional robustness checks appear in appendix I. In particular, employee stock compensation plans lead to the dilution of existing shareholders in the absence of a parallel repurchase plan. We show that the same relationships as in our main tables between human capitalist income and investment goods prices hold for the comparison between diluted and undiluted earnings per share, and stock repurchases. Both of these variables should be correlated with equity compensation grants at the firm level. We also show that our results on ownership shares are robust to expanding the sample to the entire public-firm universe by including the nonmanufacturing sectors, for which we do not have value-added data.

Table 6

Human Capital Earnings, Factor Share, and Investment Goods Prices:
Firm-Level Analysis

	Industry Level		Firm Level	
	(1)	(2)	(3)	(4)
	(Employee Stock Options, Black-Scholes Value)/VADD			
Investment goods prices	−.210***	−.168**	−.848%	−.665***
	(.067)	(.091)	(.231)	(.230)
Time effects	Yes	Yes	Yes	Yes
Industry effects	No	Yes	No	No
Firm effects	No	No	Yes	Yes
Firm controls	No	No	No	Yes
N	1,282	1,282	3,357	3,314
R^2 (%)	8.99	51.51	80.62	81.44
	(Nonexecutive Employee Stock Options, Black-Scholes Value)/VADD			
Investment goods prices	−.205***	−.171**	−.841***	−.677**
	(.067)	(.090)	(.265)	(.267)
Time effects	Yes	Yes	Yes	Yes
Industry effects	No	Yes	No	No
Firm effects	No	No	Yes	Yes
Firm controls	No	No	No	Yes
N	1,282	1,282	3,017	2,982
R^2 (%)	8.97	51.20	80.73	81.10

Note: This table reports industry- and firm-level regressions of an alternative measure of the new grants share based the Black-Scholes value of new grants of stock options for all employees (panel A), and excluding the top executives (panel B) in a given year on investment goods prices, in turn. In columns 1 and 2, we report results of industry-level analysis for a specification with industry fixed effects, which is as follows: $Y_{i,t} = \alpha + \beta X_{i,t-1} + \mu_i + \mu_t + \epsilon_{i,t}$. All specifications include time (year, μ_t) and industry (μ_i) effects. In columns 3 and 4, we report results of firm-level analysis for a specification with firm fixed effects, which is as follows: $Y_{j,i,t} = \alpha + \beta X_{j,i,t-1} + \mu_j + \mu_t + \epsilon_{j,i,t}$. All specifications include time (year, μ_t) and firm (μ_j) effects. The Black-Scholes value of new grants is relative to value added at the industry level and sales at the firm level. The independent variable is investment good prices. To ease interpretation, all variables are expressed in standard-deviation units. The interpretation of each reported coefficient is the change in standard deviations of the dependent variable associated with a one-standard-deviation change in the explanatory variable. For example, in the second column of panel A, a one-standard-deviation change in investment goods prices is associated with about 16.8% of a standard-deviation change in the new grants share. The time period is 1996–2005. See Subsection II.A and the appendix for detailed variable definitions. Standard errors are clustered by industry in the industry-level analysis and by firm in the firm-level analysis, with
* denoting significance at the 10% level.
** denoting significance at the 5% level.
*** denoting significance at the 1% level.

We also show that the cross-sectional results are robust to using a measure of employee wealth that includes the value of both new and past grants.

III. Model

In this section, we propose a simple framework to show that the stylized facts that describe factor shares in both the time series and the cross section can be explained by a unified equilibrium macroeconomic model. Our model employs a CES production function with three inputs, physical capital, human capital, and (unskilled) labor. Human capital's participation constraint accounts for the fact that human capital may earn more than its marginal product in an economy with profits to be shared and outside options to be met. However, our results indicate that almost all (91%) of equity compensation is earned in return for human capitalists' marginal product. Technological progress occurs via a standard shock to (physical) investment goods prices (see Greenwood et al. 1997; Papanikolaou 2011; Kogan and Papanikolaou 2014). We use our model to obtain quantitative estimates of the degree of complementarity between physical and human capital. We find that correcting human capitalists' income by including equity-based compensation is crucial for identifying complementarity between physical and human capital. Using wages only leads to the conclusion that physical and human capital are more substitutable than Cobb and Douglas (1928) when recent data are included. This section describes the model, and the following section discusses its estimation.

A. The Economy

The economy is populated by a continuum of symmetric firms that produce intermediate goods j using both physical capital k and human capital h. There are two sectors of households. One household sector, physical capitalists, denoted by K, owns physical capital and provides low-skilled labor, and the other household sector, human capitalists, denoted by H, produces human capital. There is no uncertainty in the economy, and the decline in investment goods prices is known by all agents in advance.

Final Goods Production

Final goods are produced using a continuum of intermediate goods, j. Final goods production is perfectly competitive, and output is produced via a Dixit–Stiglitz aggregator of intermediate goods. We have,

$$Y_t = \left[\int_0^1 y_{j,t}^{\frac{1}{\epsilon_t}} dj \right]^{\epsilon_t},\tag{1}$$

where $\epsilon_t > 1^{26}$ is the elasticity of substitution between intermediate goods j.

Each intermediate good j's price is $p_t(j)$, which is endogenous and determined by solving for its demand from the final goods producer's profit-maximization problem. Given perfect competition, there are zero profits for the final goods producer, hence we obtain the standard symmetric demand function for the intermediate goods j:

$$y_{j,t} \equiv D_t(p_t(j)) = Y_t \left(\frac{p_t(j)}{P_t^Y} \right)^{\frac{\epsilon_t}{1-\epsilon_t}}.\tag{2}$$

The final consumption good is the numeraire, and it has a price $P_t^Y = 1$.

Intermediate Goods Production

Production of intermediate goods requires both types of capital, k and h, and also (unskilled) labor, n, supplied by the households in the K sector.[27] In this simple model, we assume that there are no adjustment costs associated either with physical capital investment or with adjusting labor. The required rates of return for physical capital and human capital are R_t^k and R_t^h, respectively. Labor is compensated with a per-period market-clearing wage, w_t. Firms produce intermediate goods j using k, h, and n according to a constant-return-to-scale CES production function as in Krusell et al. (2000):

$$y_{j,t} = f(z_t, k_t(j), h_t(j), n_t(j)) = z_t \left[\alpha_c ((\alpha_k k_t(j)^\rho + (1 - \alpha_k) h_t(j)^\rho)^{\frac{\sigma}{\rho}} + (1 - \alpha_c) n_t(j)^\sigma \right]^{\frac{1}{\sigma}},\tag{3}$$

where z_t represents the level of factor-neutral productivity, and α_i, $i = k$, c are share parameters. The variable σ governs both the elasticity of substitution $(1/[1 - \sigma])$ between physical capital and labor, and the elasticity of substitution between human capital and labor. The variable ρ governs the elasticity of substitution $(1/[1 - \rho])$ between physical capital and human capital. A zero value for σ or ρ indicates the same degree of complementarity as Cobb–Douglas, and a value of 1 for σ or ρ indicates perfect substitution. A $\sigma > \rho$ indicates that physical capital is more complementary with human capital than with unskilled labor, and a negative ρ indicates that the complementarity is greater than that of Cobb–Douglas.

The profit-maximizing intermediate goods sector is owned by both physical capitalists and human capitalists. We assume that physical capitalists operate the firms in the intermediate sector. They maximize their share of firm value $V^k(j)$ subject to the participation constraint of human capitalists. A residual fraction λ of profits $\Pi_t(j)$ is owned by these physical capitalists. This fraction represents the remaining profits available for distribution after the necessary profit-sharing with human capitalists.

The profit-maximization problem $\mathcal{P}$ of each intermediate sector j is:

$$V_t^k(j) = \max_{p_t(j),k_t(j),h_t(j),n_t(j),y_{j,t},\lambda} \lambda \cdot \sum_t \beta^t \Pi_t(j) = \lambda \cdot \Pi_t(j) + \beta \cdot V_{t+1}^k(j),$$

subject to

$$\Pi_t(j) = p_t(j)y_{j,t} - R_t^k k_t(j) - R_t^h h_t(j) - w_t n_t(j) \quad (4)$$

$$y_{j,t} = p_t(j)^{\frac{\epsilon_t}{1-\epsilon_t}} Y_t \quad (5)$$

$$R_t^h h_t(j) + (1-\lambda)V_t(j) \geq \mathcal{O}_t = R_t^h h_t(j) + \eta V_t(j), \quad (6)$$

where equation (5) is the demand for intermediate goods j from equation (2), and equation (6) is the participation constraint for human capitalists. The total firm value is $V_t(j) = \Sigma_{s=t+1}\beta^s \Pi_s(j)$, which is the accumulated present value of the residual profits after the marginal products of capital and labor are paid. The fraction of firm value shared with human capitalists can be expressed as $V_t^h(j) = (1-\lambda)V_t(j)$, which is the accumulated present value of profit-sharing that physical capitalists promised to human capitalists before production. Hence, $V_t^h(j) + V_t^k(j) = V_t(j)$ for $\forall_j$. Since we will focus on a symmetric equilibrium, we will omit the index j going forward.

Equation (6) describes the participation constraint for human capitalists. If human capitalists remain with their present firm, they receive their marginal product $R^h h$ as well as some promised share of the firm $(1-\lambda)V_t^h$. Firm owners set the latter component by adjusting λ so that human capitalists' participation constraint is satisfied. This practice is consistent with observed corporate behavior in which firms retain talent by granting deferred compensation in the form of restricted equity or unvested options. If human capitalists leave to start a new firm, we assume they will still receive their marginal product $R^h h$. Note that this marginal product can be paid with wages or with equity-based compensation. In addition, at their new firm, we assume that they will accrue a fraction η of the new firm's value. Marginal products, which are the same regardless of whether the human capitalist remains with his or her existing firm or moves to a new firm, cancel out from both sides. Profit maximization by physical capitalists implies that equation (6) is always binding, and $\lambda = 1 - \eta$.

Note that the participation constraint (eq. [6]) is expressed in terms of *total* firm value shared with human capitalists, so V_t^h does not represent the flow compensation for human capitalists at period t. The share of firm value $1 - \lambda$ is promised to human capitalists in period t, but the income of human capitalists due to retention motives should only include the incremental part (i.e., the flow) of the firm shares granted in period t. For measurement, it is useful to note that the change in the share of the firm owned by human capitalists is $\Delta V_t^h \equiv \Delta(1 - \lambda)V^t \equiv \beta V_{t+1}^h - V_t^h$. Note that in a steady state, the change in shares of firm value $\Delta(1 - \lambda)V_t$ would simply be the fraction of current profit $(1 - \lambda)\Pi_t$, given the definition of V_t.

At this point, we take no stand on what fraction of human capitalists' marginal product is compensated using wages versus equity-based compensation. Equation (6) simply states that the *total* value allocated to human capitalists equals human capitalists' marginal product plus any additional shares of firm value needed to satisfy human capitalists' outside option and the participation constraint. In theory, both wages and equity-based compensation can be used for either the marginal product or the retention components of compensation. In practice, there are both accounting motivations and tax motivations for using equity-based pay, as well as retention and incentive reasons. To keep notation consistent, we denote the total flow of equity-based compensation as E^h, of which a fraction θ of E^h is used to compensate human capitalists' marginal product, and $(1 - \theta)E^h = \Delta(1 - \lambda)V_t$ is then used for retention purposes. The marginal product $R^h h$ is the sum of the flow wage payment w^h and the relevant fraction of equity-based compensation θE^h. We will use the information from the cross section to pin down the parameter θ in the second stage of our estimation.

Given η, the first-order conditions (wrt, k, h, and n) of the profit-maximizing choice yield a simple markup over marginal cost under the constant returns-to-scale technology: $p_t f_k = \mu_t R_t^k$, $p_t f_h = \mu_t R_t^h$, and $p_t f_n = \mu_t w_t$, where the markup over marginal cost is $\mu_t = \epsilon_t$. The marginal product of k is $f_k = z\alpha_c\alpha_k(y/\Psi)^{1-\sigma}(\Psi/k)^{1-\rho}$, the marginal product of h is

$f_h = z\alpha_c(1 - \alpha_k)(y/\Psi)^{1-\sigma}(\Psi/h)^{1-\rho}$, where $\Psi = (\alpha_k k^\rho + (1 - \alpha_k)h^\rho)^{\frac{1}{\rho}}$, and the marginal product of n is $f_n = z(1 - \alpha_c)(y/n)^{1-\sigma}$.

Agents

This section describes the objective functions of the two sectors of households: a sector of physical capitalists, K, that supplies physical capital k and labor n, and a sector of human capitalists, H, who supply human capital h.

Physical capitalists own the production technology that produces physical capital k. We assume a linear technology for producing capital goods. Households can invest final output goods to increase the physical capital stock k at prices determined by the level of investment-specific technological change.[28] The law of motion for physical capital is

$$k_{t+1} = (1 - \delta_k)k_t + I_t^k, \ 0 < \delta_k < 1. \tag{7}$$

Investment decisions I_t^k are made each period. The capital stock k depreciates at the rate δ_k. Define p_t^k as the relative price of physical capital investment goods over the numeraire. The price of physical capital investment goods is $\tilde{p}_t^k = p_t^k/z_t^k$, and z_t^k represents the investment-specific technological shock. Following Greenwood et al. (1997), $\tilde{p}_t^k$ represents the effective conversion rate of final output goods to equipment capital.

We assume that the physical capitalist sector owns the firms that produce intermediate goods, and it shares ownership of the profits Π_t from this production. The physical capitalist sector also has access to risk-free assets f_t with an interest rate of R_t^f. The representative physical capitalist maximizes his or her lifetime utility, defined as

$$\max_{\{c_t, I_t^k\}_{t=0}^{\infty}} \sum \beta^t U^k(c_t^k, n_t)$$

subject to the budget constraint:

$$c_t^k + \tilde{p}_t^k I_t^k + f_{t+1} - (1 + R_t^f)f_t = \int_0^1 R_t^k k_t(j)dj + \lambda\Pi_t + w_t n_t, \tag{8}$$

where $\Pi_t = \int_0^1 \Pi_t(j)dj = (\mu - 1)\int_0^1 p_t(j)y_{j,t}dj$.

Human capitalists own the production technology that produces human capital h, with the law of motion,

$$h_{t+1} = (1 - \delta_h)h_t + I_t^h, \quad 0 < \delta_h < 1. \tag{9}$$

Investment, I_t^h, can be interpreted as investing in obtaining skills or improving knowledge.

The representative human capitalist maximizes expected lifetime utility, defined as

$$\max_{\{c_t, I_t^h\}_{t=0}^{\infty}} \sum \beta^t U^h(c_t^h)$$

subject to the budget constraint:

$$c_t^h + I_t^h + f_{t+1} - (1 + R_t^f)f_t = \int_0^1 R_t^h h_t(j)dj + \beta V_{t+1}^h - V_t^h, \tag{10}$$

where the right-hand side states the sources of income of human capitalists. The marginal product of human capital is $R_t^h h_t$, and $\Delta(1 - \lambda)V_t \equiv \beta V_{t+1}^h - V_t^h$ is the change in the share of the firm value that accrues to human capitalists from t to $t + 1$ in the steady state, in which the firm grows at the risk-free rate. The change in the share of firm value accruing to human capitalists is implied by the participation constraint at consecutive dates.

Equilibrium

We consider a symmetric equilibrium defined as follows:

Definition 1: An **equilibrium** in this economy is a sequence of prices $\{p_t(j)\}_j$ and quantities such that the following optimality and market-clearing conditions hold: (a) Each household sector $i = k, h$ maximizes its lifetime utilities $\max_{\{c_t^i, I_t^i\}_{t=0}^{\infty}} \Sigma \beta^t U_t^i$ subject to the budget constraint (eq. [8]) or (eq. [10]). (b) The owner of the final consumption goods sector solves the maximization problem $\mathcal{P}$. (c) The equilibrium is symmetric: $p_t(j) = P_t = 1$, $k_t(j) = k_t$, $h_t(j) = h_t$, and $y_{j,t} = Y_t$. (d) The market clears: $Y_t = c_t^k + c_t^h + \tilde{p}_t^k I_t^k + I_t^h$.

Given the equilibrium definition, we obtain the standard intertemporal Euler equations for consumption, investment, and labor supply:

$$1 + R_{t+1}^f = \frac{U_{c,t}^i}{\beta U_{c,t+1}^i}, \quad i = k, h \tag{11}$$

$$R_{t+1}^k = \tilde{p}_t^k \frac{U_{c,t}^k}{\beta U_{c,t+1}^k} - \tilde{p}_{t+1}^k (1 - \delta_k), \tag{12}$$

$$R^h_{t+1} = \frac{U^h_{c,t}}{\beta U^h_{c,t+1}} - (1 - \delta_h), \tag{13}$$

$$w_t = \frac{U_{n,t}}{U_{c,t}}. \tag{14}$$

Equations (12) and (13) determine the investment policies for k and h. In general, households invest physical capital or human capital until the marginal benefits of capital R^i_{t+1}, $i = k, h$ equal the marginal costs of investment.

B.   Factor Shares of Income

In this subsection, we describe the factor shares of income in our economy. The final output is distributed among three sectors: physical capitalists, human capitalists, and labor. Physical capitalists receive the rental income from physical capital, $R^k_t k_t$. They also receive the residual profit share after human capitalists' equity compensation is allocated. Human capitalists receive compensation equal to their marginal product plus any additional compensation necessary to satisfy their participation constraint. The sum of wages plus equity compensation is $R^h_t h_t + \Delta(1 - \lambda)V_t$, though one cannot equate $R^h_t h_t$ to wages alone as equity can also be used to compensate marginal product. Finally, labor receives wages, $w_t n_t$. We have:

$$R^k_t k_t + R^h_t h_t + w_t n_t + \Delta V_t$$

$$= \underbrace{R^k_t k_t}_{\text{Physical Capitalists Income}} + \underbrace{R^h_t h_t + (1 - \lambda)\Delta V_t}_{\text{Human Capitalists Income}} + \underbrace{\lambda \Delta V_t}_{\text{Profit Share}} + \underbrace{w_t n_t}_{\text{Low-skilled labor share}},$$

where, in steady state, total income equals Y_t and $\Delta V_t = \Pi_t$. Note that, in our estimation, we use the full time-series data rather than comparing steady states.

The share of human capital income is then $(R^h_t h_t + \Delta[1 - \lambda]V_t)/Y_t$, and the physical capitalists' income share is $R^k_t k_t/Y_t$. The residual share of profits $\lambda \Pi_t$ is the profit share. We note that, although it is not our main focus, our model highlights the distinction between shares of value added and shares of income. Whereas shares of value added are based on current output and value-added flows, shares of income can include compensation for contributions to firm value stemming from future output. Indeed, in a dynamic model with uncertainty (e.g., Hartman-Glaser et al. 2019), ex ante income shares need not align with ex post shares of value added, and vice versa.

We now derive the relationship between the factor shares and the rate of return of each factor. For simplicity of exposition, we omit time subscripts. First, we characterize the relative shares of the two types of capital income s_k/s_h:

$$\frac{s_k}{s_h} = \frac{R^k k}{R^h h + \Delta(1-\lambda)V} = \frac{R^k k}{R^h h} \frac{R^h h}{R^h h + \Delta(1-\lambda)V} = \frac{R^k k}{R^h h} \omega_R, \quad (15)$$

where $\omega_R \equiv R^h h / R^h h + \Delta(1-\lambda)V$ is the fraction of human capital income that is the marginal product. The relative capital share of income is driven by two factors: the relative rental payment, or marginal product, of k versus h, $\mathbf{D} \equiv R^k k / R^h h$, and the composition of human capital income, ω_R. When human capitalists' outside option η is higher, human capitalists' income is driven more by the participation constraint share, $1 - \omega_R$. The elasticity of substitution between k and h is crucial for the dynamics of relative rental payments and hence the relative share of capital income.

Next, we can derive the total physical plus human capital share $s_k + s_h$ as $1 - s_n$ using the expressions of marginal products f_k and f_h:

$$1 - s_n = \frac{1}{\mu} \alpha_c^{\frac{1}{1-\sigma}} \alpha_k^{\frac{\sigma}{1-\sigma}} \mathbf{C}^{\frac{\sigma(1-\rho)}{1-\sigma}} R^{k\frac{\sigma}{\sigma-1}\%} + 1 - \frac{1}{\mu}, \quad (16)$$

where $\mathbf{C} = (\alpha_k + (1-\alpha_k)[(1-\alpha_k)R^k/\alpha_k R^h]^{\rho/1-\rho})^{1/\rho}$.[29] The total capital share of income includes the profit share $1 - (1/\mu)$ and total rental payments to h and k, and depends on σ, the capital-labor complementarity. In general, a declining rental rate of capital R^k along with capital-labor substitutability, $\sigma > 0$, leads to an increase in overall rental payments to capital.

The dynamics of factor shares of value added are captured by equations (12), (13), (15), and (16). We next confront this system with the data to estimate the production function parameters and examine their implications for the elasticities of substitution between the three input factors.

IV. Estimation

In this section, we combine our model with the data to learn about the shape of the aggregate production technology. Specifically, we estimate the elasticity of substitution between k and h, (ρ), as well as the elasticity of substitution between labor and capital, (σ) for all possible allocations of equity pay between marginal product and meeting the participation constraint. Finally, we combine a cross-section estimate of ρ with our time-series analysis to pin down the fraction of equity pay that is compensation for marginal product versus retention considerations.

A. Measurement Equations

We start with the system of first-order conditions (eqs. [15] and [16]), with error terms u_t and ϵ_t:

$$\frac{s_{k,t}}{s_{h,t}} = \left(\frac{\alpha_k}{1-\alpha_k}\right)^{\frac{1}{1-\rho}}\left[\frac{R_t^h}{R_t^k}\right]^{\frac{\rho}{1-\rho}}\omega_{R,t} + u_t \tag{17}$$

$$1 - s_{n,t} = \frac{1}{\mu}\alpha_c^{\frac{1}{1-\sigma}}\alpha_k^{\frac{\sigma}{1-\sigma}}\mathbf{C_t}^{\frac{\sigma(1-\rho)}{1-\sigma}}R_t^{k\frac{\sigma}{\sigma-1}} + 1 - \frac{1}{\mu} + \epsilon_t, \tag{18}$$

where the return to physical capitalists, R_t^k, and the return to human capitalists, R_t^h, are determined by households' intertemporal consumption and saving choices (eqs. [12] and [13]). We estimate this system via maximum likelihood. Given that there are possible omitted variables that could cause serial correlation in the error terms, we allow the error terms to be serially correlated with autocorrelation $[\psi_u, \psi_\epsilon]$. This procedure yields estimates for the constant elasticity parameters that enable the model to best fit the empirically observed trends in the relative capital share $s_{k,t}/s_{h,t}$ and the capital share $1 - s_{n,t}$.

Equation (17) is key to identifying the parameter ρ. Dividing both sides by ω_R yields:

$$\frac{s_k}{s_h \cdot \omega_R} = \frac{R^k k}{R^h h} = \left(\frac{\alpha_k}{1-\alpha_k}\right)^{\frac{1}{1-\rho}}\left(\frac{R^h}{R^k}\right)^{\frac{\rho}{1-\rho}}. \tag{19}$$

The difference between the trends of rental payments to physical capital $R^k k$ and human capital $R^h h$ identifies the parameter ρ. To see the intuition, take logs of both sides of equation (19) and consider the resulting log difference on the right-hand side. The trend in the marginal return to capital R_t^h/R_t^k equals the difference between the growth in the rental return to human capital investment R^h and the trend of investment goods prices, scaled by $\rho/(1-\rho)$. As the relative price of physical investment goods trends downward, R^k declines faster than the return to human capital investment R^h. Given that $\rho < 1$, the relative share of physical capital compared with human capital $s_{k,t}/s_{h,t}\omega_R$ can decline in $\tilde{p}^k$ only if $\rho < 0$ (i.e., only if k and h are complementary). In other words, the ratio between the two capital shares is crucial for understanding the degree of complementarity between these two types of capital in the production function.

The estimation requires data on the marginal product of human capital, $R^h h$, as an input to the left-hand side of equation (19). In practice, what is observed is total human capitalists' income, which is composed of wages w^h and equity-based compensation E^h. Each of these components may include both compensation for the marginal product $R^h h$ and any additional compensation required to satisfy human capitalists' outside option $\Delta(1 - \lambda)V$. To account for this, we assume, as in the existing literature, that all wage compensation is due to human capitalists' marginal product. For equity-based compensation, we perform a series of estimations, assigning all values between 0% and 100% for the fraction θ of equity-based pay attributable to human capitalists' marginal product. We show that the structural estimation implies more complementarity than Cobb–Douglas between physical and human capital for all but small values of the fraction of equity-based pay that is used to compensate high-skilled labor for their marginal product.

Note that we are being conservative by not assigning all equity-based pay to human capitalists' marginal product. A reasonable baseline assumption would be that equity pay has simply replaced wages but not increased overall pay. There are several reasons why firms might substitute away from wages and toward equity grants. First, equity-based pay is tax advantaged because qualified grants can avoid being taxed at income taxes. Second, before 2004, companies could use equity-based compensation without fully expensing it, thus boosting earnings.[30] Third, equity-based compensation is approved by the IRS as a justification for replacing dividends (taxed at the income tax rate) with repurchases (taxed at the capital gains rate). Finally, we note that equity-based compensation can be used to substitute for wages due to incentive alignment, retention motives, and relaxation of financial constraints by delaying a fraction of pay.

Rather than taking as a baseline that 100% of equity-based pay is simply a substitute for wages and used to compensate marginal product, we instead acknowledge that some reasons for using equity-based pay may break the standard assumption that marginal product and compensation are equated. The relative capital share on the left-hand side of equation (19) can then be represented as follows:

$$\frac{s_k}{s_h \omega_R} = \frac{R^k k}{R^h h} = \frac{R^k k}{w^h + \theta E^h}.$$

The term w^h is the measured flow wage income in the data, which represents only part of human capitalists' marginal product. The remainder of their marginal product is compensated with equity θE^h, where E^h is the observed equity-based compensation. Hence, $R^h h = w^h + \theta E^h$ is the total compensation for human capitalists' marginal product, and $(1 - \theta)E^h$ is any additional compensation, beyond the marginal product, necessary to satisfy human capitalists' outside option $\Delta(1 - \lambda)V$. Our estimation strategy then proceeds in two steps: first, we estimate our model for all $\theta \in [0, 1]$ and show the impact of varying θ on the estimated degree of complementarity between physical capital and human capital. Then, we exploit the cross-industry data to infer the value of θ from a cross-section estimate of ρ.

The correlation between the rental rate of capital k and the growth of the total capital share drives the sign of σ. To gain intuition, we can express the log growth of the total capital share as $s_c = 1 - s_n$, obtained from equation (16): $\widehat{s_c} \approx [\sigma(1 - \rho)/(1 - \sigma)]\widehat{C} + [\sigma/(\sigma - 1)] \widehat{R^k}$ where $\widehat{s_c}$ denotes the change over time in the total capital share, for example. If capital and labor are substitutes, a downward trend in the rental rate of physical capital drives up the total capital share. If physical and human capital are complements, declining capital goods prices can be accompanied by an increase in the demand for human capital despite the increase in its relative price.

B. Estimation Results

Equity-based compensation is critical when accounting for the rise in human capitalists' income share and when investigating the elasticity of substitution between physical capital and human capital. In this section, we first estimate our model using the time-series data to show that it is crucial to include equity-based compensation for the identification of the complementarity between physical and human capital. When a small fraction of equity-based compensation is included, we find greater complementarity between physical and human capital than that implied by Cobb–Douglas. However, if equity compensation is ignored completely, we find instead greater substitutability. In the final estimation step, we use cross-sectional data to estimate the elasticity of substitution between physical capital and human capital, and then we use that elasticity to pin down the fraction of equity pay that is due to human capitalists' marginal product.

We estimate our model to match the time series of factor shares for the sample period 1980–2011. The reason for focusing on this period is that the decline in investment goods prices p_t^k started in the early 1980s, and the NBER-CES sample ends in 2011. Since our identification is driven by the relative trends of prices in the data and the share series are noisy, we apply a 2-year moving average to the target moments. The set of parameters that we estimate includes physical capital's share (α_k), total capital share (α_c), the elasticity of substitution (EOS) between k and h, (ρ), and the EOS between capital and labor n, (σ). The parameters that govern the depreciation rate of capital δ_k and δ_h and the markup μ are calibrated.

For the calibrated parameters, we set the depreciation rate of capital δ_k to the average investment rate in our sample (0.08). The variable δ_h is set to 0.15, which is equal to the depreciation rate used by the BEA in its estimation of R&D capital in 2006 (Eisfeldt and Papanikolaou 2013). We set the markup parameter, μ, to be constant at 1.3 throughout the sample period.[31] The returns to human and physical capitalists are determined by equations (12) and (13), where the interest rate R_f is the time series of real rates over the sample period.

Recall that ρ measures the degree of substitutability or complementarity between physical capital and human capital, and σ measures the degree of substitutability or complementarity between physical capital and labor. Estimates below zero indicate more complementarity than Cobb–Douglas, whereas positive estimates indicate a greater degree of substitutability than Cobb–Douglas. Estimates of 1 indicate perfect substitutability. The top panel of figure 5 displays the results for the estimate of ρ.

Our estimation shows that the parameter ρ is highly sensitive to including even a small fraction of equity-based pay in the marginal product of human capitalists. When equity-based compensation is completely ignored ($\theta = 0$), the estimated parameter ρ is positive, 0.08, which implies more substitution between human capital and physical capital in the aggregate production function than Cobb–Douglas (the EOS is 1.09). As θ increases, the estimate of the EOS parameter ρ drops sharply. When only 16.7% of equity-based compensation is allocated to human capitalists' marginal product, the estimated EOS ρ becomes negative. In other words, omitting a small fraction of equity-based compensation in the human capital income share leads to an estimate of ρ with the "wrong" sign. In addition, the decline in the estimate of ρ accelerates quickly as θ increases.

By contrast, estimates of σ do not vary significantly for different assumed values of θ, as seen in the bottom panel of figure 5, which plots the estimates of the EOS between labor and capital. The average of estimate for σ is 0.22, which implies a strong degree of substitutability

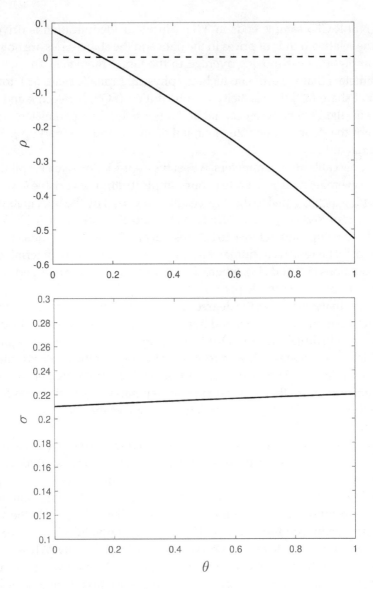

Fig. 5. Elasticities of Substitution and Equity-Based Compensation. This figure shows estimates of parameters that govern the elasticity of substitution between physical and human capital ρ and the elasticity of substitution between capital and labor, σ, when allowing for different values of θ. In the top panel, the solid line is the estimated ρ using a 2-year moving average of the target moment in the data. In the bottom panel, the solid line is the estimated σ using a 2-year moving average of the target moment in the data. The estimates of the autocorrelation coefficients for the error terms ψ_u and ψ_e vary from 0.10 to 0.69 when varying θ. Data are from Compustat Fundamental Annual, RiskMetrics (IRRC), and NBER-CES Manufacturing Industry Database. The sample period is from 1980 to 2011. A color version of this figure is available online.

between capital and labor (an EOS of 1.28). Our estimate of the EOS between capital and labor, σ, is similar to the findings in the existing literature. Karabarbounis and Neiman (2014) estimate that the EOS between
capital and labor is 1.28 on average across countries. Krusell et al.
(2000) report an EOS between capital and labor of 1.65 using their sample from the period 1963–92. Although substitution between capital and
unskilled labor can explain the declining labor share (unskilled and total)
since the 1980s, equity-based compensation is crucial for understanding
the EOS between physical capital and human capital, especially in the
last 30 years.

Thus far, we have remained relatively agnostic about what fraction, θ,
of equity-based compensation is attributable to compensation for human capitalists' marginal product. Our next estimation exercise exploits
the cross-section data to pin down our estimate of ρ, the degree of complementarity between physical and human capital. By using the estimate of ρ from the cross section, we are able to provide an estimate of
θ in our study of the time series. Our identification strategy is as follows:
recall the first-order condition (eq. [17]), which captures the dynamics of
the relative income shares of physical versus human capital for each industry at each year. We take this equation to the data by taking logs on
both sides and adding an i.i.d. error term,

$$\log s_{h,j,t} - \log s_{k,j,t} = \frac{1}{1-\rho}\log\left(\frac{1-\alpha_k}{\alpha_k}\right) + \frac{\rho}{1-\rho}\log R_{j,t}^k - \frac{\rho}{1-\rho}\log R_j^h + \log\frac{1}{\omega_{R,t}} + e_{j,t}, \quad (20)$$

where j denotes industry j. Since both $\omega_{R,t}$ and R_j^h are unobservable, we
need to assume that these variables are fixed either across time or across
industries to identify ρ from the coefficient on $\log R_{j,t}^k$. We include both
year fixed effects and industry fixed effects in the estimation and assume
that $\omega_{R,t}$ and R_j^h are absorbed by industry fixed effects and year fixed effects. We interpret the specification as assuming that (1) R_j^h is different
across industries but identical over time; and (2) $\omega_{R,t}$ is identical across
industries but varies over time. Note that because we identify ρ from
the coefficient on $\log R_{j,t}^k$, the alternative assumption that R_j^h varies over
time but is constant across industries whereas ω_R is constant over time
but varies across industries leads to the same estimation result for ρ.

We estimate equation (20) using the 4-SIC industry-level data for the
sample period from 1980 to 2011.[32] We find evidence of a strong degree
of complementarity between physical and human capital in this cross-
section regression, consistent with our findings in Subsection II.B. The estimated coefficient on $\log R_{j,t}^k$ is -0.34 and is highly significant (t-statistic

of 2.64). This estimate implies that $\rho = -0.51$, and that the EOS between physical capital and human capital is 0.66. We note that our estimate of the EOS between physical capital and human capital, using data including equity-based compensation and more recent data, delivers an almost identical estimate for complementarity to that reported in Krusell et al. (2000) (0.67) using wages only in data up to 1992. This is in stark contrast to the estimate we find using wage data alone in the full sample up to 2019.

Using this estimate of ρ, we can back out the fraction of equity-based compensation allocated to human capitalists' marginal product, θ, from the estimation results in figure 5. As can be seen in the figure, the estimate of ρ from the cross section of -0.51 implies that θ is 98%. We argue that this estimate is intuitive. It seems reasonable that, rather than increasing pay overall, firms have substituted equity-based pay for wages due to its desirable tax, accounting, incentive, and retention characteristics. Table 7 presents the complete two-step estimation results.[33]

Table 7
Two-Step Estimation

θ	ρ	α_k	α_c	σ
.98	$-.51$	.27	.61	.22
–	(.19)	(.01)	(.10)	(.12)
	$1/(1-\rho) = .66$			$1/(1-\sigma) = 1.28$

Note: This table reports estimated parameters from the two-step estimation. As the first step, we estimate the first-order condition (eq. [1]):

$$\log s_{h,j,t} - \log s_{k,j,t} = \frac{1}{1-\rho}\log\left(\frac{1-\alpha_k}{\alpha_k}\right) + \frac{\rho}{1-\rho}\log R^k_{j,t} - \frac{\rho}{1-\rho}\log R^h_j$$
$$+ \log\frac{1}{\omega_{R,t}} + e_{j,t},$$

where j stands for 4-SIC industry j. We estimate a panel regression with industry and year fixed effects. We identify ρ from the coefficient of $\log R^k_{j,t}$, and then infer θ, the fraction of equity-based compensation due to human capitalists' marginal product given the mapping between ρ and θ plotted in figure 5. Second, given the value of θ, we estimate the system of equations (17) and (18) using MLE on time-series data. This table reports the estimated parameters from the second estimation. We calibrated the following parameters: $\delta_k = 0.08$, $\delta_h = 0.15$, $\mu = 1.3$. We feed in the observed R_f using the time series of the real interest rate over the sample period. Human capitalists' income share is measured as the ratio of the sum of wage income and NG to value added in this estimation. The estimated serial correlations in the error terms are $\psi_u = 0.32$ and $\psi_e = 0.35$. The sample period is from 1980 to 2011. Standard errors are in parentheses. Implied elasticities between human and physical capital, and between all capital and labor, respectively, are given in the last row.

V.   Conclusion

Including equity-based compensation in human capitalists' total labor income is critical for accurately measuring human capitalists' contribution to economic activity as well as their share of income. In recent data, 36% of compensation to high-skilled labor appears in the form of equity-based pay. Standard data sources severely understate this compensation due to its standard deferral and to unique tax treatment at both the firm level and the individual level. We employ data from firms' SEC filings to overcome this measurement challenge. Using only wages to measure the high-skilled labor share leads to a puzzling lack of complementarity between declining capital goods prices, mainly driven by e-capital, and high-skilled labor. A comprehensive measure of human capitalists' income essentially reverses an otherwise declining trend in the high-skilled labor share and reduces the decline in the overall labor share by 32%.

Appendix

Discussion of Equity-Based Compensation in the Data and Literature

In this section, we establish facts about the measurement of equity-based compensation. First, we document that the CES wages used in this paper are wages only. The census form used to collect the responses that constitute the CES data is at https://www.census.gov/programs-surveys /asm/technical-documentation/questionnaire/2019-annual-survey-of -manufactures-forms.html, and we confirmed this with the contacts listed at https://www.nber.org/research/data/nber-ces-manufacturing-in dustry-database. We use the answer to the following question:

E. PAYROLL
What was the **annual** payroll at this establishment before deductions for:

Exclude:
- Employer-paid annual cost for fringe benefits reported in lines F1 through F3

		2019		2018	
1. Production workers reported in line B?	☐	$	,000.00	$	,000.00
2. All other employees reported in line C?	☐	$	,000.00	$	,000.00
TOTAL (Add lines E1 and E2.)	☐	$	,000.00	$	,000.00

Note that the form explicitly states that benefits reported in lines F1 to F3 should be excluded from part E, payroll, which is the CES variable "PAY" that we use to measure wages. And, in the text preceding question F, the form states: "Include: Spread on stock options that are taxable to employees at this establishment as wages." Stock options are included in question F3, which can be downloaded at the link above. Question F is preceded by the following instructions:

F. EMPLOYER-PAID ANNUAL COST FOR FRINGE BENEFITS

(This is the employer's annual cost at this establishment for legally required programs and programs not required by law. If any of the items here are maintained in your records only at the company level, allocate their costs to the manufacturing establishment. You may distribute the total on the basis of the ratio of the payroll of each manufacturing establishment to the total company payroll unless you have developed your own method of making such allocations. Specify the method used and the approximate portion that has been allocated in the Item 31: REMARKS section at the end of the instrument.)

Include:
- Premium equivalents for self-insured plans and fees paid to third-party administrators (TPAs)
- Spread on stock options that are taxable to employees at this establishment as wages

Exclude:
- Employee contributions
- Disbursements from trusts or funds to satisfy health insurance claims

Thus, the CES data provide a "wages only" labor series. This is one of the reasons that the labor share using these data is lower than in other standard sources, though the downward trend is shared with standard labor share series.

The main text (Subsec. II.C) provides detailed documentation of the fact that existing data sources (based on BEA and BLS statistics) previously employed in the literature to measure the labor share include only a small fraction of equity-based compensation. For inclusion in standard sources based on income tax data records, equity pay must satisfy both of the following two criteria. First, the pay must be nonqualified for tax purposes, because pay under qualified plans allow for taxation at the lower capital gains tax rate.[34] Second, the pay must be both vested (or unrestricted) and exercised, meaning that current tax data reflect only exercised grants from 5 or more years ago. As detailed in Subsection II.C, given the fast growth of equity pay, by the time exercised grants appear in income tax returns, these past grants are a small fraction of the current flow of new equity-pay grants. Additional email communications with the BEA and BLS staff are available upon request.

The advantage of the RS measure of equity-based pay over an expense-based measure is that it is not affected by changes in accounting rules. Starting from 1996, and up to 2004, the Financial Accounting Standards Board (FASB) recommended that firms expense compensation options using fair value (usually, Black-Scholes). However, this was only a recommendation, and firms could and did value options at the intrinsic value, which is zero if options are granted at the money. By doing so, firms boost current earnings. Due to strong incentives to inflate earnings, there is still substantial evidence in the accounting literature (e.g., Aboody, Barth, and Kasznik 2006) that firms continued to substantially undervalue their equity pay even after 2004, when FASB began requiring valuation at fair value under rule FAS 123R. In general, the value of employee stock options is reported on financial reports as a compensation expense that is spread over the period of vesting, rather than being expensed at the time it is granted.[35]

Data Construction

Data Sources

The Sample for Income Shares and Investment Goods Prices

Our main data source for constructing factor shares is the NBER-CES Manufacturing Industry Database. The NBER-CES Manufacturing Industry Database covers four-digit SIC code-level information from 1960 to 2011 on output, employment, payroll, investment goods prices, and value added. All variables are defined at an annual frequency. We extend the time series for value-added and aggregate payroll for the period 2012–19 as follows: we obtain the growth rates of manufacturing value added and employee compensation from the NIPA tables available from the BEA, and we compute the growth rates for value added and payroll for the industries comprising the manufacturing sector. We then project the CES data forward using these growth rates and the CES data from the end of our sample.

For corporate income shares (e.g., physical capital share, SG&A share) and other firm-level variables, we obtain the data from the Compustat Fundamental Annual data set from the period 1960–2019. We include only the manufacturing firms (SIC codes 2001–3999) to match the sectors covered by the NBER-CES sample.

Our main analyses are conducted in the merged sample of the public-firm data (Compustat, RiskMetrics, and hand-collection) and the NBER-CES Manufacturing Industry Database. This merged sample covers 5,271 firms and 133 industries (4-SIC) from the period 1960–2019.

The Sample for RSs

We obtain the data for RSs from publicly traded firms' accounting statements, which we gather from three sources: (*a*) the Compustat Fundamental Annual 1960–1995, (*b*) RiskMetrics 1996–2005, which covers firms from the S&P 500, S&P midcap, and S&P smallcap indices, (*c*) hand-collected data for the period 2006–19 from 10-K filings and proxy statements. We restrict our sample to US companies with headquarters located in the United States and with a native currency code of US dollars. We also restrict the sample to public firms traded in the major exchanges: New York Stock Exchange, American Stock Exchange, NASDAQ-NMS Stock Market, Midwest Exchange (Chicago), and Pacific Exchange. We exclude companies that trade ADRs (American Depositary Receipts).

Merged Sample

We merge the public-firm and NBER-CES databases using four-digit SIC codes. Since we only observe value added at the industry level, we exclude industries (4-SIC) that have one or fewer firms in the NBER-CES–public-firm merged sample. In addition, to adjust for the differential coverage of the NBER-CES data covering all firms, public and private, and the public-firm data set covering only public firms (and possibly including some pay to employees abroad), we scale our new grant series by the ratio of sales in Compustat to the ratio of sales in the NBER-CES data at the four-digit SIC code industry level. Specifically, for each year t and in each industry j, we construct the scaling factor given by $Scale_{j,t} = \Sigma_{j\in\text{Compustat}}Sales_{j,t}/\Sigma_{j\in\text{NBER-CES}}Shipment_{j,t}$. We aggregate the firm-level value of $NG_{k,t}$ to the industry-level $\widetilde{NG}_{j,t}$ by summing up over firms, $\widetilde{NG}_{j,t} = \Sigma_{k\in\text{ind }j}NG_{k,t}$. We match the industry aggregate in public-firm data to the industry aggregate in the NBER-CES data by dividing the industry-level $\widetilde{NG}_{j,t}$ by the industry-level scaling factor $Scale_{j,t}$. The adjusted industry aggregate we use in our analysis is $NG_{j,t} = \widetilde{NG}_{j,t}/Scale_{j,t}$. We construct the industry-level share of income from equity compensation as the ratio of industry-level $NG_{j,t}$ to industry-level value added.

Variable Definitions and Construction

Reserved shares. Common shares reserved for conversion and future grant of employee stock options, which are defined as follows:

1. 1960–83: CSHR (common shares reserved for conversion total) − DCPSTK (preferred stocks and convertible debt) (Compustat Fundamental Annual)
2. 1984–95: CSHRO (common shares reserved for stock options conversion). The Compustat manual states: "This item represents shares reserved for stock options outstanding as of year-end plus options that are available for future grants." During this period, there are separate data items for preferred stock and convertible bonds, as well as the data item for total common shares reserved for conversion (CSHR).
3. 1996–2005: total available shares for future grants of employee equity-based compensation + total shares reserved for outstanding employee stock option grants (RiskMetrics)
4. 2006–19: total shares reserved for both outstanding employee equity-based compensation (options, warrants and stock grants) and future grants of equity-based compensation (hand-collected data from SEC filings on Edgar)

Ownership share. The employee-owned fraction of firms is calculated as the value of RS divided by stock market capitalization.

Value added. We obtain the value-added series from NBER-CES data set from the period 1960–2011, and we extend the data to 2019 using BEA NIPA data as described above.

Human capital share. The total income to human capitalists as a share of value added.

1. Grant-based measure. Total human capital income includes the wage income of high-skilled human capitalists and their equity-based compensation. Sample period is 1960–2019.
   - Human capital wage share: skilled workers' wages/value added
   - Equity-based compensation share: NG = (number of RSs × current stock price)/(weighted-average granting period of 6 years). Equity-based compensation share = NG/value added.
   - Total human capital share = (skilled wages + NG)/value added
2. Expense-based measure (i.e., selling, general, and administrative expenses). Sample period is 1960–2019. Industry-level SG&A share: 30% of SG&A (Compustat) divided by value added (NBER-CES).

Physical capital share. Investment (NBER-CES) divided by value added (NBER-CES). This is a four-digit SIC code-level variable available from NBER-CES from 1960 to 2011 and extended using BEA NIPA as described above.

Unskilled and total labor share. The unskilled labor share is a four-digit SIC code-level variable available from NBER-CES from 1960 to 2011 and extended using BEA NIPA as described above.

1. Unskilled labor share: unskilled wages (production labor payroll)/value added (NBER-CES)
2. Total labor share = total human capital share + unskilled labor share

Constructing the New Grant Series

In this section, we provide a formal derivation of our baseline measure for the annual flow of deferred compensation. Our baseline measure is a fraction of the shares reserved for employee compensation, because the stock of RSs is available for a wide cross section of firms and a long time series of 60 years from 1960 to 2019. We calibrate our measure to RiskMetrics data, which contain information on both RSs and share-based employee compensation grants for the period 1996–2005. We also perform several robustness checks on this measure. Our measure is conservative, in the sense that we do not include capital gains or losses on share-based compensation that is granted but not vested, and share values have increased substantially, on average, over our sample (see Hall and Liebman 1998).

We start with the following law of motion for the stock of RSs:

$$RS_{t+1} = RS_t + NRS_t - EXC_t - EXP_t, \tag{A1}$$

where RS_t denotes RSs at the beginning of period t, and RS_{t+1} is the stock of RSs at the beginning of period $t + 1$. As is standard for the law of motion of any stock, there is both "investment" in the stock and "depreciation." Here, investment, or growth in RSs, is denoted by NRS_t. That is, NRS_t denotes newly authorized RSs. All newly authorized RSs are voted on by the board of directors, and they should be reported to the SEC at least annually. However, comprehensive data on new share authorizations are not reliably available electronically. The stock of RSs also depreciates due to exercised stock options and vested restricted stock (denoted EXC_t) and due to expired options or retired restricted stock (denoted by EXP_t).

In practice, the process of authorizing new RSs is lumpy. Similar to a plan for capital expenditures, firms construct a plan for new share issuances (e.g., for compensation, warrants, secondary offerings). When this plan is revised significantly, the firm authorizes a new block of RSs, NRS_t. These newly authorized shares are then used to grant options and restricted stock compensation over the next gp years, where the granting period gp denotes the time between the shares being authorized and being allocated to compensation grants. It should be noted that firms also manage their stock of RSs similar to the way firms manage their cash to ensure a sufficient supply to satisfy liquidity needs but no more than this, due to opportunity costs. They are required to reserve enough shares to satisfy compensation grants that are likely to be exercised or vested. On the other hand, firms avoid reserving too many shares because investors know that any new shares from employee compensation will result in the dilution of existing shares. Thus, firms strive to authorize new shares in a way that balances these tradeoffs.

Assume that the average granting period of the initial stock of RSs at time t, RS_t, is gp_0. This means that, on average, any previously authorized share is expected to remain on the balance sheet in the stock of RS_t for gp_0 years before being granted. We allow for the granting period to differ for any given block of newly authorized shares, NRS_t, and we denote the average granting period for NRS_t by gp_t. What will be important for determining the fraction of the stock of RSs that represents the current flow of employee compensation grants is a weighted average of the granting period for all RSs on the balance sheet. For parsimony, we assume that all newly authorized shares are evenly granted over the next gp_t periods:

$$NRS_t = \sum_{k=t}^{t+gp_t} \text{Annual Grants}(AG)_k = gp_t \cdot AG_t. \qquad (A2)$$

For further simplification, we assume that

1. On average, employees exercise a fraction e of the total RSs[36]

$$EXC_t = e \cdot RS_t \quad \forall 0 < e < 1. \qquad (A3)$$

2. On average, outstanding restricted stocks or stock options display a constant attrition rate c due to forfeiture, expiration, or

$$EXP_t = c \cdot RS_t \quad \forall 0 < c < 1. \tag{A4}$$

Using equations (A2), (A3), and (A4), we can rewrite the law of motion (A1) as

$$RS_{t+1} = (RS_t - EXC_t - EXP_t) + NRS_t$$
$$= (1 - e - c)RS_t + gp_t \cdot AG_t.$$

To correctly capture the annual share-based compensation granted to employees at time t (denoted by NG_t) for "new grants," we must include the following two components:

1. AG: annual grants from newly RSs, NRS_t
2. PG: annual grants from the stock of previously RSs, RS_t/gp_0

Note that we can rewrite the law of motion for RS_{t+1} as

$$RS_{t+1} = \underbrace{(gp_0 - e \cdot gp_0 - c \cdot gp_0)}_{\substack{\text{average remaining granting period} \\ \text{after exercising and expiration}}} \frac{RS_t}{gp_0} + gp_t \cdot AG_t.$$

Dividing both sides by $RS_{t+1}/\{[(gp_0 - e \cdot gp_0 - c \cdot gp_0)\frac{RS_t}{gp_0} + gp_t \cdot AG_t]/AG_t + \frac{RS_t}{gp_0}\}$ and multiplying by $AG_t + (RS_t/gp_0)$, we obtain

$$NG_t = AG_t + \frac{RS_t}{gp_0} = \frac{RS_{t+1}}{\frac{(gp_0 - e \cdot gp_0 - c \cdot gp_0)\frac{RS_t}{gp_0} + gp_t \cdot AG_t}{AG_t + \frac{RS_t}{gp_0}}}$$

$$= \underbrace{\frac{RS_{t+1}}{(1 - e - c)gp_0\omega_0 + gp_t\omega_1}}_{\text{weighted average granting period}}, \tag{A5}$$

where $\omega_0 = [(RS_t/gp_0)/AG_t + (RS_t/gp_0)]$ and $\omega_1 = AG_t/[AG_t + (RS_t/gp_0)]$.

Hence, the flow of share-based compensation at period t is $RS_{t+1}/\overline{gp}$, where $\overline{gp}$ denotes the average time that any existing or newly authorized RS remains on the balance sheet before being allocated to a compensation grant. Since $e, c \in (0, 1)$, the weighted-average granting period should be a value between gp_0 and gp_t.

To match the theory to the data, we note that this derivation uses t to denote values at the beginning of each period, as is standard in macro-economic notation. However, since accounting data are recorded at the end of each period, we use the end-of-period data to measure the deferred compensation flow for the annual period ending at the date of the accounting entry. That is, we use a fraction of the stock of RSs recorded at the end-of-year t to measure the flow of NG during year t.

Derivation of Equation (16)

Under the symmetric equilibrium, the returns to physical capital and human capital can be derived from the first-order conditions of the profit-maximization problem:

$$f_k = z\alpha_c\alpha_k \left(\frac{y}{\Psi}\right)^{1-\sigma} \left(\frac{\Psi}{k}\right)^{1-\rho} = \mu_t R^k, \tag{A6}$$

$$f_h = z\alpha_c(1 - \alpha_k) \left(\frac{y}{\Psi}\right)^{1-\sigma} \left(\frac{\Psi}{h}\right)^{1-\rho} = \mu_t R^h, \tag{A7}$$

where $\Psi = (\alpha_k k^\rho + (1 - \alpha_k)h^\rho)^{1/\rho}$. From the above equations, the ratio between physical and human capital is a function of the relative return to the two types of capital:

$$\frac{h}{k} = \left[\frac{(1 - \alpha_k)R^k}{\alpha_k R^h}\right]^{\frac{1}{1-\rho}} \equiv \mathbf{B}. \tag{A8}$$

We can derive the total capital share $s_k + s_h$ as $1 - s_n$ as

$$1 - s_n = s_k + s_h = \frac{(1 - \alpha_k)\left(\frac{Y}{\Psi}\right)^{1-\sigma}\Psi^{1-\rho}[\alpha_k k^\rho + (1 - \alpha_k)h^\rho]}{\mu Y} + 1 - \frac{1}{\mu}$$

$$= \frac{\alpha_c\left(\frac{Y}{\Psi}\right)^{1-\sigma}\Psi^{1-\rho}\Psi^\rho}{\mu Y} + 1 - \frac{1}{\mu} = \frac{\alpha_c}{\mu}\left(\frac{Y}{\Psi}\right)^{-\sigma} + 1 - \frac{1}{\mu}.$$

Find Y/Ψ as a function of prices:

$$h = \mathbf{B}k$$

$$\Psi = [\alpha_k k^\rho + (1 - \alpha_k)\mathbf{B}^\rho k^\rho]^{\frac{1}{\rho}} = (\alpha_k + (1 - \alpha_k)\mathbf{B}^\rho)^{\frac{1}{\rho}}k \equiv \mathbf{C}k. \tag{A9}$$

Because Ψ is linear in k, we obtain the expression of capital (nonlabor) share in the function of prices as

$$\frac{Y}{\Psi} = \frac{Y}{Ck} = \left[\frac{R^k}{\alpha_c\alpha_k \mathbf{C}^{1-\rho}}\right]^{\frac{1}{1-\sigma}} \tag{A10}$$

$$1 - s_n = \frac{\alpha_c}{\mu}\left[\frac{\alpha_c\alpha_k\mathbf{C}^{1-\rho}}{R^k}\right]^{\frac{\sigma}{1-\sigma}} + 1 - \frac{1}{\mu}$$

$$= \frac{1}{\mu}\alpha_c^{\frac{1}{1-\sigma}}\alpha_k^{\frac{\sigma}{1-\sigma}}\mathbf{C}^{\frac{\sigma(1-\rho)}{1-\sigma}}R^{k\frac{\sigma}{\sigma-1}} + 1 - \frac{1}{\mu}. \tag{A11}$$

Endnotes

Author email address: Eisfeldt (andrea.eisfeldt@anderson.ucla.edu), Falato (antonio.falato@frb.gov). We thank our discussants Gianluca Violante, Eric Zwick, Lars Alexander-Kuehn, Francois Gourio, Daniel Greenwald, and Thomas Lemieux, as well as Erik Hurst, Matthias Kehrig, Lee Ohanian, Valerie Ramey, and seminar and conference participants at the NBER Summer Institute Micro Data and Macro Models Workshop, the Society of Economic Dynamics Annual Meeting, the MIT Junior Finance Conference, ASU Sonoran Winter Finance Conference, the Macro Finance Society Biannual Meeting, Texas Finance Festival, WUSTL the Macroeconomics of Inequality Mini-Conference, AFA, Boston University, Columbia University, the University of Minnesota, the University of Illinois Urbana-Champaign, the London School of Economics, the University of Texas at Austin, MIT, Stanford, UC Davis, Northwestern University, the University of Chicago, Carnegie Mellon University, Georgetown University, Princeton University, UPenn Wharton School, and University of Toronto, London Business School for their helpful comments. Xiaolan gratefully acknowledges the financial support from the faculty excellence research grant from the McCombs School of Business at the University of Texas at Austin. For acknowledgments, sources of research support, and disclosure of the authors' material financial relationships, if any, please see https://www.nber.org/books-and-chapters/nber-macroeconomics-annual-2022-volume-37/human-capitalists.

1. We focus on the manufacturing sector because the Census of Manufacturing data provides a wages-only measure, to which we add our corresponding estimates of annual equity pay from firm-level data. Alvarez-Cuadrado et al. (2018) shows that the decline in the labor share occurred predominantly in the manufacturing sector. See also Kehrig and Vincent (2021), who use detailed microdata within the manufacturing sector to show that a reallocation of value added to lower labor share units has been a key driver of the decline in the labor share, and Acemoglu and Restrepo (2019), who argue that an important part of the declining labor share is that workers in manufacturing in particular have been displaced by automation.

2. See also Bhandari and McGrattan (2021) and McGrattan (2020).

3. See p. 2, "The current accounting assumption is to attribute the entire gross investment in business IPP to gross operating surplus (GOS), i.e., to capital income." See also Atkeson (2020) for a measure of the labor share that is unaffected by the BEA's accounting changes.

4. See table 5A of the publicly available W2 data available at https://www.irs.gov/pub/irs-soi/17inallw2.xls.

5. We show in appendix I (appendices I–V are available online) that the factor shares (excluding equity-based compensation) in our merged sample are nearly identical to those in the broader NBER-CES data set.

6. See also Kehrig and Vincent (2021) for a detailed analysis of the dynamics of the labor share in the cross section of production units.

7. See also the more recent work by Ohanian, Orak, and Shen (2021). That paper revisits the original Krusell et al. (2000) model with updated data and finds evidence of declining complementarity between high-skilled labor and capital. The authors find that the elasticity of substitution is closer to one using updated data (0.76 in updated data vs. 0.67 in

Krusell et al. [2000]). See the updated parameters in tables 5.2 and 5.3, and the related discussion.

8. See also the recent study of Jaimovich et al. (2019), who argue that incorporating the quality of goods produced is crucial for measuring the interaction between skill-biased technical change and the skill premium, as well as Caunedo, Jaume, and Keller (2019) for a study of differential occupational exposure to capital-embodied technical change.

9. See the comprehensive summary of the facts that describe executive compensation in Frydman and Jenter (2010).

10. The NBER-CES data set includes 459 (140) unique industries at the 4-SIC (3-SIC) level. Most of the variables in the NBER-CES are taken from the Annual Surveys of Manufacturing, whereas price deflators and depreciation rates are derived from other data published by the Census Bureau, the Bureau of Economic Analysis, the Bureau of Labor Statistics, and the Federal Reserve Board. NBER-CES data and documentation are available at http://www.nber.org/nberces.

11. See also https://www.census.gov/programs-surveys/asm/technical-documen tation/questionnaire/2019-annual-survey-of-manufactures-forms.html.

12. It is our understanding from accounting rules that the reserved share variable also includes shares reserved for restricted stock grants, but if not, our measure is conservative for that reason.

13. The median of the granting period across industries is 5.68 years.

14. See "Variable Definitions and Construction" in the appendix for details.

15. The cutoff for the 90th income percentile was $108,000 in 2017. See table 6A of the publicly available W2 data available at https://www.irs.gov/pub/irs-soi/17inallw2.xls. See also McGrattan and Prescott (2010), who emphasize the outsized earnings from capital gains by managerial and professional workers in the Federal Reserve's Survey of Consumer Finances.

16. Scaling the value of reserved shares by the stock market valuation helps alleviate the potential concern of market timing. Companies may issue more equity-based compensation when stock prices are high.

17. Using the sample for which we have full Compustat coverage (1970–95), we show that smaller firms (i.e., firms in the bottom quintile of the size distribution) offer 10% more equity-based compensation to employees relative to firms in the top quintile.

18. See table 5A of the publicly available W2 data available at https://www.irs.gov /pub/irs-soi/17inallw2.xls.

19. See Hall and Murphy (2003) for a detailed discussion of the tax treatment of stock options, and see Lebow et al. (1999) and Moylan (2000) for details on BLS and BEA treatment of stock options.

20. See chapter 10, "Compensation of Employees," pp. 2–3 of https://apps.bea.gov /national/pdf/chapter10.pdf.

21. See https://www.irs.gov/taxtopics/tc427.

22. The BEA wage-only series is thus BEA compensation minus $2/3 * NG_{t-5}$.

23. The modified Dickey–Fuller t-statistics is 9.53. We also perform another Engle-Granger–based cointegration Pedroni test and Westerlund test. Under both tests, we cannot reject the null hypotheses with all p values equal to zero.

24. In steady state, the physical capital share equals the investment to value-added ratio multiplied by a constant scalar: $rK/Y = I/Y(1/\beta - 1 + \delta_k/\delta_k)$. We assume the parameter β, δ_k is constant across industry at steady state. Hence, in the panel regression, this scalar is absorbed in the constant term, and we can use investment to value-added ratio to proxy physical capital share. Note that in a model with constant growth path, $I/Y = rK/Y$ as long as the real interest rate equals the growth rate of GDP.

25. We take information on stock option grants for a firm's top five executives from ExecComp, which is a standard source.

26. By assuming $\epsilon > 1$, we obtain curvature in the production of final goods: each type of intermediate good j is required for final goods production.

27. Alternatively, we can assume that labor is supplied either by the human capitalist or by both household sectors. This assumption does not affect the result for the labor share of income. The supply of labor in equilibrium is determined by the marginal cost of labor and the marginal benefit of consumption.

28. We can extend the current setup to a general environment, as in Karabarbounis and Neiman (2014), which includes an intermediate goods sector for k.

29. See "Derivation of Equation (16)" in the appendix.

30. Expensing was recommended but voluntary starting in 1996 and became mandatory in 2004.

31. De Loecker and Eeckhout (2017) estimated the average markup in the sample of publicly traded firms and showed that the average markup has increased from 1.21 in the 1980s to 1.45 around the mid-2000s. Karabarbounis and Neiman (2019) showed that the average increase in markup among the same sample is milder when including SG&A as variable costs.

32. This empirical specification is the same as in table 5 but with a different sample period. We do not use the longer sample for our estimate of ρ in aggregate since investment goods prices were increasing in our sample prior to 1980. It is the start of the IT revolution around the time investment goods prices began declining that we argue drives complementarity between physical and human capital. For reference, the estimate of ρ implied by the regression using data back to 1960 is -0.05.

33. The resulting model fit is shown in fig. IA6.

34. Qualifying dispositions, or those held by a retained employee for a sufficient time period, are reported on Schedule D and Form 8949.

35. For example, if the vesting period is 5 years, one-fifth of the value calculated at the time of the grant is expensed for each of the next 5 years.

36. Employees exercise stock options, or their stock vests, after $e_0 \cdot gp_0$ periods. We assume that one outstanding stock option has the right to purchase one common share of the firm. This is consistent with common practice.

References

Aboody, D., M. E. Barth, and R. Kasznik. 2006. "Do Firms Understate Stock Option–Based Compensation Expense Disclosed under SFAS 123?" *Review of Accounting Studies* 11:429–61.

Acemoglu, D. 2002. "Technical Change, Inequality, and the Labor Market." *Journal of Economic Literature* 40:7–72.

Acemoglu, D., D. Autor, D. Dorn, G. H. Hanson, and B. Price. 2014. "Return of the Solow Paradox? IT, Productivity, and Employment in US Manufacturing." *American Economic Review* 104:394–99.

Acemoglu, D., and P. Restrepo. 2019. "Automation and New Tasks: How Technology Displaces and Reinstates Labor." *Journal of Economic Perspectives* 33:3–30.

Alvarez-Cuadrado, F., N. Van Long, and M. Poschke. 2018. "Capital-Labor Substitution, Structural Change and the Labor Income Share." *Journal of Economic Dynamics and Control* 87:206–31.

Atkeson, A. 2020. "Alternative Facts Regarding the Labor Share." *Review of Economic Dynamics* 37:S167–S180.

Aum, S., and Y. Shin. 2020. "Why Is the Labor Share Declining?" Technical report, Federal Reserve Bank of St. Louis Review.

Autor, D. 2019. "Work of the Past, Work of the Future." Technical report, Massachusetts Institute of Technology.

Autor, D., D. Dorn, L. F. Katz, C. Patterson, and J. Van Reenen. 2020. "The Fall of the Labor Share and the Rise of Superstar Firms." *Quarterly Journal of Economics* 135:645–709.

Autor, D. H. 2014. "Skills, Education, and the Rise of Earnings Inequality among the 'Other 99 Percent.'" *Science* 344:843–51.

Bachelder, J. E. 2014. "What Has Happened to Stock Options?" Harvard Law School Forum on Corporate Governance and Financial Regulation. https://corpgov.law.harvard.edu/2014/10/02/what-has-happened-to-stock-options/.

Barkai, S. 2017. "Declining Labor and Capital Shares." Working paper, University of Chicago.

Becker, R., W. Gray, and J. Marvakov. 2013. "NBER-CES Manufacturing Industry Database." Working paper, NBER, Cambridge, MA.

Benzell, S. G., and E. Brynjolfsson. 2019. "Digital Abundance and Scarce Genius: Implications for Wages, Interest Rates, and Growth." Working Paper no. 25585, NBER, Cambridge, MA.

Berman, E., J. Bound, and Z. Griliches. 1994. "Changes in the Demand for Skilled Labor within US Manufacturing: Evidence from the Annual Survey of Manufactures." *Quarterly Journal of Economics* 109:367–97.

Bhandari, A., and E. R. McGrattan. 2021. "Sweat Equity in US Private Business." *Quarterly Journal of Economics* 136 (2): 727–81.

Black, F., and M. Scholes. 1973. "The Pricing of Options and Corporate Liabilities." *Journal of Political Economy* 81:637–54.

Caicedo, S., Robert E. Lucas Jr., and E. Rossi-Hansberg. 2016. "Learning, Career Paths, and the Distribution of Wages." Working Paper no. 22151, NBER, Cambridge, MA.

Caunedo, J., D. Jaume, and E. Keller. 2019. "Occupational Exposure to Capital-Embodied Technology." Technical report, Society for Economic Dynamics, St. Louis, MO.

Cobb, C. W., and P. H. Douglas. 1928. "A Theory of Production." *American Economic Review* 18:139–65.

Crimmel, B. L., and J. L. Schildkraut. 1999. "National Compensation Survey Collects Test Data on Stock Option Plans." *Compensation and Working Conditions* 4–5:17–20.

Cummins, J. G., and G. L. Violante. 2002. "Investment-Specific Technical Change in the United States (1947–2000): Measurement and Macroeconomic Consequences." *Review of Economic Dynamics* 5:243–84.

De Loecker, J., and J. Eeckhout. 2017. "The Rise of Market Power and the Macroeconomic Implications." Working Paper no. 23687, NBER, Cambridge, MA.

Eisfeldt, A. L., and D. Papanikolaou. 2013. "Organization Capital and the Cross-Section of Expected Returns." *Journal of Finance* 68:1365–406.

———. 2014. "The Value and Ownership of Intangible Capital." *American Economic Review* 104:189–94.

Elsby, M. W., B. Hobijn, and A. Şahin. 2013. "The Decline of the US Labor Share." *Brookings Papers on Economic Activity* 2013:1–63.

Farhi, E., and F. Gourio. 2018. "Accounting for Macro-Finance Trends: Market Power, Intangibles, and Risk Premia." *Brookings Papers on Economic Activity* 2018:147–223.

Frydman, C., and D. Jenter. 2010. "CEO Compensation." Working Paper no. 16585, NBER, Cambridge, MA.

Frydman, C., and D. Papanikolaou. 2015. "In Search of Ideas: Technological Innovation and Executive Pay Inequality." Working Paper no. 21795, NBER, Cambridge, MA.

Frydman, C., and R. E. Saks. 2010. "Executive Compensation: A New View from a Long-Term Perspective, 1936–2005." *Review of Financial Studies* 23:2099–138.

Gabaix, X., and A. Landier. 2008. "Why Has CEO Pay Increased So Much?" *Quarterly Journal of Economics* 123:49–100.

Gabaix, X., J.-M. Lasry, P.-L. Lions, and B. Moll. 2016. "The Dynamics of Inequality." *Econometrica* 84:2071–111.

Greenwald, D. L., M. Lettau, and S. C. Ludvigson. 2019. "How the Wealth Was Won: Factors Shares as Market Fundamentals." Technical report, NBER, Cambridge, MA.

Greenwood, J., Z. Hercowitz, and P. Krusell. 1997. "Long-Run Implications of Investment-Specific Technological Change." *American Economic Review* 87:342–62.

Hall, B. J., and J. B. Liebman. 1998. "Are CEOs Really Paid Like Bureaucrats?" *Quarterly Journal of Economics* 113:653–91.

Hall, B. J., and K. J. Murphy. 2003. "The Trouble with Stock Options." *Journal of Economic Perspectives* 17:49–70.

Hartman-Glaser, B., H. Lustig, and M. Z. Xiaolan. 2019. "Capital Share Dynamics When Firms Insure Workers." *Journal of Finance* 74:1707–51.

Jaimovich, N., S. Rebelo, A. Wong, and M. B. Zhang. 2019. "Trading Up and the Skill Premium." *NBER Macroeconomics Annual* 34:285–316.

Kao, C. 1999. "Spurious Regression and Residual-Based Tests for Cointegration in Panel Data." *Journal of Econometrics* 90:1–44.

Kaplan, S. N., and J. Rauh. 2010. "Wall Street and Main Street: What Contributes to the Rise in the Highest Incomes?" *Review of Financial Studies* 23:1004–50.

Karabarbounis, L., and B. Neiman. 2014. "The Global Decline of the Labor Share." *Quarterly Journal of Economics* 129:61–103.

———. 2019. "Accounting for Factorless Income." *NBER Macroeconomics Annual* 33:167–228.

Kehrig, M., and N. Vincent. 2021. "The Micro-Level Anatomy of the Labor Share Decline." *Quarterly Journal of Economics* 136 (2): 1031–87.

Kogan, L., and D. Papanikolaou. 2014. "Growth Opportunities, Technology Shocks, and Asset Prices." *Journal of Finance* 69:675–718.

Koh, D., R. Santaeulàlia-Llopis, and Y. Zheng. 2016. "Labor Share Decline and Intellectual Property Products Capital." Working Paper no. 927, Barcelona Graduate School of Economics.

———. 2020. "Labor Share Decline and Intellectual Property Products Capital." *Econometrica* 88:2609–28.

Krusell, P., L. E. Ohanian, J.-V. Rìos-Rull, and G. L. Violante. 2000. "Capital-Skill Complementarity and Inequality: A Macroeconomic Analysis." *Econometrica* 68:1029–54.

Lawrence, R. Z. 2015. "Recent Declines in Labor's Share in US Income: A Preliminary Neoclassical Account." Working Paper no. 21296, NBER, Cambridge, MA.

Lebow, D. E., L. Sheiner, L. Slifman, and M. Starr-McCluer. 1999. "Recent Trends in Compensation Practices." Finance and Economics Discussion Series 1999–32, Board of Governors of the Federal Reserve System (US), Washington, DC.

Lemieux, T., W. B. MacLeod, and D. Parent. 2009. "Performance Pay and Wage Inequality." *Quarterly Journal of Economics* 124:1–49.

McGrattan, E. R. 2020. "Intangible Capital and Measured Productivity." *Review of Economic Dynamics* 37:S147–S166.

McGrattan, E. R., and E. C. Prescott. 2010. "Unmeasured Investment and the Puzzling US Boom in the 1990s." *American Economic Journal: Macroeconomics* 2:88–123.

Moylan, C. 2000. "Treatment of Employee Stock Options in the U.S. National Economic Accounts." BEA papers, Bureau of Economic Analysis, Washington, DC.

Ohanian, L. E., M. Orak, and S. Shen. 2021. "Revisiting Capital-Skill Complementarity, Inequality, and Labor Share." Technical report, NBER, Cambridge, MA.

Papanikolaou, D. 2011. "Investment Shocks and Asset Prices." *Journal of Political Economy* 119:639–85.

Pierce, J. R., and P. K. Schott. 2016. "The Surprisingly Swift Decline of US Manufacturing Employment." *American Economic Review* 106:1632–62.

Piketty, T. 2014. *Capital in the 21st Century*. Cambridge: Harvard University.

Rognlie, M. 2015. "Deciphering the Fall and Rise in the Net Capital Share: Accumulation or Scarcity?" *Brookings Papers on Economic Activity* 2015:1–54.

Smith, M., D. Yagan, O. Zidar, and E. Zwick. 2018. "Capitalists in the Twenty-First Century." Working Paper no. 25442, NBER, Cambridge, MA.

———. 2021. "The Rise of Pass-Throughs and the Decline of the Labor Share." Technical report, NBER, Cambridge, MA.

Stokey, N. L. 2016. "Technology, Skill and the Wage Structure." Working Paper no. 22176, NBER, Cambridge, MA.

Comment

Giovanni L. Violante, Princeton University and NBER, United States of America

This insightful paper by Eisfeldt, Falato, and Xiaolan introduces the concept of "human capitalists," employees below the C-suite who receive a significant share of their pay as equity-based compensation. By collecting data on reserved shares across firms, this study documents the importance of this phenomenon in the corporate manufacturing sector. It then develops a theoretical equilibrium model to organize the correct income and value-added accounting. Finally, it argues that acknowledging the existence human capitalists can change our view on two key macroeconomic questions: (i) the recent decline in the aggregate labor share is smaller than previously estimated and (ii) the degree of capital-skill complementarity in aggregate technology is stronger than we thought.

This is a paper of general interest because its findings are relevant for a number of diverse literatures in economics: the measurement of workers' compensation, beyond wages; the prevalence of incentive-based pay and the design optimal labor contracts; the dynamics of the aggregate labor share; patterns of capital-labor substitution in the aggregate economy; intangible capital; and the nature of idiosyncratic labor market (or, as it is called in finance, background) risk. The paper provides new data, new facts, and new insights that affect all these research areas where an accurate measurement of worker compensation, and how it relates to the marginal product of labor, is crucial.

I will organize my comments in five parts: (i) quick model recap, (ii) measurement of the skilled labor share of income, (iii) model identification,

NBER Macroeconomics Annual, volume 37, 2023.

(iv) estimation of capital-skill complementarity, and (v) relation to the literature on background risk.

I. Model Recap

It is useful to recap the authors' main model. In doing so I will use, at times, a slightly different notation from the authors' one, which serves better my purposes. I will focus on a version without product differentiation and monopolistic competition. Consider directly the dynamic problem of a firm. Let k_t, h_t, and u_t be, respectively, the stock of physical and human capital and the amount of unskilled labor in the firm, and let r_t^k, r_t^h, and r_t^u denote their rental rates, that is, the compensation for services provided to the firm in period t by each of these inputs. Let $f(k_t, h_t, u_t)$ be the firm production technology, z_t be total factor productivity, and y_t be firm's output. Let V_t be the total firm value, $v_t = V_t/h_t$ the firm value per unit of human capital, and β its discount factor. The firm problem can be written as

$$V_t = \max_{h_t, k_t, u_t, \lambda, \theta} z_t f(k_t, h_t, u_t) - r_t^k k_t - r_t^h h_t - r_t^u u_t + \beta V_{t+1}$$

s.t.

$$r_t^h + (1 - \lambda)v_t \geq r_t^h + \bar{v}_t \tag{1}$$

The first three terms in the value function determine firm profits, that is, output net of remuneration to inputs k_t, h_t, and u_t, which are optimally chosen every period. All markets are competitive and frictionless, and thus the rental rates equal the marginal product of capital.

The remuneration of human capital services includes both monetary wage payments w_t and equity-based compensation. Equity-based compensation is also needed for retention purposes: the firm faces the participation constraint in equation (1) stating that the value promised by the firm to the worker (a share $1 - \lambda$ of the total firm value) must at least equal its outside option $\bar{v}_t$, for example, the value of being employed at a competing firm. To retain the worker, the firm chooses $(1 - \lambda)$ to satisfy that constraint with equality. The income from equity-based compensation accruing to the worker in period t for retention purposes is the flow value $(1 - \lambda)\Delta v_t$.

If we let e_t be the total equity-based compensation per unit of h_t in period t, a share θe_t will be paid to human capitalists as compensation for their marginal product, that is, $r_t^h = w_t + \theta e_t$. The residual share $(1 - \theta)$ is paid for retention purposes, that is, $(1 - \theta)e_t = (1 - \lambda)\Delta v_t$.

II. Measurement of the Skilled Labor Share of Income

The total income share going to human capitalists, s_t^h—or the skilled labor share—includes wage payments and all equity-based compensation paid for both labor services and retention purposes:

$$s_t^h = \frac{[w_t + \theta e_t + (1 - \lambda)\Delta v_t]h_t}{y_t} = \frac{W_t + E_t}{y_t}, \tag{2}$$

where W_t is the firm wage bill and E_t is the total equity-based compensation paid to all human capitalists in the firm. Note that, to measure the human capital share of income, θ does not matter because $(1 - \lambda)\Delta v_t = (1 - \theta)e_t$. The authors have information on the stock of shares reserved for employee compensation for a wide cross section of firms and a long time series of 60 years from 1960 to 2019. They also have information on the average vesting period. They then measure the flow of equity-based compensation in period t as

$$E_t = \underbrace{\frac{\text{\# of reserved shares}_t}{\text{average vesting period}}}_{\text{new grants}} \times \text{stock price}_t$$

This calculation, however, does not include capital gains or losses in the value of deferred compensation due to fluctuations in stock prices. Eisfeldt et al. are aware of this. In the appendix, they write: "Our measure is conservative, in the sense that we do not include capital gains or losses on share-based compensation that is granted but not vested, and share values have increased substantially, on average, over our sample." This position is shareable: the value of stocks at the time of allocation best reflects the value of labor services and the value of retention to the firm. At the same time, the current value reflects the realized earnings for the worker, and cost to the firm, if the option were to be exercised. It seems therefore of interest to ask how much their calculations would be affected by the inclusion of capital gains.

Let q_t be the number of reserved shares at t, and p_t their price. Then $E_t = \Delta q_t p_t + q_{t-1}\Delta p_t$, where the second term captures capital gains/losses during the period. The skilled labor share of income would then be augmented by the component

$$\frac{\text{capital gains}_t}{\text{income}_t} = \frac{q_{t-1}p_{t-1}}{y_t} \times \frac{\Delta p_t}{p_{t-1}}.$$

Assume $\Delta p_t/p_{t-1} = 0.05$, that is, stock prices grow by 5% per year in real terms, and abstract from short-term fluctuations. Figure 1 shows by how much the skilled labor share would change if Eisfeldt et al. had incorporated capital gains, relative to their own calculations and to a definition of the labor share that ignores altogether the equity-based component of labor earnings, such as those of the Bureau of Economic Analysis (BEA) and the Bureau of Labor Statistics (BLS). The cumulation of capital gains would have added another 2 percentage points to the Eisfeldt et al. skilled labor share between 1970 and 2000 and made the gap with the BEA/BLS one even starker.

Another important question is the following: If we add income to skilled labor we must subtract it from other factors for consistency; which share would be reduced? The answer depends on accounting practices for

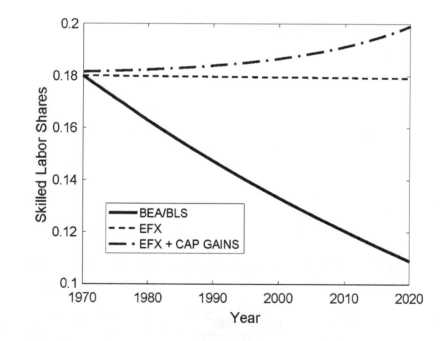

Fig. 1. The evolution of the skilled labor shares computed in three ways. BEA/BLS is the naive computation without accounting for equity-based compensation. EFX is the authors' calculation that abstracts from capital gains in the value of reserved shares. EFX + CAP GAINS includes capital gains as explained in the main text. A color version of this figure is available online.

stock-based compensation followed by firms when compiling their books. Unfortunately, over time practices have changed and even now there is no uniformly accepted rule. For example, Deloitte has a 500-page road map on how to properly account for share-based payment awards. They likely show up as profits in many books, but according to the current generally accepted accounting principles, stock-based compensation is a noncash operating expense on the income statement. As such, it could show up either in the wage bill of the firm (still, it would not be picked up by national accounts, as explained by Eisfeldt et al.) or in other operating costs related to investment in intangibles, for example, research and development, marketing, and advertising expenses. In the latter case, Eisfeldt et al. provide support for the mechanism proposed by Koh, Santaeulàlia-Llopis, and Zheng (2020). According to these authors, the decline in the labor share is directly linked to the rise of investment in intangibles because on the income side of national accounts statistical agencies attribute all the income corresponding to these intangible expenditures to capital. Eisfeldt et al. document that part of this income is, in reality, deferred compensation to skilled labor and so, as argued by Koh et al. (2020), should be added back to the labor share.

III.   Identification

The parameter θ is crucial in the analysis because it is required to compute the marginal product of skilled labor, which, in turn, is needed to estimate the parameters of the production function. Eisfeldt et al. postulate the following nested constant elasticity of substitution specification for the production function $z_t f(k_t, h_t, u_t)$:

$$y_t = z_t \left[\alpha_c (\alpha_k k_t^\rho + (1 - \alpha_k) h_t^\rho)^{\frac{\sigma}{\rho}} + (1 - \alpha_c) u_t^\sigma \right]^{\frac{1}{\sigma}},$$

where $\rho, \sigma \in (-\infty, 1)$. Combining the optimality conditions for k_t and h_t in the firm problem (eq. [1]) yields

$$\frac{r_t^k}{r_t^h} = \frac{\alpha_k k_t^{\rho-1}}{(1 - \alpha_k) h_t^{\rho-1}}. \tag{3}$$

From $r_t^h h_t = W_t + \theta E_t$, the definition of the skilled labor share in equation (2), and the definition of the capital share $s_t^k = r_t^k k_t / y_t$, we arrive at

$$\log s_t^k - \log s_t^h = \log\left(\frac{\alpha_k}{1-\alpha_k}\right) + \rho \log\left(\frac{k_t}{h_t}\right) + \log \omega_t^h(\theta), \qquad (4)$$

where

$$\omega_t^h(\theta) = \frac{W_t + \theta E_t}{W_t + E_t}.$$

This relation shows clearly that, given data on factor shares and quantity of inputs, the estimate of ρ depends on θ, and vice versa. Eisfeldt et al. approach this problem by attempting an estimation of ρ through cross-industry variation and then, given ρ, they recover the value of θ, which is consistent with the model evaluated at that estimate of ρ.

Using rental rates in equation (3) to substitute out input quantities in equation (4), and denoting industry with a subscript j, yields

$$\log s_{jt}^k - \log s_{jt}^h = \text{constant} + \frac{\rho}{1-\rho} \log r_j^h - \frac{\rho}{1-\rho} \log r_{jt}^k + \log \omega_t^h. \qquad (5)$$

Eisfeldt et al. make two assumptions reflected in the specification above: equation (A1) $r_{jt}^h = r_j^h$, that is, the marginal product of human capital is time invariant and hence can be captured by industry effects in a panel regression; equation (A2) $\omega_{jt}^h = \omega_t^h$, that is, W_t, θ, and E_t are common across industries and can be captured by time effects. Thus ρ is identified by exploiting variation of r_{jt}^k—which is directly measurable.

These two assumptions are quite strong. For example, it is quite possible that the rental rate of human capital varies over time, as aggregate supply and demand for h_t change. Let's consider what happens if this assumption is violated. The omitted variable in equation (5) is $(\rho/1 - \rho)(\log r_{jt}^h - \log r_j^h)$, which implies

$$\frac{\hat{\rho}}{1-\hat{\rho}} = \left(\frac{\rho}{1-\rho}\right)\left[1 - \frac{cov\left(\log\left(r_{jt}^h/r_j^h\right), \log r_{jt}^k\right)}{var\left(\log r_{jt}^k\right)}\right].$$

If r_{jt}^k and r_{jt}^h comove positively over time (e.g., because of aggregate productivity shocks), then the term in the square brackets is less than one and $\hat{\rho}$ is downward biased.

It is also possible that different sectors use equity-based compensation to different degrees; for example, because human capital specificity varies and, as a result, they face more or less severe retention issues. If equation (A2) is violated, then ω_{jt}^h varies across industries and the omitted variable in equation (5) is $\log \omega_{jt}^h - \log \omega_t^h$, which implies

$$\frac{\hat{\rho}}{1 - \hat{\rho}} = \left(\frac{\rho}{1 - \rho}\right) - \frac{cov\left(\log\left(\omega_{jt}^h/\omega_t^h\right), \log r_{jt}^k\right)}{var\left(\log r_{jt}^k\right)}.$$

In this case, signing the bias is more challenging without knowing more about cross-industry patterns in the data. If, for example, skill-intensive industries (which display high r_{jt}^k if physical and human capital are complements) face more severe retention issues (i.e., they feature low θ, high E_t, and low ω_{jt}), then $\hat{\rho}$ would be upward biased.

Thus, depending on which assumption is violated, the authors could under- or overestimate the degree of capital-skill complementarity. The good news is that the two biases, at least in my examples, push in opposite directions, so hopefully they offset each other.

IV. Capital-Skill Complementarity

One of the main findings of Eisfeldt et al. is that they find evidence of capital-skill complementarity only after adding equity-based compensation to the skilled labor share. Using the BEA/BLS definition of the labor share, they cannot reject a Cobb-Douglas specification in total capital and skilled labor. At first sight, this result seems to contradict the findings in Krusell et al. (2000), who used the "naive" definition of the labor share without accounting for equity-based compensation.

There is, however, a big difference between the authors' analysis and Krusell et al.'s study in the definition of capital. Eisfeldt et al. aggregate different types of capital in one capital input, whereas Krusell et al. explicitly distinguish between structures and equipment. Krusell et al.'s estimates refer to complementarity between equipment and skilled labor. It is important, I would argue, to separate these two inputs because the dynamics of their prices were vastly different over the past 60 years: equipment prices dropped dramatically, whereas the price of structures rose, relative to the price of consumption (fig. 2), a reflection of faster embodied technical change in equipment capital.

In this section, I will investigate how the Krusell et al. estimates of capital-skill complementarity are modified when the skilled labor share is

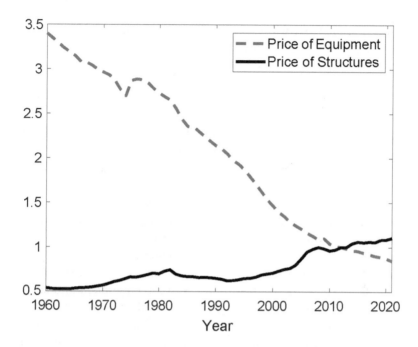

Fig. 2. Price of equipment investment and structures investment relative to the price of consumption expenditures. Data are from National Income and Product Accounts. A color version of this figure is available online.

augmented with equity-based compensation. Recall the aggregate production function in Krusell et al.,

$$y_t = z_t k_{st}^\alpha \left[\alpha_c (\alpha_k k_{et}^\rho + (1 - \alpha_k) h_t^\rho)^{\frac{\sigma}{\rho}} + (1 - \alpha_c) u_t^\sigma \right]^{\frac{1-\alpha}{\sigma}},$$

where k_{st} is structures and k_{et} is equipment. Under this technology, the expression for the skill premium is

$$\log\left(\frac{w_{ht}}{w_{ut}}\right) = \text{constant} + \frac{\sigma - \rho}{\rho} \log\left[\lambda\left(\frac{k_{et}}{h_t}\right)^\rho + (1 - \lambda)\right] \quad (6)$$

$$+ (1 - \sigma) \log\left(\frac{u_t}{h_t}\right).$$

I will use the data series in Ohanian, Orak, and Shen (2021), who extended the original data set in Krusell et al., which spanned 1963–93, up to 2019.[1] The data set contains time series for wages, quality-adjusted capital equipment, structures, skilled labor and unskilled labor, relative price of equipment, and depreciation rates. I estimate various versions of equation (6) by generalized method of moments (GMM) using as instruments lagged values for all the variables above (except wages).[2]

First, like Eisfeldt et al., I bundle all capital together and estimate equation (6) with total capital (structures plus equipment) taking the place of k_{et}. The first column in table 1 shows that I replicate their finding that using the naively computed skilled share, the data offer no support for capital-skill complementarity, that is, the estimate for ρ is slightly positive but close to zero (the Cobb-Douglas case). As claimed by Eisfeldt et al., adding equity-based compensation to skilled wages (second column) restores total capital-skill complementarity, although my point estimate for ρ is imprecise. If we, however, split capital between equipment and structures, even using the naive skilled share I do find evidence of equipment-skilled labor complementarity. The third column of table 1 shows that I estimate an elasticity of substitution between equipment and skilled labor $(1/[1 - \rho])$ of 0.69 and an elasticity of substitution between the equipment-skilled labor composite and unskilled labor $(1/[1 - \sigma])$ of 2.22. These two values are close to the original estimates in Krusell et al., respectively, 0.67 and 1.67. Finally, I augment the skilled share with equity-based compensation. I use a value of $\theta = 0.98$, the authors' estimate. Now, the relative wages of skilled workers rise even further, but the equipment-skill ratio and the skilled-unskilled labor ratio in equation (6) are the same, and thus, to account for the data, the elasticity of substitution between equipment and skilled labor must fall further to 0.589.

Overall, including equity-based pay in the compensation of skilled labor increases the estimates of capital equipment-skill complementarity,

Table 1
GMM Estimates of ρ and σ Based on Equation (6)

	Capital Aggregated		Equipment and Structures Separated	
	Naive	Adjusted	Naive	Adjusted
σ	.513 (.063)	.341 (.094)	.551 (.050)	.337 (.694)
ρ	.146 (.070)	−.467 (.219)	−.449 (.065)	−.705 (.091)
p value for J test	.755	.130	.701	.220

Note: Each column corresponds to a different combination of how capital is aggregated and how the skilled share is computed. Standard errors are in parentheses. The null hypothesis of the J test is that the instruments are valid.

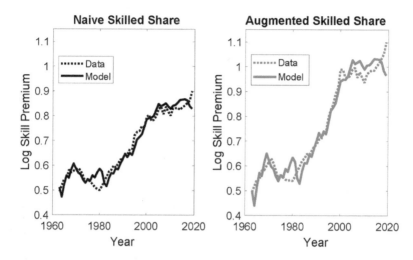

Fig. 3. Skill premium: data and fitted values as implied by estimating the Krusell et al. (2000) model. Left panel: naively computed skilled share. Right panel: skilled share augmented with equity-based compensation. A color version of this figure is available online.

but not by much. Figure 3 plots data and model-implied skill premium under the naive and adjusted data on the skilled labor share.

V. Implications for Uninsurable Labor Market Risk

The findings by Eisfeldt et al. have some interesting implications for estimates of uninsurable individual earnings risk. The measurement of unpredictable fluctuations in individual earnings is a key input for a large class of incomplete market heterogeneous agent models and an important source of welfare loss for households.

The typical empirical analysis in this literature uses data sets such as the Panel Study of Income Dynamics, Social Security Administration records, or Internal Revenue Service tax returns that, as explained by the authors, do not properly account for equity-based compensation. One would expect this component of earnings to be more cyclical and volatile than base wages.

Differential exposure of labor earnings to the business cycle can be a channel of amplification or dampening of macroeconomic shocks in heterogeneous agent New Keynesian models: the stronger the cross-sectional correlation between marginal propensity to consume and the change in household income induced by the macro shock, the more this shock gets amplified. Figure 4, reproduced from Guvenen et al. (2017),

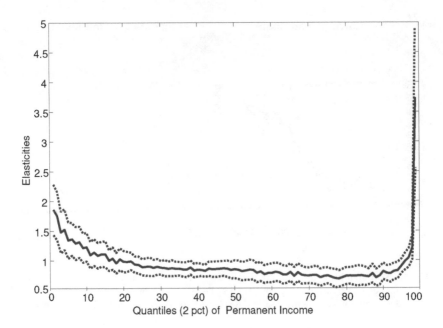

Fig. 4. The elasticity of individual earnings to aggregate earnings across the labor income distribution. Data are from Guvenen et al. (2017). A color version of this figure is available online.

shows the elasticity of individual labor income to aggregate labor income across the distribution. The elasticity is U-shaped. In particular, this elasticity is very high at the top. I conjecture that adding equity-based compensation would mostly affect the top decile of this plot and would make it even more sensitive to aggregate income fluctuations.

Turning to idiosyncratic volatility, a recent paper by Braxton et al. (2021) documents that the volatility of the persistent component of earnings shocks is higher, and it has increased more since 1990, for skilled workers than for unskilled workers. The inclusion of equity-based compensation would strengthen both conclusions because this component is more volatile than base wages and because it has become a larger share of total labor income for skilled labor over time.

Endnotes

Author email address: Violante (violante@princeton.edu). For acknowledgments, sources of research support, and disclosure of the author's material financial relationships, if any, please see https://www.nber.org/books-and-chapters/nber-macroeconomics-annual -2022-volume-37/comment-human-capitalists-violante.

1. To add equity-based compensation to skilled wages in the Ohanian et al. (2021) data set, I benchmark it to value added based on figure 4 of the Eisfeldt et al. paper.

2. As shown in table 1, the Sargan-Hansen *J* test fails to reject the null hypothesis that the instruments are orthogonal to the residuals.

References

Braxton, J. Carter, Kyle F. Herkenhoff, Jonathan L. Rothbaum, and Lawrence Schmidt. 2021. "Changing Income Risk across the US Skill Distribution: Evidence from a Generalized Kalman Filter." Working Paper no. 29567, NBER, Cambridge, MA.

Guvenen, Fatih, Sam Schulhofer-Wohl, Jae Song, and Motohiro Yogo. 2017. "Worker Betas: Five Facts about Systematic Earnings Risk." *American Economic Review* 107 (5): 398–403.

Koh, Dongya, Raül Santaeulàlia-Llopis, and Yu Zheng. 2020. "Labor Share Decline and Intellectual Property Products Capital." *Econometrica* 88 (6): 2609–28.

Krusell, Per, Lee E. Ohanian, José-Víctor Ríos-Rull, and Giovanni L. Violante. 2000. "Capital-Skill Complementarity and Inequality: A Macroeconomic Analysis." *Econometrica* 68 (5): 1029–53.

Ohanian, Lee E., Musa Orak, and Shihan Shen. 2021. "Revisiting Capital-Skill Complementarity, Inequality, and Labor Share." Working Paper no. 28747, NBER, Cambridge, MA.

Comment

Eric Zwick, Chicago Booth and NBER, United States of America

Aside from giving us a terrific title, Eisfeldt, Falato, and Xiaolan have written an important and provocative paper. They demonstrate a mastery of accounting intricacies and deftly deploy this knowledge to motivate compelling reduced-form empirical analysis and transparent structural estimation.

The basic premise of the paper is straightforward: stock-based compensation has increased in importance over time, and its measurement in the national accounts has not kept up. Accordingly, we are missing a large and increasing share of labor income in the national accounts.

This missing labor income implicates a panoply of central questions in contemporary economics. Among the key results, correcting for this mischaracterized income accounts for one-third of the labor share decline in manufacturing and all of the decline for nonproduction workers. In the structural estimation, this correction recovers the complementarity of skill and capital, explored in Krusell et al. (2000) and a rich subsequent literature. In addition, the model-implied estimates point toward substitution between wages and stock-based compensation; in other words, this compensation is better thought of as a component of the marginal product of labor rather than bargaining rents.

These are important and fascinating results. I see the paper as a major contribution with ample room for follow-on work. My comments will focus on (i) drawing some connections between these findings and other patterns in the data, (ii) providing additional data and calculations to support the basic premise of the paper, and (iii) using the paper's results to reinterpret other puzzles. In short, I see the paper as being even better than the authors do and congratulate them on this contribution.

NBER Macroeconomics Annual, volume 37, 2023.

I.   The Rise of Pass-Through Business Income

One reason I am excited about this research agenda is that it complements and reinforces some ideas I have explored in recent years. This
work began with Cooper et al. (2016), who document the dramatic rise
of business activity in the pass-through sector since the late 1980s and
connect this evolution to the beneficial tax treatment afforded such activity. In Smith et al. (2019), we find that much of the capital income
of pass-through business owners should be better thought of as compensation to owner-manager human capital, broadly defined. Accounting for this mischaracterized labor income transforms our view of the
typical top 1% earner. Smith et al. (2022) dollar-weight this result and
show that pass-through growth can account for approximately one-
third of the decline in the corporate sector labor share.

Both our pass-through story and the human capitalist story share a
common ancestor in the tax reforms of the 1980s. The key to understanding these trends is recognizing the evolving tax incentives to compensate labor over the postwar period. Figure 1 plots the top federal marginal tax rates from 1960 to 2021 for corporate income, long-term capital
gains, dividends, and personal income. I label the epoch between 1960
and the 1981 Kemp-Roth tax cuts as the *Before Times* and then label subsequent epochs using their antecedent tax changes.[1]

Consider first the incentives faced by entrepreneurs. In the Before Times,
the tax code encouraged you to leave money in your firm, to consume in
pretax dollars through your firm, and to generate paper losses to offset
economic income whenever possible. With the tax changes in the 1980s
came the incentive for traditional C-corporations to shift owner-manager

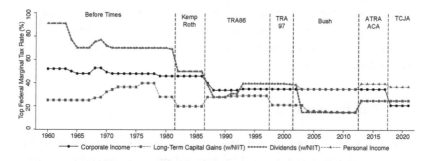

Fig. 1.   A brief history of tax policy in the United States. Data are from Tax Policy Center.
TRA86 = Tax Reform Act of 1986; TRA97 = Tax Reform Act of 1997; ATRA = American
Taxpayer Relief Act; ACA = Affordable Care Act; TCJA = Tax Cuts and Jobs Act; NIIT =
net investment income tax. A color version of this figure is available online.

compensation from corporate income to wages and bonuses to avoid the double tax on corporate income and distributions. For those entrepreneurs electing pass-through form, the lower personal income rates since the 1990s encouraged substitution to profits rather than wages to avoid payroll, Medicare, and Affordable Care Act tax surcharges.

It has always been appealing for entrepreneurs to recognize income to the extent possible as long-term capital gains. However, that incentive is stronger in recent decades because of lower corporate tax rates, which reduce the cost of leaving money in the firm, and lower interest rates, which raise the value of the option to defer. These incentives also apply to entrepreneurs in many countries across the developed world (Kopczuk and Zwick 2020).

Now consider the incentives for firms to compensate top employees. In the Before Times, the tax code encouraged you to take your pay through noncash perquisites or to defer pay through generous pension and life insurance arrangements. The same tax changes in the 1980s that encouraged owner-managers to take more pretax pay also encouraged employees to take more pay in the form of wages, bonuses, and stock. After the Clinton and Bush tax cuts, the attractiveness of stock compensation increased further due to lower long-term gains rates.

Thus, one strength of the paper is that the time series narrative nicely follows from the historical record of tax incentives for stock compensation. And this narrative comports with and extends existing evidence on entrepreneurial income. As a final note, these forces are especially important at the top. For example, they contribute to the sharp increase in top income inequality right around the Tax Reform Act of 1986 (TRA86) in the top 1% share of fiscal income (fig. 2). The series show sharp jumps in both the wage income and business income series from 1986 to 1988, which reflect the change in incentives for owner-managers and top workers.[2] One avenue for future research would be to explore the connection between rising stock compensation and top income inequality more closely.

II. Paid in Promises

The paper's main premise requires two conditions: (i) stock compensation has grown over time and (ii) it is not properly recorded as labor income in the national accounts and other data sets. The case for the former condition is strong, but how true is the latter? If stock compensation appears on Form W-2 and is therefore captured in the Bureau of

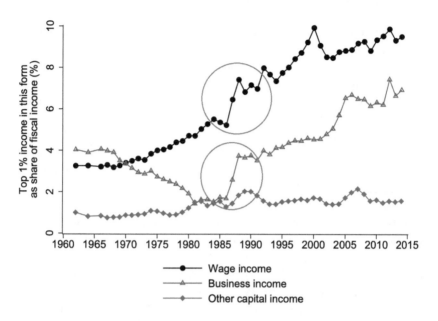

Fig. 2. Top 1% wage and business income jumps sharply around TRA86. Data are from Smith et al. (2019). A color version of this figure is available online.

Economic Analysis's (BEA) labor income measures, then perhaps the paper's claims are overstated.

To evaluate this concern, I spent some time with the tax code, Securities and Exchange Commission (SEC) filings, and practitioner reports. There are many ways in which employees are "paid in promises," in that they trade off current cash compensation for claims on future profits. First, there are nonqualified stock options (NSOs), which are recorded on Form W-2 when exercised and then treated subsequently as stock. Second, there are incentive stock options (ISOs), which are only ever recorded as capital gains. Third, there are restricted stock units (RSUs), which are recorded on Form W-2 when vested and then treated as stock. Last, there are various nonstock approaches, such as allowing special access to company stock via pension arrangements, employee stock option plans, and profit-sharing plans.

My reading of the institutional details yielded several observations in favor of the idea that this compensation is not fully recorded in BEA labor income. First, early employees and founders of companies who receive stock options can reduce the share of income that appears as W-2 and thus reduce their total tax burden by converting their options in advance of vesting, via what is called an 83(b) election. This alternative is especially attractive to higher income and wealth recipients who can afford paying taxes early upon option exercise.

Second, review of public company stock plans in financial filings supports the idea that companies retain flexibility in whether they offer NSO, ISO, or RSU compensation. For example, in PayPal's initial public offering filing (SEC Form S-1), the firm lists 60.5 million shares of common stock outstanding and 11.0 million shares of stock reserved for outstanding and future option grants.[3] This option pool thus accounts for 18% of the fully diluted outstanding share pool, a significant potential ownership claim for the company's top workers.

Importantly, the option pool allows issuance of all three kinds of stock grants listed above. My understanding is that some combination of compensation advisers, human resources, and employees negotiate the best-fit compensation arrangement subject to these stock plans. That best-fit arrangement often involves focusing on ways to reduce ordinary income tax burdens (i.e., Form W-2 income) to the extent possible. At the same time, there are fewer options for avoiding W-2 income in more mature firms, when the stock is already quite valuable and the price is not growing quickly. Note this flexibility in the choice of option and difficulty in tracking what is granted support the paper's focus on reserved shares, as it smartly avoids these accounting issues.

Third, stock option compensation is very much a standard practice in high-growth private companies. According to a survey conducted by the National Association of Stock Plan Professionals in 2019, 90% of Silicon Valley companies grant options and 80% of these companies grant the tax-favored ISO form, compared with just 20% of public companies. Thus, for this slice of the population, the missing labor income issue is especially important.

Fourth, company stock remains a favorite asset class. Figure 3 presents data from the Survey of Consumer Finances for the population of non-business owners. I partition the data into total income groups: bottom 90%, P90–99, P99–99.9, and the top 0.1%. Ownership of company stock is rare in the bottom 90% but rises to more than 50% for top 1% earners. Stock options appear to be more common for those outside the top 0.1%, with approximately 20% of top decile earners reporting some stock option ownership. For those who own stock, it accounts for between 40% and 60% of their total stock portfolios (excluding pensions) and between 20% and 40% of their non-housing wealth. Remarkably, even in the wake of Enron and the dot-com era, it appears that company stock has increased in prevalence for these groups (with some survey noise for the top 0.1% group).

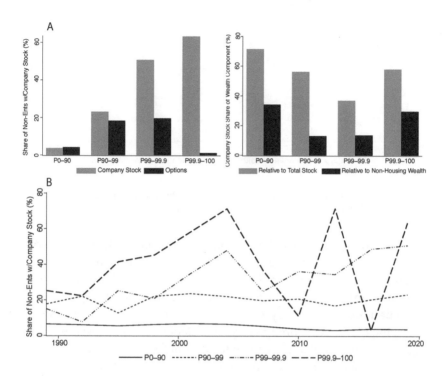

Fig. 3. Company stock in the portfolios of non-business owners: (*A*) company stock ownership in 2019; (*B*) company stock ownership over time. Calculations are author's, using the Survey of Consumer Finances. Groups are defined based on total income. A color version of this figure is available online.

Finally, and perhaps part of the explanation for the prior fact, the value of stock as a currency has increased substantially since the 1980s (fig. 4). This trend reflects a combination of discount rate declines, reduced tax burdens, and other factors. For companies with the ability to pay in stock, this trend favors doing so relative to paying in cash.

Overall, this institutional deep dive suggests there are many reasons to believe the basic premise that much of this compensation is missing from BEA labor income, with increasing importance over time. I suspect the 30%–40% assumption in the current paper may be conservative relative to the truth.

III. A Top-Down Test

Consider an alternative validation exercise for the paper's one-third-of-the-labor-share result. Whereas the authors pursue a bottom-up, constructive approach for estimating the share of labor income that's missing,

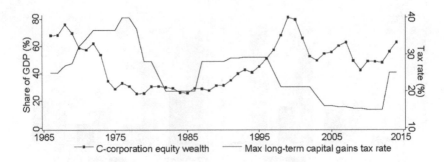

Fig. 4. Total C corporation wealth and long-term capital gains tax rates. Data are from Sarin et al. (2022). A color version of this figure is available online.

I will use aggregate data and the assumption that labor owns 10% of corporate equity to check the plausibility of their result "from the top down."

Table 1 presents data for 2017 from Smith et al. (2022) from the national accounts and our adjusted series. The latter adjusts corporate sector value added and employee compensation for the missing labor share due to the rise of pass-through business. Depending on the series, these aggregates suggest that if we want to account for 100% of the reduction in the labor share since the early 1980s, we need to find between $414B and $556B in "missing" labor compensation. These amounts, which equal 20% and 34% of profits, are too large relative to the 10% ownership share. However, if we only want to account for one-third of the reduction, then we only need to find 7%–11% of corporate profits, right in line with the bottom-up ownership share.

We can use other data to benchmark this 10% number. If workers own 10% of corporate profits via stock compensation, then this ownership

Table 1
Cumulative Labor Share Decline with and without Manufacturing

Scenario	Raw BEA	SYZZ-Adjusted
Corporate GVA ($B)	11,090	12,161
Employee comp ($B)	6,420	7,235
Corporate profits in GVA ($B)	1,650	2,119
Labor share (%)	57.9	59.5
Target labor share (%)	62.9	62.9
"Missing" labor comp ($B)	556	414
Labor share of profits for 100% of missing (%)	33.7	19.5
Labor share of profits for 1/3 of missing (%)	11.2	6.5

Note: GVA = gross value added; SYZZ = Smith, Yagan, Zidar, and Zwick.
Source: Author calculations from Smith et al. (2022), table 1.

amounts to $165B in 2017. From aggregate Internal Revenue Service tabulations, $165B equals 9.6% of the $2.7T in total W-2 income for those with more than $100K in wages. If we distribute the $165B across the top 10% of Compustat employees, of which there are 4.2 million, this ownership implies an additional $40K in pay. This ownership is 20% as large as total fiscal dividend and capital gains income, which is around $900B. It is less than 5% of total wage income of the top 10%, which equals $3.2T, and 15% if we assume that public company workers account for one-third of these workers.

The takeaway from all of these calculations is that the aggregate magnitudes required by this story are eminently plausible. Better data could help us determine whether they turn out to be too low.

IV.   The Human Capitalist Story Helps on Many Fronts

As a final comment, the reason I am so excited about this paper is that the human capitalist story helps explain many outstanding puzzles in macro labor.

First, the labor share decline in the United States was concentrated in the 2000s. This time series fact neatly aligns with the rise in the value of missing labor compensation for human capitalists (e.g., fig. 1 in the paper).

Second, with the exception of those countries emerging either partly or fully from the Soviet Union, the US labor share decline was sharper than elsewhere (fig. 5). Given the size and depth of the stock market in the United States and the large number of workers at public companies, the human capitalist story provides a mechanism that is uniquely American.

Third, the decline of the labor share features a central role played by superstar firms (Autor et al. 2020). Given such firms are typically public companies with the opportunity to pay their workers in stock, the human capitalist story applies especially to superstars.

Fourth, Koh, Santaeulàlia-Llopis, and Zheng (2020) document the rising importance of intangible capital in the secular trend away from labor. Human capitalists produce many intangible capital assets (e.g., software). A rising role for intangible capital would naturally entail more compensation to its producers. Given the dynamic considerations in incentivizing such producers to work hard, deferred compensation and stock-based pay are natural responses to the agency problems that pervade these settings.

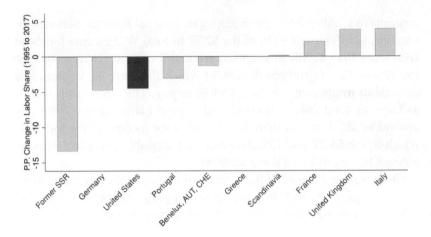

Fig. 5. The labor share decline in the United States versus the Organization for Economic Cooperation and Development. Data are from Smith et al. (2022), appendix figure A.7. SSR = Soviet Socialist Republic; AUT = Austria; CHE = Switzerland; P.P = percentage point. A color version of this figure is available online.

Fifth, the trend in the college premium in the United States flattened in the late 1990s and has remained approximately constant over the past 20 years (Finkelstein et al. 2022). If college workers are increasingly paid in stock as human capitalists and the college premium misses that income, then the trend may not have flattened after all.

Finally, the trend in the corporate sector labor share is driven by trends in manufacturing (fig. 6). In contrast to our pass-through story, the human capitalist story applies well to large, capital-intensive firms in manufacturing. It is worth noting that the manufacturing contribution

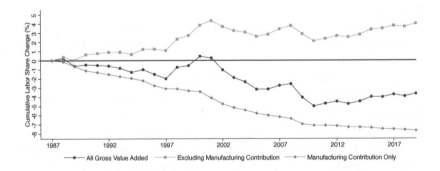

Fig. 6. Cumulative labor share decline with and without manufacturing. Data are from Smith et al. (2022), appendix figure A.6. A color version of this figure is available online.

comes along with a massive decline in the number of manufacturing workers and in the manufacturing sector's share of domestic employment and capital. These trends do not appear within the scope of the human capitalist story to explain. Thus, there remains space to learn more about the manufacturing decline and its singular contribution to trends in the labor share.

Endnotes

Author email address: Zwick (ericzwick@gmail.com). For acknowledgments, sources of research support, and disclosure of the author's material financial relationships, if any, please see https://www.nber.org/books-and-chapters/nber-macroeconomics-annual -2022-volume-37/comment-human-capitalists-2-zwick.

1. These are the Kemp-Roth tax cuts in 1981, the Tax Reform Act of 1986, the Tax Reform Act of 1997, the Bush tax cuts in 2002, the Obama tax increases in 2012, and the Tax Cuts and Jobs Act in 2017.

2. Some of this increase comes mechanically from changes in the loss limitation regime in TRA86 (Auten and Splinter 2019).

3. https://www.sec.gov/Archives/edgar/data/1103415/000091205702023923/a20820 68zs-1.htm

References

Auten, Gerald, and David Splinter. 2019. "Using Tax Data to Measure Long-Term Trends in U.S. Income Inequality." Working paper, US Department of the Treasury, Office of Tax Analysis, Washington, DC.

Autor, David, David Dorn, Lawrence F. Katz, Christina Patterson, and John Van Reenen. 2020. "The Fall of the Labor Share and the Rise of Superstar Firms." *Quarterly Journal of Economics* 135 (2): 645–709.

Cooper, Michael, John McClelland, James Pearce, Richard Prisinzano, Joseph Sullivan, Danny Yagan, Owen Zidar, and Eric Zwick. 2016. "Business in the United States: Who Owns It, and How Much Tax Do They Pay?" *Tax Policy and the Economy* 30 (1): 91–128.

Finkelstein, Amy, Casey McQuillan, Owen Zidar, and Eric Zwick. 2022. "The Health Wedge and Labor Market Inequality." In preparation.

Koh, Dongya, Raül Santaeulàlia-Llopis, and Yu Zheng. 2020. "Labor Share Decline and Intellectual Property Products Capital." *Econometrica* 88 (6): 2609–28.

Kopczuk, Wojciech, and Eric Zwick. 2020. "Business Incomes at the Top." *Journal of Economic Perspectives* 34 (4): 27–51.

Krusell, Per, Lee E. Ohanian, José-Víctor Ríos-Rull, and Giovanni L. Violante. 2000. "Capital-Skill Complementarity and Inequality: A Macroeconomic Analysis." *Econometrica* 68 (5): 1029–53.

Sarin, Natasha, Lawrence Summers, Owen Zidar, and Eric Zwick. 2022. "Rethinking How We Score Capital Gains Tax Reform." *Tax Policy and the Economy* 36:1–33.

Smith, Matthew, Danny Yagan, Owen Zidar, and Eric Zwick. 2019. "Capitalists in the Twenty-First Century." *Quarterly Journal of Economics* 134 (4): 1675–745.

———. 2022. "The Rise of Pass-Throughs and the Decline of the Labor Share." *American Economic Review: Insights* 4 (3):323–40.

Discussion

Robert Hall and Eric Swanson raised concerns about the measurement of the value of grants. In particular, Robert Hall noted that if there is high employee turnover, many shares granted to workers will fail to vest as a worker moves on before the end of the vesting period. The authors argued that their main measure, stocks reserved for compensation, was likely to be an underestimate of the expected value of grants that will vest. Although the Securities and Exchange Commission requires reporting of grants, firms are incentivized to minimize the number of shares reserved due to the dilution effect, where issuing equity to workers reduces the value of other shares as they are now a claim to a smaller portion of the firm. The authors also noted that they find a strong correlation between reserving of shares with repurchases and the difference between earnings per diluted and nondiluted shares. Eric Swanson raised concerns about the use of the Black-Scholes formula to value grants given that companies sometimes adjust the strike price if their stock price falls to ensure the employee gains some compensation from the option. This feature might make the Black-Scholes value too low compared with the actual value to the worker. The authors responded that all their results hold in specifications that do not use grant values calculated using Black-Scholes.

Robert Hall asked about the effect of equity compensation for private companies and venture capital-backed firms, as workers are often not able to sell any shares until either the company is sold or goes public. The authors responded by highlighting that most of the companies in their sample are large companies that have been public for several decades. They

NBER Macroeconomics Annual, volume 37, 2023.

hypothesized that the share of compensation that takes the form of grants would be higher in private and venture capital-owned firms based on the evidence Eric Zwick provided in his discussion.

Eric Zwick asked if household surveys could potentially be used to measure income from stock options, given how income inequality has tracked consumption inequality in these surveys. They could also resolve some of the issues about measurement raised by others in the discussion. The authors agreed that using household surveys could be a future avenue of research; however, they raised two potential issues. The first is the timing of when the grants would be considered income, as households might only report options when exercised and not when granted. The second is that households may not consider stock options when asked about income and may use their W-2 when asked about past years' income. The authors then suggested that adding a specific question about stock options to household surveys may overcome these limitations.

Guido Menzio asked about the motivation of firms to pay workers using stock options rather than wages, as the model in the paper did not contain a motivation for using it. He raised a potential concern with the empirical specification that there may be correlation between firm- or worker-specific factors and the choice to use equity-based compensation. The authors responded by noting some of the reasons that firms use equity-based compensation: tax advantages, retention, and boosting short-term profits as the grants are not immediately expensed. They explained that they were agnostic about the relative importance of these reasons in their empirical specification and try to control for correlations between firm- and worker-specific factors in their firm-level regressions.

Guido Menzio also raised the point that equity-based compensation may have implications for inequality, as workers who live paycheck to paycheck cannot afford to receive some of their compensation in tax-advantaged stock options. The authors agreed that equity compensation is more attractive for those in higher tax brackets as well as those who can afford to take on risk in their compensation.

2

A Reassessment of Monetary Policy Surprises and High-Frequency Identification

Michael D. Bauer, *Universität Hamburg and CESifo,* Germany, *and CEPR,* United Kingdom

Eric T. Swanson, *University of California, Irvine, and NBER,* United States of America

I. Introduction

Over the past two decades, high-frequency interest rate changes around the Federal Reserve's Federal Open Market Committee (FOMC) announcements, or *monetary policy surprises*, have become an important tool for identifying the effects of monetary policy on asset prices and the macroeconomy. For example, Kuttner (2001); Bernanke and Kuttner (2005); Gürkaynak, Sack, and Swanson (2005); Hanson and Stein (2015); and Swanson (2021) use monetary policy surprises to estimate the effects of monetary policy on asset prices, while Cochrane and Piazzesi (2002); Faust et al. (2003); Faust, Swanson, and Wright (2004); Gertler and Karadi (2015); Ramey (2016); and Stock and Watson (2018) use them to help estimate the effects of monetary policy on macroeconomic variables in a structural vector autoregression (SVAR) or Jordà (2005) local projections (LP) framework.

Monetary policy surprises are appealing in these applications because their focus on interest rate changes in a narrow window of time around FOMC announcements plausibly rules out reverse causality and other endogeneity problems. For example, FOMC decisions are completed an hour or two before the decision is announced, implying that the FOMC could not have been reacting to changes in financial markets in a sufficiently narrow window of time around the announcement, so the asset price changes are clearly caused by the announcements themselves, rather than vice versa. For lower-frequency changes in monetary policy and asset prices, the direction of causality is generally not clear (see, e.g., Rigobon and Sack 2003, 2004).

Monetary policy surprises are also typically viewed as being unpredictable with any publicly available information that predates the FOMC announcement. This view is supported by the standard argument that, otherwise, financial market participants would be able to trade profitably on that predictability and drive it away in the process. Thus, monetary policy surprises are plausibly exogenous with respect to all macroeconomic variables that are publicly known prior to the FOMC announcement itself, making them a valid instrument for the effects of monetary policy in SVARs and LPs, as discussed in Stock and Watson (2018).

A few recent studies, however, have questioned whether monetary policy surprises possess these desirable properties to the extent that the literature has typically assumed. For example, Cieslak (2018), Bauer and Swanson (2023), and Miranda-Agrippino and Ricco (2021) all document substantial correlation of monetary policy surprises with publicly available macroeconomic or financial market data that predate the FOMC announcement, with Bauer and Swanson (2023) reporting R^2 of 10%–40%. These results undermine the standard assumption that monetary policy surprises represent exogenous changes and call into question the results of the empirical studies cited above. In addition, Ramey (2016) finds that the macroeconomic effects of monetary policy are often poorly estimated in samples that begin after about 1984, likely because monetary policy was conducted more systematically over this period, so the set of structural monetary policy shocks (estimated using high-frequency monetary policy surprises or other methods) is much smaller and less informative than in earlier years. In other words, the results in Cieslak (2018) and the other studies cited above question the exogeneity of high-frequency monetary policy surprises, and Ramey (2016) questions whether those surprises are sufficiently relevant. As discussed in Stock and Watson (2018), both conditions are required for monetary policy surprises to be a good instrument for estimating the effects of monetary policy.

In this paper, we address these challenges in two main ways. First, we improve the relevance of monetary policy surprises by substantially expanding the set of monetary policy announcement events to include press conferences, speeches, and testimony by the Federal Reserve chair (which we will refer to as "speeches" for brevity), in addition to the FOMC announcements. As shown by Swanson and Jayawickrema (2021), speeches by the Fed chair are even more important for financial markets than FOMC announcements themselves, and thus should more than double the relevance of the monetary policy variation in our analysis, relative to previous studies that focused on FOMC announcements alone. Thus, we respond to Ramey's (2016) critique by increasing the number and total variation of monetary policy announcement shocks in our sample. Moreover, Swanson and Jayawickrema (2021) extend the sample for all of these monetary policy announcements back to 1988, giving us a few more years of data during a period when monetary policy was more variable than in the 1990s, which increases the variation in our monetary policy surprise series further still.

Second, for this expanded set of monetary policy surprises, we address the exogeneity issue by removing the component of the monetary policy surprises that is correlated with economic and financial data, following the recommendations of Bauer and Swanson (2023). In particular, we regress those surprises on the economic and financial variables that predate the announcements and are correlated with them, and take the residuals. These orthogonalized monetary policy surprises should help eliminate any attenuation bias or "price puzzle" types of effects in SVARs and LPs and provide better estimates of monetary policy's true effects on macroeconomic variables.

We thus produce a new measure of monetary policy surprises that is both more relevant and more likely to be exogenous than those used by previous researchers. We use our new measure to reassess previous empirical estimates of the effects of monetary policy on financial markets and the macroeconomy, using high-frequency event-study regressions, SVARs, and LPs. Our reassessment leads to two main findings: first, estimates of the effects of monetary policy on financial markets with high-frequency event-study regressions are largely unchanged. The correlation of monetary policy surprises with macroeconomic and financial data that predate the announcements has essentially no effect on these estimates, consistent with the simple theoretical model that we develop shortly. Second, conventional estimates of the effects of monetary policy on the macroeconomy using high-frequency identification are substantially biased, due to the econometric endogeneity of the monetary policy surprises. Using our new, improved monetary policy surprise measure produces stronger, more plausible, and more precise estimates. In addition, our correction of monetary policy surprises uses publicly available data, so our results do not support the view that Fed information effects are an important confounding factor for monetary policy surprises, in contrast to Nakamura and Steinsson (2018), Miranda-Agrippino and Ricco (2021), and others.

We begin our analysis with a simple theoretical model of private-sector learning about the Fed's monetary policy rule in Section II. The model extends an earlier model in Bauer and Swanson (2023) and helps to organize our thinking and to make testable empirical predictions. In the model, the Fed's responsiveness to the economy is both time varying and unobserved by the private sector. A key result is that monetary policy surprises arise not only from exogenous monetary policy shocks but also from incomplete information about the Fed's monetary policy rule. As a consequence, monetary policy surprises can be correlated with economic variables observed prior to the policy announcements.[1] A precondition for this effect, which Bauer and Swanson (2023) termed the "Fed response to news" channel, is that the public systematically underestimated how strongly the Fed would respond to economic news. We provide empirical evidence that the Fed has become more responsive to the economy over our sample, 1988–2019, which can explain why, on average, the Fed has responded more strongly to economic conditions than the private sector expected. Additional evidence in Cieslak (2018) and Schmeling, Schrimpf, and Steffensen (2022) also supports this view.[2] The model has additional implications for our subsequent empirical analysis: it predicts that monetary policy surprises can be used without correction for estimating asset price responses to monetary policy in high-frequency regressions, but they are unlikely to be valid instruments for monetary policy shocks in SVARs or LPs.

In Section III, we review and extend previous studies of the predictability of high-frequency monetary policy surprises. We document a strong correlation of monetary policy surprises with information that is publicly available prior to the FOMC announcements. We argue that this correlation is unlikely to be driven entirely by time-varying risk premia, because survey forecast errors for the federal funds rate are also significantly correlated with the same preannouncement information. Instead, we argue that a violation of the Full-Information Rational Expectations (FIRE) hypothesis is a more likely explanation. Monetary policy surprises were likely unpredictable ex ante but predictable ex post, consistent with our simple theoretical model and imperfect information on the part of the private sector.

We then begin our empirical reassessment of the transmission of monetary policy to financial markets and the macroeconomy. In Section IV, we revisit high-frequency empirical estimates of the effects of monetary policy announcements on financial markets, as in Kuttner (2001) and Gürkaynak et al. (2005), using our expanded set of orthogonalized monetary policy surprises. In line with previous estimates, we find very strong effects of monetary policy surprises on Treasury yields and the stock market. A comparison of the estimates using conventional versus orthogonalized monetary policy surprises shows that the two have very similar effects on asset prices, in line with the prediction of our theoretical model. The implication for empirical research is that standard event studies using conventional high-frequency monetary policy surprises can reliably estimate the financial market effects of monetary policy announcements.

In Section V, we turn to high-frequency identification of the effects of monetary policy on macroeconomic variables in an SVAR or LP framework, as in Gertler and Karadi (2015), Ramey (2016), Miranda-Agrippino and Ricco (2021), and Plagborg-Møller and Wolf (2021, 2022). Our expanded set of monetary policy surprises greatly improves the first-stage F-statistic for our high-frequency instrument, solving one of the main difficulties faced by those earlier authors. Our orthogonalized monetary policy surprises produce estimates of monetary policy's effects that do not suffer from price or activity puzzles and are up to four times larger than when conventional, unadjusted monetary policy surprises are used. Thus, we find substantial evidence that the econometric endogeneity of conventional monetary policy surprises used by previous authors leads to a significant bias that attenuates or even reverses the sign of their estimates. We collect lessons learned from revisiting previous empirical work and present new "best practice" estimates of the dynamic macroeconomic effects of monetary policy shocks using our orthogonalized monetary policy surprises.

We also revisit the role of the Fed's internal "Greenbook" forecasts for explaining the endogeneity of monetary policy surprises. Miranda-Agrippino and Ricco (2021) documented that Greenbook forecasts (and forecast revisions) have predictive power for monetary policy surprises, and that removing this correlation changes SVAR estimates that use these surprises as instruments for policy shocks. We show that there is nothing particularly special about the Greenbook forecasts in these results: both in predictions of monetary policy surprises and in SVARs that use adjusted monetary policy surprises as instruments, the use of Greenbook and Blue Chip forecasts produces almost identical results. Because Blue Chip forecasts are publicly observable, our findings challenge the view that the Fed has significant private information, consistent with the findings in Bauer and Swanson (2023) that both types of forecasts are equally (in)accurate. Hence, they call into doubt the presence of strong Fed information effects and support our interpretation in terms of a "Fed response to news" channel.

In Section VI, we conclude and discuss the implications of our results for monetary policy and central bank communication in practice. For example, we address the question of whether policy makers should be concerned about information effects or other effects that might attenuate or counteract the intended effects of monetary policy announcements. We also discuss what our new estimates imply about the effectiveness of policy communication in speeches by the Fed chair versus official communication by the FOMC itself. Finally, we lay out some ideas that hold promise for future research.

Our work is related to three different strands of the macroeconomic literature. First, several recent studies have documented that high-frequency monetary policy surprises around FOMC announcements are in fact significantly correlated ex post with information that was publicly available prior to the FOMC announcement. For example, Cieslak (2018) documents correlation with the lagged federal funds rate and employment growth; Miranda-Agrippino (2017) and Miranda-Agrippino and Ricco (2021) with broad-based macroeconomic factors from a dynamic factor model; Bauer and Swanson (2021) with major macroeconomic data release surprises— such as for nonfarm payrolls, unemployment, gross domestic product (GDP), and inflation—and changes in financial markets, such as the Standard and Poor's 500 index (S&P 500), yield curve slope, and commodity prices; Karnaukh and Vokata (2022) with the most recent Blue Chip GDP forecast revisions; Bauer and Chernov (2023) with option-implied skewness of Treasury yields; and Sastry (2021) with the consumer sentiment release, recent S&P 500 stock returns, and the most recent Blue Chip GDP forecast. Relative to these previous studies, we extend the predictability findings to additional predictors and an expanded sample. We also present new evidence that Blue Chip forecasts have predictive power for monetary policy surprises that is just as strong as the predictive power of the Fed's Greenbook forecasts documented by Miranda-Agrippino and Ricco (2021).

The above studies have also proposed a number of possible explanations for the predictability they document. For example, Karnaukh and Vokata (2022) argues that bond markets were slow to incorporate the information in the Blue Chip forecasts, although this raises the question of why competition for profits by market participants would not drive the sluggish response away. Miranda-Agrippino (2017) argues that there are substantial, predictable risk premia on short-term interest rate securities; however, Piazzesi and Swanson (2008) and Schmeling et al. (2022) estimate that the risk premia on such short-term securities is small, and Cieslak (2018) argues that those risk premia would need to be implausibly large to explain the observed predictability in the data and that a risk premium interpretation is inconsistent with a variety of other financial market evidence. Miranda-Agrippino and Ricco (2021) argue that the predictability is evidence of a "Fed information effect," according to which the Fed's monetary policy surprises reveal to the markets information about the Fed's forecast for the economy.[3] However, we show in this paper that Blue Chip forecasts have equally strong predictive power for those policy surprises, indicating that the Fed is unlikely to have significant private information, and that Fed information effects may not be an important source of that predictability. Moreover, Bauer and Swanson (2023) show that the Fed's Greenbook forecasts are no more accurate than Blue Chip forecasts, that Blue Chip forecasters do not revise their forecasts in response to FOMC announcements in a way consistent with the Fed information effect, and that previous authors' results that supported a Fed information effect can be explained by major macroeconomic data releases and financial market changes that were omitted from those previous studies.[4] Instead, in this paper and in Bauer and Swanson (2023), we argue that the predictability of monetary policy surprises is due to financial markets not having full information about the Fed's monetary policy rule and underestimating ex ante how responsive the Fed would be to economic data; this interpretation of the evidence is also very similar to Cieslak (2018) and Schmeling et al. (2022). Note, however, that our analysis in the present paper does not hinge on this particular interpretation, because we investigate the practical consequences of the predictability of monetary policy surprises, no matter what the source of that predictability is.

The second strand of literature related to the present paper uses high-frequency monetary policy surprises to estimate the effects of monetary policy on asset prices. Kuttner (2001) uses daily changes in the current-month or next-month federal funds futures rate around an FOMC announcement to measure the surprise component of the announcement and the effects of changes in the federal funds rate on short- and longer-term Treasury yields, and Bernanke and Kuttner (2005) estimate the effects of those changes on the stock market. Gürkaynak et al. (2005) extend Kuttner's analysis by focusing on intradaily changes in financial markets around FOMC announcements and by looking at interest rate futures with several months to maturity, allowing them to separately estimate the effects of changes in the federal funds rate from changes in forward guidance on bond yields and stock prices. Brand, Buncic, and Turunen (2010) extend the Gürkaynak et al. analysis to the euro area, and D'Amico and Farka (2011) consider a more detailed and updated analysis of the stock market. Swanson (2021) extends the Gürkaynak et al. analysis to separately identify the effects of the Fed's asset purchases as well as federal funds rate changes and forward guidance, and Altavilla et al. (2019) apply the analysis in Swanson to the euro area. We revisit this type of analysis in Section IV, reestimating the effects of monetary policy surprises on asset prices both with and without corrections for the predictability discussed above.

The third strand of literature related to our study uses high-frequency monetary policy surprises to help estimate and identify the effects of monetary policy on macroeconomic variables in an SVAR or LP framework. Early examples are Cochrane and Piazzesi (2002), Faust et al. (2003), and Faust et al. (2004). Stock and Watson (2012, 2018) discuss how to use high-frequency monetary policy surprises as an external instrument to identify the effects of monetary policy in a VAR, and Gertler and Karadi (2015) and Ramey (2016) follow this approach to obtain estimates that are now regarded as benchmarks. In the present paper, we reassess the VAR and LP analysis in these studies in light of our expanded set of monetary policy surprises and our corrections for the predictability of those surprises discussed above.

II.   A Simple Model with Incomplete Information

To gain intuition and guide our empirical work shown later, we present a simple theoretical model of incomplete information and private-sector learning about the Fed's monetary policy rule. Readers who are interested only in our empirical results can skip this section and proceed directly to the beginning of our empirical analysis in Section III.

The basic idea is that monetary policy surprises can arise from a discrepancy between the true and perceived responsiveness of the Fed to the state of the economy. For example, if the Fed is more responsive to the output gap than the public expects, then a high output gap will lead to a positive monetary policy surprise. If the private sector's underestimate persists for several periods, as will typically be the case in a model of learning, then the monetary policy surprises will end up being correlated with the output gap ex post even though they were unpredictable by the private sector ex ante.

A.   The Simple Model

In the interest of clarity, we make the model as simple as possible, following along the lines of the model in Bauer and Swanson (2023), but extended in two ways: first, we explicitly consider the case where the parameters of the Fed's monetary policy rule may change over time. Second, we allow for changes in the interest rate to feed back directly to the economy.

For simplicity, the state of the economy in the model is captured by a scalar variable x_t. For concreteness, x_t is taken to be procyclical (e.g., the output gap). We assume that x_t follows a simple backward-looking linear process,

$$x_t = \rho x_{t-1} - \theta i_{t-1} + \eta_t, \tag{1}$$

where time t is discrete, $|\rho| < 1$ and $\theta \geq 0$ are parameters, i_t denotes the interest rate, and η_t is an exogenous *i.i.d.* Gaussian process with mean zero and variance σ_η^2. In contrast to Bauer and Swanson (2023), we allow $\theta \neq 0$ in equation (1), which complicates the model but explicitly allows the interest rate i_t to affect future values of x_t. Intuitively, equation (1) is a simple, backward-looking IS curve, with the negative sign on θ corresponding to the standard intuition that higher interest rates reduce future economic activity.

Each period t is divided into two subperiods, with x_t realized in the first subperiod and i_t set by the Federal Reserve in the second subperiod. The Fed sets i_t according to the monetary policy rule

$$i_t = \alpha_t x_t + \varepsilon_t, \tag{2}$$

where α_t denotes the Fed's responsiveness to x_t, and ε_t is the monetary policy shock, an exogenous *i.i.d.* Gaussian process with mean zero and variance σ_ε^2. In contrast to Bauer and Swanson (2023), we explicitly allow the parameter α_t in equation (2) to be time varying; for simplicity, we assume that it follows a random walk,

$$\alpha_t = \alpha_{t-1} + u_t, \tag{3}$$

where u_t is an exogenous *i.i.d.* Gaussian process with mean zero and variance σ_u^2.

We assume that the Fed has full information and perfectly observes all variables and parameters of the model. The private sector knows the parameters ρ, θ, σ_η^2, σ_ε^2, and σ_u^2 and observes x_t and i_t each period, but does not observe α_t (or ε_t or u_t), and thus must form beliefs about α_t based on the history of the observed x_t and i_t. We assume that the private sector's belief formation is fully Bayesian and thus rational. We let $\mathcal{H}_t \equiv \{i_t, x_t, i_{t-1}, x_{t-1}, ...\}$ denote the history of variables observed by the private sector up to time t. At the beginning of period t, before x_t and i_t are realized, we assume that the private sector's prior beliefs about α_t are Gaussian with mean $a_t = E[\alpha_t | \mathcal{H}_{t-1}]$ and variance $\sigma_t^2 = \text{Var}[\alpha_t | \mathcal{H}_{t-1}]$.

Once the private sector observes x_t, it expects the interest rate to be $E[i_t | x_t, \mathcal{H}_{t-1}] = a_t x_t$. The Fed's actual interest rate decision in the second subperiod then leads to the monetary policy surprise

$$
\begin{aligned}
\text{mps}_t &\equiv i_t - E[i_t | x_t, \mathcal{H}_{t-1}] \\
&= (\alpha_t - a_t)x_t + \varepsilon_t.
\end{aligned}
\tag{4}
$$

Equation (4) illustrates that monetary policy surprises can be due either to exogenous policy shocks ε_t or to imperfect information about the Fed's monetary policy rule, $\alpha_t \neq a_t$.

After observing i_t, the private sector updates its beliefs about α_t optimally using Bayesian updating (i.e., Kalman filtering):

$$
a_{t+1} = E[\alpha_t | H_t] = a_t + k_t \text{mps}_t,
\tag{5}
$$

where the Kalman gain parameter k_t is given by

$$
k_t = \frac{\omega_t}{x_t}, \quad \omega_t = \frac{x_t^2 \sigma_t^2}{x_t^2 \sigma_t^2 + \sigma_\varepsilon^2},
\tag{6}
$$

and the belief variance evolves according to

$$
\sigma_{t+1}^2 = \sigma_t^2 (1 - \omega_t) + \sigma_u^2.
\tag{7}
$$

The direction of the parameter update naturally depends upon the signs of both x_t and mps_t: the private sector will raise its belief about α_t for a hawkish surprise ($\text{mps}_t > 0$) during an expansion ($x_t > 0$), as well as for a dovish surprise ($\text{mps}_t < 0$) during a recession ($x_t < 0$).

The model in Bauer and Swanson (2023) assumed constant $\alpha_t = \alpha$, that is, $\sigma_u^2 = 0$, for simplicity. In that case, the belief variance $\sigma_{t+1}^2 = \sigma_t^2 (1 - \omega_t)$ tends to zero as $t \rightarrow \infty$, so the private sector would gradually learn the true value of α over time. In the more general case here, the private sector can never fully learn the Fed's policy rule.

Because the updating in equations (4)–(5) is optimal, the monetary policy surprise mps_t is unpredictable ex ante, based on any information that is available to the private sector before the Fed sets the interest rate

i_t. This is evident from equation (4), which implies that $E[\text{mps}_t|x_t, H_{t-1}] = 0$. Nevertheless, the monetary policy surprises mps_t can be correlated with x_t ex post if $\alpha_t > a_t$ for several periods in a row. From equation (4), $\text{Cov}(\text{mps}_t, x_t) = (\alpha_t - a_t)\text{Var}(x_t)$, which is positive if $\alpha_t > a_t$ on average over a given sample.[5] If the private sector tends to underestimate the Fed's responsiveness to the economy, then the monetary policy surprise mps_t will be ex post positively correlated with a procyclical business cycle indicator such as x_t. Such ex post predictability in financial markets— without any true ex ante predictability due to variation in risk premia and expected returns—is a common implication of models of imperfect information and learning by investors (Timmermann 1993; Lewellen and Shanken 2002; Johannes, Lochstoer, and Mou 2016).

Our empirical analysis in Section III documents significant procyclical correlation between monetary policy surprises and macroeconomic and financial variables. The model suggests a straightforward explanation of this correlation: financial markets have underestimated how responsive the Fed would be to the economy (i.e., $\alpha_t > a_t$ on average over our sample).

One way we could have $\alpha_t > a_t$ over our sample is if the Fed became more responsive to the economy, so that α_t increased over time. In fact, several pieces of evidence presented later are consistent with such a pattern. If α_t increases, then a logical consequence of Bayesian learning is that the private sector's beliefs a_t will tend to lag behind, and thus on average $a_t < \alpha_t$. The reason is that signals about α_t are downweighted in the update of the parameter belief because $\omega_t \in [0, 1]$. To see this more clearly, rewrite the updating rule (eq. [5]) as

$$a_{t+1} = (1 - \omega_t)a_t + \omega_t\alpha_t + \frac{\omega_t}{x_t}\varepsilon_t. \qquad (8)$$

For example, suppose that at the end of period $t = 1$, the private sector's beliefs are correct, so that $a_2 = \alpha_1$, and then the Fed becomes more responsive, so that $\alpha_2 - \alpha_1 = u_2 > 0$. Assume for simplicity that there is no policy shock, so $\varepsilon_2 = 0$. After the interest rate $i_2 = \alpha_2 x_2$ is observed, the private sector's belief update is $a_3 - a_2 = \omega_2(\alpha_2 - a_2) = \omega_2 u_2$, which is smaller than the actual parameter change, u_2. This example illustrates a general pattern: if the Fed becomes more responsive over time, then the perceived responsiveness parameter will tend to be smaller than the true parameter.

There are a number of plausible reasons to think that private-sector learning about the Fed's monetary policy rule would be quite slow in practice, with the result that changes in α_t would cause a persistently large discrepancy $\alpha_t - a_t$. First, learning about a persistent component (α_t) from a noisy time series (i_t) is difficult and happens only gradually, with long-lasting biases in beliefs; see Farmer, Nakamura, and Steinsson (2021) for a recent discussion. Second, the private sector in reality faces a multidimensional learning problem: realistic policy rules are of course multivariate, requiring the public to learn about several parameters at once, which greatly slows down the learning process (Johannes et al. 2016). Third, the private sector must form beliefs about which macroeconomic and financial variables enter the Fed's monetary policy rule (i.e., about its functional form). Fourth, the Fed's monetary policy rule could contain nonlinearities—which we have also abstracted from here—so that, in practice, the Fed responds most aggressively to the economy when the economic data are most extreme. These extreme events occur only very rarely, so it is extraordinarily difficult for the private sector to learn the Fed's true responsiveness to the economy during these rare episodes.

B.   Evidence for Increasing Fed Responsiveness

Empirically, there is substantial evidence that the Fed's monetary policy has in fact become more responsive to the economy over the past few decades. First, a number of studies have investigated shifts in the parameters of the Fed's monetary policy rule, going back to the seminal work of Clarida, Gali, and Gertler (2000), who documented a substantial increase in the Fed's responsiveness to inflation and output when Paul Volcker became Fed chairman in 1979. Empirical monetary policy rules with explicitly time-varying parameters also generally suggest a tendency for the Fed's responsiveness to inflation and real activity to have increased since the 1980s (Cogley and Sargent 2005; Primiceri 2005; Boivin 2006; Kim and Nelson 2006; Bianchi, Lettau, and Ludvigson 2022). In figure 1, we report results from estimating a simple time-varying monetary policy rule for the Fed, obtained using recursive, exponentially weighted least squares estimates as described in appendix A. There is a clear upward trend in the Fed's response coefficients to both inflation and output over the past 30 years.

These empirical estimates are also supported by numerous speeches by Federal Reserve officials. For example:

- In 2001, Chairman Greenspan noted, "The Federal Reserve has seen the need to respond more aggressively than had been our wont in earlier decades" (*Wall Street Journal* 2001).

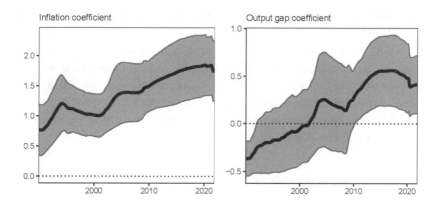

Fig. 1. Recursive least squares estimates of Fed monetary policy rule parameters. Exponentially weighted recursive least squares estimates of the Federal Reserve's monetary policy rule parameters using expanding windows beginning in 1976 and ending between 1990 and 2021, with shaded two-standard-error bands based on Newey and West (1987) with 12 lags. Regressions are estimated at monthly frequency, inflation is measured using the 1-year change in the log core Personal Consumption Expenditures price index, and the output gap is the Congressional Budget Office estimate. See text and appendix for details. A color version of this figure is available online.

- In 2008, Chairman Bernanke stated, "By way of historical comparison, this policy response stands out as exceptionally rapid and proactive" (Bernanke 2008).

- In 2012, Vice Chair Yellen introduced an "optimal control" approach to monetary policy. Under this approach, which Yellen characterized as consistent with the current strategy of the FOMC, monetary policy responds more strongly to unemployment than policy rules that had characterized past Fed behavior (Yellen 2012).

- Both Chairs Bernanke and Yellen have emphasized and elaborated on a "balanced approach" to monetary policy (e.g., Bernanke 2013; Yellen 2017), which puts more weight on resource utilization than historical policy rules. The Fed makes this explicit in its Monetary Policy Report to Congress, which regularly compares policy rules: the coefficient on the unemployment gap in the "balanced-approach rule" is two, whereas this coefficient in the classic Taylor (1993) rule is one.[6]

It is also reasonable to think that the Fed's view of optimal monetary policy has become more responsive to the economy over time. Many prominent theoretical and empirical studies of monetary policy over the past 30 years have increasingly supported the view that more systematic and proactive monetary policy leads to better macroeconomic outcomes (e.g., Taylor 1999; Clarida et al. 2000; Stock and Watson 2002; Woodford 2009).[7]

Finally, empirical evidence from surveys provides direct support for the view that the private sector has typically underestimated the responsiveness of the Fed to the economy. In particular, Cieslak (2018) and Schmeling et al. (2022) show that survey forecasts systematically underpredicted changes in the federal funds rate over our sample, particularly during easing episodes.[8]

C. Implications of the Model

The simple model of incomplete information and learning outlined above has a number of implications for empirical analysis with high-frequency monetary policy surprises. First, as discussed above, equation (4) shows that as a result of imperfect public information about the policy rule, monetary policy surprises can be correlated with information that is publicly available prior to the FOMC announcements. This is true even if the surprises are unpredictable ex ante because financial markets are perfectly rational and risk premia on short-term rate securities are negligible.

Second, the model suggests that the effects of monetary policy surprises on asset prices can be estimated using standard high-frequency regressions. The reason is that revisions to interest rate expectations—the only asset prices in this model—are affected by monetary policy announcements only through mps_t and not separately by ε_t. To show this, we introduce new notation for the change in private-sector expectations in response to the monetary policy announcement in period t, $\Delta E_t(z) = E[z|H_t] - E[z|H_{t-1}, x_t]$ for expectations about a generic variable z. Bayesian updating and the fact that α_t is a martingale imply that changes in beliefs about all future rule coefficients are simply

$$\Delta E_t(\alpha_{t+n}) = k_t \text{mps}_t, \quad \text{for all } n \geq 0. \tag{9}$$

Changes in expectations of future interest rates are

$$\begin{aligned}
\Delta E_t(i_{t+n}) &= \Delta E_t(\alpha_{t+n} x_{t+n}) \\
&\approx \Delta E_t(\alpha_{t+n}) E[x_{t+n}|\mathcal{H}_{t-1}, x_t] + \Delta E_t(x_{t+n}) E[\alpha_{t+n}|\mathcal{H}_{t-1}, x_t],
\end{aligned} \tag{10}$$

where the first equality follows from the policy rule (eq. [2]) and the fact that the policy shock ε_t is unpredictable, and the second line is a first-order approximation that simplifies the argument in the presence of an endogenous output gap ($\theta \neq 0$). In the simpler case with an exogenous output gap ($\theta = 0$), as in the model of Bauer and Swanson (2023), revisions to rate expectations are exactly equal to the first term in equation (10), which from equation (9) depends only on mps_t and not on ε_t:

$$\Delta E_t(i_{t+n}) = \Delta E_t(\alpha_{t+n})E[x_{t+n}|\mathcal{H}_{t-1}, x_t] = \rho^n \omega_t \text{mps}_t. \tag{11}$$

In the more general case, we need to account for revisions to output gap expectations, which from equation (1) and recursive substitution are

$$\Delta E_t(x_{t+n}) = -\theta \sum_{j=0}^{n-1} \rho^{n-j-1} \Delta E_t(i_{t+j}). \tag{12}$$

From induction on equations (10) and (12), with initial condition $\Delta E_t(i_t) = \text{mps}_t$, it is evident that the revisions $\Delta E_t(x_{t+1})$, $\Delta E_t(i_{t+1})$, $\Delta E_t(x_{t+2})$, $\Delta E_t(i_{t+2})$, and so forth all depend only on mps_t and not separately on ε_t. That is, up to first order, a monetary policy announcement at time t changes private-sector expectations of future interest rates i_{t+n} by an amount that is a function of the surprise mps_t, with no separate role for ε_t. Accordingly, the effects of a monetary policy shock ε_t manifest themselves entirely through mps_t.

As a result, an econometrician can use high-frequency data on monetary policy surprises mps_t to estimate the effects of those surprises on the yield curve (or other asset prices) using high-frequency regressions of the form

$$\Delta E_t(i_{t+n}) = b_0 + b_1 \text{mps}_t + e_t, \tag{13}$$

and those estimates will also be representative of the effects of an exogenous change in monetary policy ε_t. Although the high-frequency monetary policy surprises mps_t may be correlated with x_t, our model predicts that there is no omitted variable issue: once we condition on mps_t, there is no separate role for x_t or ε_t. Thus, mps_t can still be used, without adjustment, to estimate the effects of an exogenous change in monetary policy ε_t on asset prices in a narrow window of time around an FOMC announcement. This implies that the high-frequency empirical estimates in Kuttner (2001), Bernanke and Kuttner (2005), Gürkaynak et al. (2005), and others should reliably estimate the effects of an exogenous change in monetary policy (ε_t) on the yield curve, the stock market, and other asset prices. We check this prediction of our model in Section IV.

A third implication of our model is that it may be problematic to use monetary policy surprises for estimation of the dynamic effects of monetary policy on macroeconomic variables in an SVAR or LP framework. To be a valid external instrument for a monetary policy shock, mps_t must be exogenous with respect to the other structural shocks and the lagged variables of the VAR (Stock and Watson 2018). However, according to our model, mps_t can be correlated with x_t ex post, and the evidence in Section III confirms that mps_t is strongly correlated with various macroeconomic and financial variables in practice. Therefore, it is likely that the econometric exogeneity condition is violated, and mps_t is not a valid instrument for the monetary policy shock.

In Bauer and Swanson (2023), we recommend orthogonalizing mps_t with respect to the macroeconomic and financial variables that are observed before the FOMC announcement to remove this correlation. According to our model, such a procedure would: (i) isolate the component of mps_t that is due to the monetary policy shock ε_t, (ii) leave estimates of the effects of monetary policy on asset prices largely unchanged,[9] and (iii) increase the likelihood that the resulting series is a valid instrument for monetary policy shocks in a VAR. In Sections IV and V, we implement this correction and assess to what extent it affects empirical estimates typical of those in the literature.

III. Monetary Policy Surprises and Predictability

In this section, we present new evidence for the predictability of high-frequency monetary policy surprises around FOMC announcements, extending the results of previous studies such as Cieslak (2018), Bauer and Swanson (2023), and Miranda-Agrippino and Ricco (2021).[10] We expand on earlier work in three main ways: first, we use a new, more extensive data set of high-frequency monetary policy surprises from Swanson and Jayawickrema (2021). Second, we document predictive power for additional macroeconomic and financial variables, which we show to be robust across different sample periods and measures of monetary policy surprises. Third, we assess the information content in macroeconomic forecasts for subsequent monetary policy surprises and find that the Blue Chip survey consensus and the Fed's Greenbook forecasts contain the same amount of information. We interpret these results through the lens of our model and argue that they support the view that predictability arises from imperfect information in the private sector about the Fed's monetary policy rule.

A. Monetary Policy Surprises around FOMC Announcements

The Swanson and Jayawickrema (2021) data set covers the period from 1988 to 2019, which begins earlier and ends later than the studies cited above and includes 322 FOMC announcements and 880 speeches by the

Fed chair. For comparability to previous work, we focus first on FOMC announcements.

From 1994 onward, FOMC announcement dates and times are relatively easy to collect, because each announcement was communicated clearly to the markets through a press release.[11] Prior to 1994, the FOMC typically did not issue such press releases (except after a discount rate change), and market participants had to infer whether there had been a change in the federal funds rate from the size and type of open market operation conducted by the Fed each morning. In this case, the term "FOMC announcement" corresponds to the date and time of the corresponding open market operation.[12] Swanson and Jayawickrema (2021) measure intradaily interest rate changes over a 30-minute window starting 10 minutes before each FOMC announcement and ending 20 minutes afterward, using intradaily data from Tick Data.

To construct high-frequency monetary policy surprises, some authors use the change in the current-month federal funds futures contract (e.g., Kuttner 2001), some use the change in a farther-ahead federal funds futures contract (e.g., Gertler and Karadi 2015), and others use a range of federal funds and Eurodollar futures contracts (e.g., Gürkaynak et al. 2005; Nakamura and Steinsson 2018).[13] In this paper, we follow the last approach and use the first four quarterly Eurodollar futures contracts, ED1–ED4.[14] Rather than focus on two dimensions of monetary policy, as in Gürkaynak et al. (2005), we follow Nakamura and Steinsson (2018) and take just the first principal component of the changes in ED1–ED4 around FOMC announcements, which we rescale so that a one-unit change in the principal component corresponds to a 1 percentage point change in the ED4 rate. Gürkaynak et al. (2005) showed that FOMC announcements cause surprises about both the current federal funds rate target and the expected path of the federal funds rate for the next several months (i.e., their "target" and "path" factors). Because the first principal component is essentially equal to a weighted average of the target and path factors, it parsimoniously captures some of the main features of both types of monetary policy surprises.

B.   Predictability with Macroeconomic and Financial Data

The literature cited earlier has documented several variables that predict upcoming monetary policy surprises. For our analysis here, we focus on macroeconomic and financial variables that were previously found by Cieslak (2018), Bauer and Chernov (2023), and Bauer and Swanson

(2021) to be good predictors, but we also explored a number of other variables. In all cases, we make sure that the relevant data were available to financial markets prior to the FOMC announcement itself. Our goal was to choose a parsimonious and robust set of predictors that also have an intuitive relationship to the Fed's monetary policy rule, consistent with our simple model from Section II. We ultimately settled on the following six predictors:

• Nonfarm payrolls surprise: the surprise component of the most recent nonfarm payrolls release prior to the FOMC announcement, measured as the difference between the released value of the statistic minus the median expectation for that release from the Money Market Services survey.[15]

• Employment growth: the log change in nonfarm payroll employment from 1 year earlier to the most recent release before the FOMC announcement, as used in Cieslak (2018).

• S&P 500: the log change in the S&P 500 stock market index from 3 months (65 trading days) before the FOMC announcement to the day before the FOMC announcement.

• Yield curve slope: the change in the slope of the yield curve from 3 months before the FOMC announcement to the day before the FOMC announcement, measured as the second principal component of 1-to-10-year zero-coupon Treasury yields from Gürkaynak, Sack, and Wright (2007).

• Commodity prices: the log change in the Bloomberg Commodity Spot Price index from 3 months before the FOMC announcement to the day before the FOMC announcement.

• Treasury skewness: the implied skewness of the 10-year Treasury yield, measured using options on 10-year Treasury note futures with expirations in 1–3 months, averaged over the preceding month, from Bauer and Chernov (2023).

With these predictors, we estimate regressions of the form

$$\text{mps}_t = \alpha + \beta' X_{t-} + u_t, \tag{14}$$

where t indexes FOMC announcements in our sample, mps_t denotes a measure of the monetary policy surprise, X_{t-} contains the six predictors described above (which are known prior to the announcement t, indicated by the time subscript $t-$), and u_t is a regression residual.

The results from four different versions of regression (eq. [14]) are reported in table 1. The first column considers our baseline measure of the monetary policy surprise, described above, over our full sample of 322 FOMC announcements from 1988 to 2019. The R^2 is about 16%, most predictors are statistically significant, and the signs of the estimated coefficients are intuitive and, consistent with the model in Section II, indicate procyclical correlations: strong nonfarm payroll employment, a strong stock market, and high commodity prices predict a hawkish monetary policy surprise. Similarly, when the yield curve becomes more upward-sloping (i.e., when short-term interest rates fall relative to long-term rates, as they do during monetary easing cycles), or when implied skewness on the 10-year Treasury yield is negative (suggesting markets are most concerned about a decrease in interest rates), the Fed is likely to follow with an easing surprise.

Table 1
Predictive Regressions Using Macroeconomic and Financial Data

	(1)	(2)	(3)	(4)
Nonfarm payrolls	.094	.113	.082	.155
	(2.425)	(1.977)	(1.788)	(3.696)
Empl. growth (12 m)	.005	.004	.005	.003
	(2.144)	(1.402)	(1.217)	(1.601)
Δ log S&P 500 (3 m)	.084	.112	.154	.020
	(1.446)	(1.578)	(1.943)	(.350)
Δ Slope (3 m)	−.010	−.010	−.011	−.016
	(−1.393)	(−1.154)	(−1.035)	(−2.024)
Δ log Comm. price (3 m)	.119	.093	.224	.103
	(2.380)	(1.461)	(3.489)	(1.944)
Treasury skewness	.032	.035	.050	.023
	(3.017)	(2.917)	(2.127)	(2.159)
R^2	.162	.173	.192	.163
Sample	1988:1–2019:12	1994:1–2019:12	1988:1–2007:6	1990:1–2019:6
N	322	218	216	259
Policy surprise	mps	mps	mps	FF4

Note: Coefficient estimates β from predictive regressions $mps_t = \alpha + \beta' X_{t-} + u_t$, where t indexes Federal Open Market Committee (FOMC) announcements. Columns 1–3 use our baseline monetary policy surprise measure mps described in the text, and column 4 uses the change in FF4 (also used in Gertler and Karadi 2015). Predictors X are observed prior to the FOMC announcement: the surprise component of the most recent nonfarm payrolls release, employment growth over the last year, the log change in the Standard & Poor's 500 index (S&P 500) from 3 months before to the day before the FOMC announcement, the change in the yield curve slope over the same period, the log change in a commodity price index over the same period, and the option-implied skewness of the 10-year Treasury yield from Bauer and Chernov (2023). Heteroskedasticity-consistent t-statistics are in parentheses. See text for details.

The other three columns of table 1 report results for alternative estimation samples and monetary policy surprises. The second column repeats regression (eq. [14]) with the same data but begins the sample in 1994, when the FOMC started explicitly announcing its monetary policy decisions. The results over this sample are very similar to the first column, with an R^2 that is even a bit higher. The third column reports results for a sample period that stops in June 2007, before the financial crisis and zero lower bound period, again with similar estimates and a higher R^2. The last column shows results for a different measure of the monetary policy surprise: specifically, the change in the 3-month-ahead federal funds futures contract, FF4, as used by Gertler and Karadi (2015).[16] We estimate this regression over the largest sample for which we have FF4 data, 1990:1–2019:6, obtained from an extension of the Gürkaynak et al. (2005) data set used in Bauer and Swanson (2023). Again, the results in this column are very similar to the first three columns.

The results in table 1 confirm the substantial predictability of high-frequency monetary policy surprises found by previous authors, for a variety of different monetary policy surprise measures and samples. Notably, these results show ex post predictability based on full-sample estimates, and we do not claim that investors could have taken advantage of it in real time. Indeed, our model implies that monetary policy surprises are not predictable ex ante, similar to the implications of learning models for the predictability of stock returns (e.g., Timmermann 1993). In additional, unreported analysis, we have investigated the out-of-sample predictability of monetary policy surprises using expanding estimation windows, mimicking the prediction problem faced by investors at each point in time.[17] Out-of-sample predictability was generally much lower than in-sample predictability, if it was at all present, and the forecast gains from including the six predictors in table 1 were never statistically significant. This evidence is consistent with the absence of ex ante predictability.

C. Predictability with Macroeconomic Forecast Data

In an influential recent paper, Miranda-Agrippino and Ricco (2021) showed that the Fed's internal "Greenbook" forecasts contain substantial information that is correlated with the high-frequency monetary policy surprise around the subsequent FOMC announcement. The interpretation given by Miranda-Agrippino and Ricco is based on a Fed information effect, discussed above, whereby the monetary policy surprise reveals information to the private sector about the Fed's internal macroeconomic forecast. However, our predictability evidence in table 1, based on publicly available information, raises the question whether one might obtain similar results if in the Miranda-Agrippino and Ricco regressions the internal Greenbook forecasts were replaced with publicly observable forecasts from the Blue Chip survey of professional forecasters. This would then suggest a very different interpretation of the Miranda-Agrippino and Ricco monetary policy surprise predictability findings.

To investigate this question, we repeat the monetary policy surprise predictability regressions in Miranda-Agrippino and Ricco, who followed Romer and Romer (2004) closely. We use exactly the same predictors as Miranda-Agrippino and Ricco: forecasts for real GDP growth and GDP deflator inflation for the previous quarter to 3 quarters ahead; the unemployment rate forecast for the current quarter; and forecast revisions for all three macro series for the previous quarter to 2 quarters ahead. As an alternative to the Fed's Greenbook forecasts, we also consider the publicly available Blue Chip consensus forecasts and forecast revisions for the exact same macro variables and forecast horizons.[18]

The results are reported in table 2. The top panel reports results analogous to those in Miranda-Agrippino and Ricco's table 1, using the Fed's internal Greenbook forecasts, and the bottom panel repeats the analysis using the publicly available Blue Chip forecasts instead. Each column corresponds to a different sample period, along the lines of table 1, albeit ending in 2015 rather than 2019 because the Fed only releases its Greenbook forecast data with a 5-year lag. For simplicity and brevity, for each regression we report only the R^2, the adjusted R^2, and the p value for the robust Wald test that all 23 regression coefficients (aside from the intercept) are equal to zero.

The results in the top panel of table 2 confirm those of Miranda-Agrippino and Ricco (2021): there is strong evidence that the Fed's internal Greenbook forecasts are correlated with the subsequent monetary policy surprises. However, the results in the bottom panel of table 2 show that this predictability is essentially identical when we use the publicly available Blue Chip forecasts instead. Thus, the Greenbook and Blue Chip forecasts seem to contain very similar information for upcoming FOMC announcement surprises. This observation is also consistent with Bauer and Swanson (2023), who showed that Greenbook and Blue Chip forecasts are about equally accurate predictors of future macroeconomic data.

Table 2
Predictive Regressions Using Macroeconomic Forecasts

	(1)	(2)	(3)	(4)
Greenbook forecasts:				
R^2	.158	.225	.183	.153
Adjusted R^2	.085	.114	.085	.059
p value	.0003	.0002	.0010	.0225
Blue Chip forecasts:				
R^2	.144	.217	.179	.168
Adjusted R^2	.070	.105	.080	.076
p value	.0058	.0000	.0004	.0040
Sample	1988:1–2015:12	1994:1–2015:12	1988:1–2007:6	1990:1–2015:12
N	289	185	216	231
Policy surprise	mps	mps	mps	FF4

Note: Predictive regressions for monetary policy surprises using macroeconomic forecasts
and their revisions. The regressors are forecasts and forecast revisions for the same variables and horizons as in Miranda-Agrippino and Ricco (2021) (see text), using the Fed's
own Greenbook forecasts in the top panel, and the consensus forecast in the Blue Chip Economic Indicators survey in the bottom panel. We use the most recent forecasts before each
Federal Open Market Committee announcement. Columns 1–3 use our baseline monetary
policy surprise measure mps described in the text, and column 4 uses the change in FF4
(also used in Gertler and Karadi 2015). We report p values for robust Wald tests (using
White covariance estimates) of joint significance of all predictors.

The implication of these findings is that the predictive power of
Greenbook forecasts for policy surprises that was documented by
Miranda-Agrippino and Ricco does not appear to be due to a Fed information effect. Instead, it seems to be a reflection of the empirical pattern
we have documented above and in Bauer and Swanson (2023): monetary
policy surprises are systematically correlated with macroeconomic and
financial data that are publicly available prior to the monetary policy
announcement.

D.   Interpretation of the Predictability Evidence

How should we think about the predictability evidence documented
above? First, note that these high-frequency interest rate changes should
be unpredictable if (a) bond risk premia are zero or constant, and (b) investor beliefs satisfy the FIRE hypothesis.[19] We discuss deviations from
each of these two assumptions in turn.

The first possible explanation for the predictability results in table 1 is
that risk premia on the underlying interest rate securities are substantial
and time varying. Indeed, Miranda-Agrippino (2017) makes exactly this

argument. Through the lens of our model in Section II, this implies that mps_t in equation (4) should include an additional risk premium term that is time varying and correlated with x_t. One problem with this explanation is that risk premia for these short-maturity interest rate futures seem to be relatively small (Piazzesi and Swanson 2008; Schmeling et al. 2022). Cieslak (2018) argues that these risk premia would have to be implausibly large to explain the observed correlation in the data and that a risk premium interpretation is inconsistent with a variety of other financial market evidence.[20] Thus, we view this explanation as relatively implausible, although we cannot rule it out entirely.

Instead of arguing that risk premia on short-term interest rates are large, our preferred explanation is based on moderate deviations from the strong assumption of FIRE. Much empirical work in macroeconomics has documented that expectations—of households, firms, or investors—do not satisfy the FIRE assumption.[21] Directly relevant for our setting here, Cieslak (2018) shows that the forecast errors for the federal funds rate in the Blue Chip survey of professional forecasters are strongly predictable. The online appendix of Bauer and Swanson (2023) updates and extends that evidence, showing that close to one-fourth of the variation in federal funds rate survey forecast errors is predictable with information observed before the survey responses were collected.[22] Under the FIRE assumption, forecast errors should be unpredictable using information that is publicly observable at the time the forecasts are made. Thus, this body of evidence strongly supports the view that public expectations of the Fed's policy rate do not satisfy the FIRE assumption.[23]

A simple and plausible deviation from FIRE that can explain the predictability results in table 1 is that the private sector has incomplete information about the Fed's monetary policy reaction function, as in our model of Section II. Specifically, if financial markets underestimated the Fed's responsiveness to the economy, then that could explain the procyclical correlation of macroeconomic and financial variables with monetary policy surprises documented in table 1. For further arguments in support of this explanation, see Cieslak (2018), Bauer and Swanson (2023), and Schmeling et al. (2022).

An alternative explanation of the ex post predictability of monetary policy surprises relies on information effects. As the learning model in Miranda-Agrippino and Ricco (2021) shows, if the Fed's announcements reveal information that the private sector uses to update its beliefs about the state of the economy, then high-frequency monetary policy surprises can be correlated with past macroeconomic data. However, the evidence above and in Bauer and Swanson (2023) suggests that the Fed does not seem to possess an information advantage concerning the state of the economy and the future economic outlook. Thus, it seems unlikely that the Fed's monetary policy announcements reveal significant new information about the economy to the private sector.

Overall, our view is that the evidence best supports the story of imperfect information about the Fed's monetary policy rule. However, the exact reason for the predictability of the monetary policy surprises is not particularly important for the rest of our paper. What matters is that those high-frequency monetary policy surprises are correlated with macroeconomic and financial variables predating the policy announcements, which has important implications for estimating the transmission of monetary policy to financial markets and the macroeconomy using these surprises. This is what we turn to next.

IV.   Monetary Policy Effects on Asset Prices

In this section, we estimate the effects of monetary policy announcements on asset prices. Relative to previous studies, we make two contributions: first, we use a novel measure of monetary policy surprises that is orthogonal to macroeconomic and financial data observed before the announcement and compare the estimates to those obtained for a conventional measure of the monetary policy surprise. Second, we consider not only policy announcements made by the FOMC but also those communicated in post-FOMC press conferences, speeches, and testimony by the Federal Reserve chair.

A.   The Event-Study Approach

Monetary policy influences inflation and real activity through its effects on financial conditions. Changes in the current target and future expectations for the federal funds rate affect interest rates all along the yield curve, stock prices, corporate bond yields, exchange rates, and other asset prices. A large empirical literature in monetary economics estimates the transmission of monetary policy to financial markets. Starting with the landmark studies by Cook and Hahn (1989) and Kuttner (2001), event studies have been the method of choice for such empirical analysis, due to their promise to sharply identify the causal effects of monetary policy actions on interest rates and other asset prices.[24]

These event-study regressions are usually of the form

$$y_t = \alpha + \beta \text{mps}_t + u_t, \tag{15}$$

where t indexes monetary policy announcements, y_t is an asset return or interest/exchange rate change, mps_t is a measure of the policy surprise, and both y_t and mps_t are measured over tight windows around the announcement. The idea is that the monetary policy surprise mps_t captures a monetary policy shock and we can estimate the effects of this shock on financial markets using regression (eq. [15]). But accurate estimation of such causal effects on asset prices requires four crucial assumptions.

The first assumption is that there is no reverse causation; that is, that changes in asset prices do not affect the monetary policy action (Cook and Hahn 1989). With intradaily data and the usual 30-minute announcement windows, this assumption is very plausible: the policy decision is made, and the FOMC statement formulated, up to several hours in advance of the actual announcement via the release of the statement. It is therefore hard to argue that the FOMC decision could react in some way to asset price changes in a sufficiently narrow window of time around the announcement.[25]

The second assumption is that there are no omitted variables that are correlated with mps_t and independently affect y_t. News released during the event window on day t will generally affect y_t but is unlikely to be correlated with the (predetermined) policy action mps_t for the same reason as above.[26] However, information prior to the FOMC announcement may predict both mps_t and y_t, which would call this assumption into question. Previous event studies have generally not considered this possibility, based on the premise that high-frequency asset price changes are unpredictable. By contrast, our simple model in Section II predicted that mps_t may well be correlated with macroeconomic and financial variables observed before t, and our evidence in Section III confirmed this. Importantly, our model also predicted that the effects on y_t would be completely captured by the monetary policy surprise, and that once we condition on mps_t there is no separate role for monetary policy shocks (ε_t in the model) or macroeconomic and financial data (x_t). Thus, according to our model, ordinary least squares (OLS) estimates of β in equation (15) would not suffer from omitted variable bias.

Third, the surprise mps_t must be truly unanticipated.[27] If the regressor contains a component that is anticipated by financial market participants, and if asset prices do not respond to this anticipated component, then this will tend to make the estimated coefficient small and insignificant due to the presence of classical measurement error. Cook and Hahn (1989) regressed yield changes on the target rate change around FOMC decisions, but the target changes are partly anticipated by financial markets. The important contribution of Kuttner (2001) was to separate the unexpected from the expected component of the target rate change using federal funds futures, which allowed him to uncover strong and highly significant effects on bond yields. Many researchers have followed this approach since. The predictability of mps_t, documented in Section III, challenges the assumption that we have completely isolated the unexpected component of the policy surprise, and it raises the possibility of measurement error. However, estimates of the asset price response will only be affected if financial markets react differently to the predicted component of the policy surprise than to the orthogonal component. Again, our model in Section II predicts that all components of the policy surprise should lead to the same asset price reaction, so that there are no measurement error in the classical sense and no bias of the OLS estimate of β in equation (15).

The fourth and last assumption is that the surprise should not contain any information effects (Romer and Romer 2000; Campbell et al. 2012; Nakamura and Steinsson 2018). Such effects would be present if the central bank's monetary policy decision reveals private information about the economic outlook that directly affects macroeconomic expectations, in addition to the actual monetary policy shock. For some assets, such as stocks, information effects would typically have an effect opposite to that of a monetary policy shock. Thus, their presence could in principle lead to estimates of β that are smaller or even of the opposite sign than if mps_t only captured a monetary policy shock.[28] However, Bauer and Swanson (2023) found that the responses of macroeconomic surveys, stock prices, and exchange rates show little evidence of information effects.

B.   Conventional and Orthogonalized Monetary Policy Surprises

We update and extend previous results in the literature with an event study that uses our new data set of 322 FOMC announcements from 1988 to 2019, described in Section III. We estimate the event-study regression in equation (15) using two alternative measures of the policy surprise mps_t. First, as a natural starting point, we use a conventional, unadjusted high-frequency monetary policy surprise measure described in Section III: the first principal component of high-frequency changes in the

Eurodollar futures rates ED1 to ED4. This measure is essentially equal to a weighted average of the target and path factors of Gürkaynak et al. (2005) and therefore captures news about both the current federal funds rate target and the future policy path.

Our second measure of the monetary policy surprise addresses the predictability issues raised in Section III. Specifically, we construct an orthogonal measure of the monetary policy surprise by taking the residuals from the regression (eq. [14]); that is,

$$\text{mps}_t^\perp = \text{mps}_t - \hat{\alpha} - \hat{\beta}'X_{t-}, \qquad (16)$$

where X_{t-} and $\hat{\beta}$ correspond to the predictors and estimated regression coefficients in the first column of table 1. The orthogonal surprise $\text{mps}_t^\perp$ is, by construction, uncorrelated with those macroeconomic and financial data observed before the FOMC announcement, and thus is more likely to satisfy the crucial event-study assumptions noted above. In the remainder of this section we compare the effects of mps_t and $\text{mps}_t^\perp$ on asset prices, and in Section V we compare the effects of the two different monetary policy surprise measures on macroeconomic variables in an SVAR or LP framework.

C.   Asset Prices and FOMC Announcements

We estimate the effects of monetary policy surprises on Treasury yields and stock prices using high-frequency event-study regressions of the form (eq. [15]). The Treasury yield responses are measured using 30-minute changes in Treasury futures prices around each FOMC announcement, and the stock market response is measured using S&P 500 futures price changes over the same 30-minute windows.[29]

The results for the unadjusted monetary policy surprises mps are reported in the first column of table 3. All of the Treasury yields and stock prices respond very strongly to monetary policy surprises, with t-statistics of six or more. The Treasury yield responses decline with maturity, but even for the 30-year yield there is still a 25-basis-point (bp) increase per 100 bp monetary policy surprise, a t-statistic greater than 6 and an R^2 greater than 20%.[30] The same surprise leads to a 5.4% drop in the S&P 500, with a t-statistic close to 8. These large and highly statistically significant estimates are similar to those documented by previous authors, such as Kuttner (2001), Bernanke and Kuttner (2005), Gürkaynak et al. (2005), Hanson and Stein (2015), and Swanson (2021), among others.

Table 3
Asset Price Responses to Monetary Policy Surprises

	FOMC		Fed Chair Speeches	
	mps_t	$\text{mps}_t^{\perp}$	mps_t	$\text{mps}_t^{\perp}$
2-year yield:	.73	.74	.73	.72
t-statistic	(18.6)	(16.7)	(23.4)	(22.0)
R^2	.784	.689	.856	.827
5-year yield:	.63	.64	.66	.66
t-statistic	(14.4)	(13.8)	(16.5)	(15.8)
R^2	.626	.550	.737	.714
10-year yield:	.41	.41	.49	.49
t-statistic	(9.5)	(9.9)	(13.9)	(13.2)
R^2	.435	.363	.651	.627
30-year yield:	.25	.25	.39	.38
t-statistic	(6.3)	(6.7)	(10.5)	(10.1)
R^2	.206	.173	.479	.455
S&P 500:	−5.39	−5.50	−1.59	−1.56
t-statistic	(−7.7)	(−6.6)	(−2.5)	(−2.5)
R^2	.304	.266	.027	.025
Observations	322	322	295	295

Note: Estimated coefficients β and regression R^2 from high-frequency event-study regressions $y_t = \alpha + \beta \text{mps}_t + u_t$, where t indexes Federal Open Market Committee (FOMC) announcements or Fed chair speeches, y_t denotes the change in the 2-, 5-, 10-, or 30-year Treasury yield or log S&P (Standard & Poor's) 500 price index in a narrow window of time around each announcement, and the regressor mps_t is either the unadjusted high-frequency monetary policy surprise measure mps_t or $\text{mps}_t^{\perp}$, the residual from regressing mps_t on the predictors in table 1. Heteroskedasticity-consistent t-statistics are in parentheses. Sample: 1988:1–2019:12. See text for details.

Analogous results for our orthogonalized monetary policy surprise measure, $\text{mps}_t^{\perp}$, are reported in the second column of table 3, and they are similar to the first column. The point estimates are almost identical, the t-statistics are very similar, and the regression R^2 are similar, albeit a little lower in the second column. Additional, unreported estimates of an alternative regression specification that includes mps_t together with the macroeconomic and financial variables from table 1 yielded similar coefficient estimates on mps_t as in the first column of table 3, and coefficients on the additional variables that were statistically insignificant.

These estimates suggest that the predictability of monetary policy surprises does not cause any noticeable problems for standard high-frequency event-study regressions estimating the effects of monetary policy surprises on financial markets. This predictability appears to cause neither omitted variable bias nor classical measurement error in these regressions, consistent with the implications of our model in Section II. The economic and financial news variables are correlated with mps_t, but once we account for the effects of mps_t, there are no independent effects of these other variables on asset prices. In addition, the component of mps_t correlated with news variables predating t apparently leads to a similar asset price response as the orthogonal component of mps_t.

The key takeaway is that conventional monetary policy surprises can be used to estimate the effects of monetary policy on financial markets, even though these policy surprises are partly predictable. This empirical conclusion is consistent with a simple model in which the predictability of monetary policy surprises arises as a consequence of the private sector's imperfect information about the Fed's monetary policy rule.

D.   Monetary Policy Surprises around Fed Chair Speeches

News about monetary policy is released not only through FOMC announcements but also through other communication by FOMC members and the Feb. Speeches by the Fed chair are particularly important, given the influence of the chair on the committee's decisions. Leveraging the work of Swanson and Jayawickrema (2021), we construct measures of the monetary policy surprise around post-FOMC press conferences, speeches, and congressional testimony by the Federal Reserve chair and investigate their effects on asset prices. (For brevity, we refer to these types of communication by the Fed chair as "speeches.") Over our sample period, 1988–2019, there are 880 such speeches by the Fed chair (compared with 322 FOMC announcements), but many of those speeches are on topics unrelated to monetary policy.[31] To identify those speeches that did contain significant news about monetary policy, we did the following: first, we included all 40 post-FOMC press conferences and all 126 semiannual monetary policy report testimonies by the Fed chair to Congress, because these press conferences and testimonies always discuss US monetary policy at length.[32] Second, we included all 22 speeches by the Fed chair at the Fed's annual Jackson Hole symposium for central bank leaders, because these speeches also typically discuss US monetary policy in detail and are closely followed by the markets. Third, we identified all of the remaining speeches by the Fed chair that led to a substantial (3 bp or more) reaction in the 2-quarter-ahead Eurodollar futures contract (ED3). We checked whether these additional speeches contained news about monetary policy, or whether the market was moved by news unrelated to the speech, by reading the market commentary in *The Wall*

Street Journal or *New York Times* that afternoon or the following morning.[33] This resulted in an additional 107 speeches by the Fed chair that contained significant news about monetary policy.

All together, the above criteria leave us with 295 Fed chair speeches that contained significant news about monetary policy. For each of these 295 speeches, we have the exact date and time of the speech and high-frequency asset price changes around that speech from Swanson and Jayawickrema (2021).[34]

The last two columns of table 3 report the estimated effects of Fed chair speeches on financial markets. The 2- and 5-year Treasury yields respond almost identically to Fed chair speeches as they do to FOMC announcements, and 10- and 30-year Treasury yields respond even more strongly. The R^2 for Fed chair speech effects are also even higher than those for FOMC announcements. Together, these observations confirm the general point in Swanson and Jayawickrema (2021) that speeches by the Fed chair are even more important for the Treasury market than FOMC announcements themselves.

By contrast, the response of the stock market is substantially weaker, with an R^2 around 3%. The modest stock market response to Fed chair speeches is somewhat puzzling in light of the fact that monetary policy typically has pronounced effects on the stock market (Bernanke and Kuttner 2005; Gürkaynak et al. 2005). One possible explanation is based on information effects: speeches by the Fed chair could potentially have larger information effects than FOMC announcements, given the extensive conversations the chair is having with the public or Congress about the Fed's outlook for monetary policy and the US economy. For example, many of the chair's speeches are semiannual monetary policy reports to Congress, which are 3 hours long and include extensive question-and-answer sessions about many aspects of the US economy as well as monetary policy. As argued in Nakamura and Steinsson (2018), Cieslak and Schrimpf (2019), and Jarocinski and Karadi (2020), information effects could mute the negative stock market response to changes in the expected policy path, or even reverse its sign. Another explanation is that other news besides the chair's speech could have moved interest rates and stock prices during the event window. Our announcement windows for chair speeches are necessarily longer than for FOMC announcements (2 hours for regular speeches and press conferences and 3.5 hours for testimony, vs. 30 minutes for FOMC announcements) and sometimes occur in the mornings, when economic data are released.[35] Any news about employment or output would tend to move interest rates and stock prices in the same direction, in contrast to news about monetary policy (Andersen et al. 2007), explaining why the stock market response is less negative.[36] A third possible explanation is that the stock market is more sensitive to actual federal funds rate changes than to forward guidance, as found by Gürkaynak et al. (2005). The chair's speeches do not change the current federal funds rate and thus can be thought of as pure forward guidance. Of course, all of these mechanisms could be at work, and without further evidence we cannot distinguish between them.

For monetary policy surprises around Fed chair speeches, we also estimate predictive regressions using macroeconomic and financial data that predate the speeches. The predictability is generally quite a bit lower than for FOMC announcements, with R^2 in the single digits. As shown in the last column of table 3, using the orthogonalized monetary policy surprise $mps_t^\perp$ in asset price regressions has little effect on the high-frequency estimates relative to using the unadjusted mps_t itself.

V. Monetary Policy Effects on the Macroeconomy

Many recent studies use high-frequency changes in interest rates around FOMC announcements as an instrument to help estimate the effects of monetary policy on macroeconomic variables such as output and inflation; for a survey, see Ramey (2016). Our results in Section III, however, imply that these high-frequency monetary policy surprises are correlated with those economic variables, violating the standard exogeneity condition that is required for the instrument to be valid. Our orthogonalization procedure discussed above corrects the monetary policy surprises for this correlation and should alleviate the problem.

We now investigate to what extent the high-frequency identifications of the effects of monetary policy shocks in SVARs and LPs are affected by this correlation and our proposed correction. We begin, in Subsection V.A, by laying out the basic proxy-SVAR method and revisiting the analysis in Gertler and Karadi (2015), which has become a canonical benchmark specification for monetary policy SVARs. In Subsection V.B, we estimate LPs similar to those in Ramey (2016). In Subsection V.C, we consider the alternative estimation method of Plagborg-Møller and Wolf (2021) that uses a recursive SVAR with the monetary policy instrument ordered first. In Subsection V.D, we revisit some of the analysis in Miranda-Agrippino and Ricco (2021) and show that similar SVAR results are obtained when either Blue Chip consensus forecasts or Greenbook forecasts are used to orthogonalize the policy surprises. Finally, in Subsection V.E, we summarize lessons learned and present new "best practice" estimates of the macroeconomic effects of monetary policy shocks.

A. Revisiting Gertler and Karadi (2015)

Baseline VAR Specification

As in Gertler and Karadi (2015), we begin by estimating a reduced-form monthly VAR with four macroeconomic variables as our baseline specification: the log of industrial production (IP), the log of the consumer price index (CPI), the Gilchrist and Zakrajšek (2012) excess bond premium (EBP), and the 2-year Treasury yield. IP and the CPI are taken from the FRED database at the Federal Reserve Bank of St. Louis. We include the GZ EBP (available from the Federal Reserve Board's website) for comparability to Gertler and Karadi and because Caldara and Herbst (2019) found it to be important for the estimation of monetary policy VARs. The 2-year Treasury yield is from the Gürkaynak, Sack, and Wright (2007) database on the Federal Reserve Board's website. As discussed in Swanson and Williams (2014) and Gertler and Karadi (2015), the 2-year Treasury yield was essentially unconstrained during the 2009–15 zero lower bound period in the United States, making it a better measure of the stance of monetary policy than a shorter-term interest rate such as the federal funds rate. Note that Gertler and Karadi used the 1-year Treasury yield rather than the 2-year yield but only because they were unable to get a sufficiently large F-statistic for their first-stage instrumental variables regression; as shown later, we do not have this problem, which makes use of the 2-year Treasury yield feasible for our analysis.[37] We stack these four variables into a vector Y_t and estimate the reduced-form VAR

$$Y_t = \alpha + B(L)Y_{t-1} + u_t, \tag{17}$$

where $B(L)$ denotes a matrix polynomial in the lag operator, u_t is a 4×1 vector of regression residuals that are serially uncorrelated, and $\text{Var}(u_t) = \Omega$, which is not necessarily a diagonal matrix. We follow Gertler and Karadi (2015), Ramey (2016), and many others and use a specification with 12 monthly lags.

We estimate regression (eq. [17]) from January 1973 to February 2020 via OLS. The GZ EBP data begin in 1973, preventing us from beginning the sample earlier. We choose to end our sample in February 2020 to avoid the dramatic swings in IP that begin with onset of the COVID-19 pandemic in the United States. We also consider and discuss alternative sample periods, because this was a main point discussed by Ramey (2016).

We follow standard practice and assume that the economy is driven by a set of serially uncorrelated structural shocks, ε_t, with $\text{Var}(\varepsilon_t) = I$ (see, e.g., Ramey 2016). Because the dynamics of the economy are determined by $B(L)$, the effects of different structural shocks ε_t on Y_t are completely determined by differences in their impact effects on Y_t in period t, that is, by their effects on u_t. We assume that this relationship is linear,

$$u_t = S\varepsilon_t, \tag{18}$$

where S is a matrix of appropriate dimension. If the number of shocks in ε_t equals the number of variables in the VAR, a common assumption in the SVAR literature, then equation (18) implies invertibility.[38] However, we do not need to impose that restriction for our purpose of estimating impulse response functions to a monetary policy shock, so ε_t can in principle include any number of additional structural shocks.[39] We will return to the issue of invertibility in Subsection V.C.

We assume that one of the structural shocks is a "monetary policy shock," and we order that shock first in ε_t and denote it by ε_t^{mp}. The idea of a structural monetary policy shock is that sometimes the Fed is faced with a decision that is a "close call" between two options and must pick one option or the other; the difference in effects between these two choices is the outcome of a structural monetary policy shock (see Ramey 2016 for additional discussion). Given our choice of high-frequency instrument—the first principal component of the first 4 Eurodollar futures contracts, ED1–ED4—this shock should be thought of as a change in the outlook for the path of short-term interest rates over the next 4 quarters. Intuitively, this includes changes in the current federal funds rate as well as some degree of "forward guidance" about the near-term path of future values of the federal fund rate.

The first column of S describes the impact effect of the structural monetary policy shock ε_t^{mp} on u_t and Y_t. The variances of u_t and ε_t imply that

$$SS' = \Omega. \tag{19}$$

The identification problem is that there are infinitely many potential matrices S that satisfy equation (19), so that S cannot be uniquely determined by the data (even with infinitely many observations of Y_t). The econometrician must bring additional information to bear on the problem—either theoretical or empirical—to estimate S and the dynamic effects of a structural shock on Y_t. Our identification problem is simplified somewhat by the fact that estimation of the effects of monetary policy shocks does not require identification of the entire matrix S but only of its first column, s_1, and only up to scale, because we follow common practice and estimate impulse responses to a policy shock that is normalized to have a 0.25 percentage point impact effect on the interest rate.

High-Frequency Identification

To identify the impact effect s_1 of a structural monetary policy shock ε_t^{mp}, we use the high-frequency identification approach of Gertler and Karadi (2015), described in detail by Stock and Watson (2012, 2018). Let z_t denote our set of high-frequency monetary policy surprises, converted to a monthly series by summing over all of the high-frequency surprises mps within each month. For z_t to be a valid instrument for ε_t^{mp}, it must satisfy an instrument *relevance* condition,

$$E[z_t \varepsilon_t^{mp}] \neq 0, \tag{20}$$

and an instrument *exogeneity* condition,

$$E[z_t \varepsilon_t^{-mp}] = 0, \tag{21}$$

where ε_t^{-mp} denotes any element of ε_t other than the first.[40] Stock and Watson (2012, 2018) refer to z_t as an *external instrument* because it comes from information outside of the VAR—in particular, from high-frequency financial market data.

The appeal of high-frequency monetary policy surprises is that they plausibly satisfy conditions (eqs. [20]–[21]). First, consider instrument relevance: the monetary policy shock ε_t^{mp} is the total amount of exogenous news about monetary policy in month t. FOMC announcements and Fed chair speeches are an important part of this news, so it is reasonable to expect that the correlation between z_t and ε_t^{mp} is positive and may be large.[41] Crucially, monetary policy surprises that include Fed chair speeches will provide a more relevant instrument than those based solely on FOMC announcements.

Second, consider instrument exogeneity: high-frequency monetary policy surprises capture interest rate changes in very narrow windows of time around policy announcements. It would therefore appear unlikely that other structural shocks in ε_t^{-mp} can significantly affect financial markets at the same time, so that these other shocks should be uncorrelated with z_t, implying equation (21).[42]

However, the predictability documented in Section III suggests a potential violation of the exogeneity condition (eq. [21]) and calls the validity of z_t as an instrument into question. In particular, equation (21) is violated if z_t is correlated with macroeconomic news that occurs within the month, and all of the financial market predictors in table 1 are very plausibly correlated with shocks to output, inflation, and the EBP.[43] Thus, the structural VARs estimated by previous authors using high-frequency identification likely have an endogeneity problem that biases their estimates. For example, as shown in table 1, news about higher output or inflation reflected in the stock market or commodity prices tends to predict a higher value of z_t; thus, the estimated effects of a monetary policy tightening are contaminated by the fact that tighter monetary policy is correlated with news about higher output and inflation, biasing the estimated effects of a monetary policy tightening on real activity and inflation in the positive direction (attenuating or even reversing the sign of the estimated effects).[44]

To eliminate this endogeneity problem, we project out the correlation of z_t with the macroeconomic and financial predictors from Section III, as suggested by Bauer and Swanson (2023). We construct an orthogonalized version of our monthly monetary policy instrument, $z_t^{\perp}$, by regressing z_t on the predictors in table 1 and taking the residuals.[45] This instrument is more likely to satisfy the exogeneity condition (eq. [21]), leading to estimates of the effects of monetary policy on the economy that are free from the bias. Moreover, $z_t^{\perp}$ should still satisfy the relevance condition (eq. [20]), because most of the variation in mps was not predictable by macroeconomic and financial variables and represents information about the future path of monetary policy.

Given our external instrument, z_t or $z_t^{\perp}$, we estimate the impact effects s_1 in the SVAR as described in Stock and Watson (2012, 2018) and Gertler and Karadi (2015). For concreteness, order the 2-year Treasury yield last in Y_t, and denote it by Y_t^{2y}. We then estimate the regression

$$Y_t = \alpha + B(L)Y_{t-1} + s_1 Y_t^{2y} + \tilde{u}_t \tag{22}$$

via two-stage least squares, using z_t or $z_t^{\perp}$ as the instrument for Y_t^{2y}, where s_1 is the first column of S described above, α and $B(L)$ are as in equation (17), and $\tilde{u}_t$ is a regression residual.[46] Because the reduced-form residuals in equation (17) satisfy $u_t = S\varepsilon_t$, it is straightforward to show that equations (20) and (21) imply this regression produces an unbiased and consistent estimate of s_1, with the last element normalized to unity. (In our empirical results shown later, we rescale s_1 so that the last element corresponds to an impact effect of 25 basis points, rather than 1 percentage point.)

Importantly, the sample for the two-stage least squares regression (eq. [22]) used to estimate s_1 does not have to be the same as for the reduced-form VAR (eq. [17]) used to estimate α and $B(L)$, as discussed by Stock and Watson (2012, 2018) and Ramey (2016). In our data set, the high-frequency monetary policy surprises underlying z_t and $z_t^\perp$ are available only from 1988:1 to 2019:12. By contrast, we are able to estimate the reduced-form VAR coefficients α and $B(L)$ over the longer sample from 1973:1 to 2020:2.

Results Based on FOMC Announcements

Figure 2 reports impulse response functions to a 25 bp monetary policy shock in our baseline structural VAR, described above, using the unadjusted high-frequency monetary policy surprise instrument, z_t. This specification corresponds very closely to that in Gertler and Karadi (2015), Ramey (2016), and others. Column a reports the results for our full sample, January 1973 to February 2020, and columns b–c report results for two different subsamples. The solid lines report the estimated impulse response functions, and the shaded gray regions report 90% standard-error bands around those point estimates, computed using 10,000 bootstrap replications.[47]

The results in column a of figure 2 are very similar to those in Gertler and Karadi (2015), which is not surprising given the very similar specification and data, although we have used the 2-year Treasury yield instead of the 1-year yield, a longer sample (1973:1–2020:2), and a slightly different measure of the high-frequency monetary policy surprise with several more years of data (1988:1–2019:12). The 2-year Treasury yield increases 25 bp on impact, by construction, and then declines gradually back toward steady state. The EBP increases about 5 bp on impact, remains at about that level for several months, and then declines back toward steady state. IP drops slightly on impact and then declines more significantly afterward, with a trough response of about -0.35% after about 1 year. The CPI drops slightly on impact, by about 0.05%, and then declines gradually a bit more over the next several years.

Column b of figure 2 repeats the analysis in column a, but for Gertler and Karadi's sample, July 1979 to June 2012. The standard-error bands

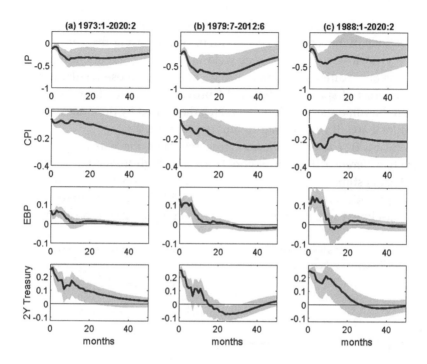

Fig. 2. Structural VAR with external instrument, different sample periods. Structural vector autoregression impulse response functions to a 25-basis-point monetary policy shock, identified using the unadjusted high-frequency mps measure around Federal Open Market Committee announcements for three different sample periods: (*a*) full sample, 1973:1–2020:2; (*b*) Gertler and Karadi's sample, 1979:7–2012:6; and (*c*) 1988:1–2020:2, because our high-frequency mps data begin in 1988. Shaded regions report bootstrapped 90% standard-error bands. EBP = excess bond premium, CPI = Consumer Price Index, IP = industrial production. See text for details. A color version of this figure is available online.

in column *b* are somewhat larger, due to the smaller sample size, but the impulse response functions are otherwise similar. Output, inflation, and the EBP respond by somewhat more on impact for this sample but have very similar shapes and are within the range of sampling variability.

Column *c* of figure 2 repeats the analysis once more, for the sample beginning in 1988, when our high-frequency mps data are first observed. Although Ramey (2016) suggests that samples beginning after the mid-1980s may not have enough variation in monetary policy to produce good estimates of its effects, we find no evidence of such a problem here: our results in column *c* are very similar to those in the first two columns, albeit with larger standard errors than in column *a*, due to the shorter sample.

The impulse response functions in figure 2 are also robust to standard variations in our baseline specification, such as using the 1-year Treasury yield instead of the 2-year yield or including the unemployment rate as an additional variable. We do not report those results here in the interest of space, but figure A1 provides them for four variations of our baseline specification that match those used by previous authors, and they are all very similar to those in figure 2.[48]

We now turn to one of the main research questions of this paper: How much difference does orthogonalizing the high-frequency surprises make for estimating the effects of monetary policy on the economy? Figure 3 provides an answer to this question, with the left column repeating the baseline results for our full sample from figure 2 column *a*, and the

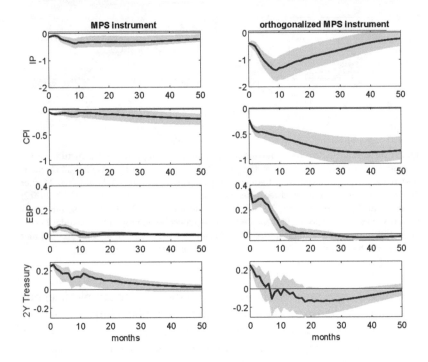

Fig. 3. Structural VAR with external instruments. Structural vector autoregression impulse response functions to a 25-basis-point monetary policy shock (MPS), identified in the left column using the unadjusted high-frequency mps measure around Federal Open Market Committee (FOMC) announcements, and in the right column using high-frequency change in mps around FOMC announcements orthogonalized with respect to economic news available prior to the announcement. Sample: 1973:1–2020:2. Shaded regions report bootstrapped 90% standard-error bands. EBP = excess bond premium, CPI = Consumer Price Index, IP = industrial production. See text for details. A color version of this figure is available online.

right column reporting results for the same specification and sample but using the orthogonalized monetary policy surprise instrument, $z_t^{\perp}$.

The first point to note in figure 3 is that the persistence of the 2-year Treasury yield response is much lower in the right-hand column, returning back to steady state in less than 1 year rather than 4 years. This is intuitive if we think of economic data as being persistent, so that the Fed's response to that data—which we have projected out in the right column—leads to an upwardly biased estimate of interest rate persistence in the left column.

The second key point to take away from figure 3 is that the responses of output, inflation, and the EBP in the right column are all larger than in the left column, by a factor of about four. For example, IP has a trough response of about -1.4% in the right column versus -0.35% in the left column. These stronger impulse responses are intuitive if we think of the right column as being free of the bias that is likely contaminating the estimates in the left column. For example, standard macroeconomic models such as Christiano, Eichenbaum, and Evans (2005) imply that positive news about output or inflation causes the Fed to raise interest rates and also causes output or inflation to increase; this is exactly opposite to the standard effects of monetary policy and leads to an upward bias in the top two panels of the left column.[49] In the right column, the monetary policy instrument is orthogonalized with respect to this news, eliminating the bias.[50]

Although our estimates in the right column of figure 3 are four times larger than in the left column, the magnitudes are quite reasonable. Coibion (2012) surveys estimates of the effects of monetary policy in the literature, with the estimates in Gertler and Karadi (2015) being similar to those from other SVARs, which Coibion regards as small.[51] In contrast, the estimates in Romer and Romer (2004) are six times larger than those in the SVARs. Coibion (2012) argues that the true effects of a monetary policy shock lie in between these two sets of estimates, which is consistent with what we estimate in the right column of figure 3.

It is also interesting to note that, in the right column of figure 3, the responses of output and the policy instrument have very different persistences, with a relatively transitory effect on the 2-year yield and a long-lasting effect on IP. This endogenous persistence of output can be explained with medium-scale dynamic stochastic general equilibrium (DSGE) models that feature, for example, consumption habits, staggered wage contracts, and variable capital utilization (e.g., Christiano et al. 2005).

Finally, a potential concern with high-frequency identification is that the instrument may be weak, with relatively little relevance. Stock and Watson (2012) use a rule of thumb according to which the instrument is weak if the first-stage F-statistic in the two-stage least squares regression is less than 10. In our SVAR results above, the first-stage F-statistic for z_t is 8.19 in the left column and only 1.83 for $z_t^{\perp}$ in the right column.[52] Thus, the orthogonalization procedure reduces the relevance of our instrument—which was already not very strong—to the point where weakness is a serious concern. Even for our unadjusted instrument z_t, the Stock and Watson rule of thumb suggests potential weakness. Indeed, it was precisely this problem that led Gertler and Karadi (2015) to modify their specification to use the month-average 1-year Treasury yield rather than the end-of-month 2-year Treasury yield we have used here. Instead of modifying our baseline specification, as Gertler and Karadi did, we propose increasing the power of our high-frequency instrument by bringing to bear additional data on high-frequency interest rate responses to speeches by the Fed chair, which Swanson and Jayawickrema (2021) showed have been an even more important source of information about monetary policy than FOMC announcements themselves.

Results Based on FOMC Announcements and Fed Chair Speeches

High-frequency monetary policy surprises around FOMC announcements are an imperfect measure of the true monetary policy shock each month, because a great deal of information about the course of monetary policy is communicated to the public outside of FOMC announcements, such as in speeches by the Fed chair and other FOMC members. To improve the relevance of our high-frequency monetary policy instrument and avoid a potential weak-instrument problem, we now include information from speeches, press conferences, and congressional testimony by the Federal Reserve chair, as discussed earlier (and recall that, for brevity, we refer to all of these communications as "Fed chair speeches").

In figure 4, we repeat the structural VAR estimation and identification from figure 3, but this time including Fed chair speeches as well as FOMC announcements in our high-frequency measure of monetary policy surprises. As before, we sum up all of the high-frequency monetary policy surprises in a given month to arrive at a monthly instrumental variable, z_t. The power of the instrument z_t is greatly increased by this addition, with the first-stage F-statistic in the two-stage least squares regression rising from 8.19 in the previous section to 30.44 here. For the

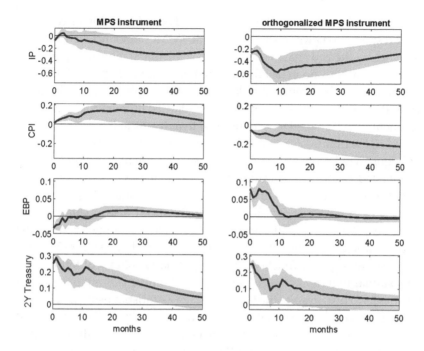

Fig. 4. Structural VAR with external instruments, including Fed chair speeches. Structural vector autoregression impulse response functions to a 25-basis-point monetary policy shock (MPS), identified in the left column using raw high-frequency mps measure around Federal Open Market Committee (FOMC) announcements and speeches by the Fed chair, and in the right column using high-frequency mps around FOMC announcements and Fed chair speeches orthogonalized with respect to economic news available prior to the announcement. Sample: 1973:1–2020:2. Shaded regions report bootstrapped 90% standard-error bands. EBP = excess bond premium, CPI = Consumer Price Index, IP = industrial production. See text for details. A color version of this figure is available online.

orthogonalized instrument $z_t^{\perp}$, the first-stage F-statistic increases from 1.83 to 12.37.

Comparing the left column of figure 4 to figure 3, the 2-year Treasury yield response is almost identical. The response of IP is also similar, albeit with a slight output puzzle for about 2 months shortly after the shock's impact. The CPI in the left column of figure 4 displays a true price puzzle, responding positively for more than 4 years after the shock, and the EBP response also displays a puzzle, dropping on impact and remaining at zero or below for about a year.

Thus, several of the impulse responses in the left-hand column of figure 3 exhibit puzzling behavior. One possible explanation for this is that speeches by the Fed chair convey more information about the economy and financial markets—either through a "Fed information effect" or a "Fed response to news" channel—than do FOMC announcements. Many speeches by the Fed chair, especially the semiannual monetary policy reports to Congress, do in fact discuss the US economy and how the Fed is responding to the economy at length, so this explanation is plausible. Thus, the endogeneity problem for the unadjusted high-frequency mps instrument may be even larger in figure 4 than it was in figure 3.

The right column of figure 4 eliminates this endogeneity by using the orthogonalized monetary policy surprise instrument $z_t^\perp$ rather than the unadjusted z_t. Orthogonalization has substantial effects on the estimated impulse responses. First, all of the output, price, and EBP puzzles are eliminated once we switch to the orthogonalized instrument. Second, the 2-year Treasury yield response is somewhat less persistent in the right column than in the left, consistent with our finding in figure 3. Third, the impulse response functions in the right-hand column of figure 4 are very similar to those in figure 3 in shape and timing, although they are a bit smaller. Thus, despite the low first-stage F-statistics using just FOMC announcements, the estimated effects of monetary policy are robust when we extend the instrument set to include speeches by the Fed chair. Overall, the differences between the columns are similar to those in figure 3 and are consistent with the orthogonalized monetary policy instrument being purged of endogenous Fed responses to economic data.

Summary

To summarize, there are three main points to take away from our reassessment of the high-frequency SVAR estimates in Gertler and Karadi (2015). First, we have consistently found that estimates using unadjusted monetary policy surprises as an external instrument are biased, leading to attenuated or "puzzling" dynamic responses. That is, estimates of the effects of monetary policy on output or inflation using unadjusted monetary policy surprises generally produce estimates that are either too small or even go in the opposite direction from what standard economic theory would predict. Using our adjusted, orthogonalized monetary policy surprise instrument consistently produced better results. This is not too surprising, given that our corrected monetary policy surprises should be largely free of the econometric endogeneity problems that we documented for the unadjusted surprises.

Second, using Fed chair speeches as well as FOMC announcements to measure the monetary policy surprise each month also helps to produce more reliable estimates. This is most evident comparing our LP esti-mates in figure 5 of Subsection V.B to figure A2, but we have also found this to be the case more generally as well. This finding is also not too sur-prising, because the larger set of monetary policy announcement events roughly doubles the explanatory power of the external instrument and leads to first-stage instrumental variables F-statistics that are much higher than those using FOMC announcements alone.

Third, the results are generally robust to variations in sample period and specification, as in figures 2 and A1, especially when using our orthogonalized monetary policy surprise measure. This robustness to using a later sample period is an important point when comparing our SVAR results to those using LPs, shown later.

B.   Revisiting Ramey's (2016) Local Projections Estimates

An alternative approach to structural VARs is to estimate the dynamic effects of a monetary policy shock via Jordà (2005) local projections (LPs). The idea is to directly regress future values of macroeconomic variables on the identified monetary policy shock, with controls for lags and other relevant macroeconomic variables. When the monetary policy shock is unobserved but we have an external instrument, such as our high-frequency monetary policy surprise measures z_t and $z_t^\perp$, we can perform the LP regressions on the 2-year Treasury yield using these in-struments. This procedure, known as LP-IV, is performed by Ramey (2016) and discussed in detail in Stock and Watson (2018). In this section, we revisit Ramey's LP estimates to assess the importance of monetary policy surprise predictability for those results.

We match our LP-IV specification to our VAR as closely as possible by using the same variables and the same number of lags (12 months). Al-though Ramey (2016) used only three monthly lags for her LP-IV spec-ification, we found that using so few lags led to substantial differences relative to using a larger number more consistent with a VAR (see also the discussion in Ramey 2022). Thus, our LP-IV regressions have the form

$$Y_{t+h} = \alpha^{(h)} + A^{(h)}(L)Y_{t-1} + \theta^{(h)}Y_t^{2y} + \eta_t^{(h)}, \tag{23}$$

where Y includes the same variables as in our VAR, $h \geq 0$ indexes the ho-rizon of the impulse response function, the regression (eq. [23]) is esti-mated separately for each horizon h, $\alpha^{(h)}$ is a constant, $A^{(h)}(L)$ is a matrix

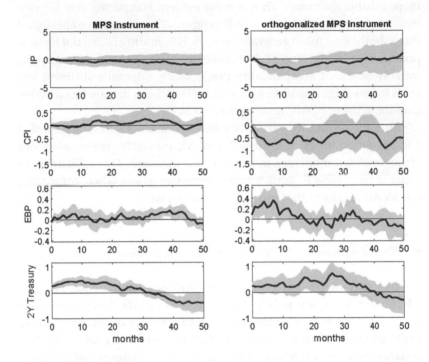

Fig. 5. Local projections. Local projections impulse response functions to a 25-basis-point monetary policy shock (MPS), identified in the left column using unadjusted high-frequency mps measure around Federal Open Market Committee (FOMC) announcements and speeches by the Fed chair, and in the right column using high-frequency mps measure around FOMC announcements and Fed chair speeches orthogonalized with respect to economic news available prior to the announcement. Sample period: 1988:1–2020:2. Shaded regions report 90% standard-error bands. EBP = excess bond premium, CPI = Consumer Price Index, IP = industrial production. See text for details. A color version of this figure is available online.

polynomial of degree 11 (allowing for 12 lags), $\theta^{(h)}$ is the coefficient of interest, Y^{2y} denotes the 2-year Treasury yield, and $\eta_t^{(h)}$ is the regression residual. Equation (23) is estimated via two-stage least squares using either the unadjusted z_t or orthogonalized $z_t^{\perp}$ as the instrument for Y_t^{2y}. Our sample period for the estimation runs from 1988:1 to 2020:2, because our high-frequency mps data begin in 1988. Standard errors are computed using Newey and West (1987) with h lags.

The results from this procedure are generally more poorly estimated than for our SVAR specifications above: they have large standard errors, suffer from month-to-month volatility, and also show large differences when speeches by the Fed chair are excluded versus included in the monetary policy surprise instrument. Figure 5 reports results for the latter case, when Fed chair speeches are included in the monetary policy surprise measure. (The corresponding results when Fed chair speeches are excluded from the instrument have even larger standard errors and are reported in fig. A2.)[53]

Although the impulse responses in figure 5 are imprecisely estimated and somewhat more erratic, they are otherwise qualitatively consistent with those for SVARs shown in figures 3–4. Comparing the left and right columns of figure 5, the estimates in the right column produce stronger responses of output, inflation, and the EBP to the monetary policy shock, and eliminate the slight output puzzle, price puzzle, and EBP puzzle that are present in the left column. Thus, as in figures 3–4, using the unadjusted high-frequency mps instrument seems to produce results that are biased, with attenuated or puzzling responses, and that bias is largely eliminated when we use the mps measure that has been orthogonalized with respect to macroeconomic and financial news.

We conclude from this exercise that the estimated impulse responses to a monetary policy shock using LP-IV are generally similar to those from a structural VAR, but substantially less precisely estimated. This conclusion contrasts somewhat with Ramey (2016), who found more substantial differences between LP-IV and SVAR impulse responses, but we found those differences to be primarily due to the shorter, 3-month lag length Ramey used for her LP-IV specification.[54] Our main point, however, is that conventional, unadjusted high-frequency surprises are a poor choice of instruments for monetary policy shocks in LPs, which agrees with Ramey's conclusions, and we have shown how one can construct instruments that are more relevant and more likely to be exogenous.

C. Revisiting Plagborg-Møller and Wolf (2021)

Plagborg-Møller and Wolf (2021) recommend an alternative procedure for estimating impulse response functions using an external instrument, which they call the "internal instrument" approach. Instead of estimating a standard proxy-SVAR or LP-IV regression, they recommend including the instrument in the VAR, ordering it first, and using a recursive (Cholesky) ordering to estimate its effects. Intuitively, this allows the other variables in the VAR to respond to the instrument on impact, and the dynamics are asymptotically the same as a conventional VAR or (in population, and for infinite lag length) LP-IV estimation.

Here we revisit the estimates of Plagborg-Møller and Wolf using our new instrument series, based on monetary policy surprises around both FOMC announcements and Fed chair speeches. Because our high-frequency surprise data run from 1988:1 to 2019:12 and are included in the VAR, the sample for the estimation is 1988:1–2019:12. As in our other SVARs and LP-IV regressions, we include 12 monthly lags in the VAR and normalize the monetary policy shock to have an impact effect of 25 bp on the 2-year Treasury yield.

The results are shown in figure 6. Overall, they are quite similar to our proxy-SVAR results in figure 4, but they are less precisely estimated due to the shorter sample and larger number of parameters (because the

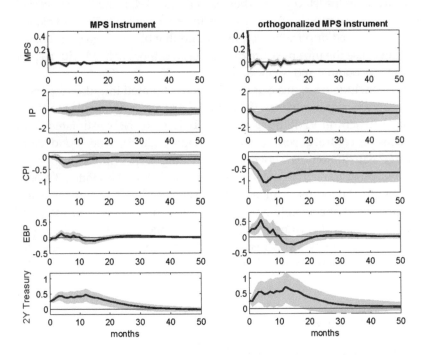

Fig. 6. Recursive structural VAR with internal instrument. Structural vector autoregression (SVAR) impulse response functions to a 25-basis-point monetary policy shock (MPS), identified in the left column using raw high-frequency mps measure around Federal Open Market Committee (FOMC) announcements and speeches by the Fed chair, and in the right column using high-frequency mps around FOMC announcements and Fed chair speeches orthogonalized with respect to economic news available prior to the announcement. Instrument is ordered first in a recursive SVAR, following the methodology of Plagborg-Møller and Wolf (2021). Sample: 1988:1–2019:12. Shaded regions report bootstrapped 90% standard-error bands. EBP = excess bond premium, CPI = Consumer Price Index, IP = industrial production. See text for details. A color version of this figure is available online.

coefficients on the lags of z_t must be estimated). Recall from our estimates across different subsamples in figure 2, starting the estimation in 1988 instead of 1973 does not substantially affect the point estimates, but it does noticeably reduce the precision. Comparing the left and right columns of figure 6, we see again that orthogonalizing the monetary policy surprises substantially increases the size of the estimated effects and removes any price puzzle types of responses in the left column.

Figure 6 is also interesting because including the instrument in the VAR automatically orthogonalizes it with respect to lags of all the variables in the VAR. Despite this, the unadjusted mps instrument in the left-hand column does a relatively poor job of estimating the effects of monetary policy on the economy, with estimates that are similar to the left column of figure 4. By contrast, our orthogonalization with respect to the predictors in table 1 seems to do a much better job of removing the econometric endogeneity. Apparently the endogeneity that is present in the mps variable is not well captured by the lags of the variables in the VAR.

As was the case with our previous SVARs in figures 3–4, the VAR structure here seems to improve the quality of our estimates, relative to unrestricted LPs. However, restricting the sample to begin in 1988, when our high-frequency data become available, reduces the precision of the estimated dynamics in figure 6. Based on these findings, an SVAR specification with identification using external instruments, as in Subsection V.A, seems preferable to a recursive SVAR with an internal instrument.

With respect to invertibility, discussed at length in Stock and Watson (2018) and Wolf (2020), we have found that the Granger-causality test suggested by Plagborg-Møller and Wolf (2022) does not reject the null of invertibility for any of the specifications and instruments that we consider.[55] Overall, lack of invertibility does not seem to be of much concern in this context, and there are good reasons to prefer the SVAR-IV approach for estimation of the dynamic effects of monetary policy with high-frequency identification.

D.   Revisiting Miranda-Agrippino and Ricco (2021)

We now turn to the SVAR analysis of Miranda-Agrippino and Ricco (2021), who orthogonalized monetary policy surprises with respect to the Fed's internal "Greenbook" forecasts and demonstrated that this leads to substantially different impulse responses to monetary policy shocks when using the resulting series for high-frequency identification.[56] They interpreted these results as supporting a strong role for a Fed information effect (Romer and Romer 2000; Campbell et al. 2012; Nakamura and Steinsson 2018), given the apparent importance of the Fed's own private forecasts. However, the results in Subsection III.C showed that the Blue Chip survey forecasts, which are publicly available on a monthly basis, have very similar predictive power for monetary policy surprises as the Fed's own Greenbook forecasts, which the public does not see until 5 years after the FOMC meeting. This raises the question of whether orthogonalizing monetary policy surprises with respect to public Blue Chip forecasts—in line with our general approach of orthogonalizing monetary policy surprises with respect to publicly available information—yields results similar to those of Miranda-Agrippino and Ricco. If so, this would raise further doubts about the Fed information effect.

Before going into the details of this analysis, it is helpful to compare, at a high level, the approach of Miranda-Agrippino and Ricco to the one we propose in this paper. Overall, Miranda-Agrippino and Ricco suggest a very similar correction to monetary policy surprises as we do. However, they recommend the use of a different set of predictors and base their approach on a different motivation. Because they document predictability of monetary policy surprises based on the information in Greenbook forecasts, they argue that this predictability is caused by a Fed information effect. They therefore recommend orthogonalizing the policy surprises with respect to the Greenbook forecasts. Our prescription is based on a different premise, and it is also practically simpler in that the data for the orthogonalization are publicly available in real time.

Most of the analysis of Miranda-Agrippino and Ricco closely follows the specification of Gertler and Karadi (2015). The key is a comparison of the impulse responses obtained using the Gertler-Karadi monetary policy surprise instrument, FF4GK, to the results obtained using a new monetary policy instrument, MPI, which Miranda-Agrippino and Ricco construct according to the following three-step approach:

1. Regress the high-frequency announcement surprises FF4 on Greenbook forecasts and forecast revisions for real GDP growth, inflation and unemployment (for details, see Subsec. III.C or Miranda-Agrippino and Ricco's table 1) and calculate the residuals.

2. Aggregate the announcement-frequency residual series to a monthly time series, with zeros for months without monetary policy announcements.

3. Regress these monthly values onto 12 lags and again calculate the residual.[57]

As a result, the Miranda-Agrippino and Ricco monthly instrument series MPI is orthogonal to the Fed's own macroeconomic forecasts and does not exhibit any serial correlation.

We construct an alternative instrument series, MPINEW_BC, using the same three-step approach, but with the Blue Chip consensus forecasts instead of the Greenbook forecasts in the first step. We use exactly the same policy surprise, sample period, variables, methods, and forecast horizons as Miranda-Agrippino and Ricco. For each FOMC announcement, we regress FF4 on the most recent available Blue Chip forecasts and revisions, as in Subsection III.C. The resulting monthly instrument series is therefore orthogonal to publicly available forecasts but does not take into account any private information that the Fed may possess, which might be contained in the Greenbook forecasts.

Figure 7 is analogous to figure 3 in Miranda-Agrippino and Ricco and shows the responses of IP, the unemployment rate, the CPI, and the 1-year Treasury yield to a 100 bp monetary policy shock. (Thus, the monetary policy shock in fig. 7 is four times larger than in figs. 2–6, for comparability to Miranda-Agrippino and Ricco.) The three different lines correspond to the three different external instruments used to identify the monetary policy shock. The lines for FF4GK and MPI exactly replicate the responses shown in Miranda-Agrippino and Ricco's figure 3.[58] One of

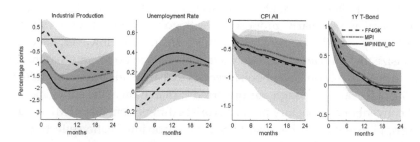

Fig. 7. Greenbook versus Blue Chip forecasts in Miranda-Agrippino and Ricco SVARs. Structural vector autoregression impulse response functions to a 100-basis-point monetary policy shock identified using three different external instrument series: the unadjusted Gertler-Karadi instrument (FF4GK), the Miranda-Agrippino and Ricco instrument orthogonalized to Greenbook forecasts (MPI), and a new instrument we construct orthogonalized to Blue Chip rather than Greenbook forecasts (MPINEW_BC). Specification, sample period, and estimation method are exactly as in figure 3 of Miranda-Agrippino and Ricco (2021). Shaded areas are 95% credibility bands based on the simulated posterior distribution. CPI = Consumer Price Index. A color version of this figure is available online.

their main points was that the response of IP and unemployment are very different for MPI than for the FF4GK instrument. In particular, using MPI they find no output or unemployment puzzle, with strong and significantly negative responses of IP and positive responses of the unemployment rate to a monetary policy tightening.

The third line in figure 7, labeled MPINEW_BC, shows the same impulse responses but using our new external instrument for identification. Strikingly, the response of IP to a monetary policy shock is at least as negative, and in fact even more negative, as when using MPI. Similarly, the response of the unemployment rate is at least as positive for our instrument as for Miranda-Agrippino and Ricco's instrument.

The results of this exercise suggest that there is nothing special in the Greenbook forecasts, and that the publicly available Blue Chip forecasts contain very similar information about upcoming monetary policy surprises. Thus, there appears to be little to no role for a Fed information effect in explaining the different macroeconomic responses to a policy shock documented by Miranda-Agrippino and Ricco. Instead, their results may well be driven by the "Fed response to news" channel of Bauer and Swanson (2023). What is clear is that their results are due to the correlation between monetary policy surprises and publicly available macroeconomic and financial news predating the FOMC announcement, which we emphasize in this paper.

The main point of Miranda-Agrippino and Ricco, however, is that one should not use unadjusted high-frequency surprises as instruments for monetary policy shocks. Our analysis very much supports this conclusion, and we similarly propose to orthogonalize the observed high-frequency surprises to construct better instruments. However, we emphasize that one can use publicly available data to do so, and that there is no need to rely on Greenbook forecasts that are made public only after a lag of 5 years. Although our preferred explanation of the endogeneity of conventional monetary policy surprises differs from that of Miranda-Agrippino and Ricco, because it does not rely on information effects, this is not crucial for the main points we make in this paper.[59]

E. Best Practice Estimates of Monetary Policy's Effects

We close our empirical analysis of the effects of monetary policy on the macroeconomy with a summary of what we have found to produce the most reliable estimates, and a final set of estimates that incorporate these lessons learned:

• High-frequency monetary policy surprises need to be orthogonalized with respect to macroeconomic and financial data observed before the policy announcements, to avoid estimation bias and create instruments that are more likely to be exogenous.

• Including additional monetary policy announcements, such as speeches by the Fed chair, improves the relevance of the instruments and the precision of the estimates.

• Estimates from SVAR models tend to be more precise and less erratic than those based on LPs, but the two are qualitatively similar.

• Using a longer sample period for estimation of the reduced-form VAR helps improve the precision of the estimates and leads to qualitatively similar results. Although there is a trade-off for using longer samples between improved efficiency and robustness to potential structural breaks, our results in figure 2 suggest that the estimated effects of monetary policy shocks are rather stable across subsamples.

• Including the instrument series in a recursive SVAR does not fix the endogeneity problem and still requires an orthogonalization of the monetary policy surprises with respect to macroeconomic and financial data.

• Invertibility of the SVAR does not seem to be an important concern in this context.

• Including additional variables in the VAR, such as the unemployment rate or commodity prices, makes relatively little difference for the other impulse responses (see, e.g., fig. A1). Nevertheless, the effects of monetary policy on these other variables may be interesting for their own sakes, and hence worth including.

Taking these lessons to heart, we report a benchmark set of impulse response functions in figure 8. These are computed using a structural VAR with external instruments, as in Subsection V.A. Because we do not reject invertibility, there are several reasons to prefer this methodology, including the ability to use longer samples for estimation of the reduced-form dynamics, higher precision, and less erratic estimates.[60] We combine FOMC announcements and Fed chair speeches to construct the monthly monetary policy surprise instrument, and we use the orthogonalized instrument series $z_t^{\perp}$. We estimate the reduced-form VAR over our full sample period from 1973:1 to 2020:2, and we use the instrument series from 1988:1 to 2019:12 to estimate the impact effects of the structural monetary policy shock on the variables of the VAR. Finally, we include the unemployment rate and an index of commodity prices in the

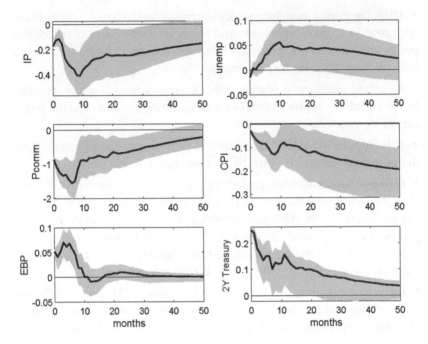

Fig. 8. Best practice estimates of structural VAR. Structural vector autoregression impulse response functions to a 25-basis-point monetary policy shock, identified using high-frequency mps measure around Federal Open Market Committee announcements and speeches by the Fed chair orthogonalized with respect to economic news available prior to the announcement. Sample: 1973:1–2020:2. Shaded regions report bootstrapped 90% standard-error bands. EBP = excess bond premium, Pcomm = commodity prices, IP = industrial production, CPI = Consumer Price Index. See text for details. A color version of this figure is available online.

VAR because the responses of these variables are often of interest and have been included by many previous authors, even though all of our other impulse response functions are very similar if unemployment and commodity prices are excluded.[61]

As in our previous estimates, we normalize the monetary policy shock in figure 8 to increase the 2-year Treasury yield 25 bp on impact. After the initial jump, we estimate that the 2-year yield gradually returns to steady state over the next several years (although only the first 4 years are plotted in fig. 8, as in our previous figures). In response to this shock, we estimate that the EBP jumps 5 bp in the impact month and commodity prices fall almost 1%. The EBP rises a bit further over the next 6 months before returning to steady state after about a year, and commodity prices fall further for the first 8 months before gradually returning to steady state over the next 4–5 years.

IP falls almost 0.2% in the impact month and declines further over the next 9 months before turning around and gradually returning to baseline over the next several years. The unemployment rate is essentially unchanged on impact, rises slightly over the next 10 months by about 0.05 percentage points, and then very slowly returns back toward steady state over the next several years. Finally, the CPI response is the most sluggish, dropping 0.05% in the impact month and then gradually decreasing about 0.2% over the next 5 years before very slowly starting to head back toward baseline.

It is interesting to compare the large and rapid response of commodity prices in figure 8 to the sluggish response of the CPI. This difference is consistent with standard medium-scale New Keynesian DSGE models that imply inflation inertia, such as Christiano et al. (2005). If we replace the CPI in the VAR with the core CPI, the core CPI response is even more sluggish.

Overall, the results in figure 8 are consistent with those we presented earlier and consistent with standard macroeconomic models. Our hope is that these may serve as a guideline and benchmark for future estimates.

VI.   Conclusion

This paper investigates the use of high-frequency monetary policy surprises to estimate the effects of monetary policy on financial markets and the real economy. This investigation is necessitated by the emerging consensus in the literature that high-frequency monetary policy surprises are significantly correlated with macroeconomic and financial data that predate the monetary policy announcements. An additional motivation is the concern that these surprises may have become less relevant over time as measures of monetary policy shocks (Ramey 2016).

We confirmed and extended previous evidence on the predictability of high-frequency monetary policy surprises. We also presented substantial evidence—and a simple theoretical model—that suggest this predictability can be attributed to the "Fed response to news" channel of Bauer and Swanson (2023), according to which financial markets simply underestimated how responsive the Fed would be to the economy. Our explanation is a plausible alternative to a "Fed information effect," according to which the Fed's monetary policy announcements reveal information about the state of the economy that the private sector did not previously have. We then investigated the consequences of the predictability of monetary policy surprises for empirical work, independent of the precise economic reason for this predictability.

When measuring the effects of monetary policy on financial markets, we found that standard, high-frequency OLS regressions using unadjusted monetary policy surprises produced reliable estimates. This observation follows both from our simple theoretical model and from our empirical reassessment comparing the effects of monetary policy surprises that are unadjusted versus orthogonalized with respect to macroeconomic and financial news that predates the announcement.

However, when estimating the effects of monetary policy on macroeconomic variables using a structural VAR or LPs, we found that unadjusted monetary policy surprises led to estimates that are biased. The bias arises because the macroeconomic data in the VAR are correlated with the monetary policy surprise, so that, for example, a monetary policy tightening is correlated with positive innovations to output and inflation, which attenuates or even reverses the estimated effects of the tightening. In this case, using our orthogonalized high-frequency monetary policy surprises provides us with an instrument that is more likely to be exogenous with respect to the other variables in the VAR and produces impulse response functions that are substantially stronger and devoid of opposite-signed puzzles such as the "price puzzle."

An additional difficulty of working with high-frequency monetary policy surprises in SVARs and LPs, especially for our orthogonalized monetary policy surprises, is that they can have low explanatory power for monthly changes in interest rates. In other words, even though our orthogonalized monetary policy surprise instrument is exogenous, it may not be very relevant, a concern that has also been expressed by Ramey (2016). We addressed this concern by bringing to bear additional monetary policy surprise data in the form of speeches, press conferences, and congressional testimony by the Federal Reserve chair. Using this larger set of monetary policy surprises avoids potential weak-instrument problems and still confirms the general pattern of the effects of monetary policy on the economy.

Our results also have important implications for central bank communication and the conduct of monetary policy. First, along with Bauer and Swanson (2023), we find little or no evidence that FOMC announcements have a substantial "Fed information effect" component. Although the minutes of recent FOMC meetings reveal that some participants worried about the potential for counterproductive information effects,[62] our results indicate that policy makers have little need to fear that information effects might attenuate the effects of their announcements, except possibly in exceptional circumstances (which our results cannot rule out).

Second, our estimates of the effects of monetary policy on financial markets confirm previous estimates in the literature, despite the fact that those monetary policy surprises are correlated with economic and financial data that predate the FOMC announcement.

Third, our estimates of the effects of monetary policy on the macroeconomy are stronger than many previous high-frequency-based estimates, because our orthogonalization of the high-frequency monetary policy surprises removes an estimation bias that was present in those studies. Thus, like Coibion (2012), we estimate larger effects of monetary policy on real activity and inflation.

Going forward, our results suggest several avenues for future research. The predictability—or rather, ex post correlation—of high-frequency monetary policy surprises with macroeconomic and financial data certainly deserves further investigation, extending the analysis to other central banks, additional predictors, and decompositions of monetary policy surprises into changes in risk premia and short-rate expectations. Explicitly incorporating empirical monetary policy rules into this analysis would also be valuable to learn more about the exact sources of this predictability. Regarding information effects, our empirical evidence here and in Bauer and Swanson (2023) suggest that they are unlikely to be strong on average, but it does not rule out that some exceptional FOMC announcements convey information about the economic outlook. Further research is needed to understand when this channel may be relevant, and recent work by Cieslak and Pang (2021) using comovement of asset prices is an important step in that direction. Regarding the macroeconomic effects of monetary policy, our analysis has documented large impulse responses to monetary policy shocks but leaves open the question of what our improved identification implies for the overall quantitative importance of monetary policy for business-cycle fluctuations. Future research could combine our identification strategy and methods for historical and variance decompositions, including methods recently developed by Plagborg-Møller and Wolf (2022), to address this important question. Finally, our SVAR analysis focused on policy surprises that shift the current target rate and expected policy path, but it did not consider the effects of forward guidance separately or of balance-sheet policies such as quantitative easing. Based on the lessons in this paper, methods for high-frequency identification may be combined with unconventional monetary policy surprises, such as those measured by Swanson (2021), to yield new insights in this area.

Appendix

Recursively Estimated Monetary Policy Rule

We estimate the following monetary policy rule:

$$i_t = r_t^* + \pi_t^* + \beta_t(\pi_t - \pi_t^*) + \gamma_t(y_t - y_t^*) + u_t,$$

according to which the Fed reacts to year-over-year core Personal Consumption Expenditures inflation, π_t, and the output gap, $y_t - y_t^*$. The dependent variable, i_t, is the 2-year Treasury yield, which we use instead of the federal funds rate to somewhat alleviate the effects of the zero lower bound. All data series are from FRED, including the Congressional Budget Office's estimates of potential GDP (y_t^*). Our data are monthly from June 1976 to July 2021, and we linearly interpolate the quarterly output gap series.[63] We estimate the response coefficients β_t and γ_t, as well as the combined intercept $r_t^* + (1 - \beta_t)\pi_t^*$, using exponentially weighted least squares and an expanding estimation window.[64] The forgetting factor is set to $\nu = 0.005$, which implies an effective sample size of 200 months. That is, estimation at time t uses data from the beginning of the sample to time t, and the weights for data at $t - j$ are proportional to $(1 - \nu)^j$. We begin our estimation in January 1990 and estimate the parameters for each month until July 2021. We obtain Newey-West standard errors using 12 lags to construct 95% confidence intervals.

Figure 1 plots the estimated response parameters $\hat{\beta}_t$ and $\hat{\gamma}_t$ and confidence intervals. An upward trend is clearly present in both estimated series. The inflation coefficient starts out slightly below 1 but increases quickly, satisfying the "Taylor principle" ($\beta_t > 1$) for most of the sample, and reaches its peak of about 1.8 near the end of the sample. The output gap coefficient is close to zero and statistically insignificant for most of the first 20 years of our sample period, and increases toward a peak around 0.6 in 2017, before declining somewhat toward the end of the sample. In both series, the estimates over the past decade are substantially higher than the earlier estimates. In sum, this evidence supports the view that the Fed has become more responsive to economic conditions, including both inflation and real activity.

Structural VAR Robustness

This section demonstrates the robustness of the results from our baseline structural VAR specification presented in the main text.

In figure A1, we present results from four variations of our baseline specification. The first column of the figure repeats the results from our baseline specification over our full sample, 1973:1–2020:2, and using the unadjusted monetary policy surprise measure mps around FOMC announcements as our high-frequency instrument, because that corresponds most closely to the instrument used by previous authors. The results in the first column of figure A1 thus are the same as in column a of figure 2 and the left-hand column of figure 3. In the second column of figure A1, we repeat the analysis using the core CPI instead of the headline CPI; in the third column, we repeat the analysis using the 1-year Treasury yield instead of the 2-year Treasury yield; and in the fourth column, we repeat the analysis including the unemployment rate as a fifth variable in the specification, as is sometimes done in the literature (e.g., Ramey 2016).

As can be seen in figure A1, the impulse response functions are very similar across all of these specifications. The different specifications also generally yield differences in the first-stage F-statistics for the regression of the reduced-form residual u_t^{2y} on the high-frequency monetary policy instrument, z_t. In the first column, the first-stage F-statistic is 8.19, in the second column 7.92, in the third column 13.12, and in the fourth column 8.12. Note that the higher first-stage F-statistic in the third column was exactly why Gertler and Karadi (2015) used that specification as their baseline. Nevertheless, Gertler and Karadi found that their estimated SVAR results were very similar using the 2-year Treasury yield instead of the 1-year yield, which we likewise find in figure A1.

Local Projections

Figure A2 reports estimated impulse response functions using the LP-IV specification (eq. [23]) with the high-frequency monetary policy instrument around FOMC announcements each month as the external instrument (excluding speeches by the Fed chair). The impulse response functions in figure A2 are larger than in figures 3–6, but the standard errors are also much larger, so we would not reject these other estimates. Ramey (2016) suggests that the later sample period may be partly responsible for the difference between the LP-IV and VAR results, but our results in figure 2 suggest that the different sample period is not a major issue. The impulse response functions for IP in particular in figure A2 are very large, especially for the orthogonalized mps instrument, although the standard errors are correspondingly large. It is likely that part of the problem here is that the orthogonalized surprises $z_t^\perp$ are a weak instrument—recall that the first-stage F-statistic for this instrument is only

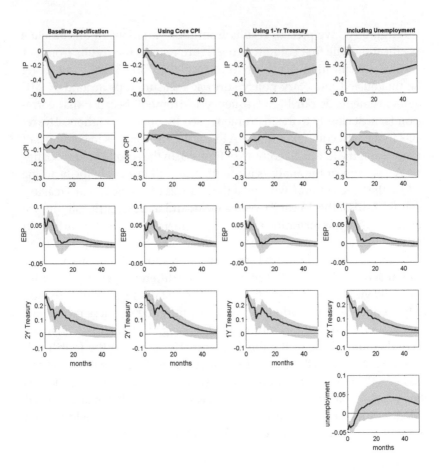

Fig. A1. Structural VAR impulse responses for four specification variations, using unadjusted monetary policy surprises around FOMC announcements. Structural vector autoregression impulse responses to a 25-basis-point monetary policy shock (MPS), identified using the unadjusted high-frequency mps measure around Federal Open Market Committee (FOMC) announcements, for four different specifications. The baseline specification includes the log of industrial production (IP), log of the Consumer Price Index (CPI), Gilchrist and Zakrajšek (2012) excess bond premium (EPB), and the 2-year Treasury yield. Sample: 1973:1–2020:2. Shaded regions report bootstrapped 90% standard-error bands. See text for details. A color version of this figure is available online.

1.83. Overall, the results in figure A2 are imprecise and should be treated very cautiously.

Miranda-Agrippino and Ricco (2021)

We noticed two issues in our reassessment of the results in Miranda-Agrippino and Ricco (2021) that are only tangentially related to our

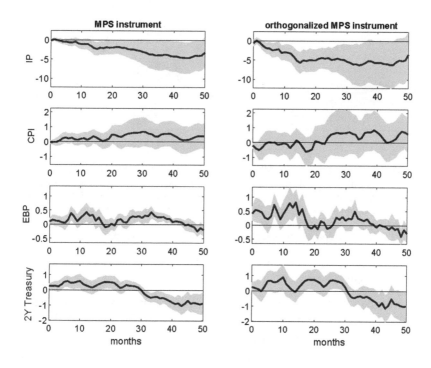

Fig. A2. Local projections impulse responses, identified using raw versus orthogonalized monetary policy surprises around FOMC announcements. Local projections impulse response functions to a 25-basis-point monetary policy shock (MPS), identified in the left column using the unadjusted high-frequency mps measure around Federal Open Market Committee (FOMC) announcements, and in the right column using high-frequency change in mps around FOMC announcements orthogonalized with respect to economic news available prior to the announcement. Sample: 1988:1–2020:2. Shaded regions report 90% standard-error bands. EBP = excess bond premium, CPI = Consumer Price Index, IP = industrial production. See text for details. A color version of this figure is available online.

main points but which are helpful for interpreting the results in their paper and in ours.

First, it is important to consider the properties of the unadjusted monetary policy surprises. As also noted by Ramey (2016), the Gertler-Karadi version of FF4, which is a 30-day moving average of the underlying high-frequency FF4 surprises, introduces serial correlation into the resulting series FF4GK. As a result, using FF4 or FF4GK leads to quite different results. In particular, impulse responses obtained using FF4 are more similar to those obtained using MPI in figure 7. Figure A3 shows that results for FF4 are more similar to results for MPI than the results for FF4GK are. That is, the orthogonalization of high-frequency surprises with respect to

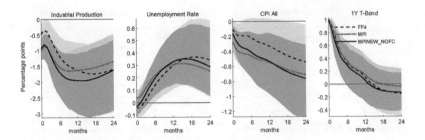

Fig. A3. Additional results for Miranda-Agrippino and Ricco. Structural vector autoregression impulse response functions to a monetary policy shock identified with three different external instrument series: raw FF4 series, Miranda-Agrippino and Ricco instruments using Greenbook forecasts (MPI), and a new instrument series that does not orthogonalize FF4 with respect to macroeconomic forecasts, and only removes serial correlation (MPINEW_NOFC). Specification, sample period, and estimation method are exactly as in figure 3 of Miranda-Agrippino and Ricco (2021). Shaded areas are 95% credibility bands based on the simulated posterior distribution. CPI = Consumer Price Index. A color version of this figure is available online.

macro forecasts and the removal of serial correlation actually makes a smaller difference for the SVAR results than it initially appeared. By contrast, our results in Subsections V.A–V.C showed that simple orthogonalization of the surprises with respect to macroeconomic and financial data makes a very substantial difference for the resulting impulse responses.

Second, we have also found that an instrument series that does not use any information in macroeconomic forecasts but only removes serial correlation leads to results not too different from those obtained using MPI or MPINEW_BC. This is evident in figure A3, which shows results for an instrument series MPINEW_NOFC obtained in exactly the same way as MPI except for the fact that we did not orthogonalize the surprises with respect to Greenbook forecasts. The similarity of the impulse response functions (IRFs) for MPI and for MPINEW_NOFC suggests that orthogonalizing with respect to macro forecasts has a very modest impact on the resulting estimates.

Overall, it appears that most of the differences in the impulse responses shown in figure 7—between those for FF4GK on the one hand, and those for MPI and MPINEW_BC on the other hand—appear to be due to the serial correlation in the FF4GK series.

Endnotes

Author email addresses: Bauer (michael.bauer@uni-hamburg.de), Swanson (eric .swanson@uci.edu). We thank Simon Gilchrist (discussant), Aeimit Lakdawala, Valerie Ramey (conference organizer), Harald Uhlig, Mark Watson (discussant), Christian Wolf, and conference participants at the NBER's 37th Annual Conference on Macroeconomics, Oslo Macroeconomics Conference, Society for Economic Dynamics Meetings, Federal Reserve Bank of Richmond Macroeconometrics Workshop, and the American Economic Association Meetings for very helpful discussions, comments, and suggestions. All remaining errors and all views expressed in the paper are ours and are not necessarily those of the individuals or groups listed above. Bauer acknowledges funding by the German Research Foundation (Deutsche Forschungsgemeinschaft), grant no. 425909451. For acknowledgments, sources of research support, and disclosure of the authors' material financial relationships, if any, please see https://www.nber.org/books-and-chapters/nber-macroeconomics-annual-2022-volume -37/reassessment-monetary-policy-surprises-and-high-frequency-identification.

1. Although there is ex post correlation between the policy surprises and economic variables predating the announcements, the monetary policy surprises were in fact unpredictable ex ante by financial market participants, according to this explanation. Imperfect information can lead to full-sample, ex post predictability even without any ex ante predictability (e.g., Timmermann 1993).

2. Bauer and Swanson (2023) show that controlling for the Fed response to news channel—by controlling for these macroeconomic and financial variables—eliminates the "Fed information effect" puzzle in survey regressions documented by Campbell et al. (2012) and Nakamura and Steinsson (2018).

3. See Romer and Romer (2000), Campbell et al. (2012), Nakamura and Steinsson (2018), and Bauer and Swanson (2023) for extensive discussions and evidence for and against the Fed information effect.

4. Using an alternative, more model-based approach, Sastry (2021) similarly concludes that there is little or no evidence of a Fed information effect in the data.

5. Although mps$_t$ would also be correlated with x_t if, on average, $\alpha_t < a_t$, the resulting negative correlation would be at odds with the procyclical correlations we document in Sec. III.

6. See, for example, the July 2021 Monetary Policy Report, available at https://www .federalreserve.gov/monetarypolicy/2021-07-mpr-part2.htm.

7. Changes in the Fed's preferences over economic outcomes or in the biases of its own forecasts could also have caused monetary policy to become more responsive to the economy. For example, Lakdawala (2016) documents changes in the Fed's preferences, and Capistrán (2008) found that the Fed underpredicted inflation before Volcker and then overpredicted inflation, which would be consistent with a shifting asymmetric loss function.

8. See also the online appendix to Bauer and Swanson (2023), which provides related evidence on the predictability of Fed funds rate survey forecast errors.

9. For high-frequency asset price regressions such as eq. (13), orthogonalizing the monetary policy surprises mps$_t$ and isolating the component due to ε_t is not necessary and may actually reduce the efficiency of the regression estimates. The reason is that, according to our model, yield changes are related to the full monetary policy surprise mps$_t$ and not just the exogenous component ε_t.

10. Throughout our paper, we use the term "monetary policy surprises" to denote high-frequency interest rate changes around FOMC announcements. Given the predictability of these changes, it may seem odd to speak of "surprises." However, this is standard terminology in the literature, so we stick with it. In addition, our simple model in Sec. II is consistent with the view that these surprises are unpredictable ex ante and that the predictability is due to imperfect information on the part of the private sector, which leads to correlation between the economy and the monetary policy surprises ex post.

11. From 1994 to May 1999, the absence of such a press release at 2:15 p.m. following an FOMC meeting indicated to the markets that there was no change in the federal funds rate target. Beginning in May 1999, the FOMC began issuing explicit press releases in those cases as well. See Swanson (2006).

12. Note that in the early years of the sample, 1988–90, changes in the federal funds rate were more frequent and there were several cases where the FOMC's decision was not immediately obvious to markets after just one open market operation. In those cases, there can effectively be two or three announcements in a row, corresponding to the consecutive days of open market operations, which gradually clarified the Fed's position to the markets. See Swanson and Jayawickrema (2021) for details.

13. Some authors have also used other measures—see Gürkaynak, Sack, and Swanson (2007) for examples.

14. Federal funds futures are also often included in the construction of monetary policy surprises but are not available in Tick Data until 2010. Gürkaynak, Sack, and Swanson (2007) show that Eurodollar futures are the best predictor of future values of the federal funds rate at horizons beyond 6 months and are virtually as good as federal funds futures at horizons less than 6 months.

15. Prior to each major macroeconomic data release, Money Market Services conducted a survey of financial market participants to determine the market expectation for the release. The survey was continued by Action Economics and is now owned by Haver Analytics. See Bauer and Swanson (2023) for additional details. The units are in thousands of workers, and the surprise is typically around 100; we divide these values by 1,000 to make the scale similar to the other predictors in our analysis.

16. Ramey (2016) and Miranda-Agrippino and Ricco (2021) also use FF4 as their primary measure of the monetary policy surprise, for comparability to Gertler and Karadi (2015). Gertler and Karadi also take a 30-day moving average of the high-frequency monetary policy surprises to create their high-frequency external instrument; we do not do that here because, as Ramey (2016) points out, the 30-day moving average induces extra serial correlation and predictability in those surprises that is not present in the underlying high-frequency changes in FF4 itself.

17. Note, however, that investors at the time had neither the same macro data as we do nor the same conceptual understanding of monetary policy surprises, which would have put them at an even bigger disadvantage.

18. The Blue Chip consensus forecasts are from the Blue Chip Economic Indicators survey and correspond to the arithmetic mean of the individual forecasts. The Blue Chip Economic Indicators forecasts, which we use in this analysis, are usually released on the tenth day of the month; we take the tenth day of the month as the date that the forecasts are publicly available. In recent years, the Blue Chip consensus forecast data do not include observations for the previous quarter when the macroeconomic data have already been released. In those cases, we add real-time data from ALFRED; see https://alfred.stlouisfed.org. The Greenbook forecasts are publicly released with a 5-year lag and are obtained from the database maintained by the Philadelphia Fed at https://www.philadelphiafed.org/surveys-and-data/real-time-data-research/philadelphia-data-set.

19. One way of seeing this is to note that high-frequency interest rate changes are essentially identical to negative excess returns on the underlying security, because over the very short holding period there is no material change in maturity or risk-free return. Excess returns are unpredictable when conditions (a) and (b) are satisfied. Schmeling et al. (2022) provide a recent discussion.

20. As discussed later, Cieslak (2018) also shows that the forecast errors for the federal funds rate in the Blue Chip survey of professional forecasters are also strongly predictable with the same variables that predict the market's forecast errors, implying that risk premia cannot be the whole story.

21. Prominent examples are Greenwood and Shleifer (2014) and Coibion and Gorodnichenko (2015).

22. Bauer and Chernov (2023) show related evidence, using conditional Treasury skewness and the shape of the yield curve as predictors for funds rate forecast errors.

23. Another possible explanation of our predictability results is the heterogeneous use of common information, as argued by Sastry (2021).

24. Event studies have been used to study the effects of both conventional monetary policy (e.g., Bernanke and Kuttner 2005; Gürkaynak et al. 2005; Bauer 2015; Hanson and Stein 2015; Nakamura and Steinsson 2018) and unconventional monetary policy such as forward guidance and large-scale asset purchases (LSAP) (e.g., Gürkaynak et al. 2005; Gagnon et al. 2011; Swanson 2011; Bauer and Neely 2014; Bauer and Rudebusch 2014; Swanson 2021). Work on unconventional monetary policy is surveyed by Kuttner (2018).

25. This assumption is possibly more problematic with daily data. However, Cook and Hahn (1989) argue that it is likely to be satisfied even with daily data, and even before the FOMC released policy statements at predetermined times (i.e., even before 1994).

26. In addition, our narrow intraday announcement windows keep the amount of other news about the economy that is released during these times to a minimum.

27. See also Kuttner (2018) for a discussion of this assumption in the context of LSAP event studies.

28. An example would be a more positive assessment of the current economic outlook by the central bank than by the public, and a hawkish policy surprise, $mps_t > 0$, as a result. Such an information effect might raise forecasts for output, inflation, and dividends, whereas a contractionary policy shock would lower them.

29. These 30-minute windows are the same as for the monetary policy surprise. The data source is Tick Data. In all cases, we use the current-quarter futures contract, which has the highest liquidity. Data for the 2-year Treasury note contract begin in January 1991 and those for the 5-year Treasury note contract begin in July 1988, so for these two Treasury yields some FOMC announcements are missing from our regressions. Changes in futures prices are converted to changes in yields using the duration of the notional underlying security obtained from Bloomberg. For the S&P 500, we use the S&P 500 futures changes up to August 1997 and switch to the e-mini S&P 500 futures changes from September 1997 onward, due to the e-mini futures having higher liquidity and longer trading hours. For additional details, see Swanson and Jayawickrema (2021).

30. Recall from Sec. III that the monetary policy surprise is normalized to move the ED4 futures rate one-for-one.

31. For example, the Fed chair has often been called on by Congress to testify about bank regulation, fiscal policy, Treasury debt policy, Social Security, Government-Sponsored Enterprises, the exchange rate, and other economic issues of national significance.

32. Although the monetary policy report testimonies are semiannual, they are given to each house of Congress, with extensive question-and-answer sessions each day. This results in a total of four of these testimonies per year.

33. Although this methodology necessarily involves some degree of personal judgment, most of the time it is quite clear from the market commentary whether the Fed chair's speech was interpreted as containing news about the likely path of monetary policy.

34. Because speeches, testimony, and press conferences take time, often an hour or more, Swanson and Jayawickrema (2021) do not use 30-minute windows for them, but instead use wider intradaily windows that are tailored to the length of the speech or testimony, typically about 90 minutes for a speech or press conference and 210 minutes for testimony. In addition, if there is a macroeconomic data release that occurs during one of these windows, they adjust the window start and end times to exclude the effects of the macro data release. See Swanson and Jayawickrema (2021) for details.

35. As discussed above, we minimized this contamination as much as possible by excluding macroeconomic data releases from our Fed chair speech event windows and by reading *The Wall Street Journal* and *New York Times* market commentary to determine whether the chair's speech was the main news moving markets, but there could always be some remaining effects of macroeconomic news in these windows.

36. A strong correlation of yield changes with the policy surprise could still be observed because interest rate changes across maturities are generally very highly correlated, and the "policy surprise" is just a measure of changes in short-term interest rates. In fact, the correlation of yield changes across maturities is even stronger for other types of news than for monetary policy news, as the latter is inherently multidimensional (Bauer 2015). The muted stock market response could be explained by the fact that the bond-stock correlation depends on the types of news.

37. Gertler and Karadi (2015) also used the month-average Treasury yield in their analysis; we use the end-of-month values. The end-of-month value corresponds more naturally to our high-frequency monetary policy surprise instrument; because Gertler and Karadi use the month-average Treasury yield, they also take a 30-day moving average of their high-frequency monetary policy surprise instrument. This 30-day moving average creates extra serial correlation and predictability in their instrument, which leads to concerns about the instrument's validity, as discussed by Ramey (2016). Nevertheless, our results shown later are all very similar whether we use the 1- or 2-year Treasury yield or the end-of-month or month-average yield in our analysis.

38. See Stock and Watson (2018) and Plagborg-Møller and Wolf (2021) for discussions of invertibility.

39. This generalization allows for a certain type of noninvertibility, but we still rule out the most common type of noninvertibility: that lagged structural shocks affect current reduced-form innovations (Wolf 2020).

40. LP estimation of impulse response functions, which we also consider later, requires an additional *lead-lag exogeneity* condition, $E[z_t \varepsilon_{t+j}] = 0 \ \forall \ j \neq 0$ (Stock and Watson 2018). In an SVAR framework, eqs. (17)–(18) and the serial independence of the ε_t make this condition unnecessary.

41. Of course, this correlation is not perfect, and $z_t \neq \varepsilon_t^{mp}$, because not all of the information about the policy shock is released in FOMC announcements and Fed chair speeches. For example, speeches by other FOMC members, minutes of FOMC meetings, interviews, and so on also contain important information about the course of monetary policy.

42. For lead-lag exogeneity, discussed in endnote 40, previous studies have typically assumed that monetary policy surprises are uncorrelated with all information that predates the FOMC announcement; thus, it is natural to view the lead-lag exogeneity condition as being satisfied for $j < 0$, and the case $j > 0$ holds due to the standard VAR assumption that the shocks ε_{t+j} are exogenous.

43. The nonfarm payrolls surprise in table 1 is also plausibly correlated with ε_t^{-mp}. Even though the released data describe month $t - 1$, the surprise is realized in month t, and a VAR which recognized this information structure would classify the surprise as an information shock in month t. In addition, the lead-lag exogeneity condition in endnote 40 is violated if z_t is correlated with macroeconomic or monetary policy shocks from previous months, which is the case for all of the macroeconomic and financial market predictors in table 1.

44. Note that this endogeneity bias could create the illusion of a "Fed information effect" (Romer and Romer 2000; Campbell et al. 2012; Nakamura and Steinsson 2018) even if there is no such information effect in the data, a point emphasized by Bauer and Swanson (2023).

45. If a month contains more than one FOMC announcement, we use the values of the predictors for the first announcement that month.

46. One can obtain the same point estimates for s_1 by regressing the reduced-form residuals u_t from eq. (17) on u_t^{2y} using z_t or $z_t^{\perp}$ as the instrument. Stock and Watson (2018) recommend using specification (eq. [22]) instead to avoid a generated regressor and correctly estimate the standard errors.

47. We compute these standard-error bands using the wild bootstrap procedure of Mertens and Ravn (2013) and Gertler and Karadi (2015). This method accounts for the uncertainty both in the estimated impact effect vector s_1 and in the reduced-form VAR coefficient matrices $B(L)$.

48. Where these specification changes make the most difference is in the first-stage F-statistics for the two-stage least squares regression. In general, the specification chosen by Gertler and Karadi (2015) (headline CPI, month-average 1-year Treasury yield, no unemployment in the VAR) helps to maximize the first-stage F-statistic. This is a problem that we generally do not have to worry about, because our data set includes Fed chair speeches as well as FOMC announcements, substantially increasing our first-stage F-statistics and helping to avoid a weak-instrument problem.

49. Similarly, good economic news about output or the EBP typically causes the Fed to raise interest rates and the EBP to fall; this is again opposite from the standard effects of monetary policy on the EBP and leads to a downward bias of the EBP response in the left column as well.

50. There are two reasons for the larger impulse response functions obtained using the orthogonalized policy surprise. Recall that the only difference between the two columns of fig. 3 is the instrument, and thus our estimate of the impact vector s_1; the reduced-form dynamics $B(L)$ are the same in both columns. The estimation procedure for s_1, described previously, amounts to a regression of the reduced-form residuals u_t on the instrument z_t, with the results scaled so that the last element of s_1 equals 0.25 (the impact effect on the 2-year yield). The first reason for the larger macro effects in the right column of fig. 3 is that the orthogonalized policy surprise has a larger impact effect on log IP, the log

CPI, and the EBP, because we eliminate bias arising from an endogenous response of monetary policy. The second reason is that the orthogonalized policy surprise has a slightly smaller impact effect on the 2-year yield, and the normalization of that effect further increases the other elements of s_1.

51. Note that most SVARs use the federal funds rate as their measure of monetary policy, and Gertler and Karadi (2015) and the present paper use the 1-year or 2-year Treasury yield. Estimates in Gürkaynak et al. (2005) imply that a 100 bp change in the federal funds rate corresponds approximately to a 50 bp or 45 bp effect on the 1-year or 2-year yield, respectively. Thus, when comparing SVAR estimates, this difference in scaling must be kept in mind: the estimated effects of a 25 bp increase in the 1- or 2-year Treasury yield are comparable to the effects of a 50 bp or 55 bp increase in the federal funds rate.

52. We compute these first-stage F-statistics as the squared t-statistic of the instrument in the regression of Y_t^{2y} on a constant, the 12 lags of Y_t, and the instrument, using Huber-White heteroskedasticity-consistent standard errors.

53. Recall that the first-stage F-statistics for the instrumental variable when we include Fed chair speeches are much higher (30.44 and 12.37) than when the chair's speeches are excluded (8.19 and 1.83), so it is not too surprising that the estimates in fig. 5 are more precisely estimated than in fig. A2.

54. See also Ramey (2022). Ramey also suggested part of the difference between her LP-IV and SVAR results was due to the later sample period for the former, but our results in fig. 2 suggest that the different sample period is not a major issue.

55. Other previously reported results of invertibility tests in the Gertler-Karadi setting are consistent with our findings: Stock and Watson (2018) used an alternative test based on impulse response function (IRF) differences between LP-IV and SVAR-IV and did not reject invertibility. Plagborg-Møller and Wolf (2022) applied their Granger-causality test in that same empirical setting, and only rejected the null when the policy instrument was taken to be the federal funds rate; in the baseline Gertler-Karadi setting with the 1-year yield they did not reject invertibility either. We thank Christian Wolf for suggesting this line of inquiry.

56. Relatedly, Lakdawala (2019) orthogonalizes monetary policy surprises with respect to the difference between Greenbook and Blue Chip forecasts.

57. Only observations with a nonzero dependent variable are used in the regression. That is, zeros in the monthly time series are not affected by this step.

58. We are grateful for excellent replication code that the authors made available via the journal's website; see https://www.openicpsr.org/openicpsr/project/116841/version/V1/view.

59. Our analysis of the Miranda-Agrippino and Ricco (2021) monetary policy instruments and results yielded some additional insights about different high-frequency surprises that are somewhat tangential to our main points; see app. D.

60. Li, Plagborg-Møller, and Wolf (2022) use simulation studies to show the advantages of SVAR-IV in the presence of invertibility and even mild noninvertibility.

61. Since Sims (1992), commodity price series have often been included in VARs to avoid a price puzzle. We emphasize that even without commodity prices, our VAR estimates do not exhibit a price puzzle, as long as orthogonalized monetary policy surprises are used as instruments for monetary policy shocks (see, e.g., figs. 3 and 4). The Bloomberg spot commodity price index is not available back to 1973, so we use the log of the Commodity Research Bureau's monthly index of commodity prices, downloaded from Bloomberg.

62. For example, in the minutes of the FOMC meeting on March 15, 2020, participants were concerned that a strong monetary easing surprise "ran the risk of sending an overly negative signal about the economic outlook." See https://www.federalreserve.gov/monetarypolicy/fomcminutes20200315.htm.

63. We use the fully revised output gap series due to the difficulties in constructing a long and consistent real-time output gap series. Although revisions to the output gap may affect estimated policy rules (Orphanides 2001), they are unlikely to affect our overall result.

64. Exponentially weighted least squares is equivalent to constant-gain recursive least squares.

References

Altavilla, Carlo, Luca Brugnolini, Refet Gürkaynak, Roberto Motto, and Guiseppe Ragusa. 2019. "Measuring Euro Area Monetary Policy." *Journal of Monetary Economics* 108:162–79.

Andersen, Torben G., Tim Bollerslev, Francis X. Diebold, and Clara Vega. 2007. "Real-Time Price Discovery in Global Stock, Bond and Foreign Exchange Markets." *Journal of International Economics* 73 (2): 251–77.

Bauer, Michael D. 2015. "Nominal Interest Rates and the News." *Journal of Money, Credit and Banking* 47 (2–3): 295–332.

Bauer, Michael D., and Mikhail Chernov. 2023. "Interest Rate Skewness and Biased Beliefs." *Journal of Finance*, forthcoming.

Bauer, Michael D., and Christopher J. Neely. 2014. "International Channels of the Fed's Unconventional Monetary Policy." *Journal of International Money and Finance* 44:24–46.

Bauer, Michael D., and Glenn D. Rudebusch. 2014. "The Signaling Channel for Federal Reserve Bond Purchases." *International Journal of Central Banking* 10 (3): 233–89.

Bauer, Michael D., and Eric T. Swanson. 2023. "An Alternative Explanation for the 'Fed Information Effect.'" *American Economic Review* 113 (3): 664–700.

Bernanke, Ben. 2008. "Federal Reserve Policies in the Financial Crisis." Remarks at the Greater Austin Chamber of Commerce, December 1. https://www.federal reserve.gov/newsevents/speech/bernanke20081201a.htm.

———. 2013. "Communication and Monetary Policy." Remarks at the National Economists Club Annual Dinner, Herbert Stein Memorial Lecture, Washington, DC, November 19. https://www.federalreserve.gov/newsevents/speech /bernanke20131119a.htm.

Bernanke, Ben, and Kenneth Kuttner. 2005. "What Explains the Stock Market's Reaction to Federal Reserve Policy?" *Journal of Finance* 60 (3): 1221–57.

Bianchi, Francesco, Martin Lettau, and Sydney C. Ludvigson. 2022. "Monetary Policy and Asset Valuation." *Journal of Finance* 77 (2): 967–1017.

Boivin, Jean. 2006. "Has US Monetary Policy Changed? Evidence from Drifting Coefficients and Real-Time Data." *Journal of Money, Credit and Banking* 38 (5): 1149–73.

Brand, Claus, Daniel Buncic, and Jarkko Turunen. 2010. "The Impact of ECB Monetary Policy Decisions and Communication on the Yield Curve." *Journal of the European Economic Association* 8 (6): 1266–98.

Caldara, Dario, and Edward Herbst. 2019. "Monetary Policy, Real Activity, and Credit Spreads: Evidence from Bayesian Proxy SVARs." *American Economic Journal: Macroeconomics* 11 (1): 157–92.

Campbell, Jeffrey, Charles Evans, Jonas Fisher, and Alejandro Justiniano. 2012. "Macroeconomic Effects of Federal Reserve Forward Guidance." *Brookings Papers on Economic Activity* 2012:1–54.

Capistrán, Carlos. 2008. "Bias in Federal Reserve Inflation Forecasts: Is the Federal Reserve Irrational or Just Cautious?" *Journal of Monetary Economics* 55 (8): 1415–27.

Christiano, Lawrence, Martin Eichenbaum, and Charles Evans. 2005. "Nominal Rigidities and the Dynamic Effects of a Shock to Monetary Policy." *Journal of Political Economy* 113 (1): 1–45.

Cieslak, Anna. 2018. "Short-Rate Expectations and Unexpected Returns in Treasury Bonds." *Review of Financial Studies* 31 (9): 3265–306.

Cieslak, Anna, and Hao Pang. 2021. "Common Shocks in Stocks and Bonds." *Journal of Financial Economics* 142 (2): 880–904.
Cieslak, Anna, and Andreas Schrimpf. 2019. "Non-Monetary News in Central Bank Communication." *Journal of International Economics* 118:293–315.
Clarida, Richard, Jordi Gali, and Mark Gertler. 2000. "Monetary Policy Rules and Macroeconomic Stability: Evidence and Some Theory." *Quarterly Journal of Economics* 115 (1): 147–80.
Cochrane, John, and Monika Piazzesi. 2002. "The Fed and Interest Rates—A High-Frequency Identification." *American Economic Review* 92 (2): 90–95.
Cogley, Timothy, and Thomas J. Sargent. 2005. "Drifts and Volatilities: Monetary Policies and Outcomes in the Post-WWII US." *Review of Economic Dynamics* 8 (2): 262–302.
Coibion, Olivier. 2012. "Are the Effects of Monetary Policy Shocks Big or Small?" *American Economic Journal: Macroeconomics* 4 (2): 1–32.
Coibion, Olivier, and Yuriy Gorodnichenko. 2015. "Information Rigidity and the Expectations Formation Process: A Simple Framework and New Facts." *American Economic Review* 105 (8): 2644–78.
Cook, Timothy, and Thomas Hahn. 1989. "The Effect of Changes in the Federal Funds Rate Target on Market Interest Rates in the 1970s." *Journal of Monetary Economics* 24 (3): 331–51.
D'Amico, Stefania, and Mira Farka. 2011. "The Fed and the Stock Market: An Identification Based on Intraday Futures Data." *Journal of Business and Economic Statistics* 29 (1): 126–37.
Farmer, Leland, Emi Nakamura, and Jón Steinsson. 2021. "Learning about the Long Run." Working Paper no. 29495, NBER, Cambridge, MA.
Faust, Jon, John Rogers, Eric T. Swanson, and Jonathan Wright. 2003. "Identifying the Effects of Monetary Policy Shocks on Exchange Rates Using High Frequency Data." *Journal of the European Economic Association* 1 (5): 1031–57.
Faust, Jon, Eric T. Swanson, and Jonathan Wright. 2004. "Identifying VARs Based on High Frequency Futures Data." *Journal of Monetary Economics* 51 (6): 1107–31.
Gagnon, Joseph, Matthew Raskin, Julie Remache, and Brian Sack. 2011. "The Financial Market Effects of the Federal Reserve's Large-Scale Asset Purchases." *International Journal of Central Banking* 7 (1): 3–43.
Gertler, Mark, and Peter Karadi. 2015. "Monetary Policy Surprises, Credit Costs, and Economic Activity." *American Economic Journal: Macroeconomics* 7 (1): 44–76.
Gilchrist, Simon, and Egon Zakrajšek. 2012. "Credit Spreads and Business Cycle Fluctuations." *American Economic Review* 102 (4): 1692–720.
Greenwood, Robin, and Andrei Shleifer. 2014. "Expectations of Returns and Expected Returns." *Review of Financial Studies* 27 (3): 714–46.
Gürkaynak, Refet, Brian Sack, and Eric T. Swanson. 2005. "Do Actions Speak Louder Than Words? The Response of Asset Prices to Monetary Policy Actions and Statements." *International Journal of Central Banking* 1 (1): 55–93.
———. 2007. "Market-Based Measures of Monetary Policy Expectations." *Journal of Business and Economic Statistics* 25 (2): 201–12.
Gürkaynak, Refet, Brian Sack, and Jonathan Wright. 2007. "The U.S. Treasury Yield Curve: 1961 to the Present." *Journal of Monetary Economics* 54 (8): 2291–304.
Hanson, Samuel, and Jeremy Stein. 2015. "Monetary Policy and Long-Term Real Rates." *Journal of Financial Economics* 115 (3): 429–48.
Jarocinski, Marek, and Peter Karadi. 2020. "Deconstructing Monetary Policy Surprises—The Role of Information Shocks." *American Economic Journal: Macroeconomics* 12:1–43.

Johannes, Michael, Lars A. Lochstoer, and Yiqun Mou. 2016. "Learning about Consumption Dynamics." *Journal of Finance* 71 (2): 551–600.

Jordà, Òscar. 2005. "Estimation and Inference of Impulse Responses by Local Projections." *American Economic Review* 95:161–82.

Karnaukh, Nina, and Petra Vokata. 2022. "Growth Forecasts and News about Monetary Policy." *Journal of Financial Economics* 146 (1): 55–70.

Kim, Chang-Jin, and Charles R. Nelson. 2006. "Estimation of a Forward-Looking Monetary Policy Rule: A Time-Varying Parameter Model Using Ex Post Data." *Journal of Monetary Economics* 53 (8): 1949–66.

Kuttner, Kenneth N. 2001. "Monetary Policy Surprises and Interest Rates: Evidence from the Fed Funds Futures Market." *Journal of Monetary Economics* 47 (3): 523–44.

———. 2018. "Outside the Box: Unconventional Monetary Policy in the Great Recession and Beyond." *Journal of Economic Perspectives* 32 (4): 121–46.

Lakdawala, Aeimit. 2016. "Changes in Federal Reserve Preferences." *Journal of Economic Dynamics and Control* 70:124–43.

———. 2019. "Decomposing the Effects of Monetary Policy Using an External Instruments SVAR." *Journal of Applied Econometrics* 34 (6): 934–50.

Lewellen, Jonathan, and Jay Shanken. 2002. "Learning, Asset-Pricing Tests, and Market Efficiency." *Journal of Finance* 57 (3): 1113–45.

Li, Dake, Mikkel Plagborg-Møller, and Christian K. Wolf. 2022. "Local Projections vs. VARs: Lessons from Thousands of DGPs." Working Paper no. 30207 (July). NBER, Cambridge, MA. https://www.nber.org/papers/w30207.

Mertens, Karel, and Morten Ravn. 2013. "The Dynamic Effects of Personal and Corporate Income Tax Changes in the United States." *American Economic Review* 103:1212–47.

Miranda-Agrippino, Silvia. 2017. "Unsurprising Shocks: Information, Premia, and the Monetary Transmission." Staff Working Paper 626, Bank of England, London.

Miranda-Agrippino, Silvia, and Giovanni Ricco. 2021. "The Transmission of Monetary Policy Shocks." *American Economic Journal: Macroeconomics* 13 (3): 74–107.

Nakamura, Emi, and Jón Steinsson. 2018. "High-Frequency Identification of Monetary Non-Neutrality: The Information Effect." *Quarterly Journal of Economics* 133 (3): 1283–330.

Newey, Whitney, and Kenneth West. 1987. "A Simple, Positive Semi-Definite, Heteroskedasticity and Autocorrelation Consistent Covariance Matrix." *Econometrica* 55 (3): 703–8.

Orphanides, Athanasios. 2001. "Monetary Policy Rules Based on Real-Time Data." *American Economic Review* 91 (4): 964–85.

Piazzesi, Monika, and Eric T. Swanson. 2008. "Futures Prices as Risk-Adjusted Forecasts of Monetary Policy." *Journal of Monetary Economics* 55:677–91.

Plagborg-Møller, Mikkel, and Christian K. Wolf. 2021. "Local Projections and VARs Estimate the Same Impulse Responses." *Econometrica* 89 (2): 955–80.

———. 2022. "Instrumental Variable Identification of Dynamic Variance Decompositions." *Journal of Political Economy* 130 (8): 2164–202.

Primiceri, Giorgio E. 2005. "Time-Varying Structural Vector Autoregressions and Monetary Policy." *Review of Economic Studies* 72 (3): 821–52.

Ramey, Valerie. 2016. "Macroeconomic Shocks and Their Propagation." In *Handbook of Macroeconomics*, Vol. 2, ed. John B. Taylor and Harald Uhlig, 71–162. Amsterdam: North-Holland.

———. 2022. "Postscript to 'Macroeconomic Shocks and Their Propagation.'" Working Paper, University of California San Diego.

Rigobon, Roberto, and Brian Sack. 2003. "Measuring the Reaction of Monetary Policy to the Stock Market." *Quarterly Journal of Economics* 118 (2): 639–69.

————. 2004. "The Impact of Monetary Policy on Asset Prices." *Journal of Monetary Economics* 51 (8): 1553–75.

Romer, Christina D., and David H. Romer. 2000. "Federal Reserve Information and the Behavior of Interest Rates." *American Economic Review* 90 (3): 429–57.

————. 2004. "A New Measure of Monetary Shocks: Derivation and Implications." *American Economic Review* 94 (4): 1055–84.

Sastry, Karthik. 2021. "Disagreement about Monetary Policy." Working Paper, Massachusetts Institute of Technology.

Schmeling, Maik, Andreas Schrimpf, and Sigurd Steffensen. 2022. "Monetary Policy Expectation Errors." *Journal of Financial Economics* 146 (3): 841–58.

Sims, Christopher A. 1992. "Interpreting the Macroeconomic Time Series Facts: The Effects of Monetary Policy." *European Economic Review* 36 (5): 975–1000.

Stock, James H., and Mark W. Watson. 2002. "Has the Business Cycle Changed and Why?" *NBER Macroeconomics Annual* 17:159–218.

————. 2012. "Disentangling the Channels of the 2007–09 Recession." *Brookings Papers on Economic Activity* 2012 (Spring): 81–130.

————. 2018. "Identification and Estimation of Dynamic Causal Effects in Macroeconomics Using External Instruments." *Economic Journal* 128 (610): 917–48.

Swanson, Eric T. 2006. "Have Increases in Federal Reserve Transparency Improved Private Sector Interest Rate Forecasts?" *Journal of Money, Credit, and Banking* 38 (3): 791–819.

————. 2011. "Let's Twist Again: A High-Frequency Event-Study Analysis of Operation Twist and Its Implications for QE2." *Brookings Papers on Economic Activity* 2011:151–88.

————. 2021. "Measuring the Effects of Federal Reserve Forward Guidance and Asset Purchases on Financial Markets." *Journal of Monetary Economics* 118:32–53.

Swanson, Eric T., and Vishuddhi Jayawickrema. 2021. "Speeches by the Fed Chair Are More Important than FOMC Announcements: An Improved High-Frequency Measure of U.S. Monetary Policy Shocks." Working Paper, University of California, Irvine.

Swanson, Eric T., and John C. Williams. 2014. "Measuring the Effect of the Zero Lower Bound on Medium- and Longer-Term Interest Rates." *American Economic Review* 104 (10): 3154–85.

Taylor, John B. 1993. "Discretion Versus Policy Rules in Practice." *Carnegie-Rochester Conference Series on Public Policy* 39:195–214.

————. 1999. *Monetary Policy Rules.* Chicago: University of Chicago Press.

Timmermann, Allan G. 1993. "How Learning in Financial Markets Generates Excess Volatility and Predictability in Stock Prices." *Quarterly Journal of Economics* 108 (4): 1135–45.

Wall Street Journal. 2001. "Fed Cuts Interest Rates by Half a Point in Attempt to Spur Second-Half Revival." WSJ.com, March 20.

Wolf, Christian K. 2020. "SVAR (Mis)identification and the Real Effects of Monetary Policy Shocks." *American Economic Journal: Macroeconomics* 12 (4): 1–32.

Woodford, Michael. 2009. "Convergence in Macroeconomics: Elements of the New Synthesis." *American Economic Journal: Macroeconomics* 1 (1): 267–79.

Yellen, Janet L. 2012. "Revolution and Evolution in Central Bank Communications." Remarks at the Haas School of Business, University of California, Berkeley, November 13. https://www.federalreserve.gov/newsevents/speech/yellen20121113a.htm.

————. 2017. "The Economic Outlook and the Conduct of Monetary Policy." Remarks at the Stanford Institute for Economic Policy Research, January 19. https://www.federalreserve.gov/newsevents/speech/yellen20170119a.htm.

Comment

Simon Gilchrist, New York University and NBER, United States of America

This is an excellent paper that reexamines the effect of monetary policy surprises on macroeconomic activity using high-frequency methods of identification. Let me say up front that the paper is well motivated, extremely clear in its findings, and a pleasure to read. There are two main innovations in this paper relative to the existing literature. First, following others in the literature, the paper shows that high-frequency monetary policy surprises are predictable based on lagged information contained in asset prices. Controlling for this predictability provides much sharper estimates of the effect of monetary policy on macroeconomic outcomes. Second, the paper incorporates information gathered in Swanson and Jayawickrema (2021) to construct monetary policy surprises based on communications by the Federal Reserve chair that occur outside of the usual Federal Open Market Committee (FOMC) announcements. This greatly expands the sample available from which to construct measures of monetary policy surprises and further increases accuracy.

The paper also extends the modeling framework considered in the authors' earlier work to motivate why monetary surprises may be predictable. In contrast to models that emphasize a "Fed information effect" regarding the state of the economy, their framework highlights the possibility that the Fed conveys information about its own policy rule.

The model in the paper is stylized but conveys two essential points. First, in an environment where the private sector learns about the monetary policy rule, high-frequency monetary surprises are predictable and impulse response estimates will be biased to the extent that there is systematic drift in the monetary policy rule. By controlling for lagged information, one can correct for such biases when estimating the impulse response. Second, the high-frequency response of asset prices to a monetary policy shock are unbiased because they reflect the same information asymmetry contained in the monetary policy surprise constructed using private-sector beliefs.

The paper provides evidence regarding drift in the policy response to output and inflation that is consistent with this argument. In particular, the Fed's monetary policy reacts more to both the output gap and inflation over time. Upward drift in the response to output and inflation implies attenuation bias in the estimated impulse responses of inflation and output to monetary policy shocks in an environment where the Fed is responding to demand shocks, as in the model described in the paper. It is less obvious that this result follows in an environment driven by supply shocks, however. Thus, one might expect the degree of bias to be time varying, both because drift in the policy rule is time varying and because the source of innovations varies over time. It would be interesting to extend the modeling framework to allow for such considerations. It is also worth noting that the two key empirical implications highlighted by the authors are also consistent with a Fed information effect, in the sense that models of a Fed information effect about the state of the economy would presumably have similar implications of no bias in the high-frequency asset price response but bias in the lower-frequency impulse responses.

In terms of the empirics, the paper confirms these key predictions: that (i) high-frequency responses of asset prices remain unchanged when controlling for lagged information and (ii) the output and inflation responses are much greater when controlling for lagged information.

Figure 3 shows this most clearly by comparing the response obtained in a structural vector autoregression (SVAR) with external instruments when one does and does not control for lagged information when constructing monetary surprises. These estimates imply that monetary policy shocks that control for lagged information have an effect that is four times larger (1.4 vs. 0.35) than the standard Gertler-Karadi estimates. The authors argue that these estimates are in line with previous studies, but it is difficult to gauge exactly because past studies benchmark the shock size using the Fed funds rate, whereas here they are benchmarked as a 25 basis point (bp) increase in the 2-year Treasury rate upon impact.

To gauge magnitudes, I find it useful to compare figure 3 to figure 7. This allows one to understand how much more we gain from using information contained in lagged asset prices relative to professional forecasts

when correcting for predictability. According to figure 7, using only information contained in the Blue Chip forecasts, a 100-bp rise in the 1-year
Treasury rate leads to a 2% drop in industrial output. As reported in
Nakamura and Steinsson (2018), the high-frequency responses of the 1-
and 2-year Treasury rates are roughly similar. They may also be considered unbiased estimates so that one can readily compare figure 3 to figure 7. Multiplying the output response in figure 3 by a factor of four
implies an output response of 5.6% to a 100-bp movement in the 2-year
Treasury rate. Thus, controlling for the information contained in lagged
asset prices leads to an output response that is nearly three times larger
than the response that one obtains by only using information contained
in professional forecasts. This suggests that the bias in beliefs about monetary policy contained in asset markets must be quite strong to obtain
such magnification.

As noted above, a major contribution of the paper is to provide additional information in the form of monetary surprises that occur in response
to speeches by the Fed chair. A key benefit of using these additional data
are that it sharpens the inference in the first stage of the external SVAR-IV
estimates. The low F-tests in these first-stage regressions have been a constant source of concern regarding inference in this literature.

There are three noteworthy empirical findings here. First, the high-
frequency response of the stock market is much weaker when using
Fed chair speeches rather than FOMC events (-1.6 vs. -5.39 according
to table 3) even though the response of the Treasury rates is essentially
unchanged across the two types of surprises. In my mind, this provides
strong suggestive evidence that Fed chair speeches convey considerable
information about the state of the economy. The second point to make
here is that it appears to be even more important to control for lagged information when using monetary policy surprises obtained from speeches
from the Fed chair. As the paper notes, this is perhaps not surprising as
such speeches are difficult to decode without incorporating prior information. Third, the implied impulse response to output that includes monetary policy surprises obtained from including Fed chair speeches is
considerably attenuated relative to the response that only uses FOMC
announcement dates. The estimates in figure 4 imply that a 25 bp rise
in the 2-year Treasury rate delivers a 0.6% drop in output rather than
the 1.4% drop obtained when using only FOMC announcements to construct monetary surprises. Moreover, the 2-year Treasury response is
quite persistent, in contrast to the case where one only looks at FOMC announcements to construct monetary policy surprises. On the whole, the

estimated responses of output and inflation obtained from using additional information from Fed chair speeches look more in line with previous estimates in the literature.

The authors do not offer an explanation as to why one would obtain an attenuated response when using speeches from the Fed chair as monetary surprises. One possibility is that Fed chair speeches convey a stronger information effect that is not reflected in lagged asset prices leading to attenuation bias. Alternatively, it is worth noting that the estimated response of the excess bond premium is significantly larger both in absolute terms and relative to output in the case of monetary surprises associated with FOMC meetings relative to the estimates that also incorporate the Fed chair speeches. Perhaps these surprises are particularly disruptive to the financial sector or, conversely, Fed chair speeches are considerably less disruptive to the financial sector.

A running theme throughout the paper is whether the predictability of monetary surprises is due to learning about policy or learning about the state of the economy. The paper does a nice job showing that Greenbook forecasts do not appear to contain information that is not already available in private-sector forecasts. On the other hand, existing evidence from the high-frequency response of asset prices to monetary policy shocks suggests a role for an information effect. Golez and Mathies (2021) show that although stock prices fall in response to monetary policy tightenings, the price of dividend strips that convey information about near-term cash flows actually rises. In ongoing research, Gilchrist, Yang, and Zhao (2022) confirm this finding and show that, adjusting for the response of interest rates, the expected cash flow component rises by 50 bp over the 1-year horizon in response to a monetary tightening of the size considered in table 2. As this paper emphasizes, we can treat these responses as an unbiased estimate of the market's change in beliefs. Thus, on average, at least over the period when dividend strip data are available (post 2004), a Fed tightening does indeed convey considerable positive news about the state of the economy.

The paper is careful to articulate that regardless of the source of predictability in monetary surprises, one should control for it using lagged information contained in private-sector forecasts and asset prices. This paper does an excellent job documenting such predictability and the effect that it has on estimates of the response of the macroeconomy to monetary policy shocks. It also provides a new time-series of monetary policy surprises based on Fed chair speeches that will be widely used in the literature. On both of these dimensions, the paper makes an outstanding contribution to the existing literature on the identification of monetary policy shocks and their estimated effects on the macroeconomy. I expect that the "best practice" methods recommended here along with the additional data will be quickly and widely adopted in the literature.

Endnote

Author email address: Gilchrist (sg40@nyu.edu). For acknowledgments, sources of research support, and disclosure of the author's material financial relationships, if any, please see https://www.nber.org/books-and-chapters/nber-macroeconomics-annual -2022-volume-37/comment-reassessment-monetary-policy-surprises-and-high-frequency -identification-gilchrist.

References

Gilchrist, Simon, Ei Yang, and Guihai Zhao. 2022. "The Fed Information Effect: Evidence from Dividend Strips." Working paper, Bank of Canada, Ottawa.
Golez, Benjamin, and Ben Mathies. 2021. "Monetary Policy and the Equity Term Structure." Working paper, University of Notre Dame.
Nakamura, Emi, and Jón Steinsson. 2018. "High-Frequency Identification of Monetary Non-neutrality: The Fed Information Effect." *Quarterly Journal of Economics* 133:1283–330.
Swanson, Eric, and Vishuddi Jayawickrema. 2021. "Speeches by the Fed Chair Are More Important Than FOMC Announcements: An Improved High-Frequency Measure of Monetary Policy Shocks." Working paper, University of California, Irvine.

Comment

Mark W. Watson, Princeton University and NBER, United States of America

Bauer and Swanson's paper is an important contribution to the literature measuring the dynamic effects of monetary policy shocks on the
macroeconomy. It shows what can go wrong using apparently exogenous high-frequency monetary policy surprises as instruments for monetary policy shocks, and it shows how to correct the faulty estimates and
inference by incorporating appropriate control variables. It is also the
first paper to use the expanded set of monetary policy surprises com-
piled by Swanson and Jayawickrema (2022), another important contribution. The culmination of the authors' work is the monthly impulse responses shown in figure 8 of the paper. These are the new benchmark
impulse response functions for the effect of Federal Reserve monetary
policy shocks on the US macroeconomy.

I.   Structural Vector Autoregressions and Local Projections
with External Instruments

In his 2008 NBER Summer Institute lectures, Stock (2008) showed how
an "external" instrument can be used in a vector autoregression (VAR)
to identify a structural shock and its impulse response function. I begin
by summarizing the external instrument framework, as this makes it
easy to explain Bauer and Swanson's contributions.

   Let Y_t denote a vector of time series variables. In Bauer and Swanson's paper, Y_t contains four variables: the 2-year Treasury bond rate,
the logarithm of the index of industrial production, the logarithm of the

NBER Macroeconomics Annual, volume 37, 2023.

Consumer Price Index, and the excess bond premium from Gilchrist and Zakrajsek (2012). The structural VAR (SVAR) is

$$Y_t = \alpha + B(L)Y_{t-1} + u_t \text{ with } u_t = S\varepsilon_t. \tag{1}$$

The elements of u_t are the VAR's one-period-ahead forecast errors, ε_t are the structural shocks, and S is a matrix linking ε and u. The term ε_t is assumed to be a white noise process with a diagonal covariance matrix. Solving the model backward shows how Y_t depends on current and lagged values of ε: $Y_t = \mu + A(L)S\varepsilon_t$, where $A(L) = [I - B(L)]^{-1}$ and $\mu = [I - B(1)]^{-1}\alpha$.

Let $Y_{j,t}$ denote the jth variable in Y_t (so $Y_{1,t}$ is the 2-year Treasury bond rate in this paper), and decompose ε_t as $\varepsilon_t = (\varepsilon_t^{MP}, \varepsilon_t^{Other})$, where ε_t^{MP} is the scalar monetary policy shock—the shock of interest in Bauer and Swanson's exercise—and ε_t^{Other} collects the other structural shocks. Let β denote the first column of S (so that β is the column of S corresponding to ε^{MP}) and Γ denote the other columns of S. Then

$$Y_t = \mu + A(L)S\varepsilon_t = \mu + A(L)\beta\varepsilon_t^{MP} + A(L)\Gamma\varepsilon_t^{Other}.$$

The parameters in μ and $A(L)$ are functions of the VAR parameters α and $B(L)$. They are identified, can be estimated using standard methods, and are unimportant for the insights provided by Bauer and Swanson. Thus, to focus on the main ideas, assume that $\mu = 0$ and $A(L) = I$, so the model becomes static with

$$Y_t = \beta\varepsilon_t^{MP} + \Gamma\varepsilon_t^{Other}. \tag{2}$$

With these simplifications, the econometric problem simplifies to estimating the value of β in equation (2). This is achieved using a scale normalization and an external instrument.

The scale normalization sets the first element of β to unity; that is,

$$Y_{1,t} = \varepsilon_t^{MP} + \gamma_1'\varepsilon_t^{Other}, \tag{3}$$

where γ_1' is the first row of Γ. This normalization says that the monetary policy shock is measured in the same units as $Y_{1,t}$, the 2-year Treasury bond rate. Rearranging equation (3), $\varepsilon_t^{MP} = Y_{1,t} - \gamma_1'\varepsilon_t^{Other}$, and substituting this into equation (2) yields

$$Y_{j,t} = \beta_j Y_{1,t} + e_t, \tag{4}$$

where $e_t = (\gamma_j - \beta_j\gamma_1)'\varepsilon_t^{Other}$ is uncorrelated with ε_t^{MP}. Conveniently, the parameter of interest, β_j, is the coefficient on $Y_{1,t}$ in equation (4). Unfortunately, though, $Y_{1,t}$ is correlated with e_t, so β_j cannot be consistently using ordinary least squares in equation (4). An instrument is needed.

Thus, consider a variable z_t that is correlated with ε_t^{MP} but uncorrelated with ε_t^{Other}. Then z_t will be correlated with $Y_{1,t}$ and uncorrelated with e_t, so it is a valid instrument for estimating β_j in equation (4). Gertler and Karadi (2015) argued that changes in federal funds rates futures contracts around Federal Open Market Committee (FOMC) announcements satisfied the conditions required for z_t. Their argument was plausible—indeed, I found it persuasive—and several subsequent papers have used these high-frequency monetary surprises as external instruments to estimate the effect of monetary policy shocks.

The resulting IV estimator is

$$\hat{\beta}_j^{IV}(z) = \frac{T^{-1}\sum z_t Y_{j,t}}{T^{-1}\sum z_t Y_{1,t}} = \beta_j + \frac{T^{-1}\sum z_t e_t}{T^{-1}\sum z_t Y_{1,t}}. \tag{5}$$

Evidently, if $T^{-1}\Sigma z_t e_t \approx 0$ and $|T^{-1}\Sigma z_t Y_{1,t}| \gg 0$, then $\hat{\beta}_j^{IV}(z) \approx \beta_j$.

II. Bauer and Swanson's Critique of Monetary Policy Surprises as Instruments

Bauer and Swanson's critique goes as follows: first, they document (following others whom they cite) that the high-frequency monetary surprises used by Gertler, Karadi, and others are correlated with information that was publicly available before FOMC meetings. Let x_t represent this information. Over the time period considered in these papers, the sample correlation between z and x is significant; that is,

$$\left|T^{-1}\sum z_t x_t\right| \gg 0. \tag{6}$$

Second, x_t is potentially correlated with ε_t^{Other} and thus potentially correlated with e_t in equation (4). Projecting e_t onto x_t yields the decomposition

$$e_t = \theta x_t + a_t,$$

where $\theta \propto cor(e_t, x_t)$. Substituting this expression for e_t in equation (5):

$$\hat{\beta}_j^{IV}(z) = \beta_j + \frac{T^{-1}\sum z_t e_t}{T^{-1}\sum z_t Y_{1,t}} = \beta_j + \frac{\theta T^{-1}\sum z_t x_t + T^{-1}\sum z_t a_t}{T^{-1}\sum z_t Y_{1,t}}. \tag{7}$$

Thus, the empirical finding that $|T^{-1}\Sigma z_t x_t| \gg 0$ suggests that $\hat{\beta}_j^{IV}(z)$ is likely to deviate significantly from β_j in the sample.

Bauer and Swanson's solution to the problem also has two parts. First, they add x_t as a control variable in equation (4). The resulting IV estimator is

$$\hat{\beta}_j^{IV}(z^{\perp}) = \beta_j + \frac{T^{-1}\sum z_t^{\perp} e_t}{T^{-1}\sum z_t^{\perp} Y_{1,t}} = \beta_j + \frac{T^{-1}\sum z_t^{\perp} a_t}{T^{-1}\sum z_t^{\perp} Y_{1,t}}, \qquad (8)$$

where $z_t^{\perp}$ is the residual from projecting z_t onto x_t. This eliminates the problematic correlation of the instrument with e_t. That is, it eliminates the problematic term in the numerator in equation (7). But it also changes the denominator, and Bauer and Swanson show $z_t^{\perp}$ is only weakly correlated with $Y_{1,t}$. Thus, β_j is only weakly identified using $z_t^{\perp}$ and $\hat{\beta}_j^{IV}(z^{\perp})$ is a weak-instrument estimator.

The second part of the solution eliminates the weak-instrument problem by adding new data, specifically by augmenting the monetary policy surprises to include surprises around speeches given by the Fed chair. These are the new data developed in Swanson and Jayawickrema (2022). Bauer and Swanson show that these additional data significantly strengthen the instrument.

Taken together, these two modifications produce credible estimates of the effect of monetary policy shocks on Y.

III.   How Can Monetary Policy "Surprises" Be Predictable?

I was puzzled by the empirical results on the predictability of monetary policy surprises documented by Bauer and Swanson and earlier papers. Why is it that changes in federal funds or Eurodollar futures contracts are so predictable? The model presented in this paper, and related arguments in Farmer, Nakamura, and Steinsson (2022), helped me understand that this predictability is a form of sampling error. Let me explain using the model presented in Bauer and Swanson's paper but incorporating some of the notation that I used above. Let i_t denote the interest rate (or the Eurodollar futures contract in Bauer and Swanson's empirical analysis) measured just after a FOMC announcement or Federal Reserve chair speech. Following the notation I used above, let x_t denote information available just before the announcement and let z_t denote the monetary policy surprise. (In Bauer and Swanson's model, the monetary policy surprise is denoted mps_t and the preannouncement information is denoted by $(x_t, \mathcal{H}_{t-1})$.) The model's monetary policy surprise is

$$z_t = i_t - \mathbb{E}(i_t|x_t),$$

so $\mathbb{E}(z_t|x_t) = 0$ and the monetary policy surprise is unpredictable. Through the lens of the model, a nonzero value of $T^{-1}\Sigma z_t x_t$ is sampling error and a "statistically significant" nonzero value of $T^{-1}\Sigma z_t x_t$ is unlikely. What, then, explains the unlikely large value of $T^{-1}\Sigma z_t x_t$ found in the data?

In the model of Bauer and Swanson, i_t and x_t are related by a parameter α, whose value changes stochastically through time. Thus,

$$\mathbb{E}(i_t|x_t) = \int \mathbb{E}(i_t|x_t, \alpha_t)p(\alpha_t|x_t)d\alpha_t,$$

where $p(\alpha_t|x_t)$ is the conditional probability density function of α_t. Figure 1 in Bauer and Swanson shows that over their sample period, the Fed's interest rate policy became increasingly more responsive to the economy, which in the model translates into an unusually long sequence of draws from the right tail of the $p(\alpha_t|x_t)$ distributions. In this sense, investors appeared to be systematically surprised by the Fed, despite using optimal predictors.

I take two lessons from this. First, from equation (7), whether $\hat{\beta}_j^{IV}(z) \approx \beta_j$ in any given sample depends on the sample covariance between monetary policy surprises and x_t; that is, $T^{-1}\Sigma z_t x_t$. Thus, it is useful to control for x_t in samples for which $T^{-1}\Sigma z_t x_t$ is large, even if $\mathbb{E}(z_t x_t) = 0$. The second lesson is that $\mathbb{E}(z_t x_t) = 0$ means that $T^{-1}\Sigma z_t x_t$ is likely to be small in future samples, so controlling for x_t in other sample periods may be unnecessary.

IV. Dynamics and Bauer and Swanson's Best Practices

Through most of my discussion, I have neglected the dynamics associated with the VAR coefficients in $B(L)$ in equation (1). Estimation of these coefficients plays a role in the Bauer and Swanson's "Best Practices" (or "Lessons Learned") at the end of their paper. The authors comment that impulse response "estimates from SVAR models tend to be more precise and less erratic that those based on local projections, but the two are qualitatively similar." This conclusion is based on unrestricted estimates of the VAR and local projection (LP) coefficients. Two recent papers—Li, Plagborg-Møller, and Wolf (2022) and Plagborg-Møller and Wolf (2021)—provide a more nuanced comparison of LP and VAR estimators. Using empirically relevant designs, these papers show that LP estimators tend to be less biased but more variable than VAR estimators, so ranking of the estimators depends on the relative weight placed on bias and variance. Consistent with Bauer and Swanson's comment, a mean squared error criterion generally favors VAR estimators. That said, shrinkage or Bayes methods improve upon the unrestricted estimators, providing significantly lower mean squared error.

Endnote

Author email address: Watson (mwatson@princeton.edu). For acknowledgments, sources of research support, and disclosure of the author's material financial relationships, if any, please see https://www.nber.org/books-and-chapters/nber-macroeconomics -annual-2022-volume-37/comment-reassessment-monetary-policy-surprises-and-high -frequency-identification-2-watson.

References

Farmer, L. E., E. Nakamura, and J. Steinsson. 2022. "Learning about the Long Run." Working Paper no. 29495, NBER, Cambridge, MA.

Gertler, M., and P. Karadi. 2015. "Monetary Policy Surprises, Credit Costs, and Economic Activity." *American Economic Journal: Macroeconomics* 7 (1): 44–76.

Gilchrist, S., and E. Zakrajsek. 2012. "Credit Spreads and Business Cycle Fluctuations." *American Economic Review* 102 (4): 1692–720.

Li, D., M. Plagborg-Møller, and C. K. Wolf. 2022. "Local Projections vs. VARs: Lessons from Thousands of DGPs." Discussion paper, Department of Economics, Princeton University.

Plagborg-Møller, M., and C. K. Wolf. 2021. "Local Projections and VARs Estimate the Same Impulse Responses." *Econometrica* 89 (2): 955–80.

Stock, J. H. 2008. "What's New in Econometrics: Time Series, Lecture 7, NBER Summer Institute." NBER, Cambridge, MA.

Swanson, E. T., and V. Jayawickrema. 2022. "Speeches by the Fed Chair Are More Important Than FOMC Announcements: An Improved High-Frequency Measure of US Monetary Policy Shocks." Discussion paper, Department of Economics, University of California, Irvine.

Discussion

Harald Uhlig opened the discussion with several comments. First, he noted that the reaction of the consumer price index is largely in the first period, so it would be interesting to see the impulse responses separately for interest rates, prices, and inflation excluding the first period. He also suggested plotting the impulse response for the real interest rate. Second, he explained that it would be useful to see how much of the variance of the price response is explained by the monetary shock. He added that he was surprised by the especially large reaction of industrial production, a comment echoed by James Stock, and that he agreed with discussant Simon Gilchrist that, if true, it might lead us to rethink the channels of monetary policy. Third, he asked whether the identification strategy relied on Fed funds futures being predictable, and, if so, whether this implied there was money to be made. Finally, he commented on how monetary policy has changed over time and how the authors deal with such issues (e.g., the zero lower bound).

The authors responded by first highlighting that the predictability is only ex post, therefore there is no money to be made. Moreover, they noted that although many papers have given reasons for this predictability (e.g., rational risk premia, irrational expectations, or imperfect information), the reasons for predictability are not important to their paper. In relation to the large responses, the authors pointed out that the monetary policy shock in their paper is a 25-basis-point (bp) shock to the 2-year US Treasury yield. This is roughly equivalent to a 55 bp shock to the Fed funds rate, which is part of the reason the estimated effects look large. Moreover, they explained

NBER Macroeconomics Annual, volume 37, 2023.

that the 2-year US Treasury was never constrained by the zero lower bound in their sample period and that this is also why Gertler and Karadi used the 1-year and 2-year US Treasury yields in their analysis.

The authors responded to comments by discussant Simon Gilchrist about information effects. They explained that the predictability regressions they showed are not a Fed information effect because all the information used is publicly available and predates the Federal Open Markets Committee announcement. They also found Simon Gilchrist's analysis of dividend strips to be very interesting and said they would need to look into it.

James Stock asked how the authors chose their controls. He suggested using a big data method, such as principal components analysis, to systematize the approach. He also asked whether the results are driven more by the orthogonalization procedure or by the inclusion of central bank speeches. In response to the latter, the authors explained that the orthogonalization procedure was the main driver of the difference with the prior literature, and the speeches helped improve the precision of the results and first-stage F-statistic.

Jonathan Parker raised some concerns about the empirical approach. He explained that if the monetary policy rule is time varying, then the authors would be estimating a vector autoregression (VAR) equivalent of a local average treatment effect (i.e., an average effect over the sample). He pointed out that the discussion by Mark Watson helped highlight this issue. In particular, if the dynamics of the system are changing, then the correlation between the control variables and the way they fit is also likely to be time varying. Therefore, including anything other than the shock in the regression will change the weighted average being estimated. He added that this would be like estimating the average treatment effect but with the weights on the different time periods changing. The authors responded that they would need to think further about this but appreciated that it is a valid concern. They pointed out that all the past monetary VAR analysis assumed a constant structure so that their analysis was consistent with previous work but suggested that an interesting avenue for future research could be to explicitly model a time-varying policy rule and place that within a VAR to see how much of a difference it makes.

Valerie Ramey pointed out that one approach to help put the magnitudes of the effects in context is to create multipliers. She suggested that one way do so, if the sign of the result does not change, is to take the cumulative response of industrial production up to a given horizon and divide that by the cumulative response of the Fed funds rate up to that horizon. She also commented that it would be useful as a credibility check to see what the results imply in a macro counterfactual; that is, how the economy would have behaved had the shocks not hit. Finally, she agreed with Jonathan Parker's point about the importance of heterogeneous treatment effects and suggested there would be significant value in having a paper on time-series regressions with heterogeneous treatment effects.

Martin Eichenbaum asked about the role of risk premia and Andrea Eisfeldt followed up with a question on the response of the prices of mortgage-backed securities. The authors argued that risk premia did not play a major role in their analysis and said they could certainly look into the impulse response of mortgage-backed securities.

3

Reparations and Persistent Racial Wealth Gaps

Job Boerma, *University of Wisconsin–Madison,* United States of America

Loukas Karabarbounis, *University of Minnesota, Federal Reserve Bank of Minneapolis, NBER, and CEPR,* United States of America

I. Introduction

According to data from the Survey of Consumer Finances (SCF), average wealth of Black households equals only 15% of average wealth of White households. In response to such a large, and persistent throughout history, racial wealth gap, various scholars and policy makers have put on the table the proposal of paying reparations to Black households. The logic underlying such proposals is that persistent racial wealth gaps do not reflect innate differences in ability, preferences, or beliefs but instead emerge from centuries-long exclusions of Black dynasties from labor and capital markets.[1]

We provide a first formal, dynamic economic analysis of the historical origins of the racial wealth gap and an initial evaluation of various reparation proposals. Our analysis aims to answer two related sets of questions. First, under the assumption of no innate racial differences in ability, preferences, or beliefs, to what extent can we account for the magnitude and persistence of the racial wealth gap when feeding into our model the history of exclusions that prevented Black households from participating in labor and capital markets? Second, will reparations today, in the form of direct wealth transfers to Black households, eliminate the racial wealth gap in the long run? If not, is there a policy that is effective in eliminating the racial wealth gap?

We answer these questions in three steps. We begin by developing a long-run equilibrium model with heterogeneous dynasties to quantify the sources of racial gaps in wealth, income, entrepreneurship, and mobility. The model shares two features with the wealth inequality literature (which we further discuss later). Motivated by the role of intergenerational transfers for persistence in wealth gaps, dynasties in our model choose how to allocate their resources between consumption for the current generation and wealth transmitted to descendants. Motivated by the observation that the top of the wealth distribution consists mostly of entrepreneurs, dynasties choose how to allocate their lifetime between labor and risky investment activities.

The innovation of our framework, relative to the wealth inequality literature, is that it generates an endogenous divergence of beliefs about risky investment returns. Entrepreneurship uses time and capital as inputs and produces uncertain output. The true return from investment is unknown, and each generation begins with a prior belief over the objective probability that investment activities are successful. Dynasties that become capitalists observe their investment outcome, update their beliefs, and transmit them to the next generation. Successful capitalists transmit more optimistic beliefs to their descendants, unsuccessful capitalists transmit more pessimistic beliefs to their descendants, and laborers do not update their beliefs because they lack investment experiences of their own. Thus, the dispersion of expected risky returns reflects differences in the accumulation of investment experiences from previous generations. This mechanism generates poverty traps, as generations with lower wealth tend to become laborers and pass more pessimistic beliefs to their descendants, who, in turn, also tend to become laborers and to realize lower wealth.[2]

We feed as driving forces into the model historical labor and capital exclusions that prohibit Black dynasties from participating in markets. By labor-market exclusions, we mean both slavery, taking place in our model between the Declaration of Independence in 1776 and the Thirteenth Amendment in 1865, and discrimination that result in lower wages for Black dynasties until today. By capital market exclusions, we mean historical events such as discrimination in patenting, redlining, Jim Crow segregation laws, and exclusion from credit markets. In our model, these policies exclude Black dynasties from becoming capitalists until the civil rights movement in the 1960s.

In the second step, we parameterize the model to evaluate its ability to account quantitatively for salient features of the data. The model is successful in accounting for the significant dispersion of wealth and income observed in the data, both for the total population and for the population of entrepreneurs. Although not targeted by our parameterization, the model matches the racial wealth gap today and its evolution since the early 1900s. Notably, the model is consistent with the observation that a large racial wealth gap still persists despite some convergence in wages. In addition, the model is consistent with observed income mobility patterns, where White dynasties are more likely than Black dynasties to see their children exceed their rank in the income distribution. Similar to the one in the data, the mobility gap in the model is more profound in the early 1900s than in recent times.

The model generates significant racial wealth gaps because Black dynasties earn lower wages than White dynasties. This disparity in turn leads to racial differences in holdings of both safe and risky assets. When White dynasties have positive investment experiences, they update upward their beliefs about risky returns and accumulate wealth over time. Black dynasties initially faced slavery and later face lower wages. They do not become capitalists, meaning that they do not update their beliefs and do not accumulate as much wealth as White dynasties. To corroborate this mechanism, we show that the model is consistent with the observed contribution of gaps in holdings of risky assets to the racial wealth gap in the SCF, when risky assets include investments such as public equity, own business assets, and real estate.

Confronted with historical labor and capital market exclusions, the model generates racial gaps without imposing differences in preferences, initial beliefs, or initial wealth. We highlight the importance of general equilibrium for the divergence of wealth. Early on, when Black dynasties are enslaved, investment returns are high because assets (such as land) are relatively unexploited. This makes risky investments worthwhile for White dynasties even if, initially, their beliefs are pessimistic and their wealth is low. As wealth in the economy accumulates, returns fall over time, and their decline dissuades Black dynasties from becoming capitalists even after emancipation.[3]

The model generates a racial gap in entrepreneurship and beliefs about risky returns in response to the same historical exclusions that prevented Black dynasties from participating in markets and accumulating as much wealth as White dynasties. We first confirm the known observation that Black households are less likely to be entrepreneurs than White households. We then evaluate whether model predictions concerning beliefs about risky returns align with available data. Using Michigan Survey data asking respondents their probability assessment of whether a diversified equity fund would increase in value, we present new evidence that Black households are more pessimistic than White households about risky returns. Despite not being targeted by the parameterization, the model generates a racial belief gap and dispersion of beliefs similar to those observed in the data.

Armed with a model that is consistent with salient observations on wealth, income, entrepreneurship, mobility, and beliefs, we perform various policy experiments to understand the predictions of the model for future racial gaps. We first clarify how we evaluate different reparation policies and why we are interested in their effects on future racial gaps. Our framework subscribes to the logic underlying reparations that persistent racial gaps do not reflect innate differences in ability, preferences, or beliefs but instead emerge from centuries-long exclusions of Black dynasties from labor and capital markets. Our criterion when evaluating reparations is that they compensate appropriately for historical exclusions only if they restore the outcomes we would have observed in a world without these exclusions. Reparation policies today that do not eliminate the racial gaps in the future do not compensate appropriately, because in the absence of exclusions, outcomes for Black and White dynasties are identical.

We evaluate reparation policies in terms of whether they achieve equal representation of Black dynasties in wealth, which is the outcome we would observe in the absence of historical exclusions. We are interested in the effects of reparations on wealth, because in our model more than half of the racial welfare gap is accounted for by differences in wealth as opposed to differences in wages. To separate the wealth effects of reparations from the wealth effects of different wages, we assume that labor-market policies are enacted to permanently close the racial wage gap at the time when reparations are given.

Our first policy experiment shows that with transfers that eliminate the racial gap in average wealth today, the average wealth of Black dynasties and that of White dynasties diverge again in the future, Black dynasties are strongly underrepresented at the top of the wealth distribution, and the racial welfare gap persists.[4] Historical labor and capital market exclusions lead Black dynasties to enter into the reparations era with more pessimistic beliefs about risky returns than White dynasties. Because this era is also characterized by a relatively low return to wealth accumulation, most Black dynasties forgo investment opportunities, despite increased wealth.

Racial outcomes differ in the long run, even with larger transfers that make the average Black dynasty significantly wealthier than the average

White dynasty today. Wealth transfers are not powerful in changing the trade-off between labor and capital activities. A policy that targets directly this trade-off is investment subsidies, which are more effective than wealth transfers in compensating Black dynasties for historical exclusions. A subsidy equal to 27 percentage points of additional return, financed with taxation of White dynasties' wealth at 100% above roughly $17 million, eliminates racial gaps in the long run. Another possibility for closing racial gaps is that after reparations, Black capitalists update their beliefs by learning from others' experiences. This possibility, however, raises the question of why learning from others' experiences did not occur earlier in history, thus leading to today's gap in wealth and entrepreneurship.

This paper contributes to three literatures. Early work by Blau and Graham (1990) concludes that racial differences in intergenerational transfers account for most of the racial wealth gap.[5] Quadrini (2000) and Cagetti and De Nardi (2006) demonstrate the importance of entrepreneurship for wealth inequality, as entrepreneurs occupy most of the top of the wealth distribution. Benhabib, Bisin, and Zhu (2011) emphasize the role of capital income risk for the upper tail of the wealth distribution, and Benhabib, Bisin, and Luo (2019) show that accounting for both inequality and mobility requires a combination of stochastic earnings, heterogeneity in saving rates, and capital income risk. Gabaix et al. (2016) show the importance of correlated returns with wealth for the fast transitions of tail inequality in the data. Our innovation relative to the wealth inequality literature is to introduce dispersion of expected returns. Unlike models that treat entrepreneurial productivity as an exogenous process, our model has differences in expected returns that emerge endogenously from accumulated investment experiences.[6]

A natural prediction of models with occupational choice is that wealth transfers lead to a rise in recipients' entrepreneurship rates and wealth relative to nonrecipients. However, Bleakley and Ferrie (2016) present historical evidence from a large wealth redistribution program, Georgia's Cherokee Land Lottery in 1832, that shows that descendants of families who received wealth transfers did not experience higher education, income, and wealth than descendants of nonrecipients. Bleakley and Ferrie (2016) conclude that financial resources play a limited role in intergenerational outcomes compared with other factors that may persist through family lines. This other factor in our model is beliefs about risky investment returns. If beliefs were homogeneous, a one-time wealth transfer would perfectly eliminate the racial wealth gap forever. Owing to the more pessimistic beliefs of Black dynasties at the time of reparations, our model instead predicts divergence of wealth after transfers.

The second related literature concerns social capital and the transmission of culture. Fogli and Veldkamp (2011) study the transition of women into the labor force in a model of learning by sampling from a small number of other women. As information about the effects of maternal employment on children accumulates, the effects of maternal employment become less uncertain and more women enter into the labor force. Fernandez (2013) demonstrates the role of cultural transmission of beliefs about wages for women's rising labor force participation. The transmission of beliefs across generations reflects both parental beliefs and a noisy observation of aggregate labor force participation. Buera, Monge-Naranjo, and Primiceri (2011) develop and estimate a model in which a country's past experiences and those of its neighbors shape policy makers' beliefs about the desirability of free-market policies.

Our baseline learning mechanism differs from some of these papers because dynasties learn about risky returns based only on their own experiences. Earlier work such as Piketty (1995) highlights the role of learning from own mobility experiences for voters' attitudes on redistribution. Similar to the model of Piketty (1995), in which experimenting is unattractive, and the cultural transmission model of Guiso, Sapienza, and Zingales (2008), in which learning occurs only upon participation, our model features persistent heterogeneity in beliefs as some dynasties do not enter into entrepreneurship.[7] We extend the baseline model to discuss learning from others' experiences and show that strengthened networks help close racial gaps.

The cultural transmission of family characteristics in our model relates to the work of Doepke and Zilibotti (2008). The authors develop a model with endogenous preference formation and occupational segregation to study the replacement of the British aristocracy by capitalists who rose from the middle class. The model of Doepke and Zilibotti (2008) features reversals of economic outcomes across generations. These occur because capitalists teach their children to appreciate leisure, anticipating that they will rely on capital income, and middle-class parents teach their children stronger work ethics and patience. Our model instead features persistence of wealth and poverty traps that are consistent with the lack of wealth convergence across races over the past 2 centuries.

Finally, our work contributes to the racial gaps literature. Darity and Frank (2003) narrate centuries-long exclusions of Black dynasties from labor and capital markets and offer proposals for the implementation of reparations.[8] Aliprantis, Carroll, and Young (2019) and Ashman and Neumuller (2020) use quantitative models to show how racial income gaps generate racial wealth gaps. Given differences in labor earnings, these models generate divergence of wealth after one-time transfers. By contrast, our model predicts wealth diverges after one-time transfers even if we eliminate forever the labor earnings gap. Hsieh et al. (2019) demonstrate that removing labor-market exclusions of Black workers increases aggregate productivity by improving the allocation of talent across occupations. Like these authors' model, our model does not feature differential changes in innate abilities by race over time and removes labor-market exclusions at the time of reparations. Unlike Hsieh et al. (2019), who do not consider wealth accumulation, we are interested in how the racial wealth gap emerged from historical events and how it will evolve after reparations.

Recent work on racial gaps includes Brouillette, Jones, and Klenow (2021), who quantify welfare differences over time, and Derenoncourt et al. (2022), who document and analyze historical wealth differences. Our approach differs from these papers in that we develop an equilibrium model that generates endogenously racial differences in saving rates and wealth returns. The benefit of this approach is that we explain how racial gaps in welfare and wealth emerged and that we allow racial gaps to respond endogenously to policies such as reparation transfers or investment subsidies.

Our conclusion that reparations in the form of transfers do not eliminate the racial wealth gap in the long run is reminiscent of the conclusion of Loury (1977) for labor-market policies aiming to equalize racial outcomes. Loury (1977) argues that equal opportunity policies may not completely eliminate racial inequality, because labor-market outcomes also depend on accumulated social capital and networks that disadvantage Black households. The parallel between our paper and the paper of Loury (1977) is that equalizing wealth in our model does not suffice to eliminate the racial wealth gap in the future, because at the time of reparations Black dynasties have accumulated fewer positive investment experiences from their network.

II. Model

We present the model and characterize its equilibrium. We then discuss key mechanisms through an example.

A. Environment

The economy is populated by a continuum of heterogeneous dynasties indexed by $\iota \in [0, 1]$. The horizon is infinite and periods $t = 1, 2, \ldots$ represent the economic life for a generation within a dynasty. We denote by Φ_t the distribution of dynasties in period t.

Demographics. Dynasty ι in period t has size $N_{\iota t}$. The evolution of $N_{\iota t}$ is given by

$$N_{\iota t+1} = (1 + n_{\iota t+1})N_{\iota t}, \tag{1}$$

where $n_{\iota t+1}$ is the population growth rate of dynasty ι between periods t and $t + 1$. The total population is $N_t = \int N_{\iota t} d\Phi_t$, and the population growth rate is $n_{t+1} \equiv N_{t+1}/N_t - 1$.

Technology. The model features an occupational choice between labor and capital, motivated by the observation that the majority of households at the top of the wealth distribution are entrepreneurs. Each generation within a dynasty is endowed with one unit of time. Generations allocate fraction $1 - k_{\iota t}$ of their lifetime to a safe technology, which we call labor, and fraction $k_{\iota t}$ to a risky technology, which we call capital or entrepreneurship. The allocation of time $k_{\iota t} \in [0, 1]$ is continuous.

The safe technology produces labor income from working and nonlabor income from saving in a risk-free asset. Dynasties that allocate fraction $1 - k_{\iota t}$ of their time to the safe technology earn income

$$(z_{\iota t} + i_t a_{\iota t})(1 - k_{\iota t}), \tag{2}$$

where $z_{\iota t}$ is the wage and i_t is the safe return on assets $a_{\iota t}$, both taken as given by dynasties.

Operating the risky technology requires time and dynasties that allocate time $k_{\iota t}$ to entrepreneurial activities forgo labor income. Entrepreneurship is risky, as $k_{\iota t}$ is chosen before an idiosyncratic investment shock is realized. Allocating time $k_{\iota t}$ produces capital income

$$\begin{aligned} r_t a_{\iota t} k_{\iota t}, & \quad \text{if } e_{\iota t} = G, \\ 0, & \quad \text{if } e_{\iota t} = B. \end{aligned} \tag{3}$$

Capital income depends on the realization of an idiosyncratic event $e_{\iota t}$. If the dynasty's experience is good, $e_{\iota t} = G$, entrepreneurship yields a net return r_t per unit of assets invested $a_{\iota t}$. If the dynasty's experience is bad, $e_{\iota t} = B$, entrepreneurship yields a net return of zero. The return r_t is determined in equilibrium and also taken as given.

Beliefs. Our modeling innovation is to introduce heterogeneity in beliefs about risky investment returns. Dynasties do not know the objective probability of a good experience, which we denote by $q^* = \mathbb{P}(e_{\iota t} = G)$. This probability is common across dynasties and constant over time. Dynasties learn about q^* from events they experience when they are capitalists.

Each dynasty ι begins period t with a prior belief, $\pi_{\iota t}(q)$, over the probability that risky investment activities are successful, q^*. The belief induces a subjective expectation of a good event, $\mathbb{E}_{\iota t} q^* = \int q \pi_{\iota t}(q) dq$. As we illustrate below, this expectation partly determines the choice to become a capitalist.

Capitalists, $k_{\iota t} > 0$, update their prior belief following their experiences using Bayes's rule:

$$
\pi_{\iota t+1}(q) = \begin{cases} \pi_{\iota t}(q) \dfrac{q}{\mathbb{E}_{\iota t} q^*}, & \text{if } e_{\iota t} = G, \\[2ex] \pi_{\iota t}(q) \dfrac{1-q}{\mathbb{E}_{\iota t}(1-q^*)}, & \text{if } e_{\iota t} = B. \end{cases} \tag{4}
$$

Following a good experience, $e_{\iota t} = G$, the posterior belief that q^* equals q, $\pi_{\iota t+1}(q)$, equals the prior belief, $\pi_{\iota t}(q)$, multiplied by the likelihood of experiencing a good event, q, divided by the probability of occurrence of a good event, $\mathbb{E}_{\iota t} q^*$. Dynasties with good experiences increase their belief about probabilities that exceed their prior mean of a good experience. Conversely, following a bad experience, $e_{\iota t} = B$, dynasties lower their belief about probabilities that exceed their prior mean of a good experience.

Capitalists, $k_{\iota t} > 0$, pass their posterior beliefs on to their children, who begin the next period with prior $\pi_{\iota t+1}$. Laborers, $k_{\iota t} = 0$, do not accumulate risky investment experiences and, therefore, do not update their prior, $\pi_{\iota t+1} = \pi_{\iota t}$. Beliefs in our model are martingale, $\mathbb{E}_{\iota t} \pi_{\iota t+1}(q) = \pi_{\iota t}(q)$. Therefore, beliefs converge to the truth in the long run, $\lim_{t \to \infty} \pi_{\iota t}(q) = 0$ for $q \neq q^*$, but only conditional on being a capitalist.

In our model, dynasties learn from their own experiences only if they become capitalists. This feature is similar to the learning assumption of Piketty (1995) in his model of income mobility. We think this is a natural benchmark, partly because it allows the model to generate persistence in returns and wealth. In Subsection IV.C, we consider alternative

assumptions under which dynasties also learn from the experiences of
other dynasties.

Timing. The timing of events in each period is as follows:

1. Dynasty ι begins period t with state $(z_{\iota t}, a_{\iota t}, \pi_{\iota t}(q), n_{\iota t+1}, T_{\iota t})$, where $z_{\iota t}$ is
the wage, $a_{\iota t}$ is assets, $\pi_{\iota t}(q)$ is the prior belief about the probability the
good event is q, $n_{\iota t+1}$ is the growth rate of the size of the dynasty, and
$T_{\iota t}$ is transfers.

2. Dynasties choose the fraction of time spent on capital activities $k_{\iota t}$
before $e_{\iota t}$ is realized.

3. Dynasties experience $e_{\iota t}$ and realize income $y_{\iota t}$.

4. Dynasties choose consumption $c_{\iota t}$ and transmit assets $a_{\iota t+1}$ and posterior beliefs $\pi_{\iota t+1}$ to the next generation $\iota t + 1$.

Preferences and budget. The model is analytically tractable because
each generation has preferences over their own consumption $c_{\iota t}$ and
over assets bequeathed per child $a_{\iota t+1}$. The utility function is

$$U = \frac{(c_{\iota t} - \bar{c}_t)^{1-\gamma} - 1}{1 - \gamma} + \beta^\gamma \frac{a_{\iota t+1}^{1-\gamma} - 1}{1 - \gamma}, \tag{5}$$

where parameter $\gamma \geq 0$ governs the curvature of the utility function for
consumption and bequests, and the discount factor $\beta > 0$ governs the
preference for bequests relative to consumption.

Preferences are nonhomothetic, with $\bar{c}_t > 0$ denoting the subsistence
level of consumption. We motivate nonhomothetic preferences with the
observation that households with higher lifetime income (e.g., Dynan,
Skinner, and Zeldes 2004; Straub 2019) and wealth (e.g., Fagereng et al.
2019) exhibit higher saving rates, leading to increased wealth inequality
(e.g., De Nardi and Fella 2017). In our quantitative analysis, $\bar{c}_t$ allows
the model to generate the low share of wealth held by the bottom half
of the population.

The budget constraint of each generation is

$$c_{\iota t} + (1 + n_{\iota t+1})a_{\iota t+1} = y_{\iota t}(k_{\iota t}, e_{\iota t}) + (1 - \delta)a_{\iota t}, \tag{6}$$

where $(1 + n_{\iota t+1})a_{\iota t+1}$ is resources saved to transfer $a_{\iota t+1}$ to each member of
the next generation, and δ is the depreciation rate of assets. Income $y_{\iota t}$ is
a function of the allocation of time $k_{\iota t}$ and the realization of experience $e_{\iota t}$

$$y_{\iota t}(k_{\iota t}, e_{\iota t}) = \begin{cases} T_{\iota t} + (z_{\iota t} + i_t a_{\iota t})(1 - k_{\iota t}) + r_t a_{\iota t} k_{\iota t}, & \text{if } e_{\iota t} = G, \\ T_{\iota t} + (z_{\iota t} + i_t a_{\iota t})(1 - k_{\iota t}), & \text{if } e_{\iota t} = B, \end{cases} \quad (7)$$

where $T_{\iota t}$ are transfers.

Interpretation of wealth, return heterogeneity, and risky investments. We interpret $a_{\iota t}$ as net worth from all assets minus liabilities, including public equity, business assets, bonds, durables, and housing, as is consistent with our model, in which wealth derives from both safe and risky investments. The ex post net return on wealth for dynasty ι at time t is

$$\rho_{\iota t} = \begin{cases} r_t k_{\iota t} + i_t(1 - k_{\iota t}) - \delta, & \text{if } e_{\iota t} = G, \\ i_t(1 - k_{\iota t}) - \delta, & \text{if } e_{\iota t} = B. \end{cases} \quad (8)$$

Equation (8) shows that there are two sources of ex post return heterogeneity across dynasties. Heterogeneity arises because of luck, as dynasties can experience either a good or a bad event $e_{\iota t}$. Heterogeneity also arises endogenously from portfolio composition, as dynasties choose to direct a different fraction of investments $k_{\iota t}$ toward risky assets and the risky return r_t differs from the safe return i_t.[9]

Our modeling of risky investments is consistent with two aspects of the data that we discuss later. In the subsection "Wealth and Income," we use the SCF to document that holdings of private business assets and public equity are quantitatively the most important drivers for the racial wealth gap. This finding is consistent with our model, in which risky investment activities amplify the racial gap in average wealth. Further, in the subsection "Beliefs about Risky Returns," we document the existence of a racial gap in beliefs about returns on a diversified equity fund, which directly maps to expected risky returns $\mathbb{E}_{\iota t} q^* r_t$.

B. Dynasty Optimization

We solve the dynasty problem backward. In the last stage, the solution for consumption and assets, given income level $y_{\iota t}$, is

$$c_{\iota t} = \bar{c}_t + \omega_{t+1}(y_{\iota t} + (1 - \delta)a_{\iota t} - \bar{c}_t), \quad (9)$$

$$a_{t+1} = \frac{1 - \omega_{t+1}}{1 + n_{t+1}}(y_{\iota t} + (1 - \delta)a_{\iota t} - \bar{c}_t), \quad (10)$$

with weight $\omega_{ut+1} \equiv (1 + n_{ut+1})^{\frac{1-\gamma}{\gamma}}/(1 + n_{ut+1})^{\frac{1-\gamma}{\gamma}} + \beta$. The solutions are constant elasticity of substitution demand functions, augmented to account for subsistence consumption. Each generation allocates a fraction ω_{ut+1} of its resources net of subsistence consumption to consumption above this subsistence level. Remaining resources are passed to the next generation in the form of assets. Because each generation is succeeded by $1 + n_{ut+1}$ members, an increase in population growth reduces the resources transferred per member of the next generation. The consumption weight ω_{ut+1} varies with population growth when $\gamma \neq 1$. With log utility, $\gamma \to 1$, the weight is independent of population growth and is inversely related to the discount factor, $\omega_{ut+1} = 1/(1 + \beta)$.

Working backward, we solve for the allocation of time k_{ut} using the optimal choice of consumption and assets in the last stage. Dynasties maximize expected utility

$$V = \max_{k_{ut}} \int (qU^*(y_{ut}(k_{ut}, G)) + (1 - q)U^*(y_{ut}(k_{ut}, B)))\pi_{ut}(q)dq, \quad (11)$$

where U^* is indirect utility given income $y_{ut} = y_{ut}(k_{ut}, e_{ut})$. The expectation is formed under the probability distribution π_{ut}. The solution for time allocated to capital is

$$k_{ut} = \begin{cases} 0, & \text{if } r_t a_{ut} \leq z_{ut} + i_t a_{ut}, \text{ or } \mathbb{E}_{ut}q^* r_t a_{ut} \leq z_{ut} + i_t a_{ut}, \\ \left(1 + \frac{T_{ut} + (1-\delta)a_{ut} - \bar{c}_t}{z_{ut} + i_t a_{ut}}\right)\left(\frac{\left[\frac{\mathbb{E}_{ut}q^*}{1-\mathbb{E}_{ut}q^*}\left(\frac{r_t a_{ut}}{z_{ut}+i_t a_{ut}} - 1\right)\right]^{\frac{1}{\gamma}} - 1}{\left[\frac{\mathbb{E}_{ut}q^*}{1-\mathbb{E}_{ut}q^*}\left(\frac{r_t a_{ut}}{z_{ut}+i_t a_{ut}} - 1\right)\right]^{\frac{1}{\gamma}} - 1 + \frac{r_t a_{ut}}{z_{ut}+i_t a_{ut}}}\right), & \text{otherwise,} \end{cases} \quad (12)$$

with $k_{ut} = 1$ if the expression in the last line exceeds one.

Figure 1 presents the policy functions for k_{ut}. Our model includes two channels affecting the decision to become a capitalist. The first is wealth, captured by a_{ut}, and the second is relative factor returns, captured by the expected return $\mathbb{E}_{ut}q^*r_t$ relative to the wage z_{ut}. Dynasties with sufficiently high wage z_{ut}, low assets a_{ut}, or pessimistic beliefs about returns $\mathbb{E}_{ut}q^*r_t$ become laborers, $k_{ut} = 0$. Conditional on a dynasty becoming capitalists, k_{ut} increases in assets and expected returns and decreases in the wage.

C. Asset Market

The return to risky investments, r_t, adjusts to clear the asset market[10]:

$$N_t \int (1 + n_{ut+1})a_{ut+1}(\cdot, r_t)d\Phi_t = \bar{A}_{t+1}/r_t^\alpha. \quad (13)$$

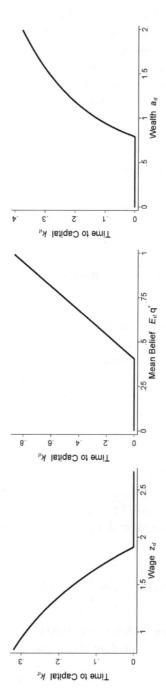

Fig. 1. Policy functions

The left-hand side of this equation is total desired assets given a return r_t. Desired assets increase in r_t because a higher return induces more dynasties to become capitalists and to transfer more assets to their children. The supply of assets has to meet a limit on investment opportunities, given by the right-hand side of equation (13). Parameter $\alpha \geq 0$ governs the magnitude of the decline in returns as wealth accumulates. In the limiting case with $\alpha = 0$, assets are in fixed supply (e.g., land) and r_t adjusts to make assets equal to the exogenous constant $\bar{A}_{t+1}$. In the other limiting case with $\alpha \to \infty$, the return to risky investment is exogenous as in a small open economy. For intermediate cases, $0 < \alpha < \infty$, the equilibrium return and assets are jointly determined as in standard closed-economy general equilibrium models.

D. Labor and Capital Market Exclusions

We treat labor and capital market exclusions as exogenous driving forces and feed them to the model in a time-varying way that we specify in the quantitative part of our analysis. In modeling these exclusions, we distinguish between Black dynasties b and White dynasties w. Black dynasties are a fraction ϕ_t of the population. We denote by Φ_t^h the distribution of dynasties $h \in \{b, w\}$ conditional on race.

We use the term "labor-market exclusion" to refer to slavery and the racial wage gap. Slavery, which we indicate by $\chi_t^\ell = 1$, forces Black dynasties to be laborers, consume subsistence consumption, and not transfer resources to their children:

$$k_{at}^b = 0, \quad c_{at}^b = \bar{c}_t, \quad a_{at+1}^b = 0. \tag{14}$$

During slavery, production of Black dynasties in excess of subsistence consumption is expropriated and evenly distributed among White dynasties:

$$(1 - \phi_t)T_{at}^w = \chi_t^\ell \phi_t \int (z_{at} - \bar{c}_t) d\Phi_t^b. \tag{15}$$

The racial wage gap means that Black dynasties draw wages from a distribution with a mean lower than the mean of the distribution of White dynasties, $\mathbb{E}z_{at}^b < \mathbb{E}z_{at}^w$.[11]

Capital market exclusions, which we indicate by $\chi_t^k = 1$, capture events such as discrimination in patenting, redlining, Jim Crow segregation laws, and exclusion from credit markets.[12] In our model, capital market exclusions prohibit Black dynasties from becoming capitalists:

$$k_{it}^b = 0. \tag{16}$$

E. Equilibrium

We conclude the description of the economy with the definition of equilibrium. Given an initial distribution over assets, beliefs, and population size by race, $\Phi_1^h(a_1, \pi_1, N_1)$, exogenous dynasty sequences $\{z_{it}, e_{it}, n_{it+1}\}_{it}$, and exogenous aggregate sequences $\{\bar{A}_t, i_t, \chi_t^\ell, \chi_t^k\}_t$, an equilibrium is a sequence of dynasty choices and beliefs $\{k_{it}, y_{it}, c_{it}, a_{it+1}, \pi_{it+1}\}_{it}$ and a return to risky investments $\{r_t\}_t$ such that (i) dynasties maximize their expected utility in equation (11) under uncertainty about e_{it} and maximize their utility in equation (5) after e_{it} is realized; (ii) beliefs are consistent with Bayes's rule in equation (4); (iii) the asset market in equation (13) clears; and (iv) the expropriation rule in equation (15) is satisfied.

F. Illustrative Example

The goal of the example is to show the mechanism by which labor-market exclusions generate wealth divergence and to highlight the role of equilibrium effects in amplifying this divergence. Figure 2 presents historical realizations for three illustrative dynasties. The first, which we label the *Rockefeller* dynasty represented by the dot-dashed line, is White and always has high wage z_{it}. The second, which we label the *Average Joe* dynasty represented by the dashed line, is White and has lower z_{it}. The third, which we label the *Boyd* dynasty represented by the solid line, has as high z_{it} as Rockefeller but is Black and hence enslaved between 1780 and 1860. All dynasties are identical in terms of their potential investment experiences e_{it} in the lower panel. We feed the realizations of z_{it} and e_{it} into the analytical solutions of Subsection II.B to generate the dynasties' evolution of occupational choice, beliefs, and wealth.[13]

Figure 3 narrates the history of the dynasties in partial equilibrium. By partial equilibrium, we mean the case with $\alpha \to \infty$ and thus a constant risky return r_t. Beginning with the Rockefeller dynasty, we see that by 1840 it has accumulated sufficient wealth to become capitalists. In 1860, during the Civil War, Rockefeller has a negative experience that discourages entrepreneurship until 1940. Thereafter, the Rockefeller dynasty continues to have positive investment experiences, resulting in its beliefs converging to the truth and a significant accumulation of

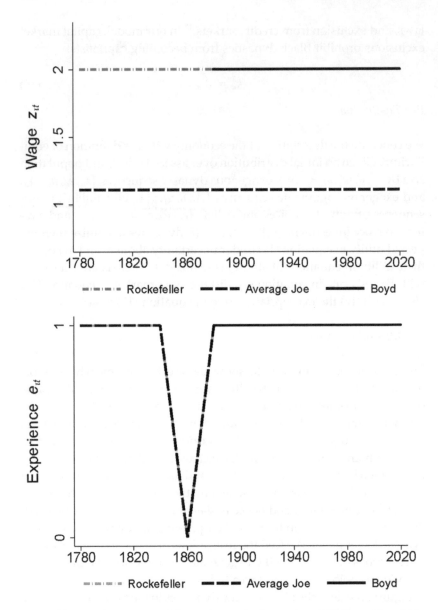

Fig. 2. Wages and entrepreneurial experiences. A color version of this figure is available online.

wealth. Average Joe differs from Rockefeller because the dynasty never accumulates enough wealth to make entrepreneurship worthwhile. Average Joe remains a laborer, does not update beliefs, and ends up with low wealth. Boyd is initially enslaved and prohibited from building

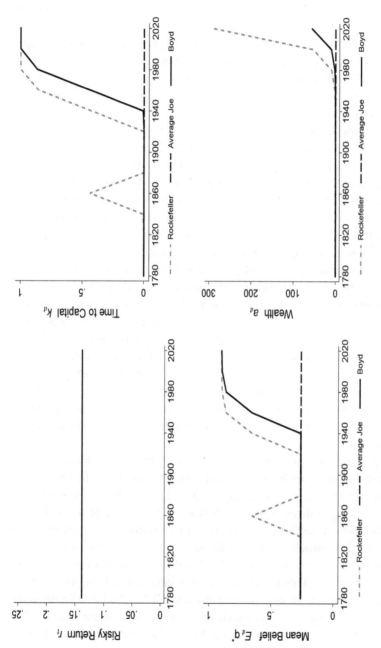

Fig. 3. Illustrative example in partial equilibrium. A color version of this figure is available online.

wealth. In partial equilibrium, Boyd eventually catches up with Rockefeller, becomes a capitalist, updates beliefs toward the truth, and accumulates wealth.

The evolution of occupational choice and wealth is different in general equilibrium, as shown in figure 4. By general equilibrium, we mean the case with $\alpha < \infty$ and, thus, a declining risky return r_t.[14] General equilibrium generates different predictions, as slavery early on coincides with higher return and the abolition of slavery coincides with lower return. Owing to the high initial return, Rockefeller becomes capitalist earlier in general equilibrium than in partial equilibrium. Good experiences encourage continued investments and wealth accumulation throughout history. Given high initial returns, even Average Joe becomes capitalist. However, after the bad experience of 1860, its wealth and the return are sufficiently low to discourage the dynasty from further investment activity. The Boyd dynasty never catches up with Rockefeller in general equilibrium, despite having the same wage. In general equilibrium, the return on risky investments is low after the abolition of slavery, discouraging Boyd from becoming capitalist and from accumulating wealth.

Equilibrium effects, through which returns on wealth accumulation during slavery are higher than returns in recent times, discourage Black dynasties from becoming capitalists. An example of an asset captured by the general equilibrium model is land, which was initially unexploited and offered high returns. The absence of early positive investment experiences for Black dynasties leads them to have more pessimistic beliefs about risky investments than White dynasties and causes a more persistent racial divergence of wealth than would occur if returns were constant.

We conclude by previewing the logic of why, in our model, a one-time transfer may not lead to wealth convergence in the future even if it eliminates the racial wealth gap today. Figure 5 shows the evolution of wealth for the three dynasties following a redistribution of wealth that eliminates wealth inequality in 2040. In partial equilibrium, Boyd accumulates as much wealth as Rockefeller after reparations. In general equilibrium, beginning in 2060, Boyd's wealth falls behind White dynasties' wealth. This result can be understood in terms of the policy function for the choice of capital in equation (12), which we summarize as $k(z, a, \mathbb{E}q^*; r)$. Despite having equal wage z and assets a with Rockefeller in 2040, relatively pessimistic beliefs $\mathbb{E}q^*$ and the relatively low return r lead Boyd to choose labor and forgo the opportunity to invest. By contrast, given optimistic beliefs, White dynasties continue to be

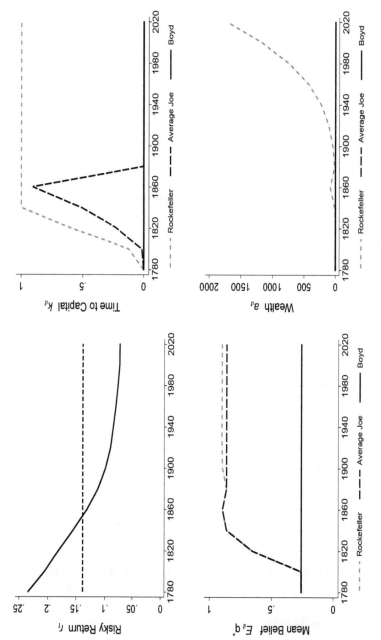

Fig. 4. Illustrative example in general equilibrium. A color version of this figure is available online.

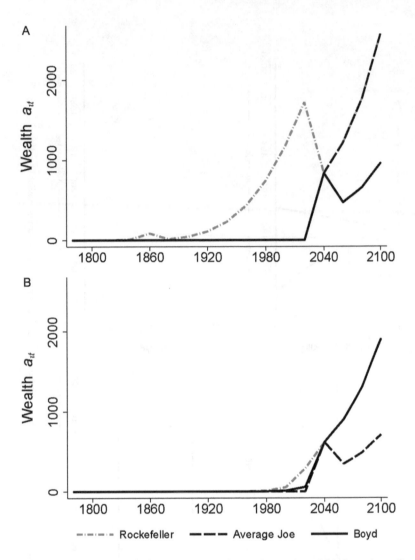

Fig. 5. Wealth transfers in the illustrative example. A color version of this figure is available online.

capitalists. As a result, wealth for the two types of dynasties diverges forever.

III. Quantitative Results

We first describe inputs to the model and the parameterization strategy. Next, we evaluate the ability of the model to account for racial gaps in wealth, income, entrepreneurship, mobility, and beliefs, none of which are targeted by the parameterization. Finally, we present welfare analyses and counterfactuals when removing labor and capital market exclusions and changing structural features of the economy.

A. Model Inputs

A model period is 20 years. We begin in 1780, which roughly corresponds to the Declaration of Independence. Slavery ends in 1860, $\chi_t^\ell = 0$, the model period closest to the time when Congress passed the Thirteenth Amendment, which abolished slavery. We remove capital market restrictions on Black dynasties in 1960, $\chi_t^k = 0$, aligning with the start of the civil rights movement. The last historical model period is 2020 and we consider policy experiments beginning in 2040.

We use tables from the US Census between 1780 and 2000 for the population of Black and White dynasties, N_t^b and N_t^w. The fraction of Black dynasties in 1780 is $\phi_1 = 0.21$. We present annualized population growth in the first two columns of table 1. The White population grows

Table 1
Population and Wages

	Population Growth		Wages			
	White	Black	Agg. Growth	Racial Gap	Persistence	Dispersion
	$(1 + n^w)^{\frac{1}{20}} - 1$	$(1 + n^b)^{\frac{1}{20}} - 1$	$(1 + g)^{\frac{1}{20}} - 1$	μ^b	ρ	σ
1780	3.40	2.81	.39	.28	.40	.71
1800	3.06	2.89	.39	.28	.40	.71
1820	2.99	2.45	1.00	.28	.40	.71
1840	3.23	2.20	1.27	.28	.40	.71
1860	2.40	1.98	1.40	.28	.40	.71
1880	2.19	1.48	1.68	.30	.40	.71
1900	1.74	.85	1.32	.32	.40	.71
1920	1.09	1.04	.82	.35	.40	.71
1940	1.39	1.93	2.29	.38	.40	.71
1960	.64	1.71	2.28	.44	.35	.63
1980	.07	1.35	2.01	.57	.32	.67
2000	.07	.07	1.43	.62	.58	.85
2020	.07	.07	1.43	.65	.58	.85

Note: This table presents the time series for population growth and for parameters of the wage process. Growth rates are in percentages and annualized. The last measured population growth rates are between 1980 and 2000; beyond 2000, we use the population growth for non-Hispanic Whites between 1980 and 2000. For the wage process, we set missing values to their closest available estimates.

more until the early 1900s, and the Black population grows faster after that.[15]

The wage of dynasty ι belonging to race h in period t is

$$z_{\iota t}^{h} = \max\{Z_t \mu_t^h \theta_{\iota t}, \bar{c}_t\}, \tag{17}$$

where Z_t is the aggregate component, μ_t^h is the race-specific component, and $\theta_{\iota t}$ is the idiosyncratic component of wages. Wages are adjusted so that they do not fall below the subsistence level of consumption $\bar{c}_t$. The idiosyncratic component follows the autoregressive process:

$$\log\theta_{\iota t} = \rho_t \log\theta_{\iota t-1} + \sigma_t \varepsilon_{\iota t}, \tag{18}$$

where ρ_t governs the persistence across generations, σ_t governs the cross-sectional dispersion of wages, and the shock $\varepsilon_{\iota t}$ is drawn from a standard normal distribution. Persistence ρ_t and dispersion σ_t are common across all dynasties.

The last four columns of table 1 present the evolution of the four parameters of the wage process. The aggregate component of wages evolves as $Z_t = (1 + g_t)Z_{t-1}$, with its growth rate g_t being equal to the growth of gross domestic product per capita from the Maddison project (Bolt and van Zanden 2020). For the race component, $\mu_t^w = 1$ for White dynasties and μ_t^b for Black dynasties is presented in the fourth column of the table. We take the racial gap in wages from Margo (2016), who uses labor force participation rates for agricultural workers and urban workers to compute Black-White relative income starting from 1870.[16] We set the persistence ρ_t from the intergenerational mobility study of Aaronson and Mazumder (2008), who match men in the census to synthetic parents in the prior generation starting from 1940. Finally, we use the American Community Survey to estimate the cross-sectional dispersion σ_t from 1940 onward.[17]

All dynasties begin with zero initial wealth, $a_{\iota 1} = 0$. We feed into the model an asset limit that evolves as $\bar{A}_t = \bar{A}_1(1 + g)^{t-1}(1 + n)^{t-1}$, where the initial value $\bar{A}_1$ is a parameter. We increase $\bar{A}_t$ at a rate equal to the growth rate of wages g and population n, allowing the model to asymptote to a balanced growth path with constant returns and factor shares.

B. Parameterization

Table 2 presents our parameter values. The upper panel shows parameter values chosen externally without solving the model. The lower panel

Table 2
Model Parameters

Parameter		Value	Source/Logic
Curvature of utility	γ	1.00	Log preferences
Returns to scale	α	1.77	Inverse of labor share
Depreciation rate (annual)	$1 - (1 - \delta)^{1/20}$	.05	NIPA fixed assets
Safe return (annual)	$(1 + i)^{1/20} - 1$	.02	Jordà et al. (2019)
Discount factor (annual)	$\beta^{1/20}$	.98	Match targets
Probability of success	q^*	.91	Match targets
Initial asset limit	$\bar{A}_1$	.23	Match targets
Subsistence consumption	$\bar{c}_t$	$.81 Z_t$	Match targets
Shape beta distribution	$\bar{q}$	.30	Match targets
Shape beta distribution	b	1.20	Match targets

Note: This table presents values of model parameters. The upper panel shows parameters' values chosen externally. The lower panel shows parameters' values chosen so that model-generated variables match their analogs in the data. NIPA = National Income and Product Accounts.

shows parameter values chosen so that model-generated moments match their data analogs. Table 3 presents the targeted moments.

Preferences are logarithmic, $\gamma = 1$. We use the inverse of the labor share from national income and product accounts to set $\alpha = 1.77$. The annual rate of depreciation, $1 - (1 - \delta)^{1/20} = 0.05$, equals the average annual depreciation rate of private fixed assets in national income and product accounts. Finally, for the real safe return, we pick $i = 0.02$ using the average return on real safe assets from Jordà et al. (2019).

The distribution of beliefs in 1780 is $\text{Beta}(b\bar{q}_{\iota1}/1 - \bar{q}_{\iota1}, b)$. The prior mean, $\bar{q}_{\iota1} = \mathbb{E}_{\iota1}q^*$, is heterogeneous across dynasties ι. Heterogeneity in initial expected returns allows the model to generate significant wealth inequality as optimistic dynasties become capitalists before pessimistic dynasties. Initial expected returns are drawn from a uniform distribution,

Table 3
Model Targets

Target (2020)		Data	Model
Wealth/lifetime income	$\int a d\Phi / \int y d\Phi$	.25	.25
Labor share	$\int z(1 - k) d\Phi / \int y d\Phi$	.56	.56
Risky return	$q^* r$	.07	.07
Top 10% wealth share	$\int_{0.9}^{1} a d\Phi / \int a d\Phi$	.76	.76
Top 50% wealth share	$\int_{0.5}^{1} a d\Phi / \int a d\Phi$	.99	.98
Entrepreneurship rate	$\int \mathbb{I}(k > 0) d\Phi$	.03	.03

Note: This table presents the moments targeted to estimate the parameters in the lower panel of table 2.

$\bar{q}_{d1} \sim U(0, \bar{q})$. Given $\bar{q}_{d1}$, parameter b governs the dispersion of beliefs and is common across dynasties. Initial beliefs vary within group, but Black and White dynasties draw from the same initial distribution so that initial beliefs are identical across race.

Besides parameters for initial beliefs, $\bar{q}$ and b, we pick the discount factor β, the objective probability of a good experience q^*, the initial asset limit $\bar{A}_1$, and subsistence levels of consumption $\bar{c}_t$ to target six moments. Table 3 shows that we target the wealth-to-income ratio, the labor share, the risky return, the share of wealth accruing to the top 10% and 50% of the wealth distribution, and the entrepreneurship rate.[18]

The model matches these targets with (annualized) discount factor $\beta^{1/20} = 0.98$ and probability of successful entrepreneurship $q^* = 0.91$. The parameter estimates favor dispersed initial beliefs around a pessimistic mean ($\bar{q}/2 = 0.15$). These beliefs imply that few initially more optimistic dynasties end up being capitalists. Given the high probability of success q^*, these few capitalists hold a significant fraction of wealth in the economy, helping the model match the high concentration of wealth at the top. Finally, the subsistence consumption value $\bar{c}_t$ implies strong nonhomotheticity in preferences, helping the model account for the observation that the bottom half of the population owns almost none of the economy's wealth.[19]

C. Comparing the Model with the Data

In this section, we evaluate the ability of the model to generate current and historical racial gaps in outcomes such as wealth, income, entrepreneurship, mobility, and beliefs about risky returns.

Wealth and Income

Table 4 compares the concentration of wealth and income in the model with the data. The measure of concentration is the share of wealth and income held by households above selected percentiles of their respective distributions. The data come from the SCF between 2010 and 2019, corresponding to model period 2020. The model accounts almost perfectly for the wealth concentration in the data up to the 5th percentile. The model also performs well in terms of matching the observed income concentration up to the 5th percentile. Above that percentile, the model overestimates wealth and income concentration relative to the data.[20]

Table 4
Wealth and Income Concentration

2020, Share of Top (%)	Wealth		Income	
	Data	Model	Data	Model
50	.99	.98	.86	.89
20	.87	.86	.62	.71
10	.76	.76	.47	.59
5	.64	.67	.37	.51
1	.37	.53	.20	.39
.1	.14	.25	.07	.18

Note: This table presents the share of wealth and income held by households above selected percentiles of their respective distributions. The data moments are calculated from the Survey of Consumer Finances between 2010 and 2019.

We next assess the ability of the model to generate racial gaps in wealth and income not targeted by the parameterization. In table 5, we report ratios of average variables for Black households relative to those of White households. In the SCF, the ratio of average wealth is 0.15 and the ratio of average income is 0.45. These large racial gaps are consistent with previous findings in the literature such as those in the recent work of Kuhn, Schularick, and Steins (2020). The model is successful in generating the large racial differences in average wealth and income observed in the data. Similar to the data, the model also generates a lower ratio for median wealth than for average wealth and a higher ratio of median income than of average income.

Wealth in the SCF is net worth from all assets minus liabilities, which includes public equity, business assets, real estate, owner-occupied

Table 5
Racial Gap in Wealth and Income

2020, Black/White	Wealth Ratio		Income Ratio	
	Data	Model	Data	Model
Mean	.15	.17	.45	.36
99th percentile	.13	.19	.25	.28
90th percentile	.19	.41	.51	.58
50th percentile	.10	.06	.57	.59

Note: This table presents the Black to White ratio of wealth and income at the mean and selected percentiles of the corresponding distributions. The data moments are calculated from the Survey of Consumer Finances between 2010 and 2019.

housing, bonds, durables, and other savings accounts. We interpret a_{it} in the model as encompassing all these forms of wealth as is consistent with this definition. To assess the relative importance of different types of assets in accounting for the racial gap in total wealth, we decompose the racial wealth gap as follows:

$$\text{Gap} = 1 - \frac{\text{Wealth}^b}{\text{Wealth}^w} = \sum_j \frac{\text{Asset}_j^w}{\text{Wealth}^w}\left(1 - \frac{\text{Asset}_j^b}{\text{Asset}_j^w}\right), \quad (19)$$

where wealth is the sum over all assets j. Equation (19) decomposes the gap between White and Black wealth into gaps arising from different asset classes, where the asset-specific gaps are weighted by the portfolio weights of White households.

The first row of table 6 applies this decomposition to the model. Wealth in our model is invested in risky assets, $k_{it}a_{it}$, and safe assets, $(1 - k_{it})a_{it}$. The portfolio weight on risky assets for White households is 58%. The contribution of risky assets to the total wealth gap is 70%. The second row performs the same decomposition in the SCF. Risky investments in our model correspond to investments in public equity, real estate investment excluding own housing, and private business assets.[21] We obtain a portfolio weight of 58% in the data, perfectly matching the portfolio weight of risky assets in the model. Further, similar to the model, we find that the racial gap in risky assets accounts for more than half of the total gap in the data.

The other rows repeat these decompositions for subcategories of assets to assess their relative importance in accounting for the total wealth gap in the data. Rows 3 and 4 present the two largest subcategories of risky assets, investments in public equity and investments in private

Table 6
Decomposition of Racial Wealth Gap

	2020	Asset Type	Portfolio Weight	Contribution to Wealth Gap
1.	Model	Risky	.58	.70
2.	Data	Risky	.58	.60
3.	Data	Public equity	.25	.26
4.	Data	Private equity	.33	.34
5.	Data	Owner-occupied housing	.18	.15
6.	Data	Bonds	.18	.18

Note: This table shows for various types of assets their contribution to the racial wealth gap defined in equation (19) and their portfolio weights. The data entries come from the Survey of Consumer Finances between 2010 and 2019.

equity, with the latter including assets used in private businesses and real estate activities excluding owner-occupied housing. Rows 5 and 6 present the two largest subcategories of safe assets, investments in owner-occupied housing and bonds. With respect to the largest types of assets, we find that for the racial wealth gap in total wealth, private equity is the most important asset and owner-occupied housing is the least important asset.

Wealth Convergence

We next assess the ability of the model to generate a realistic speed of wealth convergence across race. Matching the historical speed of convergence lends credibility to the model when analyzing how reparations affect the future evolution of the racial wealth gap. Table 7 presents the gap between Black and White average wealth in 1900 and 2020. The gap for the early period comes from the historical evidence of Higgs (1982), who uses Georgia tax assessment records to measure wealth by race, and Margo (1984), who complements this analysis with data from Arkansas, Kentucky, Louisiana, North Carolina, and Virginia. The historical data show a slow convergence of Black wealth, with the gap decreasing from 96% in 1900 to 85% in 2020. We characterize this convergence as slow compared with the convergence of wages, with the wage gap changing from 68% to 35%. Our model is successful in generating such a slow convergence of wealth, with the wealth gap changing from 98% to 83%.[22]

Entrepreneurship

The model generates significant racial wealth and income gaps partly because White dynasties are more likely to be capitalists than Black

Table 7
Evolution of Racial Wealth and Wage Gap

Gap (1 − Black/White)	Wealth		Wage	
	Data	Model	Data	Model
1900	.96	.98	.68	.68
2020	.85	.83	.35	.35

Note: This table presents the average wealth and wage gaps in 1900 and 2020. The data entry for wealth in 1900 is from Higgs (1982) and Margo (1984). The data entry for wealth in 2020 comes from the Survey of Consumer Finances between 2010 and 2019. The data entries for wages are from Margo (2016).

Table 8
Entrepreneurship

	White		Black	
	Data	Model	Data	Model
A. Fraction entrepreneurs (%)	3.1	3.6	.3	0

	Wealth		Income	
	Data	Model	Data	Model
B. Entrepreneurs share of top . . .:				
50%	.88	.96	.89	.98
20%	.66	.84	.68	.87
10%	.57	.68	.52	.71
5%	.39	.52	.40	.54
1%	.20	.23	.19	.24
.1%	.06	.06	.06	.07

Note: This table presents statistics of entrepreneurship. The first panel shows the share of households who are entrepreneurs and the second panel shows the share of wealth and income held by entrepreneurs above selected percentiles of their respective distributions. The data entries come from the Survey of Consumer Finances (SCF) between 2010 and 2019. In the SCF, we define an individual as an entrepreneur, $k > 0$, if their business assets exceed average net worth in the survey.

dynasties. Are such differences in entrepreneurship rates present in the data? Panel A of table 8 shows differences in entrepreneurship rates by race. Quantitatively, the model generates a 3.6 percentage point gap in the entrepreneurship rate, close to the 2.8 percentage point gap in the data.[23] In addition, in panel B of table 8, the model performs well in matching the observed distribution of wealth and income within entrepreneurs. For example, the top 1% of entrepreneurs hold 20% of entrepreneurial wealth in the data, compared with 23% in the model.

Income Mobility

We next assess the ability of the model to generate historical patterns of income mobility by race. The evidence comes from Collins and Wanamaker (2017), who link individual census records between 1910 and 1930 to derive historical mobility statistics and use National Longitudinal Survey of Youth data for the more recent period. Entries in table 9 show upward rank mobility probabilities by decile d:

$$\text{Upward rank mobility}(d) = \mathbb{P}(\text{rank}(y_t)$$
$$> \text{rank}(y_{t-1})|\text{rank}(y_{t-1}) \in d). \tag{20}$$

Table 9
Upward Rank Mobility

	Data		Model	
Decile d	White	Black	White	Black
(1990):				
1	.97	.80	.88	.82
3	.76	.54	.67	.50
5	.58	.51	.51	.38
7	.36	–	.39	.27
9	.31	–	.24	.16
(1930):				
1	.90	.68	.86	.59
3	.59	.31	.65	.33
5	.38	–	.50	.22
7	.28	–	.39	.13
9	.16	–	.25	–

Note: This table presents probabilities of upward rank mobility at selected deciles of the income distribution. Data entries are from Collins and Wanamaker (2017). Missing entries indicate no or very few observations to calculate probabilities.

This statistic measures the probability that a child exceeds their parents' rank in the income distribution for a parent belonging to decile d. Rank is measured within the total population, including both Black and White dynasties.

Beginning with the upper panel of table 9, we see that the model is successful in generating a racial mobility gap in the latter period. For example, starting at the third decile, 76% of White children exceed their parents' rank, whereas only 54% of Black children do so. The observed gap of 22 percentage points is close to the 17 percentage point gap generated by the model. As seen in the lower panel of table 9, the model is also successful in generating even larger mobility gaps observed during the early 1900s. For example, again at the third decile, 59% of White children exceeded their parents' rank, whereas only 31% of Black children did so. The observed gap of 28 percentage points is close to the 32 percentage point gap generated by the model.

Two features of the model allow it to generate mobility patterns similar to the patterns in the data. First, only White dynasties become entrepreneurs and, given the high returns from entrepreneurship, entrepreneurs are more likely to surpass laborers in the income distribution. Second, despite persistence parameter ρ_t and dispersion parameter σ_t

being common across all dynasties in the wage process (eq. [18]), Black dynasties are less likely to move upward in the total population's income distribution, because they draw wages from a distribution with a lower mean than the average dynasty in the population, as shown by the race component of wages μ_t^h in equation (17). Because the racial wage gap was larger in the 1900s, Black dynasties were less likely to move upward in the 1900s than today.

Beliefs about Risky Returns

The model generates a racial belief gap in response to the labor and capital market exclusions that do not allow Black dynasties to participate in markets. We now compare model predictions for beliefs about risky returns to measures of beliefs about equity returns in survey responses from the University of Michigan's Surveys of Consumers.[24] The question we use is: Think about a diversified stock fund which holds stock in many different companies engaged in a wide variety of activities. Suppose someone were to invest one thousand dollars in such a mutual fund. What do you think is the chance this one thousand dollar investment will increase in value, so that it is worth more than one thousand dollars one year from now?

We use Michigan Survey responses to this question between June 2002 and December 2015. We merge these data to microdata samples, available through the Inter-university Consortium for Political and Social Research, which contain the respondent's race. We restrict our sample to include Black and White individuals between 25 and 65 years of age. The cleaned data set contains 42,756 observations. Roughly 10% of respondents identify as Black.[25]

The response to the Michigan Survey question is a probability assessment that a diversified equity fund increases in value. The difficulty in comparing beliefs in the model with survey responses is that respondents in the data may have a benchmark return other than zero in their mind (say, because of inflation) and that dynasties in our model have the option to invest in a safe technology featuring growth. Our solution is to choose a benchmark return in the model, called $\bar{r}$, such that the model-generated average probability assessment that risky investments exceed this benchmark $\bar{r}$ matches the average probability assessment of 0.51 from the survey. Formally, for each dynasty, we calculate the probability $P_t(\pi_{it}, \bar{r})$ that the economy-wide risky return exceeds $\bar{r}$, evaluated under their model-generated belief π_{it} in 2020:

$$P_t(\pi_{it}, \bar{r}) = \int_{q:\, qr_i > \bar{r}} \pi_{it}(q) dq. \qquad (21)$$

The model-generated average probability assessment equals $\int P_{it} d\Phi = 0.51$ for $\bar{r} = 0.006$.

Having targeted the average response in the total population, we evaluate the ability of the model to generate dispersion of beliefs. Table 10 summarizes our results. In the first row, the mean probability of successful investment in the total population is the same in the model and the data by construction. The second and third rows show the mean probability for White and Black households. The racial gap in mean beliefs is 12 percentage points in the model, compared with 7 percentage points in the data.[26] At the same time, the model generates a dispersion of beliefs in the total population as large as that measured in the data. The model replicates almost perfectly the dispersion of beliefs within White households but underestimates the dispersion of beliefs within Black households.

D. Racial Welfare Gap

We calculate the racial welfare gap and decompose it into a component reflecting differences in wages and a component reflecting differences in wealth. Our welfare gap is the tax T_{it} that would make a White dynasty with $(z_{it}^w, a_{it}^w, \mathbb{E}_{it}^w q^*)$ indifferent to being a Black dynasty with $(z_{it}^b, a_{it}^b, \mathbb{E}_{it}^b q^*)$. Formally, we find the tax that solves

Table 10
Beliefs about Risky Returns

Probability of Successful Investment	Data	Model
Mean	.51	.51
Mean, White	.51	.53
Mean, Black	.44	.41
Standard deviation	.29	.28
Standard deviation, White	.29	.30
Standard deviation, Black	.29	.16

Note: This table presents statistics on the probability assessment of successful investments. Data entries show means and standard deviations of the probability of an increase in the value of a diversified stock fund as reported in the Michigan Survey. The data contain 42,756 observations. Roughly 10% of respondents identify as Black.

$$V(z_{\iota t}^b, a_{\iota t}^b, \mathbb{E}_{\iota t}^b q^*) = \hat{V}(z_{\iota t}^w, a_{\iota t}^w, \mathbb{E}_{\iota t}^w q^*; \mathcal{T}_{\iota t}), \qquad (22)$$

where V is the maximized expected utility in equation (11) that takes into account the optimal occupational choice and the allocation of resources between consumption and intergenerational transfers after the realization of the investment shock. The value $\hat{V}$ is the same value but under tax $\mathcal{T}_{\iota t}$, which subtracts resources from the income side of the budget constraint in equation (6).

In calculating $\mathcal{T}_{\iota t}$, we compare White and Black dynasties that are identical in terms of history of wage and investment shocks $\{\varepsilon_{\iota j}, e_{\iota j}\}_{j=1}^t$. In the absence of historical exclusions, the two dynasties would thus be identical.[27] When both White and Black dynasties are laborers, the solution for the racial welfare gap for dynasty ι is as follows:

$$\mathcal{T}_{\iota t} = (z_{\iota t}^w + (1 + i_t - \delta)a_{\iota t}^w) - (z_{\iota t}^b + (1 + i_t - \delta)a_{\iota t}^b). \qquad (23)$$

For laborers, the welfare gap equals the difference in available resources for consumption and intergenerational transfers in the budget constraint (eq. [6]). Because both races have the same preferences and production technologies, equalizing resources leads to identical consumption and intergenerational transfers and eliminates welfare differences.

Table 11 presents the racial welfare gap at various percentiles of the welfare gap distribution. The gaps are annualized for ease of interpretation. In the first column, the median gap equals 0.03 times average wealth in the economy. Applying an average wealth of $750,000 leads to a median welfare gap of $22,500 per year. The mean welfare gap is $105,000. What explains the significant difference between median and mean welfare gaps? As the first column shows, the distribution of welfare

Table 11
Racial Welfare Gaps

Relative to Mean Wealth (2020)	Baseline	No Wages	No Wealth
Mean	.14	.11	.10
99th percentile	1.26	1.25	1.07
95th percentile	.18	.06	.13
90th percentile	.12	.04	.09
75th percentile	.07	.02	.05
50th percentile	.03	.01	.02

Note: This table presents statistics of the welfare difference $\mathcal{T}$ in equation (22) and decompositions of the welfare difference between the component due to differences in wages and differences in assets.

gaps is significantly dispersed, with the welfare gaps at the top far exceeding the welfare gaps at the middle of the distribution.

To understand the relative importance of wages and wealth in accounting for the racial welfare gap, in the second column we present the same statistics when we equalize wages and in the third column we present the same statistics when we equalize wealth between Black and White dynasties *ι* that share the same history of shocks. The mean gap falls from 0.14 to 0.11 when we equalize wages and to 0.10 when we equalize wealth. The reductions in racial gaps do not add up to the total welfare gap, partly because wages and wealth covary positively in the cross section and partly because dynasties have different beliefs, which we do not change. For the mean welfare gap, we find a larger contribution of wealth than of wages. However, wages become the dominant source of the welfare gap for most of the distribution, as wealth differences matter most at the top of the distribution.

It is instructive to compare our results with those of Brouillette et al. (2021), who construct a measure of consumption-equivalent welfare for Black and White dynasties. The first difference between the two approaches is the sources of welfare differences. Relative to them, we incorporate utility from intergenerational transfers to descendants. Relative to us, they account for life expectancy, mortality, and leisure differences. The second difference is that we have an equilibrium framework that expresses arguments of the utility function (consumption and intergenerational transfers) as a function of primitives, and Brouillette et al. (2021) change directly inputs to the utility function (e.g., consumption) in measuring welfare differences. Although our approach comes with added complexity, it has the conceptual advantage of being able to account for dynasty responses with respect to changes in policies such as reparations.

Despite these differences, we highlight some similarities between our results and those of Brouillette et al. (2021). The authors calculate a 35% gap in consumption equivalents for the recent period, translating to a mean welfare gap of roughly $45,000. Our mean welfare gap is almost twice as large because we take into account the tail of the wealth distribution that introduces a significant deviation between mean and median welfare gap. Our welfare gap aligns with the estimate of Brouillette et al. (2021) around the 75th percentile of the welfare gap distribution.

E.   *How Historical Events Shape Today's Racial Gaps*

We conclude this section by evaluating the effects of historical events and features of the model economy on current racial gaps. Table 12

Table 12
Counterfactual History

2020, Black over White	Wealth Ratio	Income Ratio	Entrepreneurship Gap
A. All differences:	.17	.36	−3.6
− Labor exclusion	.43	.60	−3.3
− Capital exclusion	.17	.36	−3.6
− Demographics	.18	.37	−3.6
B. No differences:	1.00	1.00	0
+ Labor exclusion	.18	.37	−3.6
+ Capital exclusion	.47	.62	−3.2
+ Demographics	1.37	1.28	.9
C. Baseline:	.17	.36	−3.6
$\beta^{1/20} = .95$	.25	.47	−2.7
$q^* = .70$	.25	.48	−2.3
$\bar{c} = 0.50Z$	.24	.39	−7.6
$\gamma = 3$	.20	.40	−.6

Note: This table presents counterfactual outcomes when we remove historical events driving racial differences in the model (panel A), when we add historical events driving racial differences in the model (panel B), and when we change features of the model environment relative to the baseline (panel C).

summarizes our results. Panel A shows the racial gap in wealth, income, and the entrepreneurship rate when we remove historical events. Panel B shows racial gaps when we add historical events starting from no racial differences. Panel C shows racial gaps when we change features of the model economy.

The top panel shows that removing the history of labor-market exclusions from our baseline model results in a ratio of average wealth of 0.43 as opposed to 0.17 with these exclusions, an income ratio of 0.60 as opposed to 0.36, and a gap in entrepreneurship rate of 3.3 percentage points as opposed to 3.6. Without labor-market exclusions, we would also observe gaps today because capital market exclusions prohibit members of the Black dynasties from becoming entrepreneurs. On the other hand, removing only capital market exclusions does not affect current outcomes. Labor-market exclusions on their own put members of Black dynasties at significant disadvantage in terms of becoming capitalists and accumulating wealth, making the incremental effect of capital market exclusions in our model zero.

The middle panel confirms these conclusions by adding historical events one at a time. If there were only demographic differences, Black dynasties in our model would achieve a higher wealth, income, and entrepreneurship rate than White dynasties by 2020. As shown in table 1, in early periods, the population growth of White dynasties is higher than the population growth of Black dynasties, making it more costly for White dynasties to transfer wealth across generations on a per capita basis.

In the lower panel, we assess the role of structural parameters for racial gaps. A lower discount factor β is associated with a higher wealth and income ratio, as dynasties have a lower willingness to bequeath wealth. A lower probability of successful investments q^* is also associated with a higher wealth and income ratio, as White capitalists realize lower income from risky investments. A lower level of subsistence consumption $\bar{c}$ is associated with higher wealth and income ratios, as a smaller fraction of Black dynasties are concentrated at the bottom of the distribution where $\bar{c}$ tends to bind. Finally, wealth and income ratios increase under a higher curvature in the utility function, $\gamma = 3$, because increased risk aversion induces more dynasties to choose safe labor over risky investment activities.

IV.   Policy Experiments

We perform various policy experiments to explore the implications of our model for the future trajectory of the racial wealth gap. We begin by studying the effects of wealth transfers toward Black dynasties. Then, we analyze the alternative policy of subsidizing risky investments by Black entrepreneurs. We conclude by discussing the role of learning from others for wealth convergence.

A.   Wealth Transfers

We first discuss the financing of wealth transfers and their size. Next, we discuss the evolution of racial wage gap and how it affects the wealth gap. We then present the effects of wealth transfers on various outcomes by race.

Transfers and Financing

Wealth transfers to Black dynasties are financed by a one-time unanticipated tax on White dynasties' wealth. The wealth tax rate function, Λ, for White dynasties is

$$\Lambda(a_i^w) = \begin{cases} \lambda & \text{if } a_i^w < a^*, \\ (1-\lambda)\dfrac{a_i^w - a^*}{a_i^w} & \text{if } a_i^w \geq a^*. \end{cases} \tag{24}$$

We consider two forms of financing, which differ in their progressivity.

1. Progressive wealth taxation corresponds to $\lambda = 0$ and $a^* > 0$. Wealth below a^* is not taxed and wealth above a^* is taxed at a 100% rate.

2. Proportional wealth taxation corresponds to $\lambda > 0$ and $a^* \to \infty$. All wealth is taxed at a proportional rate λ.

We consider transfers τ to Black dynasties, resulting in average wealth of Black dynasties being a multiple m of average wealth of White dynasties. For any multiple m, we solve for the tax parameter (either λ or a^*) so that every Black dynasty receives a lump sum equal to τ

$$\int (a_i^b + \tau)\mathrm{d}\Phi^b = m \int (1 - \Lambda(a_i^w))a_i^w \mathrm{d}\Phi^w,$$

$$\text{such that} \quad \phi\tau = (1 - \phi)\int \Lambda(a_i^w)a_i^w \mathrm{d}\Phi^w, \tag{25}$$

where ϕ is the share of Black dynasties in the population.[28]

Our baseline policy is $m = 1$, so that average wealth is equalized between Black and White dynasties at the time of reparations. This is a natural policy to consider, because in the absence of historical exclusions average wealth of Black and White dynasties is equalized. The size of the required transfers is $\tau = 0.75$ relative to the average wealth in the economy. Given average household wealth of $750,000, we obtain a transfer of $562,500 per Black dynasty. Using the Census count of 18 million Black households, we find that aggregate reparation transfers equal roughly $10 trillion. To finance these wealth transfers, the progressive policy taxes at 100% all White wealth exceeding 113 times average wealth, roughly $84 million. The proportional tax rate to finance these transfers is 13%.

Our approach is to calculate the tax and transfer system that eliminates the wealth gap between Black and White dynasties today. Consistent with our approach, Darity and Mullen (2020) propose as criterion the equalization of average wealth and arrive at $8 trillion. Despite its simplicity, our approach results in total wealth transfers of similar magnitude to other estimates in the literature based on the present discounted value of forgone earnings from slavery. For example, Neal (1990) calculates wealth transfers of $1.4 trillion in 1983. Applying the average real return, $i \int (1 - k_t) a_t d\Phi / \int a_t d\Phi + q^* r \int k_t a_t d\Phi / \int a_t d\Phi = 0.05$, and adding an inflation rate of 0.02 yields \$12 trillion.

Wage Equalization

Average wealth differences between Black and White dynasties persist forever in the presence of racial differences in wages. To separate the effects of reparations from the effects of different wages on wealth, we assume that at the time of reparations, labor-market policies are enacted that permanently close the racial gap in wages. Formally, we set the racial component of wages to $\mu_t^b = 1$ in equation (17) for all periods starting in 2040.

Panel A of figure 6 presents the evolution of the ratio of average Black to average White wealth. Without any policies, the dot-dashed line shows a slow convergence of the wealth ratio toward a value of roughly 0.25. Eliminating average wage differences across races permanently increases the wealth ratio to about 0.5, as shown by the solid line. Thus, equalizing average wages permanently eliminates roughly half of the racial wealth gap.

Effects of Transfers on Wealth and Welfare Gaps

Panel A of figure 6 also shows the evolution of the wealth ratio after transfers toward Black dynasties financed either with progressive taxes (short-dashed line) or proportional taxes (long-dashed line). The transfers are enacted in addition to the wage equalization policy. Thus, the value of 0.5 is the long-run wealth ratio in the absence of reparations with which we compare the case of reparations. By construction, the racial wealth ratio is one in 2040 under our baseline policy, which calculates the tax and transfer system that equalizes average wealth. However, under both financing systems, the wealth ratio reverts back to a value of roughly 0.5, which is the long-run wealth ratio in the absence of wealth transfers. Thus, the long-run effect of one-time wealth transfers on the racial wealth gap is zero.

The logic of why transfers do not lead to wealth convergence is the same as the logic in the example of Subsection II.F. Following centuries of exclusions from labor and capital markets, Black dynasties enter the reparations era with pessimistic beliefs about investment returns. Despite having equal mean wages and wealth, the lower expected returns lead members of Black dynasties to forgo risky investments and to

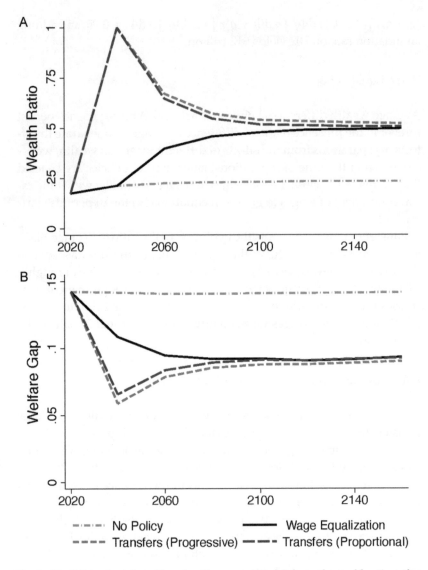

Fig. 6. Evolution of racial wealth and welfare gaps. Panel *A* shows the wealth ratio under no policy changes (dot-dashed line), after eliminating the racial wage gap in 2040 (solid line), after eliminating the racial wage gap and providing wealth transfers financed with progressive wealth taxes in 2040 (short-dashed line), and after eliminating the racial wage gap and providing wealth transfers financed with proportional wealth taxes in 2040 (long-dashed line). Panel *B* presents the average welfare gap under the same scenarios. A color version of this figure is available online.

continue to be laborers. Over time, the economy converges to the same outcome we would have observed without reparations.

Panel *B* of figure 6 shows the evolution of the racial welfare gap. Through the elimination of the wage gap, the welfare gap declines from 0.14 to 0.09. After wealth transfers to Black dynasties, the welfare gap decreases even more in the short run. However, in the longer term, the welfare gap converges to the same value we would have observed without reparations.

Next, we explore the distributional effects of wealth transfers. We define the representation index in period *t* as follows:

$$R_t(p) = \frac{\displaystyle\int_p^1 \mathbb{I}(h_t = b)a_{ut}d\Phi_t}{\phi_t \displaystyle\int_p^1 a_{ut}d\Phi_t},$$

(26)

where p denotes the percentile of the wealth distribution, $\mathbb{I}(h_t = b)$ is an indicator that selects Black dynasties, and ϕ_t is the Black population share. The index captures the Black dynasties' representation in wealth. The numerator equals the wealth of Black dynasties in the top p percentiles of the total wealth distribution. The integral in the denominator equals the wealth of all dynasties in the top p percentiles. We obtain $R_t(0) = 1$ when average wealth is equalized across race. Black dynasties are represented equally, $R_t(p) = 1$ for all p, when the Black wealth share equals the Black population share at all percentiles of the wealth distribution. When Black dynasties are underrepresented in wealth, $R_t(p) < 1$.

Figure 7 shows representation at percentiles of the wealth distribution in 2040, 2060, 2100, and the long run. After reparation transfers in 2040, average wealth is equalized and so representation equals 1 at the zero percentile. The transfers lead to an overrepresentation of Black dynasties between the 50th and the 75th percentile because every Black dynasty receives the same transfer τ, which exceeds the wealth of the median White dynasty. As is consistent with the divergence of wealth and welfare we documented before, over time the representation of Black dynasties tends to values below one. As the last panel demonstrates, Black dynasties do not have greater representation in the long run than in the absence of transfers. Wage equalization improves Black representation in wealth, but it is still significantly lower than in the case without historical exclusions.

Could larger wealth transfers lead to long-run convergence? The first row of table 13 repeats the evolution of the wealth ratio for the baseline

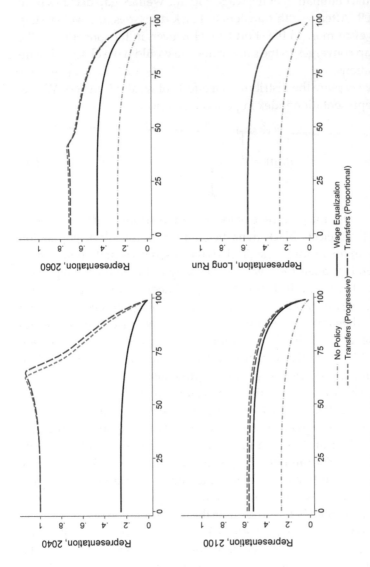

Fig. 7. Representation in wealth: transfers. Figure 7 shows representation in equation (26) as a function of the percentile of the wealth distribution in 2020, 2040, 2100, and the long run. In each panel, we demonstrate the index under no policy changes (dot-dashed line), after eliminating the racial wage gap in 2040 (solid line), after eliminating the racial wage gap and providing wealth transfers financed with progressive wealth taxes in 2040 (dashed line), and after eliminating the racial wage gap and providing wealth transfers financed with proportional wealth taxes in 2040 (long-dashed line). A color version of this figure is available online.

Table 13
Wealth Transfers versus Investment Subsidies

	Relative to Mean Wealth		Wealth Ratio (Black/White)		
	Transfer	Financing	2040	2100	∞
1.	$\tau = .75$	$a^* = 113$	1.00	.54	.52
2.	$\tau = 2.01$	$a^* = 23$	3.00	.70	.52
3.	$s = .22$	$a^* = 113$	.25	.59	.85
4.	$s = .27$	$a^* = 23$	.33	.97	1.00

Note: This table presents the wealth ratio in selected periods under four
reparation programs. The two top rows consider wealth transfers, and
the two bottom rows consider investment subsidies. Both transfers and
subsidies are financed with progressive taxes. In row 1, transfers eliminate the racial wealth gap in 2040 ($m = 1$). In row 2, the average wealth
of Black dynasties in 2040 is three times ($m = 3$) higher than the average
wealth of White dynasties. In rows 3 and 4, we use the same revenues collected in rows 1 and 2 to finance a subsidy s, which is the additional annualized return on successful risky investment activities.

policy, which equalizes wealth between Black and White dynasties. In
the second row, reparation transfers target a wealth ratio of $m = 3$,
which means that we transfer to Black dynasties enough wealth to make
them three times as wealthy as White dynasties. Under $m = 3$, the transfer per Black dynasty is $1.5 million and the progressive financing policy
taxes all wealth above $17 million. Although the divergence of wealth is
slower, the wealth ratio asymptotes again toward roughly 0.5, as with
$m = 1$.[29]

B.   Investment Subsidies

What policy can eliminate the racial wealth gap in the long run? Following centuries of labor and capital market exclusions, Black dynasties enter into reparations with pessimistic beliefs, making their entrepreneurship rates relatively inelastic to wealth transfers. This suggests that more
effective policies directly target the trade-off between labor and capital.
Instead of giving a transfer, we now use collected tax revenues to
finance an investment subsidy for Black capitalists. We calculate the
subsidy s that exhausts the revenues collected by taxing the wealth of
White dynasties:

$$\phi q^*(r + s) \int a_t^b k_t^b d\Phi^b = (1 - \phi) \int \Lambda(a_t^w) a_t^w d\Phi^w. \qquad (27)$$

The two bottom rows of table 13 summarize our results when investment subsidies are financed with progressive taxes. Tax revenues finance

an investment subsidy of 22 percentage points in row 3 and an investment subsidy of 27 percentage points in row 4. The smaller subsidy generates a racial wealth ratio of 0.25 in 2040. Although the policy does not eliminate the wealth gap at the time of the subsidy, it incentivizes risky investments by Black dynasties. Investment subsidies are more powerful than wealth transfers in increasing the wealth ratio in the long run, with the wealth ratio tending to 0.85. In row 4, a 27 percentage point subsidy toward Black capitalists eliminates the racial wealth gap in the long run. Such subsidies effectively offset the pessimistic beliefs of Black dynasties at the time of reparations and reset the conditions of Black dynasties in 2040 to the same conditions of White dynasties.

Figure 8 shows Black representation following subsidies toward risky investment activities. Compared with the wealth transfers in figure 7, subsidies do not increase the representation of Black dynasties in 2040 as much as transfers do. Consistent with the evolution of the average wealth gap, subsidies are more powerful than transfers in generating equal representation of Black dynasties in the long run. In fact, with $m = 3$, Black dynasties are equally represented in wealth in the long run.

C.   Learning from Others' Experiences

An alternative possibility for the convergence of wealth is that Black dynasties learn from others' experiences after reparations. To understand the importance of networks for the speed of learning and the convergence of wealth, we let dynasties learn from others' experiences. Our formulation of learning from others is that dynasties observe outcomes of other dynasties around them, which we label "friends." Every dynasty has a number of own-race friends F^o and a number of cross-race friends F^c. The number of friends is the number of additional experiences that each dynasty potentially observes in a given period, in addition to its own experience. Dynasties observe the entrepreneurial experiences of friends who are entrepreneurs but do not learn from friends who are laborers. As in our baseline model, dynasties do not learn from aggregate variables.[30]

Table 14 summarizes our results when transfers are financed with progressive taxes. The first row repeats the baseline results without learning from others. In row 2, we allow dynasties to potentially observe the experience of one additional dynasty from their own race, $F^o = 1$. The next three rows increase the number of friends from a dynasty's own race F^o to 2, 4, and 10. When dynasties learn from the experiences of others, they update their beliefs at a faster rate toward the objective

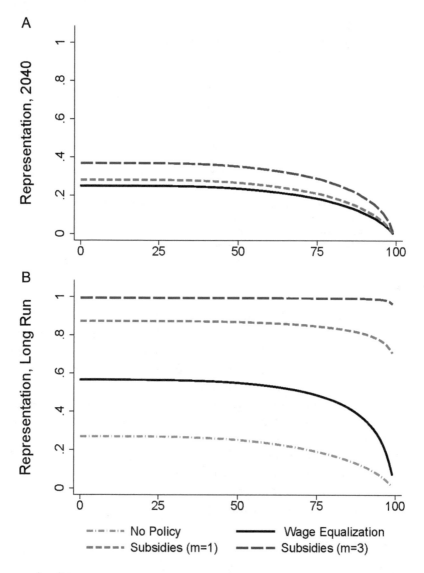

Fig. 8. Representation in wealth: subsidies. Figure 8 shows representation in equation (26) as a function of the percentile of the wealth distribution in 2040 and the long run. In each panel, we demonstrate the index under no policy changes (dot-dashed line), after eliminating the racial wage gap in 2040 (solid line), after eliminating the racial wage gap and providing investment subsidies financed with progressive wealth taxes in 2040 (dashed line), and after eliminating the racial wage gap and providing larger investment subsidies financed with progressive wealth taxes in 2040 (long-dashed line). A color version of this figure is available online.

Table 14
Learning from Others' Experiences after Reparations

	Friends		Wealth Ratio (Black/White)		
	F^o	F^c	2040	2100	∞
1.	0	0	1.00	.54	.52
2.	1	0	1.00	.54	.52
3.	2	0	1.00	.53	.55
4.	4	0	1.00	.53	.63
5.	10	0	1.00	.52	.94
6.	1	1	1.00	.55	1.00

Note: This table presents the wealth ratio under wealth transfers financed with progressive taxes. Each dynasty has a number of own-race friendships F^o and a number of cross-race friendships F^c. The total number of friends equals the number of additional experiences that each dynasty observes in a given period, in addition to their own experience.

probability of success in entrepreneurship q^*. As the table shows, the wealth ratio increases as we increase the number of friends. To eliminate the racial wealth gap in the long run, the model requires more than 10 additional observations. As the wealth ratio in 2100 demonstrates, the speed of convergence is in all cases quite slow.

Another possibility is that dynasties learn from dynasties of the other race. In row 6 of table 14, the racial wealth gap is eliminated after reparations if Black dynasties can observe at least one White dynasty. We interpret this result as showing the importance of interracial networks. To the extent that networks are amenable to policy or technological change, increased learning from others' experiences can complement reparations in closing the racial wealth gap.[31]

V. Conclusion

In this paper, we develop a dynamic, quantitative framework that helps us understand the historical origins of the racial wealth gap and policies that can affect this gap in the future. The model features heterogeneous dynasties, an occupational choice, and bequests, all of which are standard elements in the wealth inequality literature. To these elements, we add learning about risky returns. Our model features endogenous dispersion of beliefs about risky returns, as some dynasties learn from investment experiences of previous generations and other dynasties do not because their members are laborers. Methodologically, our model contributes to the wealth inequality literature by highlighting the importance of heterogeneous expected returns for wealth accumulation and inequality.

We reach a positive answer to the first question we pose: "Under the assumption of no innate racial differences in ability, preferences, or beliefs, to what extent can we account for the magnitude and persistence of the racial wealth gap when feeding into our model the history of exclusions that prevented Black households from participating in labor and capital markets?" When we feed historical events that exclude Black dynasties from labor and capital markets into the model, we find that it is consistent with salient features of the data such as current and historical racial gaps in wealth, income, entrepreneurship, and mobility. We also present evidence that suggests there exists a racial gap in beliefs about risky returns and show that our model is consistent with such a gap.

We reach a negative answer to the second question we pose: "Will reparations today, in the form of direct wealth transfers to Black households, eliminate the racial wealth gap in the long run?" Transfers eliminating the racial wealth gap today do not generate convergence of wealth and welfare and an equal representation in the long run. The logic of the divergence result is that centuries-long exclusions lead members of Black dynasties to enter into the reparations era with pessimistic beliefs about risky returns and to forgo risky investment opportunities. Thus, wealth transfers do not meet our definition of compensating appropriately for historical exclusions, because in the absence of exclusions there would be no racial gaps in our model. However, there are alternative policies that can change the future trajectory of the racial gaps in our model. We show that investment subsidies toward Black dynasties can achieve convergence of racial outcomes in the long run. We also highlight the possibility that dynasties may learn faster after reparations if information networks are stronger than they were in the past. Stronger networks can complement other forms of reparations to eliminate racial gaps in the future.

Endnotes

Authors' email addresses: Boerma (job.boerma@wisc.edu), Karabarbounis (loukas@ umn.edu). The views expressed herein are those of the authors and not necessarily those of the Federal Reserve Bank of Minneapolis or the Federal Reserve System. The authors declare no conflicts of interests and no funding related to this study. For acknowledgments, sources of research support, and disclosure of the authors' material financial relationships, if any, please see https://www.nber.org/books-and-chapters/nber-macroeconomics-annual -2022-volume-37/reparations-and-persistent-racial-wealth-gaps.

1. In April 2019, Senator Booker introduced a bill to "address the fundamental injustice, cruelty, brutality, and inhumanity of slavery in the United States and the 13 American

colonies between 1619 and 1865 and to establish a commission to study and consider a national apology and proposal for reparations for the institution of slavery." Although most policy makers have not explicitly endorsed wealth transfers to descendants of slaves yet, prominent cosponsors of the bill expressed their support to study reparations and make policy recommendations. The bill is available at https://bit.ly/3oyNG9p. Prominent cosponsors include Vice President Harris and Senators Klobuchar, Sanders, and Warren.

2. An example we use to illustrate model mechanisms is the Rockefeller dynasty. When asked how the Rockefellers have managed to preserve wealth over centuries, David Rockefeller Jr., chairman of Rockefeller & Co., stated (https://cnb.cx/2YwePiE) that the family has developed a system of values, traditions, and institutions that have helped the family stay together and preserve its wealth. The family meets twice per year in a forum where heirs talk about the family's direction, projects, and other news related to careers or important milestones.

3. Consistent with our mechanism, Kuvshinov and Zimmermann (2021) document a decline in US expected risky returns since 1890, and Schmelzing (2020) documents a decline in long-term US yields since the late eighteenth century.

4. We calculate transfers to Black dynasties that total $10 trillion and consider progressive and proportional wealth taxes on White dynasties that finance these transfers. Wealth transfers are the most commonly discussed reparation policy (Darity and Mullen 2020). The long-run equalization of average wealth is viewed as a goal from proponents of reparations. For example, Darity and Mullen in their discussion of reparations (https://brook.gs/3j1soQs) argue, "The wealth gap will not persist if the target of well-executed reparations is direct elimination of it."

5. Quantitative work on wealth inequality, such as De Nardi (2004), highlights the role of bequests and nonhomothetic preferences in the emergence of large estates and the transmission of wealth across generations. Nonhomothetic preferences allow models to account for the observation that households with higher lifetime income (Dynan et al. 2004; Straub 2019) or higher wealth (Fagereng et al. 2019) exhibit higher saving rates.

6. Consistent with our model that generates a positive correlation between wealth and expected returns, Bach, Calvet, and Sodini (2020) use asset pricing models to document that households with higher wealth exhibit higher expected returns. Although a novel part of our model is heterogeneity in expected returns, the model is also consistent with "scale dependence," as emphasized by Gabaix et al. (2016), because wealthier dynasties are more likely to be capitalists and realize higher ex post returns. Fagereng et al. (2020) document a positive correlation of ex post returns with wealth and, consistent with our model, persistence of returns across generations.

7. In our model, learning depends directly on own investment experiences and indirectly on the aggregate risky return. In their study of perceptions of intergenerational mobility, Alesina, Stantcheva, and Teso (2018) offer evidence that individuals who have experienced upward mobility in their own life are more optimistic about mobility. In the context of forming inflation expectations, Malmendier and Nagel (2016) present evidence that individuals put more weight on personal experiences than on other available historical data, especially following periods of volatile inflation.

8. We confront quantitatively the model with historical evidence on racial gaps in wealth, wages, and mobility from Higgs (1982), Margo (1984, 2016), and Collins and Wanamaker (2017).

9. Recent work by Kermani and Wong (2021) on housing documents that rate of returns may differ for reasons other than luck and portfolio composition. Adding exogenous differences in returns to our environment, for example by assuming that r_t is higher for White dynasties than for Black dynasties, would increase even more the racial wealth gap.

10. The demand for safe assets is perfectly elastic, implying an exogenous return i_t. In our quantitative results, we set i_t to a constant, but the results are not sensitive to feeding in the time-varying return from Jordà et al. (2019).

11. Our model focuses on physical capital accumulation and does not explicitly consider human capital accumulation. We believe that human capital can be analyzed similar to physical capital, as our model would predict that centuries of exclusions lead Black dynasties to underinvest in human capital and to have more pessimistic beliefs about schooling returns.

12. Cook (2014) uses patent records matched with census data and other survey data from the US Patent Office to argue that the decline in Black patents occurred in areas with higher incidence of race riots and segregation laws between 1870 and 1940. Fairlie, Robb, and Robinson (2020) present evidence from the Kauffman Firm Survey that Black start-ups face more difficulty raising external capital. Even controlling for credit scores and net worth, Black entrepreneurs are significantly more likely than White entrepreneurs to report fear of denial as the reason for not applying for loans.

13. Although some readers may be familiar with Rockefeller, we suspect the story of Henry Boyd is not well known among economists. Boyd was born into slavery in 1802 in Kentucky and later was apprenticed out to a cabinetmaker. Boyd was very skilled and earned money to buy his freedom. He moved to Cincinnati in 1826 as a free man but faced discrimination finding a job. His first job was to unload iron, and eventually he was promoted to janitor. According to historical accounts, one day a White carpenter showed up drunk at work and Boyd substituted. Impressing his boss, Boyd earned enough money as a carpenter to buy the freedom of two of his siblings and open his own business. Unable to patent his bed frame invention, he stamped bedsteads with his name and eventually partnered with a White businessman. Although Boyd expanded his business, arsonists burned his shop three times and companies denied him insurance, resulting in business closure in 1862. In the early 1990s, Boyd's estate in Cincinnati was torn down and turned into a garage. See https://bit.ly/3iULZBY and https://bit.ly/2Ny8AII for some original sources on these historical accounts.

14. Kuvshinov and Zimmermann (2021) document a decline in expected risky returns for many countries, including the United States, since 1890. The 2 percentage points decline in r_t during the twentieth century in figure 4 is quantitatively consistent with the decline in expected returns documented by these authors.

15. For periods 2020 and after, we extrapolate population figures using the average annual growth rate of non-Hispanic Whites between 1980 and 2000 and set $1 + n = 1.0007^{20}$ for both Black and White dynasties. Our model population excludes American Indian, Hispanic, and Asian individuals, as well as individuals who identify with multiple races. In our model, every Black dynasty is enslaved until 1860. According to census sources, roughly 90% of the Black population in the United States was enslaved by 1860.

16. The first observations in Margo (2016) are for 1870, 1900, and 1940. We interpolate linearly to set the racial wage gap in 1880 and 1920. We use the 1870 observation for the racial wage gap in model period 1860 and before. The more recent data after 1940 come from census records. Aizer et al. (2020) study the role of defense production during World War II for closing the racial wage gap after 1940. Derenoncourt and Montialoux (2021) study the role of expansions of the federal minimum wage for closing the racial earnings and income gap during the civil rights era. Bayer and Charles (2018) document that, despite the narrowing of the racial gap in median earnings between 1940 and 1970, the median Black man's rank in the total earnings distribution did not improve significantly.

17. Our estimates are dispersion of log income and control for age and race fixed effects.

18. Average wealth to income equals household net worth over gross domestic product from the Flow of Funds. The risky return is taken from Jordà et al. (2019) and is adjusted for inflation. The shares of wealth accruing to the top 10% and 50% and the entrepreneurship rate are calculated from the SCF between 2010 and 2019. For the entrepreneurship rate, we define an individual as an entrepreneur, $k > 0$, if their business assets exceed average net worth in the survey.

19. We parameterize $\bar{c}_t = 0.81 Z_t$, ensuring that subsistence consumption per capita grows at rate g over time. With this parameterization, $\bar{c}$ equals 49% of the average wage in 2020.

20. Our estimates of the share of wealth held by the top 1% and top 0.1% are consistent with other estimates in the literature. Using Internal Revenue Service data, Saez and Zucman (2016) estimate these shares are 38% and 20%. Using the same data, but a different capitalization approach, Smith, Zidar, and Zwick (2020) estimate they are 30% and 14%. For our SCF data, these authors report a share of 13% for the top 0.1%.

21. In the SCF, we split asset classes with an ambiguous asset mix (non-money-market mutual funds, quasi-liquid individual retirement accounts, and pensions) between stocks and bonds in proportion to their unambiguous shares.

22. Recent work by Derenoncourt et al. (2022) has extended the time series of the racial wealth gap back to 1860. They document a racial wealth gap of roughly 98%. We have adopted the simplified assumption that all Black dynasties are enslaved before 1860, which implies that the wealth gap in our model period 1860 is 100%.

23. Fairlie and Meyer (2000) document that the self-employment rate is lower for Black than for White men and the ratio of self-employment rates has remained remarkably stable since the early 1900s. Bogan and Darity (2008) argue that, although much of the literature tries to account for the entrepreneurship gap by appealing to cultural differences, the comparison of Black with immigrant groups suggests a more important role for discriminatory practices, institutions, and legislation restricting Black entrepreneurship. Our model is compatible with a more elaborate version of the Bogan and Darity (2008) view, as the historical exclusions they describe endogenously lead to differences in beliefs about entrepreneurship.

24. We also observe a racial gap in public equity holdings, similar to the racial gap in entrepreneurship. For example, using the SCF surveys between 1992 and 2019, we find that the portfolio share of public equities for White households averages around 0.23, as compared with a portfolio share of around 0.14 for Black households. Chiteji and Stafford (1999) use data from the Panel Study of Income Dynamics to document that stock market participation is correlated across generations.

25. Responses to this question were studied by Dominitz and Manski (2011) for the period between June 2002 and August 2004. The authors find results nearly identical to the results we report in table 10. Dominitz and Manski (2011) also report similar results for their Survey of Economic Expectations. Because the Survey of Economic Expectations has only 85 Black respondents, we focus on the Michigan Survey.

26. Consistent with the model in which the probability assessment P depends on other variables that differ by race, table 10 shows mean probabilities by group without controls. A regression of the probability assessment on a race dummy controlling for a host of observables (age, time, sex, marital status, region, education, number of children, number of adults, and income) produces an estimated coefficient for the race dummy equal to 5 percentage points with a standard error of 0.5. Thus, the difference in mean probabilities reflects a race component conditional on other observables.

27. More precisely, the dynasties are identical up to population differences. However, we eliminate population growth differences in table 1 starting in 2000, so that the two dynasties are identical in the absence of exclusions starting in 2000.

28. Every Black dynasty receives the same transfer τ. We have experimented with two alternative transfer functions: proportional transfers and transfers that generate the same dispersion of wealth between Black and White dynasties. Both alternatives generate an evolution of the racial gap in average wealth that is similar to the evolution under the same transfer τ.

29. The long-run outcomes refer to the median outcome over the last 300 model periods from a simulation of 600 model periods.

30. We formalize learning as follows. Friends of dynasty ι are denoted f_ι. To construct the set of friends, we order dynasties along a unit circle and denote a dynasty's location by $\iota \in \mathbb{I} \equiv [0, 1]$. Dynasties in the interval $\mathbb{I}^w \equiv [0, \phi)$ are White, and dynasties in the interval $\mathbb{I}^b \equiv [\phi, 1]$ are Black. Similarly, every dynasty has an identity $\iota^h \in [0, 1]$ along a race-specific unit circle, where $\iota^w \equiv \iota/\phi$ for every $\iota \in \mathbb{I}^w$ and $\iota^b \equiv \iota - \phi/1 - \phi$ for every $\iota \in \mathbb{I}^b$. Friends are drawn from the set of dynasties who are within distance d on the circle. By construction, the friendships are not mutual. Dynasties draw F^o friends along the circle specific to their race, $f_\iota^o \sim U([\iota^h, \iota^h + d]^{F^o})$, and F^c friends along the circle for the cross-race, $f_\iota^c \sim U([\iota^h, \iota^h + d]^{F^c})$. For White dynasties, the identities of friends along the unit circle are given by the union $f_\iota = \phi f_\iota^o \cup (\phi + (1 - \phi) f_\iota^c)$, and for Black dynasties, friends are $f_\iota = \phi f_\iota^c \cup (\phi + (1 - \phi) f_\iota^o)$.

31. An example of such a policy is the Gates Scholarship, which is geared toward outstanding minority students from low-income backgrounds by the Bill & Melinda Gates Foundation. The foundation organizes a summer institute and uses an online platform to enable current and former recipients to directly connect with and learn from one another.

References

Aaronson, D., and B. Mazumder. 2008. "Intergenerational Economic Mobility in the United States, 1940 to 2000." *Journal of Human Resources* 43 (1): 139–72.
Aizer, A., R. Boone, A. Lleras-Muney, and J. Vogel. 2020. "Discrimination and Racial Disparities in Labor Market Outcomes: Evidence from WWII." Working Paper no. 27689, NBER, Cambridge, MA.
Alesina, A., S. Stantcheva, and E. Teso. 2018. "Intergenerational Mobility and Preferences for Redistribution." *American Economic Review* 108 (2): 521–54.
Aliprantis, D., D. Carroll, and E. Young. 2019. "The Dynamics of the Racial Wealth Gap." Working Paper no. 19-18, Federal Reserve Bank of Cleveland, OH.
Ashman, H., and S. Neumuller. 2020. "Can Income Differences Explain the Racial Wealth Gap? A Quantitative Analysis." *Review of Economic Dynamics* 35:220–39.
Bach, L., L. Calvet, and P. Sodini. 2020. "Rich Pickings? Risk, Return, and Skill in Household Wealth." *American Economic Review* 110 (9): 2703–47.
Bayer, P., and K. Charles. 2018. "Divergent Paths: A New Perspective on Earning Differences between Black and White Men Since 1940." *Quarterly Journal of Economics* 133 (3): 1459–501.
Benhabib, J., A. Bisin, and M. Luo. 2019. "Wealth Distribution and Social Mobility in the US: A Quantitative Approach." *American Economic Review* 109 (5): 1623–47.
Benhabib, J., A. Bisin, and S. Zhu. 2011. "The Distribution of Wealth and Fiscal Policy in Economies with Finitely Lived Agents." *Econometrica* 79 (1): 123–57.
Blau, F., and J. Graham. 1990. "Black-White Differences in Wealth and Asset Composition." *Quarterly Journal of Economics* 105 (2): 321–39.
Bleakley, H., and J. Ferrie. 2016. "Shocking Behavior: Random Wealth in Antebellum Georgia and Human Capital across Generations." *Quarterly Journal of Economics* 131 (3): 1455–95.
Bogan, V., and W. Darity. 2008. "Culture and Entrepreneurship? African American and Immigrant Self-Employment in the United States." *Journal of Socio-Economics* 37:1999–2019.
Bolt, J., and J. L. van Zanden. 2020. "Maddison Style Estimates of the Evolution of the World Economy. A New 2020 Update." Working Paper no. WP-15, Maddison-Project.
Brouillette, J.-F., C. Jones, and P. Klenow. 2021. "Race and Economic Well-Being in the United States." Working paper, Stanford University.
Buera, F., A. Monge-Naranjo, and G. Primiceri. 2011. "Learning the Wealth of Nations." *Econometrica* 79 (1): 1–45.
Cagetti, M., and M. De Nardi. 2006. "Entrepreneurship, Frictions, and Wealth." *Journal of Political Economy* 114 (5): 835–70.
Chiteji, N., and F. Stafford. 1999. "Portfolio Choices of Parents and Their Children as Young Adults: Asset Accumulation by African-American Families." *American Economic Review* 89:377–80.
Collins, W., and M. Wanamaker. 2017. "Up from Slavery? African American Intergenerational Economic Mobility since 1880." Working Paper no. 23395, NBER, Cambridge, MA.
Cook, L. 2014. "Violence and Economic Activity: Evidence from African American Patents, 1870–1940." *Journal of Economic Growth* 19:221–57.

Darity, W., and D. Frank. 2003. "The Economics of Reparations." *American Economic Review Papers and Proceedings* 93 (2): 326–29.

Darity, W., and K. Mullen. 2020. *From Here to Equality: Reparations for Black Americans in the Twenty-First Century.* Chapel Hill: University of North Carolina Press.

De Nardi, M. 2004. "Wealth Inequality and Intergenerational Links." *Review of Economic Studies* 71:743–68.

De Nardi, M., and G. Fella. 2017. "Saving and Wealth Inequality." *Review of Economic Dynamics* 26:280–300.

Derenoncourt, E., C. H. Kim, M. Kuhn, and M. Schularick. 2022. "The Racial Wealth Gap, 1860–2020." Working paper, Princeton University.

Derenoncourt, E., and C. Montialoux. 2021. "Minimum Wages and Racial Inequality." *Quarterly Journal of Economics* 136 (1): 169–228.

Doepke, M., and F. Zilibotti. 2008. "Occupational Choice and the Spirit of Capitalism." *Quarterly Journal of Economics* 123 (2): 747–93.

Dominitz, J., and C. Manski. 2011. "Measuring and Interpreting Expectations of Equity Returns." *Journal of Applied Econometrics* 26 (3): 352–70.

Dynan, K., J. Skinner, and S. Zeldes. 2004. "Do the Rich Save More?" *Journal of Political Economy* 112 (2): 397–444.

Fagereng, A., L. Guiso, D. Malacrino, and L. Pistaferri. 2020. "Heterogeneity and Persistence in Returns to Wealth." *Econometrica* 88 (1): 115–70.

Fagereng, A., M. B. Holm, B. Moll, and G. Natvik. 2019. "Saving Behavior across the Wealth Distribution: The Importance of Capital Gains." Working paper, London School of Economics.

Fairlie, R., and B. Meyer. 2000. "Trends in Self-Employment among White and Black Men during the Twentieth Century." *Journal of Human Resources* 35 (4): 643–69.

Fairlie, R., A. Robb, and D. Robinson. 2020. "Black and White: Access to Capital among Minority-Owned Startups." Working Paper no. 28154, NBER, Cambridge, MA.

Fernandez, R. 2013. "Cultural Change as Learning: The Evolution of Female Labor Force Participation over a Century." *American Economic Review* 103 (1): 472–500.

Fogli, A., and L. Veldkamp. 2011. "Nature or Nurture? Learning and the Geography of Female Labor Force Participation." *Econometrica* 79 (4): 1103–38.

Gabaix, X., J.-M. Lasry, P.-L. Lions, and B. Moll. 2016. "Heterogeneity and Persistence in Returns to Wealth." *Econometrica* 84 (6): 2071–111.

Guiso, L., P. Sapienza, and L. Zingales. 2008. "Social Capital as Good Culture." *Journal of the European Economic Association* 6 (2–3): 295–320.

Higgs, R. 1982. "Accumulation of Property by Southern Blacks before World War I." *American Economic Review* 72 (4): 725–37.

Hsieh, C.-T., E. Hurst, C. Jones, and P. Klenow. 2019. "The Allocation of Talent and US Economic Growth." *Econometrica* 87 (5): 1439–74.

Jordà, Ò., K. Knoll, D. Kuvshinov, M. Schularick, and A. Taylor. 2019. "The Rate of Return on Everything, 1870–2015." *Quarterly Journal of Economics* 134 (3): 1225–98.

Kermani, A., and F. Wong. 2021. "Racial Disparities in Housing Returns." Working Paper no. 29306, NBER, Cambridge, MA.

Kuhn, M., M. Schularick, and U. Steins. 2020. "Income and Wealth Inequality in America, 1949–2016." *Journal of Political Economy* 128 (9): 3469–519.

Kuvshinov, D., and K. Zimmermann. 2021. "The Expected Return on Risky Assets: International Long-Run Evidence." Discussion Paper no. 15610, CEPR, Paris.

Loury, G. 1977. "A Dynamic Theory of Racial Income Differences." In *Women, Minorities, and Employment Discrimination*, ed. P. A. Wallace and A. LaMond, 153–86. Lanham, MD: Lexington.

Malmendier, U., and S. Nagel. 2016. "Learning from Inflation Experiences." *Quarterly Journal of Economics* 131 (1): 53–87.

Margo, R. 1984. "Accumulation of Property by Southern Blacks before World War I: Comment and Further Evidence." *American Economic Review* 74 (4): 768–76.

———. 2016. "Obama, Katrina, and the Persistence of Racial Inequality." *Journal of Economic History* 76 (2): 301–41.

Neal, L. 1990. "A Calculation and Comparison of the Current Benefits of Slavery and the Analysis of Who Benefits." In *The Wealth of Races*, ed. R. F. America, 91–106. Westport, CT: Greenwood.

Piketty, T. 1995. "Social Mobility and Redistributive Politics." *Quarterly Journal of Economics* 110 (3): 551–84.

Quadrini, V. 2000. "Entrepreneurship, Saving, and Social Mobility." *Review of Economic Dynamics* 3 (1): 1–40.

Saez, E., and G. Zucman. 2016. "Wealth Inequality in the United States since 1913: Evidence from Capitalized Income Tax Data." *Quarterly Journal of Economics* 131 (2): 519–78.

Schmelzing, P. 2020. "Eight Centuries of Global Real Interest Rates, R-G, and the 'Suprasecular' Decline, 1311–2018." Working paper, Bank of England, London.

Smith, M., O. Zidar, and E. Zwick. 2020. "Top Wealth in America: New Estimates and Implications for Taxing the Rich." Working paper, Princeton University.

Straub, L. 2019. "Consumption, Savings, and the Distribution of Permanent Income." Working paper, Harvard University.

Comment

Ellora Derenoncourt, *Princeton University and NBER*, United States of America

The topic of long-standing US racial inequality is experiencing a revival in mainstream economics literature. Numerous studies released in recent years document the prevalence and persistence of racial gaps across several economic domains, analyze the heterogeneous impact of policies across racial groups, or develop new theoretical frameworks for understanding racial gaps. This paper makes a timely intervention in this last literature, focusing on one of the most striking forms of racial inequality, the Black-White wealth gap.

This paper models the persistence of racial wealth inequality as arising from endogenous beliefs about returns on risky assets. In the authors' model, beliefs update through learning, which is assumed to occur solely through participation in the market for risky assets (an assumption that is later relaxed to allow for learning through social networks). In the model setup, Black and White households hold equally pessimistic initial beliefs. During slavery, capital returns were very high—high enough that the expected gains exceeded that of eschewing investment even when beliefs were pessimistic. Under these circumstances, White households participated in risky asset markets and thus learned more about the true distribution of good and bad outcomes after investment. But because slavery barred Black Americans from participation in labor and capital markets, only White households were able to experiment and thus update their beliefs about returns. After slavery, Black Americans could in theory participate, but by then, returns had fallen and were no longer sufficiently

NBER Macroeconomics Annual, volume 37, 2023.

high to overcome expected low returns due to pessimistic beliefs. The long-run result of this is that there are no Black capitalists today.

The model is well able to match the fact that risky assets are an important driver of today's racial wealth gap. The policy implications of the model are that investment subsidies have the power to close the racial wealth gap in the infinite time horizon, and transfers such as one-time reparations payments do not close the racial wealth gap in the long run because they do not affect beliefs. Indeed, relative to a world with wage equalization, which reduces the racial wealth gap through low-risk asset building, reparations have no additional impact on the long-run racial wealth gap.

There is much to admire in this paper. First, the authors take the history of racial oppression seriously and carefully develop a model that highlights one way the past can cast a long shadow on racial wealth inequality today. They formalize capital- and labor-market exclusion under slavery as well as racial wage gaps in the Jim Crow era. These exclusions, combined with the historical dynamics of capital returns, give rise to a situation where Black households opt for safe returns over risky ones, generation after generation, leading to low wealth levels today. Second, the model reproduces several key facts about racial inequality. For example, the model matches the average racial wealth gap today as well as the intergenerational mobility gap in the past and present. In addition, the model matches the contribution of risky assets to the racial wealth gap overall. Finally, racial differences in beliefs about risky asset returns in the model are corroborated by consumer survey evidence.

I focus my commentary on three questions. First, one of the contributions of the paper is to incorporate endogenous beliefs about risky asset returns as drivers of the racial wealth gap. In the paper, such differences arise from Black Americans not updating their beliefs. What if racial differences in beliefs about risky asset returns stem from actual differences in the returns themselves?

A substantial literature documents that there are racial differences in returns on assets of various types. This raises the question of whether Black beliefs are not so much pessimistic as simply reflective of reality. In illustrating the model's mechanisms, the authors give the example of Henry Boyd, a former slave who purchases his freedom and attempts to run a business. Though Boyd is able to secure initial capital to start his business by partnering with a White business partner (as Boyd himself is legally and socially barred from borrowing money), his shop is burned down so many times by White supremacists that he eventually closes his business altogether. Far from being an example of exclusion that prevents further learning, the case seems to exemplify learning itself, thus changing the interpretation of the key mechanism for persistent gaps.

After slavery, there were many further instances of the destruction of Black wealth, from the burning of Black homes in White neighborhoods to the very salient example of the destruction of the Greenwood district in Tulsa, Oklahoma, in 1921. Albright et al. (2021) find that the Tulsa Massacre had long-run effects on the local Black community, with increased labor force participation by women and suppressed rates of homeownership. The authors further find that news of Tulsa sent a chill throughout the Black community, with reductions in homeownership in those places connected to the massacre through newspaper coverage. Kroeger and Wright (2021) find that Black-owned businesses have lower survival rates than White-owned ones, and business closure is associated with downward economic mobility. Thus, focusing solely on the entry margin—encouraging business ownership by Black Americans—may not lead to lower racial wealth gaps if Black businesses have a lower success rate. To be effective at reducing racial gaps in business wealth, policies fostering entrepreneurship must address the sources of racial differences in success.

The second question has to do with the time to convergence. I would argue that it too must be considered when evaluating policies that purport to close racial wealth gaps. Reparations may be insufficient for closing racial wealth gaps in the infinite time horizon, yet this type of policy closes the gap by construction, once implemented. This is an important outcome in and of itself, because the full evolution of the racial wealth gap suggests that a long convergence path is itself a legacy of slavery and initial conditions in the wealth gap.

In Derenoncourt et al. (2022), we provide a new time series of the racial wealth gap since 1860. We build the time series by combining census data from 1860 and 1870 with southern state tax reports from the 1860s to the 1910s, statistical reports on Black economic progress, household survey data, the censuses of population and agriculture, and finally historical and modern waves of the survey of consumer finances. This time series is illustrative, as it shows that the biggest reductions in racial wealth inequality occurred in the first 50 years after emancipation. Over the past 160 years, the wealth gap exhibits a "hockey-stick" shape over time that aligns with standard wealth accumulation frameworks where savings, capital gains, and income growth are the determinants of wealth for Black and White Americans. Even under equal parameters for wealth accumulation in terms of savings rates and capital gains, and under observed income convergence, the wealth gap would remain sizable today (a gap of 3 to 1) and would not converge, even in the next near 200 years. Given observed differences in savings and capital-gains-induced wealth accumulation across the two groups, convergence is indeed no longer in sight. In fact, the past few decades show the wealth gap widening again, not closing.

This long-run perspective puts today's wealth gap in context. It would take large advantages in savings rates, capital gains, or income growth rates to bring about racial wealth convergence in a short time frame. Policies such as reparations in the amount of the wealth gap bring the wealth ratio to one at the time the transfer is made. Although it is true that the wealth gap would reemerge if such a transfer does not change the parameters of wealth accumulation, such as capital returns or savings (whether stemming from differences in behavior or not), there may be reason for considering the time to convergence in the design of wealth equalization policies.

The final strand of this discussion focuses on the determinants of beliefs in the model. In the authors' baseline model, beliefs depend first on direct participation in the market. Historical institutions and the dynamics of capital returns mean that Black Americans never believe it is worth it to become capitalists. The authors then relax this assumption and allow social networks to influence beliefs. However, they note that segregated social networks mean that beliefs can remain relatively pessimistic even with a large number of ties, if networks are segregated by race. They find that including even just one White "friend" in the network can eliminate the wealth gap in the infinite time horizon.

However, it would be interesting for future research to consider other ways beliefs might be influenced. For example, it is possible that a policy such as reparations and the type of society in which such a policy is realized would also affect Black beliefs about returns. Historical abuses that erode trust in institutions can dampen economic convergence. Whether or not policies such as reparations can restore that trust is a difficult question to answer empirically. But one case study may be illustrative. Miller (2020) studies land and capital redistribution in the Cherokee Nation after the Civil War. The Cherokee Nation joined the Confederacy during the Civil War. Afterward, the nation signed a treaty with the US federal government that gave freed Black persons in the Cherokee Nation citizenship of the nation and the right to claim land. New landowners were allocated equipment to assist in farming. Studying the impact of this policy, the author found that racial wealth gaps fell in the Cherokee Nation relative to the rest of the South. Furthermore, the author found that human capital investment in the next generation increased, and that Black farmers in the nation planted fruit trees as opposed to staple crops only.

This change in investment choices may signify updated beliefs on the returns to a relatively riskier investment. Fruit trees have a long gestational period compared with staples and are only remunerative if landowners believe their property rights to be secure. Thus, this evidence raises the question of whether certain forms of reparations policy can also change beliefs. This would then allow reparations to have a more lasting effect on the racial wealth gap relative to a world in which reparations do not affect beliefs.

Endnote

Author email address: Derenoncourt (ellora.derenoncourt@princeton.edu). For acknowledgments, sources of research support, and disclosure of the author's material financial relationships, if any, please see https://www.nber.org/books-and-chapters/nber-macroeconomics -annual-2022-volume-37/comment-persistent-racial-wealth-gaps-derenoncourt.

References

Albright, Alex, Jeremy A. Cook, James J. Feigenbaum, Laura Kincaide, Jason Long, and Nathan Nunn. 2021. "After the Burning: The Economic Effects of the 1921 Tulsa Race Massacre." Working Paper no. w28985, NBER, Cambridge, MA.
Derenoncourt, Ellora, Chi Hyun Kim, Moritz Kuhn, and Moritz Schularick. 2022. "Wealth of Two Nations: The US Racial Wealth Gap, 1860–2020." Working Paper no. w30101, NBER, Cambridge, MA.
Kroeger, Teresa, and Graham Wright. 2021. "Entrepreneurship and the Racial Wealth Gap: The Impact of Entrepreneurial Success or Failure on the Wealth Mobility of Black and White Families." *Journal of Economics, Race, and Policy* 4 (3): 183–95.
Miller, Melinda C. 2020. "'The Righteous and Reasonable Ambition to Become a Landholder': Land and Racial Inequality in the Postbellum South." *Review of Economics and Statistics* 102 (2): 381–94.

Comment

Jonathan A. Parker, *Massachusetts Institute of Technology and NBER,*
United States of America

This paper is an insightful and important social-scientific analysis of the
legacy of slavery on wealth accumulation and the efficacy of policies designed to close this gap. The paper uses a state-of-the-art, general equilibrium model of the type previously used to study wealth inequality over
time and across generations to study the racial wealth gap. At the broadest
level, I read the paper as a cautionary tale.

In the model, all agents, Black and White, choose how much to invest
in a high-risk, high-return activity and, if they end up with enough wealth,
leave bequests to their heirs. But all households in the model have to learn
about the return to the high-risk opportunity. The key assumption is that
all agents update optimally but based only on their own dynasty's past
experiences. Because slavery and economic discrimination prohibit learning about high-return activities and investments, Black agents, in the model's version of the present, start with a prior belief that the probability of
success in these high-risk opportunities is low.

As a result, even a transfer of wealth from White agents to Black agents
that completely equalizes average wealth—an extreme policy relative to
almost any historical precedent—fails to equalize economic outcomes by
race. Over time, Black agents, having not been allowed to learn the probability of success in high-risk, high-return activity, invest less in high-risk,
high-return activity than White agents and so leave lower bequests to
their heirs. Thus, the racial wealth gap reemerges even as the "belief gap"
closes. This is the cautionary tale: treating the current symptom directly—
wealth inequality—without treating other residual inequalities of slavery
may not succeed in closing the wealth gap prospectively. In the paper, the

NBER Macroeconomics Annual, volume 37, 2023.

residual inequality is the information gap about the high returns that comes from (restricted) past experience. And addressing this inequality as well—the belief gap—through a policy that subsidizes the returns to investing in high-risk, high-return activity for Black agents, is a policy that can permanently eliminate the Black-White wealth gap.

In the remainder of my discussion, I briefly review the model, emphasizing the assumption that people's learning overweights their own dynasty's past experiences. This assumption implies that beliefs are a state variable that differs by race and that propagate the damaging effects of slavery and discrimination. Second, I discuss how important it is to measure well what I just called "other residual inequalities" from slavery and discrimination. There are two important high-return investments in which there are large racial gaps that appear at first pass consistent with racial differences in beliefs. But are they? One cannot randomly assign race or beliefs to infer their roles; however, one can investigate the correlates of differences in investment behavior besides race. I will argue that for these two investment opportunities, most gaps in investment behavior are driven by differences in actual returns, some of which appear to be driven by liquidity shocks rather than racial differences in beliefs independently. That is, in these cases, there is little evidence that racial differences in behavior or beliefs are inconsistent with reality in the present. Liquidity shocks—that is, lack of wealth itself—appear to cause most of the racial gap in these investments.

Does this liquidity channel also cause differences in the paper's central example, entrepreneurship? If so, then these gaps would be eliminated by reparations alone because they would close the investment behavior gap and the ex post return gap. In sum, although this paper raises an important warning—that beliefs based on own experiences may propagate inequality—the evidence that I discuss suggests that reparations would be more effective than in this model.

I. Key Model Components and Findings

The core of the model is a relatively standard, heterogeneous agent, overlapping generations model with uninsurable, idiosyncratic risk and in which bequests are a luxury good. There are two types of agents, Black and White, that are identical in terms of preferences but are treated unequally. The (lifetime) wage is stochastic with race-specific (serially correlated across generations) distributions based on historical data. Each generation chooses what fraction of its time to devote to working and earning its wage and what faction to devote to a high-risk, high-return activity. Each generation also chooses what fraction of its wealth to invest in a safe asset and what faction to invest in a high-risk, high-return investment. These fractions must be the same—labor time must be allocated in equal proportion to wealth—so that the activity is most analogous to entrepreneurship. The model is solved with either exogenous or endogenous aggregate (average) asset returns, and in each case, returns on the high-risk activity decline over time as more agents accumulate wealth.

In terms of beliefs, all agents know all model parameters except the probability of success of the risky activity/investment. Agents update this probability based on their own dynasty's individual experience. This assumption is critical for propagating wealth inequality. The assumption of rational expectations would make reparations completely effective (conditional on equalizing all other factors as assumed in the model experiments). Given its importance, is this a good assumption? The paper shows that its main results still hold when agents can learn also from the others as long as they still overweight their own experiences. There is a large (cited) literature that shows individuals overweight their own experiences in forming their beliefs. In particular, Malmendier and Nagel (2011, 2016) show that individual past experiences shape investment behaviors (also see Malmendier and Wachter, forthcoming). My reading is that this evidence is sufficiently convincing that we absolutely should consider whether policies that are effective under rational expectations are robust to the alternative assumption that learning occurs as the authors posit. Before implementing the authors' suggested policy, however, I would also want to consider whether there are teaching or information interventions that might make reparations fully effective. I suggest one such possibility when discussing the findings below.

In sum, in the model, wealth inequality is propagated across generations by lower Black wages, higher White bequest, and each generations' choices about how much to consume and how much of savings and labor effort to invest in the high-risk, high-return activity.

The model is parameterized so as to fit to the past evolution of Black-White wealth gaps given historical expropriation of Black earnings by White households during slavery (1780–1860) and Black exclusion from high-risk, high-return investments and lower earnings (as in earning data) in the pre–civil rights era. The model is simulated into the future and various policies considered under the assumption that the economic opportunities of Black and White households are equalized going forward given their inherited wealth. That is, both types of agents have equal access to high-risk, high-return investment options and equal wage distributions. There are two main lessons from the model.

First, even under the extreme assumption of equal opportunities in the future, the model implies that, absent policy interventions, the Black-White wealth gap is extraordinarily persistent. In the model, this occurs in part because convergence of wealth distributions is slow even in standard models. Convergence is further slowed in this model because Black agents make safer, lower-return portfolio choices because they have less wealth (and bequests are a luxury good) and because past discrimination has blocked Black agents from learning about the high-risk, high-return investment activity.

This finding echoes Derenoncourt et al. (2022), who find the same result in a much simpler model without any differences in portfolio choices or returns by race. This is an important and underappreciated point: wealth distributions are very slow moving over time. Even under optimal behavior and no discrimination, Black-White wealth distributions will take many, many generations to converge. We do not need to look for further explanations. The fact that we have persistent large wealth gaps does not itself imply ongoing discrimination or failures of Black households to take advantage of opportunities. Standard economic models imply that the impact of past slavery and discrimination on relative wealth will fade only very slowly, even if we could eliminate all discrimination and wage gaps. Anything remotely close to equalization in any of our lifetimes requires policy interventions (broadly defined).

The second, and more novel, finding of the paper is where I read the paper as a cautionary tale. In the model, equalizing wealth by race through reparations causes only a temporary elimination of the wealth gap by race. Primarily because Black agents have not learned about the high probability of success in the high-return investment, they invest less in the high-risk, high-return activity than White agents. These different choices lead to lower returns by Black agents than White agents, and so Black agents accumulate relatively less wealth. And the wealth gap opens up again. The point: even in the model where we can eliminate disparate racial treatment going forward, wealth reparations are not enough.

Give that the central problem for reparations is the initial racial gap in beliefs about returns to the risky activity, a more effective policy subsidizes these returns for Black agents and speeds learning. The paper shows this point with a nice experiment, so that there is a policy route to equalizing wealth distributions. Nicely, in the experiment the subsidy does not change the learning technology. But, as I noted above, it might be possible to provide information—contracts, promises, et cetera—along with reparations so that behavior changes more than just through learning about underlying returns. For example, I conjecture that in the model, a policy that promised an after-subsidy distribution of returns equal to that believed by White agents could cost nothing ex post and would make reparations fully effective under both rational expectations and the learning model assumed by the paper (as long as one allows a fully credible version of my policy).

One reaction to the paper might be concerns that slavery and lack of civil rights has caused other differences between Black and White households besides belief differences. This paper shows that the efficacy of policies to equalize the distribution of outcomes is critically dependent on how people update beliefs about the returns to the high-risk, high-return activities and investments. Should we be worried about beliefs about other opportunities from which Black households have not had equal access? What about other "residual inequalities" caused by slavery and discrimination?

II.   How Is the Past Persistent? Liquidity and Investment Choices

I will begin by characterizing two entire fields with a complete lack of nuance.

First, economics studies human behavior from the starting point that people are ex ante identical and behave differently due to different economic circumstances. As examples, in the classic Becker models of taste-based discrimination and statistical discrimination, Black and White agents are economically similar except for differential treatment. Empirically, economics has also focused on both inputs (access to schooling, loans, jobs) and outputs (wage differentials, skill gaps, wealth gaps) that are more measurable.

In contrast, sociology studies the way in which group experiences shape culture, and how culture shapes individual behavior and group outcomes. There is a substantial amount of work in sociology about the way Black American culture in part derives from the shared experiences of slavery and lack of equal rights. I am very much not an expert in this literature (or at least my familiarity with it is out of date), but this line of argument often implies that increasing wealth alone does not address completely the problems caused by past discrimination and persistently low wealth. Sociological approaches instead often recommend a richer and broader array of policy interventions that address directly other ills associated with low wealth and the legacy of slavery.

Although this paper sits in the economics tradition, in that Black and White agents in the model are identical except for their experience, the inequality in the treatment of Black and White agents in the slavery and pre–civil rights era is propagated over generations not only through wealth handed down from generation to generation but also through beliefs about the returns to different types of working and investing. I laud the warning provided by the paper, but (in part as an economist) I am skeptical of any model in which slavery and discrimination persistently change behavior (beliefs are part of the specification of preferences). In my role as discussant, I want to propose a different channel that seems to propagate a racial investment gap in high-return assets and may be addressed by simple reparations.

Let me first emphasize how careful this paper is about evidence and how rigorous it is in its analysis. As I noted above, there is a substantial literature documenting that people overweight their own past experiences in updating their beliefs, and that this behavior occurs in this exact domain, in risk-taking in investment choices. The model is fit to historical data. The paper provides survey evidence on a racial belief gap.

But there is also evidence in two important areas of wealth accumulation that a lot of the racial gap in investment in high-return investments is driven by lack of wealth rather than racial differences in beliefs.

First, consider evidence from Choukhmane et al. (2022) on retirement saving. Saving into an employer-sponsored retirement plan is a high-return investment that White households invest in much more than Black households. It is a high-return investment because contributions to employer-sponsored retirement saving plans are both tax advantaged and typically subsidized by the employer. In 80% of plans, employers match employee contributions, and the most common matching rate is 50% up to 6% of income. These subsidies are roughly the equivalent of an additional 4% per annum risk-free return above and beyond the actual returns on the funds that the employee invests in.

Choukhmane et al. (2022) show that on average Black workers contribute 1.4% less of their income to retirement plans than White workers, a large racial investment gap in a high-return activity. This difference would cumulate into White households having 30% more defined contribution retirement wealth than Black households at retirement even if incomes were equalized. Comparing workers at the same firms—and thus with the same match rates and so forth—at the same ages, earning similar incomes, and in the same occupations, this gap declines to 0.9% of income, still quite different.

But this measured gap can be cut by more than a third by controlling for rough proxies for lack of liquidity, spousal income, home ownership, and parental income. That is, the racial gap in investment rates for similar workers is more than a third explained by a just a few factors related to other sources of income and wealth. A plausible interpretation of this finding is that Black households are less able to take advantage of illiquid, high-return saving opportunities due to lower family earnings and wealth and so a higher need for liquidity.

Choukhmane et al. (2022) further show that, in contrast, a measure related to beliefs—parental investment in retirement saving plans—does not appear related to the racial gap in retirement contribution rates.

A similar conclusion follows from Kermani and Wong (2022), who show that ex post annual returns on houses are 3.7% lower for Black than White households, implying a 16.5% lower return on equity investment (accounting for leverage) for Black households relative to White households. This huge gap does not appear to be driven by beliefs, despite quite differential treatment of Black and White homeowners historically. Instead, this gap is almost entirely accounted for by the higher propensity of Black homeowners to have distressed sales. Excluding distressed sales lowers the racial gap in (unlevered) returns from 3.7% to 0.1%.

In sum, much of the observed racial gaps in investment in at least these two central channels of wealth accumulation, retirement saving and housing, are in a correlational sense explained by proximate measures of low liquidity and actual low liquidity as indicated by distressed sales, respectively. Low liquidity would be directly addressed by reparations. This evidence does not imply that a belief gap plays no role in these domains. But this evidence does raise the question whether a greater propensity to suffer low liquidity might account for some of the survey evidence on beliefs presented by this paper and a larger share of the wealth gap than implied by this model. These two domains are not the central example of the paper, which is entrepreneurship, but we also know that liquidity and wealth are important determinants of entrepreneurship. In sum, these two examples are cautionary tales for this paper's cautionary tale.

Endnote

Author email address: Parker (JAParker@MIT.edu). For acknowledgments, sources of research support, and disclosure of the author's material financial relationships, if any,

please see https://www.nber.org/books-and-chapters/nber-macroeconomics-annual
-2022-volume-37/comment-persistent-racial-wealth-gaps-2-parker.

References

Choukhmane, Taha, Jorge Colmenares, Cormac O'Dea, Jonathan Rothbaum,
    and Lawrence Schmidt. 2022. "Who Benefits from Retirement Saving Incen-
    tives in the US? Evidence on Racial Gaps in Retirement Wealth Accumula-
    tion." Working paper, Massachusetts Institute of Technology.
Derenoncourt, Ellora, Chi Hyun Kim, Moritz Kuhn, and Moritz Schularick.
    2022. "Wealth of Two Nations: The U.S. Racial Wealth Gap, 1860–2020." Work-
    ing Paper no. 30101 (May), NBER, Cambridge, MA.
Kermani, Amir, and Francis Wong. 2021. "Racial Disparities in Housing Re-
    turns." Working Paper no. 29306 (September), NBER, Cambridge, MA.
Malmendier, Ulrike, and Stefan Nagel. 2011. "Depression Babies: Do Macroeco-
    nomic Experiences Affect Risk-Taking?" *Quarterly Journal of Economics* 126 (1):
    373–416.
———. 2016. "Learning from Inflation Experiences." *Quarterly Journal of Eco-
    nomics* 131 (1): 53–87.
Malmendier, Ulrike, and Jessica A. Wachter. Forthcoming. "Memory of Past Ex-
    periences and Economic Decisions." In *Oxford Handbook of Human Memory*,
    ed. M. Kahana and A. Wagner. Oxford: Oxford University Press.

Discussion

Guido Menzio opened the discussion with two points. First, he suggested that, because beliefs do not enter the future value function, there is no benefit to experimentation. Second, he was concerned that all the wealth in the model is from bequests, but the data the authors use are cross-sectional wealth at a given point in time, rather than at death. The authors responded by saying that to rationalize the belief gaps we see today, one needs learning from experimentation to be noisy. They agreed that the wealth data are not specifically bequests, and they could certainly look at the wealth of older people (e.g., 65-year-olds). The authors further responded that there a lot of work has been done highlighting the importance of bequests for wealth inequality generally and that, statistically, bequests are an important factor affecting the Black-White wealth gap.

Robert Hall asked about an alternative mechanism: the health trap. He said earlier work by himself and Chad Jones showed that health is a luxury good. Therefore, a health trap could lead to a model with two equilibria where some people are poor and have poor health. He noted that we also know there are substantial differences in health outcomes between Black and White people. The authors welcomed the suggestion and noted that they should think more about this.

Eric Swanson asked about another alternative mechanism: education. He argued that some of the empirical evidence of differential beliefs about equity returns could be explained by education differences, given that there is evidence of a Black-White education gap and that less-educated households typically have lower expectations for equity returns. He added

NBER Macroeconomics Annual, volume 37, 2023.

that if less-educated households earn lower returns, one way to reduce wealth inequality is to focus on reducing the Black-White education gap. Finally, he asked why the Black-White education gap has persisted. He argued that if there are concerns about expropriation (e.g., because of events like the Tulsa race massacre), we would expect greater investment in human capital, because it is not subject to expropriation risk in the same way as other forms of capital. He cited the Jewish community as another example of a historically marginalized group that was subject to expropriation risk (especially from pogroms in Europe, which occurred many times over history). This led Jewish people to invest heavily in human capital. The authors agreed that human capital can play an important role. They highlighted that in their model, when they close the wage gap, which proxies for the human-capital gap, they eliminate most of the wealth differences. However, they pointed out that wealth differences remain for the right tail (i.e., above the 95th percentile).

Eric Zwick commented that to the extent the authors are focused on settings where entrepreneurial wealth is important, he has ongoing work that shows not only expected returns differing across groups but also realized returns. In his work, he shows that upfront barriers to entry are unable to explain the differences in returns. It seems ongoing barriers (such as discrimination in the product or labor markets) or the accumulation of human capital appears more likely to generate the right tail of entrepreneurial outcomes. The authors responded that in their model, the right tail is driven by high-return entrepreneurs. They added that their model is also consistent with returns varying by size of the business.

Martin Eichenbaum then asked how the authors distinguish between different hypotheses. He argued that although the experience of Black people in the United States is unique, there are many other immigrant groups that have come to the country, but it is not clear whether they have converged as slowly. He noted that immigration might be prone to selection issues, as highlighted by discussant Jonathan Parker, but there are periods of time where there is little choice (e.g., during World War II). The authors responded that they specifically looked at different race identifiers. They found that the beliefs of both Hispanic and Asian Americans aligned with the mean wealth across these racial groups, which lends support to their model.

Andrea Eisfeldt said she found the evidence presented by Parker compelling. Specifically, that much of the return differential between Black and White people comes from downside risk. As such, she asked whether policies such as the social safety net would be worth exploring. The authors explained that one way to think about such policies is the return subsidy in their model. This subsidy protects against some downside risk by effectively acting as a guarantee.

Joel Mokyr commented that previous work by Bruce Meyer found little evidence that liquidity constraints prevented Black people from pursuing self-employment or that Black people concentrated in capital-light self-employment. He suggested that there must be some unobserved cultural differences. Mokyr added that there is also a role for discrimination in housing. He pointed out that this is exacerbated by education being funded by local taxes in the United States. Therefore, being discriminated against in housing may also result in worse educational outcomes. The authors explained that they had cited Meyer's paper, and the missing cultural factor in their model is beliefs.

The authors concluded by thanking the discussants and responding to an overarching comment about what is driving the difference in returns. They suggested that this difference has two components. The first is compositional differences, which is the story of their model. That is, Black people invest in low-risk assets and White people invest in high-risk assets. The second component relates to within-asset differences. The authors agreed that this could be a potential factor driving wealth gaps, and said they would try to look into it.

4

Stubborn Beliefs in Search Equilibrium

Guido Menzio, *New York University and NBER*, United States of America

I. Introduction

In search-theoretic models of the labor market (e.g., Pissarides 1985), the expectations that the workers hold about their future job-finding probability and their future wages have a direct impact on the determination of current labor-market outcomes. Consider, for example, a worker and a firm that have just met and are bargaining over the worker's wage. Whether the worker accepts or rejects an offer from the firm depends on his expectations about how quickly he could find another job and what wage he could earn at another job. That is, the worker's bargaining strategy depends on his expectations about his future labor-market outcomes. For this reason, the result of the bargaining game between the worker and the firm depends on the worker's expectations about his future labor-market outcomes. Because the workers' expectations about their future affect current wages, they also affect the firms' current incentives to create vacancies, the current tightness of the labor market, and the workers' current job-finding probability.

In the literature, it is standard to assume that workers have full information and rational expectations about their future labor-market outcomes (see, e.g., Pissarides 1985; Mortensen and Pissarides 1994; Shimer 2005). That is, workers know the current realization and the stochastic process of all the time-varying fundamentals of the economy—such as, say, productivity and monetary or fiscal policy—as well as the time-invariant fundamentals—such as, say, the factor at which firms

NBER Macroeconomics Annual, volume 37, 2023.

discount future profits, the cost that firms have to incur to maintain vacancies, and the bilateral matching process that brings unemployed workers and vacant jobs together. Using these pieces of information, workers can recover the mapping between realizations of the fundamentals and equilibrium outcomes and, thus, form correct expectations about their labor-market prospects. The assumption of full-information rational expectations is very convenient for modeling. Because workers have full information, the modeler does not need to specify the workers' prior beliefs about the fundamentals nor the information that the workers use to update such beliefs. Because workers have rational expectations, the modeler does not need to exogenously specify the workers' expectations.

The assumption that workers have full-information rational expectations, however, need not be realistic. Mueller, Spinnewijn, and Topa (2021) find that, among workers who have just become unemployed, the average expected job-finding probability is quite close to the average realized job-finding probability. Yet, the workers who have the highest expected job-finding probability tend to be too optimistic, and the workers who have the lowest expected job-finding probability tend to be too pessimistic. This finding is inconsistent with the assumption of full information. Moreover, Mueller et al. (2021) find that the expected job-finding probability of an individual worker does not change throughout a spell of unemployment—even for those workers who were too optimistic. Similarly, they find that the workers' expected job-finding probability does not respond to changes in macroeconomic conditions. These findings are inconsistent with the assumption of rational expectations. Overall, the picture that emerges from Mueller et al. (2021) is that workers have "stubborn beliefs" about their labor-market prospects: beliefs that are correct on average but do not respond to either new individual information (the length of an unemployment spell) or to new aggregate information (the state of the business cycle).

In this paper, I propose a simple search-theoretic model of the labor market in which workers have stubborn beliefs.[1] The fundamentals of the economy are constant over time, except for the aggregate component of productivity, which follows a stochastic process. Yet, workers believe that all the fundamentals of the economy, including the aggregate component of productivity, are constant over time and equal to their unconditional mean. Based on their view of the economy, workers compute the equilibrium outcomes and, in turn, form expectations about labor-market tightness, job-finding probability, firms' bargaining strategy, and the outcome of the bargaining game. In contrast, firms have rational expectations and complete information about the fundamentals of the economy, including how workers form their expectations. When an individual worker meets an individual firm, I consider two alternative scenarios. In the first scenario, the worker observes the productivity of the firm with which he is bargaining and interprets any difference between the firm's productivity and the average of the aggregate component of productivity as a permanent, firm-specific component of productivity. In the second scenario, the worker does not observe the productivity of the firm with which he is bargaining and believes it to be given by the average of the aggregate component of productivity. In both scenarios, workers' expectations about their labor-market prospects are correct on average, but they do not change in response to aggregate productivity shocks.

An equilibrium of the model with stubborn workers is given by a system of equations for the actual value functions and equilibrium outcomes, and by a system of equations for the workers' perception of the value functions and the workers' expected equilibrium outcomes. The two systems of equations are linked by the outcome of the bargaining game. The bargaining game follows the same protocol as in Binmore, Rubinstein, and Wolinsky (1986), in which the firm and the worker alternate in making wage offers and wage demands, and the negotiation may break down after a proposal is rejected. The wage outcome of the bargaining game is a weighted average between the worker's perception of the productivity of the firm and the worker's perception of his value of unemployment. In the first scenario, the worker's perception of the productivity of the firm is the firm's actual productivity. Hence, in this scenario, the wage is sticky, in the sense that it is affected by aggregate productivity fluctuations only though their impact on the firm's actual productivity, not through their impact on the worker's actual value of unemployment. In the second scenario, the worker's perception of the productivity of the firm is the unconditional mean of aggregate productivity. Hence, in this scenario, the wage is rigid, in the sense that it is completely unresponsive to aggregate productivity fluctuations. In both scenarios, the wage is entirely pinned down by the worker's beliefs. The intuition is simple. Because the firm knows that the worker's beliefs cannot be changed, it has no choice but to accommodate them.

The properties of equilibrium are different when workers have stubborn beliefs rather than rational expectations. If the aggregate component of productivity is at its unconditional mean, the labor-market tightness, the job-finding probability, and the unemployment and vacancy rates are the same in an stubborn belief equilibrium (SBE) as in an rational expectation equilibrium (REE). This is because the wage is the same in an SBE and in an REE. The elasticities of labor-market tightness, job-finding probability, and the unemployment and vacancy rates with respect to aggregate productivity are, however, higher in an SBE than in an REE. This is because the wage responds less to deviations of aggregate productivity from its unconditional mean in an SBE than in an REE. Moreover, because the wage in an SBE is sticky in the first scenario and rigid in the second scenario, the elasticity of labor-market outcomes in an SBE is larger in the second scenario than in the first.

The welfare properties of equilibrium are also different when workers have stubborn beliefs rather than rational expectations. An REE is generically inefficient because, when a firm decides to create a vacancy, it does not internalize the negative effect of its decision on the probability that other vacancies are filled—the so-called congestion externality—and it does not internalize the positive effect of its decision on the worker who is eventually hired to fill the vacancy—the so-called thick-market externality. An REE can be made efficient by means of an unemployment subsidy designed to make the firm internalize the congestion and the thick-market externalities. An SBE is also inefficient because there is a gap between the actual surplus of a firm-worker match and the surplus perceived by the worker—which is the one that determines the wage and the allocation of the gains from trade between the firm and the worker. An SBE can be made efficient by adding a countercyclical component to the unemployment subsidy that is optimal for an REE. For instance, when the Hosios condition holds, the REE is efficient and the optimal unemployment subsidy is zero. The SBE, however, is still inefficient, and the optimal unemployment subsidy involves making transfers to firms in recessions and taxing firms in expansions.

I then consider an extension of the baseline model in which some workers have stubborn beliefs and some workers have rational expectations. When a firm and worker bargain over the wage, the firm knows the probability that the worker is stubborn and the probability that the worker is rational, but it does not know the type of the worker. Thus, the bargaining game between the firm and the worker is one of asymmetric information. The outcome of the bargaining game depends on whether a stubborn worker is more optimistic than a rational worker, which is the case when aggregate productivity is below its unconditional mean;

or vice versa, which is the case when aggregate productivity is above its unconditional mean. When a stubborn worker is more optimistic, the outcome of the bargaining game is such that both types of workers earn the wage that a stubborn worker would earn if the firm knew his type—that is, both types earn the same wage as in the baseline SBE. When a rational worker is more optimistic, the outcome of the bargaining game is such that each type of worker earns the same wage that he would earn if the firm knew his type—that is, a rational worker earns the same wage as in an REE and a stubborn worker earns the same wage as in the baseline SBE. Even though asymmetric-information bargaining games are typically plagued by a multiplicity of equilibria, I show that this is the unique Perfect Sequential Equilibrium—a natural equilibrium concept proposed by Grossman and Perry (1986a, 1986b).

The intuition behind the asymmetry of the bargaining outcomes is relatively simple. When a stubborn worker is more optimistic than a rational worker, the symmetric-information wage is higher for a stubborn worker than for a rational one.[2] For this reason, the rational worker finds it optimal to hide his type and make the same wage demands as a stubborn worker. The firm could screen the two types by making a wage offer that is acceptable only to the rational worker. The firm, however, does not find it optimal to do so, as the screening offer would have to be close to the symmetric-information wage of a stubborn worker, which the rational worker can attain by rejecting the screening offer. This is the same logic behind the Coase conjecture (see, e.g., Gul and Sonnenschein 1988). When a rational worker is more optimistic than a stubborn worker, the symmetric-information wage for a rational worker is higher than the symmetric-information wage for a stubborn worker. For this reason, the rational worker would like to signal his type to the firm and can do so by making a wage offer that the firm could only credibly interpret as coming from him.

The asymmetric outcomes of the bargaining game cause the labor market to behave differently when the aggregate component of productivity is lower or higher than its unconditional mean. When aggregate productivity falls below its unconditional mean, the response of the wage paid by firms to both stubborn and rational workers—hence, the average wage paid by firms—is just as downward sticky or as rigid as in the baseline SBE. As a result, the response of the labor-market tightness, job-finding probability, and unemployment and vacancy rates is just as large as in the baseline SBE, even though only a fraction of workers are stubborn. When aggregate productivity rises above its unconditional mean, the response of the wage paid by firms to stubborn workers is as sticky or rigid as in the baseline SBE, but the response of the wage paid by firms to rational workers is fully flexible as in an REE. As a result, the response of the average wage paid by firms is not as sticky as in the baseline SBE and not as flexible as in an REE. Consequently, the response of the labor-market tightness, job-finding probability, and unemployment and vacancy rates is higher than in an REE but lower than in the baseline SBE, and whether the response is closer to one or the other extreme depends on the fraction of stubborn workers in the population. If, for example, the fraction of stubborn workers is small, the labor market features the same large response to negative productivity shocks as in an SBE and the same small response to positive productivity shocks as in an REE.

The paper makes two contributions. The first is to build a search-theoretic equilibrium model of the labor market in which workers have stubborn beliefs. To build a model in which workers do not have rational expectations, I have to specify how workers form their expectations about equilibrium outcomes. I assume that workers form their expectations by solving the equilibrium of a model in which all of the fundamentals of the economy—including those that are stochastic—are constant and equal to their unconditional means. Given this specification of the workers' expectations, the equilibrium of the model can be represented by a system of equations describing the actual value functions and the actual equilibrium outcomes coupled with a system of equations describing the value functions perceived by the workers and the equilibrium outcomes expected by the workers. The two systems of equations come together in the solution of the bargaining game between a firm and a worker and, hence, in the equilibrium condition for the wage. The equilibrium is such that, on average, workers' expectations are correct, but they do not respond to fluctuations in fundamentals, as documented by Mueller et al. (2021). The analysis of the bargaining game between a firm with rational expectations and a worker that may or may not have stubborn beliefs is the central intellectual contribution of the paper.

The paper departs from the assumption of rational expectations and, in this sense, relates to the behavioral macro literature (see Gabaix 2019 for an excellent survey and Gabaix 2020 for a modeling approach that is similar to mine). Behavioral macro, however, mainly focuses on models where trade is centralized and frictionless; hence, it does not deal with the issue of characterizing the outcome of a strategic game between agents that may have different expectations. There are some papers that consider search-theoretic models where workers have nonrational expectations (e.g., Conlon et al. 2018; Mueller et al. 2021). These models, however, take the distribution of wages offered by firms to be exogenous. Hence, these models also do not deal with the issue of characterizing the outcome of a game between agents that may have different expectations.

The second contribution of the paper is to show that stubborn beliefs cause wages to be sticky. In a version of the model where all workers have stubborn beliefs, wages are sticky if workers observe the productivity of the firm with which they are bargaining and rigid if they assume such productivity to be the unconditional mean of aggregate productivity. In a more general version of the model where only some workers have stubborn beliefs, wages are as sticky/rigid downward as they are when all workers have stubborn beliefs; they are sticky upward only in proportion to the fraction of workers who have stubborn beliefs.

Therefore, the paper is related to theories of wage stickiness in frictional labor markets. Hall (2005) proposes a simple but radical theory of wage rigidity. When a firm and a worker meet, the wage is not determined by some bargaining game. Instead, the wage is given by some social norm that does not respond to cyclical fluctuations in fundamentals. Hall and Milgrom (2008) and Christiano, Eichenbaum, and Trabandt (2016) propose a theory of wage stickiness based on an alternative bargaining protocol. The bargaining protocol behind the wage equation in standard search-theoretic models of the labor market is such that, if the negotiations between the firm and the worker break down, the two parties separate forever. Hall and Milgrom (2008) assume instead that, if the negotiations between the firm and the worker break down, the two parties do not trade in the current period but remain matched in the next period. This alternative protocol leads to an equilibrium wage that does not depend on the worker's value of unemployment and is therefore less responsive to aggregate fluctuations. Gertler and Trigari (2009) obtain aggregate wage stickiness by assuming that firms can adjust the wage paid to their employees—including the newly hired ones—only occasionally.

Menzio (2005) and Kennan (2010) propose theories of wage stickiness that are based on asymmetric information. In both theories, the premise is that, when a firm and a worker bargain over the wage, the worker knows the state of the economy but does not know how the state of the economy affects the productivity of the firm. Menzio (2005) shows that, if the outcome of the negotiation is observed by the other employees of the firm, the firm wants to mimic the bargaining strategy of a low-productivity firm to avoid revealing information to other employees and renegotiating their wage. As a result, the wage paid by the firm is rigid. Kennan (2010) shows that, if the gains from trade between the worker and the firm are large and the output gap between a high- and a low-productivity firm is small, the worker finds it optimal to make a pooling wage demand. As a result, the wage paid by the firm is sticky, in the sense that it does not fully respond to changes in average productivity caused by aggregate shocks.

Menzio and Moen (2010) propose a theory of wage stickiness that borrows from the theory of implicit contracts (see, e.g., Azariadis 1975). When workers are risk averse and firms are risk neutral, firms want to insure workers against aggregate shock by offering them acyclical wages. If the firms cannot commit not to replace incumbent employees with new hires, though, the firms must commit to downward sticky wages for new hires to credibly provide insurance to incumbent employees. Fukui (2021) turns the theory of Menzio and Moen (2010) on its head. In a model where workers search on and off the job, the firm's optimal wage offered to new hires depends on the distribution of wages earned by employed workers as well as by the reservation wage of unemployed workers. If the wages earned by employed workers are sticky because firms want to insure their risk-averse employees against productivity fluctuations, firms find it optimal to offer sticky wages to new hires.

Ljungqvist and Sargent (2017) argue that search-theoretic models that produce a high elasticity of unemployment to productivity shocks often rely on a small "fundamental surplus"—that is, a small share of the flow of output produced by a firm-worker pair that "the invisible hand can allocate to vacancy creation." Because the notion of fundamental surplus is somewhat fuzzy—as pointed out by Christiano, Eichenbaum, and Trabandt (2021)—one might be able to interpret stubborn beliefs as making the fundamental surplus smaller than it would be under rational expectations. I believe, however, that this would not be a fruitful approach. The mechanism at work here is conceptually different. Workers' stubborn beliefs about labor-market prospects affect their bargaining strategy and, in turn, make the bargained wage less responsive to productivity shocks. As a result, the profit margin enjoyed by firms becomes more responsive to productivity shocks. It is also worth pointing out that a small fundamental surplus and wage stickiness are not the only way to go from small productivity shocks to large unemployment fluctuations (see, e.g., Menzio and Shi 2011; Kaplan and Menzio 2016; Kehoe, Midrigan, and Pastorino 2019; Golosov and Menzio 2020).

II. Environment and Definition of Equilibrium

In this section, I propose a search-theoretic model of the labor market in which the workers' expectations about the probability of finding a job and the wage they would earn after finding a job are stubborn—in the sense that they do not change in response to fluctuations in aggregate productivity. In terms of preferences, technology, and search frictions, I make the same assumptions as Pissarides (1985). In terms of expectations, I assume that workers believe that aggregate productivity is always equal to its "normal" value and they form expectations about the tightness of the labor market, the probability of finding a job, and the wage they will earn once they find a job by computing the equilibrium outcomes of a hypothetical labor market without aggregate productivity shocks. The workers' expectations have an impact on the equilibrium outcomes of the actual labor market because they affect the worker's bargaining strategy and, in turn, the wage and the tightness of the labor market.

A. Environment

The labor market is populated by a measure one of workers and by a positive measure of firms. A worker maximizes the present value of income discounted at some factor β, where $\beta \in (0, 1)$. A worker's income is given by some wage w when he is employed, and by some value of leisure b when he is unemployed. A firm maximizes the present value of profits discounted at the factor β. A firm operates a constant return-to-scale technology that turns one unit of labor into y units of output. I will refer to y as aggregate productivity.

The labor market is subject to search frictions. Unemployed workers search the labor market to locate vacant jobs, and firms search the labor market to locate unemployed workers by opening and maintaining job vacancies at some unit cost $k > 0$. The outcome of the search process is a number $M(u, v)$ of random bilateral meetings between unemployed workers and vacant jobs, where u denotes the measure of unemployed workers, v denotes the measure of vacant jobs, and M is a constant return-to-scale function of u and v. An unemployed worker meets a vacancy with probability $p(\theta) \equiv M(1, \theta)$, where $\theta \equiv v/u$ denotes the tightness of the labor market and $p(\theta)$ is a strictly increasing and concave function with $p(0) = 0$ and $p(\infty) = 1$. A vacancy meets an unemployed worker with probability $q(\theta) = p(\theta)/\theta$, where $q(\theta)$ is a strictly decreasing function with $q(0) = 1$ and $q(\infty) = 0$.

Upon meeting, a worker and a firm bargain over the wage. The bargaining game follows the alternating-offer protocol of Binmore et al. (1986). Without loss in generality, assume that the game starts with the worker making a wage demand. If the firm accepts the worker's demand, the game ends. If the firm rejects the worker's demand, the negotiation breaks down with probability $1 - \exp(-\lambda\Delta)$, and it continues with probability $\exp(-\lambda\Delta)$, where $\lambda > 0$ and $\Delta > 0$. If the negotiation breaks down, the game ends. If the negotiation continues, the firm makes a wage offer. If the worker accepts the wage offer, the game ends. If the worker rejects, the negotiation breaks down with probability $1 - \exp(-\mu\Delta)$, where $\mu > 0$. With probability $\exp(-\mu\Delta)$, the negotiation continues with the worker making another wage demand. The firm and the worker keep taking turns until either they reach an agreement or the negotiation breaks down. As standard in the bargaining literature, I will focus on the outcome of the bargaining game in the limit for $\Delta \to 0$.

If the bargaining game ends with a breakdown, the worker moves back into unemployment and the firm's job remains vacant. If the bargaining game ends with an agreement at some wage w, the firm and the worker start producing output y and the firm pays the wage w to the worker. The employment relationship between the firm and the worker continues until it is dissolved with some probability $\delta \in (0, 1)$.

Aggregate productivity follows a simple stochastic process. If $y = y^*$ in the current period, then next period's aggregate productivity y_+ is equal to y^* with probability ϕ_s and to some $\tilde{y}$ with probability $1 - \phi_s$, where $\phi_s \in [0, 1]$ and $\tilde{y}$ is a drawn from a cumulative distribution function $H(\tilde{y})$ with support $[y_\ell, y_h]$ and mean y^*. If $y \neq y^*$ in the current period, then next period's aggregate productivity y_+ is equal to y with probability ϕ_r and to y^* with probability $1 - \phi_r$, with $\phi_r \in [0, 1]$. The unconditional mean of the stochastic process for aggregate productivity is y^*. The parameter ϕ_s controls the frequency at which productivity shocks happen, and the parameter ϕ_r controls the duration of productivity shocks.

When a worker is negotiating with a firm and deciding whether to accept or reject a wage offer, he makes an intertemporal calculation—a calculation that involves comparing the value of being employed at the wage offered by the firm and the value of remaining unemployed and having to search for another firm. For this reason, the worker's expectations about future labor-market outcomes affect his current bargaining strategy and, in turn, the result of the current bargaining game. In the search-theoretic literature, it is standard to assume that the worker's expectations about future labor-market outcomes are correct—that is, the worker knows the law of motion and the current realization of aggregate productivity, and he correctly computes the mapping between aggregate productivity and labor-market tightness, job-finding probability, firms' bargaining strategies, and wage outcomes.

Motivated by the empirical evidence in Mueller et al. (2021), I assume that a worker's expectations about labor-market outcomes are incorrect. Specifically, a worker incorrectly believes that aggregate productivity is always equal to y^*. Based on this belief, the worker forms expectations about the tightness of the labor market, the job-finding probability, the firm's bargaining strategy, and the wage by computing the equilibrium outcomes of a hypothetical labor market in which aggregate productivity is always equal to y^*. When a worker finds himself negotiating with a particular firm, I consider two alternative scenarios, which, as I will show, lead to different outcomes of the bargaining game. In the first scenario, the worker observes the actual productivity y of the firm and, if different from y^*, he rationalizes $y - y^*$ as a permanent firm-specific component of productivity. In the second scenario, the worker does not observe the actual productivity y of the firm and, instead, believes it to be y^*. In contrast to workers, firms have correct expectations about aggregate productivity, labor-market tightness, worker's bargaining strategy, and wages. In particular, firms know that the worker's beliefs are incorrect.

B. Equilibrium Conditions and Bargaining Outcomes

To define an equilibrium, I need some notation. Let $V_0(y)$ denote the worker's actual value of unemployment, and $\hat{V}_0$ the worker's perceived value of unemployment—that is, the value of unemployment calculated based on the worker's beliefs. Let $V_1(w, y)$ denote the worker's actual value of employment at the wage w, and $\hat{V}_1(w)$ the worker's perceived value of employment at the wage w. Let $J(w, y)$ denote the firm's value from employing a worker at the wage w, and $\hat{J}(w, y)$ the worker's perception of that value. Let $\theta(y)$ denote the actual tightness of the labor market, and $\hat{\theta}$ the tightness expected by the worker. Last, let $w(y)$ denote the actual wage outcome of the bargaining game between a worker and a firm, and $\hat{w}$ the wage outcome expected by the worker.

The worker's actual and perceived values of unemployment are, respectively, given by

$$V_0(y) = b + \beta \mathbb{E}_{y_+} [p(\theta(y_+))V_1(w(y_+), y_+) + (1 - p(\theta(y_+)))V_0(y_+)], \qquad (1)$$

$$\hat{V}_0 = b + \beta [p(\hat{\theta})\hat{V}_1(\hat{w}) + (1 - p(\hat{\theta}))\hat{V}_0]. \qquad (2)$$

Consider equation (1). In the current period, the worker's income is b. In the next period, the worker meets a firm with probability $p(\theta(y_+))$. In this case, the worker and the firm agree to the wage $w(y_+)$ and the worker's continuation value is $V_1(w(y_+), y_+)$. With probability $1 - p(\theta(y_+))$, the worker does not meet a firm. In this case, the worker remains unemployed and his continuation value is $V_0(y_+)$. Now, consider equation (2). In the current period, the worker's income is b. In the next period, the worker expects to meet a firm with probability $p(\hat{\theta})$. Conditional on meeting a firm, the worker expects to agree to the wage $\hat{w}$ and to enjoy the continuation value $\hat{V}_1(\hat{w})$. The worker expects to not meet a firm with probability $1 - p(\hat{\theta})$. Conditional on not meeting a firm, the worker expects a continuation value of $\hat{V}_0$.

The worker's actual and perceived values of employment at the wage w are given by

$$V_1(w, y) = w + \beta \mathbb{E}_{y_+} [(1 - \delta)V_1(w, y_+) + \delta V_0(y_+)], \qquad (3)$$

$$\hat{V}_1(w) = w + \beta [(1 - \delta)\hat{V}_1(w) + \delta \hat{V}_0]. \qquad (4)$$

Consider the Bellman equation for $V_1(w, y)$. In the current period, the worker's income is w. In the next period, the worker becomes unemployed with probability δ. In this case, the worker's continuation value is $V_0(y_+)$. The worker remains employed with probability $1 - \delta$. In this case, the worker's continuation value is $V_1(w, y_+)$. The Bellman equation for $\hat{V}_1(w)$ is the same as for $V_1(w, y)$, except that the worker expects continuation values $\hat{V}_0$ and $\hat{V}_1(w)$ rather than $V_0(y_+)$ and $V_1(w, y_+)$.

The firm's actual value from having an employee and the worker's perception of such value are given by

$$J(w, y) = y - w + \beta \mathbb{E}_{y_+} [(1 - \delta)J(w, y_+)], \qquad (5)$$

$$\hat{J}(w, \hat{y}) = \hat{y} - w + \beta(1 - \delta)\hat{J}(w, \hat{y}). \qquad (6)$$

Consider equation (5). In the current period, the firm earns a profit of $y - w$ from the employee. In the next period, the firm loses the employee with probability δ, in which case its continuation value is zero. The firm retains the employee with probability $1 - \delta$, in which case its continuation value is $J(w, y_+)$. Now, consider equation (6). Let $\hat{y}$ denote the worker's perception of the firm's productivity. In the current period, the worker perceives the firm's profit to be $\hat{y} - w$. In the next period, the worker expects the firm to retain the employee with probability $1 - \delta$, in which case he expects the firm's continuation value to be $\hat{J}(w, \hat{y})$.

The actual tightness of the labor market is given by

$$k = q(\theta(y))J(w(y), y). \qquad (7)$$

That is, the actual tightness $\theta(y)$ is such that the firm's cost from opening a vacancy, k, is equal to the benefit, $q(\theta(y))J(w(y), y)$—which is the product between the firm's probability of filling the vacancy and the firm's value of having an extra worker employed at the wage $w(y)$.

In contrast, the tightness of the labor market expected by the worker is given by

$$k = q(\hat{\theta})\hat{J}(\hat{w}, y^*). \qquad (8)$$

That is, the tightness $\hat{\theta}$ is such that, from the worker's perspective, the firm's cost from opening a vacancy, k, is equal to the benefit, $q(\hat{\theta})\hat{J}(\hat{w}, y^*)$—which is the product between the firm's probability of filling a vacancy and the firm's value of having an extra worker employed at the wage $\hat{w}$, as perceived by the worker.

Up to this point, the equilibrium conditions that describe the actual agents' values and the actual aggregate outcomes of the economy do not interact with the equilibrium conditions that describe the workers' perception of the agents' values and the workers' expectations about aggregate outcomes. The two blocks of conditions interact in the outcome of the bargaining game between a worker and a firm, which I characterize next.

I start with the characterization of the outcome of the bargaining game for the scenario in which the worker observes the productivity of the firm y and rationalizes the difference $y - y^*$ as a permanent, firm-specific component of productivity. In this scenario, the worker's bargaining strategy is the best response to the strategy that he expects the firm to follow—which is the strategy that a firm with productivity y would follow in an economy in which the aggregate component of productivity is always equal to y^*. As known from Binmore et al., the strategy of this hypothetical firm is to make the wage offer $\hat{w}_o$ and to accept any wage demand $w_d \leq w_d^*$, where w_d^* and $\hat{w}_o$ are such that

$$\hat{J}(w_d^*, y) = e^{-\lambda\Delta}\hat{J}(\hat{w}_o, y), \tag{9}$$

$$\hat{V}_1(\hat{w}_o, y) = (1 - e^{-\mu\Delta})\hat{V}_0 + e^{-\mu\Delta}\hat{V}_1(w_d^*, y). \tag{10}$$

Equation (9) states that w_d^* is such that the hypothetical firm is indifferent between accepting w_d^* (left-hand side) and rejecting w_d^* (right-hand side). The hypothetical firm's value of rejecting w_d^* is equal to the probability that the negotiation continues times the firm's value of reaching an agreement at the wage $\hat{w}_o$. Equation (10) states that $\hat{w}_o$ is such that the worker is indifferent between accepting $\hat{w}_o$ (left-hand side) and rejecting $\hat{w}_o$ (right-hand side). The value of rejecting $\hat{w}_o$ is equal to the probability that the negotiation breaks down times the value of unemployment plus the probability that the negotiation continues times the value of reaching an agreement at the wage w_d^*. The worker's bargaining strategy is the best response to the strategy of this hypothetical firm. It is easy to see that the worker's best response is to make the wage demand w_d^* and to accept any wage offer $w_o \geq \hat{w}_o$.

The actual firm's bargaining strategy is the best response to the worker's bargaining strategy. Assuming that $J(\hat{w}_o, y) \geq 0$, the firm finds it optimal to offer the wage $w_o^* = \hat{w}_o$. It is easy to see why this is the case. If the firm offers a wage $w_o = \hat{w}_o$, the worker accepts $\hat{w}_o$ and the firm's payoff is $J(\hat{w}_o, y)$. If the firm offers any wage $w_o > \hat{w}_o$, the worker accepts w_o and the firm's payoff is $J(w_o, y)$, which is strictly smaller than $J(\hat{w}_o, y)$). If the firm offers any wage $w_o < \hat{w}_o$, the worker rejects w_o and demands the wage w_d^*. If the firm accepts w_d^*, its payoff is $\exp(-\mu\Delta)J(w_d^*, y)$, which is strictly smaller than $J(\hat{w}_o, y)$ because equation (9) implies that $w_d^* > \hat{w}_o$. If the firm rejects w_d^*, the firm finds itself again in the position of making a wage offer. Because the worker's strategy is stationary, the firm has nothing to gain from having delayed the trade.

The firm finds it optimal to accept any wage demand w_d such that

$$J(w_d, y) \geq e^{-\lambda\Delta}J(w_o^*, y). \tag{11}$$

Because $J(w, y) \neq \hat{J}(w, y)$, the firm may find it optimal to reject the worker's equilibrium wage demand w_d^*. In particular, if $y < y^*$ and $\phi_r < 1$, $J(w, y) > \hat{J}(w, y)$ because the worker believes y to be a permanent component of productivity and y is an aggregate component of productivity that reverts back to the mean. Therefore, if $y < y^*$, the firm finds it optimal to accept w_d^*. Conversely, if $y > y^*$, the firm finds it optimal to reject w_d^*.

Given the bargaining strategy of the worker and the bargaining strategy of the firm, I can characterize the outcome of the bargaining game.

For $\Delta \to 0$, the outcome of the bargaining game is such that the worker and the firm reach an agreement with probability 1 at the wage

$$w(y) = \frac{\lambda}{\lambda + \mu} y + \frac{\mu}{\lambda + \mu} (1 - \beta) \hat{V}_0. \tag{12}$$

In words, the wage demanded by the worker and the wage offered by the firm are identical, and they are equal to a weighted average between the worker's annuitized value of unemployment and the firm's current productivity, as perceived by the worker. The weight on the worker's value of unemployment is $\mu/(\lambda + \mu)$ and the weight on the firm's productivity is $\lambda/(\lambda + \mu)$. I will denote $\lambda/(\lambda + \mu)$ as γ and refer to it as the worker's bargaining power. I will denote $\mu/(\lambda + \mu)$ as $1 - \gamma$ and refer to it as the firm's bargaining power. Similarly, in the scenario where the worker does not observe the firm's productivity y and instead believes it to be equal to y^*, the firm and the worker reach an agreement with probability 1 at the wage $w(y) = w(y^*)$. In both scenarios, it is easy to show that the worker's expected wage upon meeting a firm is $\hat{w} = w(y^*)$.

I summarize the characterization of the bargaining game in the following proposition.

Proposition 1. (Bargaining outcomes.) The equilibrium outcome of the bargaining game is as follows:

1. If the worker observes the firm's productivity y, the worker and the firm reach an agreement with probability 1 at the wage $w(y)$, where $w(y)$ is given by equation (12);
2. If the worker believes that the firm's productivity is y^*, the worker and the firm reach an agreement with probability 1 at the wage $w(y^*)$;
3. When searching the market, the worker expects to earn the wage $\hat{w} = w(y^*)$ upon meeting a firm.

A few comments about Proposition 1 are in order. The equilibrium wage is determined entirely by the worker's beliefs. The worker's optimal bargaining strategy is the best response to the firm's bargaining strategy expected by the worker—that is, the bargaining strategy that a firm would follow if the worker's and firm's agreement payoffs were $\hat{V}_1(w)$ and $\hat{J}(w, \hat{y})$ and the disagreement payoffs were $\hat{V}_0$ and 0. The worker's best response to the firm's bargaining strategy expected by the worker is to demand the wage w_d^* and to accept any wage offer above $\hat{w}_o$, with $w_d^* = \hat{w}_o = w(\hat{y})$ and $\hat{y} = y$ in the first scenario and $\hat{y} = y^*$ in the second scenario. The firm understands that the worker's beliefs are incorrect and therefore anticipates the worker's strategy. Given the worker's strategy, the firm has no choice but to trade at the wage $w(\hat{y})$. In some sense, its awareness of the worker's beliefs forces the firm to passively respond to the worker's bargaining strategy.

The equilibrium wage is an average between the worker's annuitized value of unemployment and the firm's productivity, as perceived by the worker. In the first scenario, the equilibrium wage does not respond to changes in the worker's actual value of unemployment caused by aggregate productivity fluctuations. Because the worker's actual value of unemployment moves in the same direction as aggregate productivity, the equilibrium wage tends to be "sticky." This is the same type of stickiness obtained in Hall and Milgrom (2008), albeit through an entirely different channel. Hall and Milgrom (2008) assume that, when the negotiation between the worker and the firm breaks down, the two parties cannot trade in the current period, but they enter the next period matched. For this reason, the worker's and firm's bargaining strategies and, in turn, the wage outcome are independent from the worker's value of unemployment and, hence, from its changes. Here, the equilibrium wage does not respond to changes in the worker's value of unemployment because the worker believes that the value of unemployment to be constant.

In the second scenario, the equilibrium wage does not respond to changes in the firm's productivity nor to changes in the worker's value of unemployment caused by fluctuations in aggregate productivity. Hence, in the second scenario, the equilibrium wage is "rigid." Hall (2005) obtains the same result through a different mechanism. Hall (2005) assumes that the wage is not given by the outcome of a bargaining game between the worker and the firm, but rather it is determined by a social norm. Because the social norm is assumed to be invariant to aggregate productivity fluctuations, the wage is rigid. Here, the wage is rigid because the worker—no matter what aggregate productivity might be—is convinced that the aggregate state of productivity and the productivity of the firm with which he is bargaining are always equal to y^*.

Finally, note that the equilibrium wage equation (12) links the conditions that describe the workers' perception of the agents' values and the worker's expectations of aggregate outcomes with the conditions that describe the actual agents' values and aggregate outcomes. In fact, the equilibrium wage—which is entirely determined by the workers' beliefs—affects the firms' benefit from opening vacancies and, in turn, the actual market tightness.

I am now in the position to define a Stubborn Beliefs Equilibrium (SBE).

Definition 1.   (SBE.) An SBE is given by actual and perceived values $\{V_0, V_1, J,$ $\hat{V}_0, \hat{V}_1, \hat{J}\}$, actual and expected market tightness $\{\theta, \hat{\theta}\}$, and actual and expected wages $\{w, \hat{w}\}$ such that:

1. The values $\{V_0, V_1, J, \hat{V}_0, \hat{V}_1, \hat{J}\}$ satisfy conditions (eqs. [1]–[6]);
2. The tightnesses θ and $\hat{\theta}$ satisfy conditions (eq. [7]) and (eq. [8]);
3. The wage w satisfies condition (eq. [12]) and $\hat{w} = w(y^*)$.

It will be useful to compare the SBE with the standard Rational Expectations Equilibrium (REE), in which the workers' expectations are correct. An REE is defined as follows.

Definition 2.   (REE.) An REE is given by values $\{V_0, V_1, J\}$, tightness θ, and wage w such that:

1. The values $\{V_0, V_1, J\}$ satisfy conditions (eq. [1]), (eq. [3]), and (eq. [5]);
2. The tightness θ satisfies condition (eq. [7]);
3. The wage w is such that the gains from trade accruing to the firm, $J(w(y), y)$, are equal to a fraction $1 - \gamma$ of $V_1(w(y), y) + J(w(y), y) - V_0(y)$.

Before moving to the characterization of an SBE and its comparison with an REE, let me point out a couple of properties of equilibrium. First, the worker's beliefs about market tightness, job-finding probability, and wages are all correct when aggregate productivity y is equal to y^*. To see why this is the case, note that the worker's expected wage $\hat{w}$ is equal to $w(y^*)$—which, up to a first-order approximation, is equal to the wage that would emerge in an REE when $y = y^*$. Moreover, the worker's perception of the firm's value $\hat{J}(w, y^*)$ is equal to the firm's actual value $J(w, y^*)$, which, through equilibrium conditions (eq. [7]) and (eq. [8]), implies that the worker's expected market tightness $\hat{\theta}$ is equal to $\theta(y^*)$ and, hence, the worker's expected job-finding probability $p(\hat{\theta})$ is equal to $p(\theta(y^*))$. Because the unconditional mean of aggregate productivity is y^*, the fact that the worker's expectations are correct when $y = y^*$ implies that, up to a first-order approximation, the worker's expectations are correct on average.

Thus, there are two alternative interpretations for an SBE: (i) the worker believes aggregate productivity y is always equal to y^*, and he forms expectations about tightness, job-finding probability, and wages by solving for the equilibrium outcomes of a hypothetical labor market in which y never moves away from y^*; (ii) the worker believes that aggregate productivity is always equal to y^*, and he forms expectations about tightness, job-finding probability, and wages based on their actual long-run averages. Although I defined an SBE based on the first interpretation, it turns out to be consistent with the second interpretation as well.

Second, when $y = y^*$, the market tightness, job-finding probability, and wages in an SBE coincide with the market tightness, job-finding probability, and wages in an REE. To see why this is the case, it is sufficient to notice that, when $y = y^*$, the equilibrium conditions for an SBE coincide—up to a first-order approximation—with the equilibrium conditions for an REE. This property of an SBE implies that—when the economy is in its "normal" state y^*—the equilibrium outcomes in an SBE are the same as in a version of the model where workers have rational expectations.

III. Properties of Equilibrium

In this section, I characterize the properties of an SBE and compare them with the properties of an REE. I am particularly interested in comparing the elasticity of the market tightness, the job-finding probability, and the unemployment and vacancy rates with respect to aggregate productivity when workers have stubborn or rational beliefs about their labor-market prospects. I find that the elasticity of the market tightness, job-finding probability, and unemployment and vacancy rates are all higher in an SBE than in an REE.

A. Properties of an REE

Let me start with the characterization of an REE. Let me denote as $S(y)$ the surplus of a match between a worker and a firm, which is defined as the difference between the sum of the values to a worker and a firm if they do trade, $V_1(w, y) + J(w, y)$, and the sum of their values if they do not trade, $V_0(y)$. Using equations (1), (3), (5), and the outcome of the bargaining game, I can write $S(y)$ as

$$S(y) = y - b - \beta\mathbb{E}_{y_+}[p(\theta(y_+))\gamma S(y_+)] + \beta\mathbb{E}_{y_+}[(1 - \delta)S(y_+)]. \quad (13)$$

Equation (13) is a Bellman equation for the surplus of a match. In the current period, the flow of surplus is given by the difference between the joint income of a worker and a firm if they are matched and their joint income if they are not matched, $y - b$, net of the worker's option value of searching, $\beta\mathbb{E}_{y_+}[p(\theta(y_+))\gamma S(y_+)]$. In the next period, the match breaks with probability δ and survives with probability $1 - \delta$. In the first case, the continuation surplus is zero. In the second case, the continuation surplus is $S(y_+)$.

Using the definition of surplus and the outcome of the bargaining game, I can write equation (7) as

$$k = q(\theta(y))(1 - \gamma)S(y). \tag{14}$$

Equation (14) states that the market tightness $\theta(y)$ is such that the firm's cost of opening a vacancy is equal to the firm's probability of filling the vacancy times the firm's value of filling the vacancy—which, given the outcome of the bargaining game, is equal to a fraction $1 - \gamma$ of the surplus of the match between the firm and a worker.

Taken together, equations (13) and (14) characterize an REE. To understand the cyclical properties of an REE, I differentiate equations (13) and (14) with respect to the aggregate productivity y and derive expressions for the elasticities of the surplus of a match and the tightness of the labor market with respect to y in a neighborhood of y^*. Differentiating equation (13) with respect to y yields

$$\frac{S'(y^*)y^*}{S(y^*)} = \frac{1 - \beta[1 - \delta - p(\theta(y^*))\gamma]}{1 - \beta\phi_r[1 - \delta - p(\theta(y^*))\gamma]} \cdot \frac{y^*}{y^* - b}$$
$$- \frac{\beta\phi_r p(\theta(y^*))\gamma\epsilon}{1 - \beta[1 - \delta - p(\theta(y^*))\gamma]} \cdot \frac{\theta'(y^*)y^*}{\theta(y^*)}, \tag{15}$$

where ϵ denotes the elasticity of the job-finding probability p with respect to θ. Equation (15) states that the elasticity of the surplus with respect to y is given by the difference of two terms. The first term is proportional to the elasticity of $y - b$ with respect to y, and it captures the effect of an increase in y on the difference between the joint income generated by a firm and a worker when they are matched rather than unmatched. The second term is proportional to the elasticity of θ with respect to y and captures the effect of an increase in y on a worker's option value of searching.

Differentiating equation (14) with respect to y yields

$$\frac{\theta'(y^*)y^*}{\theta(y^*)} = \frac{1}{1 - \epsilon} \cdot \frac{S'(y^*)y^*}{S(y^*)}, \tag{16}$$

where $1 - \epsilon$ is the elasticity of the job-filling probability q with respect to θ. Equation (16) states that the elasticity of the labor-market tightness with respect to y is proportional to the elasticity of the surplus with respect to y. The constant of proportionality is the inverse of the elasticity of q with respect to θ and captures the extent to which the tightness needs to move for the job-filling probability to absorb a given change in the surplus of a match.

Using equations (15) and (16), I can solve for the elasticity of the surplus and the elasticity of the market tightness. Specifically, these elasticities are

$$\frac{S'(y^*)y^*}{S(y^*)} = \frac{1 - \beta[1 - \delta - p(\theta(y^*))\gamma]}{1 - \beta\phi_r[1 - \delta - p(\theta(y^*))\gamma/(1 - \epsilon)]} \cdot \frac{y^*}{y^* - b} \quad (17)$$

and

$$\frac{\theta'(y^*)y^*}{\theta(y^*)} = \frac{1}{1 - \epsilon} \cdot \frac{1 - \beta[1 - \delta - p(\theta(y^*))\gamma]}{1 - \beta\phi_r[1 - \delta - p(\theta(y^*))\gamma/(1 - \epsilon)]} \cdot \frac{y^*}{y^* - b}. \quad (18)$$

The elasticity of the job-finding probability, $p(\theta(y))$, the elasticity of the stationary unemployment rate, $u(y) = \delta/(\delta + p(\theta(y)))$, and the elasticity of the stationary vacancy rate, $v(y) = u(y)\theta(y)$, are all proportional to the elasticity of the market tightness. Specifically, these elasticities are

$$\frac{p'(\theta(y^*))\theta'(y^*)y^*}{p(\theta(y^*))} = \epsilon \cdot \frac{\theta'(y^*)y^*}{\theta(y^*)}, \quad (19)$$

$$\frac{u'(y^*)y^*}{u(y^*)} = -\epsilon \cdot \frac{p(\theta(y^*))}{\delta + p(\theta(y^*))} \cdot \frac{\theta'(y^*)y^*}{\theta(y^*)}, \quad (20)$$

$$\frac{v'(y^*)y^*}{v(y^*)} = \frac{\theta'(y^*)y^*}{\theta(y^*)} + \frac{u'(y^*)y^*}{u(y^*)}. \quad (21)$$

B. Properties of an SBE

I now characterize an SBE in the first scenario—that is, when workers observe the productivity y of the firm with which they are bargaining and rationalize any difference between y and y^* as a permanent and firm-specific component of productivity.

Let me denote as $\hat{S}(y)$ the worker's perceived surplus of a match with a firm. I define $\hat{S}(y)$ as the worker's perceived difference between the sum of his and the firm's value if they do trade, $\hat{V}_1(w) + \hat{J}(w, y)$, and the sum of the their values if they do not trade, $\hat{V}_0$. Using equations (4) and (6), it follows that $\hat{S}(y)$ is given by

$$\hat{S}(y) = \frac{y - (1 - \beta)\hat{V}_0}{1 - \beta(1 - \delta)}. \quad (22)$$

Using equations (22) and (12), it follows that the outcome of the bargaining game is such that, from the worker's perspective, he captures a fraction γ of the surplus and the firm captures a fraction $1 - \gamma$ of the surplus. That is,

$$\hat{V}_1(w(y)) - \hat{V}_0 = \gamma\hat{S}(y), \text{ and } \hat{J}(w(y), y) = (1 - \gamma)\hat{S}(y). \tag{23}$$

Using equations (2) and (23) and the fact that $\hat{\theta} = \theta(y^*)$, it follows that the worker's perceived value of unemployment $\hat{V}_0$ is such that

$$(1 - \beta)\hat{V}_0 = b + \beta p(\theta(y^*))\gamma\hat{S}(y). \tag{24}$$

Combining equations (22) and (24), I can write the worker's perceived surplus as

$$\hat{S}(y) = y - b - \beta p(\theta(y^*))\gamma\hat{S}(y^*) + \beta(1 - \delta)\hat{S}(y). \tag{25}$$

Equation (25) is a Bellman equation for the perceived surplus of a match. In the current period, the perceived flow of surplus is given by the difference between the income produced by the worker and the firm when they are matched rather than unmatched, $y - b$, net of the worker's perceived option value of searching, $\beta p(\theta(y^*))\gamma\hat{S}(y^*)$. In the next period, the match breaks up with probability δ and continues with probability $1 - \delta$. In the first case, the perceived continuation surplus is zero. In the second case, the perceived continuation surplus is $\hat{S}(y)$.

Combining equations (7) and (23), I can write equation (7) as

$$k = q(\theta(y)) \left[(1 - \gamma)\hat{S}(y) - \frac{\beta(1 - \delta)(1 - \phi_r)}{1 - \beta\phi_r(1 - \delta)} \cdot \frac{y - y^*}{1 - \beta(1 - \delta)} \right]. \tag{26}$$

Equation (26) states that the tightness of the labor market is such that the firm's cost of opening a vacancy is equal to the firm's probability of filling a vacancy times the firm's value of filling a vacancy. In turn, the firm's value of filling a vacancy is equal to a fraction $1 - \gamma$ of the perceived surplus $\hat{S}(y)$ plus the difference between the firm's actual value of filling a vacancy and the worker's perception of it—a difference that exists because the worker interprets $y - y^*$ to be a permanent firm-specific component of productivity, and $y - y^*$ is a transitory aggregate component of productivity.

Taken together, equations (25) and (26) characterize an SBE. To understand the cyclical behavior of an SBE, I differentiate equations (25) and (26) with respect to y and derive expressions for the elasticities of the perceived surplus of a match and the actual tightness of the market with respect to aggregate productivity y in a neighborhood of y^*. Differentiating equation (25) with respect to y yields

$$\frac{\hat{S}'(y^*)y^*}{\hat{S}(y^*)} = \frac{1 - \beta[1 - \delta - p(\theta(y^*))\gamma]}{1 - \beta(1 - \delta)} \cdot \frac{y^*}{y^* - b}. \tag{27}$$

Differentiating equation (26) with respect to y yields

$$\frac{\theta'(y^*)y^*}{\theta(y^*)} = \frac{1}{1 - \epsilon} \cdot \frac{1 - \beta(1 - \delta)(1 + (1 - \phi_r)\gamma/(1 - \gamma))}{1 - \beta\phi_r(1 - \delta)} \cdot \frac{\hat{S}'(y^*)y^*}{\hat{S}(y^*)}. \tag{28}$$

Using equation (27) to substitute out $\hat{S}'(y^*)y^*/\hat{S}(y^*)$ in equation (28), I can write the elasticity of the labor-market tightness as

$$\frac{\theta'(y^*)y^*}{\theta(y^*)} = \frac{1}{1 - \epsilon} \cdot \frac{1 - \beta(1 - \delta)(1 + (1 - \phi_r)\gamma/(1 - \gamma))}{1 - \beta\phi_r(1 - \delta)}$$

$$\cdot \frac{1 - \beta[1 - \delta - p(\theta(y^*))\gamma]}{1 - \beta(1 - \delta)} \cdot \frac{y^*}{y^* - b}. \tag{29}$$

Equation (29) states that the elasticity of the labor-market tightness is proportional to the elasticity of the difference $y - b$ between the income generated by the worker and the firm when they are matched and the income generated by the worker and the firm when they are not matched. The constant of proportionality is the product of three terms. The first term captures the extent to which the market tightness needs to change for the firm's probability of filling a vacancy to absorb changes in the firm's value of filling a vacancy. The second term captures the relationship between changes in the firm's value of filling a vacancy and changes in the perceived surplus of a match. The last term captures the relationship between changes in the perceived surplus of a match and changes in $y - b$.

The elasticity of the labor-market tightness in an SBE is different than in an REE because of two misperceptions by workers. First, in an SBE, the worker does not recognize the existence of fluctuations in aggregate productivity and, hence, believes that his option value of searching is constant. For this reason, the worker's bargaining strategy is unaffected by the changes in the option value of searching caused by aggregate productivity fluctuations. This misperception tends to make the wage less sensitive and the market tightness more sensitive to aggregate productivity shocks. Second, in an SBE, the worker believes a firm has productivity $y \neq y^*$, because $y - y^*$ is a permanent firm-specific component of productivity rather than a transitory shock to the aggregate component of productivity. For this reason, the worker's bargaining strategy responds too much to the changes in the current productivity of the firm caused by aggregate productivity fluctuations. This misperception tends to make the wage more sensitive and the market tightness less sensitive to aggregate productivity shocks. Overall, the elasticity of the market tightness in an SBE may be higher or lower than in an REE. Yet, if aggregate productivity shocks are persistent enough, the second misperception is small and the elasticity of the market tightness is higher than in an SBE.

Next, I characterize the properties of an SBE in the second scenario—that is, when workers do not observe the productivity y of the firm with which they are bargaining and instead believe the productivity to be equal to y^*. In this scenario, the worker's perceived surplus from a match is given by

$$\hat{S} = y^* - b - \beta p(\theta(y^*))\gamma\hat{S} + \beta(1 - \delta)\hat{S}. \tag{30}$$

Equation (30) is a Bellman equation for the perceived surplus. In the current period, the perceived flow of surplus is given by the difference between the perceived income generated by the worker and the firm when they are matched rather than unmatched, $y^* - b$, net of the worker's perceived option value of searching, $\beta p(\theta(y^*))\gamma\hat{S}$. In the next period, the match breaks up with probability δ, in which case the perceived continuation surplus is zero, and survives with probability $1 - \delta$, in which case the perceived continuation surplus is $\hat{S}$.

The tightness of the labor market is given by

$$k = q(\theta(y))\left[(1 - \gamma)\hat{S} + \frac{1 - \beta(1 - \delta)(1 - \phi_r)}{1 - \beta\phi_r(1 - \delta)} \cdot \frac{y - y^*}{1 - \beta(1 - \delta)}\right]. \tag{31}$$

Equation (31) states that the market tightness is such that the firm's cost of opening a vacancy is equal to the probability of filling a vacancy times the value of filling a vacancy. In turn, the firm's value of filling a vacancy is equal to a fraction $1 - \gamma$ of the perceived surplus $\hat{S}$ plus the difference between the firm's actual value of filling a vacancy and the worker's perception of such value. The difference exists because the worker believes the firm's productivity to be y^* now and in the future; the firm's productivity is y now and possibly in the future.

Differentiating equation (31) with respect to y yields the following expression for the elasticity of the market tightness with respect to y in a neighborhood of y^*:

$$\frac{\theta'(y^*)y^*}{\theta(y^*)} = \frac{1}{1 - \epsilon} \cdot \frac{1}{1 - \gamma} \cdot \frac{1 - \beta[1 - \delta - p(\theta(y^*))\gamma]}{1 - \beta\phi_r(1 - \delta)} \cdot \frac{y^*}{y^* - b}. \tag{32}$$

The elasticity of the market tightness is again proportional to the elasticity of $y - b$ with respect to y. The constant of proportionality is the product of three terms. The first term captures the extent to which the market tightness needs to change for the firm's probability of filling a vacancy to absorb changes in the firm's value of filling a vacancy. The second and third terms capture the relationship between changes in $y - b$ and changes in the firm's value of filling a vacancy.

Also in the second scenario, the elasticity of the market tightness is different than in an REE because of two misperceptions by workers. First, the worker does not recognize the existence of fluctuations in aggregate productivity and therefore believes that his option value of searching is constant. For this reason, the worker's bargaining strategy is unaffected by changes in the option value of searching caused by aggregate productivity fluctuations. Second, the worker believes that the firm's productivity is y^* rather than y. For this reason, the worker's bargaining strategy is also unaffected by the changes in the productivity of the firm caused by aggregate productivity fluctuations. Overall, in the second scenario, the worker's bargaining strategy and the bargained wage do not respond at all to changes in aggregate productivity and, hence, the elasticity of the market tightness is higher than in an REE. The elasticity of the market tightness in the second scenario is also higher than in the first scenario, as workers make the same mistake in calculating the option value of searching but underestimate, rather than overestimate, the present value of the changes in the productivity of the firm with which they are bargaining.

Because the elasticities of the job-finding probability, the unemployment rate, and the vacancy rate depend on the elasticity of the market tightness in exactly the same way in an SBE and in an REE, the proof of the following proposition is complete.

Proposition 2. (Labor-market fluctuations.) There exists a $\phi_r^* \in (0, 1)$ such that for all $\phi_r > \phi_r^*$:

1. The elasticity of $\theta(y)$, $p(\theta(y))$, $u(y)$, and $v(y)$ with respect to y is greater in an SBE than in an REE;
2. In an SBE, the elasticity of $\theta(y)$, $p(\theta(y))$, $u(y)$, and $v(y)$ with respect to y is higher if workers do not observe the productivity y of the firm with which they are bargaining but rather believe such productivity to be y^*.

A simple back-of-the-envelope calibration reveals the importance of different assumptions about workers' beliefs on the elasticity of the labor-market variables with respect to aggregate productivity shocks. Assume that the average transition rate from unemployment to employment (UE) $p(\theta(y^*))$ is 30% per month, the average transition rate from employment to unemployment (EU) δ is 2% per month, the elasticity ϵ of the job-finding probability with respect to tightness is 0.5, the worker's bargaining power γ is 0.5, and the unemployment income b is half of the unconditional mean of aggregate productivity y^*. Although these values are somewhat arbitrary, they are similar to the values typically used to calibrate search-theoretic models of the labor market (see, e.g., Shimer 2005; Menzio and Shi 2011; Martellini, Menzio, and Visschers 2021). For the sake of simplicity, let me assume that the discount factor β is close to 1. Moreover, let me assume that productivity shocks are rare and permanent, in the sense that ϕ_s and ϕ_r are close to 1.

For $\beta, \phi_s, \phi_r \to 1$, the elasticity of the market tightness with respect to aggregate productivity shocks in an REE simplifies to

$$\frac{\theta'(y^*)y^*}{\theta(y^*)} = \underbrace{\frac{1}{1-\epsilon}}_{2} \cdot \underbrace{\frac{\delta + p(\theta(y^*))\gamma}{\delta + p(\theta(y^*))\gamma/(1-\epsilon)}}_{.53} \cdot \underbrace{\frac{y^*}{y^* - b}}_{2} = 2.12. \qquad (33)$$

The elasticity is equal to 2.12. That is, a 1% decline in the aggregate productivity of labor leads to a 2.12% decline in the tightness of the labor market. In turn, the elasticity of the UE rate is about 1%, and so are the elasticities of the unemployment and vacancy rates. As a point of comparison, note that the ratio of the standard deviation of the cyclical component of the labor-market tightness to the standard deviation of the cyclical component of productivity is about 20 in the postwar United States. The relative elasticity of the cyclical component of the UE rate is about 6, and the relative elasticities of the unemployment and vacancy rates are both close to 10.

For $\beta, \phi_s, \phi_r \to 1$, the elasticity of the market tightness in an SBE where workers observe the productivity of their employer simplifies to

$$\frac{\theta'(y^*)y^*}{\theta(y^*)} = \frac{1}{1-\epsilon} \cdot \underbrace{\frac{\delta + p(\theta(y^*))\gamma}{\delta}}_{8.5} \cdot \frac{y^*}{y^* - b} = 34. \qquad (34)$$

The elasticity is equal to 34. That is, a 1% decline in the aggregate productivity of labor leads to a 34% decline in the tightness of the labor market. The elasticity of the UE rate is about 17, and the elasticities of the unemployment and vacancy rates are both close to 16. All these elasticities are 16 times higher than in an REE.

For $\beta, \phi_s, \phi_r \to 1$, the elasticity of the market tightness in an SBE where workers do not observe the productivity of their employer simplifies to

$$\frac{\theta'(y^*)y^*}{\theta(y^*)} = \underbrace{\frac{1}{1-\epsilon}}_{2} \cdot \frac{1}{1-\gamma} \cdot \underbrace{\frac{\delta + p(\theta(y^*))\gamma}{\delta}}_{8.5} \cdot \frac{y^*}{y^* - b} = 68. \qquad (35)$$

The elasticity is equal to 68. In turn, the elasticity of the UE rate is about 34, and so are the elasticities of the unemployment and vacancy rates. These elasticities are 30 times higher than in an REE.

IV. Optimal Policy

In this section, I analyze the efficiency properties of an SBE and derive a formula for the optimal employment subsidy—that is, the subsidy that makes an SBE efficient. I start the analysis by solving the problem of a utilitarian social planner and deriving the efficient tightness of the labor market as a function of aggregate productivity. I then solve for the SBE in the presence of an arbitrary employment subsidy that is allowed to depend on aggregate productivity. Last, I derive a formula for the employment subsidy that makes an SBE efficient. I find that, even at the Hosios condition, the SBE is inefficient and the optimal employment subsidy is countercyclical.

A. Social-Planner Problem

A utilitarian social planner controls the tightness of the labor market to maximize the present value of aggregate income discounted at the factor β. Given a measure e of employed workers, a measure u of unemployed workers, and an aggregate productivity of y, the value $W(e, u, y)$ of the social plan is such that

$$W(e, u, y) = ey + ub + \beta \mathbb{E}_{y_+} \left[\max_{\theta \geq 0} - k\theta u + W(e_+, u_+, y_+) \right], \qquad (36)$$

$$\text{s.t. } e_+ = e(1 - \delta) + up(\theta), \text{ and } u_+ = u(1 - p(\theta)) + e\delta.$$

In the current period, aggregate income is the sum of the income produced by the workers who are employed, ey, and the income produced by the workers who are unemployed, ub. In the next period, $k\theta u$ units of income are spent to create vacancies, and the continuation value of the social plan is $W(e_+, u_+, y_+)$, where e_+ and u_+ denote next period's measures of employed and unemployed workers. As shown in Menzio and Shi (2011), $W(e, u, y)$ is linear in u and e.

Let $S_P(y)$ denote the difference between the value to the planner of an additional employed worker and the value to the planner of an additional unemployed worker. It is easy to verify that $S_P(y)$ is such that

$$S_P(y) = y - b - \beta \mathbb{E}_{y_+} [p(\theta_P(y_+))S_P(y_+) - k\theta_P(y_+)] \tag{37}$$
$$+ \beta \mathbb{E}_{y_+} [(1 - \delta)S_P(y_+)].$$

In the current period, the difference between the social value of an employed worker and the social value of an unemployed worker is the difference in the income they produce, $y - b$, net of the social value generated by the search of the unemployed worker, $p(\theta_P(y_+))S_P(y_+) - k\theta_P(y_+)$. In the next period, the employed worker becomes unemployed with probability δ, in which case the continuation difference in the social value of the two workers is zero, and he remains employed with probability $1 - \delta$, in which case the continuation difference in the social value of the two workers is $S_P(y_+)$.

Let $\theta_P(y)$ denote the optimal market tightness. It is easy to verify that $\theta_P(y)$ is such that

$$k = p'(\theta_P(y))S_P(y)$$
$$= q(\theta_P(y))\epsilon(\theta_P(y))S_P(y). \tag{38}$$

The optimal market tightness is such that the marginal cost of increasing the tightness, k, is equal to the marginal benefit—which is given by the increase in the probability that an unemployed worker becomes employed, $p'(\theta_P(y))$, times the difference between the social value of an employed worker and the social value of an unemployed worker, $S_P(y)$. The second line makes use of the fact that $q(\theta) = p(\theta)/\theta$ and of the definition of $\epsilon(\theta)$.

It is useful to take a linear approximation of equation (37) around $y = y^*$, which yields

$$S_P(y^*) = y^* - b - \beta p(\theta_P(y^*))(1 - \epsilon(\theta_P(y^*)))S_P(y^*) + \beta(1 - \delta)S_P(y^*), \tag{39}$$

$$S_P'(y^*) = 1 - \beta \phi_r p(\theta_P(y^*))S_P'(y^*) + \beta \phi_r (1 - \delta)S_P'(y^*). \tag{40}$$

The expression in equation (39) is derived from a linear approximation of equation (37) making use of the fact that equation (38) implies that $p(\theta_P(y^*))S_P(y^*) - k\theta_P(y^*)$ is equal to $p(\theta_P(y^*))(1 - \epsilon(\theta_P(y^*)))S_P(y^*)$. The expression in equation (40) is derived from a linear approximation of equation (37) making use of the fact that equation (38) implies that k is equal to $p'(\theta_P(y))S_P(y)$.

B. Optimal Employment Subsidy

I now want to derive a formula for the optimal employment subsidy $t(y)$. The subsidy is a flow transfer from the government to every firm that is currently employing a worker. The subsidy is financed through a lump-sum tax levied on all workers, irrespective of whether they are currently employed or unemployed. The subsidy is optimal when it is such that the market tightness in the equilibrium, $\theta(y)$, coincides with the market tightness in the solution of the social planner's problem, $\theta_P(y)$. To simplify the characterization of the optimal employment subsidy, I will assume that the elasticity $\epsilon(\theta)$ of the job-finding probability with respect to the market tightness is a constant ϵ in a neighborhood of $\theta_P(y^*)$.

Let me start by characterizing the optimal employment subsidy $t(y)$ in an REE. Given the subsidy $t(y)$, the surplus $S(y)$ and the tightness $\theta(y)$ are such that

$$S(y) = y + t(y) - b - \beta\mathbb{E}[p(\theta(y_+))\gamma S(y_+)] + \beta\mathbb{E}[(1-\delta)S(y_+)], \quad (41)$$

$$k = q(\theta(y))(1-\gamma)S(y). \quad (42)$$

A linear approximation of equation (41) around y^* yields

$$S(y^*) = y^* + t(y^*) - b - \beta p(\theta(y^*))\gamma S(y^*) + \beta(1-\delta)S(y^*), \quad (43)$$

$$S'(y^*) = 1 + t'(y^*) - \beta\phi_r p'(\theta(y^*))\theta'(y^*)\gamma S(y^*)$$
$$- \beta p(\theta(y^*))\gamma S'(y^*) + \beta\phi_r(1-\delta)S'(y^*). \quad (44)$$

A comparison between equations (38) and (42) reveals that the employment subsidy $t(y)$ is optimal if and only if the firm's benefit from opening a vacancy, $q(\theta(y))(1-\gamma)S(y)$, is equal to the planner's benefit from opening a vacancy, $q(\theta_P(y))\epsilon S_P(y)$, for $\theta(y) = \theta_P(y)$. Using the fact that $S(y^*)$ is approximately equal to equation (43) and $S_p(y^*)$ is approximately equal to the expression in equation (39), the optimal $t(y)$ for $y = y^*$ can be written as

$$t(y^*) = \left\{\frac{\epsilon}{1-\gamma} \cdot \frac{1 - \beta[1 - \delta - p(\theta_P(y^*))\gamma]}{1 - \beta[1 - \delta - p(\theta_P(y^*))(1-\epsilon)]} - 1\right\}(y^* - b). \quad (45)$$

Using the fact that $S'(y^*)$ is approximately equal to equation (44) and that $S_P'(y^*)$ is approximately equal to equation (40), the optimality condition for $t(y)$ in a neighborhood of y^* can be written as

$$1 + t'(y^*) = \frac{\epsilon}{1 - \gamma} \cdot \frac{1 - \beta\phi_r[1 - \delta - p(\theta_P(y^*))\gamma/(1 - \epsilon)]}{1 - \beta\phi_r[1 - \delta - p(\theta_P(y^*))]}. \qquad (46)$$

The formula in equation (45) implies that the optimal employment subsidy $t(y^*)$ is positive if $\epsilon > 1 - \gamma$, negative if $\epsilon < 1 - \gamma$, and zero if $\epsilon = 1 - \gamma$. The properties of $t(y^*)$ are an immediate consequence of the well-known efficiency properties of search-theoretic models (e.g., Mortensen 1982; Hosios 1990). When a firm opens a vacancy, it creates a negative congestion externality on the other firms searching the labor market. The congestion externality is equal to the difference between the probability that the vacancy is filled, $M(u, v)/v$, and the number of additional matches created by the vacancy, $M_v(u, v)$, times the firm's share of the surplus, $(1 - \gamma)S(y)$. When a firm opens a vacancy, it also creates a positive thick-market externality on the workers searching the labor market. The thick-market externality is equal to the number of additional matches created by the vacancy, $M_v(u, v)$, times the worker's share of the surplus, $\gamma S(y)$. Therefore, if the elasticity of the matching function with respect to vacancies, ϵ, exceeds the firm's bargaining power, $1 - \gamma$, the thick-market externality dominates and the equilibrium market tightness is inefficiently low. In this case, the optimal employment subsidy is positive. If $\epsilon < 1 - \gamma$, the congestion externality dominates, the equilibrium market tightness is inefficiently high, and the optimal employment subsidy is negative. At the Hosios condition, where $\epsilon = 1 - \gamma$, the equilibrium is efficient and the optimal employment subsidy is zero.

The formula in equation (46) implies that the derivative $t'(y^*)$ of the optimal employment subsidy is positive if $\epsilon > 1 - \gamma$, negative if $\epsilon < 1 - \gamma$, and zero if $\epsilon = 1 - \gamma$. The properties of $t'(y^*)$ are also easy to understand. An increase in aggregate productivity y leads to an increase in the surplus. If $\epsilon > 1 - \gamma$, the increase in the surplus magnifies the difference between the thick-market and the congestion externalities, and the optimal employment subsidy increases. If $\epsilon < 1 - \gamma$, the increase in the surplus magnifies the difference between the congestion and the thick-market externalities, and the optimal employment subsidy decreases. If $\epsilon = 1 - \gamma$, the equilibrium remains efficient, and the optimal employment subsidy remains equal to zero.

Now, let me characterize the optimal employment subsidy in an SBE. I begin by considering the scenario in which the worker observes the productivity y as well as the employment subsidy $t(y)$ of the firm with which he is bargaining. In this scenario, the worker's perceived surplus $\hat{S}(y)$ and the market's actual tightness $\theta(y)$ are such that

$$\hat{S}(y) = y + t(y) - b - \beta p(\theta(y^*))\gamma\hat{S}(y^*) + \beta(1 - \delta)\hat{S}(y), \tag{47}$$

$$k = q(\theta(y))\left[(1 - \gamma)\hat{S}(y) - \frac{\beta(1 - \delta)(1 - \phi_r)}{1 - \beta\phi_r(1 - \delta)} \cdot \frac{1 + t'(y^*)}{1 - \beta(1 - \delta)} \cdot (y - y^*)\right], \tag{48}$$

where the second term on the right-hand side of equation (48) is the difference between the firm's actual value of filling a vacancy and the worker's perception of such value, computed using a linear approximation of $t(y)$ around y^*.

The optimal employment subsidy is such that the firm's value of filling a vacancy (i.e., the right-hand side of eq. [48]) is equal to the planner's value of filling a vacancy (i.e., the right-hand side of eq. [38]). For $y = y^*$, the optimality condition for the employment subsidy yields equation (45). For $y = y^*$, the equilibrium conditions for an SBE coincide with the equilibrium conditions for an REE and, hence, the optimal employment subsidy is the same in an SBE as in an REE. For y in a neighborhood of y^*, the optimality condition for the employment subsidy yields

$$1 + t'(y^*) = \frac{\epsilon}{1 - \gamma} \cdot \frac{1 - \beta\phi_r[1 - \delta - p(\theta_P(y^*))\gamma/(1 - \epsilon)]}{1 - \beta[1 - \delta - p(\theta_P(y^*))]}$$

$$\cdot \frac{1 - \beta\phi_r(1 - \delta)}{1 - \beta\phi_r[1 - \delta - p(\theta_P(y^*))\gamma/(1 - \epsilon)]} \tag{49}$$

$$\cdot \frac{1 - \beta(1 - \delta)}{1 - \beta(1 - \delta)[1 + (1 - \phi_r)\gamma/(1 - \gamma)]}.$$

The first term on the right-hand side of equation (49) is equal to $1 + t'(y^*)$ in an REE. The second term on the right-hand side of equation (49) is equal to the elasticity of the market tightness with respect to y in an REE relative to the elasticity of the market tightness with respect to y in an SBE. If the market tightness is less elastic in an SBE than in an REE, the second term is larger than 1. This is the case if the persistence ϕ_r of aggregate productivity shock is smaller than ϕ_r^*. If the market tightness is more elastic in an SBE than in an REE, the second term is smaller than 1. This is the case if ϕ_r is greater than ϕ_r^*.

The formula in equation (49) implies that, as long as $\phi_r > \phi_r^*$, the optimal employment subsidy in an SBE is the given by the product between the optimal employment subsidy in an REE and a countercyclical term. For $\epsilon > 1 - \gamma$, the derivative of the optimal employment subsidy with respect to aggregate productivity y is positive in an REE, and it is either positive but smaller or altogether negative in an SBE. For $\epsilon < 1 - \gamma$, the derivative of the optimal employment subsidy with respect to y is negative in an REE, and it is more negative in an SBE. For $\epsilon = 1 - \gamma$, the case in which the optimal employment subsidy in an REE is equal to zero for all y, the derivative of the optimal employment subsidy with respect to y is negative. These properties are easy to understand. In an SBE, workers incorrectly perceive that the value of searching the labor market is acyclical and, hence, they bargain wages that are less procyclical than in an REE. As a result of the lower procyclicality of wages, the labor-market tightness is more procyclical than in an REE. To correct for the higher procyclicality of the labor-market tightness, the employment subsidy must incorporate an additional countercyclical term.

Last, I consider the scenario in which the worker observes neither the productivity y nor the employment subsidy $t(y)$ of the firm with which he is bargaining but rather believes that the firm's productivity is y^* and the employment subsidy is $t(y^*)$. In this scenario, the worker's perceived surplus $\hat{S}$ and the market's actual tightness $\theta(y)$ are such that

$$\hat{S} = y^* + t(y^*) - b - \beta p(\theta(y^*))\gamma\hat{S} + \beta(1 - \delta)\hat{S}, \tag{50}$$

$$k = q(\theta(y))\left[(1 - \gamma)\hat{S} + \frac{1 + t'(y^*)}{1 - \beta(1 - \delta)} \cdot (y - y^*)\right], \tag{51}$$

where the second term on the right-hand side of equation (51) is the difference between the firm's actual value of filling a vacancy and the worker's perception of such value, computed using a linear approximation of $t(y)$ around y^*.

The optimal employment subsidy is such that the firm's value of filling a vacancy (i.e., the right-hand side of eq. [51]) is equal to the planner's value of filling a vacancy (i.e., the right-hand side of eq. [38]). For $y = y^*$, the optimality condition for the employment subsidy yields equation (45). For y in a neighborhood of y^*, the optimality condition for the employment subsidy yields

$$1 + t'(y^*) = \frac{\epsilon}{1 - \gamma} \cdot \frac{1 - \beta\phi_r[1 - \delta - p(\theta_P(y^*))\gamma/(1 - \epsilon)]}{1 - \beta[1 - \delta - p(\theta_P(y^*))]}$$

$$\cdot (1 - \gamma)\frac{1 - \beta\phi_r(1 - \delta)}{1 - \beta\phi_r[1 - \delta - p(\theta_P(y^*))\gamma/(1 - \epsilon)]}. \tag{52}$$

The first term on the right-hand side of equation (52) is equal to $1 + t'(y^*)$ in an REE. The second term on the right-hand side of equation (52) is equal to the elasticity of the market tightness with respect to y in an REE relative to the elasticity of the market tightness with respect to y in an SBE. The second term is smaller than 1. Hence, the optimal employment subsidy is more countercyclical in an SBE than in an REE. The second term is also smaller than its analog in equation (49). Hence, the optimal employment subsidy is even more countercyclical in an SBE if workers do not observe the productivity of the firm with which they are bargaining.

The following proposition summarizes the characterization of the optimal employment subsidy.

Proposition 3. (Optimal policy.) For all $\phi_r > \phi_r^*$:

1. In an REE, the optimal employment subsidy is positive and procyclical if $\epsilon > 1 - \gamma$, negative and countercyclical if $\epsilon < 1 - \gamma$, and always equal to zero if $\epsilon = 1 - \gamma$;
2. In an SBE, the optimal employment subsidy is more countercyclical than in an REE. The optimal employment subsidy is more countercyclical if workers do not observe the productivity y of the firm with which they are bargaining but rather believe such productivity to be y^*.

To appreciate the impact of different assumptions about workers' expectations on the design of the optimal employment subsidy, it is useful to return to our back-of-the-envelope calibration. Recall that we calibrate the model to an average UE rate $p(\theta(y^*))$ of 30% per month, an average EU rate δ of 2% per month, an elasticity ϵ of the job-finding probability with respect to tightness of 0.5, a worker's bargaining power γ of 0.5, and an unemployment income b equal to half of y^*.

Because the Hosios condition $\epsilon = 1 - \gamma$ holds, the optimal employment subsidy at y^* is equal to zero both in an REE and in an SBE. For β, ϕ_s, $\phi_r \to 1$, the derivative of the optimal employment subsidy in an REE simplifies to

$$t'(y^*) = \underbrace{\frac{\epsilon}{1 - \gamma} \frac{\delta + \frac{\gamma}{1-\epsilon}p(\theta_P(y^*))}{\delta + p(\theta_P(y^*))}}_{1} - 1 = 0. \qquad (53)$$

The derivative of the optimal employment subsidy in an SBE where workers observe the productivity of their employer simplifies to

$$t'(y^*) = \underbrace{\frac{\epsilon}{1 - \gamma} \frac{\delta + \frac{\gamma}{1-\epsilon}p(\theta_P(y^*))}{\delta + p(\theta_P(y^*))}}_{1} \cdot \underbrace{\frac{\delta}{\delta + \frac{\gamma}{1-\epsilon}p(\theta_P(y^*))}}_{0.06} - 1 = -0.94. \qquad (54)$$

The derivative of the optimal employment subsidy in an SBE where workers do not observe the productivity of their employer simplifies to

$$t'(y^*) = \underbrace{\frac{\epsilon}{1-\gamma} \frac{\delta + \frac{\gamma}{1-\epsilon} p(\theta_P(y^*))}{\delta + p(\theta_P(y^*))}}_{1} \cdot \underbrace{\frac{\delta(1-\gamma)}{\delta + \frac{\gamma}{1-\epsilon} p(\theta_P(y^*))}}_{0.03} - 1 = -0.97. \quad (55)$$

In an REE, the optimal employment subsidy remains equal to zero in response to changes in aggregate labor productivity. In an SBE where workers observe the productivity of their employer, the optimal employment subsidy decreases by 94 cents for any \$1 increase in the aggregate component of productivity. In other words, the optimal employment subsidy is such that the postsubsidy output of a firm-worker match increases by only 6 cents for every \$1 of increase in presubsidy output. In an SBE where workers do not observe the productivity of their employer, the optimal employment subsidy decreases by 97 cents for any \$1 of increase in the aggregate component of productivity. In other words, the optimal employment subsidy is such that the postsubsidy output of a firm-worker match increases by only 3 cents for every \$1 of increase in presubsidy output. These findings show that almost all of the volatility of the labor market induced by productivity shocks in an SBE is inefficient, and the optimal employment subsidy is tasked with undoing almost all of productivity fluctuations.

V. Rational and Stubborn Workers

I now study a version of the model in which workers with stubborn beliefs coexist with workers with rational expectations. The extension is natural, because presumably some workers are aware of aggregate shocks and adjust accordingly their expectations about their probability of finding a job and the wage they would earn when hired. More importantly, the extension provides new and surprising insights. It would be natural to conjecture that a model in which some workers have stubborn beliefs and some workers have rational expectations behaves like a mixture of an REE and an SBE. The conjecture, however natural, turns out to be wrong. A model in which some workers have stubborn beliefs and some workers have rational expectations behaves exactly like an SBE in recessions, and it behaves like a mixture of an REE and an SBE only in expansions. The intuition behind this result is relatively simple. In recessions, a firm cannot successfully wage discriminate between rational and stubborn workers, because a rational worker can mimic the strategy of a stubborn worker and earn the same wage. As a result, in response to a negative productivity shock, the average wage is as downward sticky or rigid as in an SBE and the market tightness, job-finding probability, and unemployment and vacancy rates are as elastic as in an SBE. In expansions, a rational worker will signal his type to the firm and, hence, earn a different wage than a stubborn worker. As a result, in response to a positive productivity shock, the average wage is upward sticky or rigid proportionally to the fraction of stubborn workers in the economy. Therefore, the market tightness, job-finding probability, and unemployment and vacancy rates are not as elastic as in an SBE.

A. Equilibrium Conditions

I consider a version of the model in which there are two types of workers: stubborn and rational. Stubborn workers (S) believe that the aggregate component of productivity y is always equal to y^* and, based on such belief, they compute the equilibrium of a hypothetical labor market and use it to form expectations about the tightness of the labor market, the job-finding probability, the firm's bargaining strategy, and the wage. Rational workers (R) know the actual law of motion for aggregate productivity, the current realization of aggregate productivity, and the economic environment—including the measure and beliefs of workers of type S. Therefore, they know the actual equilibrium mapping between aggregate productivity, market tightness, job-finding probability, firm's bargaining strategy, and wages. The measure of workers of type S is σ, and the measure of workers of type R is $1 - \sigma$, with $\sigma \in (0, 1)$. Firms, like workers of type R, know the law of motion, the current realization of aggregate productivity, and the economic environment—including the measure and beliefs of workers of type S and R. However, when they meet a worker, firms do not know his type.

To define an equilibrium for this version of the model, I need some extra notation. Let $V_{i,0}(y)$ and $V_{i,1}(w, y)$ denote the actual values of unemployment and employment for a worker of type i, and let $\hat{V}_{S,0}$ and $\hat{V}_{S,1}(w)$ denote the values of unemployment and employment perceived by a worker of type S. Let $J(w, y)$ denote the actual value of a worker to a firm, and let $\hat{J}_S(w, y)$ denote the firm's value as perceived by a worker of type S. Let $\theta(y)$ and $\hat{\theta}$ denote the actual tightness of the labor market and the tightness of the labor market expected by a worker of type S. Last, let $w_i(y)$ denote the actual wage for a worker of type i, and let $\hat{w}_S$ denote the wage expected by a worker of type S.

The worker's actual and perceived values of unemployment, $V_{i,0}(y)$ and $\hat{V}_{S,0}$, are

$$V_{i,0}(y) = b + \beta\mathbb{E}_{y_+}[p(\theta(y_+))V_{i,1}(w_i(y_+), y_+) + (1 - p(\theta(y_+)))V_{i,0}(y_+)], \quad (56)$$

$$\hat{V}_{S,0} = b + \beta[p(\hat{\theta})\hat{V}_{S,1}(\hat{w}_S) + (1 - p(\hat{\theta}))\hat{V}_{S,0}]. \quad (57)$$

The worker's actual and perceived values of employment, $V_{i,1}(w, y)$ and $\hat{V}_{S,1}(w)$, are

$$V_{i,1}(w, y) = w + \beta\mathbb{E}_{y_+}[(1 - \delta)V_{i,1}(w, y_+) + \delta V_{i,0}(y_+)], \quad (58)$$

$$\hat{V}_{S,1}(w) = w + \beta[(1 - \delta)\hat{V}_{S,1}(w) + \delta\hat{V}_{S,0}]. \quad (59)$$

The firm's actual and perceived values of employing a worker, $J(w, y)$ and $J_S(w, \hat{y})$, are

$$J(w, y) = y - w + \beta\mathbb{E}_{y_+}[(1 - \delta)J(w, y_+)], \quad (60)$$

$$\hat{J}_S(w, \hat{y}) = \hat{y} - w + \beta(1 - \delta)\hat{J}_S(w, \hat{y}). \quad (61)$$

The values for workers of type S and the values for the firm are the same as in the definition of an SBE in Section II and need no further comment. The values for workers of type R are the same as in the definition of an REE, because these workers have rational expectations.

The actual market tightness, $\theta(y)$, and the market tightness expected by workers of type S, $\hat{\theta}_S$, are such that

$$k = q(\theta(y))[\sigma J(w_S(y), y) + (1 - \sigma)J(w_R(y), y)], \quad (62)$$

$$k = q(\hat{\theta}_S)\hat{J}_S(\hat{w}_S, y^*). \quad (63)$$

Consider equation (62). The firm pays the cost k to open a vacancy. The firm fills the vacancy with probability $q(\theta(y))$. With probability σ, the firm fills the vacancy with a worker of type S, to whom it pays a wage $w_S(y)$. With probability $1 - \sigma$, the firm fills the vacancy with a worker of type R, whom it pays a wage $w_R(y)$. The actual market tightness is such that the firm's cost and benefit from opening a vacancy are equal. Now consider equation (63). From the S-worker's perspective, the firm's cost of opening a vacancy is k. The firm's benefit of opening a vacancy is the probability of filling the vacancy, $q(\hat{\theta}_S)$, times the value of filling the vacancy, which is $\hat{J}_S(\hat{w}_S, y^*)$ because the worker expects the firm to have productivity y^* and to pay the wage $\hat{w}_S$. The market tightness expected by a worker of type S is such that, from his perspective, the firm's cost and benefit from opening a vacancy are equal.

B. Bargaining Outcomes

I now turn to the analysis of the bargaining game between a firm and a
worker. The protocol of the game is the same as in Section II. Now,
though, the game is one of asymmetric information, because the firm
knows that there is a probability σ that the worker with whom it is bargaining is of type S and a probability $1 - \sigma$ that the worker with whom it
is bargaining is of type R, but it does not know the worker's actual type.
To simplify the analysis of the game, I restrict attention to the case in
which productivity shocks are nearly permanent (i.e., $\phi_r \to 1$ and
$\phi_s \to 1$).

As an equilibrium concept, I adopt the Perfect Sequential Equilibrium
(PSE) proposed by Grossman and Perry (1986a, 1986b). A PSE consists
of metastrategies for the firm and the workers, and of a belief-updating
rule for the firm. The metastrategy of an agent specifies the actions of the
agent conditional on any history and on any firm's belief. The metastrategy of an agent is required to be optimal after any history and for
any firm's belief, conditional on the metastrategy of the other agents.
The belief-updating rule specifies the evolution of the firm's beliefs after
any history and for any firm's prior belief.[3] The belief-updating rule is
given by Bayes' rule if the firm observes an action from the worker that
occurs with positive probability given the firm's beliefs and the worker's
metastrategy. When the firm observes an action from the worker that
occurs with probability zero given the firm's belief and the worker's
metastrategy, the posterior belief must be credible—that is, the firm
must seek a subset of the worker types in the support of its prior belief
that would be better off taking the off-equilibrium action rather than
playing the equilibrium action if the firm were to believe that the action
comes from that subset of types. If there is no such subset of types, the
only restriction on the posterior belief is that its support should be contained in the support of the prior belief.[4] The above definition of a PSE
needs to be amended to account for workers of type S. In particular, I
do not require the metastrategy of an S-worker to be optimal. Rather,
the metastrategy of an S-worker is the best response to the strategy of
the firm that he expects, that is, the strategy that the firm would follow
in a world where aggregate productivity was always equal to y^*.

I start by characterizing a PSE in the scenario where the S-worker observes the productivity y of the firm and interprets the difference $y - y^*$
as a permanent firm-specific component of productivity. As a preliminary step, it is useful to define some wages. Let $w_{S,d}$ and $w_{S,o}$ denote

the wage demand and the wage offer in the equilibrium of the bargaining game between a firm and a worker of type S under symmetric information, that is, the game between a firm and an S-worker in which the firm believes that the worker is of type S with probability 1. This is the game analyzed in Section II and, given $\phi_r \to 1$ and $\phi_s \to 1$, the equilibrium wages are

$$w_{S,d} = \frac{1 - e^{-\lambda\Delta}}{1 - e^{-(\lambda+\mu)\Delta}} y + \frac{1 - e^{-\mu\Delta}}{1 - e^{-(\lambda+\mu)\Delta}} e^{-\lambda\Delta}(1 - \beta)\hat{V}_{S,0}, \tag{64}$$

$$w_{S,o} = \frac{1 - e^{-\lambda\Delta}}{1 - e^{-(\lambda+\mu)\Delta}} e^{-\mu\Delta}y + \frac{1 - e^{-\mu\Delta}}{1 - e^{-(\lambda+\mu)\Delta}} (1 - \beta)\hat{V}_{S,0}. \tag{65}$$

Similarly, let $w_{R,d}$ and $w_{R,o}$ denote the wage demand and the wage offer in the equilibrium of the bargaining game between the firm and a worker of type R under symmetric information; that is, the game between a firm and an R-worker in which the firm believes that the worker is of type R with probability 1. This is the same game analyzed by Binmore et al. (1986) and the equilibrium wages are

$$w_{R,d} = \frac{1 - e^{-\lambda\Delta}}{1 - e^{-(\lambda+\mu)\Delta}} y + \frac{1 - e^{-\mu\Delta}}{1 - e^{-(\lambda+\mu)\Delta}} e^{-\lambda\Delta}(1 - \beta)V_{R,0}(y), \tag{66}$$

$$w_{R,o} = \frac{1 - e^{-\lambda\Delta}}{1 - e^{-(\lambda+\mu)\Delta}} e^{-\mu\Delta}y + \frac{1 - e^{-\mu\Delta}}{1 - e^{-(\lambda+\mu)\Delta}} (1 - \beta)V_{R,0}(y). \tag{67}$$

Notice that $w_{S,o} < w_{S,d}$ and $w_{R,o} < w_{R,d}$. Furthermore, under the conjecture that $V_{R,0}(y)$ is continuous and increasing in y and such that $V_{R,0}(y) < \hat{V}_{S,0}$ for $y < y^*$ and $V_{R,0}(y) > \hat{V}_{S,0}$ for $y > y^*$, $w_{R,d} < w_{S,o}$ for $y < y^*$ and $w_{S,d} < w_{R,o}$ for $y > y^*$ for all Δ small enough.

Consider a continuation game in which the firm's belief is $\hat{\sigma} = 0$. Because in a PSE the support of the posterior belief is always contained in the support of the prior, the firm's updated belief is at $\hat{\sigma}_+ = 0$. In this continuation game, the strategy of a worker of type S is, as always, to accept a wage offer w_o if and only if $w_o \geq w_{S,o}$ and to make the wage demand $w_{S,d}$. The strategy of a worker of type R is to accept a wage offer w_o if and only if $w_o \geq w_{R,o}$ and to make the wage demand $w_{R,d}$. The strategy of the firm is to accept a wage demand w_d if and only if $w_d \leq w_{R,d}$ and to make the wage offer $\leq w_{R,o}$. It is immediate to verify that the above strategies and belief updates are the unique PSE for the continuation game with $\hat{\sigma} = 0$.

Consider a continuation game in which the firm's belief is $\hat{\sigma} = 1$. Because in a PSE the support of the posterior belief is always contained by the support of the prior belief, the firm's updated belief is $\hat{\sigma}_+ = 1$. In this continuation game, the strategy of a worker of type S is, as always, to accept a wage offer w_o if and only if $w_o \geq w_{S,o}$ and to make the wage demand $w_{S,d}$. The strategy of the firm is to accept a wage demand w_d if and only if $w_d \leq w_{S,d}$ and to make the wage offer $w_{S,o}$. The strategy of a worker of type R is to accept a wage offer w_o if and only if $w_o \geq \tilde{w}_R$ and to make the wage demand $w_{S,d}$, with $\tilde{w}_R$ such that

$$V_{R,1}(\tilde{w}_R, y) = (1 - e^{-\mu\Delta})V_{R,0}(y) + e^{-\mu\Delta}V_{R,1}(w_{S,d}, y). \qquad (68)$$

It is immediate to verify that the above strategies and belief updates are the unique PSE for the continuation game with $\hat{\sigma} = 1$.

Consider the game in which the firm's belief is $\hat{\sigma} = \sigma$. The outcome of the game depends on whether y is smaller or greater than y^*. Suppose that $y < y^*$, so that $w_{R,o} < w_{R,d} < w_{S,o} < w_{S,d}$ and $\tilde{w}_R \in (w_{R,d}, w_{S,o})$ for all Δ small enough. The belief updates are as follows. The firm's updated belief is $\hat{\sigma}_+ = 0$ if the worker makes a wage demand $w_d < w_{S,d}$, and it is $\hat{\sigma}_+ = \sigma$ if the worker makes a wage demand $w_d \geq w_{S,d}$. The firm's updated belief is $\hat{\sigma}_+ = \sigma$ if the worker rejects a wage offer $w_o < \tilde{w}_R$, and it is $\hat{\sigma}_+ = 1$ if the worker rejects a wage offer $w_o > \tilde{w}_R$. The strategy of a worker of type S is to accept a wage offer w_o if and only if $w_o \geq w_{S,o}$ and to make the wage demand $w_{S,d}$. The strategy of a worker of type R is to accept a wage offer w_o if and only if $w_o \geq \tilde{w}_R$ and to make the wage demand $w_{S,d}$. The strategy of the firm is to accept a wage demand w_d if and only if $w_d \leq w_{R,d}$ or $w_d = w_{S,d}$ and to make the wage offer $w_{S,o}$. These strategies and belief updates are illustrated in figures 1 and 2.

I now need to check that the strategies of the firm and of a worker of type R are optimal. Let me consider the acceptance strategy of the firm. If

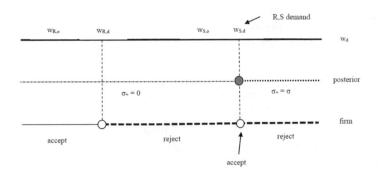

Fig. 1. Strategies and belief updates when $\hat{\sigma} = \sigma$ and $y < y^*$. A color version of this figure is available online.

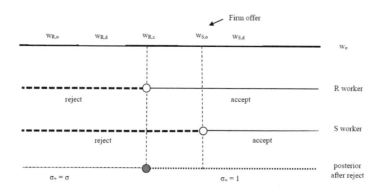

Fig. 2. Strategies and belief updates when $\hat{\sigma} = \sigma$ and $y < y^*$. A color version of this figure is available online.

the worker makes a wage demand $w_d < w_{S,d}$, the firm updates its belief to $\hat{\sigma}_+ = 0$. If the firm accepts the demand, it gets the payoff $J(w_d, y)$. If the firm rejects the demand, it expects the payoff $\exp(-\lambda\Delta)J(w_{R,o}, y)$, where $J(w_{R,o}, y)$ is the firm's equilibrium payoff in the continuation game in which the firm's belief is $\hat{\sigma} = 0$ and the firm makes an offer. Because $J(w_d, y) = \exp(-\lambda\Delta)J(w_{R,o}, y)$ for $w_d = w_{R,d}$ and is decreasing in w_d, the firm finds it optimal to accept w_d if $w_d \leq w_{R,d}$ and to reject w_d if $w_d \in (w_{R,d}, w_{S,d})$. If the worker makes a wage demand $w_d \geq w_{S,d}$, the firm updates its belief to $\hat{\sigma}_+ = \sigma$. If the firm accepts the demand, its payoff is $J(w_d, y)$. If the firm rejects the demand, it expects the payoff $\exp(-\lambda\Delta)$ $J(w_{S,o}, y)$, where $J(w_{S,o}, y)$ is the firm's equilibrium payoff in the continuation game in which the firm's belief is $\hat{\sigma} = \sigma$ and the firm makes an offer. Because $J(w_d, y) = \exp(-\lambda\Delta)J(w_{S,o}, y)$ for $w_d = w_{S,d}$, the firm finds it optimal to accept w_d if $w_d = w_{S,d}$ and to reject w_d if $w_d > w_{S,d}$.

Consider the optimality of the firm's wage-offer strategy. If the firm makes the offer $w_o \geq w_{S,o}$, every worker accepts and the firm gets the payoff $J(w_o, y)$. If the firm makes an offer $w_o < \tilde{w}_R$, every worker rejects, and the firm gets the payoff $\exp(-\mu\Delta)J(w_{S,d}, y)$, where $J(w_{S,d}, y)$ is the firm's equilibrium payoff in the continuation game in which the firm's belief is $\hat{\sigma} = \sigma$ and the worker makes a demand. If the firm makes an offer $w_o \in [\tilde{w}_R, w_{S,o})$, a worker of type R accepts, a worker of type S rejects, and the firm gets the payoff $(1 - \sigma)J(w_o, y) + \sigma \exp(-\mu\Delta)J(w_{S,d}, y)$, where $J(w_{S,d}, y)$ is the firm's equilibrium payoff in the continuation game in which the firm's belief is $\hat{\sigma} = 1$ and the worker makes a demand. Because $J(w_o, y)$ is decreasing in w_o and $J(w_{S,o}, y) > J(w_{S,d}, y)$, the firm prefers making the offer $w_{S,o}$ rather than any offer $w_o > w_{S,o}$ or any offer $w_o < \tilde{w}_R$. Because $J(w_o, y)$ is decreasing in w_o, the firm prefers making the offer $\tilde{w}_R$ rather than any offer $w_o \in (\tilde{w}_R, w_{S,o})$. The firm prefers making the offer $w_{S,o}$ rather than the offer $\tilde{w}_R$ if $J(w_{S,o})$ is greater than $(1 - \sigma)J(\tilde{w}_R, y) + \sigma \exp(-\mu\Delta)J(w_{S,d}, y)$. This is the case as long as

$$\sigma(y - (1 - \beta)\hat{V}_{S,0}) \geq (1 - \sigma)(1 - \beta)(\hat{V}_{S,0} - V_{R,0}(y)). \tag{69}$$

Notice that, under the conjecture that $V_{R,0}(y)$ is continuous and increasing in y and $V_{R,0}(y) = \hat{V}_{S,0}$ for $y = y^*$, condition (eq. [69]) holds for all y that are smaller than y^* and sufficiently close to y^*. In particular, for any given fraction $\sigma > 0$ of S-workers, there exists a left neighborhood of y^* such that condition (eq. [69]) holds.

I now turn to the optimality of the acceptance strategy for a worker of type R. Suppose that the firm makes a wage offer w_o. If the worker accepts the offer, he gets the payoff $V_{R,1}(w_o, y)$. If the worker rejects the offer, the firm's posterior belief is $\hat{\sigma}_+ = \sigma$ if $w_o < \tilde{w}_R$ or $\hat{\sigma}_+ = 1$ if $w_o \geq \tilde{w}_R$. In either case, if the worker rejects the offer w_o, he makes the wage demand $w_{S,d}$ and the firm accepts it. Therefore, if the worker rejects the offer w_o, he gets the payoff $(1 - \exp(-\mu\Delta))V_{R,0}(y) + \exp(-\mu\Delta)V_{R,1}(w_{S,d}, y)$. Because the acceptance and rejection payoffs are equal for $w_o = \tilde{w}_R$, the worker finds it optimal to accept w_o if and only if $w_o \geq \tilde{w}_R$.

Consider the proposal strategy for a worker of type R. If the worker makes a wage demand $w_d \leq w_{R,d}$, the firm accepts, and the worker gets the payoff $V_{R,1}(w_d, y)$. If the worker makes a wage demand $w_d \in (w_{R,d}, w_{S,d})$, the firm rejects, and the worker gets the payoff $(1 - \exp(-\lambda\Delta))V_{R,0}(y) + \exp(-\lambda\Delta)V_{R,1}(w_{R,o}, y)$, which is the worker's equilibrium payoff in the continuation game where the firm's belief is $\hat{\sigma} = 0$ and the firm makes an offer. If the worker makes a wage demand $w_d = w_{S,d}$, the firm accepts, and the worker gets the payoff $V_{R,1}(w_{S,d}, y)$. If the worker makes a wage demand $w_d > w_{S,d}$, the firm rejects, and the worker gets the payoff $(1 - \exp(-\lambda\delta))V_{R,0}(y) + \exp(-\lambda\Delta)V_{R,1}(w_{S,o}, y)$, where $V_{R,1}(w_{S,o}, y)$ is the worker's equilibrium payoff in the continuation game in which the firm's belief is $\hat{\sigma} = \sigma$ and the firm makes an offer. Clearly, the worker finds it optimal to demand the wage $w_{S,d}$.

Finally, I need to check that the firm updates its belief according to Bayes' rule if possible, and credibly otherwise. Consider the way in which the firm updates its belief after a wage offer w_o is rejected. For $w_o < \tilde{w}_R$, the firm updates its belief from $\hat{\sigma} = \sigma$ to $\hat{\sigma}_+ = \sigma$, which is consistent with Bayes' rule. For $w_o \in [\tilde{w}_R, w_{S,o})$, the firm updates its belief from $\hat{\sigma} = \sigma$ to $\hat{\sigma}_+ = 1$, which is also consistent with Bayes' rule. For

$w_o > w_{S,o}$, no worker is expected to reject the offer, and Bayes' rule is not applicable. In this case, the firm should seek a subset of types that would be better off rejecting the offer than accepting it, if the firm believed that the rejection came from this subset of types. If the firm were to believe the rejection comes from an S-worker, the S-worker would be better off accepting than rejecting w_o and getting $w_{S,d}$. If the firm were to believe that the rejection comes from an R-worker, the R-worker would be better off accepting than rejecting w_o and getting $w_{R,d}$. If the firm were to believe that the rejection comes from both S- and R-workers, both types would be better off accepting it. Overall, the credibility condition does not impose any further constraint on the firm's off-equilibrium beliefs.

Now, consider the way in which the firm updates its belief after a wage demand w_d. For $w_d = w_{S,d}$, the firm updates its belief from $\hat{\sigma} = \sigma$ to $\hat{\sigma}_+ = \sigma$ in accordance with Bayes' rule. For $w_d \neq w_{S,d}$, Bayes' rule is not applicable. In this case, the firm should seek a subset of types that would be better off making the wage demand w_d rather than $w_{S,d}$, if the firm believed that the demand w_d came from this subset of types. Notice that, no matter how the firm updates its belief, a worker of type R and a worker of type S are better off making the wage demand $w_{S,d}$ than any wage demand $w_d < w_{S,d}$, which might be either accepted or rejected by the firm, and then countered with an offer nongreater than $w_{S,o}$. Hence, the credibility condition does not impose any constraint on the firm's off-equilibrium beliefs for $w_d < w_{S,d}$. Similarly, irrespective of how the firm updates its belief, the firm rejects a wage demand $w_d > w_{S,d}$. Hence, a worker of type R and a worker of type S are better off demanding $w_{S,d}$ than demanding $w_d > w_{S,d}$ and then settling for at most $w_{S,o}$. Also for $w_d > w_{S,d}$, the credibility condition does not impose any further constraint on the firm's off-equilibrium beliefs.

I have thus shown that the strategies and belief updates above constitute a PSE for $y < y^*$ and y close enough to y^*. It is straightforward to compute the outcome of the PSE. In particular, in the limit for $\Delta \to 0$, the outcome of the PSE is such that the firm and a worker of type i reach an agreement with probability 1 at the wage $w_{S,d} = w_{S,o} = w_i(y)$, with

$$w_i(y) = \gamma y + (1 - \gamma)(1 - \beta)V_{S,0}, \tag{70}$$

where $\gamma \equiv \lambda/(\lambda + \mu)$ is the worker's bargaining power and $1 - \gamma = \mu/(\lambda + \mu)$ is the firm's bargaining power.

Now, I analyze the game in which the firm's belief is $\hat{\sigma} = \sigma$, for the case $y > y^*$. In this case, for all Δ small enough, $w_{S,o} < w_{S,d} < w_{R,o} < w_{R,d}$ and

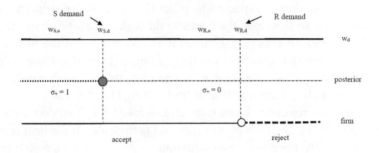

Fig. 3. Strategies and belief updates when $\hat{\sigma} = \sigma$ and $y < y^*$. A color version of this figure is available online.

$\tilde{w}_R \in (w_{S,d}, w_{R,o})$. The belief updates are as follows. The firm's updated belief is $\hat{\sigma}_+ = 1$ if the worker makes a wage demand $w_d \leq w_{S,d}$, and $\hat{\sigma}_+ = 0$ if the worker makes a wage demand $w_d > w_{S,d}$. The firm's updated belief is $\hat{\sigma}_+ = \sigma$ if the worker rejects a wage offer $w_o < w_{S,o}$, and $\hat{\sigma}_+ = 0$ if the worker rejects a wage offer $w_o \geq w_{S,o}$. The strategy of a worker of type S is to accept a wage offer w_o if and only if $w_o \geq w_{S,o}$ and to make the wage demand $w_{S,d}$. The strategy of a worker of type R is to accept a wage offer w_o if and only if $w_o \geq w_{R,o}$ and to make the wage demand $w_{R,d}$. The strategy of the firm is to accept a wage demand w_d if and only if $w_d \leq w_{R,d}$ and to make the wage offer $w_{S,o}$. These strategies and belief updates are illustrated in figures 3 and 4.

I now check that the acceptance strategy of the firm is optimal. If the worker makes a wage demand $w_d \leq w_{S,d}$, the firm updates its belief to $\hat{\sigma}_+ = 1$. If the firm accepts the demand, its payoff is $J(w_d, y)$. If the firm rejects the demand, its payoff is $\exp(-\lambda\Delta)J(w_{S,o}, y)$, where $J(w_{S,o}, y)$ is the firm's equilibrium payoff in the continuation game in which the firm's belief is $\hat{\sigma} = 1$ and the firm makes an offer. Because $J(w_d, y) \geq \exp(-\lambda\Delta)J(w_{S,o}, y)$ for all $w_d \leq w_{S,d}$, the firm finds it optimal to accept any wage demand $w_d \leq w_{S,d}$. If the worker makes a wage demand $w_d > w_{S,d}$, the firm updates its belief to $\hat{\sigma}_+ = 0$. If the firm accepts the demand, its payoff is $J(w_d, y)$. If the firm rejects the demand, it expects the payoff $\exp(-\lambda\Delta)J(w_{R,o}, y)$, where $J(w_{R,o}, y)$ is the firm's equilibrium payoff in the continuation game in which the firm's belief is $\hat{\sigma} = 0$ and the firm makes an offer. Because $J(w_d, y) = \exp(-\lambda\Delta)J(w_{R,o}, y)$ for $w_d = w_{R,d}$, the firm finds it optimal to accept w_d if $w_d \in (w_{S,d}, w_{R,d}]$ and to reject if $w_d > w_{R,d}$.

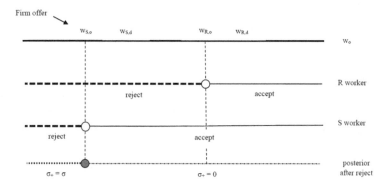

Fig. 4. Strategies and belief updates when $\hat{\sigma} = \sigma$ and $y < y^*$. A color version of this figure is available online.

Consider the optimality of the firm's wage-offer strategy. If the firm makes an offer $w_o < w_{S,o}$, every worker rejects, and the firm's payoff is $\exp(-\mu\Delta)\{\sigma J(w_{S,d}, y) + (1 - \sigma)J(w_{R,d}, y)\}$. If the firm makes an offer $w_o \in [w_{S,o}, w_{R,o})$, a worker of type R rejects, a worker of type S accepts, and the firm's payoff is $\sigma J(w_o, y) + (1 - \sigma) \exp(-\mu\Delta)J(w_{R,d}, y)$. If the firm makes an offer $w_o \geq w_{R,o}$, every worker accepts, and the firm's payoff is $J(w_o, y)$. Because $J(w_o, y)$ is decreasing in w_o and $w_{S,o} < w_{S,d}$, the firm prefers making the offer $w_{S,o}$ rather than any other offer $w_o < w_{R,o}$. Because $J(w_o, y)$ is decreasing, the firm prefers making the offer $w_{R,o}$ rather than any offer $w_o > w_{R,o}$. To figure out whether the firm prefers making the offer $w_{S,o}$ or the offer $w_{R,o}$, notice that the distance between $w_{R,d}$ and $w_{R,o}$ vanishes for $\Delta \to 0$, but the distance between $w_{R,o}$ and $w_{S,o}$ is bounded away from zero for $\Delta \to 0$. Hence, for all Δ small enough, the firm prefers making the offer $w_{S,o}$ rather than the offer $w_{R,o}$.

Consider the optimality of the acceptance strategy for a worker of type R. Suppose that the firm makes a wage offer w_o. If the worker accepts the offer, he attains the payoff $V_{R,1}(w_o, y)$. If the worker rejects the offer, the firm's posterior belief is $\hat{\sigma}_+ = \sigma$ if $w_o < w_{S,o}$ or $\hat{\sigma}_+ = o$ if $w_o \geq w_{S,o}$. In either case, after rejecting the wage offer w_o, the worker makes the wage demand $w_{R,d}$ and the firm accepts it. Hence, if the worker rejects w_o, he gets the payoff $(1 - \exp(-\mu\Delta))V_{R,0}(y) + \exp(-\mu\Delta)V_{R,1}(w_{R,d}, y)$. Because the acceptance and rejection payoffs are equal for $w_o = w_{R,o}$, the worker finds it optimal to accept w_o if and only if $w_o \geq w_{R,o}$.

Consider the optimality of the proposal strategy for a worker of type R. If the worker makes a wage demand $w_d \leq w_{R,d}$, the firm accepts and the

worker's payoff is $V_{R,1}(w_d, y)$. If the worker makes a wage demand $w_d >
w_{R,d}$, the firm rejects and the worker's payoff is $(1 - \exp(-\lambda\Delta))V_{R,0}(y) +
\exp(-\lambda\Delta)V_{R,1}(w_{R,o}, y)$. Because $V_{R,1}(w_d, y)$ is increasing in w_d and equals
$(1 - \exp(-\lambda\Delta))V_{R,0}(y) + \exp(-\lambda\Delta)V_{R,1}(w_{R,o}, y)$ for $w_d = w_{R,d}$, the worker
finds it optimal to demand the wage $w_{R,d}$.

Finally, I need to check that the firm updates its belief according to
Bayes' rule if possible, and credibly otherwise. Consider the way in
which the firm updates its belief after a wage offer w_o is rejected. For
$w_o < w_{S,o}$, the firm updates its belief from $\hat{\sigma} = \sigma$ to $\hat{\sigma}_+ = \sigma$, which is consistent with Bayes' rule. For $w_o \in [w_{S,o}, w_{R,o})$, the firm updates its belief
from $\hat{\sigma} = \sigma$ to $\hat{\sigma}_+ = 0$, which is also consistent with Bayes' rule. For
$w_o \geq w_{R,o}$, no worker is expected to reject the offer and Bayes' rule is
not applicable. Suppose that the firm were to believe that the rejection
of w_o comes from an S-worker. In this case, the S-worker would be better
off accepting w_o rather than rejecting it and trading at $w_{S,d}$. Suppose that
the firm were to believe that the rejection of w_o comes from an R-worker.
In this case, the R-worker would be better off accepting w_o rather than
rejecting it and trading at $w_{R,d}$. If the firm were to believe that the rejection of w_o comes from both S- and R-workers, then both S- and R-
workers would be better off accepting w_o rather than rejecting it. Overall, the credibility condition does not impose any further constraint on
the firm's off-equilibrium beliefs.

Consider the way in which the firm updates its belief after a wage de-
mand w_d. For $w_d = w_{S,d}$, the firm updates its belief from $\hat{\sigma} = \sigma$ to $\hat{\sigma}_+ = 1$,
which is consistent with Bayes' rule. For $w_d = w_{R,d}$, the firm updates its
belief from $\hat{\sigma} = \sigma$ to $\hat{\sigma}_+ = 0$, which is also consistent with Bayes' rule.
For $w_d \neq w_{S,d}$ and $w_{R,d}$, Bayes' rule is not applicable. Notice that a worker
of type S is better off making the equilibrium wage demand $w_{S,d}$ rather
than any off-equilibrium wage demand w_d, irrespective of how the firm
updates its beliefs. If the worker demands $w_d < w_{S,d}$, the worker expects
the firm to accept w_d. Hence, the worker is worse off demanding
$w_d < w_{S,d}$ than $w_{S,d}$. If the worker demands $w_d > w_{S,d}$, the worker expects
the firm to reject w_d and counter with $w_{S,o}$. Hence, the worker is worse off
demanding $w_d > w_{S,d}$ rather than $w_{S,d}$. Similarly, a worker of type R is
better off making the equilibrium wage demand $w_{R,d}$ rather than any
off-equilibrium wage demand w_d, irrespective of how the firm updates
its beliefs. If the worker demands $w_d < w_{R,d}$, the firm may accept w_d
or reject it and counter with an offer nongreater than $w_{R,o}$. Hence, the
worker is worse off demanding $w_d < w_{R,d}$ rather than $w_{R,d}$. If the worker
demands $w_d > w_{R,d}$, the firm rejects w_d and counters with an offer

nongreater than $w_{R,o}$. Hence, the worker is worse off demanding $w_d > w_{R,d}$ rather than $w_{R,d}$. Because there is no type of worker that is better off making an off-equilibrium demand, irrespective of how the firm updates its belief, the credibility condition does not impose any further constraint on the firm's off-equilibrium beliefs.

I have thus shown that the strategies and belief updates above constitute a PSE for $y > y^*$. It is straightforward to compute the outcome of the PSE. In particular, in the limit for $\Delta \to 0$, the outcome of the PSE is such that the firm and a worker of type S reach an agreement with probability 1 at the wage $w_{S,d} = w_{S,o} = w_S(y)$, with

$$w_S(y) = \gamma y + (1 - \gamma)(1 - \beta)\hat{V}_{S,0}. \tag{71}$$

In contrast, in the limit for $\Delta \to 0$, the outcome of the PSE is such that the firm and a worker of type R reach an agreement with probability 1 at the wage $w_{R,d} = w_{R,o} = w_R(y)$, with

$$w_R(y) = \gamma y + (1 - \gamma)(1 - \beta)V_{R,0}(y). \tag{72}$$

I summarize the characterization of the bargaining game in the following proposition.

Proposition 4. (Asymmetric-information bargaining I.) Consider the scenario in which a worker of type S observes the productivity y of the firm with which he is bargaining. For any $\sigma > 0$, there exists a unique PSE of the bargaining game. The PSE is such that:

1. For any $y < y^*$ with y sufficiently close to y^*, the firm and the worker reach an agreement with probability 1. The worker is paid $w_S(y)$ if his type is S, and $w_R(y)$ if his type is R, where $w_S(y)$ and $w_R(y)$ are such that $w_S(y) = w_R(y)$ and given by equation (70);
2. For any $y > y^*$, the firm and the worker reach an agreement with probability 1. The worker is paid $w_S(y)$ if his type is S, and $w_R(y)$ if his type is R, where $w_S(y)$ and $w_R(y)$ are such that $w_S(y) < w_R(y)$ and given by equations (71) and (72);
3. When searching the market, a worker of type S expects to earn the wage $\hat{w}_S = w_S(y^*)$ upon meeting a firm.

Some comments about Proposition 4 are in order. For $y < y^*$, an R-worker and an S-worker earn the same wage. This common wage is the same as in the symmetric-information game between a firm and an S-worker. For $y > y^*$, an R-worker and an S-worker earn different wages. An R-worker earns the same wage as in the symmetric-information game between a firm and an R-worker. An S-worker earns the same wage as in the symmetric-information game between a firm and an S-worker. Note that the symmetric-information wage of an R-worker is fully flexible, in the sense that it responds to changes in the productivity of the firm and changes in the value of unemployment that are caused by aggregate productivity shocks. In contrast, the symmetric-information wage of an S-worker is sticky, in the sense that it does not respond to changes in the value of unemployment caused by aggregate productivity shocks. Therefore, under asymmetric information, the responsiveness of the average wage paid by the firm to a worker is different depending on whether shocks are negative or positive. In response to a negative shock, the average wage features the same degree of stickiness as in a version of the model where every worker is of type S. In response to a positive shock, the degree of stickiness of the average wage is proportional to the fraction of S-workers in the population. Overall, the average wage is stickier downward than upward. When the fraction of S-workers in the population is small, the average wage is only downward sticky.

Let me now provide some intuition for the properties of the equilibrium wages. When $y < y^*$, the symmetric-information wage of an R-worker is lower than the symmetric-information wage of an S-worker. For this reason, an R-worker does not want to reveal his type to the firm, and it can do so by making the same wage demand $w_{S,d}$ as an S-worker. The firm can then try to screen the two types of workers by making a wage offer $\tilde{w}_R$ that is acceptable to an R-worker but not to an S-worker, or it can pool the two types of workers by making a wage offer $w_{S,o}$ that is acceptable to both types. Because an R-worker has the option to reject the screening offer $\tilde{w}_R$ and thus convince the firm he is an S-worker, $\tilde{w}_R$ must be close to the symmetric-information wage of an S-worker. Because $\tilde{w}_R$ is close to the symmetric-information wage of an S-worker, the return to the firm from screening the two types is small and, under condition equation (69), the firm prefers making the pooling offer $w_{S,o}$.

When $y > y^*$, the symmetric-information wage of an R-worker is higher than the symmetric-information wage of an S-worker. For this reason, an R-worker wants to reveal his type to the firm, and he can do so by making a wage offer $w_{R,d}$. Indeed, after observing the wage offer $w_{R,d}$, the firm must believe that the offer is coming from an R-worker, because it realizes that making such an offer would be in the interest of an R-worker if the firm interpreted as coming from an R-worker, though making such an offer would never be in the interest of an S-worker—because the S-worker expects the offer to be rejected. Once the R-worker has revealed his type by offering $w_{R,d}$, the firm finds it optimal to accept. Once the S-worker has revealed his type by offering $w_{S,d}$, the firm finds it optimal to accept. The asymmetry between the nature of the equilibrium in the case of $y < y^*$—where the R-worker mimics the S-worker—and in the case of $y > y^*$—where the S-worker does not mimic the R-worker—is because S-workers do not understand that aggregate productivity and, in turn, the value of unemployment is different in the two cases.

It is easy to show that the PSE is unique—up to the specification of some off-equilibrium belief updates that do not affect the equilibrium payoffs. Consider the case in which $y < y^*$. In any PSE, an R-worker and an S-worker make the same wage demand, $w_{S,d}$. To see why this is the case, suppose there were a PSE in which the R-worker made a different wage demand than an S-worker. In such a PSE, the firm would accept the wage demand $w_{S,d}$ of an S-worker, and it would either accept or reject the wage demand of an R-worker. In either case, the R-worker would not earn more than $w_{R,d}$. Because $w_{R,d} < w_{S,d}$, an R-worker would be better off deviating from the equilibrium by making the wage demand $w_{S,d}$. In any PSE, the firm makes the pooling wage offer, $w_{S,o}$. To see why this is the case, suppose there were a PSE in which the firm makes a screening wage offer that is accepted by an R-worker and rejected by an S-worker. If an R-worker rejects the offer, the firm believes that the worker is of type S and accepts $w_{S,d}$. Therefore, the screening offer cannot be lower than $\tilde{w}_R$. And, under condition (69), the firm prefers making the pooling offer $w_{S,o}$ rather than any screening offer greater or equal to $\tilde{w}_R$.

In the case of $y > y^*$, uniqueness follows immediately from the credibility restriction on belief updating. In any PSE, an R-worker and an S-worker make different wage demands. To see why this is the case, suppose there were a PSE in which an R-worker and an S-worker make the same wage demand $w_{S,d}$. If the firm accepted $w_{S,d}$, an R-worker would be better off deviating from the equilibrium and making the wage offer $w_{R,d}$, which—because of the credibility restriction on the belief updates—the firm must interpret as coming from an R-worker and therefore accept. For the same reason, if the firm rejected $w_{S,d}$, an R-worker would be better off making the wage offer $w_{R,d}$. Because, in any PSE, an R-worker reveals his type by making a wage offer different from $w_{S,d}$, his payoff is the same as in a full-information game. In turn, the payoff of an S-worker is the same as in a full-information game.

Finally, let me comment on the existence of a PSE. For $y > y^*$, a PSE always exists and is unique. For $y < y^*$, a PSE exists and is unique as long as condition (eq. [69]) holds. If the condition does not hold, the firm prefers making the screening offer $\tilde{w}_R$ rather than the pooling offer $w_{S,o}$. Because the firm prefers offering $\tilde{w}_R$ rather than $w_{S,o}$, it does reject the wage demand $w_{S,d}$ when its belief is $\hat{\sigma} = \sigma$. Now, consider a wage offer w_o that is slightly lower than $\tilde{w}_R$. Suppose the firm believes that w_o is rejected by both type of workers. In this case, an R-worker who rejects the offer will make the demand $w_{S,d}$, which the firm will reject, and he will end up accepting $\tilde{w}_R$. Therefore, if the firm believes that w_o is rejected by both types of workers, an R-worker should accept it, and the firm's belief would violate Bayes' rule. Suppose the firm believes that w_o is rejected only by S-workers. In this case, an R-worker who rejects the offer will make the wage demand $w_{S,d}$, which the firm will accept. Therefore, if the firm believes that w_o is rejected by S-workers, an R-worker would reject it too, and the firm's belief would violate Bayes' rule. This argument suggests that, when condition (eq. [69]) does not hold, a pure-strategy PSE may not exist. A mixed-strategy PSE could be quite complicated and involve multiple rounds of screening. Yet, by the logic of the Coase conjecture (see Gul and Sonnenschein 1988), one would expect that, even in a mixed-strategy PSE, an R-worker would end up with a wage that is arbitrarily close to the symmetric-information wage of an S-worker.

Without going into details, let me briefly discuss the outcome of the bargaining game in the scenario where a worker of type S believes that the productivity of the firm with which he is bargaining is y^*. In this alternative scenario, the unique PSE of the bargaining game is similar to the one described above, in terms of both metastrategies and belief-updating rules. The two PSE differ because, in the alternative scenario, the strategy of an S-worker is to accept any wage offer $w_o \geq w_{S,o}$, where $w_{S,o}$ is given by equation (65) with y^* replacing y and to make the wage demand $w_{S,d}$, where $w_{S,d}$ is given by equation (64) with y^* replacing y. Hence, in the alternative scenario, the symmetric-information wage for an S-worker is different. For $y > y^*$, this leads to a different wage paid to S-workers. For $y < y^*$, this leads to a different wage paid to both R- and S-workers. Moreover, the condition under which the firm prefers making the pooling offer $w_{S,o}$ rather than the screening offer $\tilde{w}_R$ becomes

$$(\sigma - \gamma)(y - (1 - \beta)\hat{V}_{S,0}) \geq \sigma(y^* - y) + (1 - \sigma)(1 - \beta)(\hat{V}_{S,0} - V_{R,0}(y)). \quad (73)$$

The following proposition contains a characterization of the bargaining outcomes.

Proposition 5. (Asymmetric-information bargaining II.) Consider the scenario in which a worker of type S does not observe the productivity y of the firm with which he is bargaining and believes such productivity to be y^*. For any $\sigma > \gamma$, there exists a unique PSE of the bargaining game. The PSE is such that:

1. For any $y < y^*$ with y sufficiently close to y^*, the firm and the worker reach an agreement with probability 1. The worker is paid $w_S(y)$ if his type is S and $w_R(y)$ if his type is R, where $w_S(y)$ and $w_R(y)$ are such that $w_S(y) = w_R(y)$ and are given by

$$w_i(y) = \gamma y^* + (1 - \gamma)(1 - \beta)\hat{V}_{S,0}; \qquad (74)$$

2. For any $y > y^*$, the firm and the worker reach an agreement with probability 1. The worker is paid $w_S(y)$ if his type is S, and $w_R(y)$ if his type is R, where $w_S(y)$ and $w_R(y)$ are such that $w_S(y) < w_R(y)$ and are given by

$$w_R(y) = \gamma y + (1 - \gamma)(1 - \beta)V_{R,0}(y), \qquad (75)$$

$$w_S(y) = \gamma y^* + (1 - \gamma)(1 - \beta)\hat{V}_{S,0}; \qquad (76)$$

3. When searching the market, a worker of type S expects to earn the wage $\hat{w}_S = w_S(y^*)$ upon meeting a firm.

Let me comment on Proposition 5. For $y < y^*$, an R-worker and an S-worker both earn the symmetric-information wage of an S-worker. For $y > y^*$, an R-worker earns the symmetric-information wage of an R-worker, and an S-worker earns the symmetric-information wage of an S-worker. The symmetric-information wage of an R-worker is fully flexible, in the sense that it responds to the changes in the productivity of the firm and the changes in the value of unemployment that are caused by aggregate shocks. In contrast, the symmetric-information wage of an S-worker is rigid, as it responds to neither the changes in the productivity of the firm nor the changes in the value of unemployment that are caused by aggregate shocks. Therefore, under asymmetric information, the average wage paid by the firm to a worker does not respond at all to negative shocks to aggregate productivity. The average wage is rigid downward. In contrast, the average wage paid by the firm responds to positive shocks in proportion to the fraction of R-workers in the population. If the fraction is large, the average wage is essentially fully flexible upward.

I am now in the position to formally define an equilibrium for the model in which some workers have rational expectations and some workers have stubborn beliefs. I refer to this equilibrium as a Partially Rational Expectations Equilibrium (PREE).

Definition 3. (PREE.) A PREE is given by actual and perceived values $\{V_{i,0}, V_{i,1}, J, \hat{V}_{S,0}, \hat{V}_{S,1}, \hat{J}_S\}$, actual and expected market tightness $\{\theta, \hat{\theta}_S\}$, and actual and expected wages $\{w_i, \hat{w}_S\}$ such that:

1. The values $\{V_{i,0}, V_{i,1}, J, \hat{V}_{S,0}, \hat{V}_{S,1}, \hat{J}_S\}$ satisfy conditions (eqs. [56]–[61]);
2. The tightnesses θ and $\hat{\theta}_S$ satisfy conditions (eqs. [62]) and ([63]);
3. The wage w_i is given in Proposition 4 or Proposition 5, and $\hat{w}_S = w_S(y^*)$.

C. Properties of Equilibrium

I now want to characterize the properties of a PREE and compare them
with the properties of an SBE and with the properties of an REE. Let
me start with the analysis of the scenario in which an S-worker observes
the productivity y of the firm with which he is bargaining and interprets
the difference $y - y^*$ as a permanent and firm-specific component of
productivity.

Let $S_R(y)$ denote the surplus of a match between a firm and an R-worker.
That is, $S_R(y)$ denotes $V_{R,1}(w, y) + J(w, y) - V_{R,0}(y)$. Similarly, let $\hat{S}_S(y)$ denote the surplus of a match between a firm and an S-worker, as perceived
by the worker. That is, $\hat{S}_S(y)$ denotes $\hat{V}_{S,1}(w) + \hat{J}_S(w, y) - \hat{V}_{S,0}$. Inserting
the equilibrium wages $w_R(y)$ and $w_S(y)$ for $y < y^*$ into $V_{R,1}(w, y)$, $\hat{V}_{S,1}(w)$,
and $J(w, y)$ and using the definitions of $S_R(y)$ and $\hat{S}_S(y)$ yield

$$\hat{V}_{S,1}(w_S(y)) - \hat{V}_{S,0} = \gamma \hat{S}_S(y), \tag{77}$$

$$V_{R,1}(w_R(y), y) - V_{R,0}(y) = \gamma \hat{S}_S(y) + S_R(y) - \hat{S}_S(y), \tag{78}$$

$$J(w_S(y), y), J(w_R(y), y) = (1 - \gamma)\hat{S}_S(y). \tag{79}$$

For $y < y^*$, the outcome of the bargaining game between a firm and an
S-worker is such that the firm captures a fraction $1 - \gamma$ of the surplus
perceived by the worker, and the worker captures a fraction γ of it.
The outcome of the bargaining game between a firm and an R-worker
is such that the firm captures a fraction $1 - \gamma$ of the surplus perceived
by an S-worker, and the worker captures a fraction γ of the surplus perceived by an S-worker plus the difference between the actual and perceived surpluses.

Let $y > y^*$. Inserting the equilibrium wages $w_R(y)$ and $w_S(y)$ into $V_{R,1}(w,
y)$, $\hat{V}_{S,1}(w)$, and $J(w, y)$ and using the definitions of $S_R(y)$ and $\hat{S}_S(y)$ yield

$$\hat{V}_{S,1}(w_S(y)) - \hat{V}_{S,0} = \gamma \hat{S}_S(y), \tag{80}$$

$$V_{R,1}(w_R(y), y) - V_{R,0}(y) = \gamma S_R(y), \tag{81}$$

$$J(w_S(y), y) = (1 - \gamma)\hat{S}_S(y), \tag{82}$$

$$J(w_R(y), y) = (1 - \gamma)S_R(y). \tag{83}$$

For $y > y^*$, the outcome of the bargaining game between a firm and an
S-worker is such that the firm captures a fraction $1 - \gamma$ of the surplus
perceived by the worker, and the worker captures a fraction γ of it.

The outcome of the bargaining game between a firm and an R-worker is such that the firm captures a fraction $1 - \gamma$ of the actual surplus, and the worker captures a fraction γ of the actual surplus.

Using the definition of the surplus and the outcome of the bargaining game, I can characterize the equilibrium values for $S_R(y)$, $\hat{S}_S(y)$, and $\theta(y)$. For $y < y^*$, they are

$$S_R(y) = y - b - \beta p(\theta(y))\left[\gamma\hat{S}_S(y) + S_R(y) - \hat{S}_S(y)\right] + \beta(1 - \delta)S_R(y), \quad (84)$$

$$\hat{S}_S(y) = y - b - \beta p(\theta(y^*))\gamma\hat{S}_S(y^*) + \beta(1 - \delta)\hat{S}_S(y), \quad (85)$$

$$k = q(\theta(y))(1 - \gamma)\hat{S}_S(y). \quad (86)$$

For $y > y^*$, $S_R(y)$, $\hat{S}_S(y)$, and $\theta(y)$ are given by

$$S_R(y) = y - b - \beta p(\theta(y))\gamma S_R(y) + \beta(1 - \delta)S_R(y), \quad (87)$$

$$\hat{S}_S(y) = y - b - \beta p(\theta(y^*))\gamma\hat{S}_S(y^*) + \beta(1 - \delta)\hat{S}_S(y), \quad (88)$$

$$k = q(\theta(y))(1 - \gamma)\left[\sigma\hat{S}_S(y) + (1 - \sigma)S_R(y)\right]. \quad (89)$$

The expressions (eqs. [85]) and ([88]) for the surplus perceived by an S-worker make use of the fact that $\hat{\theta}_S = \theta(y^*)$ and that $\hat{w}_S = w_S(y^*)$. It is immediate to verify that the system of equations (84)–(86) and the system of equations (87)–(89) are identical at $y = y^*$, and they are both equal to the system of equations that describes a Rational Expectation Equilibrium.

To characterize the cyclical properties of a PREE, I differentiate $S_R(y)$, $\hat{S}_S(y)$, and $\theta(y)$ with respect to y around y^* and derive expressions for their elasticities with respect to y. Because $S_R(y)$, $\hat{S}_S(y)$, and $\theta(y)$ satisfy different conditions for $y < y^*$ and for $y > y^*$, I need to distinguish between left and right derivatives. Let me start with the left derivatives. Differentiating equations (85) and (86) with respect to y yields

$$\frac{\hat{S}_S'(y^*-)y^*}{\hat{S}_S(y^*)} = \frac{1 - \beta[1 - \delta - p(\theta(y^*))\gamma]}{1 - \beta(1 - \delta)} \cdot \frac{y^*}{y^* - b}, \quad (90)$$

$$\frac{\theta'(y^*-)y^*}{\theta(y^*)} = \frac{1}{1 - \epsilon} \cdot \frac{1 - \beta[1 - \delta - p(\theta(y^*))\gamma]}{1 - \beta(1 - \delta)} \cdot \frac{y^*}{y^* - b}. \quad (91)$$

Now consider the right derivatives. Differentiating equations (87), (88), and (89) yields

$$\frac{\theta'(y^*+)y^*}{\theta(y^*)} = \frac{1}{1-\epsilon} \cdot \left[\sigma \frac{\hat{S}_S'(y^*+)y^*}{\hat{S}_S(y^*)} + (1-\sigma) \frac{S_R'(y^*+)y^*}{S_R(y^*)} \right], \qquad (92)$$

$$\frac{\hat{S}_S'(y^*+)y^*}{\hat{S}_S(y^*)} = \frac{1 - \beta[1 - \delta - p(\theta(y^*))\gamma]}{1 - \beta(1-\delta)} \cdot \frac{y^*}{y^* - b}, \qquad (93)$$

$$\frac{S_R'(y^*+)y^*}{S_R(y^*)} = \frac{y^*}{y^* - b} - \frac{\beta p(\theta(y^*))\gamma\epsilon}{1 - \beta[1 - \delta - p(\theta(y^*))\gamma]} \cdot \frac{\theta'(y^*+)y^*}{\theta(y^*)}, \qquad (94)$$

where the expression in equation (92) makes use of the fact that the surplus perceived by an S-worker, $\hat{S}_S(y)$, is equal to the actual surplus of an R-worker, $S_R(y)$, at $y = y^*$. Substituting equations (93) and (94) into equation (92) gives

$$\frac{\theta'(y^*+)y^*}{\theta(y^*)} = \frac{1}{1-\epsilon} \cdot \frac{1 - \beta[1 - \delta - p(\theta(y^*))\gamma\sigma]}{1 - \beta(1-\delta)}$$
$$\cdot \frac{1 - \beta[1 - \delta - p(\theta(y^*))\gamma]}{1 - \beta[1 - \delta - p(\theta(y^*))\gamma\frac{1-\epsilon\sigma}{1-\epsilon}]} \cdot \frac{y^*}{y^* - b}. \qquad (95)$$

The elasticity (eq. [91]) of the market tightness with respect to a negative shock to aggregate productivity is the same as the elasticity (eq. [29]) in an SBE, irrespective of what the fraction σ of S-workers in the population might be. This property of equilibrium is easy to understand. When the economy is hit by a negative productivity shock, an S-worker overestimates the value of unemployment and therefore insists on making wage demands and accepting wage offers that are too high. An R-worker knows that the strategy of the S-worker is suboptimal, but he is better off mimicking the strategy of an S-worker than revealing his own type. In response to the strategy of the workers, the firm ends up agreeing to the wage demand of both types of worker. Because the wage demanded by both types of workers is the wage demanded by an S-worker and does not depend on the fraction of S-workers in the population, the wage is just as downward sticky as in an SBE. Hence, the elasticity of the market tightness is just the same as in an SBE, and so are the elasticities of the job-finding probability, the unemployment, and the vacancy rates.

The elasticity (eq. [95]) of the market tightness with respect to a positive shock to aggregate productivity lies between the elasticity (eq. [18]) in an REE and the elasticity (eq. [29]) in an SBE, and its exact value depends on the fraction σ of S-workers in the population. In particular, the elasticity (eq. [95]) converges to the elasticity (eq. [18]) in an REE for

$\sigma \to 0$, converges to the elasticity (eq. [29]) for $\sigma \to 1$, and is increasing in σ. These properties of equilibrium are also intuitive. When the economy is hit by a positive productivity shock, an S-worker underestimates the value of unemployment and therefore insists on making wage demands and accepting wage offers that are too low. An R-worker knows this and signals its type to the firm by making higher wage demands. The firm ends up paying each type of worker their symmetric-information wage. Because the symmetric-information wage of an S-worker is sticky, but the symmetric-information wage of an R-worker is flexible, it follows that the average wage paid by the firm has an intermediate degree of stickiness. Hence, the market tightness, the job-finding probability, and the unemployment and vacancy rates have an elasticity that is in between an REE and an SBE. If σ is low, the average wage is upward flexible, and the elasticity of the labor-market outcomes with respect to a positive shock to productivity is close to an REE.

The asymmetric response of wages and, in turn, of market tightness, job-finding probability, and unemployment and vacancy rates calls for an asymmetric employment subsidy. The optimal subsidy when $y = y^*$ is the same as in an REE or in an SBE. The optimal subsidy when $y < y^*$ is the same as in an SBE, which is more countercyclical (i.e., higher) than the optimal subsidy in an REE. The optimal subsidy when $y > y^*$ is between the optimal subsidy in an REE and the optimal subsidy in an SBE, which is more countercyclical (i.e., lower) than the optimal subsidy $t(y)$ in an REE. For instance, if the Hosios condition holds and σ is small, the optimal subsidy is zero for $y = y^*$ (i.e., $t(y^*) = 0$), positive for $y < y^*$ (i.e., $t'(y^*-) < 0$), and approximately equal to zero for $y > y^*$ (i.e., $t'(y^*+) = 0$).

For the sake of completeness, let me now characterize the properties of a PREE in the second scenario—the one where an S-worker does not observe the productivity y of the firm with which he is bargaining and believes such productivity to be equal to y^*. In this second scenario, the equilibrium value for $\hat{S}_S$ is such that

$$\hat{S}_S = y^* - b - \beta p(\theta(y^*))\gamma \hat{S}_S + \beta(1 - \delta)\hat{S}_S. \qquad (96)$$

For $y < y^*$, $S_R(y)$ and $\theta(y)$ are such that

$$S_R(y) = y - b - \beta p(\theta(y))[\gamma \hat{S}_S + S_R(y) - \hat{S}_S] + \beta(1 - \delta)S_R(y), \qquad (97)$$

$$k = q(\theta(y))\left[(1 - \gamma)\hat{S}_S + \frac{y - y^*}{1 - \beta(1 - \delta)}\right]. \qquad (98)$$

For $y > y^*$, $S_R(y)$ and $\theta(y)$ are such that

$$S_R(y) = y - b - \beta p(\theta(y))\gamma S_R(y) + \beta(1 - \delta)S_R(y), \tag{99}$$

$$k = q(\theta(y))\left\{\sigma\left[(1 - \gamma)\hat{S}_S(y) + \frac{y - y^*}{1 - \beta(1 - \delta)}\right] + (1 - \sigma)(1 - \gamma)S_R(y)\right\}. \tag{100}$$

Differentiating equation (98) with respect to y, I find that the elasticity of the market tightness with respect to a negative productivity shock is

$$\frac{\theta'(y^* -)y^*}{\theta(y^*)} = \frac{1}{1 - \epsilon} \cdot \frac{1}{1 - \gamma} \cdot \frac{1 - \beta[1 - \delta - p(\theta(y^*))\gamma]}{1 - \beta(1 - \delta)} \cdot \frac{y^*}{y^* - b}. \tag{101}$$

Differentiating equations (99) and (100) with respect to y, I find that the elasticity of the market tightness with respect to a positive productivity shock is

$$\frac{\theta'(y^* +)y^*}{\theta(y^*)} = \frac{1}{1 - \epsilon} \cdot \frac{1 - \beta[1 - \delta - p(\theta(y^*))\gamma]}{1 - \beta[1 - \delta - p(\theta(y^*))\gamma\frac{1 - \sigma\epsilon}{1 - \epsilon}]}$$

$$\cdot \left\{\frac{\sigma}{1 - \gamma} \frac{1 - \beta[1 - \delta - p(\theta(y^*))\gamma]}{1 - \beta(1 - \delta)} + 1 - \sigma\right\} \cdot \frac{y^*}{y^* - b}. \tag{102}$$

Also in this scenario, the elasticity of the market tightness with respect to a negative shock to y is the same in a PREE as in an SBE, irrespective of the fraction σ of S-workers in the population. Because the elasticity of market tightness in an SBE is higher in this scenario than in the previous one, so is the elasticity of the market tightness with respect to a negative shock to y in a PREE. The elasticity of the market tightness with respect to a positive shock to y in a PREE is between the elasticity in an REE and the elasticity in an SBE, and the elasticity increases with the fraction σ of S-workers in the population. It is easy to check that the elasticity of the market tightness in response to a positive shock to y is higher in the second scenario than in the first one.

The following proposition summarizes the characterization of a PREE.

Proposition 6. (Asymmetric labor-market fluctuations.) Let $\phi_r \to 1$ and $\phi_s \to 1$:

1. The elasticity of $\theta(y)$, $p(\theta(y))$, $u(y)$, and $v(y)$ with respect to a negative y-shock is the same in a PREE as in an SBE, is greater than in an REE, and does not depend on σ;
2. The elasticity of $\theta(y)$, $p(\theta(y))$, $u(y)$, and $v(y)$ with respect to a positive y-shock is greater in a PREE than in an REE, is smaller than in an SBE, and goes from one extreme to the other as σ increases;

3. The elasticity of $\theta(y)$, $p(\theta(y))$, $u(y)$, and $v(y)$ with respect to y in a PREE is higher if S-workers do not observe the productivity y of the firm with which they are bargaining.

To assess the extent of the asymmetry of labor-market fluctuations in response to negative and positive shocks to aggregate productivity, let me return to our back-of-the-envelope calibration. As a reminder, the calibration targets an average UE rate of 30%, an average EU rate of 2%, an elasticity of the job-finding probability with respect to tightness of 0.5, a worker's bargaining power of 0.5, and an unemployment income that is half of the unconditional mean of labor productivity.

In an REE, the elasticity of the labor-market tightness is the same with respect to positive and negative shocks to productivity, and it is equal to 2.1 for β, ϕ_s, $\phi_r \to 1$. Now consider a PREE in which stubborn workers observe the productivity of their employer. For β, ϕ_s, $\phi_r \to 1$ and for a fraction σ of stubborn workers equal to 10% of the population, the elasticity of the market tightness with respect to a negative shock to aggregate productivity is

$$\frac{\theta'(y^*-)y^*}{\theta(y^*)} = \frac{1}{1-\epsilon} \cdot \underbrace{\frac{\delta + p(\theta(y^*))\gamma}{\delta}}_{8.5} \cdot \frac{y^*}{y^*-b} = 34, \qquad (103)$$

and the elasticity of the market tightness with respect to a positive shock is

$$\frac{\theta'(y^*+)y^*}{\theta(y^*)} = \frac{1}{1-\epsilon} \cdot \underbrace{\frac{\delta + p(\theta(y^*))\gamma}{\delta} \cdot \frac{\delta + p(\theta(y^*))\gamma\sigma}{\delta + p(\theta(y^*))\gamma\frac{1-\epsilon\sigma}{1-\epsilon}}}_{.94} \cdot \frac{y^*}{y^*-b} = 3.7. \quad (104)$$

The elasticity of the labor-market tightness is about 10 times larger in response to a negative shock than in response to a positive shock, and about 15 times larger than in an REE. Similarly, the elasticity of the UE rate, the unemployment rate, and the vacancy rate are also 15 times larger in response to a negative shock than in response to a positive shock, and 10 times larger than in an REE.

Next, consider a PREE in which stubborn workers do not observe the productivity of their employer. For $\sigma = 0.1$, the no-screening condition does not hold. This does not necessarily mean that the bargaining outcome would be different, only that the characterization of the equilibrium would be different and involve mixed strategies. To be on the safe side, however, let me choose $\sigma = 0.55$, a value for which the no-screening condition holds. For $\beta, \phi_s, \phi_r \to 1$, the elasticity of the market tightness with respect to a negative shock to aggregate productivity is

$$\frac{\theta'(y^*-)y^*}{\theta(y^*)} = \underbrace{\frac{1}{1-\epsilon} \cdot \frac{1}{1-\gamma}}_{2} \cdot \underbrace{\frac{\delta + p(\theta(y^*))\gamma}{\delta}}_{8.5} \cdot \frac{y^*}{y^*-b} = 68, \qquad (105)$$

and the elasticity of the market tightness with respect to a positive shock is

$$\frac{\theta'(y^*+)y^*}{\theta(y^*)} = \frac{1}{1-\epsilon} \cdot \underbrace{\frac{\delta + p(\theta(y^*))\gamma}{\delta + p(\theta(y^*))\gamma \frac{1-\alpha\epsilon}{1-\epsilon}}(\ldots)}_{7} \frac{y^*}{y^*-b} = 28. \qquad (106)$$

The elasticity of the labor-market tightness is about three times larger in response to a negative shock than in response to a positive shock, and about 30 times larger than in an REE, and so are the elasticities of the UE, unemployment, and vacancy rates.

VI. Conclusions

In this paper, I developed a search-theoretic model of the labor market in which workers have incorrect expectations about their probability of finding a job and about the wage they will earn once they are hired. I modeled workers with incorrect expectations as agents who believe that aggregate productivity in the economy is always at its normal level, and who construct expectations about the tightness of the labor market, the job-finding probability, the firms' bargaining strategy, and the wage according to such beliefs. The worker's expectations are correct on average, but they are irrationally optimistic when aggregate productivity is below its normal level and irrationally pessimistic when aggregate productivity is above its normal level. The worker's expectations affect bargaining outcomes, specifically leading to wages that are either too sticky or outright rigid. On the positive side, the behavior of wages leads to excess cyclical volatility of the tightness of the labor market, job-finding probability, unemployment, and vacancies. On the normative side, the behavior of wages calls for a countercyclical employment subsidy, even when firms happen to internalize the congestion and thick-market externalities associated with vacancy creation.

The model is amenable to several natural extensions. In the paper, I considered a version of the model in which some workers have rational expectations, some workers have stubborn beliefs, and firms cannot observe the type of worker with which they are bargaining. In this version

of the model, the outcome of the bargaining game is qualitatively different depending on whether aggregate productivity is below or above its
normal level. When aggregate productivity is below its normal level,
the outcome of the bargaining game is such that both types of workers
earn the same wage that a worker with stubborn beliefs would earn if
the firm knew his type. When aggregate productivity is above its normal
level, the outcome of the bargaining game is such that each type of worker
earns the same wage that he would earn if the firm knew his type. As a
result, when aggregate productivity falls below its normal level, the average wage is as sticky or as rigid as it would be in a model where all workers have stubborn beliefs. When aggregate productivity rises above its
normal level, the average wage is sticky or rigid only in proportion to
the fraction of workers with stubborn beliefs. The asymmetry in the response of wages leads to a response of market tightness, job-finding probability, unemployment, and vacancies that is more pronounced in response to negative than in response to positive shocks.

Other extensions of the model seem worth exploring. Let me mention
two of them. For example, it would be interesting to consider a version
of the model in which the output produced by a firm-worker pair depends on a component of productivity that is aggregate and one that
is specific to the firm-worker pair (as in, say, Mortensen and Pissarides
1994). In this version of the model, the stubbornness of the workers' beliefs would lead to inefficiencies not only in job creation but also in job
destruction. In particular, when aggregate productivity is below its normal level, a stubborn worker would have expectations about his job-
finding probability that are too optimistic, and he would quit matches
that have positive surplus. When aggregate productivity is above its
normal level, a stubborn worker would have expectations that are overly
pessimistic, and he would stay in matches that have a negative surplus.
As a result, job destruction would be amplified in response to negative
shocks and muted in response to positive shocks.

Another interesting extension would be to consider workers who all
believe that the job-finding probability and the wage are constant, but
who differ with respect to the level of job-finding probability and wage
that they expect. This version of the model would be especially interesting when job destruction is endogenous. The most optimistic workers
would be the most likely to quit a job and the least likely to find a job.
The least optimistic workers would be the least likely to keep a job
and the most likely to find a job. Therefore, heterogeneity in workers'
beliefs could provide an explanation for the systematic heterogeneity

in the workers' pattern of transitions across employment states observed in the data (see, e.g., Hall and Kudlyak 2019; Gregory, Menzio, and Wiczer 2021).

Endnotes

Author email address: Menzio (gm1310@nyu.edu). I am grateful to Andrew Caplin, Marty Eichenbaum, Xavier Gabaix, John Kennan, Ilse Lindenlaub, Elliot Lipnowski, Simon Mongey, Andi Mueller, Richard Rogerson, and Venky Venkateswaran for useful comments and suggestions. For acknowledgments, sources of research support, and disclosure of the author's material financial relationships, if any, please see https://www
.nber.org/books-and-chapters/nber-macroeconomics-annual-2022-volume-37/stub
born-beliefs-search-equilibrium.
1. In this paper, I will focus on a search-theoretic model of the labor market in which wages are determined through a bargaining game. It is clear, though, that many of the insights would apply to a search-theoretic model of the labor market in which wages are posted by firms.
2. By "symmetric-information wage," I mean that wage that would obtain in a bargaining game between the firm and the worker where the firm knew the worker's type.
3. I only consider PSE in pure strategies. For this reason, I restrict attention to firm's beliefs $\hat{\sigma} \in \{0, \sigma, 1\}$.
4. The credibility requirement for the updating of beliefs is designed to avoid situations in which the firm can insist on a particular wage offer by threatening to revise its beliefs optimistically whenever a different wage offer is made.

References

Azariadis, C. 1975. "Implicit Contracts and Underemployment Equilibria." *Journal of Political Economy* 83:1183–202.
Binmore, K., A. Rubinstein, and A. Wolinksy. 1986. "The Nash Bargaining Solution in Economic Modelling." *RAND Journal of Economics* 17:176–88.
Christiano, L., M. Eichenbaum, and M. Trabandt. 2016. "Unemployment and Business Cycles." *Econometrica* 84:1523–69.
———. 2021. "Why Is Unemployment So Countercyclical?" *Review of Economic Dynamics* 41:4–37.
Conlon, J., L. Pillosoph, M. Wiswall, and B. Zafar. 2018. "Labor Market Search with Imperfect Information and Learning." Working paper, Federal Reserve Bank of New York.
Fukui, M. 2021. "A Theory of Wage Rigidity and Unemployment Fluctuations with On-the-Job Search." Working paper, Massachusetts Institute of Technology.
Gabaix, X. 2019. "Behavioral Inattention." In *Handbook of Behavioral Economics*, ed. D. Bernheim, S. DellaVigna, and D. Laibson, 2:261–343. Amsterdam: Elsevier.
———. 2020. "A Behavioral New Keynesian Model." *American Economic Review* 110:2271–327.
Gertler, M., and A. Trigari. 2009. "Unemployment Fluctuations with Staggered Nash Wage Bargaining." *Journal of Political Economy* 117:38–85.
Golosov, M., and G. Menzio. 2020. "Agency Business Cycles." *Theoretical Economics* 15:123–58.
Gregory, V., G. Menzio, and D. Wiczer. 2021. "The Alpha Beta Gamma of the Labor Market." Working Paper no. 28663, NBER, Cambridge, MA.

Grossman, S., and M. Perry. 1986a. "Perfect Sequential Equilibrium." *Journal of Economic Theory* 39:97–119.

———. 1986b. "Sequential Bargaining under Asymmetric Information." *Journal of Economic Theory* 39:120–54.

Gul, F., and H. Sonnenschein. 1988. "On Delay in Bargaining with One-Sided Uncertainty." *Econometrica* 56:601–11.

Hall, R. 2005. "Employment Fluctuations with Equilibrium Wage Stickiness." *American Economic Review* 95:50–65.

Hall, R., and M. Kudlyak. 2019. "Job-Finding and Job-Losing: A Comprehensive Model of Heterogeneous Individual Labor-Market Dynamics." Working paper, Stanford University.

Hall, R., and P. Milgrom. 2008. "The Limited Influence of Unemployment on the Wage Bargain." *American Economic Review* 98:1653–74.

Hosios, A. 1990. "On the Efficiency of Matching and Related Models of Search and Unemployment." *Review of Economic Studies* 57:279–98.

Kaplan, G., and G. Menzio. 2016. "Shopping Externalities and Self-Fulfilling Unemployment Fluctuations." *Journal of Political Economy* 124:771–825.

Kehoe, P., V. Midrigan, and E. Pastorino. 2019. "Debt Constraints and Employment." *Journal of Political Economy* 127:1926–91.

Kennan, J. 2010. "Private Information, Wage Bargaining and Unemployment Fluctuations." *Review of Economic Studies* 77:633–64.

Ljungqvist, L., and T. Sargent. 2017. "The Fundamental Surplus." *American Economic Review* 107:2630–65.

Martellini, P., G. Menzio, and L. Visschers. 2021. "Revisiting the Hypothesis of High Discounts and High Unemployment." *Economic Journal* 131:2203–32.

Menzio, G. 2005. "High Frequency Wage Rigidity." Working paper, Northwestern University.

Menzio, G., and E. Moen. 2010. "Worker Replacement." *Journal of Monetary Economics* 57:623–36.

Menzio, G., and S. Shi. 2011. "Efficient Search on the Job and the Business Cycle." *Journal of Political Economy* 119:468–510.

Mortensen, D. 1982. "Property Rights and Efficiency in Mating, Racing and Related Games." *American Economic Review* 72:968–79.

Mortensen, D., and C. Pissarides. 1994. "Job Creation and Job Destruction in the Theory of Unemployment." *Review of Economic Studies* 61:397–415.

Mueller, A., J. Spinnewijn, and G. Topa. 2021. "Job Seekers' Perceptions and Employment Prospects: Heterogeneity, Duration Dependence, and Bias." *American Economic Review* 111 (1): 324–63.

Pissarides, C. 1985. "Short-Run Equilibrium Dynamics of Unemployment, Vacancies, and Real Wages." *American Economic Review* 75:676–90.

Shimer, R. 2005. "The Cyclical Behavior of Equilibrium Unemployment and Vacancies." *American Economic Review* 95:25–49.

Comment

Ilse Lindenlaub, Yale University, United States of America

I. Summary

Guido Menzio's paper, "Stubborn Beliefs in Search Equilibrium," provides a new and provocative approach to a set of long-standing questions in the macro labor literature. What is the source of downward wage rigidity? And how can one of the workhorse models in this literature—the random-search model pioneered by Diamond, Mortensen, and Pissarides (DMP)—generate realistic cyclical fluctuations in vacancies and unemployment?

Menzio proposes a novel mechanism for wage rigidity, which relies on the presence of nonrational workers in an otherwise standard DMP model. These "stubborn" workers do not have rational expectations but instead have biased beliefs about the aggregate state of the economy. More specifically, they believe that aggregate productivity is constant and equal to its unconditional mean of the productivity distribution, failing to recognize booms or recessions. In a downturn, workers who contemplate forming a match with a firm therefore have beliefs about their outside option—the value of search—that are too optimistic, which affects the wages they bargain. In fact, wages are entirely pinned down by workers' beliefs, because firms have no choice but to accommodate these biased beliefs as they cannot be changed. Wages are therefore too high compared with what a recession would call for; that is, they are downward sticky/rigid. As a result, firms' incentives to post vacancies strongly diminish. In the presence of stubborn workers, aggregate productivity

NBER Macroeconomics Annual, volume 37, 2023.

movements then translate into larger shifts in vacancies and unemployment, as well as in labor-market tightness, which is the ratio between the two. On the normative side, the paper shows that these fluctuations can be inefficiently large and that this inefficiency can be corrected by a countercyclical employment subsidy.

Although in the baseline model, all workers are stubborn, the extension features a more realistic setting, in which some workers are stubborn (i.e., a fraction σ) and some are "rational." Firms do not know the type of the particular worker that they bargain with. But they know the distribution of beliefs (i.e., they know σ), and they try to learn about the individual worker's type they bargain with. In a recession, the focus is on a pooling equilibrium. Compared with rational workers, stubborn workers are more optimistic about the economy's state and their outside option. Hence, they bargain wages that are too high compared with what is justified in a state of poor aggregate fundamentals. Rational workers understand this and have an incentive to mimic stubborn workers' bargaining strategy to get paid higher wages. If the fraction of stubborn workers is relatively large or the negative productivity shock is relatively small, then screening is too costly and firms have no incentive to disentangle the two worker types. A pooling equilibrium results, in which both worker types obtain the wage that reflects stubborn beliefs. Conditional on pooling, this wage is independent of the amount of stubborn workers σ. In turn, the boom features a separating equilibrium. Rational workers are more optimistic about the state of the economy and their outside option than stubborn ones. As a result, they have an incentive to signal to firms their true rational type. Higher wages will be paid to rational than to stubborn workers, and the extent of upward sticky wages will depend on the fraction of stubborn workers σ.

II. Contribution to the Literature

The main contribution of this paper is to provide a new mechanism for rigid wages. This mechanism has the potential to generate large cyclical fluctuations of unemployment and vacancies in models that have struggled to do so.

As more accurate information on wages, along with rich worker and job characteristics, has become available, the empirical literature on wage rigidity has experienced a revival. Recent work tries to overcome the challenge posed by worker and job selection over the business cycle for the measurement of wage rigidities. Using administrative wage data from the largest US payroll processing company, Grigsby, Hurst, and Yildir-maz (2021) find that wages of incumbent workers and new hires are similarly rigid. Hazell and Taska (2020) measure the extent of wage rigidity of new hires based on job postings from the Burning Glass online vacancy platform. When controlling for cyclical changes in job composition, they also find that new-hire wages are downward rigid (and flexible upward). Although wage rigidity for incumbent workers may be natural, wage rigidity for new hires is more surprising and also more difficult to rationalize in models. Menzio contributes a new mechanism that generates (new-hire) wage rigidity.

Understanding the sources and degree of rigid wages is especially important for the analysis of business-cycle fluctuations in vacancies and unemployment. In fact, the most common way to generate realistic business-cycle fluctuations in unemployment in the DMP model is through rigid wages. Under the standard assumption of period-by-period Nash bargained wages (and under a standard calibration), this model features wages that are too flexible, absorbing a large chunk of aggregate productivity shifts. This excess volatility in wages is the main reason the standard DMP model has failed to generate realistic fluctuations in quantities, a phenomenon known as the unemployment volatility puzzle (see Shimer 2005).

Why do flexible wages dampen the cyclical fluctuations of unemployment, vacancies, and market tightness in the standard DMP model? First, note that what determines the amount of vacancies v and ultimately the labor-market tightness θ (which is the ratio of vacancies over unemployment u) as well as unemployment in this model is a free-entry condition for firms. It says that firms (or vacancies) should enter the labor market up to the point where the cost (k) and benefit of posting a vacancy are equalized. This benefit is the expected value of filling the vacancy, given by the job-filling rate $q(\theta(y))$ times the firm's value of a filled job $J(w(y), y)$, where both market tightness θ and the wage w depend on the economy's aggregate productivity y:

$$k = q(\theta(y))J(w(y), y) \approx q(\theta(y))(y - w(y)).$$

The value of a filled job is an increasing function of flow profits $y - w(y)$. Thus, if the wage $w(y)$ is very responsive to aggregate productivity shocks to y, then $y - w(y)$ is roughly constant. As a result, the incentives to post vacancies do not vary over the business cycle, so that $\theta = \theta(y)$ is approximately constant, and so is the unemployment rate.

What makes wages responsive to aggregate productivity y in this model in the first place? The standard way to pin down wages in the

DMP model is through Nash bargaining. The axiomatic Nash solution maximizes the product of the worker and job surplus, with weights that are equal to the worker (firm) bargaining power γ $(1 - \gamma)$. The resulting wage is given by a weighted average of productivity and the worker's outside option:

$$w(y) = \gamma y + (1 - \gamma)(1 - \beta)V_0(y),$$

where β is the discount factor and $V_0(y)$ is the value of search (i.e., the value of unemployment). The value of search is what the worker would get if the match did not happen (i.e., his outside option). It depends on the aggregate state because it is affected by labor-market tightness θ (a tight labor market increases the job-finding rate for workers and thus the value of search) and the wages in other jobs (higher wages lead to a higher value of search). This equation illustrates why in this type of model, wages strongly depend on aggregate productivity. There is a direct effect of aggregate productivity through surplus sharing, weighted by the worker's bargaining power; there is an indirect effect through the worker's outside option, which is increasing in y as well.

Much research has been dedicated to develop ways that make wages more rigid in this model.[1] Some approaches focus on solutions that maintain the Nash bargaining assumption, and others abandon Nash bargaining altogether.

For instance, Hall (2005) lets go of Nash bargaining and makes wages rigid by assumption $w(y) = \bar{w}$, substantially increasing the cyclical fluctuations of firms' profits and thus the incentives to post vacancies based on the free-entry condition.

Hall and Milgrom (2008) also abandon Nash bargaining. They replace it with alternating-offer bargaining (Binmore, Rubinstein, and Wolinsky 1986). One side of the market makes a wage offer. If accepted, this offer will be the agreed wage. If rejected by the other side, then a counteroffer is made. If accepted, then the match will form at that wage. Workers and firms keep making alternative offers until they agree or the negotiations (exogenously) break down. The key difference with Nash bargaining is that this bargaining game puts the disagreement payoff (as opposed to the outside option) at its center stage. The disagreement payoff is what the two sides obtain while bargaining before the agreement is reached. The workers' outside option is still in the picture, but it only becomes relevant in the unlikely case of a negotiation breakdown. This loosens the connection between the wage and the value of search, and therefore the connection between wages and aggregate productivity. As a result, unemployment responds more strongly to aggregate shocks.

Gertler and Trigari (2009) replace the period-by-period Nash bargaining with staggered multiperiod Nash bargaining, according to which in each period only a subset of firms and workers negotiate wage contracts. Workers hired in between wage bargaining periods receive the same wage as the firm's existing workers. As a result, wages are more rigid than in the baseline model, producing larger responses of unemployment to productivity shocks.

Menzio's solution to the problem of excessively flexible wages is different but can be understood within this framework as well. He assumes, similar to Hall and Milgrom (2008), that wages are set by alternating-offer bargaining. Contrary to Hall and Milgrom, he focuses on the limit case, in which the cost of delaying the agreement by one period becomes negligible. In this limit, the alternating-offer bargaining solution becomes the axiomatic Nash solution, so in principle there is a strong transmission of aggregate productivity to wages through the workers' outside option. Menzio's twist to prevent this is to make the outside option of workers independent of the aggregate state, weakening the feedback effect from the current state of the economy to the current wage. Stubborn workers do not update their beliefs about the aggregate state of the economy; they think it is always the same, $y = y^*$. As a result, the value of search does not depend on aggregate productivity $V_0(y) = \bar{V}_0$, and wages are given by

$$w(y) = \gamma y + (1 - \gamma)(1 - \beta)\bar{V}_0.$$

This leads to a smaller transmission (or no transmission at all, if workers in addition do not observe the firm productivity realization y, which is equal to the aggregate productivity) of aggregate shocks to wages, and thereby to larger fluctuations in vacancies and unemployment in response to these shocks.

III. Discussion

In this discussion, I will examine several of the model's key ingredients that underlie the mechanism for wage rigidity. My main focus will be on the nonrational (stubborn) beliefs. What does the analyst need to know about the workers' beliefs when applying this model and what do we actually know about individuals' beliefs in the labor-market context? I will also discuss the importance of two other assumptions, of wage bargaining (versus posting), and of hiring from unemployment only (versus from employment also), for generating the desired wage rigidity. I base my discussion on the model extension that features a mix of stubborn and rational workers, as I believe it will be the main candidate for applications and quantitative analysis.

A. Workers' Biased Beliefs

As a first comment, note that the information requirements for the analyst of this model are nonnegligible. To apply this model both in a positive way (to understand the extent of business-cycle fluctuations of unemployment and the market tightness they can generate) and in a normative way (to design the optimal employment subsidy that corrects the excess volatility of unemployment), the researcher needs to know the distribution of workers' beliefs. She needs to know not only how the deviations from rationality look like but also what the fraction of nonrational workers in the economy is.

For a start, I will take the particular deviations from rationality that the paper proposes as given, and I will come back to this point later. Let me focus for now on the point that the researcher needs to know the share of stubborn workers, σ, to work with this model. Consider the pooling equilibrium of a recession. The attractive feature of the model is that if pooling materializes, then the equilibrium wage will be downward rigid, independent of the level of σ. But checking that the condition for pooling is satisfied (i.e., that firms have no incentive to screen rational and stubborn workers) requires knowledge of σ. Using a slightly simplified model (with a two-point process for aggregate productivity) and a calibration that mimics the one in this paper, one can compute the (candidate) pooling equilibrium and check whether the condition for pooling holds.[2] I illustrate this condition for the calibrated (simplified) model in figure 1, which graphs the fraction of stubborn workers σ as a function of the productivity realization in the recession y (the "normal" state of the economy is $y^* = 1$).[3] Pooling happens in the parameter set that is northeast to the solid-line curve. For any given shock y with $y < y^*$, the fraction of stubborn workers needs to be large enough so that screening out the rational workers is too costly for firms. But the larger the negative productivity shock (i.e., the larger the deviations of y from $y^* = 1$), the more stubborn workers (higher σ) are needed to prevent firms from screening out rational workers and from paying them lower wages. Pooling makes wages particularly rigid in a recession, which amplifies the response

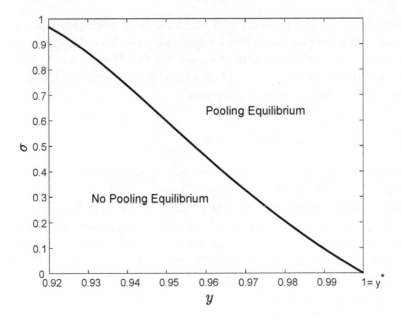

Fig. 1. Recession: parameter restrictions for pooling. A color version of this figure is available online.

of unemployment and vacancies to a negative shock. But whether pooling materializes depends on the distribution of stubborn/rational workers, captured by σ.[4]

Knowledge of the distribution of beliefs is also required for assessing the qualitative and, especially, quantitative implications of the boom equilibrium. In the boom, stubborn workers are relatively pessimistic and therefore bargain a wage that is lower than the state of the economy calls for. Rational workers have therefore no incentive to mimic stubborn workers' wage bargaining strategy. Instead, they signal their rational type to firms to obtain higher wages. Rational workers' wages therefore reflect the favorable aggregate state. The extent of wage rigidity (and the extent of fluctuations of labor-market tightness in response to productivity shocks) will thus depend on the fraction of stubborn workers, σ.

Figure 2 illustrates this point by graphing the model-implied elasticity of labor-market tightness with respect to aggregate productivity as a function of the fraction of stubborn workers, σ. The more stubborn workers there are, the more rigid wages will be in a boom, translating into a larger elasticity of labor-market tightness with respect to aggregate productivity. The horizontal dashed line indicates the empirical

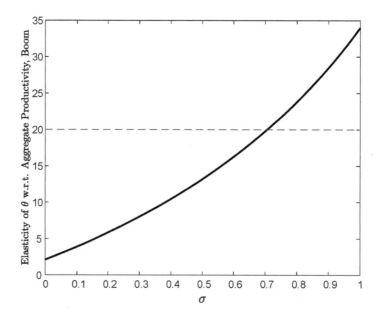

Fig. 2. Boom: elasticity of market tightness with respect to aggregate productivity as a function of σ. A color version of this figure is available online.

elasticity, which is around 20.[5] To achieve realistic fluctuations of tightness (and unemployment) with respect to aggregate productivity, this simple calibration suggests that what is required is that the majority of workers (about 70%) are ignorant of the aggregate state.

Given that the level of σ is central to whether the model can generate a sufficient degree of wage rigidity that renders realistic business-cycle fluctuations in tightness, it is important to discipline these beliefs in a credible way. Otherwise, anything goes: if σ is a free parameter, one can always choose it such that the model matches the observed volatility. Can the data help us discipline those beliefs? This is the question I will turn to next.

Data on workers' beliefs about labor-market prospects are still rare. To date, only a few surveys elicit individuals' beliefs in the labor-market context. Among the best data sources for this purpose is the Survey of Consumer Expectations (SCE), administered by the Federal Reserve Bank of New York. This is a monthly panel, interviewing 1,000–2,000 workers about their perceived probabilities of job loss and job finding. The survey seeks answers from around 200–300 unemployed workers per year. Data collection started in 2012 and is ongoing (data from 2012 to the beginning of 2022 are publicly available at https://www.newyorkfed.org/micro economics/databank.html).

Apart from issues with small sample size and (so far) limited time dimension, this survey—like any survey that elicits beliefs of individuals—wrestles with a few known challenges. As discussed in detail in Mueller and Spinnewjin (2022), it is intrinsically difficult to elicit beliefs about the economy's primitives. This is because the respondents' answers reflect both beliefs about primitives and behavioral responses. A respondent may be optimistic about his job-finding rate because he expects the economy to be in a good aggregate state going forward, or because he expects to search hard for a job in the coming months. Furthermore, not every deviation between elicited belief and actual outcome is a sign of a bias. The reason is that the object of elicitation may not perfectly coincide with the realized outcome; moreover, unexpected aggregate shocks can drive a wedge between beliefs and outcomes without any bias.

Bearing these limitations in mind, let us take a look at the evidence on elicited beliefs in the labor-market context, based on the SCE. I am interested in (a) whether workers adjust their beliefs to the aggregate state and (b) what we can learn about the nature of their biases and the distribution of the biased beliefs from these data.

A first look at the data suggests that workers do adjust their beliefs to the aggregate state of the economy, at least to some extent. The top panel in figure 3 plots the expected rise in unemployment 1 year ahead, and the bottom panel plots the expected job-finding rate during the next 3 months if the worker becomes unemployed.[6] Beliefs about both statistics become more optimistic as the United States leaves the Great Recession further behind, with more respondents expecting a decline or no shift in the future unemployment rate and an increase in the future job-finding rate. In turn, both trends are disrupted by the pandemic recession, with beliefs about future unemployment spiking and beliefs about future job finding plummeting. As the pandemic recession wanes, beliefs about unemployment and the job-finding rate quickly approach pre-recession levels.

In a second step, to get a sense of whether beliefs are biased and of the nature of this bias (i.e., too optimistic or too pessimistic), I compare elicited beliefs about job finding to actual outcomes, replicating the findings from Mueller and Spinnewjin (2022) (see their fig. 1, left panel). However, I focus on a sample of unemployed workers to make it comparable with the figure that follows. Figure 4 plots the expected and realized job-finding rate from 2013 to 2019. There is comovement between expectation

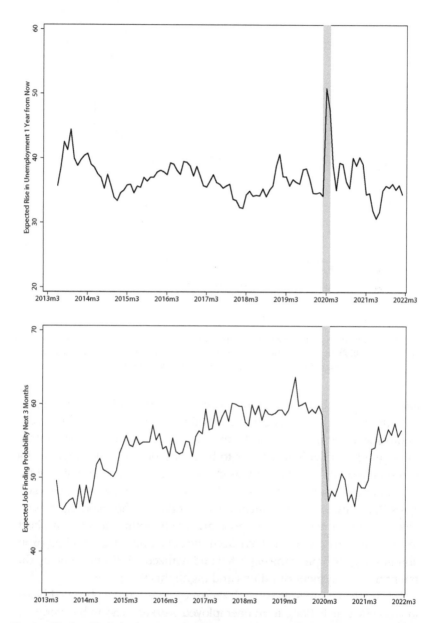

Fig. 3. Workers' beliefs about unemployment and job finding. Author's calculations are based on the Survey of Consumer Expectations, Federal Reserve Bank of New York, 2013–22. Numbers are reported in percent.

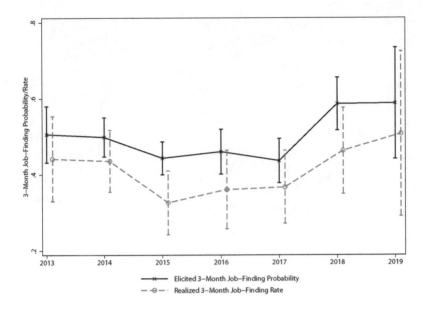

Fig. 4. Expectation and realization of job finding. Author's replication of Mueller and Spinnewjin (2022), figure 1*a*, is based on a sample of only unemployed workers in the Survey of Consumer Expectations, Federal Reserve Bank of New York, 2013–19.

and realization, but throughout, the expected job-finding rate is higher than the realized one, suggesting that unemployed workers are overly optimistic about their prospects (but this bias is imprecisely estimated). Interestingly, individuals appear to be overly optimistic throughout the entire period 2013–19, which was characterized by an economic boom.[7]

Zooming further into these biased beliefs of unemployed workers suggests that only long-term unemployed workers, who make up around 25% of the US unemployment pool, are overly optimistic. In turn, short-term unemployed workers have accurate beliefs about job-finding probabilities. Figure 5 plots the expected and realized job-finding rate by different unemployment durations and highlights this point.

This evidence suggests some discrepancy between the observed biases in workers' beliefs (long-term unemployed workers tend to be overly optimistic during a boom and short-term unemployed workers have accurate beliefs) and the model's specification of stubborn beliefs, according to which all those unemployed workers that are stubborn are overly optimistic in a recession and overly pessimistic in a boom. But, due to the small sample and short time horizon, the evidence is not sufficiently sharp to draw strong conclusions either in support of or against the model's

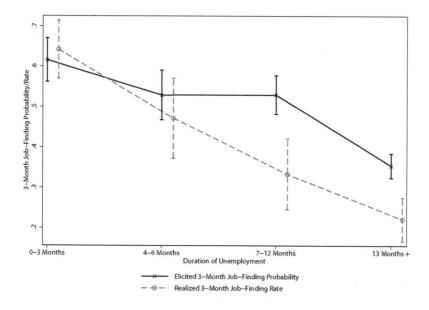

Fig. 5. Expectation and realization of job finding, by unemployment duration. Author's replication of Mueller, Spinnewijn, and Topa (2021), figure 3, is based on the Survey of Consumer Expectations, Federal Reserve Bank of New York, 2013–19.

assumptions on the nature of the bias. What this analysis suggests, however, is that it may be difficult to infer the value of the model's central parameter, namely the level of σ that indicates the fraction of stubborn workers, from these data on workers' expectations.

Apart from the presence of nonrational workers whose beliefs do not vary with the aggregate state, there are additional model ingredients I would like to discuss that support the proposed mechanism behind wage rigidity.

B. Wage Bargaining

One of them is the assumption of wage bargaining. Menzio's model relies on the alternating-wage bargaining game (Binmore et al. 1986), which in the limit—when the negotiation intervals become very small—converges to the axiomatic Nash bargaining solution. As discussed above, the Nash solution yields wages that generally show a strong comovement with aggregate productivity. One reason for this is their dependence on workers' outside option that varies significantly with the aggregate state in standard models. This makes profits and, thus, the incentive to create vacancies inelastic with respect to aggregate productivity. Menzio obtains rigid wages despite his focus on the Nash limit of the bargaining game by making (stubborn) workers' outside option sticky. The sticky outside option translates into sticky wages, by breaking an important channel through which aggregate productivity affects wages. What seems important for this mechanism is that there is a strong impact of the outside option on wages, and the assumed wage bargaining protocol delivers this.

Overall, there is not much evidence on how wages are set. Existing findings give a mixed picture. Hall and Krueger (2012) collect data on this issue and find that around a third of all workers bargain over their wages. More recently, Lachowska et al. (2022) document that only 25% of workers bargain over their wages, based on a clever identification strategy that uses dual jobholders in administrative data from Washington State. Moreover, those who bargain tend to be educated, high-income individuals that are employed.

It is therefore worth asking whether the model mechanism would be robust to replacing wage bargaining by the common alternative of wage posting. How would the model implications for wage rigidity change if firms made take-it-or-leave-it offers, leaving little if any of the match surplus to the worker? In this scenario, firms adjust their wages in each period optimally to the aggregate state of the economy, dampening the effect of individual workers' outside options on wages and thus leaving less room for biased beliefs to generate rigid wages and strong responses of tightness to productivity shocks. It would still be true that workers' beliefs affect their reservation wages, which firms take into account in their wage-posting strategies. But one conjecture is that individual workers' outside options affect wages less compared with the current setting, potentially weakening the proposed mechanism for wage rigidity.

C.   Search Only from Unemployment

A second assumption that amplifies the role of workers' beliefs in wage setting is that only the unemployed search for jobs. When unemployed workers bargain for wages, their outside option—the value of search—strongly depends on their beliefs about the economy's aggregate state. This gives a prominent role to workers' beliefs in wage bargaining and thus in aggregate fluctuations of unemployment.

When it comes to the evidence, it is well known that hiring from employment is as important as hiring from unemployment. The average poaching share (i.e., the fraction of hires that are made from employment) is almost 50% in the United States (Haltiwanger, Hyatt, and McEntarfer 2015).

For employed workers, the role of beliefs in wage outcomes is potentially smaller. Employed workers' outside option is the current wage, which, at that stage, does not depend on their beliefs about the aggregate state. I conjecture that additional features, such as a mobility cost for job switchers or endogenous search intensity, could restore the important role of beliefs for employed job seekers' outcomes. But adding employed workers' search to the current model would likely dampen the impact of stubborn beliefs on wage rigidity and aggregate fluctuations.

IV.   Conclusion

This paper provides a new and provocative take on a set of long-standing questions that have shaped the macro labor literature in important ways. First, what underlies (downward) wage rigidity? Second, and related, how can the DMP model produce realistic fluctuations in labor-market tightness and unemployment?

Existing literature has offered several answers over the years. However, none of them seem perfectly satisfactory. Depending on the approach, the proposed models imply a labor share that is too high or too strongly countercyclical and unemployment that is too responsive to flow unemployment benefits. It therefore seems worthwhile to revisit these important questions with a fresh perspective.

This is what Menzio's paper is about. He proposes an intriguing, novel mechanism for wage rigidity, which hinges on workers' biased beliefs about the aggregate economy. One could check in a quantitative application of his model whether it can overcome some of the mentioned challenges of existing approaches. But to do so, one would need to discipline the agents' beliefs in the model in a data-driven way. The agenda of relaxing the rational-expectations assumption will likely hinge on how well and convincingly this can be done.

Endnotes

Author email address: Lindenlaub (ilse.lindenlaub@yale.edu). For acknowledgments, sources of research support, and disclosure of the author's material financial relationships, if any, please see https://www.nber.org/books-and-chapters/nber-macroeconomics-annual -2022-volume-37/comment-stubborn-beliefs-search-equilibrium-lindenlaub.

1. A solution to the unemployment volatility puzzle that does not rely on wage rigidity is proposed by Hagedorn and Manovskii (2008), who maintain Nash bargaining in the

DMP model but choose a different calibration than Shimer (2005): they set a high level of unemployment flow income, which makes firms' profit margin small. This implies that small productivity shocks have a relatively large proportional impact on profits, affecting the incentive to post vacancies even with relatively flexible wages.

2. Formally, the condition for pooling is given by

$$\sigma(y - (1 - \beta) > \hat{V}_{S,0}) \geq (1 - \sigma)(1 - \beta)(\hat{V}_{S,0} - V_{R,0}(y)),$$

where $\hat{V}_{S,0}$ is the perceived value of search of unemployed workers, which is independent of the aggregate productivity y, and $V_{R,0}(y)$ is the value of search of rational workers, which depends on y. See equation (69) in Menzio (2022).

3. The figure is based on a model with two-point productivity process, with $y^* = 1$, $\gamma = 0.5$, $\delta = 0.02$, $b = 0.5$, $\phi_R = 0.98$, and $\phi_S = 0.95$; k is chosen such that the average monthly job-finding rate is around 30%.

4. Menzio (2022) makes the plausible conjecture that even when the equilibrium is separating in the recession, rational workers' wages will be close to the wages of stubborn workers. But even in this case, σ needs to be known for grasping the extent of wage rigidity in the boom.

5. This is in between the targets of Shimer (2005), who uses 17, and Hornstein, Krusell, and Violante (2005), who use 27.

6. The unemployment beliefs reflect the mean probability that US unemployment rate will be higher 1 year from the interview date among respondents in a given year. Respondents are asked for the percent chance that within the next 12 months the US unemployment rate will be higher than it is now. In turn, the beliefs about the job-finding probability give the mean probability of finding and accepting a job among the respondents in a given year. Respondents who report not being self-employed but working full time, working part time, being temporarily laid off, or being on sick leave are asked for the percent chance that within the following 3 months they will find a new job they will accept (considering the pay and type of work) if they were to lose their job this month.

7. Overoptimism of unemployed workers has also been documented by Spinnewijn (2015).

References

Binmore, K., A. Rubinstein, and A. Wolinsky. 1986. "The Nash Bargaining Solution in Economic Modelling." *RAND Journal of Economics* 17 (2): 176–88.
Gertler, M., and A. Trigari. 2009. "Unemployment Fluctuations with Staggered Nash Wage Bargaining." *Journal of Political Economy* 117 (1): 38–86.
Grigsby, J., E. Hurst, and A. Yildirmaz. 2021. "Aggregate Nominal Wage Adjustments: New Evidence from Administrative Payroll Data." *American Economic Review* 111 (2): 428–71.
Hagedorn, M., and I. Manovskii. 2008. "The Cyclical Behavior of Equilibrium Unemployment and Vacancies Revisited." *American Economic Review* 98 (4): 1692–706.
Hall, R. E. 2005. "Employment Fluctuations with Equilibrium Wage Stickiness." *American Economic Review* 95 (1): 50–65.
Hall, R. E., and A. B. Krueger. 2012. "Evidence on the Incidence of Wage Posting, Wage Bargaining, and On-the-Job Search." *American Economic Journal: Macroeconomics* 4 (4): 56–67.
Hall, R. E., and P. R. Milgrom. 2008. "The Limited Influence of Unemployment on the Wage Bargain." *American Economic Review* 98 (4): 1653–74.
Haltiwanger, J., H. Hyatt, and E. McEntarfer. 2015. "Cyclical Reallocation of Workers across Employers by Firm Size and Firm Wage." Working Paper no. 21235, NBER, Cambridge, MA.

Hazell, J., and B. Taska. 2020. "Downward Rigidity in the Wage for New Hires." *ERN: Wages; Intergenerational Income Distribution (Topic).* https://papers.ssrn.com/sol3/papers.cfm?abstract_id=3728939.

Hornstein, A., P. Krusell, and G. L. Violante. 2005. "Unemployment and Vacancy Fluctuations in the Matching Model: Inspecting the Mechanism." *FRB Richmond Economic Quarterly* 91 (3).

Lachowska, M., A. Mas, R. Saggio, and S. A. Woodbury. 2022. "Wage Posting or Wage Bargaining? A Test Using Dual Jobholders." *Journal of Labor Economics* 40 (S1): 469–93.

Menzio, G. 2022. "Stubborn Beliefs in Search Equilibrium." NBER Macroeconomics Annual 2022, vol. 37, NBER, Cambridge, MA.

Mueller, A. I., and J. Spinnewijn. 2022. "Expectations Data, Labor Market and Job Search." In *Handbook of Economic Expectations,* ed. Rüdiger Bachmann, Giorgio Topa, and Wilbert van der Klaauw, 677–713. Cambridge, MA: Academic Press.

Mueller, A. I., J. Spinnewijn, and G. Topa. 2021. "Job Seekers' Perceptions and Employment Prospects: Heterogeneity, Duration Dependence, and Bias." *American Economic Review* 111 (1): 324–63.

Shimer, R. 2005. "The Cyclical Behavior of Equilibrium Unemployment and Vacancies." *American Economic Review* 95 (1): 25–49.

Spinnewijn, J. 2015. "Unemployed but Optimistic: Optimal Insurance Design with Biased Beliefs." *Journal of the European Economic Association* 13 (1): 130–67.

Comment

Richard Rogerson, Princeton University and NBER, United States of America

I. Introduction

At a general level, this paper is an exploration of the effect of departures from rational expectations in frictional models of the labor market. More specifically, it studies a handful of examples in which some (or all) workers are assumed to exhibit a very specific form of irrational expectations that Menzio labels as stubborn beliefs.

As one would expect with this author, the modeling features a high level of artistry and craftsmanship, the analysis is clear and elegant, and all of the results are accompanied with strong intuition. The examples illustrate that these departures from rational expectations can have interesting effects on aggregate labor-market outcomes, and some of the results are quite provocative. In particular, he shows in one of his examples that a small subset of workers with stubborn beliefs can make labor-market outcomes more volatile for all workers in the labor market. That is, workers with incorrect perceptions are not just hurting themselves, they are hurting all workers. The paper also offers a methodological contribution in showing how to formulate equilibrium in frictional models with strategic wage setting and irrational beliefs.

There are two key components to the exercises carried out in the paper. One component is the specification of the departure from rational expectations. The second component is the mechanism through which the specific departure from rational expectations is propagated into aggregate labor-market outcomes. In what follows, I will discuss each of these in turn.

NBER Macroeconomics Annual, volume 37, 2023.

II.   The Departure from Rational Expectations

Menzio studies a model in which there are aggregate shocks to productivity. In a rational-expectations equilibrium, all agents in the economy know the stochastic process for aggregate productivity and the mapping from aggregate productivity to the endogenous variables that they take parametrically. Menzio considers a departure from rational expectations in which some or all workers believe that there are no aggregate shocks to the economy, with aggregate productivity always equal to its mean value. These workers solve for the equilibrium that would result if there were no shocks and use it to forecast the values that they take parametrically. This specification amounts to these workers essentially using past long-run average values in the economy to forecast future values. Because these workers do not adjust their beliefs about the existence of aggregate shocks, Menzio refers to them as having "stubborn beliefs."

One of the issues with considering departures from rational expectations, or rational behavior more broadly, is that there are just so many ways to depart from rationality. This remains true even when one restricts attention to departures that one might label as empirically or intuitively plausible. Moreover, as I describe later in the context of one example, I think it is often the case that one can find two equally plausible departures that give opposite results. For this reason, any analysis that focuses on one specific departure will be most compelling if it offers strong evidence to support the specific departure being considered.

Menzio appeals to the recent interesting paper by Mueller, Spinnewijn, and Topa (2021) to support his assumption about stubborn beliefs. This paper analyzes evidence from the Survey of Consumer Expectations administered by the Federal Reserve Bank of New York to assess the properties of workers' perceived job-finding rates. It documents several facts. First, there is significant heterogeneity in both perceived and actual job-finding rates. Second, perceived and actual job-finding rates are highly positively correlated. Third, there is little bias in average perceived rates for individuals that are beginning unemployment spells. Fourth, perceived rates seem to "underreact" to actual rates, in that individuals with high (low) actual job-finding rates tend to be overly pessimistic (optimistic). Fifth, perceived job-finding rates do not adjust over the course of an unemployment spell.

Menzio interprets these findings as supporting his assumption of stubborn beliefs, but my reading of the evidence in Mueller et al. (2021) is much less conclusive on this point. The fact that average perceived rates for individuals at the beginning of a spell are roughly equal to average observed job-finding rates seems inconsistent with Menzio's specification of stubborn beliefs. In his model, these two values are equal when averaged across all business cycles, or at a point in time if the economy is in its steady-state position. But neither of these conditions holds in the data analyzed by Mueller and coauthors.

The finding that perceived job-finding rates do not change over an unemployment spell might be interpreted as some sort of inertia or stubbornness in beliefs but is not really informative about Menzio's notion of stubborn beliefs. What is key for Menzio's exercise is how expectations of job-finding probabilities vary over the business cycle in response to aggregate shocks. Ideally, one would want to see what happens to the distribution of perceived rates over the business cycle, but an important limitation of the data in Mueller et al. (2021) is that it does not contain an entire business-cycle episode and so cannot provide this evidence.

Although they do not have data that cover an entire business-cycle episode, Mueller and coauthors can assess the correlation of changes in aggregate variables with changes in perceived job-finding rates. The main body of Mueller et al. (2021) does not report any evidence on this issue, though there are some results in the online appendix. There they report no statistically significant relation between perceived job-finding probabilities and the level of unemployment (though with large standard errors), but they find significant correlations between perceived job-finding probabilities and expected changes in the stock market and unemployment.

Two of the reported regressions suggest that perceived probabilities do respond to some changes in the aggregate economic environment. The regression result about unemployment strikes me as very inconclusive. Viewed through the lens of a standard Mortensen and Pissarides model, the aggregate level of unemployment is not a state variable and so need not be correlated with the job-finding rate during a recovery period; unemployment rate dynamics could be driven by transition dynamics following a shock. It would be more interesting to study the relationship between time-series changes in observed job-finding rates and perceived job-finding rates, controlling for potential composition effects, but I did not see these results reported.

Although my reading of the evidence does not lead me to conclude that there is no basis for the departure from rationality that Menzio considers, I do not see a strong case for elevating it beyond the category of "empirically plausible." As I mentioned earlier, I think the set of empirically plausible departures is a very large one. For this reason, it is unclear how much weight we want to attach to the results associated with this departure. In fact, I think there are other empirically plausible departures that can generate very different results. One of the examples considered in this paper is an economy in which all workers believe that there are no aggregate shocks to the economy. The result of these beliefs is that wages are completely rigid, and in particular fluctuate less than they would in the rational-expectations equilibrium.

Consider an alternative set of beliefs for workers. In particular, instead of workers believing that the future state of the economy will always look like the time-series average of the past, suppose we assume that workers always believe that the future state of the economy (i.e., aggregate productivity) will be the same as it is today. Such expectations are not rational but seem no less plausible than the case considered in the previous paragraph. Menzio does not consider this set of beliefs in his paper, and I have not worked through the details, but it is intuitive that this will generate the opposite pattern. That is, wages will now fluctuate more than they would in the economy with rational expectations.[1]

III. The Mechanism

Let me now turn to the second component of the paper: the mechanism through which the specific departures from rational expectations that Menzio considers are translated into effects on aggregate labor-market outcomes. How one views this component depends heavily on one's view of how wages are determined. Menzio considers only the possibility that wages are determined via an alternating-offer bargaining game. As he makes very clear in the paper, worker expectations have an impact on labor-market outcomes only to the extent that they affect strategic interactions through the bargaining game. With the exception of the bargaining game, workers are completely passive: they have zero cost of search, so whenever unemployed they search. Once matched, they remain employed until their match is exogenously destroyed.

Although the bargaining game that Menzio assumes is common in the literature, it is not the only way in which the literature models wage determination. Consider the wage-posting model of Burdett and Mortensen (1998). The physical environment in this paper is somewhat different from the one in Menzio's paper; it allows for on-the-job search but assumes that meeting rates are exogenous, though it can easily be extended to include a matching function and have meeting rates determined endogenously. For concreteness, I will focus on the case in which meeting rates are the same

for unemployed and employed workers. The key result I want to highlight
is that in the rational-expectations equilibrium of this model, everything is
determined on the firm side. All that matters from the worker side is the
disutility of working, and in equilibrium, workers are completely passive.
They search whether employed or unemployed. When unemployed, they
accept their first job, and when employed, they accept any job that offers a
higher wage than their existing job. Importantly, assuming that workers
perceive meeting rates to be the same when unemployed or employed,
worker expectations about meeting rates have no impact on the equilibrium wage distribution or allocations in this economy. That is, there is no
channel by which worker misperceptions about meeting rates would affect outcomes.

To be sure, one can extend this model in ways that would create a channel through which worker perceptions of meeting rates would affect equilibrium outcomes. For example, one could add a worker decision regarding search intensity. Importantly, this channel is quite distinct from the
channel that Menzio studies.

The main point from the previous discussion is that the effect of worker
expectations is very much dependent on what one assumes about wage-
setting protocols. I think which wage-setting protocol best fits the data remains an open question. Wage-setting protocols in the spirit of Cahuc,
Postel-Vinay, and Robin (2006) are perhaps of particular interest. Consider
a model like Burdett and Mortensen but assume that firms differ in their
productivity level. Rather than assuming that firms post wages, now assume the following protocol. If an unemployed worker meets a firm,
the firm makes a take-it-or-leave-it offer in which the outside option for
the worker is being unemployed. If the worker is employed and meets another firm, then the two firms play a Bertrand game in which the worker
chooses the firm with the higher productivity, and the wage is such that it
is the maximum of the worker's current wage and the wage that would
leave the lower productivity firm with zero payoff from the match. This
protocol does not attribute a role to worker perceptions of meeting rates.
But this need not be the case for other protocols. In fact, like Menzio, the
Cahuc et al. (2006) paper assumes that when an unemployed worker meets
a firm, the two play an alternating-offer bargaining game. There is a rich
set of possibilities here.

Quite apart from the issue of how different wage-setting protocols fit
the patterns in the wage data, there is one feature of the equilibrium in
Menzio's paper that I find somewhat unappealing from an aesthetic point
of view. Given how he sets up the strategic bargaining game, agents with

rational expectations must know how many individuals have irrational beliefs and the exact nature of those irrational beliefs. The reason I find this somewhat unappealing is that one rationale for considering departures from rationality stems from the perspective that rationality requires a large capacity for accessing and processing information. If this is costly to the individual, it creates an incentive for them to find simple "rules" that are easy to implement and have relatively low cost in terms of foregone utility. But in Menzio's framework, the informational demands on a large subset of agents can become much greater as we move to the equilibrium with departures from rational expectations.

Viewed from this perspective, and starting from the rational-expectations equilibrium in Menzio's model, one might argue that his departure from full rationality has things backward. That is, the most complicated elements of decision-making in the rational-expectations equilibrium are the strategic considerations associated with wage determination, so that if one were looking to adopt simple rules to avoid the most complicated calculations, it might make sense to vary the wage-setting protocol rather than have workers fail to realize the existence of business cycles. Having said this, I should note that Menzio does not explicitly offer a rationale for why individuals might have stubborn beliefs, and so in particular does not appeal to information-processing capacity as a rationale.

IV. Discussion

I wrote at the beginning of my comment that I view the general objective of this paper to be the exploration of how departures from rational expectations can affect aggregate outcomes in models with frictional labor markets. All the examples in the paper focus on the beliefs of workers. This is perhaps understandable given that the evidence in Mueller et al. (2021) focuses on worker perceptions. But from a broader perspective, the focus on worker expectations in these models is somewhat curious.

In the class of models that Menzio studies, the only allocation decision for the economy is the number of vacancies that are posted by firms. Because the posting cost is incurred today and the potential returns come in the future, the vacancy-posting decision is essentially an investment decision. If one is interested in exploring how departures from rational expectations matter for equilibrium outcomes, it seems natural to focus on the expectations of those agents that make dynamic allocation decisions. As noted earlier, worker expectations matter in this economy purely through their impact on the outcome of the bargaining game.

One response to this comment is that there is no novelty in assessing how expectations affect investment decisions. Although I do not disagree with this, I think the power of firm expectations to influence wages in benchmark models of frictional labor markets is something worth noting in the context of the exploration that Menzio undertakes. In what follows, I will assume that rather than wages being determined via a bargaining game, firms make take-it-or-leave-it offers to workers. (Alternatively, I could assume that firms post wages.) This serves to make workers completely passive. The physical environment is the same as that studied by Menzio; the only difference is the assumption about wage setting. Note that as in Menzio, there is no on-the-job search. The unique rational-expectations equilibrium for this economy will have the property that the wage rate is always equal to the disutility of working. This outcome emerges because firms have correct beliefs about a worker's disutility of work, or equivalently, have true beliefs about a worker's reservation wage.

Now assume that all firms are endowed with the same irrational expectations regarding this parameter. The equilibrium wage will then be whatever one assumes about firms' beliefs. Put somewhat differently, if the modeler is free to endow firms with irrational beliefs about workers' preference parameters (and hence indirectly about their reservation wages), then the modeler has immense freedom to rationalize wage outcomes.

V. Conclusion

I begin my concluding remarks by viewing this paper in relation to Mueller et al. (2021). Those authors interpret their evidence on perceived and actual job-finding rates to be prima facie evidence that some workers have incorrect beliefs about job-finding rates. They go on to explore how this might affect the decisions that individuals make. In particular, they are interested in the possibility that this might help explain the incidence of long-duration unemployment spells. The intuition is clear: an individual with a low job-finding rate will tend to experience a longer unemployment duration, but if that individual is also overly optimistic about the probability of receiving an offer, they may set too high a reservation wage, thereby amplifying the effect of the low job-offer arrival rate. The authors evaluate this effect quantitatively in the context of a standard McCall-style search problem, in which unemployed workers receive offers from a wage distribution with cumulative distribution function $F(w)$ with some probability λ, where λ is allowed to vary across workers. The authors show that allowing some low λ individuals to have overly optimistic beliefs in accordance with those found in the survey data can generate a nontrivial increase in the incidence of long-duration unemployment spells.

Menzio's key insight is that the consequences of misperceptions about job-finding rates may go well beyond the individual workers. If worker expectations of future outcomes affect wages, and wages in turn affect vacancy-posting decisions, there is a possibility that a group of workers with incorrect beliefs about future job-finding probabilities may affect job-finding rates for everyone. That is, incorrect beliefs held by one group of workers may affect the employment volatility that all workers face via general equilibrium effects mediated through wage setting.

Menzio develops this idea in a set of models that impose a particular structure on expectations and assume a particular protocol for wage setting. The analysis in the paper serves to establish the theoretical plausibility of such effects. But I think the question of whether these effects are playing an important role in shaping outcomes in labor markets remains an open one.

Endnotes

Author email address: Rogerson (rdr@princeton.edu). For acknowledgments, sources of research support, and disclosure of the author's material financial relationships, if any, please see https://www.nber.org/books-and-chapters/nber-macroeconomics-annual-2022-volume-37/comment-stubborn-beliefs-search-equilibrium-2-rogerson.

1. If the aggregate shock is quite persistent, the quantitative magnitude of this effect could be quite small. But even so, a result of no effect on wage variability is quite distinct from the result that Menzio finds.

References

Burdett, K., and D. Mortensen. 1998. "Wage Differentials, Employer Size, and Unemployment." *International Economic Review* 39:257–73.
Cahuc, P., F. Postel-Vinay, and J. Robin. 2006. "Wage Bargaining with On-the-Job Search: Theory and Evidence." *Econometrica* 74:323–64.
Mueller, A., J. Spinnewijn, and G. Topa. 2021. "Job Seekers' Perceptions and Employment Prospects: Heterogeneity, Duration Dependence, and Bias." *American Economic Review* 111:324–63.

Discussion

Guido Menzio started by explaining his motivation for writing the paper, in response to the discussants who had expressed skepticism about the strength of the evidence for the belief formation he had assumed and about the realism of the bargaining process. He argued that several papers have used surveys that document worker beliefs as less than full-information, rational expectations. He said he wanted to work out the implications for wage bargaining as a strategic interaction in which beliefs play an important role. Having found the implication of wage stickiness, he decided to allow for the coexistence of strategic and nonstrategic agents; the strategic implications were clear, because strategic agents can always mimic nonstrategic agents, leading to asymmetries. He argued that the results would qualitatively generalize to similar settings without the exact bargaining structure, because the potential for strategic agents to sometimes mimic nonstrategic workers would still be present.

Robert Hall noted that the macro labor literature contains many proposed solutions to the Shimer puzzle and raised the concern that the evidence from A. Mueller, J. Spinnewijn, and G. Topa ("Job Seekers' Perceptions and Employment Prospects: Heterogeneity, Duration Dependence, and Bias," *American Economic Review* 111, no. 1 [2021]: 324–63) is not strong enough to support the assumptions made in Menzio's paper. Although Robert Hall thought the analysis was interesting and could be learned from, he expressed skepticism about its usefulness as a solution to the Shimer puzzle. He mentioned evidence from his work with Marianna Kudlyak that suggests consumer perceptions of the state of the labor

NBER Macroeconomics Annual, volume 37, 2023.

market track the actual state quite well over the business cycle (Section 5.3 of Robert E. Hall and Marianna Kudlyak, "The Unemployed with Jobs and without Jobs" [Economics Working Paper no. 21110, Hoover Institution, 2022]).

Jonathan Parker found the core ideas interesting: that some agents are less sophisticated or informed, other agents may seek to gain by mimicking the less-sophisticated agents, and this can generate asymmetries between increases and decreases if the degree of mimicking varies over the cycle. He argued that this result might be more robust than Richard Rogerson had suggested in his comment. He hypothesized that the qualitative results might still hold if the behavior of less-sophisticated agents were closer to rational, and if the more sophisticated agents followed simpler (and therefore less perfectly designed) mimicking strategies, such as lower bounds on accepted wages.

Menzio responded to some technical points made by the discussants. He agreed with Rogerson that in dynamic asymmetric-information games such as the bargaining game in the paper, much is possible due to one part of the game being a signaling game—the party with private information takes an action interpreted by the other party that could be anything off equilibrium. However, the solution concept of perfect sequential equilibrium suggested by Grossman and Perry specifies a theory for off-equilibrium beliefs that delivers a unique equilibrium in the paper from S. Grossman and M. Perry ("Perfect Sequential Equilibrium," *Journal of Economic Theory* 39 [1986a]: 97–119; "Sequential Bargaining under Asymmetric Information," *Journal of Economic Theory* 39 [1986b]:120–54).

The author addressed the existence of equilibria as raised in Ilse Lindenlaub's comment. He said the technical conditions under which the equilibrium exists are not a no-screening condition but rather conditions under which a pure-strategy equilibrium exists. If the condition is violated, the logic of the Coase conjecture—that the informed agent will extract all the rents—still holds. However, it will be a mixed-strategy equilibrium in which one type will randomize their actions along the equilibrium path. This would require solving for the evolution of the mixing and the posterior distribution of beliefs of the firm, so he focused on the simpler cases in which a pure-strategy equilibrium exists. He then explained the reason for not requiring a no-screening condition. If a firm screens, workers with correct beliefs will be paid less in bad states than workers with stubborn beliefs. As the time interval between offers shrinks, then the gap must shrink, because the worker with correct beliefs can obtain the stubborn workers' wage when the next offer arrives.

Menzio then expressed surprise at the results Ilse Lindenlaub had shown during her discussion of beliefs over the business cycle; Mueller et al. find only a small correlation between beliefs and the business cycle. Menzio asked if this was due to composition. Lindenlaub said the difference is that she included both unemployed and employed workers. The beliefs of employed workers move much more over the business cycle.

Rogerson added that the regressions of beliefs on the business cycle in Mueller et al. paper have large point estimates and large standard errors; they cannot be interpreted as no variation. Menzio agreed with that comment and said his paper is more of an intellectual exercise in understanding the impact of small or no movement in beliefs.

Harald Uhlig suggested that a potential empirical strategy would be to compare the behavior of wages in industries with more or less individual-level bargaining. He suggested industries with high levels of unionization as ones in which there is little to no individual-level bargaining.

5

Excess Savings and Twin Deficits: The Transmission of Fiscal Stimulus in Open Economies

Rishabh Aggarwal, *Stanford University,* United States of America
Adrien Auclert, *Stanford University, CEPR, and NBER,* United States of America
Matthew Rognlie, *Northwestern University and NBER,* United States of America
Ludwig Straub, *Harvard University, CEPR and NBER,* United States of America

I. Introduction

Governments around the world responded to the economic fallout from the COVID pandemic with unprecedented transfers to households and firms, financing these transfers with large fiscal deficits that will have a long-lasting effect on public debt levels.[1] During this period, private saving rates rose everywhere, and there were important movements in current accounts, including a notable increase in the US current-account deficit (see fig. 1). In this paper, we ask: To what extent were these changes related? How do fiscal deficits affect the world's balance of payments in the short and the long run?

The standard Ricardian paradigm asserts that deficit-financed transfers raise private savings, with no effect on the current account or any other macroeconomic outcome. According to this view, households should save all of their transfers. This, however, is inconsistent with the substantial marginal propensities to consume (MPCs) out of transfers documented during the pandemic.[2] Moreover, even among households that initially saved their transfers, there is increasing evidence of a "spending-down" phenomenon. For instance, figure 2 shows that, in the United States, middle-class households—as proxied by the bottom 80% of the distribution of checking-account balances—rapidly depleted the excess balances they built from each of the three rounds of stimulus payments.[3] To date, however, the analysis of fiscal policy in the open economy has been largely limited to models that either satisfy Ricardian equivalence or feature no spending down of past savings.

NBER Macroeconomics Annual, volume 37, 2023.

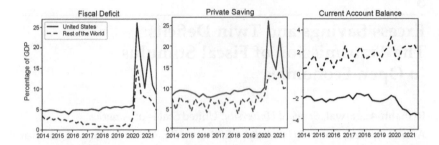

Fig. 1. Recent developments in the world's balance of payments. For this graph, "Rest of the World" consists of 16 advanced economies, as listed in table D1. Data are from US National Income and Product Accounts, International Monetary Fund International Financial Statistics, and Organization for Economic Cooperation and Development Quarterly Sector Accounts. GDP = gross domestic product. A color version of this figure is available online.

In this paper, we revisit the effects of debt-financed fiscal transfers in a model of the world economy that is consistent with both high MPCs and a spending-down effect. We show that incorporating these features of the micro data dramatically changes the standard view of the effects

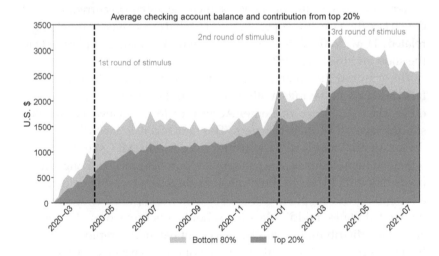

Fig. 2. Increase in mean checking-account balance and contribution from the top 20%. This graph, courtesy of the JPMorgan Chase Institute, shows the average checking-account balance relative to the first week of 2020 and the contributions to this mean from the top 20% and the bottom 80% of the distribution of balances. These contributions are estimated from information about the 25th, 50th, 75th, and 90th percentiles by fitting a spline through the cumulative distribution function. These percentiles are reported here. We thank Erica Deadman, Peter Ganong, Fiona Greig, and Pascal Noel for sharing the data. A color version of this figure is available online.

of fiscal deficits on the balance of payments. In the long run, increases in government debt anywhere increase private wealth everywhere. In the short run, a country with a larger-than-average fiscal deficit experiences both a large increase in private savings ("excess savings") and a small but persistent current-account deficit (a "slow-motion twin deficit"). These predictions are qualitatively consistent with the patterns in figure 1: the United States runs a large fiscal deficit relative to the rest of the world, has a larger-than-average increase in private savings, and shows a small, delayed deterioration in its current account. We show that our model is in fact quantitatively consistent with the cross-country relationship between fiscal deficits, private savings, and current accounts observed since the beginning of the pandemic. We further show that our model's distributional dynamics are consistent with those of figure 2: in both model and data, a few quarters after a fiscal transfer, most of the excess savings are held by the rich.

Our model is a merger of two heterogeneous-agent models from previous work: the closed-economy fiscal-policy model in Auclert, Rognlie, and Straub (2018) and the open-economy model in Auclert et al. (2021c). It has three key features. First, households have buffer-stock behavior: in response to a fiscal transfer that raises their wealth above target, they try to spend down the additional wealth over time. This leads to large MPCs and a spending-down effect, as in the data. Second, the model has open economies with substantial home bias in spending, also in line with the data. Third, going beyond the Galí and Monacelli (2005) small-open-economy assumption adopted in our earlier work, domestic fiscal policy affects the worldwide demand for goods as well as the world interest rate, as in Frenkel and Razin (1986).

We use this model to study the consequences of a worldwide increase in fiscal transfers financed by a permanent increase in countries' debt levels. Our model formalizes the following mechanism. When households in one country receive transfers, they spend out of those transfers according to their MPCs and initially save the rest, driving up private savings. Most of their spending is on domestic goods, which they earn back as income, further boosting private savings—but these savings pile up disproportionately among the rich, who earn income but have low MPCs.

The rest of household spending is on imported goods, leading to an increase in aggregate imports. But because the same phenomenon also happens in other countries, aggregate exports increase as well. On balance, countries that give larger-than-average transfers run current-account deficits, and other countries run current-account surpluses. In either case, the share of spending on foreign goods is small everywhere, and so the initial magnitude of the change in current accounts is also small. This implies that, initially, each country finances its own fiscal deficit through a similar increase in private savings.

The model's dynamics, however, do not stop when the transfers end. Instead, households keep spending out of their initial excess savings. Some fraction of this later spending goes into imports and exports too, prolonging the current-account patterns. In other words, the spending-down phenomenon implies that the effects of fiscal deficits on current accounts are very persistent: twin deficits happen in slow motion.

In the paper, after setting up the model in Section II, we formalize this mechanism in two parts. First, in Section III, we analytically characterize the effects of fiscal deficits in a small economy within our world-economy model. There, assuming a world interest rate of $r = 0$, we prove a stark result: in the long-run natural allocation, private wealth is unchanged, so any new debt issued by the government must be entirely held abroad. In other words, eventually, fiscal deficits translate one-for-one into current-account deficits. In the short run, however, private savings absorb the vast majority of the initial transfer. The speed of convergence is dictated by the degree of openness α and the matrix $\mathbf{M}$ of "intertemporal MPCs" (Auclert et al. 2018), formalizing the role of home bias and the spending-down effect for the transmission of fiscal deficits.

Then, in Section IV, we show that the outcomes of symmetric countries in a worldwide fiscal expansion can be decomposed into two parts: (a) aggregate worldwide outcomes, given by treating the world as a closed economy running the world average fiscal deficit, and (b) relative cross-country outcomes, given by treating each country as if it were a small economy faced with its deficits net of the world average. Part (a) implies that increases in government debt anywhere raise the world interest rate and increase private wealth everywhere. Part (b), combined with our small-economy results, implies that large-deficit countries run slow-motion twin deficits, and that eventually any debt issuance they have above the world average is held abroad. It also implies that, after a one-off fiscal expansion in all countries, a cross-country regression of cumulative private savings on cumulative fiscal deficits delivers a coefficient that starts around 1 and decays toward 0 over time, and a cross-country regression of cumulative current accounts on cumulative fiscal deficits delivers a coefficient that starts around 0 and decays toward -1 over time.

In Section V, we test this prediction of our model using recent data on the world's balance of payments. We construct measures of cumulative private savings, current accounts, and fiscal deficits since 2020Q1. After five quarters, the regression coefficients on fiscal deficits are 0.79 for private savings and −0.34 for current accounts, compared with our baseline model's predictions of 0.81 and −0.19, respectively. We discuss potential confounders from nonfiscal shocks over this period, including the concern that fiscal policy may be correlated with the severity of the pandemic across countries. We find that the resulting bias to our empirical estimates is likely to be modest, because variables that directly measure the severity of the pandemic in each country have limited association with excess savings or current accounts in the data. We show that this is consistent with theory: in general equilibrium, a COVID shock that does not involve a fiscal deficit cannot increase aggregate savings very much, and may in fact lower savings.

Finally, in Section VI, we turn to a quantitative version of our model that addresses the main limitations of our prior analysis. First, we relax the symmetry assumption, calibrating to data on openness and fiscal policy for 26 countries. Second, we relax the assumption that the fiscal-policy shock was a one-off shock in 2020Q1, instead feeding in the realized time path of fiscal deficits since that date. Finally, and most importantly, we explicitly add a COVID shock to each country, inferring the magnitude of this shock from the realized levels of consumption worldwide, similar to the procedure in Gourinchas et al. (2021). Simulating the effect of both the fiscal and the COVID shocks,[4] we find that the model still replicates the cross-country fiscal pass-through coefficients documented in our empirical section very well. In addition, we show that fiscal-deficit shocks explain the vast majority of the observed level of excess savings, with the COVID shock playing essentially no role. By contrast, and consistent with a slow-motion twin-deficit effect, there is a role for other shocks in explaining current accounts, at least over the short horizon we study.

Our paper refines the original twin-deficit hypothesis, according to which fiscal deficits cause (contemporaneous) current-account deficits. This hypothesis was popular in the 1980s, when the Reagan tax cuts were followed by a large dollar appreciation and increase in the current-account deficit, consistent with the predictions of the Mundell-Fleming model (e.g., Feldstein 1993; Ball and Mankiw 1995). It then fell out of fashion in the 1990s and 2000s, because the Clinton years featured both a fiscal surplus and a current-account deficit—a so-called twin divergence. Empirically, Bernheim (1988), Chinn and Prasad (2003), and Chinn and Ito (2007) find a generally positive correlation between fiscal and current-account deficits in a panel of countries, but it is well under-stood that the data are driven by many shocks beyond fiscal policy.[5] More recent work using identified tax shocks has reached mixed conclu-sions: using a structural vector autoregression, Kim and Roubini (2008) find evidence for twin divergence, and, using narratively identified tax shocks, Feyrer and Shambaugh (2012) and Guajardo, Leigh, and Pescatori (2014) find evidence for the causal twin-deficit hypothesis. Our slow-motion twin-deficit result can help interpret these findings: it suggests that a causal twin-deficit relationship may not be detectable over the short run, where it can be swamped by other shocks in the data, but that it should start to appear as one considers longer horizons.

As mentioned at the beginning of the paper, the usual open-economy analysis of fiscal policy is conducted in models featuring Ricardian equivalence. In this context, twin deficits emerge only when governments finance government spending, not transfers (e.g., Corsetti and Müller 2006). Models with hand-to-mouth agents a la Galí, López-Salido, and Vallés (2007), Bilbiie (2008), Farhi and Werning (2016), and House, Proeb-sting, and Tesar (2020) imply some twin deficits, but, as explained in Bilbiie, Eggertsson, and Primiceri (2021), these occur only contemporane-ously with the fiscal deficit, with excess savings sticking around forever after that: in these models, there is no spending down of past savings. Our model, by contrast, predicts a prolonged effect of fiscal deficits on current accounts.

The finite-horizon Blanchard (1985) model and its descendants (e.g., Ghironi 2006; Kumhof and Laxton 2013) behave more similarly to ours in the aggregate. Blanchard (1985) pointed out that the net foreign asset (NFA) position of a country deteriorated in response to a permanent in-crease in the public debt, and that this involved a transition to the new steady state, but he overstated the speed of this transition for two rea-sons. First, in his model, there is no selection of the set of spenders at any point in time: households that have saved their transfers until today remain equally likely to spend them today. Second, and more impor-tantly, he worked with a model with no home bias.

Finally, our paper contributes to the Heterogeneous-Agent New Keynesian (HANK) literature. This literature has so far studied mone-tary policy in closed economies (Werning 2015; McKay, Nakamura, and Steinsson 2016; Kaplan, Moll, and Violante 2018; Auclert 2019), fis-cal policy in closed economies (Oh and Reis 2012; McKay and Reis 2016; Auclert et al. 2018; Hagedorn, Manovskii, and Mitman 2019) and mon-etary policy in open economies (Auclert et al. 2021c; Guo, Ottonello, and

Perez 2021).[6] To our knowledge, we are the first paper to study fiscal policy in open economies in this class of models, and also the first to write a many-country model of large open economies.

II. Model

We now describe our many-country HANK model. The general structure of the model is borrowed from Galí and Monacelli (2005)'s small-open-economy, representative-agent New Keynesian model. We add three elements to this model. First, as in Auclert et al. (2021c), in each country there are heterogeneous agents facing idiosyncratic income uncertainty and borrowing constraints. Second, as in Auclert et al. (2018)'s closed-economy model, agents are taxed according to a progressive tax schedule, and the government conducts fiscal policy by changing transfers, purchasing local goods, and issuing or retiring public debt. Finally, an innovation of this paper is to modify the Galí and Monacelli (2005) environment to consider an integrated world economy made of any number of countries, interacting in frictionless capital markets but subject to home bias in spending. Asset market clearing at the world level is essential to understand the implications of a worldwide fiscal expansion such as the one that motivates this paper.

We write down the model by assuming that individuals have perfect foresight over aggregate variables and solve the model to first order in these aggregates. As Auclert et al. (2021a) show, this delivers the first-order perturbation solution of the equivalent model with aggregate shocks.

World economy setup. There are K countries. Consumption c_{it}^k of consumer i in country $k = 1 \dots K$ aggregates a "home" good H, produced by country k itself, and a "world" good W, made up of goods produced by all countries. The elasticity of substitution between the home and the world good is η, with $1 - \alpha^k$ measuring the extent of home bias in consumption:

$$c_{it}^k = \left[(1 - \alpha^k)^{\frac{1}{\eta}} \left(c_{iHt}^k \right)^{\frac{\eta-1}{\eta}} + (\alpha^k)^{\frac{1}{\eta}} \left(c_{iWt}^k \right)^{\frac{\eta-1}{\eta}} \right]^{\frac{\eta}{\eta-1}}. \tag{1}$$

The world good basket W is common to all countries and given by

$$c_{iWt}^k = \left(\sum_{l=1}^{K} (\omega^l)^{\frac{1}{\gamma}} \left(c_{iWt}^{k,l} \right)^{\frac{\gamma-1}{\gamma}} \right)^{\frac{\gamma}{\gamma-1}}, \tag{2}$$

where $c^{k,l}_{iWt}$ the consumption of world goods from country l by consumer i in country k.[7] We assume that $\gamma > 0$, $\eta > 0$, $\omega^l \geq 0$, and $\Sigma^K_{l=1}\omega^l = 1$. Note that the weights $\{\omega^l\}$ are the same in each country k.

Domestic agents. We now describe the domestic economy in any given country k. To simplify notation, we call that country "home" and drop the superscript k whenever there is no ambiguity. Home households have preferences over goods described by equation (1). They work hours N_t at disutility $v(N_t)$ but take these hours as given in the short run. A union occasionally resets their nominal wage W_t, denoted in home currency. Households invest in a mutual-fund asset with nominal value A subject to a borrowing constraint, which we assume to be equal to zero for simplicity. This asset pays a real return r^p_t in terms of the consumer price index (CPI) P_t, denoted in home currency. Households are also subject to a CPI-indexed tax schedule a la Heathcote, Storesletten, and Violante (2017), with intercept v_t and degree of progressivity λ. Their Bellman equation is therefore

$$V_t(A, e) = \max_{c_F, c_H, A'} u(c(c_H, c_W)) - v(N_t) + \beta\mathbb{E}_t[V_{t+1}(A', e')]$$

$$\text{s.t. } P_{Ht}c_H + \sum^K_{l=1}P_{lt}c^l_W + A' = (1 + r^p_t)\frac{P_t}{P_{t-1}}A + P_t \cdot v_t\left(e\frac{W_t}{P_t}N_t\right)^{1-\lambda}, \quad (3)$$

$$A' \geq 0$$

where $u(c) = c^{1-\sigma}/(1 - \sigma)$, with $c(c_H, c_W)$ described in equation (1), and $v(n) = \varphi(n^{1+\phi}/(1 + \phi))$. We define aggregate real posttax income as the cross-sectional average:

$$Z_t \equiv \mathbb{E}_e\left[v_t\left(e\frac{W_t}{P_t}N_t\right)^{1-\lambda}\right].$$

Because labor is not a choice, Z_t is taken as given by the household. Defining $a \equiv A/P_{t-1}$ as the real value of household assets, and using standard two-step budgeting arguments with constant elasticity of substitution utility, we can solve for policy functions as follows. First, rewrite equation (3) as

$$V_t(a, e) = \max_{c, a'} u(c) + \beta\mathbb{E}_t[V_{t+1}(a', e')]$$

$$\text{s.t. } c + a' = (1 + r^p_t)a + \frac{e^{1-\lambda}}{\mathbb{E}[e^{1-\lambda}]}Z_t. \quad (4)$$

$$a' \geq 0$$

The solution to this problem gives households' optimal choice of consumption versus savings for given aggregate sequences $\{r^p_t, Z_t\}$. Denote by $c = c_t(a, e)$ the resulting consumption policy and $a' = a_t(a, e)$ the resulting asset policy. Then, the demand for home goods (respectively, for country l goods) for a household in state (a, e) is given by

$$c_{Ht}(a, e) = (1 - \alpha)\left(\frac{P_{Ht}}{P_t}\right)^{-\eta} c(a, e)$$

$$c_{Wt}^l(a, e) = \alpha \omega^l \left(\frac{P_{lt}}{P_{Wt}}\right)^{-\gamma} \left(\frac{P_{Wt}}{P_t}\right)^{-\eta} c(a, e),$$

where $P_t = [(1 - \alpha)(P_{Ht})^{1-\eta} + \alpha(P_{Wt})^{1-\eta}]^{1/1-\eta}$ is the CPI and $P_{Wt} = [\Sigma_{l=1}^K \omega^l (P_{lt})^{1-\gamma}]^{1/1-\gamma}$ the price of the world good, both expressed in home currency. Aggregating up, and writing C_t for the aggregate consumption policy across the distribution of agents, total domestic demand for home goods and for country l goods is given by

$$C_{Ht} = (1 - \alpha)\left(\frac{P_{Ht}}{P_t}\right)^{-\eta} C_t \tag{5}$$

$$C_{Wt}^l = \alpha \omega^l \left(\frac{P_{lt}}{P_{Wt}}\right)^{-\gamma} \left(\frac{P_{Wt}}{P_t}\right)^{-\eta} \dot{C}_t \tag{6}$$

Production and prices. Firms in the home economy produce using a linear production function with productivity Θ that is country specific but constant over time (i.e., $\Theta_t^k = \Theta^k$ for each k, generating level differences across countries):

$$Y_t = \Theta N_t. \tag{7}$$

They have flexible prices and there is perfect competition in the goods market. This implies that the home-currency price of home goods is

$$P_{Ht} = \frac{W_t}{\Theta} = \frac{w_t P_t}{\Theta}, \tag{8}$$

where $w_t \equiv W_t/P_t$ denotes the real wage. Firms make zero profits. A standard derivation of the New Keynesian wage Phillips curve (e.g., Auclert et al. 2018) implies that wage inflation, $\pi_{wt} = (W_t/W_{t-1}) - 1$, is given by

$$\pi_{wt} = \kappa_w \left(\frac{v'(N_t)N_t}{\frac{\epsilon_w}{\epsilon_w - 1}(1 - \lambda)Z_t u'(C_t)} - 1 \right) + \beta \pi_{wt+1}, \tag{9}$$

where ϵ_w is the elasticity of substitution between unions in labor demand and λ is the progressivity of taxes (taxes are distortionary for labor supply when $\lambda > 0$). Because, from equation (8), $P_{Ht+1}/P_{Ht} = W_{t+1}/W_t$, producer price inflation is equal to wage inflation at all times,

$$\pi_{Ht} = \pi_{wt}. \tag{10}$$

We assume there is frictionless trade for each individual good so that the law of one price holds everywhere.[8]

Because the world good is identical in all countries, it acts as a natural world numeraire. To implement this numeraire in a consistent and intuitive way, we introduce an infinitesimal reference country, the "star country," whose monetary policy is set to keep the price of the numeraire world good in its currency, the "star currency," always equal to 1. We further assume that the CPI in the star country consists entirely of world goods. By assumption, then, $P_{Wt}^* = P_t^* = 1$. We then let $\mathcal{E}_t$ be the nominal exchange rate relative to the star currency—the number of domestic currency units per units of star currency—such that an increase in $\mathcal{E}_t$ represents a depreciation of the currency relative to the star currency. The star currency is then a useful unit of account for exchange rates: the bilateral exchange rate between any two countries k and l is given by $\mathcal{E}_t^k/\mathcal{E}_t^l$.

The law of one price implies that, in each country k, the price of good l is equal to country l's home-good price once expressed in country k's currency; that is, $P_{lt}^k = (\mathcal{E}_t^k/\mathcal{E}_t^l)P_{Ht}^l$. Because, in the star currency, $P_{Wt}^* = 1$, this implies in particular that, for the home economy (where, recall, we drop the country superscript k):

$$P_{Wt} = \mathcal{E}_t. \tag{11}$$

That is, the price of world goods is equal to the exchange rate in the home currency. Finally, writing Q_t for the real exchange rate between the home and the star currency, we have

$$Q_t = \frac{\mathcal{E}_t}{P_t}. \tag{12}$$

To first order, CPI inflation is given by $\pi_t = (1 - \alpha)\pi_{Ht} + \alpha\pi_{Wt}$. Combining this with equations (10), (11), and the definition of the price index, we obtain

$$\pi_t = \pi_{wt} + \frac{\alpha}{1 - \alpha}(q_t - q_{t-1}), \tag{13}$$

where $q_t = \log Q_t$ is the log of the real exchange rate. Equation (13) shows how real exchange-rate depreciations pass through to CPI inflation, over and above domestic inflation.

Government. Fiscal policy sets exogenous paths for real government debt B_t and spending G_t, which it spends entirely on local goods. It then levies taxes T_t by changing the slope ν_t of the retention function, with fixed progressivity λ, as in Auclert et al. (2018). Bonds are denominated in units of the domestic consumption bundle, and government spending and tax revenue are denominated in units of home goods. Bonds are short term, and promise to pay at t the ex ante real interest rate r_{t-1} that prevails between time $t - 1$ and time t. The government budget constraint is then

$$B_t = (1 + r_{t-1})B_{t-1} + \frac{P_{Ht}}{P_t}(G_t - T_t). \qquad (14)$$

The government taxes labor income $w_t N_t$ and lets individuals retain Z_t in the aggregate, so that $(P_{Ht}/P_t)T_t = w_t N_t - Z_t$. Combining equations (7) and (8), aggregate pretax wage income is

$$w_t N_t = \frac{P_{Ht}}{P_t}\Theta N_t = \frac{P_{Ht}}{P_t}Y_t. \qquad (15)$$

We therefore have the following relationship between posttax income Z_t, output Y_t, and taxes T_t:

$$Z_t = \frac{P_{Ht}}{P_t}(Y_t - T_t). \qquad (16)$$

Monetary policy sets the ex ante real rate for $t \geq 0$. We consider three different rules. The first is a real-interest-rate rule,

$$r_t = r. \qquad (17)$$

We think of this rule as capturing the case of "no monetary response," because it holds fixed the vehicle of monetary transmission to the real economy, which is the domestic-CPI-based real interest rate. By contrast, a Taylor rule allows for a response of the real interest rate to local economic conditions captured by the aggregate inflation rate:

$$i_t = r^* + \phi_\pi \pi_t. \qquad (18)$$

The third rule we consider simply implements the path of "natural" interest rates, which ensures there is no wage inflation at any time; that is, $\pi_{wt} = \pi_{wt}^n = 0$,

$$r_t = r_t^n. \qquad (19)$$

This path corresponds to the flexible-wage limit of the model, in which unions can flexibly set wages.[9]

In our analysis below, we will at times consider the limit of a perfectly open economy, $\alpha \to 1$, that follows the constant-r monetary-policy rule (eq. [17]). We spell out this limit in Section A4, where we show that this is identical to a monetary policy that targets a constant path for the terms of trade P_{Ht}/P_{Wt}.[10]

World demand for home goods. Section A1 shows that, combining each country's demand system with the law of one price, world demand for the home good is given by

$$C_{Ht}^* = \omega \left(\frac{P_{Ht}}{P_{Wt}} \right)^{-\gamma} C_t^*, \tag{20}$$

where C_t^* is world import demand, defined as

$$C_t^* \equiv \sum_{l=1}^{K} \alpha^l \left(Q_t^l \right)^{-\eta} C_t^l. \tag{21}$$

Asset-pricing equations. The domestic mutual fund's assets consist of home real bonds B_t and star-country bonds B_t^*. The latter pay a nominal interest rate of i_t^* in star currency. Because $P_{Wt}^* = 1$ at all times, i_t^* is also equal to the real interest rate in terms of the world goods bundle, which is common across all countries. At every point in time, the liquidation value of the mutual fund's liabilities equals the value of its assets, which implies

$$(1 + r_t^p)A_{t-1} = (1 + r_{t-1})B_{t-1} + \left(1 + i_{t-1}^* \right) Q_t B_{t-1}^*.$$

Optimization implies that, for all $t \geq 0$, ex ante CPI-based real interest rates across countries are related by the real uncovered interest-rate parity (UIP) condition

$$1 + r_t = \left(1 + i_t^* \right) \frac{Q_{t+1}}{Q_t} \tag{22}$$

as well as the domestic no-arbitrage condition $r_{t+1}^p = r_t$ for all $t \geq 0$. We further assume that gross-foreign-asset positions are zero initially; that is, $A_{ss} = B_{ss}$, implying $r_0^p = r_{ss} = r_{-1}$.[11] We therefore have

$$r_t^p = r_{t-1} \qquad \forall t \geq 0. \tag{23}$$

Finally, assuming that the mutual fund can also invest in zero-net-supply domestic nominal bonds, we obtain the nominal UIP equation, as well as the Fisher equation:

$$1 + i_t = \left(1 + i_t^*\right) \frac{\mathcal{E}_{t+1}}{\mathcal{E}_t} \qquad (24)$$

$$1 + r_t = \frac{1 + i_t}{1 + \pi_{t+1}}. \qquad (25)$$

Equilibrium. We define equilibrium in two steps. First, we define an open-economy equilibrium for given world "star" interest rate and export demand $\{i_t^*, C_t^*\}$. Second, we define an integrated world equilibrium, in which $\{i_t^*, C_t^*\}$ are endogenously determined. Because a small open economy is too small to affect $\{i_t^*, C_t^*\}$, it can be analyzed as an open-economy equilibrium given these two aggregates. This formulation therefore provides a natural extension of the Galí and Monacelli (2005) model to an integrated world economy in which global asset and goods markets clear.

Definition 1. Given sequences for star currency monetary policy and world exports $\{i_t^*, C_t^*\}$, as well as paths for fiscal policy $\{G_t, B_t\}$, an *open-economy equilibrium* is a sequence of aggregates $\{Q_t, Y_t, C_t, A_t, T_t, Z_t, r_t\}$ as well as mutually consistent policy functions and distributions of individuals over their state variables (a, e), such that: (*a*) the real-interest-rate parity condition (eq. [22]) holds, (*b*) the relative prices P_{Ht}/P_t and P_{Ht}/P_{Wt} are consistent with the real exchange rate Q_t and the pricing equation for world goods (eq. [11]), (*c*) taxes T_t ensure that equation (14) holds and real income Z_t by equation (16), (*d*) household choices are optimal given $\{Z_t, r_t\}$, and their aggregation is given by $\{C_t, A_t\}$, (*e*) domestic wage inflation and CPI inflation satisfy equations (9) and (13), (*f*) r_t is consistent with the country's monetary-policy rule—that is, one of equations (17), (18), or (19)—and (*g*) the domestic goods market clears:

$$Y_t = C_{Ht} + C_{Ht}^* + G_t. \qquad (26)$$

In an open-economy equilibrium, any excess of demand for assets domestically A_t relative to its supply B_t is held abroad in the form of an NFA position, which we write as nfa$_t$:

$$A_t = B_t + \text{nfa}_t. \qquad (27)$$

The trade deficit of the economy is given by

$$\text{TD}_t \equiv C_t - \frac{P_{Ht}}{P_t}(Y_t - G_t). \qquad (28)$$

Section A2 shows that, in equilibrium, the trade deficit is related to the current account CA$_t$ (the change in the NFA position) via the standard balance-of-payments identity:

$$CA_t \equiv nfa_t - nfa_{t-1} = r_{t-1}nfa_{t-1} - TD_t. \qquad (29)$$

Because we ruled out initial gross positions, there are no valuation effects in equation (29).

We now turn to the world economy. In it, C_t^* and i_t^* are endogenously determined, as per the following definition.

Definition 2. *A world-economy equilibrium*, given country-specific productivity level Θ^k, preference parameters $\{\alpha^k, \omega^k, \beta^k\}$, income processes e_t^k, monetary-policy rules, and fiscal-policy paths $\{G_t^k, B_t^k\}$, is a set of world variables $\{i_t^*, C_t^*\}$ and country-specific aggregates $\{Q_t^k, Y_t^k, C_t^k, A_t^k, T_t^k, Z_t^k, r_t^k\}$ such that, in each country, $\{Q_t^k, Y_t^k, C_t^k, A_t^k, T_t^k, Z_t^k, r_t^k\}$ is an open-economy equilibrium given country-specific parameters and $\{i_t^*, C_t^*\}$, world export demand equals world import demand

$$C_t^* = \sum_{k=1}^{K}\alpha^k \left(Q_t^k\right)^{-\eta} C_t^k, \qquad (30)$$

and the price of world goods in the star currency P_{Wt}^* is constant and equal to 1:

$$\sum_{k=1}^{K}\omega^k \left(\frac{P_{Ht}^k}{\mathcal{E}_t^k}\right)^{1-\gamma} = 1. \qquad (31)$$

In Section A3, we show that these conditions are equivalent to world asset market clearing, which reads

$$\sum_{k}\frac{A_t^k}{Q_t^k} = \sum_{k}\frac{B_t^k}{Q_t^k}, \qquad (32)$$

or alternatively, by equation (27), the world's NFA position is zero:

$$\sum_{k}\frac{nfa_t^k}{Q_t^k} = 0. \qquad (33)$$

In a world-economy equilibrium, the world goods market also clears, which reads

$$\sum_{k}\frac{P_{Ht}^k}{\mathcal{E}_t^k}\left(Y_t^k - G_t^k\right) = \sum_{k}\frac{P_t^k C_t^k}{\mathcal{E}_t^k}. \qquad (34)$$

Calibration. We next calibrate the world-economy equilibrium of our model. We use this calibration to analyze the open-economy equilibrium of an individual small country in Section III, and the full-world equilibrium in Section IV.

We start from an initial steady state with no NFA position in any country, $nfa^k = 0$, and where all relative prices are 1. In particular,

$Q^k = (P_H/P)^k = 1$. (We omit the subscript "t" when discussing steady-state values.) By equation (29), the trade deficit is zero in each country k, so imports and exports are equal; that is,

$$\alpha^k C^k = \omega^k C^*, \tag{35}$$

where $C^* = \Sigma_{l=1}^K \alpha^l C^l$.

Our baseline calibration assumes that all countries are perfectly symmetric except for size. (We relax this assumption in Section VI.) That is, countries have identical preferences, openness α, income processes, government spending G/Y, and debt B/Y relative to their gross domestic product (GDP), and only differ in their baseline productivity level Θ^k and weight ω^k in the world basket.

In this symmetric-country calibration, export weights are also consumption and GDP weights; that is, $\omega^k = C^k/\Sigma_{l=1}^K C^l = Z^k/\Sigma_{l=1}^K Z^k = Y^k/\Sigma_{l=1}^K Y^l = \Theta^k/\Sigma_{l=1}^K \Theta^l$ and world import demand is simply $C^* = \alpha\Sigma_{l=1}^K C^l$. Symmetry also requires that $\nu^k/(\omega^k)^\lambda$ and $\varphi^k/(\omega^k)^{1-\sigma}$ are equalized across countries, to ensure that steady-state after-tax income Z^k scales with Θ^k and labor supply N^k is independent of Θ^k.

We calibrate each of these symmetric countries as a scaled version of the United States economy. In particular, we choose the income process and the degree of tax progressivity as in Auclert et al. (2018) and allow for heterogeneity in discount factors with a spread δ. We take our calibration targets to be consistent with our US targets in our world-economy quantitative exercise of Section VI. Government spending is $G/Y = 14\%$ of GDP, public debt is $B/Y = 82\%$ of GDP, and openness (backed out from the ratio of imports and exports to GDP) is $\alpha = 16\%$. We then calibrate β, δ to hit a real interest rate of $r = 0\%$ annually, as in recent experience, and a quarterly MPC of 0.25, consistent with evidence from a large literature on MPCs. Our calibrated parameters are summarized in table 1.

Small-open-economy case ($\Theta^k \to 0$). In Section III, we study an individual small open economy in our model. Mathematically speaking, a small open economy corresponds to a country with small productivity

Table 1
Baseline Calibration

Parameter	r	σ	η	γ	A	ϕ	λ
Value	0	1	1	1	.16	2	.181
Parameter	G/Y	B/Y	nfa/Y	β	Δ	κ_w	ϕ_π
Value	.14	.82	0	.992	.098	.1	1.5

relative to the rest of the world ($\Theta^k \to 0$) and a correspondingly small demand for its goods in the world consumption basket ($\omega^k \to 0$). In this limit, all domestic aggregates scale with Θ^k and are therefore small themselves.[12] In particular, C^k and A^k are too small to affect any world aggregates in equations (30)–(34). Hence, any policy change in that country does not affect C_t^* or i_t^*. This result allows us to interpret the equations for an open-economy equilibrium given $\{C_t^*, i_t^*\}$ as relevant to understand the response to fiscal-policy changes in small open economies.

Closed-economy case ($K = 1$). When there is a single country ($K = 1$), then equation (31) reduces to $P_{Ht} = \mathcal{E}_t$, implying that $Q_t = 1$ and that $P_{Ht} = P_{Wt} = P_t$ at all times. By equation (13), $\pi_t = \pi_{wt}$. Combining equations (5), (20), and (21), total demand for domestic goods is simply domestic demand, $C_{Ht} + C_{Ht}^* = C_t$, and equation (32) reduces to domestic asset market clearing $A_t = B_t$. Hence, this case collapses to a standard closed-economy heterogeneous-agent model with wage rigidities, the same as in Auclert et al. (2018).

Intertemporal MPCs (iMPCs). An important part of our analysis is to characterize household behavior in any given country. We do so by summarizing aggregate saving and consumption choices in terms of two functions, $\mathcal{A}_t$ and $\mathcal{C}_t$. These functions map the only two endogenous aggregate sequences that matter for household decisions—ex ante[13] interest rates $\{r_s\}$ and after-tax incomes $\{Z_s\}$—into aggregate assets held by households and aggregate consumption,

$$A_t = \mathcal{A}_t(\{r_s, Z_s\}), \qquad C_t = \mathcal{C}_t(\{r_s, Z_s\}). \qquad (36)$$

The two functions are naturally homogeneous of degree one in $\{Z_s\}$ and satisfy the aggregate budget constraint

$$\mathcal{C}_t + \mathcal{A}_t = (1 + r_{t-1})A_{t-1} + Z_t. \qquad (37)$$

Following Auclert et al. (2018), we define **M** as the matrix derivative (Jacobian) of the consumption sequence to the after-tax income sequence, evaluated at the steady state. That is, the entries of **M** are given by

$$M_{t,s} \equiv \frac{\partial \mathcal{C}_t}{\partial Z_s}(\{r, Z\}).$$

We call those entries *intertemporal marginal propensities to consume* (iMPCs). iMPCs are a richer set of moments than standard MPCs, in that they capture both the entire dynamic response of consumption to unanticipated income changes—the entries in the first column $(M_{.,0})$ of $\mathbf{M}$—and the entire dynamic response of consumption to anticipated income changes—the entries in column s, $(M_{.,s})$, for an anticipated income change at date $s > 0$.

This information is critical to understanding the propagation of fiscal policy, because agents that do not immediately spend a given transfer may do so in later periods, and because agents may spend in anticipation of future transfers or income changes.

Figure 3 displays several columns of the iMPC matrix $\mathbf{M}$ in our baseline calibration. Each line corresponds to a different column s, giving the dynamic response of aggregate consumption to a one-time income change at date s. For example, the standard MPC is the immediate response to an unanticipated one-time unit income change and thus corresponds to the quarter-0 element of the darkest "$s = 0$" line. For future reference, we call this number mpc $\equiv M_{0,0}$; our calibration targets mpc $= 0.25$. The remaining unspent 0.75 of the unit income change is then endogenously spent in later periods. For instance, the iMPC in quarter 1 is around 0.10, and the total MPC in the first year is around 0.45. For income changes at later dates s, we see that despite some spending in anticipation of the income change, most of the spending

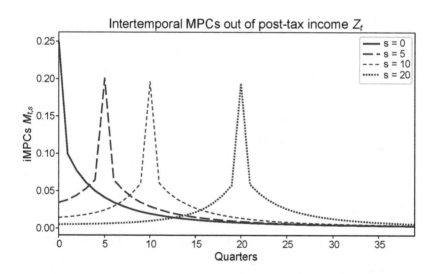

Fig. 3. Intertemporal marginal propensities to consume $M_{t,s}$ (baseline calibration). A color version of this figure is available online.

response happens when the income is actually received. This is consistent with existing empirical evidence.

We next show that the iMPC matrix **M**, together with the degree of openness α, are critical determinants of the propagation of fiscal policy in open economies.

III. Excess Savings and Twin Deficits in a Small Open Economy

In this section, we analyze fiscal policy in a small open economy (ω, $\Theta \approx 0$), with the world remaining at a steady state, with $i_t^* = r$ and $C_t^* = C^*$. In the next section, we will show that the outcomes of this small-open-economy model map directly to relative cross-country outcomes in the world-economy model.

In addition to the standard effects of fiscal policy on output, inflation, and exchange rates, we pay particular attention to the model's predictions for private saving and the current account. We will argue that these predictions are unique to models such as ours that combine stable long-run asset demand and home bias.

Specifically, we are interested in tracing out the response of private wealth A_t and the NFA position nfa_t to a change in fiscal policy, as captured in our model by changes in the exogenous time paths of government spending G_t and debt B_t. We will say that an increase in public debt ($\Delta B_t \geq 0$) causes excess savings when it increases private wealth ($\Delta A_t \geq 0$) and that it causes a twin deficit when it leads to a deterioration in the NFA position ($\Delta nfa_t \leq 0$). By the asset market clearing condition (eq. [27]), the equilibrium response to an increase in B must involve a combination of excess savings and twin deficits. Our goal is to study which of these two prevails and over what horizon.

A convenient way to describe this dynamic relationship is to study flows (i.e., saving and the current account) rather than stocks. These are determined in the model by goods market clearing and can also naturally be mapped to the data. To this end, we define private saving PS_t, the current account CA_t and the fiscal deficit FD_t, respectively, as the change in the stocks of private wealth, the NFA position, and public debt:

$$PS_t \equiv A_t - A_{t-1} \qquad CA_t \equiv nfa_t - nfa_{t-1} \qquad FD_t \equiv B_t - B_{t-1}.$$

It follows from asset market clearing equation (27) that $FD_t = PS_t - CA_t$, so an increase in the fiscal deficit must be matched by an increase in private saving or a decline in the current account.

We focus on the case of a zero steady-state net interest rate, $r = 0$, for now. This is consistent with our calibration and greatly simplifies the analytical expressions.[14] We relax this assumption in Section B4.

A. Long-Run Result

Our first result concerns the long-run effects of fiscal policy. Assume that the economy is initially at a steady state, with government spending G_{ss}, debt level B_{ss}, real interest rate r_{ss}, and posttax income Z_{ss}. Suppose that there is a change in fiscal policy, such that in the long run government spending is $G = G_{ss} + \Delta G$ and debt is $B = B_{ss} + \Delta B$. How does this affect the economy's steady state?

The key to answering this question is to consider the determinants of the long-run level of private wealth. In any steady state, equation (36) shows that this level is a function $A(r, Z)$ of the long-run real interest rate r and the level of posttax income Z. Combining this observation with the steady-state market clearing condition (eq. [27]), we obtain

$$A(r, Z) = B + \text{nfa}. \qquad (38)$$

The left-hand side of equation (38) is long-run domestic asset demand, determined by the long-run real interest rate and level of posttax income. The right-hand side is domestic asset supply, here made of bonds, plus the NFA position. Building on this observation, the following proposition solves for the long-run effect of fiscal policy.

Proposition 1. Assume that $r = 0$ and that the economy converges back to the natural allocation in the long run. Suppose that long-run government spending is unchanged $\Delta G = 0$, and that government debt increases by ΔB. Then, the long run features an unchanged real exchange rate $\Delta Q = 0$, an unchanged level of real income $\Delta Z = 0$, zero excess savings, and a perfect twin deficit:

$$\Delta A = 0 \qquad \Delta \text{nfa} = -\Delta B.$$

In particular, the long-run pass-through (LRPT) of public debt into the NFA position is LRPT $= -\Delta \text{nfa}/\Delta B = 1$.

If government spending increases by a small amount dG in addition to a small debt increase of dB, then to first order, the real exchange rate changes by $dQ/Q = -(1 - \alpha)/(\chi - 1) \, \epsilon \, dG/Y$ and excess savings and twin deficits are given by

$$dA = -\epsilon \cdot A \cdot dG \qquad d\text{nfa} = -(dB + \epsilon \cdot A \cdot dG),$$

where $\epsilon \equiv ((\sigma - 1)/(1 + \varphi) + (1 - G/Y)(1 + \alpha/(\chi - 1)))^{-1}$ and $\chi \equiv \eta(1 - \alpha) + \gamma$.

The key to this proposition is that, under our assumptions, a change in long-run B at constant long-run G does not change either the long-run real interest rate or the level of after-tax income ($r = r_{ss}$, $Z = Z_{ss}$). The real interest rate is unaffected because the economy is too small for its fiscal policy to affect the rest of the world, and after-tax income is unaffected because, at $r = 0$, no local tax increase is necessary to finance the increase in B. Hence, irrespective of how much fiscal policy affects private wealth in the short run, the long-run level of private wealth is unchanged at $A(r, Z)$, and the increase in B is therefore entirely absorbed by foreigners.

Note that this result is true irrespective of the monetary policy that is followed along the path (assuming that it gets the economy back to the natural allocation), and irrespective of what is done with the fiscal expansion along the path (government spending or transfers, provided that government spending is back at steady state in the long run). The logic behind it is very general and only relies on the existence of a stable long-run asset demand function $A(r, Z)$. For instance, an identical result would hold if we added capital to our model, or if the household model generated a long-run asset demand function $A(r, Z)$ for some other reason than our benchmark of precautionary savings and borrowing constraints. We come back to the question of which models fit this bill in subsection "Alternative Models: RANK, TANK, and Blanchard (1985)."

If government spending G changes in the long run, the real exchange rate Q, consumption C, and real income Z are affected. If real income declines as a result of this increase in G, as happens under plausibly high long-run elasticities (e.g., $\sigma \geq 1$ and $\chi \geq 1$), then the LRPT of public debt into the NFA position $\text{LRPT} = -d\text{nfa}/dB$ is even greater than 1, due to the combination of reduced asset demand and increased asset supply.

B.   Short-Run Dynamics without a Monetary-Policy Response

Proposition 1 shows that any increase in public debt in a small open economy with a well-defined long-run asset demand function $A(r, Z)$ is eventually entirely held abroad. However, this cannot happen right away. By the balance-of-payments identity (eq. [29]), a deterioration in the NFA position requires a sequence of trade deficits, in the form of higher imports or lower exports. In turn, the change in imports and exports must be induced by the change in fiscal policy.

Here, we characterize analytically this transition. We stack the entire paths of government spending $\{dG_t\}$ and public debt $\{dB_t\}$ into vectors, which we denote by $d\mathbf{G} = (dG_0, dG_1, ...)$ and $d\mathbf{B} = (dB_0, dB_1, ...)$, and similarly for other variables. We then solve for the first-order impulse response of all macroeconomic aggregates to this change.

Solving for the transition requires an assumption about monetary policy. In this section, we consider the case of "no monetary response," in which monetary policy maintains a constant r throughout; that is, equation (17), with $r = 0$. We also assume that any government spending change is transitory, so that $\lim_{t \to \infty} dG_t = 0$. Under these conditions, we know from Proposition 1 that the long-run real exchange rate $\lim_{t \to \infty} Q_t$ is unchanged and equal to $Q = 1$. Combined with the real UIP condition (eq. [22]), and given $i_t^* = r = 0$, it then follows that the entire path of real exchange rates is unchanged, as well:

$$Q_t = \frac{P_{Ht}}{P_t} = 1 \quad \forall t. \tag{39}$$

This result implies that any causal effect of fiscal policy on the trade balance must go through changes in import demand, rather than through expenditure switching. In Subsection III.D, we consider alternative monetary-policy rules, in which expenditure switching also plays a role.

Because $r_t = 0$ for all t, the government budget constraint (eq. [22]) implies that the fiscal deficit FD_t is also the primary deficit:

$$FD_t = B_t - B_{t-1} = \frac{P_{Ht}}{P_t}(G_t - T_t) = G_t - T_t. \tag{40}$$

Recall that our equilibrium takes as exogenous the path of government spending and the path of public debt B_t (or, equivalently, fiscal deficits FD_t). By equation (40), any increase in the fiscal deficit that is not used to finance government spending leads to lower taxes; that is, transfers to households.

The next two propositions consider the first-order effect of exogenous changes in $d\mathbf{G}$ and the fiscal deficit $d\mathbf{FD}$. We begin with the case without home bias, and then consider the case with home bias.

Case with No Home Bias ($\alpha \to 1$)

In the limit with no home bias $\alpha \to 1$, the following proposition summarizes the effect on our outcomes of interest.

Proposition 2. Assume constant-r monetary policy, $r = 0$, $\lim_{t \to \infty} dG_t = 0$, and no home bias $\alpha \to 1$. Then, the first-order responses of output $d\mathbf{Y}$, the current account $d\mathbf{CA}$, and the trade deficit $d\mathbf{TD}$ are given by

$$dY = dG \qquad (41)$$

$$-dCA = dTD = \mathbf{M}d\mathbf{FD} \qquad (42)$$

$$d\mathbf{PS} = (I - \mathbf{M})d\mathbf{FD}. \qquad (43)$$

Equation (41) shows that the effect on domestic output only depends on local government spending, with a fiscal multiplier of 1. Equation (42) shows that fiscal deficits cause a current-account and trade deficit (a twin deficit) with a dynamic pass-through exactly equal to the iMPC matrix $\mathbf{M}$. Equation (43) shows that fiscal deficits cause a rise in private saving (excess saving) with a pass-through given by the matrix of intertemporal marginal propensities to save, $I - \mathbf{M}$.

The logic behind these results is as follows. Consider first the case where local government spending changes without a change in the fiscal deficit, so that the government raises taxes contemporaneously. Equation (41) shows that this affects local GDP one for one with the rise in spending. This result is made possible by our monetary-policy assumption; see Woodford (2011) for the representative-agent case and Auclert et al. (2018) for the heterogeneous-agent case in a closed-economy setting. The additional spending causes pretax incomes to increase by as much as taxes do, and because these have the same incidence across the population, there is no effect on posttax incomes for anyone and therefore no effect on either private savings or private spending.

Next, consider the case where the fiscal deficit changes. Combining equations (16) and (40), we see that this change affects posttax incomes by the magnitude of the fiscal deficit, $dZ = dY - dT = dG - dT = d\mathbf{FD}$. The matrix of intertemporal MPCs then determines how much is saved and goes into private saving $(I - \mathbf{M})d\mathbf{FD}$, and how much of it is spent $(\mathbf{M}d\mathbf{FD})$. Importantly, because there is no home bias, all spending is on foreign goods and therefore affects the trade and current-account deficits one for one.[15]

The solid line in figure 4 illustrates this logic in the case of a one-time, permanent shock to the debt level, as visualized in the top left panel. This is an especially instructive case to understand equilibrium adjustment, and it corresponds to the typical case in which public debt rises because the government sends one-off transfers to households. Here, the path of current-account deficits is exactly equal to that of iMPCs out of unanticipated transfers in figure 3. In particular, the impact effect on the current-account deficit of a unit change in dB is equal to 0.25. The NFA position follows the cumulative iMPCs $\Sigma_{s=0}^{t} M_{0s}$. Because

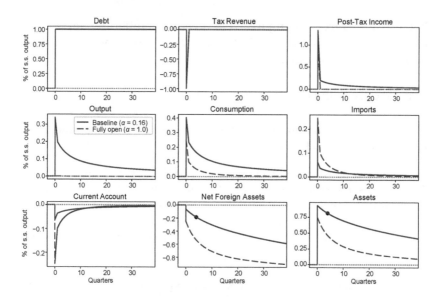

Fig. 4. Impulse response to a debt-financed transfer under different degrees of openness α. The solid dots on the Net Foreign Asset and Asset impulse responses correspond to the predictions of the baseline model for the empirical regressions discussed in Section V. S.S. = steady state. A color version of this figure is available online.

households' intertemporal budget constraints imply that $\Sigma_{s=0}^{\infty}M_{0s} = 1$, in the long run we obtain a pass-through of 1, confirming Proposition 1.

The reason why MPCs matter here is straightforward: in the aggregate, a fiscal-deficit increase of $1 leads households to receive $1 in transfers, out of which they immediately spend $M_{0,0}$ dollars. Because there is no home bias, all of this is extra spending is on imports, leading to a current-account deterioration on impact of $M_{0,0}$. Taking stock, the short-run pass-through of the fiscal deficit into the current-account deficit when there is no home bias is

$$\text{SRPT}^{\alpha=1} = \frac{-d\text{CA}_0}{d\text{FD}} = \frac{-d\text{nfa}_0}{d\text{FD}} = M_{0,0}.$$

As households keep spending down, their excess savings and the spending response builds up, imports remain elevated, and the current account remains in deficit, until the point at which the country has accumulated a foreign debt equal to the increase in government debt.

This discussion illustrates the importance of iMPCs in disciplining the time path of twin deficits. There is a great deal of evidence that iMPCs are elevated not just at times when households receive the transfers but also afterward, as in figure 3. One general-equilibrium implication of this fact for open economies is that we expect current-account deficits to be more persistent than fiscal deficits.

General Case with Home Bias ($0 < \alpha < 1$)

The next proposition provides the impulse responses in the more general case with home bias $0 < \alpha < 1$.

Proposition 3.   Assume constant-r monetary policy, $r = 0$, and $\lim_{t \to \infty} dG_t = 0$. Then, the first-order responses of output $d\mathbf{Y}$, the current account $d\mathbf{CA}$, and the trade deficit $d\mathbf{TD}$ are related to the iMPC matrix $\mathbf{M}$ and openness α via:

$$d\mathbf{Y} = d\mathbf{G} + (1 - \alpha)\mathbf{M}\left(\sum_{k \geq 0}(1 - \alpha)^k\mathbf{M}^k\right)d\mathbf{FD} \qquad (44)$$

$$-d\mathbf{CA} = d\mathbf{TD} = \alpha\mathbf{M}\left(\sum_{k \geq 0}(1 - \alpha)^k\mathbf{M}^k\right)d\mathbf{FD} \qquad (45)$$

$$d\mathbf{PS} = (I - \mathbf{M})\left(\sum_{k \geq 0}(1 - \alpha)^k\mathbf{M}^k\right)d\mathbf{FD} \qquad (46)$$

The proof is in Section B2. This result can be seen as a combination of the closed-economy analysis of fiscal policy in Auclert et al. (2018) and the open-economy analysis of exchange rates and monetary policy in Auclert et al. (2021c).

Just as in Proposition 2, and for the same reason, a balanced-budget change in government spending has a one-for-one effect on output. However, with home bias, the response to fiscal deficits is different. Consider now a change in the time path of fiscal deficits with no change in government spending $d\mathbf{G} = 0$, so that all that changes is transfers to households $-d\mathbf{T} = d\mathbf{FD}$. Households still spend these transfers according to their MPCs. But now, a fraction $1 - \alpha$ of this additional spending is used to purchase domestic goods, which boosts country income and is therefore spent again. The resulting effect on output is that of a standard Keynesian cross, but here each round of spending affects the time path of output according to $((1 - \alpha)\mathbf{M})^k$. This explains the right-hand sides of equations (44)–(46), which correspond to the general-equilibrium change in total posttax income induced by the change in the fiscal deficit.

Apart from these general-equilibrium effects on income, the key difference to Proposition 2 is that now the response of the current-account deficit is characterized by $\alpha\mathbf{M}$ rather than $\mathbf{M}$. This effect is critical to slow down the pass-through of the fiscal deficit to the current deficit. To understand this effect quantitatively, consider again a one-time, permanent shock to the debt level, as visualized in the dashed line of figure 4 for our baseline calibration to $\alpha = 0.16$.

Here also, the direct effect of a fiscal deficit of \$1 is that households receive \$1, of which they spend $M_{0,0}$ \$. However, only $\alpha \times M_{0,0}$ \$ is spent on imports. This is much smaller in practice than $M_{0,0}$. This explains why the impact effect on the current-account deficit in figure 4 is much below 0.25. Because of the general-equilibrium effect on output, however, this effect is higher in absolute value than $\alpha \times M_{0,0}$. One simple way to understand this adjustment process is to think about a case where households do not anticipate any future increases in income.[16] In this case, the short-run pass-through (SRPT) parameter would be

$$\mathrm{SRPT}^{na} = \frac{\alpha \cdot M_{0,0}}{1 - (1 - \alpha)M_{0,0}}. \tag{47}$$

This is still much smaller than $M_{0,0}$ for any realistic calibration of mpc and α. Taking account of the dynamic effects requires using the full expression for the current account in equation (45). If we let $\mathbf{e}_0' = (1 \quad 0 \quad 0 \quad \cdots)$ be the vector with one as the first element and zeros everywhere else, the full expression for the pass-through is

$$\mathrm{SRPT} = -\alpha\mathbf{e}_0'(I - (1 - \alpha)\mathbf{M})^{-1}\mathbf{Me}_0 dB. \tag{48}$$

In practice, the SRPT from this expression is only slightly above $\alpha \times M_{0,0}$ (see fig. 4). This implies a slow buildup of the foreign ownership of debt.

Taking stock, the combination of limited MPCs and home bias leads to slow transition dynamics in response to increases in public debt.

C.   Who Holds the New Assets? The Three Phases of Ownership

An advantage of our HANK model is that it allows us to trace out the cross-sectional patterns that underlie any fiscal expansion. Figure 5 traces out the dynamics of ownership that underlie the one-time debt-expansion experiment in figure 4. The medium gray area corresponds to the increase in wealth for the top 20% of the wealth distribution at each point in time (henceforth, "the rich"). The light gray area corresponds to the wealth increase for the next 80% (henceforth, "the middle class"). Together, these two sum to the "Asset" line in figure 4. Finally, the dark

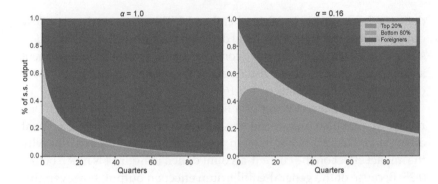

Fig. 5. Three phases of asset ownership in the small open economy. S.S. = steady state. A color version of this figure is available online.

gray area corresponds to the negative of the NFA position, which is the amount of the marginal public debt held by foreigners.

The left panel of figure 5 considers the case with no home bias, $\alpha \rightarrow 1$. Initially, the middle class and rich both increase their savings in response to the transfers, but the middle class spends down these savings much more quickly than the rich. One can summarize these dynamics in three phases: first, private wealth rises for all households; then, it remains elevated only for rich households; and eventually, all debt is held by foreigners.

The right panel of figure 5 displays the same outcomes in our baseline calibration with $\alpha = 0.16$. Here, the three phases are even more pronounced: as the middle class initially spends down their transfers, economic activity rises, which allows the rich to keep increasing their savings as the middle class spends theirs down. This phenomenon relies on the output boom from the spending and is therefore not present in the left panel.[17]

D. Extensions

We now consider two extensions. In the appendix, we also consider the case where $r \neq 0$, as well as alternative distributions for transfers.

Monetary-Policy Response

We next consider alternative monetary policies, deviating from the constant-r rule in equation (17). We study a Taylor rule targeting home-goods inflation (eq. [18]), and the natural allocation that induces

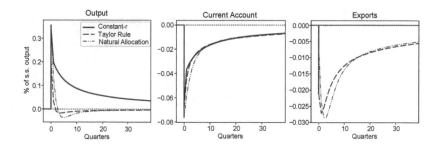

Fig. 6. Impulse response to a debt-financed transfer under alternative monetary-policy rules. S.S. = steady state. A color version of this figure is available online.

a zero domestic inflation path at all times (eq. [19]). Figure 6 shows the results of simulations under these alternative monetary-policy rules. Because the fiscal shock is inflationary, under these rules it induces a monetary tightening whose main effect is to reduce the output response. Import demand is consequently reduced. However, the current-account dynamics (and therefore those of NFAs) are very similar to the constant-r case. This is because the appreciation of the real exchange rate from the monetary tightening reduces net exports via expenditure switching.

It is possible to further understand these dynamics by considering the separate effects of the real exchange rate $d\mathbf{Q}$ and total consumption demand $d\mathbf{C}$ on the trade and current-account deficit. Section B2 shows that we always have

$$-d\mathbf{CA} = \frac{-\alpha}{1 - \alpha}C(\chi - 1)d\mathbf{Q} + \alpha d\mathbf{C}, \qquad (49)$$

where $\chi = (1 - \alpha)\eta + \gamma$ is the sum of import and export elasticities. Other things equal, the appreciation deteriorates the current account provided that $\chi > 1$, an effect that can counterbalance the decline in import demand from the direct effect of monetary policy on spending. In our calibration, these two effects almost exactly offset each other.[18]

Note that the natural allocation features a twin-deficit phenomenon exactly like the one under our constant-r monetary rule. This shows that nominal rigidities are not important for our main results.

Alternative Models: RANK, TANK, and Blanchard (1985)

Having discussed the time paths of asset ownership in our baseline model, we now consider the implications of alternative widely used

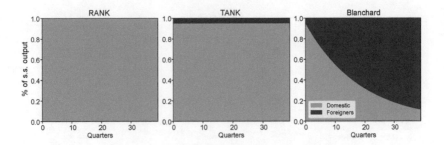

Fig. 7. Impulse response of assets to a debt-financed transfers in alternative models. S.S. = steady state. A color version of this figure is available online.

models, beginning with a representative-agent model. There, Ricardian equivalence implies that any increase in debt immediately results in excess savings, as illustrated in the left panel of figure 7. A_t tracks B_t perfectly.[19]

A more involved question is whether alternative non-Ricardian models also deliver a similar response. We consider two of the main leading non-Ricardian models in the literature, which act as tractable alternatives to heterogeneous-agent models: a TANK model as in Galí et al. (2007) and Bilbiie (2008), and a perpetual-youth model along the lines of Blanchard (1985).

In Section B6, we study the TANK model, which is made up of a fraction μ of hand-to-mouth agents and a fraction $1 - \mu$ of standard infinitely lived unconstrained consumers. We show that, in this model, the twin-deficit equation (45) reduces to

$$-d\mathbf{CA} = \frac{\mu\alpha}{1 - \mu(1 - \alpha)} d\mathbf{FD}.$$

Here, the "no-anticipation" logic that governed equation (47) applies not only to the impact effect but also at every point in time. Therefore, the TANK model provides backing for the classical twin-deficit hypothesis, in which fiscal deficits translate into current-account deficits at the same point in time. However, the quantitative magnitudes from this particular microfounded model are difficult to reconcile with the "rules of thumb" typically used by policy institutions. For realistic calibration, even if $\mu = 0.25$, at our US-calibrated value for openness of $\alpha = 0.157$, we find a pass-through of only about 5%, much smaller than the 30%–50% range often assumed. In the limit with $\mu = 0$, this becomes the representative-agent model with Ricardian equivalence and no impact of the fiscal deficit on the current-account deficit.

Note further that the TANK model has very different dynamic behavior from our HANK model. In the TANK model, the current-account deficit only lasts for as long as the transfers last (when hand-to-mouth agents spend it), so the LRPT is just $\mu\alpha/(1 - \mu(1 - \alpha)) = 1$. This is illustrated in the middle panel of figure 7.

A model that behaves much closer to the HANK model is the well-known Blanchard (1985) model, which was first introduced to study analytically the effects of debt on the current account, albeit in a one-good setting. In Section B7, we write down the discrete-time counterpart of this model. We show that it features a consumption and asset function as in equation (36), whose $\mathbf{M}$ matrix can be characterized in closed form, as well as a closed-form long-run asset demand function $A(r, Z)$. The model's parameters can be calibrated to hit $M_{0,0}$ directly. The model also features a LRPT of 1, and its main difference in dynamics is because it has a different $\mathbf{M}$ even when calibrating to the same $M_{0,0}$. Figure 7 illustrates how similar the Blanchard model is to the baseline HANK model once matched to the same mpc and α. Here, the decay in NFAs is faster than in the HANK model, because $M_{0,1}$ is larger in the Blanchard model.[20]

E. Can a COVID Shock Explain Excess Savings and the Current Account?

We have seen that a fiscal-deficit shock does a good job at qualitatively matching the patterns of figures 1 and 2: it is accompanied by a large increase in private savings with realistic distributional dynamics and by a limited decline in the current-account deficit that happens in slow motion.

It is often argued that the increase in private savings documented in figure 1 is not just the result of fiscal policy but also of pandemic restrictions (e.g., European Central Bank 2021; Goldman Sachs 2021; TD Bank 2021). Here, we show that this argument misses an important part of general equilibrium: COVID restrictions that depress consumption also depress income, so that the effects of these restrictions on aggregate excess saving were likely small.[21] We demonstrate this logic in our model using two different types of shocks to proxy for the idea that the COVID shock depressed spending.

We first consider a shock to overall spending, in the form of a shock to the discount factor β of all households in the small open economy. This shock depresses desired spending and therefore equilibrium spending, with households cutting back on domestic and foreign spending alike.

We solve for the response of the model under the constant-r monetary-policy scenario, under our baseline calibration of $\alpha = 0.16$.

We calibrate this shock such that it implies a realistic decline in the level of output. In the United States, in 2020Q2, the level of output was 9% below where it had been in 2020Q1, and it had essentially entirely recovered by 2021Q2. Of course, some of this recovery was the sustained effect of the US fiscal stimulus. Using our quantitative model from Section VI, we infer that fiscal policy sustained the level of output by around 3% for about 2 years. This implies that the pure effect of the COVID shock, absent fiscal policy, would have been to lower output by 12% in 2020Q2 and 3% in 2021Q2. We fit the standard deviation and persistence of an AR(1) shock to β to match these numbers. The resulting effect is displayed in the top panels of figure 8.

We do find that a shock to overall spending can lead to aggregate excess savings. The shock implies a decline in both home and foreign spending. The decline in home spending lowers GDP and domestic income, with no net effect on saving. The decline in foreign spending, however, leads to a current-account surplus. In the aggregate, absent a rise in fiscal deficits or investment, a current-account surplus is the only way the country can build up excess savings. Note, however, from the right panel, that the magnitude of this effect is very small: a 12% decline in

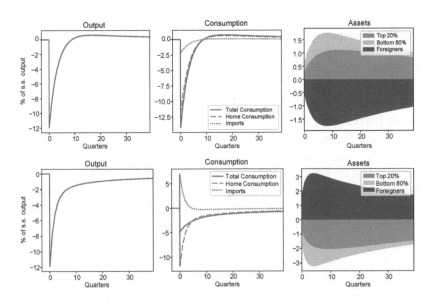

Fig. 8. Impulse responses to two COVID shocks. S.S. = steady state. A color version of this figure is available online.

GDP leads to a peak increase of cumulative excess savings of only about 1.5%, which is small compared with the observed increase of about 11%.

A widely noted aspect of the pandemic is that it has unequally hit sectors, with services being much harder hit, such that the pandemic created a reallocation of activity toward goods and away from services (e.g., Baqaee and Farhi 2022; Guerrieri et al. 2022). This suggests that an overall shock to desired spending is not the most appropriate way of modeling the COVID shock. We therefore modify equation (1) to feature a shock ζ_t to home spending

$$c_{it} = \left[(1-\alpha)^{\frac{1}{\eta}}(\zeta_t c_{iHt})^{\frac{\eta-1}{\eta}} + \alpha^{\frac{1}{\eta}}(c_{iWt})^{\frac{\eta-1}{\eta}}\right]^{\frac{\eta}{\eta-1}}$$

and solve for the general-equilibrium effect of this shock.[22] We recalibrate the model to feature a low intratemporal elasticity relative to the intertemporal elasticity ($\eta = 0.5 < 1 = \sigma^{-1}$) such that the shock has a general-equilibrium effect on home output (see Guerrieri et al. 2022 for a similar condition.) We calibrate an AR(1) ζ_t shock to match the same output decline as described previously.

The bottom panels of figure 8 display the effect of this shock. As expected, the shock leads to a decline in home spending and a reallocation of spending toward imports. Hence, now in equilibrium the current account and excess savings actually decline in equilibrium, with "excess dissavings" of about 3% of GDP at the peak.

Overall, this shows that the COVID shock itself may have limited general-equilibrium effects on saving, because it reduces income along with consumption. Whether income or consumption declines more depends on the exact details of the shock, but the magnitude of the rise in saving falls well short of the data even in the (somewhat unrealistic) scenario that gives the most chance to this idea.

IV. Fiscal Deficits in the World Economy

In the last section, we discussed a small open economy changing fiscal policy in isolation. In practice, however, the COVID fiscal expansion that motivates this paper happened simultaneously across all countries. This renders the small-open-economy analysis incomplete. For instance, although one country can borrow from the rest of the world—as predicted by Proposition 1—to finance its new debt, collectively the world cannot. Instead, after an increase in world debt, some mechanism must convince agents collectively to buy the new debt. In our model, that mechanism is a rising world interest rate.

In this section, we characterize the world-economy equilibrium. We maintain our baseline symmetric-country calibration, with export weights ω^k equal to GDP weights. In this environment, we show analytically that our small-open-economy results remain highly relevant, because they characterize the deviations of each country from the world average. They can either be combined with closed-economy results to obtain the world equilibrium or brought directly to the cross-sectional data.

A. A Decomposition Result for the World Economy

In our symmetric-country calibration, all variables are either constant across countries k in the steady state (e.g., i^k or Q^k) or scale with each country's relative GDP ω^k (e.g., C^k or Y^k). We define aggregate and demeaned versions of both kinds of variables.

Definition 3. Define aggregate and demeaned variables as follows:

- For all variables that are constant across countries in the symmetric steady state, (e.g., i_t), the *aggregate* is the weighted sum (e.g., $i_t \equiv \Sigma_k \omega^k i_t^k$), and the *demeaned* is the deviation from the aggregate (e.g., $\tilde{i}_t^k = i_t^k - i_t$).

- For all variables that scale with ω^k across countries in the symmetric steady state (e.g., C_t^k), the *aggregate* is the overall sum across countries (e.g., $C_t \equiv \Sigma C_t^k$), and the *demeaned* is the scaled deviation from the aggregate (e.g., $\tilde{C}_t^k = (C_t^k/\omega^k) - C_t$).

We then have the following first-order decomposition result for the world equilibrium.

Proposition 4. Consider a symmetric world-economy hit by shocks (e.g., $d\mathbf{B}^k$), in each country k. The first-order impulse responses of variables in each country satisfy the following property. First, aggregate variables are given by the closed-economy model in response to the aggregate shocks (e.g., $d\mathbf{B}$). Second, all demeaned variables in country k are given by the small-open-economy model in response to the demeaned shocks (e.g., $d\tilde{\mathbf{B}}^k$).

This powerful result decomposes the response to shocks in the world economy into two simpler cases introduced in Section II: first, the closed economy, which characterizes the response of world aggregates; and second, the small open economy, which characterizes the response of deviations relative to the world. The former allows us to draw on existing closed-economy work to understand the evolution of the world as a whole, and the latter allows us to reinterpret the results of Section III as characterizing relative outcomes across countries.

The intuition for Proposition 4 is that collectively, the world cannot run a current-account deficit against itself, nor can it change its real exchange rate relative to itself. Hence, when we combine variables across countries to obtain world aggregates, the world behaves like a closed economy. At the same time, all countries face the same world import demand C_t^* and interest rate i_t^* at every date. Hence, to first order, relative outcomes across countries should be unaffected by changes in C_t^* and i_t^*, and should be the same as implied by the small-open-economy model, which holds C_t^* and i_t^* fixed.

In the next two sections, we apply Proposition 4 to study the transmission of fiscal shocks, both in the long run and in the transition.

B. Application: Long Run

We now assume that each country conducts a small, permanent fiscal expansion of dB^k. In the interest of space, we focus on the case where we initially have $r = 0$ and countries do not increase long-run government spending, $dG^k = 0$. We then have the following corollary of Propositions 1 and 4.

Corollary 1. Assume that $r = 0$; that $dG^k = 0$; that the government of country k with GDP weight ω^k expands its long-run debt by dB^k; and that all economies go back to the natural allocation in the long run. Then, to first order, in each country the long-run real exchange rate is unchanged ($dQ^k = 0$), real income changes by the same proportion everywhere, $d \log Z^k = d \log Z$, and letting $B = \Sigma_k B^k$, we have the same amount of excess savings everywhere and a twin deficit in higher-debt countries:

$$d \log A^k = d \log B \qquad \mathrm{dnfa}^k = -\left(dB^k - \omega^k dB\right). \qquad (50)$$

In particular, the LRPT of public debt to the NFA is $LPRT = 1 - \omega^k$. Letting $a(r) \equiv A(r, Z)/Z$ denote normalized asset demand, the increase in the world interest rate that sustains this equilibrium is

$$dr^n = \frac{d \log B}{\dfrac{d \log a(r)}{dr} - \dfrac{1 + \frac{1}{1-\frac{G}{Y}}\frac{\sigma}{1+\phi}}{1 - \frac{1}{1-\frac{G}{Y}}\frac{1-\sigma}{1+\phi}}a(r)}. \qquad (51)$$

Proof. It follows from Proposition 4 that demeaned variables will have the impulses characterized in the small open economy by Proposition 1, so that steady-state demeaned assets, real exchange rates, real interest rates, and real incomes are all unchanged. It follows that the change dA^k in assets in each country must equal its share ω^k of the aggregate increase dB in asset supply, so that $\mathrm{dnfa}^k = dA^k - dB^k = \omega^k dB - dB^k$. It also follows that real incomes must change by the same proportion everywhere, and real exchange rates are unchanged (because the change in the closed economy is $dQ = 0$). The common change dr^n in real interest rate is calculated in Section C2 from the closed-economy aggregate model.

Corollary 1 shows that in response to a global fiscal expansion, each country in the long run increases its asset holdings by the same proportional amount: the newly created assets are spread evenly, regardless of which countries issued the debt. This is because the long-run real interest rate r is equalized across all countries—and in the symmetric calibration, a uniform increase in r leads to a uniform expansion in long-run assets. The twin-deficit result in Proposition 1 now characterizes deviations from the world average: an increase in a country's debt over and above its share of the world's debt leads to a one-for-one deterioration in its long-run NFA.

To apply this result in practice, consider the recent COVID fiscal expansion. As we will document in more detail in Section V, this expansion was very unequal, with countries such as the United States expanding their deficits, relative to pre-COVID GDP, by much more than countries such as Denmark. Applying Corollary 1, we can obtain the implied long-run change in NFAs in each country by taking its cumulative increase in deficits relative to the world average. These predictions are given by the bars in figure 9. For instance, because it had a very limited increase in public debt, Denmark's NFA position is projected to increase by around 11 percentage points of GDP, and the US NFA is projected to deteriorate by around 2 percentage points. Note that, for most large

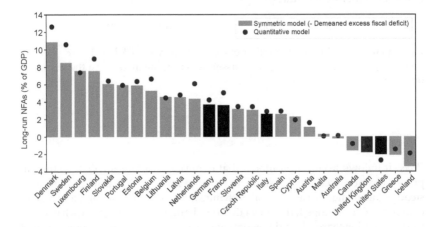

Fig. 9. Accounting for fiscal deficits in the United States and the rest of the world. GDP = gross domestic product. A color version of this figure is available online.

Table 2
Effect on the Long-Run World Interest Rate from the World Fiscal Shock

		Symmetric Countries	Quantitative Model
Increase in debt (% of initial)	$d \log B$	14.5	14.5
Interest semielasticity of savings	$d \log a/dr$	21.3	21.3
Tax adjustment (with $\sigma = 1$)	$a(r)(1-1/(1-G/Y) \times 1/(1+\phi))$	1.3	1.3
First-order approximation	dr^n	72 bp	72 bp
Actual change	$r - r^n$	71 bp	68 bp

Note: This table implements equation (51) and compares the effect to solution in the full quantitative model of Section VI with asymmetric countries. Semielasticities and interest-rate effects are annualized. bp = basis points.

countries, these long-run NFAs are relatively modest, because the fiscal expansions tended to be large in all of these countries.

At the same time, the world real interest rate must increase by enough to clear the world asset market in the long run, with the first-order effect given by equation (51). The first column of table 2 reports numbers for our symmetric model in the context of the recent COVID fiscal expansion. The average cumulative deficit (dB) is 12% of GDP, which is a proportional change of $d \log B = 14\%$ given an initial level of 82%. The interest semielasticity of asset demand in the model is around 21, implying a first-order effect on interest rates of 72 basis points—very close to the true, nonlinear effect in the model.[23]

C. Application: Transitional Dynamics

We now assume that countries announce an entire fiscal expansion path $\{dB_t^k\}$, eventually settling at $dB^k = \lim_{t \to \infty} dB_t^k$. We also allow for an arbitrary path of changes to government spending $\{dG_t^k\}$ in each country but continue to assume steady-state $r = 0$ for simplicity.

In Section III, we had simple analytical results for impulse responses to fiscal shocks in the small open economy, assuming that monetary policy follows a constant-r rule. By Proposition 4, these results also describe demeaned impulse responses in the world economy, assuming that demeaned r is constant at zero—that is, that countries across the world maintain the same path of real interest rates in response to the shock, perhaps motivated by a desire to avoid real exchange-rate movements.

At the aggregate world level, the response of output is the same as in the standard closed-economy case, with an intertemporal Keynesian cross as described in Auclert et al. (2018), augmented with a consumption response $ZM^rd\mathbf{r}$ to the average real interest-rate change (which can come from an arbitrary monetary rule).[24]

We summarize these observations in the following corollary.

Corollary 2. If monetary policy implements the same path $d\mathbf{r}$ in all countries, then the demeaned impulses in each country are given by equations (44)–(46), in response to the demeaned shocks $\widetilde{d\mathbf{FD}}^k$ and $\widetilde{d\mathbf{G}}^k$ to deficits and government spending. More generally, for any monetary rules in each country, the aggregate response is characterized by the equations $dY = dG + M(dPD - dG) + ZM^rd\mathbf{r} + MdY$ tand $d\mathbf{PS} = d\mathbf{FD}$, where $d\mathbf{r}$ is the average world real interest rate.

Applying the first part of Corollary 2 to the simple fiscal experiment we contemplated in Section III—where each country permanently increases its debt by some amount—gives the following simple prediction for a cross-sectional regression.

Corollary 3. Consider the data $(dA^k, d\mathbf{nfa}^k)$ generated by the model hit by a one-time permanent shock to debt in each country, $dB^k = dB^k\mathbf{1}$, assuming that all countries have a common monetary response $d\mathbf{r}$. Then, a regression of dA_t^k on dB^k delivers the time path in the bottom right panel of figure 4, and a regression of $d\mathbf{nfa}_t^k$ on dB^k delivers the time path in the bottom center panel of figure 4.

In the next section, we take Corollary 3 directly to the data.

It is worth noting that Proposition 4 also applies for other specifications of monetary policy, such as Taylor rules, or rules that replicate the natural flexible-wage allocation. The impulse responses of our small-open-economy model in Section III under these rules will continue to give, by Proposition 4, demeaned impulse responses in the world economy, with cross-sectional predictions as in Corollary 3. For our dependent variables of interest (dA_t^k and $d\mathbf{nfa}_t^k$), however, figure 6 suggests little effect from alternative monetary rules: the current-account response, and therefore $d\mathbf{nfa}_t^k$ and dA_t^k, is nearly identical for the three.

A similar generalization also applies for other shocks and other variables of interest. For instance, we could look at the cross-sectional impact of deficit-financed government spending shocks on output, and compare to cross-sectional multipliers estimated in the data as in Nakamura and Steinsson (2014) and Chodorow-Reich (2019).[25]

V. Excess Savings and Twin Deficits during the Pandemic

Our analysis predicts a distinctive cross-country time path of excess savings and current accounts in response to a worldwide fiscal expansion. In this section, we test this prediction using the COVID pandemic as a natural experiment. Although this is not an ideal experiment because the pandemic was a shock in itself, it is nevertheless a promising episode to study the causal effect in our model, because the fiscal-policy response to the pandemic was largely unrelated to the size of the pandemic shock across countries.[26]

We are specifically interested in testing the predictions of Corollary 3, which suggests running a simple regression. To do this, we first construct the empirical counterparts of the dA^k, $dnfa^k$, and dB^k variables for a set of 26 advanced economies. We then run the regression implied by Corollary 3 directly in these data and show that the empirical regression results support our model predictions. We conclude by discussing potential sources of bias in our regression, and how we address these.

A. Data

We focus on advanced economies, following the International Monetary Fund (IMF) definition. These economies are a natural starting point for our analysis, because they constitute a large and highly financially integrated part of the world.

For advanced economy k, we collect data on (net) private saving PS_t^k, (net) investment I_t^k, the current account CA_t^k, the fiscal deficit FD_t^k, and GDP Y_t^k over the period 2014Q1–2021Q2. Private saving (respectively, net investment) is constructed by subtracting depreciation from gross private saving (respectively, gross investment) in the Organization for Economic Cooperation and Development (OECD) Quarterly Sector Accounts; the other three variables are from the IMF International Financial Statistics (IFS) database. We find that 28 advanced countries have both current-account and fiscal-deficit data for the entire period. We exclude Ireland and Norway, whose current accounts are known to be heavily influenced by tax-haven flows, and oil and natural-gas prices, respectively. This determines our baseline set of 26 countries. We define a reduced set of 17 countries that also have private saving data and investment data, so that the full balance of payments is available.[27] Appendix D lists all the countries in our baseline and reduced sample and provides more details about the variables we use. We refer to the set of remaining 16 advanced economies in the reduced sample, excluding the United States, as the "rest of the world."

To test Corollary 3, we need to construct the empirical analogues of dA^k, $dnfa^k$, and dB^k. We do this as follows. We define "excess private savings" as the accumulated stock of assets from private saving above the pre-COVID trend. That is, taking $t = 0$ to be 2020Q1, we define for any quarter $t \geq 1$:

$$\text{Excess Private Savings}_t^k \equiv \sum_{s=1}^{t} \left(\frac{PS_s^k}{Y_0^k (1 + \bar{g}^k)^s} - \overline{\left(\frac{PS}{Y} \right)}^k \right), \quad (52)$$

where $\bar{g}^k \equiv Y_{t+1}^k / Y_t - 1$ is nominal GDP growth, and bars denote the 5-year prepandemic average (2015Q2–2020Q1).[28] We then define cumulative "excess current-account surpluses" and "excess fiscal deficits" in an exactly analogous way. These three excess metrics are natural counterparts of dA_t^k, $dnfa_t^k$, and dB_t^k, respectively, because they capture the additional stock of private wealth, the additional NFA position, and the additional public debt, all relative to potential GDP, that countries have incurred up until quarter t, relative to a baseline in which the corresponding flows had remained at their average level.[29] We then verify that our fiscal-deficit measure lines up well with an independent measure of the fiscal response to COVID by the IMF.[30] Finally, we analogously construct "excess capital accumulation" by cumulating net investment. If we enriched our model with capital, this would be the counterpart of the capital stock in each country.

The balance-of-payments identity relates the four excess metrics we construct in a natural way. In each country k, modulo the statistical discrepancy, the fiscal deficit must be equal to private savings, net of the current account and investment:

$$FD_t^k = PS_t^k - CA_t^k - I_t^k. \quad (53)$$

Because this equation holds in every time period, it also holds for the cumulative measures we construct at each t. Hence, equation (53) provides us with a natural way of visualizing our data. Figure 10 performs this exercise for the United States and the rest of the world: at each quarter t, it shows how much of the fiscal deficit up to that date was empirically accounted for by private saving, investment, and the current account. We find that private saving accounted for the most, that current-account deficits are smaller and more delayed, and that investment moved little.[31] These patterns are qualitatively consistent with those implied by our model in response to a shock to fiscal deficits that is larger in the United States than the rest of the world. We next show that they are also quantitatively consistent with the model's predictions given the excess fiscal deficits we measure.

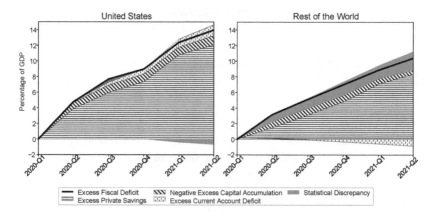

Fig. 10. Long-run NFAs in quantitative model versus predictions from Proposition 1. Bars indicate predictions from Corollary 1: long-run net foreign assets (NFAs) in the symmetric model are equal to the demeaned excess fiscal deficit. Black dots indicate the long-run NFAs in our quantitative model of Section VI. A color version of this figure is available online.

B. Testing the Symmetric Model

We start by running the simple regression implied by Corollary 3. Specifically, we regress excess savings, current-account surpluses, and capital accumulation on excess fiscal deficits after t quarters. For instance, we run in the cross section of countries k:

$$\text{Excess Private Savings}_t^k = \alpha^k + \beta_t \text{Excess Fiscal Deficits}_t^k + \epsilon^k.$$

The results as of 2021Q2 ($t = 5$) are displayed in the left column of figure 11.

The figure confirms that larger fiscal deficits are associated with larger savings and a current-account deficit after five quarters, with limited effect on investment. In addition, it shows that the model and the data pass-through coefficients are quantitatively consistent: the point estimate on excess savings is 0.81 in the model versus 0.79 in the data, and that on current accounts is −0.19 in the model versus −0.34 in the data, although it is not precisely estimated.[32] The dashed lines in the figure visualize this quantitative success, which is unique to our model with realistic home bias and MPCs. Without home bias, for instance, our model implies a pass-through of 0.4 on savings and −0.6 for current accounts (see fig. 4), which is much too fast relative to the data.[33] In figure D1, we further show that the time path of the empirical pass-through coefficients is also consistent with that predicted by the model: the

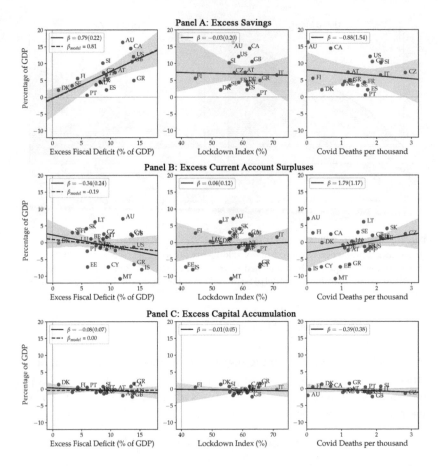

Fig. 11. Cross-country determinants of excess savings and current accounts. β indicates the regression coefficient of the y-axis on the x-axis variable. The standard error around this coefficient is in parentheses. Shaded areas correspond to 68% bootstrapped confidence intervals. The dashed lines in the left panels represent the prediction from the baseline model, with slopes for excess savings and current accounts given by the black dots of figure 4. GDP = gross domestic product. Country codes defined in tables D1 and E1. A color version of this figure is available online.

savings pass-through starts close to 1 and declines over time, and the current-account pass-through starts close to 0 and declines over time.

Although we view the fact that the simple regression coefficients match up in the data and the model as an important success of our model, in principle, the simple regression is biased if the fiscal shock is correlated with another shock at the country level and if that shock in turn has a meaningful effect on excess savings and current accounts. The main shocks that we have to worry about during this period are those related to the disruptions caused by COVID. In Subsection III.E, we argued that, in theory, a COVID shock alone can only have a modest effect on savings or the current account. We now show that this also appears to be the case in the data.

To this end, the middle and right columns of figure 11 rerun our simple regressions, substituting the fiscal-deficit variable with two country-level metrics of COVID intensity: a lockdown index (where 0 indicates laxest and 100 strictest) and the cumulative number of deaths per thousand individuals.[34] These graphs show that the COVID-shock story has a difficult time explaining the cross section of excess savings. The lockdown has no association with savings, with a point estimate of zero. COVID deaths correlate with the wrong sign: an increase in deaths by 2 per thousand, from the Finnish to the Italian level, reduces excess savings by 2%. Similarly, lockdowns and COVID deaths have a difficult time explaining the cross section of current accounts: the point estimates are positive but insignificant.[35]

This limited empirical association between measures of the COVID shock and excess savings or current accounts suggests that controlling for the size of the COVID shock directly should not change our main regression coefficients much. Figure D2 verifies this is in fact the case. The next section provides a model-based way of extracting the magnitude of the COVID shock in each country.

VI. Quantitative Model

In this section, we turn to a quantitative version of our model that relaxes the main limitations of our analysis so far. First, we relax the symmetry assumption, calibrating to openness and fiscal-policy data for 26 countries. Second, we relax the assumption that the fiscal-policy shock was a one-off shock in 2020Q1, instead feeding in the realized time path of fiscal deficits since that date. Finally, and most importantly, we explicitly add a COVID shock to each country, inferring the magnitude of this shock from the realized level of consumption in each country, similar to Gourinchas et al. (2021).

A. Calibration, Shocks, and Solution Method

Instead of assuming symmetric countries, we now calibrate each economy to hit its own degree of openness α^k, government debt B^k/Y^k, and spending G^k/Y^k. Section E1 provides details of these calibration targets.

Although the specification of monetary policy was unimportant for
our cross-country pass-through predictions, it becomes important in these
simulations. We assume a reasonable specification of monetary policy,
where the authority in each country follows a Taylor rule,

$$i_t = r_t^* + \phi_\pi \pi_t,$$

with r_t^* phasing in the transition between the initial natural rate of interest and the long-run natural rate. Our assumption here is that monetary
authorities are recognizing the pressure of fiscal policy on interest rates
and acting accordingly to avoid long-run inflationary pressure. In particular, this monetary-policy rule ensures that the economy reaches the natural allocation in the long run, as in the assumption of Corollary 1.

Our model allows us to recognize the presence of two shocks in each
country: a fiscal shock and a COVID shock. Our measure of the fiscal
shock dB_t^k in country k is the realized time paths of excess fiscal deficits
computed in Section V. Our measure of the COVID shock in each country is inferred from the realized time path of consumption, as follows.
We simulate the counterfactual effect of the fiscal shock on consumption
in each country. This effect is positive everywhere, and larger in countries with bigger fiscal interventions, reflecting the fact that fiscal policy
supported spending. We then subtract this effect from the actual consumption path in each country and find the time path of COVID shocks
in all 26 countries that rationalizes these paths. Specifically, we assume
that the COVID shock is an AR(1) discount factor shock as discussed in
Subsection III.E, with country-specific magnitude σ^k and a common persistence ρ. We then pick (σ^k, ρ) to hit consumption in each country perfectly in 2020Q1 and to minimize the square distance of the time path
of consumption in the model and the data afterward. Figure E1 visualizes this procedure, showing the actual time path of consumption in
each country, the effect implied by the fiscal shocks, and the effect implied by the COVID shocks.

Because the countries are no longer symmetric, we can no longer rely
on our results from Section IV to derive the world allocation and instead
must solve for the 26-country allocation simultaneously. We instead use
a novel approach to do this, adapting the ideas of Auclert et al. (2021a),
which we discuss further in Section E2.

B.   *Testing the Quantitative Model*

Figure 12 compares the pass-through coefficients of fiscal deficits on
excess savings and current accounts in the data relative to our model,

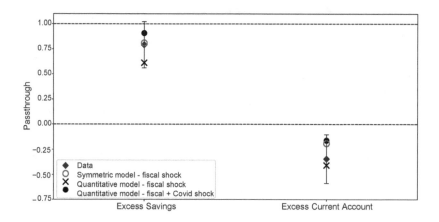

Fig. 12. Pass-through regression coefficients in the data and the model. "Data" correspond to our cross-country regressions on excess fiscal deficits as of 2021Q2 ($t = 5$), with 68% confidence intervals. "Model" corresponds to the same regression coefficients in each of the three models we consider. A color version of this figure is available online.

both at quarter 5. The data line corresponds to empirical regression in figure 11, together with 68% confidence intervals. The open circle labeled "symmetric model – fiscal shock" corresponds to the prediction from the symmetric model, per Corollary 3 and the black dots in figure 4.

The cross in the figure, labeled "quantitative model – fiscal shock," shows that considering a nonsymmetric world and the empirical time path for fiscal deficits does not significantly change these results. The main effect stems from the fact that the world as a whole is more open than the United States, which we used to calibrate our baseline model. As a consequence, the model converges to its long-run steady state faster: by quarter 5, the pass-through is closer to 0 for savings and closer to −1 for current accounts.

The solid circle in the figure, labeled "quantitative model – fiscal + COVID shock," shows that considering country-specific COVID shocks still keeps our two regression coefficients within the 68% error band. Our procedure infers that countries with larger fiscal shocks also experienced a larger COVID shock, consistent with the view that the fiscal shock was in part a response to the COVID shock. Given our discussion in Subsection III.E, a larger COVID shock increases savings and creates a current-account surplus. The net effect is to push up the regression coefficients on both excess savings and the current account, back toward the top of the error band. Overall, these three versions of the model are

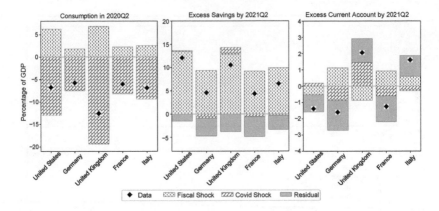

Fig. 13. Share of consumption, excess savings, and current accounts explained by each shock. GDP = gross domestic product. A color version of this figure is available online.

consistent with the data, and a model without home bias or high MPCs is not.[36]

We next turn to the model's ability to explain the overall variation in the data. For the largest five countries by GDP in our sample, figure 13 considers how much of consumption in 2020Q2, excess savings in 2021Q2, and current accounts in 2021Q2 can be explained by our model, and it splits the model contribution into the independent contribution of COVID shocks and fiscal shocks. By construction, our model can explain the level of consumption in 2020Q2 in each country: it finds that the COVID shock explains the decline in consumption everywhere, and fiscal policy boosted consumption in all countries. Turning to excess savings, which is not targeted by our procedure, the model does a very good job at explaining this outcome across countries overall, with a limited role for the residual. Our key finding is that the fiscal shock explains the vast majority of excess savings in the data, with almost no role for the COVID shock. This is for two reasons. First, the fiscal shock is calibrated to the data and has a realistic pass-through to savings. Second, a COVID shock alone cannot affect savings much, as demonstrated in Subsection III.E.

Finally, we find that the model has limited explanatory power for current-account movements. Hence, although the pass-through coefficient of fiscal deficits to current accounts has the right magnitude, there is a role for additional shocks to explain the data. Our COVID shock is one of these, but even after it is added, much of the variation in current accounts remains unexplained. We conjecture that this is for two reasons. First, most theories have a difficult time explaining empirical movements in current accounts. Second, if our theory that twin deficits take

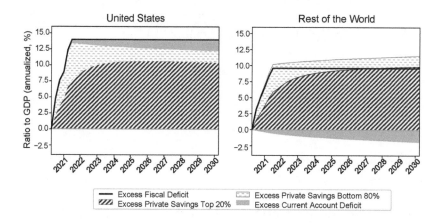

Fig. 14. Excess savings and their distribution: United States versus the rest of the world. GDP = gross domestic product. A color version of this figure is available online.

place in slow motion is correct, then fiscal deficits should in fact have limited explanatory power for current accounts over short horizons.

VII. Conclusion

We show that a multicountry HANK open-economy model is consistent with the initial phases of excess savings and twin deficits that followed the COVID epidemic worldwide. Our model suggests that excess savings are here to last, but that they will be held increasingly by the world's rich, with twin deficits continuing to pool them across countries. Figure 14, which shows the empirical dynamics of asset ownership predicted by our model going forward, illustrates this conclusion.

Appendix A

A1. World Demand

In each country, imports are given by equation (6). Therefore, the total demand received by country l, summing all countries k, is

$$\left(C_{Ht}^{*}\right)^{l} = \omega^{l} \cdot \left(\sum_{k=1}^{K}\alpha^{k}\left(\frac{P_{lt}^{k}}{P_{Wt}^{k}}\right)^{-\gamma}\left(\frac{P_{Wt}^{k}}{P_{t}^{k}}\right)^{-\eta}C_{t}^{k}\right). \tag{A1}$$

Using the law of one price $P_{lt}^{k} = (\mathcal{E}_{t}^{k}/\mathcal{E}_{t}^{l})P_{Ht}^{l}$, which for country k reads $P_{Wt}^{k} = \mathcal{E}_{t}^{k}$ (see eq. [11]), and the definition of the real exchange rate (eq. [12]), which for country k reads $Q_{t}^{k} = \mathcal{E}_{t}^{k}/P_{t}^{k}$, we have

$$\left(C_{Ht}^*\right)^l = \omega^l \cdot \sum_{k=1}^{K} \alpha^k \left(\frac{P_{Ht}^l}{\mathcal{E}_t^l}\right)^{-\gamma} \left(\frac{\mathcal{E}_t^k}{P_t^k}\right)^{-\eta} C_t^k$$

$$= \omega^l \cdot \left(\frac{P_{Ht}^l}{\mathcal{E}_t^l}\right)^{-\gamma} \sum_{k=1}^{K} \alpha^k (Q_t^k)^{-\eta} C_t^k$$

$$= \omega^l \cdot \left(\frac{P_{Ht}^l}{P_{Wt}^l}\right)^{-\gamma} C_t^*$$

where we have defined world import demand as $C_t^* \equiv \Sigma_{k=1}^{K} \alpha^k (Q_t^k)^{-\eta} C_t^k$. This gives equations (20) and (21).

A2. Deriving the Current-Account Equation

Start from the aggregate budget constraint (eq. [37]) and use the market clearing condition (eq. [27]) at t and $t-1$ to find

$$C_t + B_t + \text{nfa}_t = (1 + r_{t-1})A_{t-1} + Z_t$$

$$= (1 + r_{t-1})B_{t-1} + (1 + r_{t-1})\text{nfa}_{t-1} + \dot{Z}_t$$

Use the government budget constraint (eq. [14]) to obtain

$$C_t + \frac{P_{Ht}}{P_t} G_t + \text{nfa}_t = (1 + r_{t-1})\text{nfa}_{t-1} + Z_t + \frac{P_{Ht}}{P_t} T_t.$$

Using the definition of posttax income (eq. [16]), we obtain

$$C_t + \frac{P_{Ht}}{P_t} G_t + \text{nfa}_t = (1 + r_{t-1})\text{nfa}_{t-1} + \frac{P_{Ht}}{P_t} Y_t.$$

Let the trade deficit be defined as in equation (28). The NFA position evolves as

$$\text{nfa}_t = (1 + r_{t-1})\text{nfa}_{t-1} - \text{TD}_t.$$

In a model with valuation effects on the NFA, there would be an additional term $(r_t^p - r_{t-1})A_{t-1}$ on the right-hand side of this expression. We obtain the relationship between the current account and the trade deficit:

$$CA_t \equiv \text{nfa}_t - \text{nfa}_{t-1} = r_{t-1}\text{nfa}_{t-1} - \text{TD}_t,$$

which is equation (29). Observe, moreover, that

$$\text{TD}_t = \frac{P_{Ht}}{P_t} C_{Ht} + \frac{P_{Wt}}{P_t} C_{Wt} - \frac{P_{Ht}}{P_t} \left(C_{Ht} + C_{Ht}^*\right)$$

$$= \frac{P_{Wt}}{P_t} C_{Wt} - \frac{P_{Ht}}{P_t} C_{Ht}^* \tag{A2}$$

that is, it is the difference between the value of imports $(P_{Wt}/P_t)C_{Wt}$ and exports $(P_{Ht}/P_t)C^*_{Ht}$.

A3.   Walras's Law for the World

In this appendix, we show that the world export market clearing condition (eq. [30]) is equivalent to a world goods market condition and a world asset market clearing condition. Start from country-level goods market clearing

$$Y_t^k - G_t^k = (1 - \alpha^k)\left(\frac{P_{Ht}^k}{P_t^k}\right)^{-\eta} C_t^k + \omega^k \cdot \left(\frac{P_{Ht}^k}{\mathcal{E}_t^k}\right)^{-\gamma} C_t^*,$$

multiply by $P_{Ht}^k/\mathcal{E}_t^k$, and sum,

$$\sum_k \frac{P_{Ht}^k}{\mathcal{E}_t^k}(Y_t^k - G_t^k) = \sum_k (1-\alpha^k)\frac{P_{Ht}^k}{\mathcal{E}_t^k}\left(\frac{P_{Ht}^k}{P_t^k}\right)^{-\eta} C_t^k + \sum_k \left(\omega^k \cdot \left(\frac{P_{Ht}^k}{\mathcal{E}_t^k}\right)^{1-\gamma}\right)C_t^*;$$

using the price-consistency condition (eq. [31]) and export market clearing (eq. [30]), we find

$$\begin{aligned}\sum_k \frac{P_{Ht}^k}{\mathcal{E}_t^k}(Y_t^k - G_t^k) &= \sum_k \left\{(1-\alpha^k)\frac{P_{Ht}^k}{\mathcal{E}_t^k}\left(\frac{P_{Ht}^k}{P_t^k}\right)^{-\eta} + \alpha^k(Q_t^k)^{-\eta}\right\}C_t^k \\ &= \sum_k \left\{(1-\alpha^k)\frac{P_{Ht}^k}{\mathcal{E}_t^k}\frac{\mathcal{E}_t^k}{P_t^k}\left(\frac{P_{Ht}^k}{P_t^k}\right)^{-\eta} + \alpha^k(Q_t^k)^{1-\eta}\right\}\frac{C_t^k}{Q_t^k} \\ &= \sum_k \left\{(1-\alpha^k)\left(\frac{P_{Ht}^k}{P_t^k}\right)^{1-\eta} + \alpha^k(Q_t^k)^{1-\eta}\right\}\frac{C_t^k}{Q_t^k} \\ &= \sum_k \frac{C_t^k}{Q_t^k}\end{aligned}$$

where the last line follows from the definition of the price index P_t^k in each country. We therefore obtain world goods market clearing (eq. [34]).

From the current account identity in each country, we have

$$\text{nfa}_t^k = (1 + r_{t-1}^k)\text{nfa}_{t-1}^k + \frac{P_{Ht}^k}{P_t^k}(Y_t^k - G_t^k) - C_t^k,$$

so

$$\frac{1}{Q_t^k}\text{nfa}_t^k = (1+r_{t-1}^k)\frac{1}{Q_t^k}\text{nfa}_{t-1}^k + \frac{P_{Ht}^k}{\mathcal{E}_t^k}(Y_t^k - G_t^k) - \frac{P_t^k C_t^k}{\mathcal{E}_t^k}.$$

But from the UIP condition in country k, we have $(1 + r_{t-1}^k)/Q_t^k = (1 + i_{t-1}^*)/Q_{t-1}^k$, where i_t^* is the star interest rate, which is common across countries. Hence, NFAs in units of the common world good satisfy

$$\frac{\text{nfa}_t^k}{Q_t^k} = \left(1 + i_{t-1}^*\right) \frac{\text{nfa}_{t-1}^k}{Q_{t-1}^k} + \frac{P_{Ht}^k}{\mathcal{E}_t^k}\left(Y_t^k - G_t^k\right) - \frac{P_t^k C_t^k}{\mathcal{E}_t^k}. \tag{A3}$$

Given world goods market clearing condition (eq. [34]), and initial asset market clearing $\Sigma \text{nfa}_{-1}^k/Q_{-1}^k = 0$, we therefore have at each date

$$\sum_k \frac{\text{nfa}_t^k}{Q_t^k} = 0,$$

or equivalently, given $\text{nfa}_t^k = A_t^k - B_t^k$, world asset market clearing

$$\sum_k \frac{A_t^k}{Q_t^k} = \sum_k \frac{B_t^k}{Q_t^k}. \tag{A4}$$

A4. $\alpha \to 1$ Limit

In the $\alpha \to 1$ limit, the economy is perfectly open. We have the following relations:

$$P_t = P_{Ft} = \mathcal{E}_t$$

$$Q_t = \frac{\mathcal{E}_t}{P_t} = 1$$

$$C_{Ft} = C_t$$

$$C_{Ht} = 0$$

$$r_t = r_t^*$$

Monetary policy has no control over the real interest rate or the real exchange rate. The Fisher equation is also the UIP equation,

$$1 + i_t = \left(1 + r_t^*\right) \frac{\mathcal{E}_{t+1}}{\mathcal{E}_t},$$

so the central bank can set the nominal interest rate, which affects the nominal exchange rate through the standard overshooting mechanism, and therefore the price index (residents only buy foreign goods, but the country is still producing goods for the rest of the world).

Real after-tax income is now

$$Z_t = \frac{P_{Ht}}{P_t}\left(Y_t - T_t\right) = \frac{P_{Ht}}{\mathcal{E}_t}\left(Y_t - T_t\right).$$

The goods market clearing condition now reads

$$Y_t = \left(\frac{P_{Ht}}{\mathcal{E}_t}\right)^{-\gamma} C^* + G_t$$

so real income is

$$Z_t = \left(\frac{P_{Ht}}{\mathcal{E}_t}\right)^{1-\gamma} C^* + \frac{P_{Ht}}{\mathcal{E}_t}(G_t - T_t).$$

In other words, it is the sum of export income (a constant when $\gamma = 1$), plus any real value of the primary deficit.

The government budget constraint is

$$B_t = (1 + r_{t-1})B_{t-1} + \frac{P_{Ht}}{\mathcal{E}_t}(G_t - T_t).$$

Substituting into real income, we obtain

$$Z_t = \left(\frac{P_{Ht}}{\mathcal{E}_t}\right)^{1-\gamma} C^* + PD_t.$$

Domestic price inflation is

$$\pi_{Ht} = \kappa_w \left(\frac{v'(Y_t/\Theta)Y_t}{\frac{\epsilon_w}{\epsilon_w - 1}(1 - \lambda)\Theta Z_t u'(C_t(\{r, Z_s\}))} - 1 \right) + \beta \pi_{Ht+1},$$

and NFA dynamics are

$$\mathrm{nfa}_t - \mathrm{nfa}_{t-1} = r_{t-1}\mathrm{nfa}_{t-1} + \underbrace{\frac{P_{Ht}}{\mathcal{E}_t}(Y_t - G_t) - C_t}_{NX_t}.$$

$$= r_{t-1}\mathrm{nfa}_{t-1} + \left(\frac{P_{Ht}}{\mathcal{E}_t}\right)^{1-\gamma} C^* - C_{Ft}(\{r, Z_s\})$$

We consider a monetary policy that targets a constant path for the terms of trade, $P_{Ht}/\mathcal{E}_t = 1$. These equations show that this corresponds to the $\alpha \to 1$ limit of the economy with home bias where monetary policy sets a constant Q.

A5. Details on the US Calibration

Table A1 plots moments of the distribution of wealth in the model versus the data.

Table A1
Wealth Distribution: Data versus Model

% of Total Wealth Held	Top 50%	Top 20%	Top 10%	Top 5%	Top 1%	Gini Coefficient
Data (SCF 2019)	98.5	87.4	76.5	64.9	37.2	.85
Model (US)	99.2	84.0	63.2	42.8	13.7	.79

Note: SCF = Survey of Consumer Finances.

Appendix B

B1.   Proof of Proposition 1

Proof. Start from the steady-state version of equation (16),

$$Z = \frac{P_H}{P}(Y - T).$$

We also have the long-run government budget constraint (eq. [14]), which at $r = 0$ just reads

$$G = T.$$

Moreover, from the steady-state budget constraint (eq. [37]) at $r = 0$, we know that we have $C = Z$. Combining the three previous equations, we find that

$$C = Z = \frac{P_H}{P}(Y - G). \tag{B1}$$

From steady-state goods market clearing (eq. [26]), we find

$$Y - G = (1 - \alpha)\left(\frac{P_H}{P}\right)^{-\eta} C + \omega\left(\frac{P_H}{\mathcal{E}}\right)^{-\gamma} C^* \tag{B2}$$

where the two relative prices that enter are simple functions of the real exchange rate Q,

$$\frac{P_H}{P} = p_H(Q) \qquad \frac{P_H}{\mathcal{E}} = p_H^*(Q). \tag{B3}$$

Multiplying equation (B2) by P_H/P, and combining with equation (B1), we obtain

$$C = \frac{\omega p_H(Q)\left(p_H^*(Q)\right)^{-\gamma} C^*}{1 - (1 - \alpha)(p_H(Q))^{1-\eta}}. \tag{B4}$$

We can also rewrite equation (B1) as

$$Y = \frac{G + C}{p_H(Q)}. \tag{B5}$$

Finally, from equation (9), and noting that the natural allocation requires $\pi_w = 0$, we get after plugging in production $N = Y/\Theta$ and $C = Z$, the equation

$$\frac{Y}{\Theta} v'\left(\frac{Y}{\Theta}\right) = \frac{\epsilon_w}{\epsilon_w - 1}(1 - \lambda)Cu'(C). \tag{B6}$$

Equations (B4), (B5), and (B6) determine long-run C, Y, and Q. If long-run G is unchanged from the initial steady state, then these equations tell us that long-run (C, Y, Q) also are. Then, equation (B1) implies that Z is also unchanged, so equation (27) shows that $A(r, Z)$ is unchanged. It follows that $\Delta B + \Delta \text{nfa} = 0$.

In the case where G changes, we have, log-differentiating equations (B4)–(B6),

$$\hat{C} = \frac{\chi - \alpha}{1 - \alpha}\hat{Q}$$

$$\hat{Y} = \frac{G}{Y}\hat{G} + \left(1 - \frac{G}{Y}\right)\left(\hat{C} + \frac{\alpha}{1 - \alpha}\hat{Q}\right).$$

$$(1 + \phi)\hat{Y} = (1 - \sigma)\hat{C}$$

Solving these equations, we obtain

$$\hat{C} = -\frac{\frac{G}{Y}}{\frac{\sigma-1}{1+\phi} + \left(1 - \frac{G}{Y}\right)\left(\frac{\chi+\alpha-1}{\chi-1}\right)}\hat{G}$$

$$\hat{Y} = \frac{\frac{\sigma-1}{1+\phi}\frac{G}{Y}}{\frac{\sigma-1}{1+\phi} + \left(1 - \frac{G}{Y}\right)\left(\frac{\chi+\alpha-1}{\chi-1}\right)}\hat{G}$$

$$\hat{Q} = -\frac{\frac{1-\alpha}{\chi-1}\frac{G}{Y}}{\frac{\sigma-1}{1+\phi} + \left(1 - \frac{G}{Y}\right)\left(\frac{\chi+\alpha-1}{\chi-1}\right)}\hat{G}$$

$$= -\frac{1 - \alpha}{\chi - 1}\frac{1}{\frac{\sigma-1}{1+\phi} + \left(1 - \frac{G}{Y}\right)\left(\frac{\chi+\alpha-1}{\chi-1}\right)}\frac{dG}{Y}$$

From market clearing, we further have

$$dB + dnfa = a(r)dZ = a(r)dC = A\frac{dC}{C}$$

$$= -A \cdot \frac{\frac{G}{Y}}{\frac{g-1}{1+\phi} + \left(1 - \frac{G}{Y}\right)\left(\frac{x+\alpha-1}{x-1}\right)} \hat{G}$$

$$= -A \cdot \frac{1}{\frac{g-1}{1+\phi} + \left(1 - \frac{G}{Y}\right)\left(\frac{x+\alpha-1}{x-1}\right)} \frac{dG}{Y}$$

This implies

$$\frac{-dnfa}{dB} = 1 + \frac{A}{Y} \frac{1}{\frac{g-1}{1+\phi} + \left(1 - \frac{G}{Y}\right)\left(\frac{x+\alpha-1}{x-1}\right)} \frac{dG}{dB},$$

which delivers the LRPT formula in the case where $dG \neq 0$.

B2. Proof of Proposition 3

Here, we consider the general case where $r \neq 0$ and any monetary policy. We then specialize our results to the case of constant-r monetary policy and $r = 0$.

Preliminaries. Start from the definition of the consumer price index,

$$P_t = \left[(1 - \alpha)(P_{Ht})^{1-\eta} + \alpha(P_{Wt})^{1-\eta}\right]^{\frac{1}{1-\eta}}.$$

Use equations (11) and (12) to find

$$1 = \left[(1 - \alpha)\left(\frac{P_{Ht}}{P_t}\right)^{1-\eta} + \alpha(Q_t)^{1-\eta}\right]^{\frac{1}{1-\eta}}.$$

Differentiating around a steady state with $P_H/P = Q = 1$, we find

$$d\left(\frac{P_{Ht}}{P_t}\right) = -\frac{\alpha}{1 - \alpha}dQ_t. \qquad (B7)$$

From equations (11) and (12), we also have

$$\frac{P_{Ht}}{P_{Wt}} = \frac{P_{Ht}}{\mathcal{E}_t} = \frac{P_{Ht}/P_t}{Q_t},$$

so we also have

$$d\left(\frac{P_{Ht}}{P_{Wt}}\right) = \frac{-1}{1-\alpha} dQ_t. \tag{B8}$$

Next, define the primary deficit as

$$PD_t \equiv \frac{P_{Ht}}{P_t}(G_t - T_t) \tag{B9}$$

and note that, from the government budget constraint (eq. [14]), we have

$$PD_t = B_t - (1 + r_{t-1})B_{t-1}. \tag{B10}$$

Combining the definition of real income (eq. [16]) with equation (B9), we can write real income as

$$Z_t \equiv \frac{P_{Ht}}{P_t}(Y_t - G_t) + PD_t. \tag{B11}$$

Finally, we have the following lemma.

Lemma 1.   We have that

$$\frac{\partial C_t}{\partial r_s}(\{Z, r\}) = Z\frac{\partial C_t}{\partial r_s}(\{1, r\}) = ZM_{t,s}^r$$

where $M_{t,s}^r \equiv \partial C_t/\partial r_s(\{1, r\})$ is defined as the response of spending to interest rates when steady-state posttax income is 1, and also

$$\frac{\partial C_t}{\partial Z_s}(\{Z, r\}) = \frac{\partial C_t}{\partial Z_s}(\{1, r\}) = M_{t,s}$$

where $M_{t,s} \equiv \partial C_t/\partial Z_s(\{1, r\})$ is defined as the response of spending to income when steady-state posttax income is 1.

Proof. Follows from the homotheticity of the consumption function $C_t(\{Z_s, r_s\})$ in Z, in the sense that, for any $\lambda \geq 0$, we have

$$C_t(\{\lambda Z_s, r_s\}) = \lambda C_t(\{Z_s, r_s\}). \tag{B12}$$

This equation, in turn, follows from standard homotheticity arguments.

International fiscal Keynesian cross. Differentiate equation (B11) around the steady state with $P_H/P = 1$, $Y - G = C$, and $PD = -rB$ (the primary balance is a surplus large enough to pay for the interest on the debt), to find

$$dZ = d\left(\frac{P_H}{P}Y\right) - d\left(\frac{P_H}{P}G\right) + dPD$$

$$= Cd\left(\frac{P_H}{P}\right) + dY - dG + dPD \qquad (B13)$$

$$= -\frac{\alpha}{1-\alpha}CdQ + dY - dG + dPD$$

Next, differentiate the aggregate consumption function $C_t(\{r_s^p, Z_s\})$, using the fact that $r_s^p = r_s$ everywhere from equation (23), together with Lemma 1, to find

$$dC = ZM'dr + MdZ. \qquad (B14)$$

Substituting equations (5), (20), and (11) into the goods market clearing condition (eq. [26]), we obtain

$$Y_t = (1 - \alpha)\left(\frac{P_{Ht}}{P_t}\right)^{-\eta}C_t + \omega\left(\frac{P_{Ht}}{P_{Wt}}\right)^{-\gamma}C_t^* + G_t.$$

Differentiating this equation around the steady state where $\alpha C = \omega C^*$, and using equations (B7)–(B8) give

$$dY_t = \left(\alpha C\eta + \omega C^* \cdot \frac{\gamma}{1-\alpha}\right)dQ_t + (1-\alpha)dC_t + \omega dC_t^* + G_t$$

$$= \alpha\left(\eta + \frac{\gamma}{1-\alpha}\right)CdQ_t + (1-\alpha)dC_t + \omega dC_t^* + G_t$$

hence, denoting $dY = (dY_0, dY_1, ...)$, we have

$$dY = \frac{\alpha}{1-\alpha}\left(\underbrace{(1-\alpha)\eta + \gamma}_{\chi}\right)CdQ + (1-\alpha)dC + \omega dC^* + dG \quad (B15)$$

where χ is the trade elasticity, also known as the Marshall-Lerner elasticity (Auclert et al. 2021c).

Collecting equations, we have

$$dC = ZM'dr - \frac{\alpha}{1-\alpha}CMdQ + M(dY - dG + dPD)$$

$$dY = \frac{\alpha}{1-\alpha}\chi CdQ + (1-\alpha)dC + \omega dC^* + dG$$

(B16)

we can combine to obtain the general equation

$$dY = \left(\underbrace{\frac{\alpha}{1-\alpha}\chi}_{\text{exp. switching}} - \underbrace{\alpha\,M}_{\text{real income}}\right)CdQ + \underbrace{(1-\alpha)ZM'dr}_{\text{intertemp. substitution}}$$

$$+ \underbrace{(I - (1-\alpha)M)dG + (1-\alpha)MdPD}_{\text{fiscal impulse}} + \underbrace{\omega\,dC^*}_{\text{export demand impulse}} \cdot \quad \text{(B17)}$$

$$+ \underbrace{(1-\alpha)MdY}_{\text{multiplier}}$$

Moreover, the real exchange rate is related to i^* via the UIP condition

$$dQ = -\frac{U}{1+r}(dr - di^*),$$

where U is a matrix with 1's on and above the diagonal. Finally, combining equation (A2) with equations (6) and (20), we obtain

$$TD_t = \frac{P_{Wt}}{P_t}C_{Wt} - \frac{P_{Ht}}{P_t}C^*_{Ht} = \alpha(Q_t)^{1-\eta}C_t - \omega(Q_t)\left(\frac{P_{Ht}}{P_{Wt}}\right)^{1-\gamma}C^*_t.$$

Linearizing, and using equation (B8), we find

$$dTD_t = \alpha C(1-\eta)dQ_t + \alpha dC_t - \omega C^*\left(dQ_t - \frac{(1-\gamma)}{1-\alpha}dQ_t\right) - \omega dC^*_t$$

$$= \alpha C\left(1 - \eta - 1 + \frac{1-\gamma}{1-\alpha}\right)dQ_t + \alpha dC_t - \omega dC^*_t$$

$$= \frac{\alpha}{1-\alpha}C\left(1 - \underbrace{\eta(1-\alpha) + \gamma}_{\chi}\right)dQ_t + \alpha dC_t - \omega dC^*_t$$

,

hence

$$dTD = \frac{-\alpha}{1-\alpha}C(\chi - 1)dQ + \alpha dC - \omega dC^*. \quad \text{(B18)}$$

Other things equal, a depreciation worsens the trade deficit if $\chi > 1$. More local demand $d\mathbf{C}$ also worsens the trade deficit because it increases imports. An exogenous increase in foreign demand $d\mathbf{C}^*$ raises exports and lowers the trade deficit.

Constant-r monetary policy. In the case of a small open economy, with $d\mathbf{i}^* = d\mathbf{C}^* = 0$ and constant-r monetary policy, we have $d\mathbf{r} = d\mathbf{Q} = 0$. Then equation (B17) specializes to

$$d\mathbf{Y} = (I - (1 - \alpha)\mathbf{M})d\mathbf{G} + (1 - \alpha)\mathbf{M}d\mathbf{PD} + (1 - \alpha)\mathbf{M}d\mathbf{Y}. \qquad \text{(B19)}$$

Solving this delivers

$$d\mathbf{Y} = d\mathbf{G} + (1 - \alpha)(I - (1 - \alpha)\mathbf{M})^{-1}\mathbf{M}d\mathbf{PD}. \qquad \text{(B20)}$$

Using this solution into equation (B16) gives

$$\begin{aligned} d\mathbf{C} &= \mathbf{M}(d\mathbf{Y} - d\mathbf{G} + d\mathbf{PD}) \\ &= \mathbf{M}(I - (1 - \alpha)\mathbf{M})^{-1}((1 - \alpha)\mathbf{M} + I - (1 - \alpha)\mathbf{M})d\mathbf{PD} \\ &= \mathbf{M}(I - (1 - \alpha)\mathbf{M})^{-1}d\mathbf{PD} \end{aligned}$$

and using this into (B18) gives the general twin-deficit equation relating the primary deficit to the trade deficit:

$$d\mathbf{TD} = -\alpha\mathbf{M}(I - (1 - \alpha)\mathbf{M})^{-1}d\mathbf{PD}.$$

Special case with $r = 0$. Around $r = \text{nfa} = 0$, we have from equation (29) that

$$d\mathbf{CA} = -d\mathbf{TD}.$$

Moreover, differentiating equation (B10) we find $dPD_t = dB_t - dB_{t-1} - Bdr_{t-1} = d\text{FD}_t - Bdr_{t-1}$. In turn, with $dr = 0$ we obtain

$$d\mathbf{PD} = d\mathbf{FD}.$$

Plugging this into equation (B19) gives equation (44), hence in this case, the twin-deficit equation can also be written as a relationship between the current-account deficit $-d\mathbf{CA}$ and the fiscal deficit $d\mathbf{FD}$,

$$-d\mathbf{CA} = -\alpha\mathbf{M}(I - (1 - \alpha)\mathbf{M})^{-1}d\mathbf{FD},$$

which is equation (45).

B3.   No-Anticipation Model

Here we describe the no-anticipation model. The **M** matrix is given by

$$\mathbf{M}^{na} = \begin{pmatrix} M_{00} & 0 & 0 & \\ M_{01} & M_{00} & 0 & \\ M_{02} & M_{01} & M_{00} & \\ \vdots & \vdots & \vdots & \ddots \end{pmatrix}. \qquad (B21)$$

Figure B1 shows the iMPCs in this case. This would be the outcome, for instance, of adding sticky expectations to our baseline model as in Auclert, Rognlie, and Straub (2020), if expectations were perfectly sticky.

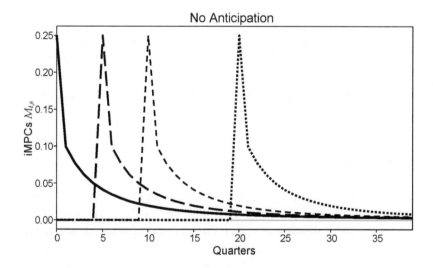

Fig. B1.   Intertemporal marginal propensities to consume in the no-anticipation model. A color version of this figure is available online.

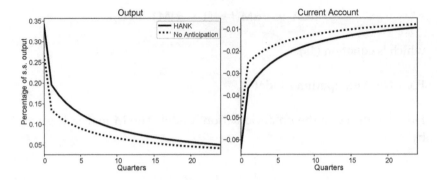

Fig. B2. Impulse response to a transfer: main HANK model versus model with $\mathbf{M}^{na}$. S.S. = steady state. A color version of this figure is available online.

Applying equations (44)–(45) to this model, we find

$$dY_0 = \frac{(1-\alpha)\cdot \mathrm{mpc}}{1-(1-\alpha)\mathrm{mpc}}dB$$

$$dCA_0 = -\frac{\alpha \cdot \mathrm{mpc}}{1-(1-\alpha)\mathrm{mpc}}dB$$

Now we see the exact effect of income adjustment on both GDP and the current account. Figure B2 provides the general-equilibrium simulation. We see that the no-anticipation model has slightly lower output and current response throughout, but the time paths are otherwise similar.

B4. Case with $r \neq 0$

Here, we revisit Propositions 1–3 in the case with $r \neq 0$. The steady-state result is similar, but the LRPT is no longer exactly 1. With $r > 0$, the LRPT is typically above 1, as a government debt expansion leads to a reduction in posttax income and therefore asset demand. The dynamic equations, however, are the same, provided that, in Propositions 2 and 3, we replace $-d\mathbf{CA}$ with the trade deficit $d\mathbf{TD}$, and $d\mathbf{FD}$ with the primary deficit $d\mathbf{PD}$.

Long-run pass-through. We mirror the proof of Proposition 1, high-lighting the places where $r \neq 0$ makes a difference. Start from

$$a(r)Z = \text{nfa} + B$$

and use the fact that the budget constraint implies $C = rA + Z$, so $Z = C - rA$. Hence, we get

$$a(r)(C - r(\text{nfa} + B)) = \text{nfa} + B,$$

so

$$A = \frac{a(r)}{1 + ra(r)}C = \text{nfa} + B.$$

The long-run government budget constraint (eq. [14]) is now

$$\frac{P_H}{P}(T - G) = rB.$$

The steady-state budget constraint (eq. [37]) now implies

$$C = rA + Z$$

$$= rA + \frac{P_H}{P}(Y - T) \qquad , \tag{B22}$$

$$= r\text{nfa} + p_H(Q)(Y - G)$$

where we have substituted in the government budget constraint, asset market clearing $A = B + \text{nfa}$, and the relation $p_H(Q)$ between the relative price P_H/P and the real exchange rate Q. Multiplying the goods market clearing condition (eq. [B2]) by P_H/P, and combining, we now have

$$C = \frac{r\text{nfa} + \alpha p_H(Q)\left(p_H^*(Q)\right)^{-\gamma}C^*}{1 - (1 - \alpha)(p_H(Q))^{1-\eta}}, \tag{B23}$$

which replaces equation (B4). We can also write (B22) as

$$Y = G + \frac{(C - r\text{nfa})}{p_H(Q)}, \tag{B24}$$

which replaces equation (B5). Finally equation (9) at $\pi_w = 0$, replacing $Z = C/1 + ra(r)$,

$$\frac{Y}{\Theta}v'\left(\frac{Y}{Y}\right) = \frac{\epsilon_w}{\epsilon_w - 1}(1 - \lambda)\frac{C}{1 + ra(r)}u'(C), \tag{B25}$$

which replaces equation (B6). Differentiating starting from $\text{nfa} = 0$, we get

$$\hat{C} = \frac{r}{\alpha}\, dnfa + \frac{\chi - 1}{1 - \alpha}\hat{Q}$$

$$\hat{Y} = \frac{G}{Y}\hat{G} + \left(1 - \frac{G}{Y}\right)\left(\hat{C} - r\, dnfa + \frac{\alpha}{1 - \alpha}\hat{Q}\right),$$

$$\hat{Y} = \frac{1 - \sigma}{1 + \phi}\hat{C}$$

$$dB + dnfa = A \cdot \hat{C}$$

which gives us a system of four equations in four unknowns ($\hat{C}$, $\hat{Q}$, $\hat{Y}$, dnfa) as a function of dB, dG. The solution is given by

$$dnfa\left(\frac{rA\left(1 - \frac{G}{Y}\right)\left(1 + \frac{1}{\chi-1}\right)}{\frac{\sigma-1}{1+\phi} + \left(1 - \frac{G}{Y}\right)\left(1 + \frac{\alpha}{\chi-1}\right)} - 1\right)$$
$$= dB + \frac{A}{\frac{\sigma-1}{1+\phi} + \left(1 - \frac{G}{Y}\right)\left(1 + \frac{\alpha}{\chi-1}\right)}\frac{dG}{Y}$$

which gives, in the case of $dG = 0$,

$$\mathrm{LRPT} = \frac{dnfa}{dB} = \frac{1}{1 - \frac{rA\left(1-\frac{G}{Y}\right)\left(1+\frac{1}{\chi-1}\right)}{\frac{\sigma-1}{1+\phi}+\left(1-\frac{G}{Y}\right)\left(1+\frac{\alpha}{\chi-1}\right)}},$$

which is, in general, greater than 1.

Dynamics. Section B2 covered the proof in the general case with $r \neq 0$. To summarize, Proposition 3 holds provided that we replace the fiscal deficit dFD by the primary deficit dPD and the current-account deficit $-d$CA by the trade deficit dTD.

B5.   Lump-Sum Transfers

So far, we have studied debt-financed transfer increases that occur through the regular tax schedule and therefore benefit the rich more in absolute terms. This allows for simple analytics, but many transfer programs (such as stimulus checks) are distributed more progressively. We now study this type of case, extending Proposition 3. The dynamics of output, private saving, and the current account after these alternative distributions of transfers are determined by

$$dY = (1 - \alpha)\left(\sum_{k \geq 0}(1 - \alpha)^k \mathbf{M}^k\right)\widetilde{\mathbf{M}}d\mathbf{FD} \qquad (B26)$$

$$d\mathbf{CA} = -\alpha\left(\sum_{k \geq 0}(1 - \alpha)^k \mathbf{M}^k\right)\widetilde{\mathbf{M}}d\mathbf{FD}, \qquad (B27)$$

$$d\mathbf{PS} = \left(\sum_{k \geq 0}(1 - \alpha)^k \mathbf{M}^k\right)\left(I - \widetilde{\mathbf{M}}\right)d\mathbf{FD} \qquad (B28)$$

where $\widetilde{M}_{t,s} = \partial C_t / \partial Tr_s$ is now the consumption response to transfers Tr_s, which can have a different incidence than after-tax income. For instance, in the case of lump-sum transfers, $\widetilde{\mathbf{M}}$ corresponds to an equal-weighted rather than income-weighted average MPC. These equations show that the MPCs that matter for the effect of the policy, $\widetilde{\mathbf{M}}e_0$, are different from those that matter in aggregate for the dynamic propagation of shocks, which are still given by $\mathbf{M}$.

Figure B3 shows that, compared with proportional transfers, lump-sum transfers have a larger output effect because they benefit higher-MPC households, on average. However, the current-account and savings dynamics are very similar. In other words, although the exact distribution of transfers is critical to understanding which agent is affected and how much of an immediate effect on output we obtain (with better-targeted transfers boosting output by more), the aggregate dynamics of domestic and foreign wealth accumulation conditional on a given path of government debt are governed by the same general forces, irrespective of how the transfers are distributed.

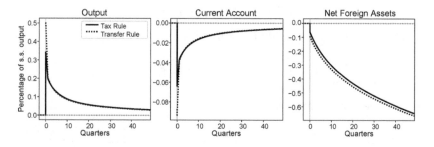

Fig. B3. Impulse response to a transfer under alternative transfer-distribution rules. S.S. = steady state. A color version of this figure is available online.

B6.   TANK Model

In the TANK model, a fraction $1 - \mu$ behaves like infinitely lived unconstrained agents (u) and fraction μ behaves like hand-to-mouth constrained agents. The Euler equation and budget constraint for the unconstrained households are, respectively:

$$C_{u,t}^{-\sigma} = \beta(1 + r_{t+1}^p)C_{u,t+1}^{-\sigma}$$
$$A_{u,t} = (1 + r_t^p)A_{u,t-1} + Z_t - C_{u,t}$$

and constrained households just consume their income,

$$C_{c,t} = Z_t.$$

Aggregation implies

$$C_t = \mu Z_t + (1 - \mu)C_{u,t}$$
$$A_t = \mu \times 0 + (1 - \mu)A_{u,t}$$

In steady state, $C_t = C$, $Z_t = Z$, and $C_{u,t} = C_u$, implying $\beta(1 + r^p) = 1$. With $r = 0$, we have

$$C_{u,t} = \overline{C}_u = C_u^{ss}$$
$$A_{u,t} = A_{u,t-1} + Z_t - C_u^{ss} \tag{B29}$$

because $Z_t = Y_t - T_t$ where $T_t = B_{t-1} - B_t + G_t$. As a result, we have

$$C_t = \mu Z_t + (1 - \mu)C_u^{ss}$$
$$= \mu(Y_t - T_t) + (1 - \mu)C_u^{ss} \tag{B30}$$

At constant r, we have $Q = 1$. Goods market clearing

$$\omega C^* + (1 - \alpha)C_t = Y_t - G_t$$

combined with equation (B30) implies

$$\frac{1}{1 - \alpha}(Y_t - G_t - C^*C^*) = \mu(Y_t - T_t) + (1 - \mu)C_u^{ss};$$

solving out, we obtain

$$Y_t = \frac{1 - \alpha}{1 - \mu(1 - \alpha)}\left((1 - \mu)C_u^{ss} + \frac{\omega}{1 - \alpha}C^* + \frac{1}{1 - \alpha}G_t - \mu T_t\right).$$

We can write this in terms of the fiscal deficit $FD_t = G_t - T_t$ as $T_t = G_t - FD_t$, as

$$Y_t = \frac{(1-\alpha)(1-\mu)C_u^{ss} + \omega C^*}{1 - \mu(1-\alpha)} + G_t + \frac{\mu(1-\alpha)}{1 - \mu(1-\alpha)} FD_t,$$

which implies in particular

$$dY = dG + \frac{\mu(1-\alpha)}{1 - \mu(1-\alpha)} d\mathbf{FD} \tag{B31}$$

as claimed in the text. Moreover, we have

$$
\begin{aligned}
Z_t &= Y_t - T_t \\
&= \frac{(1-\alpha)(1-\mu)C_u^{ss} + \omega C^*}{1 - \mu(1-\alpha)} + \left(1 + \frac{\mu(1-\alpha)}{1 - \mu(1-\alpha)}\right) FD_t \\
&= \frac{(1-\alpha)(1-\mu)C_u^{ss} + \omega C^*}{1 - \mu(1-\alpha)} + \frac{1}{1 - \mu(1-\alpha)} FD_t
\end{aligned}
$$

Substitute in asset dynamics equation (B29) to get

$$
\begin{aligned}
A_t - A_{t-1} &= (1-\mu)(A_{u,t} - A_{u,t-1}) \\
&= (1-\mu)(Z_t - C_u^{ss}) \\
&= \frac{1-\mu}{1 - \mu(1-\alpha)} FD_t
\end{aligned}
$$

This implies that the current account is

$$
\begin{aligned}
CA_t = nfa_t - nfa_{t-1} = A_t - A_{t-1} - FD_t &= \left(\frac{1-\mu}{1 - \mu + \alpha\mu} - 1\right) \\
&= \frac{-\mu\alpha}{1 - \mu(1-\alpha)} FD_t,
\end{aligned}
$$

implying in particular

$$-d\mathbf{CA} = \frac{\mu\alpha}{1 - \mu(1-\alpha)} d\mathbf{FD}. \tag{B32}$$

Equations (B31) and (B32) show that, for TANK, Proposition 3 applies with $M = \mu\mathbf{I}$.

To see what this implies for the steady state, integrate the asset equation. This shows

$$\Delta A = \frac{1 - \mu}{1 - \mu(1 - \alpha)} \Delta B \qquad \qquad (B33)$$

$$\Delta \mathrm{nfa} = \frac{-\mu\alpha}{1 - \mu(1 - \alpha)} \Delta B \qquad \qquad (B34)$$

where the Δ applies between any time t and the initial steady state, and in particular between the initial and the final steady state.

In particular, we have

$$\mathrm{LPRT} = -\frac{\Delta \mathrm{nfa}}{\Delta B} = \frac{\mu\alpha}{1 - \mu(1 - \alpha)}.$$

To draw figure 7, we calibrate μ to a certain $\mathrm{mpc}_0 = 0.25$ and $\alpha = 0.16$, as in our main model. The TANK model does not have another degree of freedom for MPCs.

B7. Blanchard Model

Here we consider a discrete-time version of the Blanchard (1985) model. This is one of the simplest models of non-Ricardian agents that can be consistent with the data on iMPCs.

The model is as follows. Agents have infinite planning horizons, discount the future at rate β, and have a constant probability of death each period. Specifically, their probability of surviving to period t is $\Phi_t = \phi^t$, where ϕ is the (constant) period survival probability. This setting implies that agents' expected lifetime is $1/(1 - \phi)$. Moreover, in a stationary distribution, the size of a cohort of age j is proportional to ϕ^j. Because $\Sigma_j \phi^j = 1/(1 - \phi)$, the share of agents of age j is $\pi_j = (1 - \phi)\phi^j$.

The model is set up such that there is no within-cohort heterogeneity: all agents aged j at time t (so from the same cohort $k = t - j$) receive the same income $z_{j,t}$. However, there is a lot of heterogeneity across cohorts.

Specifically, the problem of an agent born in cohort k, going through ages $j = t - k$ (where t denotes calendar time) is

$$\max \; \mathbb{E}_k \left[\sum_j \beta^j \phi^j \log(c_{jt}) \right] \qquad \qquad (B35)$$

$$\text{s.t.} \quad c_{j,t} + a_{j+1,t} = \frac{(1 + r_t)}{\phi} a_{j,t-1} + z_{j,t}$$

where $z_{j,t}$ is posttax income of an agent aged j at time t. Here, agents have access to annuities $a_{j,t-1}$ that pay a return $(1 + r_t)/\phi$ conditional on not dying, such that the assets of the dying are distributed equally among the remaining members of the cohort.

We consider the extension of the canonical Blanchard model in which age profiles decay with age at rate ς:

$$z_{j,t} \propto (1 - \varsigma)^j Z_t, \tag{B36}$$

where Z_t denotes aggregate income. This front-loaded income profile generates a life-cycle motive to save, which is essential to deliver positive asset accumulation in the steady state at $r = 0$ (the canonical Blanchard model then corresponds to $\varsigma = 0$).

Given log utility and the presence of annuities, individual consumption follows

$$c_{j,t} = (1 - \phi\beta)\left(\frac{(1 + r_t)}{\phi} a_{j,t-1} + h_{j,t}\right), \tag{B37}$$

where human capital is given by

$$h_{j,t} = z_{j,t} + \frac{\phi}{1 + r_{t+1}} h_{j+1,t+1}. \tag{B38}$$

This leads us the following proposition.

Proposition 5. Aggregate dynamics in the Blanchard model are given by the asset demand function $A_t = A_t(\{r_s, Z_s\})$ and the consumption function $C_t = C_t(\{r_s, Z_s\})$ that solve the system of three equations:

$$H_t = Z_t + (1 - \varsigma)\frac{\phi}{1 + r_{t+1}} H_{t+1} \tag{B39}$$

$$C_t = (1 - \phi\beta)((1 + r_t)A_{t-1} + H_t). \tag{B40}$$

$$C_t + A_t = (1 + r_t)A_{t-1} + Z_t \tag{B41}$$

Moreover, the long-run asset demand curve is given by

$$A = a(r)Z \quad \text{where} \quad a(r) = \frac{1}{1 - (1 + r)\beta\phi}\left(1 - \frac{(1 - \phi\beta)}{1 - (1 - \varsigma)\frac{\phi}{1+r}}\right).$$

Proposition 5, which follows from aggregation of equations (B38), (B37), and (B35), respectively, using the stationary distribution $\pi_j = (1 - \phi)\phi^j$, is the discrete-time counterpart of equations (19)–(21) in Blanchard (1985). We derive it as follows.

Since $Z_t = \Sigma_j \pi_j z_{j,t}$, if follows from equation (B36) that $z_{j,t} = (1 + \frac{\varsigma\phi}{1-\phi})(1 - \varsigma)^j Z_t$. Let $A_{t-1} \equiv \frac{1}{\phi}\Sigma_j\pi_j a_{jt-1}$ denote incoming aggregate assets, and $C_t \equiv \Sigma_j \pi_j c_{jt}$ denote aggregate consumption. Aggregating the budget constraints in equation (B35), and using the fact that newly-born agents have no assets, $a_{0,t} = 0$, we have

$$(1 + r_t)A_{t-1} + Z_t = C_t + \frac{1}{\phi}\left((1 - \phi)\cdot 0 + \sum_{j=1}^{\infty}(1 - \phi)\phi^{j+1}a_{j+1,t}\right).$$

$$= C_t + A_t$$

Aggregating the consumption policies in equation (B37) we have $C_t = (1 - \phi\beta)((1 + r)A_t + H_t)$, where we define aggregate human capital as $H_t \equiv \Sigma_j \pi_j h_{j,t}$. Finally, aggregating the dynamics of individual human capital in equation (B38), and noting that new each generation earns $(1 + \frac{\varsigma\phi}{1-\phi})$ times average income so has $(1 + \frac{\varsigma\phi}{1-\phi})$ times the average human capital, we get

$$H_t = Z_t + \frac{\phi}{1 + r_{t+1}}\sum_{j\geq 0}(1 - \phi)\phi^j h_{j+1,t+1}$$

$$= Z_t + \frac{1}{1 + r_{t+1}}(H_{t+1} - (1 - \phi)h_{0t+1})$$

$$= Z_t + \frac{1}{1 + r_{t+1}}\left(1 - (1 - \phi)\left(1 + \frac{\varsigma\phi}{1 - \phi}\right)\right)H_{t+1}$$

$$= Z_t + \frac{1}{1 + r_{t+1}}\phi(1 - \varsigma)H_{t+1}.$$

We now characterize analytically the dynamic response of assets and consumption to a given path of aggregate income Z_t at constant real interest rate r. Combining equations (B40) and (B41), we have:

$$(1 - \phi\beta)H_t + A_t = \phi\beta(1 + r)A_{t-1} + Z_t,$$

and then using $1 - \phi\beta$ times equation (B39), we find

$$\phi\beta(1 + r)A_{t-1} + Z_t - A_t = (1 - \phi\beta)Z_t$$
$$+ (1 - \varsigma)\frac{\phi}{1 + r}(\phi\beta(1 + r)A_t + Z_{t+1} - A_{t+1}),$$

rearranging, this gives the second-order difference equation

$$A_{t+1} - \frac{(1+r)}{(1-\zeta)\phi}(1 + (1-\zeta)\phi^2\beta)A_t + \beta\frac{(1+r)^2}{1-\zeta}A_{t-1}$$

$$= -\beta\frac{1+r}{1-\zeta}Z_t + Z_{t+1}. \tag{B42}$$

Consider the quadratic equation

$$C(X) = X^2 - \frac{(1+r)}{(1-\zeta)\phi}(1 + (1-\zeta)\phi^2\beta)X + \beta\frac{(1+r)^2}{1-\zeta}.$$

We have that

$$C((1+r)\phi\beta) = (1+r)^2\phi^2\beta^2 - \frac{(1+r)^2}{(1-\zeta)}\beta(1 + (1-\zeta)\phi^2\beta) + \beta\frac{(1+r)^2}{1-\zeta}$$

$$= (1+r)^2\left(\phi^2\beta^2 - \frac{\beta}{1-\zeta} - \phi^2\beta^2 + \frac{\beta}{1-\zeta}\right)$$

$$= 0.$$

Hence, this equation has a root $\lambda \equiv (1+r)\phi\beta$, and $\lambda \in (0,1)$ provided that $(1+r)\phi\beta < 1$. Define $\hat{\beta} \equiv 1/(\beta(1+r)) \cdot ((1-\zeta)/(1+r))$, so that the other root is $(1/\hat{\beta}\lambda) = ((1+r)/(1-\zeta)\phi) > 1$. Then, equation (B42) rewrites as:

$$A_{t+1} - \left(\lambda + \frac{1}{\hat{\beta}\lambda}\right)A_t + \frac{1}{\hat{\beta}}A_{t-1} = -\frac{1}{\hat{\beta}(1+r)}Z_t + Z_{t+1}. \tag{B43}$$

By standard results, this implies the asset dynamics:

$$A_t = \lambda A_{t-1} + \sum_{s=0}^{\infty}(\hat{\beta}\lambda)^{s+1}\left\{\left(\frac{1}{\hat{\beta}(1+r)}\right)dZ_{t+s} - dZ_{t+s+1}\right\}$$

Finally, we solve for consumption using using the aggregate budget constraint (eq. [B41]), and from this obtain the consumption Jacobian $M_{ts} \equiv (\partial C_t/\partial Z_s)$. In particular, the consumption response to a date-0 shock is given by $(\partial C_0/\partial Z_0) = 1 - (\partial A_0/\partial Z_0) = 1 - (\lambda/(1+r)) = 1 - \phi\beta$, and subsequent dynamics are given by $(\partial C_t/\partial Z_0) = (1 + r - \lambda)(\partial A_{t-1}/\partial Z_0) = (1 - (\lambda/(1+r)))\lambda^t = (1 - \phi\beta)((1+r)\phi\beta)^t$. This leads us to the following proposition.

Proposition 6. In the Blanchard model, the first column of the **M** matrix is given by

$$M_{t,0} = \frac{\partial C_t}{\partial Z_0} = \begin{cases} (1 - \beta\phi) & t = 0 \\ (1 - \beta\phi)(\phi\beta(1 + r))^t & t > 0 \end{cases}.$$

Note that ζ does not appear in these equations—instead, ζ controls the degree of anticipation of future income shocks, through its effect on $\hat{\beta}$.

Given Proposition 6, we calibrate the household side of the Blanchard model by picking $\beta\phi$ to hit mpc $= M_{0,0} = 0.25$. This implies in particular that $M_{1,0} = $ mpc$(1 - $ mpc$) = 0.19$. We then pick $\beta = 0.8$, $\zeta = 0.98$, and finally $\alpha = 0.16$ as in our main calibration. This delivers figure 7.

B8. Bond-in-Utility Model

Here, we set up a bond-in-utility (BU) model. We then show that, for its response to income, this model is first-order equivalent to the Blanchard model.

The agent maximizes the objective

$$\sum \beta^t \{u(C_t) + v(A_t)\},$$

where v is a love-of-asset function, subject to the same aggregate budget constraint as in our main HANK model, equation (37). The Euler equation for this problem is

$$u'(C_t) = \beta(1 + r_{t+1})u'(C_{t+1}) + v'(A_t) \tag{B44}$$

and the steady state is characterized by

$$u'(rA + Z)(1 - \beta(1 + r)) = v'(A).$$

Assuming homothetic utility $u'(c) = c^{-\sigma}$, $v'(a) = a^{-\sigma}$, this can be rewritten as

$$\left(r + \frac{Z}{A}\right) = (1 - \beta(1 + r))^{\frac{1}{\sigma}}.$$

Hence, the steady-state asset demand function is

$$A = a(r)Z,$$

where, here,

$$a(r) = \frac{A}{Z} = \frac{1}{(1 - \beta(1 + r))^{\frac{1}{\sigma}} - r}.$$

The dynamics at a constant real rate r can be characterized by differentiating equations (B44) and (37). This delivers

$$u''(C)dC_t = \beta(1 + r)u''(C)dC_{t+1} + v''(A)dA_{t+1}$$
$$dC_t + dA_t = (1 + r)dA_{t-1} + dZ_t$$

Combining, we obtain

$$\beta(1 + r)dA_{t+1} - \left(1 + \frac{v''(A)}{u''(C)} + \beta(1 + r)^2\right)dA_t + (1 + r)dA_{t-1}$$
$$= -dZ_t + \beta(1 + r)dZ_{t+1},$$

which we rearrange as

$$dA_{t+1} - \frac{1}{\beta(1 + r)}\left(1 + \frac{v''(A)}{u''(C)} + \beta(1 + r)^2\right)dA_t + \frac{1}{\beta}dA_{t-1} = -\frac{1}{\beta(1 + r)}dZ_t + dZ_{t+1}. \text{ (B45)}$$

Let λ and $1/\beta\lambda$ be the roots of

$$C(X) = X^2 - \frac{1}{\beta(1 + r)}\left(1 + \frac{v''(A)}{u''(C)} + \beta(1 + r)^2\right)X + \frac{1}{\beta}.$$

Then equation (B45) rewrites as

$$dA_{t+1} - \left(\lambda + \frac{1}{\beta\lambda}\right)dA_t + \frac{1}{\beta}dA_{t-1} = -\frac{1}{\beta(1 + r)}dZ_t + dZ_{t+1}. \quad \text{(B46)}$$

Comparing equations (B46) and (B43), and using the fact that the budget constraints equations (37) and (B41) are identical, we see that the two models are identical provided that $\beta^{BU} = \hat{\beta}^{OLG} \equiv (1/(\beta(1 + r)) \cdot ((1 - \varsigma)/(1 + r))$, and $\lambda^{BU} = \lambda^{OLG}$. This delivers:

Proposition 7. Assume that the bond-in-utility model is parameterized such that

$$\beta^{BU} = \frac{1}{(1 + r)}\frac{(1 - \varsigma)}{\beta(1 + r)}$$

and that $v''(A)/u''(C)$ is picked so that $\lambda^{BU} = (1 + r)\phi\beta$. Then, the BU model and the Blanchard model share the same **M** matrix; that is, to first order they have identical responses to income shocks at any date.

B9. COVID Shock to Home Spending

As mentioned in the text, to model the COVID shock to home spending, we modify the household problem so that consumption is defined as

$$c_{it}^k = \left[(1 - \alpha^k)^{\frac{1}{\eta}} (\zeta_t c_{iHt}^k)^{\frac{\eta-1}{\eta}} + (\alpha^k)^{\frac{1}{\eta}} (c_{iWt}^k)^{\frac{\eta-1}{\eta}} \right]^{\frac{\eta}{\eta-1}}.$$

Given this new definition, equation (3) is modified to be

$$V_t(A, e) = \max_{c_F, c_H, A'} u(c_t(c_H, c_W)) - v(N_t) + \beta \mathbb{E}_t [V_{t+1}(A', e')]$$

$$\text{s.t.} \quad P_{Ht} c_H + \sum_{l=1}^{K} P_{lt} c_W^l + A' = (1 + r_t^p) \frac{P_t}{P_{t-1}} A + P_t \cdot \nu_t \left(e \frac{W_t}{P_t} N_t \right)^{1-\lambda}. \tag{B47}$$

$$A' \geq 0$$

This gives rise to a new demand system

$$c_H = (1 - \alpha) \left(\frac{P_H}{\zeta P^{\text{mod}}} \right)^{-\eta} \frac{c}{\zeta} \qquad c_F = \alpha \left(\frac{P_{Ft}}{P^{\text{mod}}} \right)^{-\eta} c, \tag{B48}$$

where P^{mod}, the modified price index, is given by

$$P^{\text{mod}} = \left[(1 - \alpha) \left(\frac{P_H}{\zeta} \right)^{1-\eta} + \alpha (P_W)^{1-\eta} \right]^{\frac{1}{1-\eta}} \tag{B49}$$

with the Cobb Douglas limit $\eta = 1$ being $P^{\text{mod}} = (P_H/\zeta)^{1-\alpha} (P_W)^{\alpha}$.

We can modify the household problem as follows. The household perceives real posttax income to be equal to

$$\frac{e^{1-\lambda}}{\mathbb{E}[e^{1-\lambda}]} \frac{Z_t}{P_t^{\text{mod}}/P_t},$$

which effectively implies that it perceives real income to be $Z_t^{\text{mod}} = Z_t/(P_t^{\text{mod}}/P_t)$. Similarly, it perceives the ex post real interest rate to be

$$1 + r_t^{\text{mod,post}} = (1 + r_t^{\text{post}}) \cdot \frac{P_{t-1}^{\text{mod}}/P_{t-1}}{P_t^{\text{mod}}/P_t}.$$

Given the paths $\{r_t^{\text{mod}}, P_t^{\text{mod}}\}$, households solve their problem to determine consumption c^{mod}, then allocates demand per equation (B48); that is,

$$c_H = (1 - \alpha)\left(\frac{P_H}{\varsigma P^{mod}}\right)^{-\eta}\frac{c^{mod}}{\varsigma} \qquad c_F = \alpha\left(\frac{P_{Ft}}{P^{mod}}\right)^{-\eta}c^{mod}.$$

We obtain P^{mod}/P from

$$\frac{P^{mod}}{P} = \left(\frac{(1 - \alpha)\left(\frac{P_H}{\varsigma}\right)^{1-\eta} + \alpha(P_W)^{1-\eta}}{(1 - \alpha)(P_H)^{1-\eta} + \alpha(P_W)^{1-\eta}}\right)^{\frac{1}{1-\eta}}$$

$$= \left(\frac{(1 - \alpha)\left(\frac{1}{\varsigma}\right)^{1-\eta} + \alpha\left(\frac{P_W}{P_H}\right)^{1-\eta}}{(1 - \alpha)(1)^{1-\eta} + \alpha\left(\frac{P_W}{P_H}\right)^{1-\eta}}\right)^{\frac{1}{1-\eta}}$$

as well as the relevant relative prices from

$$\frac{P_H}{P^{mod}} = \frac{P_H}{P}\cdot\frac{1}{P^{mod}/P} \qquad \frac{P_F}{P^{mod}} = \frac{P_F}{P}\cdot\frac{1}{P^{mod}/P}.$$

Finally we can recreate aggregate c using

$$\frac{P_H}{P}c_H + \frac{P_F}{P}c_F.$$

Appendix C

C1. Proof of Proposition 4

We start by proving the following two more abstract lemmas.

Lemma 2. Suppose that we have a number of countries k, for all of which some vectors $\mathbf{X}^k$ and $\mathbf{Y}^k$ obey some equation

$$F(\mathbf{X}^k, \mathbf{Y}^k) = 0, \qquad (C1)$$

which is either homogeneous of degree 1 or homogeneous of degree 0 in $\mathbf{X}^k$. Furthermore, suppose that in steady state, each country satisfies $\mathbf{X}^{k,ss} = \omega^k\mathbf{X}^{ss}$ for scalars ω^k summing to 1 and some $\mathbf{X}^{ss}$; it also satisfies $\mathbf{Y}^{k,ss} = \mathbf{Y}^{ss}$ for some common $\mathbf{Y}^{ss}$.

Away from the steady state, for any $\mathbf{X}^k$ and $\mathbf{Y}^k$ all satisfying equation (C1) above, define $\mathbf{X} \equiv \Sigma_k\mathbf{X}^k$ and $\mathbf{Y} \equiv \Sigma_k\omega^k\mathbf{Y}^k$. Then to first order around the steady state $(\mathbf{X}^{ss}, \mathbf{Y}^{ss})$, $F(\mathbf{X}, \mathbf{Y}) = 0$.

Proof. First, note that our assumptions imply $F(\mathbf{X}^{ss}, \mathbf{Y}^{ss}) = 0$ regardless of whether F is homogeneous of degree 1 or 0.

Next, totally differentiate equation (C1) for each k to obtain

$$dF(\mathbf{X}^k, \mathbf{Y}^k) = \frac{\partial F}{\partial \mathbf{X}^k} d\mathbf{X}^k + \frac{\partial F}{\partial \mathbf{Y}^k} d\mathbf{Y}^k = 0, \qquad (C2)$$

where $\partial F/\partial \mathbf{X}^k$ and $\partial F/\partial \mathbf{Y}^k$ denote derivatives taken around the country-k steady state $(\mathbf{X}^{k,ss}, \mathbf{Y}^{k,ss})$. Then we have two cases:

- If F is homogeneous of degree 1 in $\mathbf{X}^k$, then $\partial F/\partial \mathbf{X}^k = \partial F/\partial \mathbf{X}$ and $\partial F/\partial \mathbf{Y}^k = \omega^k \partial F/\partial \mathbf{Y}$, where $\partial \Gamma/\partial \mathbf{X}$ and $\partial F/\partial \mathbf{Y}$ are taken around $(\mathbf{X}^{ss}, \mathbf{Y}^{ss})$. Summing equation (C2) across all k we get

$$\sum_k \frac{\partial F}{\partial \mathbf{X}} d\mathbf{X}^k + \frac{\partial F}{\partial \mathbf{Y}} \omega^k d\mathbf{Y}^k = \frac{\partial F}{\partial \mathbf{X}} d\mathbf{X} + \frac{\partial F}{\partial \mathbf{Y}} d\mathbf{Y}.$$

- If F is homogeneous of degree 0 in $\mathbf{X}^k$, then $\partial F/\partial \mathbf{X}^k = (1/\omega^k)(\partial F/\partial \mathbf{X})$ and $\partial F/\partial \mathbf{Y}^k = \partial F/\partial \mathbf{Y}$. Summing equation (C2) across all k, weighted by ω^k, we get

$$\sum_k \omega^k \left(\frac{1}{\omega^k} \frac{\partial F}{\partial \mathbf{X}} d\mathbf{X}^k + \frac{\partial F}{\partial \mathbf{Y}} d\mathbf{Y}^k \right) = \frac{\partial F}{\partial \mathbf{X}} d\mathbf{X} + \frac{\partial F}{\partial \mathbf{Y}} d\mathbf{Y}.$$

Hence, in both cases we obtain $(\partial F/\partial \mathbf{X}) d\mathbf{X} + (\partial F/\partial \mathbf{Y}) d\mathbf{Y} = 0$ for the aggregate economy, validating our claim that $F(\mathbf{X}, \mathbf{Y}) = 0$ holds to first order.

Lemma 3. Under the same assumptions as in Lemma 2, define $\widetilde{\mathbf{X}}^k = (\mathbf{X}^k/\omega^k) - \mathbf{X}$ and $\widetilde{\mathbf{Y}}^k = \mathbf{Y}^k - \mathbf{Y}$. Then to first order around the steady state $(\mathbf{X}^{ss}, \mathbf{Y}^{ss})$, $F(\mathbf{X}^{ss} + \widetilde{\mathbf{X}}^k, \mathbf{Y}^{ss} + \widetilde{\mathbf{Y}}^k) = 0$.

Proof. Now taking all derivatives around the aggregate steady state $(\mathbf{X}^{ss}, \mathbf{Y}^{ss})$, we want to show $(\partial F/\partial \mathbf{X}) d\widetilde{\mathbf{X}}^k + (\partial F/\partial \mathbf{Y}) d\widetilde{\mathbf{Y}}^k = 0$. We can write

$$\frac{\partial F}{\partial \mathbf{X}} d\widetilde{\mathbf{X}}^k + \frac{\partial F}{\partial \mathbf{Y}} d\widetilde{\mathbf{Y}}^k = \frac{1}{\omega^k} \frac{\partial F}{\partial \mathbf{X}} d\mathbf{X}^k + \frac{\partial F}{\partial \mathbf{Y}} d\mathbf{Y}^k - \frac{\partial F}{\partial \mathbf{X}} d\mathbf{X} - \frac{\partial F}{\partial \mathbf{Y}} d\mathbf{Y}. \quad (C3)$$

We note that $(\partial F/\partial \mathbf{X}) d\mathbf{X} + (\partial F/\partial \mathbf{Y}) d\mathbf{Y} = 0$ is what we have already proven in Lemma 2, and $1/\omega^k (\partial F/\partial \mathbf{X}) d\mathbf{X}^k + (\partial F/\partial \mathbf{Y}) d\mathbf{Y}^k$ is proportional to $(\partial F/\partial \mathbf{X}^k) d\mathbf{X}^k + (\partial F/\partial \mathbf{Y}^k) d\mathbf{Y}^k = 0$, either by a factor of $1/\omega^k$ (if F homogeneous of degree 1) or a factor of 1 (if F homogeneous of degree 0), and this holds by our assumption (eq. [C1]). Hence the right of equation (C3) is zero, as desired.

Next, we apply these two lemmas to prove the claims of Proposition 4.

We start by observing that any open-economy equilibrium in any country k, as defined in Definition 3, is fully characterized by equations (7)–(19), (22)–(29), demands equations (5) and (20), and the sequence-space equation (36) for aggregate assets and consumption, all conditional on some given world $\{i_t^*\}$ and $\{C_t^*\}$. All these equations satisfy the assumption stated in Lemma 2, being either homogeneous of degree 1 in the variables that scale with ω^k (e.g., the government budget constraint [eq. (14)]) or homogeneous of degree 0 (e.g., the relationship [eq. (13)] between price and wage inflation).

It follows immediately from Lemma 2 that if each of these equations holds for each country k, then to first order around the aggregate steady state, they each hold in aggregates as well. Hence, to first order, the path of aggregates satisfies the equations for an open economy.

We further argue that equations (31) and (33), which together characterize world-economy equilibrium, will also hold in aggregates as if in a one-country world. This is clearly true in steady state, where given the normalizations $P_H^k, \mathcal{E}^k, Q^k \equiv 1$, equation (31) immediately holds and equation (33) is just nfa = 0 for the aggregate nfa $\equiv \Sigma \text{nfa}^k$. This is also true to first order away from the steady state, where linearizing equation (31) gives $\Sigma_k \omega^k (dP_{Ht}^k - d\mathcal{E}_t^k) = 0$, reducing to just $dP_{Ht} - d\mathcal{E}_t = 0$ in aggregates, and linearizing equation (33) gives $\Sigma_k d\text{nfa}_t^k = 0$, reducing to just $d\text{nfa}_t = 0$ in aggregates.

We conclude that to first order around the steady state, aggregate variables obey all the equations of the world-equilibrium model with a single country. This proves the first part of Proposition 4.

For the second part, it follows immediately from Lemma 3 that the demeaned variables satisfy, to first order around the world steady state, all the equations of an open economy. We further note that the global variables i_t^* and C_t^* have demeaned values always equal to zero, because their value in each country equals their mean: $\tilde{i}_t^* = \tilde{C}_t^* = 0$. Hence, the demeaned response is equivalent to a small-open-economy response, where i_t^* and C_t^* are held constant, as desired.

C2. Proof of Corollary 1

All that remains is to derive the formula (51) for the change dr^n in steady-state real interest rate. Letting $a(r)$ denote steady-state asset demand normalized by after-tax income, asset market clearing is

$$Za(r) = B.$$

In the steady state, posttax income is

$$Z = Y - G - rB$$

and the natural allocation with zero wage inflation, equation (9) implies that the condition

$$v'(N)N = v'\left(\frac{Y}{\Theta}\right)\frac{Y}{\Theta} = \frac{\epsilon_w}{\epsilon_w - 1}(1 - \lambda)Zu'(C)$$

must hold for each individual country, with steady-state $C = Z + rB = (1 + ra(r))Z$.

Using our functional forms for v and u and combining these equations, we obtain

$$\varphi\left(\frac{Y}{\Theta}\right)^{1+\phi} = \frac{\epsilon_w}{\epsilon_w - 1}(1 - \lambda)\left(\frac{B}{a(r)}\right)^{1-\sigma}(1 + ra(r))^{-\sigma} \qquad \text{(C4)}$$

$$(Y - G)a(r) = (1 + ra(r))B. \qquad \text{(C5)}$$

Log-differencing and assuming $d \log G = 0$, we find

$$(1 + \phi)d \log Y = (1 - \sigma)(d \log B - d \log a(r)) - \sigma d \log(1 + ra(r))$$

$$\frac{1}{1 - \frac{G}{Y}}d \log Y = d \log(1 + ra(r)) + (d \log B - d \log a(r)) \qquad '$$

which gives

$$d \log B - d \log a(r) = -\frac{1 + \frac{1}{1-\frac{G}{Y}}\frac{\sigma}{1+\phi}}{1 - \frac{1}{1-\frac{G}{Y}}\frac{1-\sigma}{1+\phi}}d \log(1 + ra(r)).$$

Noting finally that, around $r = 0$, we have $d \log(1 + ra(r)) = (a(r) + ra'(r))/(1 + ra(r))dr = a(r)dr$, we obtain

$$dr = \frac{d \log B}{\frac{d \log a(r)}{dr} - \frac{1 + \frac{1}{1-\frac{G}{Y}}\frac{\sigma}{1+\phi}}{1 - \frac{1}{1-\frac{G}{Y}}\frac{1-\sigma}{1+\phi}}a(r)},$$

which is the formula in the main text.

Appendix D

D1. Data Sources and Country List

Table D1 lists the 26 economies in our study, which are the advanced economies that have nonmissing data on fiscal deficits (general government net lending and borrowing) and current accounts between 2020Q1 and 2021Q2. The table also indicates, under the column labeled "R?," whether countries are part of our "reduced sample" that also includes private savings and investment data over this period.

The data used in appendix D is collected as follows. General government net lending and borrowing are from the IMF IFS. Current-account data are from the IMF Balance of Payments and International Investment Position Statistics.[37] Private savings are from the OECD Quarterly Non-Financial Sector Accounts and are computed as gross savings net of consumption of fixed capital for the private sector.[38] Net investment data are from the OECD Quarterly National Accounts, computed as gross fixed-capital formation net of the consumption of fixed capital. For the United States, all data are taken from National Income and Product Accounts. We use seasonally adjusted data when available; otherwise, we use nonseasonally adjusted data. To construct figure 1, we also construct the trade balance by subtracting imports from exports in the IMF IFS.

The data used to construct the remaining columns of table D1 are constructed as follows. Nominal GDP is from the IMF IFS database; we report nominal GDP weights based on 2020Q1 values as share of total nominal GDP for our 26 countries.

Openness averages the import-to-GDP and export-to-GDP ratio from the World Development Indicators (WDI) over 2015–19; government spending to GDP is the WDI average over the same period. We use the net debt to GDP from the IMF Fiscal Monitor averaged over 2015–19. For Greece, this number is missing; we calculate it by taking general government gross debt from the World Bank Quarterly Public Sector Debt database and subtracting financial assets from the IFS.

Table D1
Countries in our Sample and Their Characteristics

Country	R?	Code	GDP Weight Y^k	Openness $(X^k + I^k)/2Y^k$	Spending G^k/Y^k	Debt B^k/Y^k
United States	Y	US	52.36	13.5	14.1	81.9
Germany	Y	DE	9.32	43.4	19.9	46.3
United Kingdom	Y	GB	7.00	30.1	18.8	76.8
France	Y	FR	6.27	31.4	23.5	88.6
Italy	Y	IT	4.55	29.1	18.9	121.8
Canada	Y	CA	4.12	32.9	20.8	26.4
Australia	Y	AU	3.24	21.4	19.0	24.1
Spain	Y	ES	3.19	32.9	18.9	84.4
Netherlands	Y	NL	2.19	77.7	24.6	46.8
Sweden	Y	SE	1.29	43.2	26.0	7.2
Belgium	N	BE	1.27	80.7	23.2	88.6
Austria	Y	AT	1.05	52.4	19.5	53.9
Denmark	Y	DK	.85	52.5	24.6	15.0
Finland	Y	FI	.65	37.5	23.4	22.6
Czech Republic	Y	CZ	.61	74.6	19.1	22.5
Portugal	Y	PT	.56	41.7	17.3	115.9
Greece	Y	GR	.48	36.3	20.3	150.5
Slovakia	N	SK	.25	92.9	18.9	45.5
Luxembourg	N	LU	.17	179.4	16.4	−11.2
Lithuania	N	LT	.13	71.6	16.8	31.9
Slovenia	Y	SI	.13	77.1	18.6	48.6
Latvia	N	LV	.08	60.9	18.5	30.1
Estonia	N	EE	.07	73.9	19.5	−1.9
Cyprus	N	CY	.06	72.5	15.4	71.5
Iceland	N	IS	.05	44.5	23.7	62.1
Malta	N	MT	.04	141.3	16.2	37.5

Note: R = reduced sample; GDP = gross domestic product.

D2. Dynamic Regression versus Model Predictions

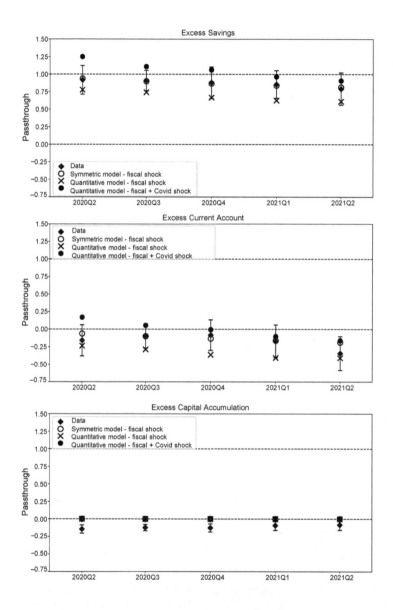

Fig. D1. Dynamic pass-through regressions versus model predictions. These figures provide the dynamic counterpart to figure 12, regressing dA_t^k, $dnfa_t^k$, and dK_t^k on dB_t^k for $t = 1, ..., 5$ in our three models and comparing to the empirical counterpart. The empirical regression coefficients are reported with 68% confidence bands. A color version of this figure is available online.

D3.   Regression with Controls

Figure D2 repeats the exercise from figure 11, but it adds controls by residualizing each x-axis variable with the other two variables. For instance, the fiscal deficit is residualized with the lockdown index and COVID deaths, and so on. The patterns from figure 11 are almost identical.[39]

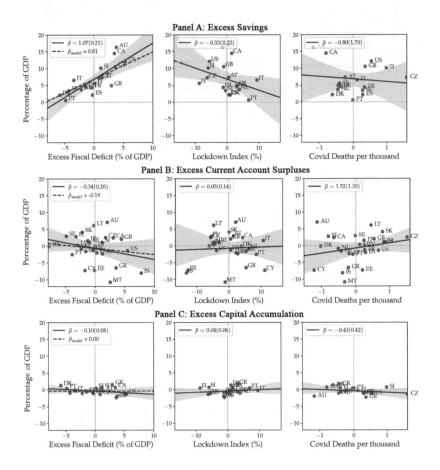

Fig. D2.   Determinants of excess savings, investment, and current accounts (with controls). β indicates the regression coefficient of the y-axis on the x-axis variable. The latter is the original x-axis variable purged of the other two, so that the regression coefficient corresponds to the one in a regression that directly controls for these other variables. The standard error around this coefficient is in parentheses. Shaded areas correspond to 68% bootstrapped confidence intervals. A color version of this figure is available online.

D4. Accounting for Fiscal Deficits in the Rest of the World

Figure D3 repeats the exercise from figure 10 for the 16 countries that make up the rest of the world in our reduced sample, for which all balance-of-payment data are available.

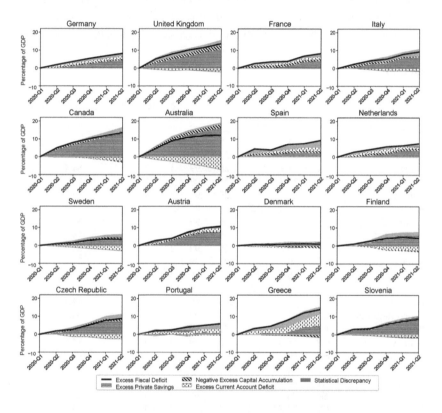

Fig. D3. Accounting for fiscal deficits in the rest of the world. GDP = gross domestic product. A color version of this figure is available online.

Appendix E

E1. Nonsymmetric World-Economy Calibration

Table E1 displays our calibration targets, as well as the outcomes of the model. We take openness α and GDP shares from the data. We then infer the parameter ω so that equation (35) holds. We look for β, δ to simultaneously hit an mpc of 0.25 and an r of 0. Each country has its own wealth

Table E1
Calibration Outcomes

Country	Code	A	ω	mpc	β	δ	$M_{1,0}$	Top 20% Wealth Share
United States	US	15.7	27.8	.25	.99	.1	.1	83.9
Germany	DE	54.2	16.2	.25	.99	.1	.1	84.2
United Kingdom	GB	37	8.6	.25	.99	.1	.1	84.2
France	FR	41.1	7.9	.25	.99	.1	.1	84.4
Italy	IT	35.8	5.1	.25	.99	.1	.1	84.1
Canada	CA	41.5	5.2	.25	.99	.1	.1	84.3
Australia	AU	26.4	2.7	.25	.99	.1	.1	84.1
Spain	ES	40.6	4.1	.25	.99	.1	.1	84.2
Netherlands	NL	90	5.9	.25	.99	.1	.1	84.5
Sweden	SE	58.3	2.2	.25	.99	.1	.1	84.5
Belgium	BE	90	3.5	.25	.99	.1	.1	84.4
Austria	AT	65.1	2.2	.25	.99	.1	.1	84.3
Denmark	DK	69.6	1.8	.25	.99	.1	.1	84.5
Finland	FI	49	.9	.25	.99	.1	.1	84.4
Czech Republic	CZ	90	1.7	.25	.99	.1	.1	84.2
Portugal	PT	50.5	.9	.25	.99	.1	.1	84.1
Greece	GR	45.6	.6	.25	.99	.1	.1	84.3
Slovakia	SK	90	.7	.25	.99	.1	.1	84.2
Luxembourg	LU	90	.5	.25	.99	.1	.1	84.1
Lithuania	LT	86	.4	.25	.99	.1	.1	84.2
Slovenia	SI	90	.4	.25	.99	.1	.1	84.2
Latvia	LV	74.7	.2	.25	.99	.1	.1	84.2
Estonia	EE	90	.2	.25	.99	.1	.1	84.3
Cyprus	CY	85.7	.2	.25	.99	.1	.1	84.1
Iceland	IS	58.4	.1	.25	.99	.1	.1	84.4
Malta	MT	90	.1	.25	.99	.1	.1	84.1

distribution; the table reports the top 20% wealth share in each. Given its importance for aggregate dynamics, we also report the second entry of the **M** matrix, $M_{1,0}$, across countries.

E2.   Solution Method for Nonsymmetric 26-Country Model

In principle, computation here should be very difficult: we have a 26-country model with a separate wealth distribution in each country. However, we observe that countries only interact through the two aggregates (C_t^*, i_t^*). This makes it feasible to solve the model to first order efficiently by adapting the ideas developed in Auclert et al. (2021a).

Briefly, the idea is to first calculate separately and once and for all, in each country k, sequence-space Jacobians $J^{A,C^*,k}$ and $J^{A,i^*,k}$ as well as $J^{Q,C^*,k}$ and $J^{Q,i^*,k}$ of asset demand A and the real exchange rate Q to the world aggregates C^*, i^*. We can then aggregate these Jacobians into a world Jacobian using, for instance, $J^{A,C^*} = \Sigma \omega^k J^{A,C^*,k}$. Second, we calculate the change in net asset supply $d\mathbf{B}^{k,0} - d\mathbf{A}^{k,0}$ and the real exchange rate $d\mathbf{Q}^{k,0}$ that results from the fiscal shock specific to country k. Finally, we differentiate the two equations, (31) and (32), through which countries interact. This gives us a simple linear system in $2T$ unknowns, where T is the truncation horizon of the sequence-space Jacobians:

$$J^{Q,C^*} d\mathbf{C}^* + J^{Q,i^*} d\mathbf{i}^* = -\sum \frac{\omega^k}{1 - \alpha^k} d\mathbf{Q}^{k,0}$$
$$J^{A,C^*} d\mathbf{C}^* + J^{A,i^*} d\mathbf{i}^* = \sum_k \left(d\mathbf{B}^{k,0} - d\mathbf{A}^{k,0} \right)$$

Inverting this system delivers the first-order solution for $(d\mathbf{C}^*, d\mathbf{i}^*)$. This type of procedure is helpful to solve models any time multiple groups of heterogeneous agents interact via a limited set of aggregates.

E3.   COVID-Shock Matching Procedure

Figure E1 illustrates the procedure we use to recover the COVID shock in each country. As discussed in the main text, we first use our model with only the fiscal shock to back out the counterfactual effect of the fiscal shock on consumption in each country. This delivers the thin dashed line. Then, assuming that, in each country, the COVID shock is an AR(1) discount factor shock, with country-specific magnitude σ^k and a common persistence ρ, we pick (σ^k, ρ) so that the combined effect of the fiscal and the COVID shock matches the data in the solid line. The dot-dashed line visualizes the resulting effect of the COVID shock alone on consumption. The thick dashed line visualizes the combined effect of the COVID shock and the fiscal shock, to compare to our target in the solid line.

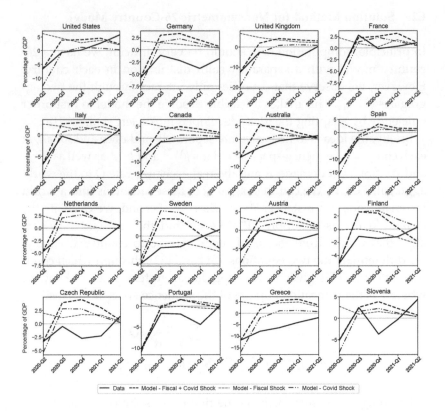

Fig. E1. Recovering a COVID shock in each country. GDP = gross domestic product. A color version of this figure is available online.

Endnotes

Authors' email addresses: Aggarwal (arishabh@stanford.edu), Auclert (aauclert@stanford.edu), Rognlie (matthew.rognlie@northwestern.edu), Straub (ludwigstraub@fas.harvard.edu). This research is supported by National Science Foundation grant numbers SES-1851717 and SES-2042691. We thank our discussants Oleg Itskhoki, Fabrizio Perri, and Linda Tesar as well as Luigi Bocola, Larry Christiano, Marty Eichenbaum, Pierre-Olivier Gourinchas, Calvin He, Kilian Huber, Anders Humlum, Şebnem Kalemli-Özcan, Greg Kaplan, Rohan Kekre, Thibaut Lamadon, Elisa Rubbo, Giovanni Sciacovelli, Daan Struyven, and Christian Wolf for helpful comments. We thank Agustin Barboza for excellent research assistance. We thank Erica Deadman, Peter Ganong, Fiona Greig, and Pascal Noel for sharing JPMorgan Chase Institute data. For acknowledgments, sources of research support, and disclosure of the authors' material financial relationships, if any, please see https://www.nber.org/books-and-chapters/nber-macroeconomics-annual-2022-volume-37/excess-savings-and-twin-deficits-transmission-fiscal-stimulus-open-economies.

1. Congressional Budget Office (2020) and IMF Fiscal Affairs Department (2021) show that fiscal deficits were largely used to finance furlough pay, extended unemployment-insurance benefits, stimulus checks, and so on. Projections in IMF (2021) imply a permanent effect of these deficits on levels of debt/gross domestic product.

2. Coibion, Gorodnichenko, and Weber (2020), Ganong et al. (2022), and Parker et al. (2022) study MPCs from pandemic stimulus checks.

3. See also *New York Times*, "Americans' Pandemic-Era 'Excess Savings' Are Dwindling for Many," December 7, 2021.

4. This step is technically challenging because we solve a world-economy model keeping track of 26 wealth distributions, but we show how to adapt the sequence-space Jacobian method (Auclert et al. 2021a) to deal with this challenge.

5. For instance, a business-cycle boom typically is associated with a current-account deficit as import demand rises, as well as a fiscal surplus due to higher tax revenue and reduced transfer payments.

6. See also de Ferra, Mitman, and Romei (2020), Oskolkov (2021), and Zhou (2022).

7. Note that consumers from country k value two types of goods from their own country: the home good c_{iHt}^k and the world good $c_{iWt}^{k,k}$. In equilibrium, these two goods have the same price so contribute in the same way to domestic aggregate demand.

8. It would be interesting to extend this setting to allow for imperfect pass-through, such as in a local or dollar currency-pricing paradigm (Devereux and Engel 2003; Gopinath et al. 2020; Gopinath and Itskhoki 2021).

9. This limit is close, but not identical, to the model in which all agents are individually on their labor supply curves at all times. The difference comes from the fact that (*a*) unions still have monopoly power, and (*b*) the relationship $v'(N_t)/u'(C_t) = \epsilon_w/\epsilon_w - 1(1 - \lambda)Z_t/N_t$ holds in the aggregate but not for each individual.

10. By contrast, in this limit, the real exchange rate Q_t is outside of the control of monetary policy.

11. This would be different if the mutual fund invests in international assets/liabilities, there is an initial NFA position, or government bonds are long term. See Auclert et al. (2021c) for a model in which this is the case.

12. Mathematically, as $\Theta^k \to 0$, $\{Y_t^k/\Theta^k, C_t^k/\Theta^k, A_t^k/\Theta^k, T_t^k/\Theta^k, Z_t^k\Theta^k, Q_t^k\}$ continues to constitute an open-economy equilibrium given $\{C_t^*, i_t^*\}$.

13. Although it is the ex post return r_t^p that directly enters the household's problem, in this model we have $r_t^p = r_{t-1}$ by eq. (23).

14. Because the counterpart of this condition in a model with long-run growth is r equal to the growth rate, this is also empirically relevant, as has been widely argued (see, e.g., Blanchard 2019).

15. The same logic would prevail in an endowment economy with a single worldwide good, as in the canonical Blanchard (1985) model, rather than in our model with a produced good and our particular assumption about monetary policy.

16. We explicitly spell out this "no-anticipation" model in Sec. B3.

17. If a monetary response—such as in subsection "Monetary-Policy Response"—limits the output boom, we still see a similar effect now because the rich increase their savings in response to the higher interest rate.

18. This result is specific to our calibration of trade elasticities to $\eta = \gamma = 1$. Under this parameterization, and in a setting with $\sigma = 1$ (i.e., the Cole-Obstfeld case) and assets that represent capitalized claims on the (constant) share of future profits, Proposition 6 in Auclert et al. (2021c) shows that in general equilibrium, changes in the real interest rate dr have no effect on the current account (echoing a similar result in Galí and Monacelli 2005). Here, assets are bonds rather than capitalized profits, so this result does not hold exactly, but fig. 6 shows that it holds approximately.

19. Observe that $r = 0$ is, strictly speaking, not possible to achieve in a representative-agent model, but $A_t = B_t$ holds irrespective of the steady-state interest rate assumed in a representative-agent model.

20. This is due to the lack of selection into spending: unlike in TANK and HANK, where households that choose not to spend have lower propensities to spend in the future, the MPC out of excess savings is constant in the Blanchard model. We could improve the Blanchard model's fit to the **M** matrix by adding hand-to-mouth agents, because as Sec. B8

shows it is locally isomorphic to a bond-in-utility model, and Auclert et al. (2018) show that a mixture of bond-in-utility and hand-to-mouth agents (a "TABU" model) closely approximates the **M** matrix of a HANK model.

21. To simplify the argument, in this section, we focus on levels in a small open economy rather than on cross-country outcomes.

22. Details are provided in Sec. B9.

23. There is reason to believe that this effect on the world interest rate may be a little high. First, although the semielasticity of asset demand is similar to the one calculated by Auclert et al. (2021b) using a realistic life-cycle model, our model underestimates total assets because it ignores other components of wealth beyond public debt: hence, in practice, an increase of world public debt of 12% as a share of GDP represents a much smaller proportional increase in assets. Second, the literature review in Mian, Straub, and Sufi (2022) suggests that a 10% increase in public debt raises the world interest rate by only around 20 basis points.

24. Here, $M_{t,s}^r \equiv \partial C_t / \partial r_s(\{1, r\})$, where C is the consumption function defined in Sec. II. The full result for $d\mathbf{Y}$ in the corollary can be derived from eq. (B17), substituting $\alpha = 0$ for the closed economy. Note that we cannot write $d\mathbf{Y}$ as an infinite series as in eq. (44), because with $\alpha = 0$ it is no longer guaranteed that this series will converge.

25. If, as in these papers, the setting is one of a currency union where monetary policy follows a common nominal interest-rate path, the analogue to Corollaries 2 and 3 states that cross-sectional fiscal multipliers are equal to multipliers in a small open economy with a constant nominal interest-rate rule $i_t \equiv i$.

26. An alternative approach to testing the model would be to study the dynamic effect on worldwide savings and current accounts after an identified deficit-financed tax shock in one country, in the spirit of Guajardo et al. (2014).

27. Countries for which we are missing saving or investment data make up a relatively small fraction of advanced economy GDP: Belgium, Cyprus, Estonia, Iceland, Latvia, Lithuania, Luxembourg, Malta, and Slovakia.

28. We rebase the level of private savings using potential GDP $Y_0^k (1 + \overline{g^k})^s$ rather than actual GDP Y_s^k to avoid the mechanical effect of the recession on the savings-to-GDP ratio.

29. Although all three stocks in principle could be measured directly, in practice measured wealth-to-GDP and NFA-to-GDP ratios are heavily influenced by valuation effects (Gourinchas and Rey 2007; Saez and Zucman 2016; Atkeson, Heathcote, and Perri 2022). Our metric of excess savings corresponds more directly to the increase in wealth that resulted from additional saving by private agents, rather than from changes in the prices of the assets they held.

30. Source is "Fiscal Policies Database in Response to COVID-19," entry "Additional spending or foregone revenues in nonhealth sector, as % of GDP, covering measures for implementation in 2020, 2021, and beyond."

31. As fig. D3 shows, these patterns are broadly the same in all of the 16 "rest of the world" countries in our sample.

32. Given eq. (53), the coefficients on private savings, minus those on capital accumulation and current accounts, must be 1. This is not exactly true in fig. 11, because we have more countries with data on current accounts and because of the statistical discrepancy in the data.

33. In a Ricardian model, the pass-through is 1 for savings and 0 for current accounts. Although this is not technically rejected by the macro data in fig. 11, this model is clearly inconsistent with the micro MPC and spending-down evidence that motivate this paper.

34. The lockdown index is "a composite measure based on nine response indicators including school closures, workplace closures, and travel bans, rescaled to a value from 0 to 100." COVID deaths per thousand are cumulated between 2020Q1 and 2021Q2 (source: "Our World in Data" stringency index and COVID deaths).

35. Investment also has very limited association with either fiscal deficits or COVID severity. This suggests that it is not a limitation for our model to abstract away from it altogether.

36. Fig. D1 shows that different versions of our model still compare favorably to the data when we consider the dynamic pass-through regressions: the regression coefficients

then start at 1 and decay toward those of fig. 12 for savings, and they start at 0 and decay toward those of fig. 12 for current accounts.

37. We take US dollar values for the current account and convert them to domestic currency using period average exchange rates from the IMF IFS.

38. The private sector consists of households, nonprofits serving households, financial corporations, and nonfinancial corporations.

39. The excess-savings point estimate is somewhat higher, now 1.07, but this is due to the statistical discrepancy in the national accounts, which is correlated with the residualized fiscal-deficit shock. Inferring excess savings from the identity (eq. [53]) would imply a point estimate of 0.56 rather than 1.07.

References

Atkeson, Andrew, Jonathan Heathcote, and Fabrizio Perri. 2022. "The End of Privilege: A Reexamination of the Net Foreign Asset Position of the United States." Working Paper no. 29771 (February), NBER, Cambridge, MA.

Auclert, Adrien. 2019. "Monetary Policy and the Redistribution Channel." *American Economic Review* 109 (6): 2333–67.

Auclert, Adrien, Bence Bardóczy, Matthew Rognlie, and Ludwig Straub. 2021a. "Using the Sequence-Space Jacobian to Solve and Estimate Heterogeneous-Agent Models." *Econometrica* 89 (5): 2375–408.

Auclert, Adrien, Hannes Malmberg, Frederic Martenet, and Matthew Rognlie. 2021b. "Demographics, Wealth, and Global Imbalances in the Twenty-First Century." Working Paper no. 29161 (August), NBER, Cambridge, MA.

Auclert, Adrien, Matthew Rognlie, Martin Souchier, and Ludwig Straub. 2021c. "Exchange Rates and Monetary Policy with Heterogeneous Agents: Sizing Up the Real Income Channel." Working Paper no. 28872 (May), NBER, Cambridge, MA.

Auclert, Adrien, Matthew Rognlie, and Ludwig Straub. 2018. "The Intertemporal Keynesian Cross." Working Paper no. 25020 (September), NBER, Cambridge, MA.

———. 2020. "Micro Jumps, Macro Humps: Monetary Policy and Business Cycles in an Estimated HANK Model." Working Paper no. 26647 (January), NBER, Cambridge, MA.

Ball, Laurence, and N. Gregory Mankiw. 1995. "What Do Budget Deficits Do?" *Proceedings of the Jackson Hole Economic Policy Symposium* 1995:95–119.

Baqaee, David, and Emmanuel Farhi. 2022. "Supply and Demand in Disaggregated Keynesian Economies with an Application to the COVID-19 Crisis." *American Economic Review* 112 (5): 1397–436.

Bernheim, B. Douglas. 1988. "Budget Deficits and the Balance of Trade." *Tax Policy and the Economy* 2:1–31.

Bilbiie, Florin O. 2008. "Limited Asset Markets Participation, Monetary Policy and (Inverted) Aggregate Demand Logic." *Journal of Economic Theory* 140 (1): 162–96.

Bilbiie, Florin, Gauti Eggertsson, and Giorgio Primiceri. 2021. "US 'Excess Savings' Are Not Excessive." *VoxEU Column*, March.

Blanchard, Olivier J. 1985. "Debt, Deficits, and Finite Horizons." *Journal of Political Economy* 93 (2): 223–47.

———. 2019. "Public Debt and Low Interest Rates." *American Economic Review* 109 (4): 1197–229.

Chinn, Menzie D., and Hiro Ito. 2007. "Current Account Balances, Financial Development and Institutions: Assaying the World 'Saving Glut.'" *Journal of International Money and Finance* 26 (4): 546–69.

Chinn, Menzie D., and Eswar S. Prasad. 2003. "Medium-Term Determinants of Current Accounts in Industrial and Developing Countries: An Empirical Exploration." *Journal of International Economics* 59 (1): 47–76.

Chodorow-Reich, Gabriel. 2019. "Geographic Cross-Sectional Fiscal Spending Multipliers: What Have We Learned?" *American Economic Journal: Economic Policy* 11 (2): 1–34.

Coibion, Olivier, Yuriy Gorodnichenko, and Michael Weber. 2020. "How Did US Consumers Use Their Stimulus Payments?" Working Paper no. 27693 (August), NBER, Cambridge, MA.

Congressional Budget Office. 2020. "The Effects of Pandemic-Related Legislation on Output." September. Congressional Budget Office, Washington, DC.

Corsetti, Giancarlo, and Gernot J. Müller. 2006. "Twin Deficits: Squaring Theory, Evidence and Common Sense." *Economic Policy* 21 (48): 598–638.

de Ferra, Sergio, Kurt Mitman, and Federica Romei. 2020. "Household Heterogeneity and the Transmission of Foreign Shocks." *Journal of International Economics* 124:1–18.

Devereux, Michael B., and Charles Engel. 2003. "Monetary Policy in the Open Economy Revisited: Price Setting and Exchange-Rate Flexibility." *Review of Economic Studies* 70 (4): 765–83.

European Central Bank. 2021. "The Implications of Savings Accumulated during the Pandemic for the Global Economic Outlook." Prepared by Maria Grazia Attinasi, Alina Bobasu and Ana-Simona Manu. *ECB Economic Bulletin* Issue 5, September.

Farhi, Emmanuel, and Iván Werning. 2016. "Fiscal Multipliers: Liquidity Traps and Currency Unions." In *Handbook of Macroeconomics*, vol. 2, ed. Harald Uhlig and John B. Taylor, 2417–92. Amsterdam: North Holland.

Feldstein, Martin. 1993. "The Dollar and the Trade Deficit in the 1980s: A Personal View." Working Paper no. 4325, NBER, Cambridge, MA.

Feyrer, James, and Jay Shambaugh. 2012. "Global Savings and Global Investment: The Transmission of Identified Fiscal Shocks." *American Economic Journal: Economic Policy* 4 (2): 95–114.

Frenkel, Jacob A., and Assaf Razin. 1986. "Fiscal Policies in the World Economy." *Journal of Political Economy* 94 (3, Part 1): 564–94.

Galí, Jordi, J. David López-Salido, and Javier Vallés. 2007. "Understanding the Effects of Government Spending on Consumption." *Journal of the European Economic Association* 5 (1): 227–70.

Galí, Jordi, and Tommaso Monacelli. 2005. "Monetary Policy and Exchange Rate Volatility in a Small Open Economy." *Review of Economic Studies* 72 (3): 707–34.

Ganong, Peter, Fiona E. Greig, Pascal J. Noel, Daniel M. Sullivan, and Joseph S. Vavra. 2022. "Spending and Job-Finding Impacts of Expanded Unemployment Benefits: Evidence from Administrative Micro Data." Working Paper no 30315 (August), NBER, Cambridge, MA.

Ghironi, Fabio. 2006. "Macroeconomic Interdependence under Incomplete Markets." *Journal of International Economics* 70 (2): 428–50.

Goldman Sachs. 2021. "The Boost from Pent-up Savings." By Sid Bhushan and Daan Struyven. *Global Economics Analyst*, July.

Gopinath, Gita, Emine Boz, Camila Casas, Federico J. Díez, Pierre-Olivier Gourinchas, and Mikkel Plagborg-Møller. 2020. "Dominant Currency Paradigm." *American Economic Review* 110 (3): 677–719.

Gopinath, Gita, and Oleg Itskhoki. 2021. "Dominant Currency Paradigm: A Review." Working Paper no. 29556 (December), NBER, Cambridge, MA.

Gourinchas, Pierre-Olivier, Şebnem Kalemli-Özcan, Veronika Penciakova, and Nick Sander. 2021. "Fiscal Policy in the Age of COVID: Does It 'Get in All of the Cracks'?" Working Paper no. 29293 (September), NBER, Cambridge, MA.

Gourinchas, Pierre-Olivier, and Hélène Rey. 2007. "International Financial Adjustment." *Journal of Political Economy* 115 (4): 665–703.

Guajardo, Jaime, Daniel Leigh, and Andrea Pescatori. 2014. "Expansionary Austerity? International Evidence." *Journal of the European Economic Association* 12 (4): 949–68.

Guerrieri, Veronica, Guido Lorenzoni, Ludwig Straub, and Iván Werning. 2022. "Macroeconomic Implications of COVID-19: Can Negative Supply Shocks Cause Demand Shortages?" *American Economic Review* 112 (5): 1437–74.

Guo, Xing, Pablo Ottonello, and Diego Perez. 2021. "Monetary Policy and Redistribution in Open Economies." Working Paper no. 28213 (March), NBER, Cambridge, MA.

Hagedorn, Marcus, Iourii Manovskii, and Kurt Mitman. 2019. "The Fiscal Multiplier." Working Paper no. 25571 (February), NBER, Cambridge, MA.

Heathcote, Jonathan, Kjetil Storesletten, and Giovanni L. Violante. 2017. "Optimal Tax Progressivity: An Analytical Framework." *Quarterly Journal of Economics* 132 (4): 1693–754.

House, Christopher L., Christian Proebsting, and Linda L. Tesar. 2020. "Austerity in the Aftermath of the Great Recession." *Journal of Monetary Economics* 115:37–63.

IMF. 2021. *Fiscal Monitor: Strengthening the Credibility of Public Finances.* Washington, DC: International Monetary Fund.

IMF Fiscal Affairs Department. 2021. "Fiscal Monitor Database of Country Fiscal Measures in Response to the COVID-19 Pandemic." October. International Monetary Fund, Washington, DC.

Kaplan, Greg, Benjamin Moll, and Giovanni L. Violante. 2018. "Monetary Policy According to HANK." *American Economic Review* 108 (3): 697–743.

Kim, Soyoung, and Nouriel Roubini. 2008. "Twin Deficit or Twin Divergence? Fiscal Policy, Current Account, and Real Exchange Rate in the U.S." *Journal of International Economics* 74 (2): 362–83.

Kumhof, Michael, and Douglas Laxton. 2013. "Fiscal Deficits and Current Account Deficits." *Journal of Economic Dynamics and Control* 37 (10): 2062–82.

McKay, Alisdair, Emi Nakamura, and Jón Steinsson. 2016. "The Power of Forward Guidance Revisited." *American Economic Review* 106 (10): 3133–58.

McKay, Alisdair, and Ricardo Reis. 2016. "The Role of Automatic Stabilizers in the U.S. Business Cycle." *Econometrica* 84 (1): 141–94.

Mian, Atif R., Ludwig Straub, and Amir Sufi. 2022. "A Goldilocks Theory of Fiscal Deficits." Working Paper no. 29707 (January), NBER, Cambridge, MA.

Nakamura, Emi, and Jón Steinsson. 2014. "Fiscal Stimulus in a Monetary Union: Evidence from US Regions." *American Economic Review* 104 (3): 753–92.

Oh, Hyunseung, and Ricardo Reis. 2012. "Targeted Transfers and the Fiscal Response to the Great Recession." *Journal of Monetary Economics* 59 (Supplement): S50–S64.

Oskolkov, Aleksei. 2021. "Exchange Rate Policy and Heterogeneity in Small Open Economies." Working paper (March), University of Chicago.

Parker, Jonathan A., Jake Schild, Laura Erhard, and David Johnson. 2022. "Household Spending Responses to the Economic Impact Payments of 2020: Evidence from the Consumer Expenditure Survey." Working Paper no. 29648 (January), NBER, Cambridge, MA.

Saez, Emmanuel, and Gabriel Zucman. 2016. "Wealth Inequality in the United States since 1913: Evidence from Capitalized Income Tax Data." *Quarterly Journal of Economics* 131 (2): 519–78.

TD Bank. 2021. "Where the Road of Excess [Saving] Leads." By Maria Solovieva. *TD Economics*, September.

Werning, Iván. 2015. "Incomplete Markets and Aggregate Demand." Working Paper no. 21448 (August), NBER, Cambridge, MA.

Woodford, Michael. 2011. "Simple Analytics of the Government Expenditure Multiplier." *American Economic Journal: Macroeconomics* 3 (1): 1–35.

Zhou, Haonan. 2022. "Open Economy, Redistribution, and the Aggregate Impact of External Shocks." Working paper (February), Princeton University.

Comment

Oleg Itskhoki, *UCLA and NBER,* United States of America

The heterogeneous agent New Keynesian (HANK) framework has become a leading framework for the analysis of both monetary and, especially, fiscal policy transmission in a closed economy. What are the implications of HANK for open economy dimensions such as the magnitude and the composition of current account deficits? In particular, what were the open economy implications—for capital flows, current account imbalances, and exchange rate adjustment—of the massive fiscal policy response to the COVID-19 pandemic?

The current paper addresses these questions by adopting a version of an open economy HANK model developed in the earlier work of the authors, which features household heterogeneity in terms of wealth and marginal propensity to consume, nominal wage rigidities, and home bias in consumption that leads to equilibrium real exchange rate dynamics.[1] The paper then asks what the implications are of a HANK framework for current account adjustment in response to a pandemic shock and the fiscal policy that accommodated it. In my discussion, I instead ask what the patterns of current account and exchange rate adjustment are in response to these shocks in the data, and what the likely first-order theoretical mechanisms needed to explain them are.

The HANK model provides sharp intuitive predictions for the macroeconomic response of aggregate savings to a differential fiscal transfer shock across countries, as summarized in the concluding figure 14 in the paper. A larger local fiscal transfer turns into increased local consumption expenditure by high marginal propensity to consume agents, spread over

NBER Macroeconomics Annual, volume 37, 2023.

time, and results only in a small medium-term increase in private savings among the bottom 80% of the households in terms of wealth. In contrast, the top 20% of households globally increase their savings considerably, and this international spread of high-wealth private savings sustains the increased home current account deficit. These equilibrium dynamics are associated with an elevated world interest rate, as well as an appreciated home currency due to home bias in local consumption.

The paper uses microdata from JPMorgan Chase Institute on private checking account balances to show that the three waves of fiscal stimulus in the United States in 2020–21 were indeed associated with the predicted patterns of savings dynamics among the top 20% and bottom 80% of households (see fig. 1), providing support for the HANK mechanism. In my discussion, instead, I focus on the aggregate data series and cross-country comparisons, extending the analysis in Section V of the paper.

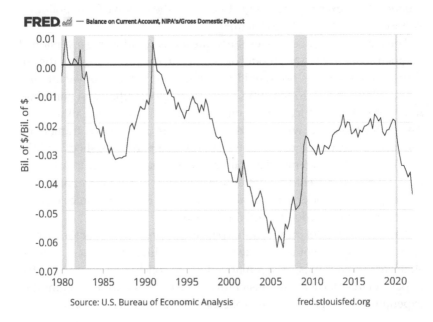

Fig. 1.   Dynamics of the US current account as a share of gross domestic product. NIPA = National Income and Product Accounts. Data are from US Bureau of Economic Analysis, "Balance on Current Account, NIPA's (NETFI)," https://fred.stlouisfed.org/series /NETFI, and "Gross Domestic Product (GDP)," https://fred.stlouisfed.org/series /GDP, retrieved from Federal Reserve Economic Database (FRED), Federal Reserve Bank of St. Louis. A color version of this figure is available online.

I.   International Macroeconomic Dynamics

We first examine US current account dynamics displayed in figure 1 here. The United States has run a series of unprecedented current account deficits in the first decade of the twenty-first century, reaching a peak of 6% of gross domestic product (GDP) just before the 2008–9 global financial crisis (GFC), at which point the deficit shrank to 2% of GDP and remained there through the 2010s. Since the start of the pandemic in the end of 2019, there was indeed an increase in the US current account deficit from 2.2% in 2019 to 2.9% in 2020 and 3.6% in 2021. Although this is a noticeable increase, the 2020–21 current account deficits are by no means unusually large in historical perspective. Indeed, one may wonder whether 2010–19 was a special period of low current account imbalances due to general deleveraging of the economies after the GFC, which ended with the fiscal expansion of 2020–21.

We next examine the dynamics of the US dollar nominal exchange rate against a basket of major currencies displayed in figure 2. The 2008–9

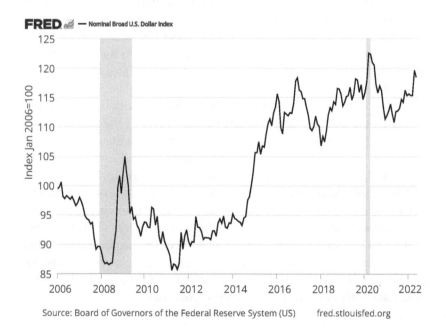

Source: Board of Governors of the Federal Reserve System (US)   fred.stlouisfed.org

Fig. 2.   US dollar nominal exchange rate (trade weighted against major trade partners). Data are from Board of Governors of the Federal Reserve System (US), "Nominal Broad U.S. Dollar Index (DTWEXBGS)," retrieved from FRED, Federal Reserve Bank of St. Louis; https://fred.stlouisfed.org/series/DTWEXBGS. A color version of this figure is available online.

GFC was associated with strong and persistent appreciation of the dollar, triggered by the international capital flight to safety toward the US Treasury bonds. The sharp economic slowdown from the pandemic in early 2020 was also associated with a US dollar appreciation on impact, albeit considerably smaller than that in 2008–9, which then quickly mean-reverted and turned further into a mild depreciation of the dollar, all within 2020 and before the second and third waves of fiscal stimulus. Overall, the limited swings in the currency market perhaps suggest that exchange rates were not the main mechanism of adjustment to the large pandemic shocks.

Global interest rates, of course, also remained at their zero levels, which persisted throughout the 2010s. Instead, the unprecedented nature of the pandemic crisis is clearly visible in the national income accounts and, in particular, in personal consumption expenditure, GDP, and investment, which all declined sharply and then partially recovered in 2020. What is particularly striking about 2020 is the very sharp decline in consumption, a series that remained largely smooth through the 2008–9 GFC. This is not surprising given the nature of the pandemic crisis, which limited consumer behavior and, in particular, the ability to safely obtain many personal services. What I emphasize here is that we did not observe any comparable sharp swings in the international dimension of the data, that is, neither in exchange rates nor in current accounts.

Finally, a quick look at the international comparisons in figure 3 suggests that the United States was not an outlier among the rich countries in terms of the current account response. The United States had a comparable deterioration in the current account to Japan, Germany, France, Spain, and the Netherlands, whereas the United Kingdom, Italy, Canada, and Belgium saw a current account improvement. Any of these movements, however, are again considerably smaller than current account "imbalances" that were a persistent feature of international capital flows in the first decade of the twenty-first century. This again suggests that the international dimension was not a key part of the macroeconomic adjustment mechanism to the COVID pandemic, which was largely a symmetric set of shocks across all developed countries.

II. Intertemporal Approach to Current Account

Next, I briefly consider theoretical implications of a neoclassical model that features Ricardian equivalence—the intertemporal approach to the

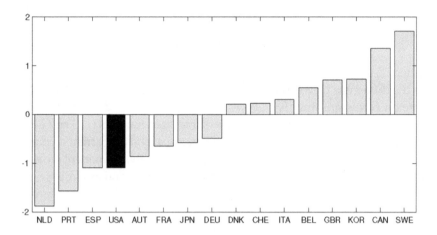

Fig. 3. Current account as percentage of GDP, change between 2018–19 and 2020–21. NLD = Netherlands; PRT = Portugal; ESP = Spain; USA = United States; AUT = Austria; FRA = France; JPN = Japan; DEU = Germany; DNK = Denmark; CHE = Switzerland; ITA = Italy; BEL = Belgium; GBR = United Kingdom; KOR = South Korea; CAN = Canada; SWE = Sweden. A color version of this figure is available online.

current account, as laid out in Obstfeld and Rogoff (1996, chap. 1). The National Income and Product Accounts (NIPA) definition of the current account can be formalized as

$$CA_t = r_t B_t + (Y_t - C_t - I_t - G_t),$$

where $r_t B_t$ are net factor income from abroad, Y_t is GDP, C_t is private consumption, I_t is investment, and G_t is government consumption. Note that the term in brackets is net exports, $NX_t = Y_t - C_t - I_t - G_t$, and thus current account differs from net exports by net factor income from abroad. In other words, net exports characterize net movement of goods across borders, whereas current account characterizes net capital flows. We therefore can write the accumulation of net foreign assets of the country as

$$B_{t+1} - B_t = CA_t = S_t - I_t,$$

where $S_t = r_t B_t + Y_t - C_t - G_t$ is national savings. In other words, an excess of national savings over investment results in capital outflows, which in turn results in net foreign asset accumulation, and vice versa.

Net foreign assets of the country could be held by private agents or by the public sector. With some simplification, we can write the evolution of private assets B_t^p and public debt D_t^g as follows:

$$B_{t+1}^p = (1 + r_t)B_t^p + Y_t - T_t - C_t - I_t,$$
$$D_{t+1}^p = (1 + r_t)D_t^g + G_t - T_t,$$

where T_t is net transfers from the private sector to the government equal to the difference between collected taxes and government transfers. Net foreign assets are thus $B_t = B_t^p - D_t^g$. We are interested, in particular, whether the pandemic policy response of increased transfers ($T_t\downarrow$) and government debt accumulation ($D_{t+1}^p \uparrow$) had an impact on the current account.

A useful benchmark to make further progress is the permanent income hypothesis under Ricardian equivalence. In this case, and assuming $r_t \equiv r = 1/\beta - 1$, consumption must equal the expected disposable permanent household income:

$$C_t = rB_t + \bar{Y}_t - \bar{I}_t - \bar{G}_t = rB_t + \mathbb{E}_t \sum_{j=0}^{\infty} \frac{Y_{t+j} - I_{t+j} - G_{t+j}}{(1 + r)^j},$$

where the first term is the flow value of net foreign wealth and the second term is the expected present value of net household income equal to the difference between real GDP and investment and government consumption. Ricardian equivalence implies that households' choices are shaped by aggregate net foreign assets B_t and the path of government consumption expenditure G_t, and not by government debt D_t^g or the path of taxes and transfers T_t.

Substituting the expression for permanent income consumption into the expression for current account, we obtain the fundamental current account equation (Obstfeld and Rogoff 1995):

$$CA_t = (Y_t - \bar{Y}_t) - (I_t - \bar{I}_t) - (G_t - \bar{G}_t).$$

This equation has simple yet powerful implications. In particular, the current account deteriorates when output is below its long-run expected average level and investment and/or government consumption expenditure are above their long-run expected average levels. Furthermore, the current account does not depend on taxes, transfers, and government debt—a consequence of Ricardian equivalence. An increase in transfers and government debt results in a reduction in private savings but does not affect real allocations including the path of current account and net foreign assets. Although there is abundant evidence that Ricardian equivalence does not hold in general, we evaluate below whether it provides a useful approximation for thinking about international dimensions of the response to the pandemic shock.

To summarize, the neoclassical intertemporal approach to the current account suggests that a pandemic shock that resulted in a decline in output Y_t and an increase in government consumption G_t should lead to a current account deficit, whereas changes in fiscal transfers T_t should not affect the current account. Note, however, that the global current account—global savings net of global investment—must be balanced at all times, which we write as $CA_t + CA_t^* = 0$, where * denotes the rest of the world. Because all countries experienced a decline in output, it is not possible for all countries to run a current account deficit in response to a pandemic shock. Indeed, interest rates must adjust—in this case, increase to offset increased global desire to borrow—to ensure equilibrium in the international financial market.[2]

Nonetheless, countries that experience larger declines in output Y_t or larger increases in government consumption G_t are the ones whose current accounts we expect to see deteriorate, which is a testable implication of the model.

III. Another Look at the Data

The authors describe the empirical relationship between changes in current account and government debt accumulation in the cross section of developed countries in 2020 (see fig. 11 in the paper). Here the picture is that of a glass half full or half empty. Indeed, there is some relationship between current account deterioration and fiscal deficits, which is quantitatively consistent with the predictions of a HANK model. At the same time, this relationship is weak, and the hypothesis of no statistical relationship cannot be rejected at any conventional significance level. Therefore, the data do not reject predictions of a Ricardian model as well. Furthermore, the authors show that fiscal deficits do not crowd out investment and result in additional private savings—somewhat less than one-for-one consistent with HANK but again not statistically different from the full offset predicted by a Ricardian model.

We now look at two additional implications of a neoclassical model, namely the association between current accounts and output declines and government consumption expenditure, as we report in figure 4. We use the data from 2019 to 2020 on Organization for Economic Cooperation and Development countries from World Bank's World Development Indicators database, and we regress the change in the current account balance $\Delta CA_t/Y_{t-1}$ first on the change in GDP $\Delta Y_t/Y_{t-1}$ and second on the change in government consumption expenditure $\Delta G_t/Y_{t-1}$,

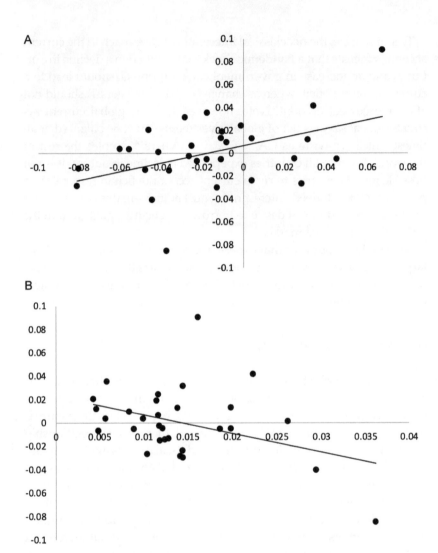

Fig. 4. Current account against gross domestic product (GDP) and government consumption expenditure. Panel *A* projects the current account on GDP and panel *B* projects the current account on government consumption expenditure. All variables measured as change in 2020 relative to 2019 scaled by GDP in 2019, World Bank World Development Indicators database. Each dot corresponds to one of the 40 high-income countries in the sample. β is the slope coefficient with its standard error in brackets. A color version of this figure is available online.

all as a share of the prepandemic GDP. We see strong and statistically significant relationships between these variables, as predicted by the simple current account theory. Specifically, current accounts deteriorate more in countries that have larger declines in output and larger increases in government consumption expenditure. Furthermore, these relationships are statistically strong and, in particular, stronger than the statistical association between current account and fiscal deficits reported in the paper.

IV.   Conclusion

My take from this analysis is that a baseline neoclassical model with Ricardian equivalence does a surprisingly good job at accounting for the main international macroeconomic features of adjustment to the pandemic shocks, at least as a first approximation. Additional features such as sticky prices and home bias appear to be of limited importance in understanding international dimensions of transmission in this episode. It is, of course, interesting to evaluate whether these ingredients improve our understanding of the differential exchange rate and inflation dynamics to the extent distinct asymmetries across countries can be identified for these variables.

Household heterogeneity and non-Ricardian features central to HANK models are essential to make sense of the micro-level consumption and savings dynamics. At the same time, I remain to be convinced that these features have first-order implications for aggregate savings and current account dynamics at the country level during the COVID pandemic. This is not to say that I am generally skeptical about the usefulness of HANK's application to international transmission and business cycles. It is rather a consequence of the particular nature of the pandemic shock, which was driven by a large fiscal expansion to support private incomes in response to severe consumption (and hence output) restrictions imposed by the pandemic. This was largely a set of symmetric shocks across all developed countries, and consequently the international dimension of the response via current account and exchange rate adjustment was limited, and thus both Ricardian and HANK models can be consistent with these aggregate patterns.

It is also conceivable that HANK models, although similar in terms of aggregate international implications, predict important distributional differences at the micro level. We provide such an example in Itskhoki and Mukhin (2022), where we study the policy of domestic financial repression in response to capital outflow shocks. Although aggregate implications are the same in representative and heterogeneous agent models, the predictions of these models differ vastly in terms of desirability of financial repression. Although financial repression is unambiguously welfare-reducing in a representative agent model, it is redistributive in a heterogeneous agent model and improves welfare when the planner puts sufficient weight on poor hand-to-mouth agents who benefit from exchange rate appreciation as a result of repressed savings of the Ricardian agents.

Endnotes

Author email address: Itskhoki (itskhoki@econ.UCLA.edu). For acknowledgments, sources of research support, and disclosure of the author's material financial relationships, if any, please see https://www.nber.org/books-and-chapters/nber-macroeconomics-annual -2022-volume-37/comment-excess-savings-and-twin-deficits-transmission-fiscal-stimulus -open-economies-itskhoki.

1. The paper also provides a detailed reference list for both closed economy and more recent open economy HANK literature.

2. The data, however, do not feature increased interest rates during the pandemic, which is likely due to a combination of two different forces: (i) precautionary savings, decreased safe rates, and increased risk premia due to uncertainties associated with the pandemic and (ii) consumption restrictions (and thus excess savings) that were the source of output declines rather than the opposite. Both of these forces can be modeled in a reduced form as a patience shock that results in lower consumption and greater savings, and a decline in the interest rate as a consequence.

References

Itskhoki, O., and D. Mukhin. 2022. "Sanctions and the Exchange Rate." Working Paper no. 30009, NBER, Cambridge, MA.
Obstfeld, M., and K. S. Rogoff. 1995. "The Intertemporal Approach to the Current Account." In *Handbook of International Economics*, ed. G. Grossman and K. Rogoff, 1731–99. Vol. 3 of *Handbooks in Economics*. Amsterdam: Elsevier.
———. 1996. *Foundations of International Macroeconomics*. Cambridge, MA: MIT Press.

Comment

Linda Tesar, University of Michigan and NBER, United States of America

During the COVID pandemic, governments undertook large fiscal interventions—initially to support households and firms during mandated shutdowns and then, as the need for social distancing abated, to revive economic activity. Beginning in early 2020, the US government passed a sequence of bills to provide COVID support, totaling some $5.8 trillion and increasing the federal debt to gross domestic product (GDP) ratio from 107% in 2019 to 136% in 2021. Governments in Europe similarly enacted an ambitious set of fiscal policies, including an expansion of social safety nets, loan guarantees to firms to protect workers and jobs, and expanded flexibility in national and local debt limits. Over the same 2019–21 period, euro area government debt increased from 84% to 96% of GDP (International Monetary Fund, n.d.). The debt figures for the euro area as a whole mask large differences across Europe, as the countries hardest hit by the pandemic (such as Spain and Italy) saw debt increases comparable to that of the United States. Relative to the United States, European governments tended to provide more above-the-line support such as loan guarantees, whereas US fiscal interventions relied more heavily on direct transfer payments to individuals.

The focus of Aggarwal et al. is the transmission of these unprecedented, COVID-related fiscal expenditures across the set of advanced economies. The paper argues that debt-financed transfers during COVID resulted in predictable changes in the current account that persist over time. Countries that made larger-than-average transfers tended to run current account surpluses, whereas those below the average ran deficits.[1] In the model, fiscal deficits are initially funded by increases in private saving, but over time households begin to unwind the unexpected windfall of transfers. Depending on the magnitude of the fiscal transfer and preferences for home and foreign goods, this dissipation of savings generates a persistent shift in the current account.

The model in the paper is a many-country extension of Auclert et al. (2021) and Auclert, Rognlie, and Straub (2018). The baseline case is a small open economy, where the government can borrow on international markets at a fixed world interest rate. Because the economy is small, there is no impact on the global interest rate and the government can undertake a one-time rollover of debt and transfer purchasing power to households. The increase in borrowing effectively relaxes the national budget constraint, making it possible to consume more of both home and foreign goods. The paper briefly considers an extension to a global economy with asymmetric countries and examines the relative importance of pure COVID shocks relative to COVID-induced fiscal shocks.

I. How Well Does This Theory Explain the Data?

The emphasis of the paper is the extension of their theoretical framework to the COVID shock. The emphasis of my comments will be to ask, How well does the theoretical framework help us understand the data? To make the discussion simple, I will focus on the United States and Europe, with Europe measured by the euro area.

Figure 1 shows the evolution of net private and government savings in the United States and Europe since 2000. The plots are both in $US trillions and are on the same scale for ease of comparison. The bars in light gray show household net saving, and the dark gray bars show government dissaving. The magnitude of the US fiscal intervention starting in 2020Q2 is clear, roughly quadrupling in one quarter. As the paper suggests, dissaving by the government is nearly matched by saving on the part of the private sector. Private saving stays high and gradually decreases over time. Figure 1B shows that spending by euro area governments also increased, though less dramatically than in the United States. For Europe, private saving jumps quite a bit more than the increase in government spending. One possibility, advanced by the paper, is that the difference in the magnitude of the fiscal shock will result in different saving and consumption behavior across countries. An alternative, one I will consider below, is that differences in the way that governments provided COVID

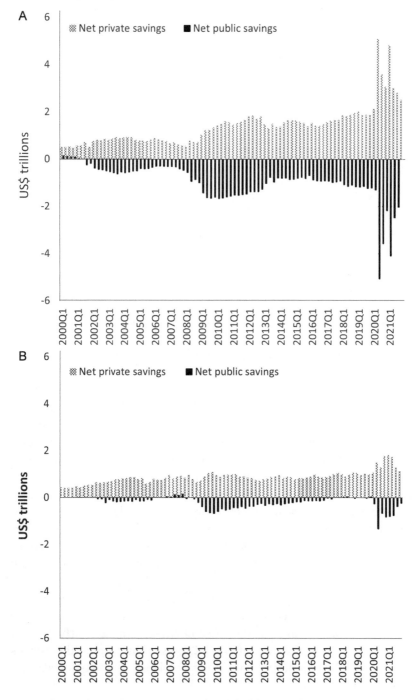

Fig. 1. Net private and government savings: (*A*) United States (source: BEA); (*B*) euro area (source: Eurostat). A color version of this figure is available online.

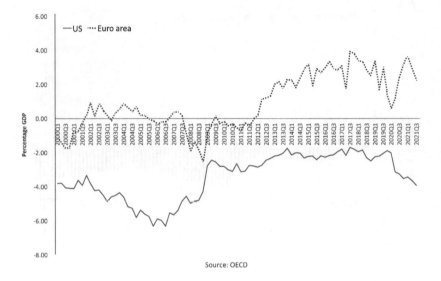

Source: OECD

Fig. 2. Balance on the current account: US and euro area. Data are from Organization for Economic Cooperation and Development. A color version of this figure is available online.

support generated differences in consumption as well as employment and output.

The second part of the paper's story is the impact of fiscal expenditures on the current account. Figure 2 illustrates the current account for the United States and the euro area, again over the 2000–21 period. Both current accounts are scaled by GDP, consistent with the paper's emphasis on the dynamics of saving and consumption and not the direct impact of COVID on economic activity. The connection between the dramatic fiscal interventions that occurred after 2020Q1 and the current account is not at all clear. The US current account deficit deteriorates a bit, but the drop is rather small compared with the unprecedented, fourfold increase in government spending. The euro area current account improves a bit in the early stages of the pandemic but again is in the range of 2%–4% of GDP that is observed for the euro area since 2013. Overall, it is a stretch to see the COVID period as a dramatic change from previous movements in the current account. It is also hard to see a dynamic "unwinding" of the COVID shock—though perhaps with just eight quarters of data that is a lot to ask. The authors themselves concede that their model has only limited explanatory power for changes in the current account.

Is it a puzzle that we don't see much action in the current account during COVID? Neoclassical theory suggests no. Current accounts move in response to country-specific, asymmetric, transitory shocks. The COVID pandemic was (still is?) a global shock that depressed output and disrupted markets worldwide. It certainly affected some countries more than others, and the timing was not exactly synchronous. But as shocks go, COVID was a big, global shock. In the face of such a shock, governments effectively borrowed from the future by running deficits and issuing debt, but there was little scope for countries to borrow from each other.

II. Fiscal Policy in the United States and Europe

This is not to suggest that there was no impact on the current accounts of the major countries of the world. The COVID shock affected countries at different points in time, and governments responded with different types of economic policies, generating asymmetries in income, consumption, and demand for home and foreign goods. The paper emphasizes the size of the fiscal shock and differing degrees of home bias, but there are likely other asymmetries that could also be important. As suggested above, fiscal policy in Europe tended to come in the form of loan guarantees and efforts to keep workers connected with firms, whereas much of the US fiscal response tolerated higher unemployment along with direct transfers of income to households.

In a speech on the nascent recoveries of the United States and the euro area, Organization for Economic Cooperation and Development (OECD) chief economist Laurence Boone (2022) highlights the asymmetric role of fiscal policy in the two regions. As figure 3 shows, the decline in economic activity during the COVID crisis was deeper in the euro area than in the United States. At the same time, euro area employment remained almost constant, whereas it declined sharply in the United States. As Boone emphasizes, this is likely a consequence of the fiscal policies in Europe that kept idle workers in their jobs. Fiscal policy in the United States tended to support income, and this is evident in figure 4. Although the contraction in overall consumption in the two regions is similar at 10%–15% of the pre-COVID level, household disposable income in the United States increased during the COVID pandemic, remaining flat in the euro area. Figure 4 indicates where that income went—US demand for both durables and nondurables surged, whereas demand in the euro area remained flat. As durables and nondurables both contain a significant component of tradable inputs (or are directly importable as final goods), this surge in demand likely put strong downward pressure on the US current account.

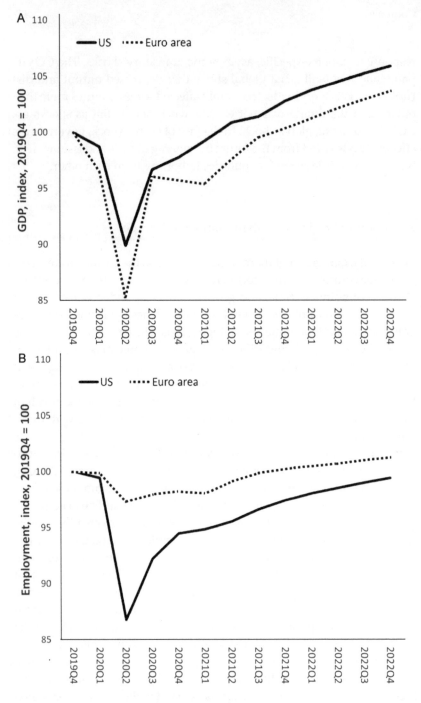

Fig. 3. Output and employment, United States versus euro area: (*A*) GDP fell less in the United States (source: Organization for Economic Cooperation and Development [OECD]); (*B*) employment has hardly contracted in the euro area (source: OECD). A color version of this figure is available online.

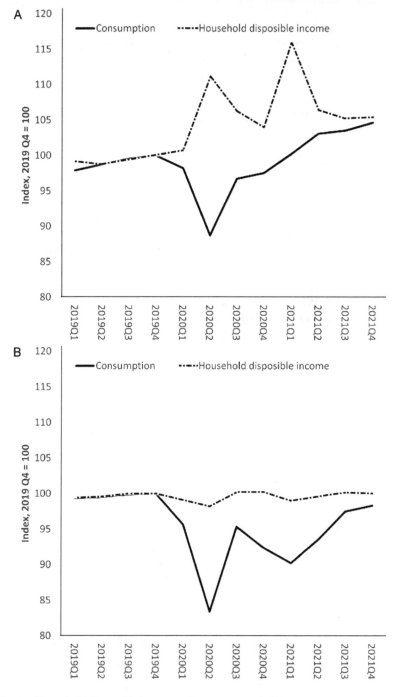

Fig. 4. Household disposable income and consumption: (*A*) United States (source: Organization for Economic Cooperation and Development [OECD]); (*B*) euro area (source: OECD). A color version of this figure is available online.

A generous interpretation of the paper would be that the fiscal shock, which was bigger in the United States and spread across more households, indeed resulted in more consumption spending and current account deficit. A less generous interpretation is that it is important to take into account the impact of fiscal policy on output, investment, and employment to say something about the current account.

III.   What about China?

Although a paper cannot be expected to explain everything, a paper about US and European current accounts probably should address China. China accounts for nearly 20% of US imports and 12% of euro area imports. More importantly, the economic impact of COVID hit China earlier than in the United States and Europe. Figure 5 illustrates industrial production in the United States, Germany, the United Kingdom, and China, all indexed to 2019:12 = 100. Whereas the United Kingdom, Germany, and the United States move almost in lockstep, China both contracts earlier and recovers earlier. Again, neoclassical theory would suggest that China, not Europe, is a more likely counterpart for US trade imbalances.

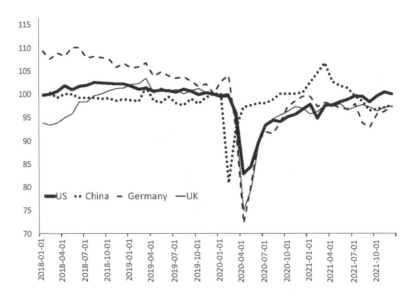

Fig. 5.   Industrial production: United States, China, United Kingdom, Germany. 2019: 12 = 100. Data are from Federal Reserve Economic Database. A color version of this figure is available online.

IV. Conclusion

This contribution is part of a larger set of papers that have helped shed light on the dynamics of consumption and saving both within and across countries. In some ways, the theory is very simple and elegant. There are exogenous changes to government spending, there is no role for production or investment, and the theory yields a simple mechanism to deliver dynamic adjustments in consumption and the current account. In other ways, however, the model is quite complicated, with heterogeneous agents, monetary policy, sticky wages, incomplete markets, and dynamic asset positions. In the end, however, it is not clear that the details of the model are central for understanding the impact of the fiscal responses to the COVID shock and the implications for international borrowing and lending.

Endnotes

Author email address: Tesar (ltesar@umich.edu). For acknowledgments, sources of research support, and disclosure of the author's material financial relationships, if any, please see https://www.nber.org/books-and-chapters/nber-macroeconomics-annual -2022-volume-37/comment-excess-savings-and-twin-deficits-transmission-fiscal-stimu lus-open-economies-2-tesar.
1. Note that the "twin deficits" phenomenon emphasized in the title—that countries with high fiscal deficits also run current account deficits—can, by definition, only apply to some countries in the world. Virtually all countries experienced fiscal deficits during COVID, but only a subset can run current account deficits.

References

Auclert, Adrien, Matthew Rognlie, Martin Souchier, and Ludwig Straub. 2021. "Exchange Rates and Monetary Policy with Heterogeneous Agents: Sizing up the Real Income Channel." Working Paper no. 28872 (May), NBER, Cambridge, MA.
Auclert, Adrien, Matthew Rognlie, and Ludwig Straub. 2018. "The Intertemporal Keynesian Cross." Working Paper no. 25020 (September), NBER, Cambridge, MA.
Boone, Laurence. 2022. "The EA and the US in the COVID-19 Crisis: Implications for the 2022–2023 Policy Stance." *Ecoscope* (blog). https://oecdecoscope .blog/2022/01/18/the-ea-and-the-us-in-the-covid-19-crisis-implications-for -the-2022-2023-policy-stance/.
International Monetary Fund. n.d. "Policy Responses to COVID-19." https:// www.imf.org/en/Topics/imf-and-covid19/Policy-Responses-to-COVID-19.

Discussion

Multiple audience members raised concerns about how much of the increase in private savings was in response to governments' fiscal transfers as opposed to responses to shocks more directly related to COVID prevalence. Erik Hurst asked how we should think about savings responses in a world with health shocks and consumption restrictions. In particular, he noted that the micro evidence showed a strong link between COVID cases and consumption at the local level. Jonathan Parker asked if the consumption dynamics as well as the high real interest rate could be explained by a process that affects marginal utility, lowering marginal utility during times when COVID was prevalent. This might be consistent with the empirical interest rate dynamics as well the evidence on COVID restrictions. The authors responded by saying they look exactly at these shocks to the discount rate/marginal utility overall, and that they also look at shocks to just the marginal utility of domestic services. They said these shocks account for the fall in consumption and output worldwide but that they are not able to explain both the increase in private savings and the fall in the current account in the United States. With no increase in public borrowing, any increase in private savings would have to lead to an increase in either investment or the current account, but investment moved very little, and the current account fell as part of the observed twin deficits in the United States. Oleg Itskhoki added that shocks to a household's desire for consumption would lead to an increase in desired savings, but in a closed economy model either output would have to decline or investment would have to increase, so that there may not

NBER Macroeconomics Annual, volume 37, 2023.

be much of an increase in equilibrium saving. The authors noted that their quantitative model was a large open economy model, so that the global economy is closed and so Oleg Itskhoki's reasoning from a closed economy model applied to thinking about the world economy. This was the key reason why consumption shocks alone could not explain the global increase in household savings. They further added that you would need large differential consumption shocks across countries to generate the movements in current accounts seen in the data.

Guido Menzio asked two questions. The first was about how the authors modeled the income process and how it was affected by COVID. The authors responded that different income processes would affect their calibration of the intertemporal marginal propensities to consume (MPCs) of the household sector, which in their model are all that matter for the macroeconomic predictions. They said they were using a standard calibration to MPCs but could recalibrate using evidence from Jonathan Parker's work on MPCs during the pandemic. The second question was about different forms of fiscal transfers with different distributional implications such as lump sum versus unemployment benefits. Guido Menzio noted that these distributional implications have been found to matter a lot for the predictions of heterogeneous agent models. The authors mentioned that they had considered various distributional rules for transfers in the paper, including rebates through the tax system versus lump-sum transfers. They found that transfers targeted to lower wealth and thus higher MPC agents did cause a larger short-run output response but that the qualitative implications for dynamics were unchanged because the long-run steady state was dependent only on the amount of debt issued. They gave the intuition, because rich agents spend fiscal transfers slower than poor agents, debt-financed transfers that are targeted toward the rich are absorbed by domestic savings for longer, and so aggregate dynamics are slower than if transfers are targeted toward the poor.

Eric Swanson asked about the implications for inflation given the large increases in inflation after the COVID fiscal stimulus packages. The authors said that their main simulation implies that fiscal policy caused inflation to rise by 4%–5% on average across countries, lasting for a couple of years. Moreover, countries with a larger fiscal response, such as the United States and the United Kingdom, had higher inflation rates, consistent with the data.